PAGE 36

ON THE ROAD

YOUR COMP...
In-depth reviews, detailed listings
and insider tips

KT-489-495

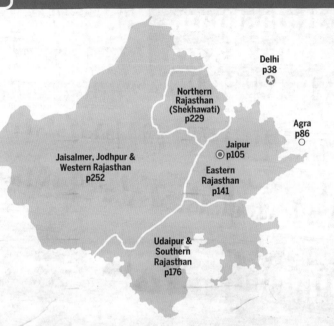

Delhi
p38

Northern
Rajasthan
(Shekhawati)
p229

Agra
p86

Jaisalmer, Jodhpur &
Western Rajasthan
p252

Jaipur
p105

Eastern
Rajasthan
p141

Udaipur &
Southern
Rajasthan
p176

PAGE 343

SURVIVAL GUIDE

VITAL PRACTICAL INFORMATION TO
HELP YOU HAVE A SMOOTH TRIP

Scams & Touts

THIS EDITION WRITTEN AND RESEARCHED BY

Lindsay Brown

Abigail Hole, Daniel McCrohan, John Noble

Welcome to Rajasthan, Delhi & Agra

The Golden Triangle

This book's first steps take in the famous Golden Triangle, a traveller's trigonometric survey of emblematic India. It starts at the daunting mega-metropolis of Delhi with its majestic Mughal heritage, and then directs you to Agra, where one of the world's most famous tombs, the Taj Mahal, defines a city. The third apex is the gateway to Rajasthan, Jaipur – a city painted pink with the Palace of the Winds and some of the most colourful bazaars in India. From here, the rest of Rajasthan beckons. The colours of this region are impossible to ignore and the effect of emerald green, canary yellow and fire-engine red turbans and saris is simply dazzling. Rajasthan is

India's major drawcard and once you step into a palace, stare up at a fort or see your first lac bangle being made, you will soon appreciate why this is so.

Magnificent Monuments

Most travellers to this region will arrive by air in the nation's capital. Delhi is an overwhelming, bursting-at-the-seams city that still manages to charm visitors with its magnificent heritage and heady cocktail of old and new. The former capital of Shahjahanabad, the seventh city on this ancient site, anchors the Old City with its massive Red Fort while evocative tombs of empires past are islands in the sprawl of New Delhi. A short train journey to the south, the Taj

Against a backdrop of desert sands, fairy-tale palaces and massive forts, modern and traditional India puts on its greatest show. From elephant rides to colourful festivals, this is India at its high-definition, surround-sound best.

(left) Jagdish Temple (p201), Udaipur
(below) Image of the goddess Parvati, Mewar Festival (p177)

Mahal lives up to its hype with its perfect proportions and marble tones. For many, though, it's Agra's red-stone fort and its sorrowful gaze across the Yamuna River towards the Taj Mahal that captures their imagination.

Land of Kings

Rajasthan is literally the Land of the Kings. It is home to the chivalrous Rajputs, and its battle-scarred heritage has bestowed legacies of pride and tradition. The upper echelons of this medieval society built magnificent palaces and forts, many of which are now glorious hotels and museums. In addition, stunning handicrafts and fine arts were developed and nurtured through patronage of the maharajas. At the other end, village Rajasthan is so steeped in tradition that it has been one of the slowest segments of Indian society to modernise. But, just like the rest of India, the pace of change is ever accelerating. Witnessing turbaned men bartering for decorated camels brings history to life, even if the successful deal is relayed home by a mobile phone. Snapshots of the everyday in Rajasthan capture India at its most evocative – the twirl of a moustache, a veiled glance or a puff of blue hashish smoke. It will fill your memory card many times over.

›Rajasthan, Delhi & Agra

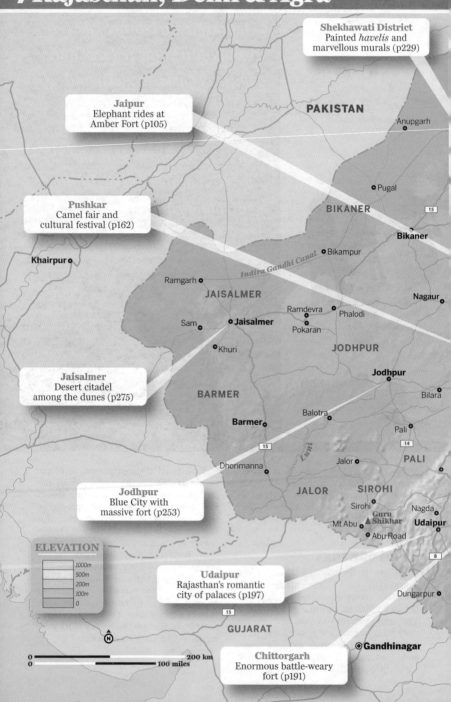

Shekhawati District
Painted *havelis* and
marvellous murals (p229)

Jaipur
Elephant rides at
Amber Fort (p105)

Pushkar
Camel fair and
cultural festival (p162)

Jaisalmer
Desert citadel
among the dunes (p275)

Jodhpur
Blue City with
massive fort (p253)

Udaipur
Rajasthan's romantic
city of palaces (p197)

Chittorgarh
Enormous battle-weary
fort (p191)

PAKISTAN

Anupgarh

Pugal

BIKANER

15

Bikaner

Khairpur

Indira Gandhi Canal Bikampur

Nagaur

Ramgarh

JAISALMER

Ramdevra Phalodi

Sam **Jaisalmer** Pokaran

Khuri

JODHPUR

Jodhpur

Bilara

BARMER

Balotra

Barmer

Pali

15 *Luni* 14

Dhorimanna Jalor **PALI**

JALOR SIROHI

Sirohi Nagda

Mt Abu Guru
Shikhar **Udaipur**

Abu Road

8

ELEVATION

	1000m
	500m
	200m
	100m
	0

Dungarpur

Udaipur
Rajasthan's romantic
city of palaces (p197)

15

GUJARAT

Ⓝ

0 200 km
0 100 miles

◉**Gandhinagar**

Chittorgarh
Enormous battle-weary
fort (p191)

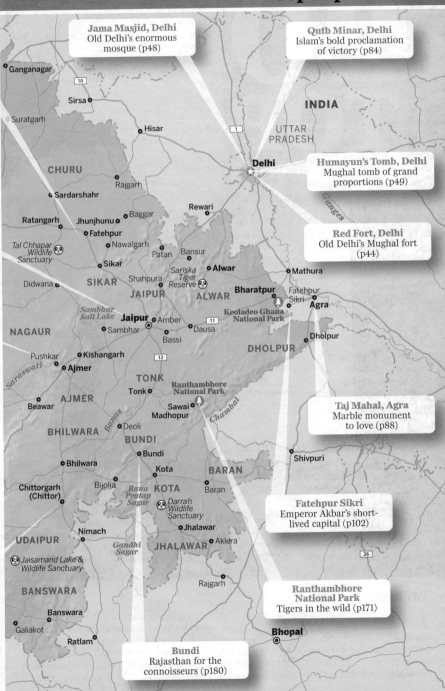

Jama Masjid, Delhi
Old Delhi's enormous mosque (p48)

Qutb Minar, Delhi
Islam's bold proclamation of victory (p84)

Humayun's Tomb, Delhi
Mughal tomb of grand proportions (p49)

Red Fort, Delhi
Old Delhi's Mughal fort (p44)

Taj Mahal, Agra
Marble monument to love (p88)

Fatehpur Sikri
Emperor Akbar's short-lived capital (p102)

Ranthambhore National Park
Tigers in the wild (p171)

Bundi
Rajasthan for the connoisseurs (p180)

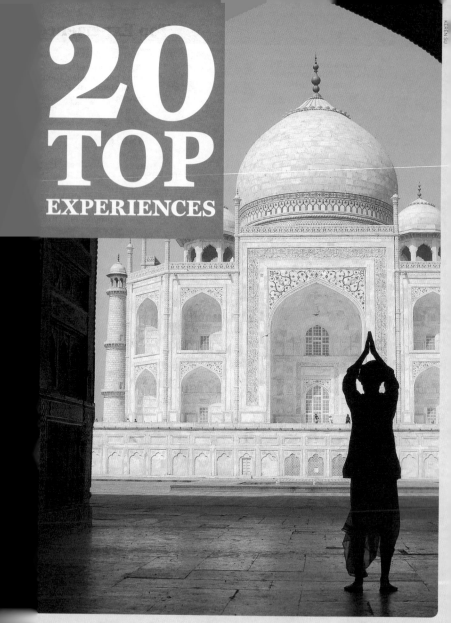

20 TOP EXPERIENCES

j Mahal, Agra

ramed in its arched gateway, the full-frontal vision of the Taj Mahal (p88) is stunning – a paint-
ng somehow made real for you to enter. Even the maddening crowds don't spoil this vision
oportion and symmetry reflected in the mirror-like watercourses of the surrounding Mughal
en. Translucent white marble softly glows at dawn, dusk and under moonlight. Closer inspection
als delicate designs and beautiful calligraphy inlaid with coloured stone, and the two cenotaphs,
of Mumtaz Mahal, the inspiration for the Taj Mahal, and the second of Shah Jahan, its creator.

Jaisalmer Fort

2 The 12th-century Jaisalmer Fort (p278) defiantly rises from the flat desert lands, a vision from childhood memories of tales such as 'Ali Baba and the Forty Thieves'. The reality is no less romantic. Castellated stone bastions and elephant-size doors protect a warren of narrow bazaars and Jain and Hindu temples, all bustling with life – a quarter of the city's population lives inside the fort. Overseeing the bazaars is the former Maharaja's seven-storey palace, now a fascinating museum.

Jodhpur

3 The ancient capital of the kingdom of the Marwar, Jodhpur (p253) rewards the traveller with Rajasthan's most spectacular fort and from its ramparts one of India's iconic views. Mehrangarh seems to emerge organically from its rocky pedestal to protect the Blue City. From this elevated perch the old city of Jodhpur, a maze of blue-block houses, is like an ocean surrounding an island fortress. Beyond the teeming city, jeep safaris explore the home of the desert-dwelling Bishnoi, a people who have been protecting the natural environment for aeons.

Red Fort, Delhi

4 The massive Red Fort (p44) of Delhi is the heart of Shahjahanabad, the walled city constructed by Shah Jahan and now known as Old Delhi. Though little remains of the glorious interiors, the massive Mughal architecture and geometric gardens evoke the centuries-old magnificence of this imperial throne. From Lahore Gate, through which the visitor can easily imagine the grand processions of day's past, you can wander the covered market, trimmed gardens, water features and elegant buildings, and then take in a sound and light show. Diwan-i-Am, left

Camel Safari, Thar Desert

5 For an unbeatable cultural experience, hop aboard a ship of the desert for an extended safari or simple overnight jaunt into the windswept dunes of Rajasthan's Thar Desert. From a camel's back you can see herds of gazelles and meet desert-dwelling villagers. At the end of the day you can make chapatis over an open fire, witness a cultural show and fall blissfully asleep under a Persian carpet of glittering stars. You can organise a camel safari in the cities of Jaisalmer (p291), Bikaner (p297) and Osian (p271).

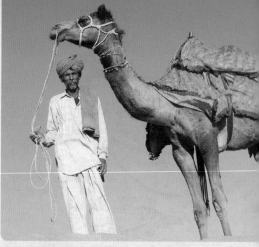

DIANA MAYFIELD

Ranthambhore National Park

6 There are only a handful of places left to see the magnificent tiger in the wild. Ranthambhore National Park (p171) is one such place and your chances of spotting a tiger are good. This former hunting reserve of the maharajas of Jaipur is a majestic setting for a tiger safari. There are lush ravines and crocodile-infested lakes, and a crumbling fort straight out of the *Jungle Book*. Spotted deer graze in the dappled light of an open wood, their eyes, nostrils and ears twitching for the sight, smell or sound of a striped predator.

ANDERS BLOMQVIST

Amber Fort, Jaipur

7 Before the capital was moved to Jaipur, the fort palace of Amber (p136) was the capital of the Kachwaha. The honey-coloured citadel rises from a sloping ridge surrounded by higher ridges capped with battlements and watchtowers. From the beautiful geometric gardens and Maota Lake, you can ride an elephant to the main square, Jaleb Chowk. From here, wander freely through the palace grounds, halls of audience, the magnificent three-storey Ganesh Pol, the once-taboo zenana (women's quarters), and the still-glittering Jai Mandir.

HUW JONES

Bundi

8 Bundi isn't really 'undiscovered' (Lieutenant-Colonel James Tod gave it a good write-up in his *1829 Annals & Antiquities of Rajasthan*), yet it is a sufficient backwater for those escaping the crowds of Delhi, Jaipur and Agra. The picturesque, decaying palace (p180) tumbles down a rocky slope beneath the ramparts of the fort of Taragarh. Inside the once-luxurious palace are evocative but fading gold-and-turquoise murals. Come evening, the palace is floodlit and today's tenants, bats by the score, fly out through the spotlights and into the night.

Fatehpur Sikri, Agra

9 Not far from Agra, on a rocky ridge where a Sufi saint had lived in a cave, Emperor Akbar built his new capital of Fatehpur Sikri (p102). This move from Agra was short-lived, however. Wandering the beautiful complex you can only be amazed that after just 14 years the great sandstone metropolis was abandoned, probably due to a lack of water. Dominating the palace complex is the expansive Jama Masjid fronted by the immense Buland Darwaza (Victory Gate) commemorating Akbar's victory in Gujarat.

Humayun's Tomb, Delhi

10 The splendid Humayun's tomb (p49) graciously sits on a multiarched plinth rising from the neat lawns of its extensive *charbagh* (formal Persian garden), of which this was the first example in India. The garden is a perfect escape from Delhi's crowds. Sparkling water features, tidy cypresses and swaying palm trees are set against the symmetrical pink sandstone tomb built for Humayan, the second Mughal emperor, by his Persian-born senior wife, Haji Begum, who also lays here.

CHRISTER FREDRIKSSON

APRIL MACIBORKA

Colours of Rajasthan

12 Against a canvas of muted desert tones, Rajasthan is a region generously splashed with vibrant colour. Bedazzling saris float through bazaars like a swarm of multicoloured butterflies, elephants lumber tourists up to Amber Fort self-consciously sporting gaudy body paint and camels are clipped with intricate patterns and capped with colourful bridles. Turbans take on a luminous glow, lac bangles sparkle with ground glass, while gold and silver links dripping with diamonds, emeralds and rubies enchant the most prosaic of hearts.

Fantastic Festivals

11 Barely a week goes by when there isn't some form of festival being celebrated in Rajasthan (p24). Hindu, Muslim, Jain and Christian – each contributes to the festival calendar. Whenever there's an opportunity to prepare culinary treats, throw on colourful saris or turbans, ignite fireworks or paint an elephant, almost everyone likes to join in. Though many festivals are age-old and deeply spiritual, others have evolved to celebrate the rich traditions and unique characteristics of Rajasthan in a rapidly modernising world. Jaipur Elephant Festival, above

Jantar Mantar, Jaipur

13 If you have the inclination for cosmology, astronomy or even astrology, take a detour at Jaipur's City Palace to observe the remarkable Jantar Mantar (p111). The carefully laid-out observatory was constructed in 1728, one of five such complexes built by Jaipur's Maharaja Jai Singh. Pride of place goes to a massive sundial, the Brihat Samrat Yantra. Wandering around the grounds you will also discover instruments used to forecast weather and eclipses, and measure the zodiac star clusters and the intensity of the coming monsoon.

Qutb Minar, Delhi

14 The magnificent sandstone-and-marble tower known as the Qutb Minar (p84) is an imposing symbol of the beginnings of an Islamic ruling dynasty in Delhi. Its impressive five storeys taper upwards to reach almost 73m and its fluted form is embellished with verses from the Quran. Its tilt means that you can't climb its stairs and will have to be content with a view from the grounds, which contain a mosque and an extraordinary iron pillar with its own fascinating story.

Jama Masjid, Delhi

15 The largest mosque in India, the red-sandstone Jama Masjid (p48) dominates the bazaars of Old Delhi with its towering 40m-high twin minarets and trio of marble domes. Grand flights of stairs lead up from the street to the imposing gates that separate the secular from the sacred. The vast, enclosed courtyard of Emperor Shah Jahan's last architectural extravagance can host more than 20,000 worshippers at a single prayer session. Climb the southern minaret for an unforgettable view.

Chittorgarh

16 The enormous rambling fortress of Chittorgarh (p192) epitomises the romanticism of Rajput myth and legend, with tales of chivalry, heroism and tragedy all intricately entwined within its architecture. As Rajasthan's greatest fort, it was the capital of the Sisodia rulers of Mewar and attracted numerous invaders, particularly Delhi's sultans and emperors – though its spectacular defensive walls were not as effective as expected. Virtually a ruin now, Chittorgarh crowns the top of a rocky hill, its crenellated battlements protecting palaces, temples and extraordinary towers.

ANDERS BLOMQVIST

Udaipur

TIM MAKINS

17 Following the fall of Chittorgarh, Maharana Udai Singh II moved the Mewar capital to Udaipur (p197) in 1568. The city is dominated by the sprawling City Palace that hugs the eastern shoreline of Udaipur's centrepiece, Lake Pichola. The enormous complex houses a museum, a couple of swish heritage hotels and the erstwhile royals. The mirror-surfaced lake, in turn, hosts one of Rajasthan's most renowned palaces, the wedding-cake Lake Palace, now also an exclusive five-star hotel and occasional movie set. City Palace, left

Simply Shekhawati

18 In the arid plains of northern Rajasthan, the district known as Shekhawati (p229) has a seemingly incongruous treasure of once-lavish *havelis*. The walls of these grand homes built by wealthy traders can't speak, but they certainly tell a damn good story with their colourful and often whimsical murals. Shekhawati is a lot more than its celebrated *havelis* and murals, however. It also has a rich and deeply conservative village culture that rewards travellers who take time out to immerse and listen.

ANDERS BLOMQVIST

19 You can eat your way around Rajasthan, Delhi and Agra and never have the same dish twice, but chances are you will find a few favourites that you will habitually seek out on the menu or in the bazaar. It may be a freshly squeezed *mosambi* (sweet lime), a fiery dahl or a delicate butter chicken from one of Delhi's swishest restaurants. In the bazaars, freshly fried samosas and puffed-up *kachori*, or sticky sweet *jalebis* (orange-coloured, fried batter in syrup) and *gulab jamun* (deep-fried milk dough in rose-flavoured syrup) pull you in by the nostrils. *Jalebis*, left

Pushkar Camel Fair

20 Some come for the camels, some come to bathe away their sins, some come just for the fun. Pushkar's extraordinary camel fair (p144) is Rajasthan's signature event, combining Hindu spiritulism, camel commerce and cultural celebration. The camels, cattle and Mawaristeeds arrive early so that the dealing can be done before the frivolity of the fair takes over, and before the full-moon ceremony of Kartik Purnima, when pilgrims bathe and set candles afloat in a holy lake.

Taj Mahal

TIMELINE

1631 Emperor Shah Jahan's beloved third wife, Mumtaz Mahal, dies in Buhanpur while giving birth to their 14th child. Her body is initially interred in Buhanpur itself, where Shah Jahan is fighting a military campaign, but is later moved, in a golden casket, to a small building on the banks of the Yamuna River in Agra.

1632 Construction of a permanent mausoleum for Mumtaz Mahal begins.

1633 Mumtaz Mahal is interred in her final resting place, an underground tomb beneath a marble plinth, on top of which the Taj Mahal will be built.

1640 The white-marble mausoleum is completed.

1653 The rest of the Taj Mahal complex is completed.

1658 Emperor Shah Jahan is overthrown by his son Aurangzeb and imprisoned in Agra Fort.

1666 Shah Jahan dies. His body is transported along the Yamuna River and buried underneath the Taj, alongside the tomb of his wife.

1908 Repeatedly damaged and looted after the fall of the Mughal empire, the Taj receives some long-overdue attention as part of a major restoration project ordered by British viceroy Lord Curzon.

1983 The Taj is awarded Unesco World Heritage Site status.

2002 Having been discoloured by pollution in more recent years, the Taj is spruced up with an ancient recipe known as *multani mitti* – a blend of soil, cereal, milk and lime once used by Indian women to beautify their skin.

Today More than three million tourists visit the Taj Mahal each year. That's more than twice the current population of Agra.

DANIEL MCCROHAN

Go Barefoot
Help the environment by entering the mausoleum barefoot instead of using the free disposable shoe covers.

Pishtaqs
These huge arched recesses are set into each side of the Taj. They provide depth to the building while their central, latticed marble screens allow patterned light to illuminate the inside of the mausoleum.

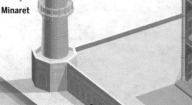

Minaret

Entrance

Plinth

Marble Relief Work
Flowering plants, thought to be representations of paradise, are a common theme among the beautifully decorative panels carved onto the white marble.

DANIEL MCCROHAN

Be Enlightened
Bring a small torch into the mausoleum to fully appreciate the translucency of the white marble and semiprecious stones.

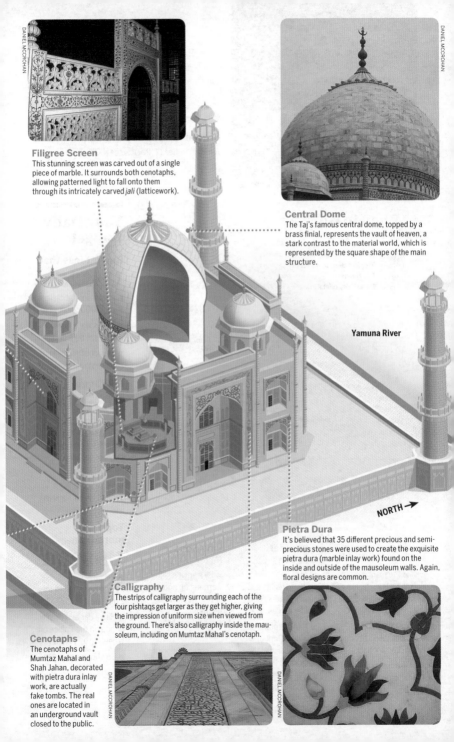

Filigree Screen
This stunning screen was carved out of a single piece of marble. It surrounds both cenotaphs, allowing patterned light to fall onto them through its intricately carved *jali* (latticework).

Central Dome
The Taj's famous central dome, topped by a brass finial, represents the vault of heaven, a stark contrast to the material world, which is represented by the square shape of the main structure.

Yamuna River

NORTH →

Pietra Dura
It's believed that 35 different precious and semi-precious stones were used to create the exquisite pietra dura (marble inlay work) found on the inside and outside of the mausoleum walls. Again, floral designs are common.

Calligraphy
The strips of calligraphy surrounding each of the four pishtaqs get larger as they get higher, giving the impression of uniform size when viewed from the ground. There's also calligraphy inside the mausoleum, including on Mumtaz Mahal's cenotaph.

Cenotaphs
The cenotaphs of Mumtaz Mahal and Shah Jahan, decorated with pietra dura inlay work, are actually fake tombs. The real ones are located in an underground vault closed to the public.

DANIEL MCCROHAN

need to know

Language
» Hindi and English. There are five regional dialects of Hindi spoken in Rajasthan; see p377

Currency
» Indian Rupee (₹, INR)

When to Go

Warm to hot summers, mild winters
Tropical climate, wet & dry seasons
Dry climate
Desert, dry climate

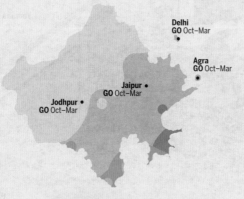

Delhi
GO Oct–Mar

Agra
GO Oct–Mar

Jaipur •
GO Oct–Mar

Jodhpur •
GO Oct–Mar

High Season
(Dec–Feb)
» Pleasant daytime temperature, but can get cold at night
» Peak tourists, peak prices – pre-book all flights and accommodation
» Domestic flights often get delayed owing to fog

Shoulder Seasons (Sep–Nov & Feb–Mar)
» Warm nights suit many visitors fleeing colder climes
» Ranthambhore National Park opens in October and the migratory birds arrive at Keoladeo Ghana National Park

Low Season
(Apr–Aug)
» By April it's warming up and June is very hot awaiting the monsoon, which brings the rain in July and August
» Ranthambhore National Park closes at the end of June

Your Daily Budget

Budget less than
US$25
» Accommodation less than ₹1000 for double
» Thalis are a healthy way to eat on a budget
» Drink bottled beer as an occasional treat

Midrange
US$100
» Accommodation ₹1000 to ₹5000 (allows for occasional stays in heritage hotels)
» Consider hiring a car and driver for short sightseeing jaunts

Top End more than
US$200
» Palatial accommodation fit for a maharaja at ₹5000
» Hire a car and driver or hop on the Palace on Wheels luxury train
» Go shopping

Money

» Most urban centres have ATMS. Carry cash or travellers cheques as back-up. MasterCard and Visa are the most widely accepted credit cards.

Visas

» Most people travel on the standard six-month tourist visa. Tourist visas are valid from the date of issue, not the arrival date.

Mobile Phones

» Getting connected can involve time-consuming identity checks. Avoid high roaming costs by hooking up to a local network.

Driving

» Don't do it. Hiring a car with driver doesn't cost a fortune and India has expansive rail, bus and air connections.

Websites

» **Festivals of India** (www.festivalsofindia. in) All about Indian festivals.

» **Incredible India** (www.incredibleindia. org) Official India tourism site.

» **IndiaMike** (www. indiamike.com) Popular travellers forum.

» **Lonely Planet** (www.lonelyplanet. com/india) Destination information, the popular Thorn Tree Travel Forum and more.

» **Rajasthan Tourism Development Corporation** (www.rtdc.in) Rajasthan government tourism site.

Exchange Rates

Australia	A$1	₹45.52
Bangladesh	Tk 100	₹63.85
Canada	C$1	₹46.05
Euro zone	E1	₹61.35
Japan	¥100	₹54.55
New Zealand	NZ$1	₹34.35
UK	UK1	₹72.75
US	US$1	₹45.45

For current exchange rates see www.xe.com.

Important Numbers

To dial numbers in this book from outside India, dial your international access code, India's country code then the number (minus the '0' used for dialling domestically).

Country code	☑91
International access code (in India)	☑00
Ambulance	☑102
Police	☑100

Arriving in New Delhi

» **Indira Gandhi International Airport** There is a prepaid-taxi booth at Delhi airport where you can book a taxi for a fixed price (including luggage), thus avoiding commission scams. Many hotels will arrange airport pick-ups with advance notice – these are often complimentary with top-end hotels but for a fee at others. Because of the late-night arrival of many international flights, a hotel-room booking and airport pick-up is advised.

DON'T LEAVE HOME WITHOUT...

» Getting a visa (p356), travel insurance (p350) and required vaccinations (p372)

» Nonrevealing clothes (women and men) and slip-on shoes for visiting holy sites

» Well-concealed money belt

» Sunscreen, sunglasses and mosquito repellent

» Small flashlight for poorly lit streets and/or power cuts

» Earplugs – noise can be a nuisance

» Tampons – sanitary pads are widely available, tampons restricted to larger towns

» Water bottle and water-purification tablets or filters

» Sleeping-bag sheet (to cover hotel linen and for overnight train journeys)

if you like...

Wildlife

If you are interested in India's wildlife – particularly its legendary tigers and amazing birdlife – then Rajasthan should be high on your list of Indian states to visit. The national parks of Rajasthan started out as hunting reserves for the maharajas. The animal populations were fiercely protected until the maharajas and their guests went on a shooting spree. In later years, with modern weapons, this turned into wholesale slaughter and led to a conservation ethos and establishment of national parks.

Ranthambhore National Park This remains one of the best places to spot a wild tiger in India and has amazing scenery and a spooky fort (p171)

Keoladeo Ghana National Park An internationally recognised wetland attracting scores of seasonal migrants – a bird-watchers paradise (p148)

Sariska Tiger Reserve Tigers were reintroduced here after controversially losing its own population to poaching – Sariska is now at the forefront of tiger conservation (p152)

Bazaar Shopping

Rajasthan (and Delhi) really is one of the easiest places to spend money, with its bustling and vibrant bazaars, colourful arts and crafts, gorgeous fabrics, miniature paintings, blue pottery, magic carpets and much more. The cardinal rule is to bargain and bargain hard.

Delhi The capital has it all, from modern shopping malls with international designer goods down to the pestering purveyors of Chandni Chowk (p76)

Agra Artisans create marble inlaid with coloured stones in the pietra dura technique used on the Taj Mahal (p99)

Jaipur A shopper's dream – arts and crafts abound in the bazaars of the Old City and top of the list is the amazing jewellery (p129)

Pushkar Explore the cluttered Sadar Bazaar, chock-a-block full with arts and crafts such as exquisite embroidered textiles from the desert town of Barmer (p129)

Fancy Festivals

Rich in religion and tradition, Rajasthan has scores of vibrant festivals. Most festivals follow either the Indian lunar calendar (a complex system determined by astrologers) or the Islamic calendar (which falls about 11 days earlier each year; 12 days earlier in leap years), and therefore change annually relative to the Gregorian calendar.

Diwali The liveliest festival of the Hindu calendar, celebrated on the 15th day of Kartika (Oct/Nov), featuring crazy amounts of fireworks (p26)

Holi Probably the most exuberant Hindu festival – people celebrate the beginning of spring (Feb/Mar) by throwing brightly coloured water and gulal (powder) at one another (p24)

Pushkar Camel Fair Rajasthan's biggest event – part agricultural show, part cultural festival and part Hindu pilgrimage (p144)

Jaipur Elephant Festival A celebration of all things pachyderm – pampered elephants are decorated and games include elephant-versus-human tug-of-war (p107)

CHRISTER FREDRIKSSON

» Holi festival (p25)

Sleeping in a Palace

The phenomenal wealth of the feudal kings and princes was as exclusive as it was vast. At that time only by luck of birth or special invitation could one have experienced the splendid interiors. But now the erstwhile royals rely on tourism and the palaces have become luxury hotels where you can sleep like a maharaja.

Jaipur Regional nobles built palaces around this city, so you'll find an embarrassment of palatial digs – the former maharaja's own palace, the Rambagh, is one of India's best hotels (p119)

Udaipur This ticks all the boxes for the most romantic setting with the picture-perfect Lake Palace, a floating wedding cake hotel (p209)

Jodhpur Boasts one of the last palaces to be built before the royals lost their gravy trains – the Umaid Bhawan Palace is an Art Deco colossus with stunning rooms (p122)

Deserts & Camels

Rajasthan's great Thar Desert is criss-crossed by ancient trade routes and dotted with traditional villages where life continues in a fashion very similar to more romantic times. Slow loping camels remain an important method of transport even in this frantic era, and they remain integral to traditional desert culture.

Jaisalmer Home to the very popular but still evocative overnight camel safari – sweeping sand dunes, traditional dance and food and a charpoy under the stars (p291)

Jodhpur The centre for exploring the desert homelands of the Bishnoi, a people who hold all animals sacred, particularly the blackbuck, India's desert antelope (p269)

Bikaner Travel in a traditional camel cart through the arid scrubland, while visiting villages and sleeping on dunes (p297)

Mighty Forts

The feudal past of Delhi, Agra and Rajasthan has left a sturdy architectural legacy of defensive fortresses. These massive buildings evoke the past and are quite rightly the focus of tourists and would-be time travellers.

Delhi The home of Shah Jahan's Red Fort, where the famous Peacock Throne once resided (p44)

Agra View the older and bigger red sandstone fort that was started by Akbar and became the prison of his grandson Shah Jahan (p90)

Chittorgarh A massive citadel capping a mountain plateau – its battle-scarred bastions embrace palaces, temples and towers (p191)

Jodhpur A blue city spread beneath the ramparts of the hulk of Mehrangarh, Rajasthan's most commanding fort (p257)

Jaisalmer Travellers are rewarded with a golden sandstone castle that drifts in the desert and is still inhabited (p275)

Rajasthani Colour

The most vivid impression on visitors to Rajasthan is that of colour: brilliant, bright tribal dress, glittering gold jewellery and rainbow-coloured bangles adorn the locals and illuminate the bazaars. Inside the palaces, *havelis* and even humble homes, this trend continues.

The people of Rajasthan have a passion for decoration, having taken advantage of their position on trade routes to acquire artistic skills from many lands. This passion is evident in the manifold variations of Rajasthani turbans and in the attire of the state's women, from their block-printed *odhnis* (headscarves) right down to their brilliantly embroidered *jootis* (leather shoes). Utilitarian items are transported into the world of art with ceramics such as the famous blue-glazed pottery from Jaipur.

Tie-dyed, block-printed and embroidered textiles and hand-woven carpets are functional yet decorative and colourful. Traditionally, all Rajasthan's textile colours were derived from natural sources such as vegetables, minerals and even insects. Yellow, for instance, came from turmeric and buttermilk; green from banana leaves; orange from saffron and jasmine; blue from the indigo plant; and purple from the kermes insect. Today, however, the majority are synthetically dyed; while they may not possess the subtlety of the traditional tones, they will, at least, stand a better chance in a 40°C machine wash.

THOR VAZ DE LEON

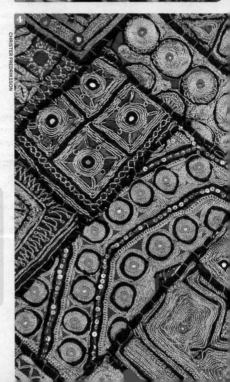

CHRISTER FREDRIKSSON

BEST PLACES TO SEE...

» **Block-printed textiles** Sanganer (p138)
» **Blue pottery** Jaipur (p129)
» **Carpets** Jaipur (p129)
» **Embroidery** Jaisalmer (p287)
» **Jewellery** Jaipur (p129)
» **Miniature Paintings** Udaipur (p211)

Clockwise from top left
1. Carpet weaving, Jodhpur 2. House adorned with mural
3. Block-printing textiles, Jaipur 4. Mirrored embroidery

1. Mosaics
An ornate peacock mosaic is one of many eleborate visual delights within Udaipur's City Palace (p200).

2. Mehndi
Women participate in the *mehndi* (ornate henna) competition during the Shekhawatin Festival (p231).

3. Bracelets

Sparkling bracelets add to a colourful ensemble during the Mewar Festival (p177).

4. Puppets

Puppetry is a dying art in Rajasthan, but these rich characters retain their value as souvenirs.

5. Murals

Detail of one of the distinctive turquoise and gold murals within Bundi Palace (p180).

month by month

Top Events

1 **Pushkar Camel Fair**, October or November

2 **Diwali**, October or November

3 **Jaipur Literature Festival**, January

4 **Jaisalmer Desert Festival**, January or February

5 **Jaipur Elephant Festival**, February or March

Many festivals follow the Indian lunar calendar (a complex system determined by astrologers) or the Islamic calendar (which falls about 11 days earlier each year; 12 days earlier in leap years, and therefore change annually relative to the Gregorian calendar. Contact local tourist offices for exact festival dates, as many are variable.

January

Mid-winter cool lingers throughout the north, and it's downright cold in the desert night air. Pleasant daytime weather and several festivals make it a popular time to travel, so book ahead.

 Kite Festival

Sankranti, the Hindu festival marking the sun's passage across the Tropic of Capricorn, is celebrated in many ways throughout India. In Jaipur it's the mass kite-flying that steals the show.

Jaipur Literature Festival

In just a handful of years the Jaipur Literature Festival (jaipurliteraturefestival. org) has grown into Asia's most talked-about literary feast, attracting local and international authors and poets. Readings, debates and workshops and even the odd controversy keep it energised.

Jaisalmer Desert Festival

A three-day celebration of desert culture, with many events taking place in the Sam sand dunes. Camel races, turban-tying contests, traditional puppetry, folk dances and the famous Mr Desert competition are part of the fun. It may fall in February.

Vasant Panchami

Hindus dress in yellow and place books, musical instruments and other educational objects in front of idols of Saraswati, the goddess of learning, to receive her blessing. It may fall in February.

February

The weather remains comfortable in Delhi and Rajasthan, with very little rain and plenty of festivals. The days are getting marginally warmer but it's still ideal travelling weather.

The Prophet Mohammed's Birthday

The Islamic festival of Eid-e-Milad-un-Nabi celebrates the birth of the Prophet Mohammed with prayers and processions. It falls in the third month of the Islamic calendar: around 4 February (2012), 24 January (2013) and 13 January (2014).

Shivaratri

This day of Hindu fasting recalls the *tandava* (cosmic victory dance) of Lord Shiva. Temple processions are followed by the chanting of mantras and anointing of linga (phallic images symbolising Shiva). Shivaratri can also fall in March.

Jaipur Elephant Festival

Taking place on the day before Holi (and so both can fall in March), the Jaipur Elephant Festival celebrates the pachyderm's place in Indian culture. There are elephant dress parades and competitions such as polo and tug-of-war.

Holi

One of North India's most exuberant festivals; Hindus celebrate the beginning of spring, in either February or March, by throwing coloured water and *gulal* (powder) at anyone within range. On the night before Holi, bonfires symbolise the demise of the demoness Holika.

March

The last month of the main travel season, March sees the last of the cool days of the winter as daytime temperatures creep above 30°C.

Wildlife-Watching

As the weather warms up and water sources dry out, animals tend to congregate at the few remaining sources of water. This can improve your chances of spotting tigers and leopards.

Rama's Birthday

During Ramanavami, which lasts anywhere from one to nine days, Hindus celebrate the birth of Rama with processions, music, fasting and feasting, readings and enactments of scenes from the Ramayana and ceremonial weddings of Rama and Sita idols.

May

The region heats up with daytime temperatures over 40°C. Life slows down as the humidity builds up in anticipation of the monsoon.

Summer Festival

Rajasthan's very own hill station, the delightful Mt Abu, celebrates summer (or perhaps the town's climatological defiance of summer) with a three-day carnival. There are boat races on Nakki Lake, fireworks and traditional music and dances.

Mango Madness

Mangoes are indigenous to India, which might be why they're so ridiculously good here. The season starts in March, but in May the fruit is sweet, juicy and everywhere. A hundred varieties grow here, but the Alphonso is known as 'king'.

July

Now it's really raining, with many a dusty road becoming an impassable quagmire. But you may be tempted by the reduced accommodation rates and smaller crowds.

Brothers and Sisters

On Raksha Bandhan (Narial Purnima), girls fix amulets known as *rakhis* to the wrists of brothers and close male friends to protect them in the coming year. Brothers reciprocate with gifts and promises to take care of their sisters.

Ramadan (Ramazan)

Thirty days of dawn-to-dusk fasting mark the ninth month of the Islamic calendar. Muslims traditionally turn their attention to God, with a focus on prayer and purification. Ramadan begins around 20 July (2012), 9 July (2013) and 28 June (2014).

August

It's very much monsoon season and the relief is palpable. In a good season there's copious but not constant rainfall, and temperatures are noticeably lower but still steamy.

Independence Day

This public holiday on 15 August marks the anniversary of India's independence from Britain in 1947. Celebrations are a countrywide expression of patriotism, with flag-hoisting ceremonies – the biggest one is in Delhi – parades and patriotic cultural programs.

Teej

The festival of Teej celebrates the arrival of the monsoon and of the marriage of Parvati to Shiva. Three-day celebrations across Rajasthan, particularly Jaipur, culminate in a street procession of the Teej idol.

Eid al-Fitr

Muslims celebrate the end of Ramadan with three days of festivities, starting 30 days after the start of the fast.

September

The rain begins to ease, though temperatures are still high. By the end of September, Rajasthan and Delhi are all but finished with the monsoon.

Ganesh's Birthday

Hindus celebrate Ganesh Chaturthi, the birth of the elephant-headed god, with verve, particularly in Ranthambhore Fort (p171). Thousands gather at the abandoned fort and clay idols of Ganesh are paraded. Ganesh Chaturthi may also be in August.

Navratri

This Hindu 'Festival of Nine Nights' leading up to Dussehra celebrates the goddess Durga in all her incarnations. Special dances are performed, and the goddesses Lakshmi and Saraswati are also celebrated. Festivities are particularly vibrant in Gujarat and Maharashtra. Navratri may fall in October.

Dussehra

Colourful Dussehra celebrates the victory of the Hindu god Rama over the demon-king Ravana and the triumph of good over evil. Dussehra is big in Kota (p186), where effigies of Ravana are ritually burned. This festival may fall in October.

October

Occasional heavy showers aside, this is when North India starts to get its travel mojo on. October brings festivals, national park openings and more comfortable temperatures, with post-monsoon lushness.

Gandhi's Birthday

The national holiday of Gandhi Jayanti is a solemn celebration of Mohandas Gandhi's birth, on 2 October, with prayer meetings at his cremation site in Delhi (Raj Ghat; p49). Schools and businesses close for the day.

Dewali

In the lunar month of Kartika, in October or November, Hindus celebrate Diwali (Deepavali) for five days, giving gifts, lighting fireworks, and burning lamps to lead Lord Rama home from exile. This is India's main holiday time and it is hard to get a seat or a room without a booking.

November

The climate is blissful, with warm days and cooler nights. The peak season is getting into full swing. Lower temperatures mean higher prices and more tourist buses.

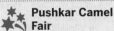 Pushkar Camel Fair

Rajasthan's premier cultural event takes place in the Hindu lunar month of Kartika (October or November). As well as camel trading, there is horse and cattle trading and an amazing fairground atmosphere. It culminates with ritual bathing in Pushkar's holy lake.

December

December is peak tourist season for a reason: the daytime weather is glorious, the humidity is low and the nights are cool. The mood is festive and it seems everyone is getting married.

Weddings!

Marriage season peaks in December, and you may see a *baraat* (bridegroom's procession), replete with white horse and brass band, on your travels. Across the country, loud music and spectacular parties are the way they roll, with brides in *mehndi* (orante henna) and pure gold.

Bird-watching

Many of India's spectacular winter migrants complete their winter travels and have set up nesting colonies. Keoladeo Ghana National Park (p148) is an internationally renowned wetland and bird-watching mecca.

Camel Treks in Rajasthan

The cool winter (November to February) is the time to mount a camel and ride through the Rajasthani sands. See the Thar Desert from a whole new perspective: observe gazelles, make dinner over an open fire and camp out in the dunes.

itineraries

Whether you've got six days or 60, these itineraries provide a starting point for the trip of a lifetime. Want more inspiration? Head online to lonelyplanet. com/thorntree to chat with other travellers.

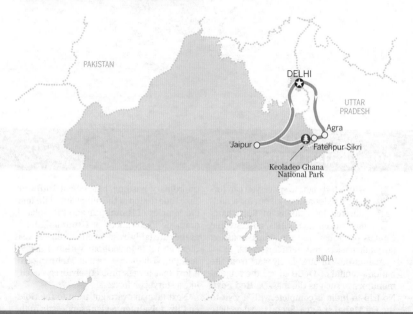

One Week
The Golden Triangle

> One route is so well loved it even has a name: the Golden Triangle. This classic Delhi–Agra–Jaipur trip can be squeezed into a single week.

Spend a day or two in **Delhi** finding your feet and seeing the big-draw sights, such as the magnificent Mughal **Red Fort** and **Jama Masjid**, India's largest mosque. Then catch a convenient train to **Agra** to spend a day being awed by the world's most extravagant monument to love, the **Taj Mahal**, and exploring the mighty **Agra Fort**. Only an hour away is **Fatehpur Sikri**, a beautiful Mughal city dating from the apogee of Mughal power. It is amazingly well preserved and deserves a full day of exploring.

If you have time, take a rural respite at **Keoladeo Ghana National Park**, one of the world's foremost bird reserves. Having relaxed at this beautiful and rewarding place, you can then take a train to **Jaipur**. Spend a couple of days in and around Rajasthan's hectic, dusky-pink capital, seeing the **City Palace** and **Amber Fort**, and stocking up on blue pottery, dazzling jewellery and Rajasthani puppets before heading back to Delhi.

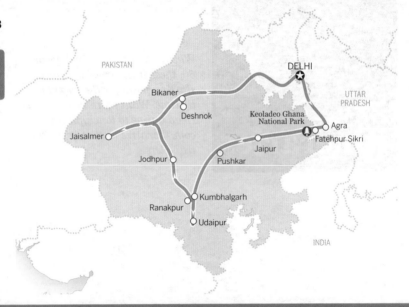

Two Weeks
Royal Rajasthan

With a fortnight to spare, you can forget triangles and go all out for a multifaceted loop taking in Rajasthan's most spectacular cities, all erstwhile capitals of former princely states, boasting fairy-tale palaces and stern fortresses.

Again, you will most likely start from the nation's capital of **Delhi** to see the Mughal monuments, such as the massive **Red Fort**. No trip to India is complete with a visit to the **Taj Mahal** at **Agra**. Spend two days here viewing the Taj during the day, at night and from the maze-like **Agra Fort**. Spend a day exploring the ghost city of **Fatehpur Sikri**, before heading to the bird-watching mecca that is at **Keoladeo Ghana National Park**. Next stop is the pink city of **Jaipur** where you will want to spend two or three days exploring the palaces of Jaipur and **Amber**.

From Jaipur, take a short trip to the sacred lake of **Pushkar**, where you can release your inner hippie or attend the camel fair. Move on to the romantic lake-town of **Udaipur**, visiting the fine **City Palace** and the impressive **Jagdish Temple** as well as doing some shopping and relaxing on rooftops while peering at the lake and its famous palace. From Udaipur head towards the ex-

traordinary, bustling, blue city of **Jodhpur**. Take time to stop at the milk-white Jain temple complex of **Ranakpur** and the isolated, dramatic fortifications of **Kumbhalgarh** – as they are fairly close together, you can visit them en route to Jodhpur within a day. In Jodhpur, visit the spectacular **Mehrangarh**, a fort that towers protectively over the city like a storybook fortress.

Next take an overnight train to the Golden City, **Jaisalmer**, a giant sandcastle in the desert, with its beautiful Jain temples and exquisite merchants' *havelis* (traditional, ornately decorated mansions). Take a short camel safari through the bewitching landscape of sweeping dunes and sleep under the stars. If you have the time, break your journey back to Delhi with a stop in the desert city of **Bikaner**, home of the impregnable **Junagarh Fort**, and nearest city to the famous rat temple of **Deshnok**.

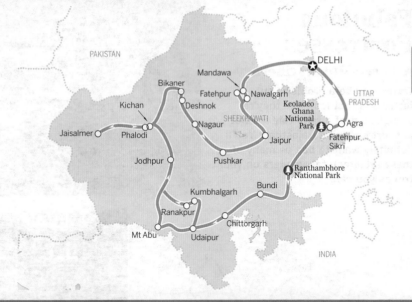

A Month-Long Sojourn

After arriving in **Delhi** and exploring the city sights, take the train down to **Agra** to gaze at the picture-perfect **Taj Mahal**, explore **Agra Fort** and have a day-trip out to the abandoned Mughal city of **Fatehpur Sikri**. To experience Rajasthan's wild side, first head to the World Heritage–listed bird-watching paradise of **Keoladeo Ghana National Park**, where the sheer numbers of nesting birdlife will astound you. This can be followed by a tiger safari or three at **Ranthambhore National Park**, one of your best bets of spotting a tiger in all India.

Take a Kota-bound train southwest for a stop at the charming small town of **Bundi**, to explore the crumbling palace. From here, it is a short train ride to **Chittorgarh** where one of Rajasthan's most impressive fortresses occupies a mountain plateau. Next stop is **Udaipur**, where you can relax from your travels with a few easy days of sightseeing, elegant dining and souvenir shopping.

From Udaipur it's worth side-tripping to **Mt Abu** to see the magnificent **Dilwara Temples** before going north to **Jodhpur**. Alternatively, head north to Jodhpur, stopping on the way to see the Jain temples of **Ranakpur** and the magnificent fort at **Kumbhalgarh**. From Jodhpur it's an easy train or bus ride to **Jaisalmer**, the desert town with a romantic picturesque fort rising from the golden sands. Here you can spend a few days exploring *havelis* and palaces, before taking an overnight camel trek into the desert. After Jaisalmer, head to **Bikaner** via **Phalodi** and **Kichan**, where you can observe the fearless flocks of the village's renowned demoiselle cranes.

Travel south from Bikaner, stopping at the fascinating rat temple of **Deshnok** and the sleepy cattle-fair town of **Nagaur** before coming to rest at the sacred pilgrimage town of **Pushkar**. At Pushkar you may be in time for the famous camel festival; otherwise, just put your feet up for a few days and soak in the serenity.

From Pushkar it's a short hop to **Jaipur** with its fabulous citadel at Amber and great shopping. Head north to **Shekhawati** for a few days, inspecting *havelis* at **Mandawa**, **Nawalgarh** and **Fatehpur**, before returning to Delhi.

Fabulous Fortresses

A Three-Week Itinerary

Water may be a problem, but fortresses that look like they're straight out of a fairy tale are not in short supply in Rajasthan. You'll definitely want to bag as many of these architectural wonders on your trip as you can.

» Start your fort appreciation in **Delhi** (p38), with the city-centre Red Fort introducing you to massive Mughal architecture.

» Head south to **Agra** (p86), where the red-sandstone Agra Fort has exquisite architecture and views to the Taj Mahal.

» From Agra, it is a short day-trip to the fortified ghost city of **Fatehpur Sikri** (p102).

» Spend a couple of days in **Jaipur** (p105) to visit the citadel of Amber and the ridge-top forts of Jaigarh and Nahargarh.

» For something straight out of the *Jungle Book,* head to **Ranthambhore National Park** (p171), where Ranthambhore Fort perches on a craggy mountain, surrounded by jungle (and the odd tiger).

» Slow down the pace at **Bundi** (p180), where Taragarh is an overgrown, crumbling fortress for a ramble.

» Take the train to **Chittorgarh** (p178), where Rajasthan's most legendary fort covers a mountain plateau.

» Even more evocative is **Kumbhalgarh** (p216), a remote edifice between the tourist centres of Udaipur and Jodhpur.

» The prize for most dramatic fort goes to Mehrangarh in **Jodhpur** (p253), rising from a sheer rock above a blue-washed city.

» Looking like an *Arabian Nights* movie set is the still-inhabited, golden-sandstone fortress in the desert city of **Jaisalmer** (p275).

» On the way back to Delhi, drop into **Bikaner** (p292), where the never-conquered Junagarh boasts spectacular interiors.

Clockwise from top left
1. Mehrangarh, Jodhpur 2. Jaisalmer Fort, Jaisalmer
3. Agra Fort, Agra

Travel with Children

Best Regions for Kids

Agra & Fatehpur Sikri
Give them a few stories of the Arabian Nights before they lay eyes on the Taj Mahal and let their imaginations soar. A visit to nearby Fatehpur Sikri will also please the creative young mind.

Keoladeo Ghana National Park
Here, the kids can let go of your hand and jump on a bike. Let them ride along the car-free road and tick off as many feathered species as they can.

Ranthambhore National Park
What kid won't be thrilled to see a wild tiger? And to top it off there's a mesmerising jungle fortress straight out of Kipling's *Jungle Book* to explore.

Amber
The highlight for young and old at Amber will probably be the elephant ride to the entrance of the glorious citadel.

Sam Sand Dunes
Riding a camel across the sand dunes should be easy after mastering an elephant...surely?

Fascinating, frustrating, thrilling and fulfilling – India is as much of an adventure for children as it is for parents. Though the sensory overload may be, at times, overwhelming for younger kids, the colours, scents, sights and sounds of India more than compensate by setting young imaginations ablaze. Gaze at riotous Diwali fireworks, tuck into family-sized thalis at a bus station lunch joint or ride a camel through the dunes: moments like these can make the predictable aches and pains of Indian travel worthwhile. Taking your children along for the ride will create fantastic childhood memories and foster a lasting fascination and fondness for this incredible, riotous country.

India for Kids

Being a family-oriented society, India is a very child-friendly destination. That doesn't necessarily translate into a travelling-with-children-friendly destination, however. Smaller children, in particular, will be constantly coddled, offered treats and smiles and warm welcomes. And while all this is fabulous for outgoing children it may prove tiring, or even disconcerting or frightening, for those of a more retiring disposition. Remember, though, that the attention your children will inevitably receive is almost always good-natured; kids are the centre of life in many Indian households, and your own will be treated – usually for better rather than worse – just the same.

Before You Go
Remember to visit your doctor to discuss vaccinations, health advisories and other health-related issues involving your children well in advance of travel. For helpful hints, see Lonely Planet's *Travel with Children*, and the Kids To Go section of Lonely Planet's Thorn Tree forum (lonelyplanet.com/thorntree).

What to pack
If you're travelling with a baby or toddler, there are several items worth packing in quantity: nappies, nappy rash cream, extra bottles, wet wipes, infant formula and jars or dehydrated packets of favourite foods. You can get these items in many parts of India too, but often at premium prices and brands may be unfamiliar. Another good idea is a fold-up baby bed; a pushchair, though, is superfluous, since there are few places with pavements even enough to use it. For older children, make sure you bring sturdy footwear, a hat, child-friendly insect repellent and sun lotion.

Eating

Feeding your brood is fairly easy in the well-touristed parts of India and you'll find Western dishes with a bit of searching. Look out for multicuisine restaurants, should your little one be saying: 'Not curry again.'

Adventurous eaters will delight in experimenting with a vast range of tastes and textures: paneer (unfermented cheese) dishes, simple dhal (curried lentil dish), creamy korma, buttered naan (tandoor-baked bread), pilau (rice) and *momos* (steamed or fried dumplings) are all firm favourites. Few children, no matter how culinarily unadventurous, can resist the finger-food fun of a vast South Indian *dosa* (rice pancake).

Sleeping

India offers such an array of accommodation – from budget boxes to former palaces of the maharajas – that you're bound to be able to find something that will appeal to the whole family. Hotels will almost always come up with an extra bed or two for a nominal charge. Most places won't mind fitting one or maybe two children into a regular-sized double room along with their parents. Any more is pushing your luck – look for two rooms that have an adjoining door.

On the Road

Travel in India can be arduous for the whole family. Plan fun, easy days to follow longer car, bus or train rides, and pack plenty of diversions. Portable iPods and iPads or laptops with a stock of movies downloaded make invaluable travel companions, as do books, light toys and games. The golden rule is to expect your best-laid plans to take a hit every now and then. Travelling on the road with kids in India requires constant vigilance. Be especially cautious of road traffic – pedestrians are at the bottom of the feeding chain and road rules are routinely ignored.

Health

A decent standard of healthcare, even in the most traveller-frequented parts of India, is not as easily available as you might be used to. The recommended way to track down a doctor at short notice is through your hotel. In general, the most common concerns for on-the-road parents include heat rash, skin complaints such as impetigo, insect bites or stings and diarrhoea. If your child takes special medication, bring along an adequate stock in case it's not easily found locally. For more information on health, see p371.

Children's Highlights
Fortress Splendours

» Jaipur – Take an elephant ride into the majestic citadel of Amber.

» Jaisalmer – Re-create the *Arabian Nights* in Jaisalmer's desert fortress.

» Jodhpur – Amaze their imaginations with the story-book fort and palace.

Cats & Birds

» Ranthambhore National Park – Tigers, jungles, jeep safaris and an abandoned mountain-top fort.

» Keoladeo Ghana National Park – The chance to go cycling on car-free roads.

regions at a glance

Delhi

Mughal Sites ✓✓
Bazaars ✓✓
Food ✓

Mughal Sites
Wander around Delhi's sprawling Red Fort and Jama Masjid, and the streets of labyrinthine Old Delhi, and you'll soon gain a sense of the glories of the Mughal empire. Humayan's domed tomb was the precursor to the Taj Mahal.

Bazaars
All of India's riches sparkle in Delhi's bazaars and emporiums but you need to be prepared to haggle. You can also browse designer boutiques, 19th-century musical instrument shops and some of the country's best bookstores.

Food
Delhi is one of the better places in India to taste everything from cutting-edge creative Indian cuisine in luscious five-star hotels, to fresh-from-the-fire, delectable *Dilli-ka-chaat* (Delhi street food).

p38

Agra

Architecture ✓✓✓
History ✓✓✓
Shopping ✓✓

Architecture
The Taj Mahal is as breathtakingly proportioned and serenely beautiful as the brochures would have you believe. Follow its moods throughout the day and into the night with a viewing under a full moon.

Mughal History
Peering at the Taj from where Shah Jahan was imprisoned in Agra Fort gives a whole new perspective to the famous tomb. While wandering the empty spaces of Fatehpur Sikri, Emperor Akbar's spectacular but poorly sited city is also evocative.

Shopping
Agra is renowned for marble items inlaid with semi-precious stones, recreating the amazing pietra dura work that embellishes the Taj Mahal.

p86

Jaipur

Palaces ✓✓✓
Arts & Crafts ✓✓✓
Festivals ✓✓

Palaces
The Rajput palaces of Jaipur and Amber demonstrate the wealth and power of the former royals. They boast magnificent architecture and accessories such as the Hawa Mahal and Jantar Mantar.

Arts & Crafts
The maharajas of Jaipur bestowed great importance on the arts, and generations later many of artisans of the very same castes ply their skilled trade in crafts such as jewellery, pottery, carpet weaving and embroidery.

Festivals
Jaipur is a great place to witness national celebrations such as Teej and Diwali – viewing the city's fireworks from Nahargarh is unforgettable. Jaipur's own festivals include its famous literature festival.

p105

Eastern Rajasthan

Festivals ✓✓✓
Wildlife ✓✓✓
Forts, Palaces ✓✓

Festivals
Heading the list is the celebrated camel fair in the tiny Hindu pilgrimage town of Pushkar. It is a very different scene at the Urs, the anniversary of the death of a sufi saint in nearby Ajmer.

Wildlife
Your chance of seeing a tiger is pretty decent in Ranthambhore National Park. Some of the park's tigers have been transferred to Sariska Tiger Reserve. Birdwatchers should make a bee-line to Keoladeo Ghana National Park.

Forts & Palaces
Ranthambhore National Park protects the ancient, jungle-clad Ranthambhore Fort, while Suraj Mahl's Palace in Deeg is set in manicured pleasure-palace gardens.

p141

Udaipur & Southern Rajasthan

Forts, Palaces ✓✓
Temples ✓✓
Romance ✓✓

Forts & Palaces
Chittorgarh, Rajasthan's greatest fortress, sprawls over a mountain plateau and its stories epitomise Rajput chivalry and aggression – as does remote Kumbhalgarh. Bundi's crumbling palace assumes a gentler pose.

Temples
The flawless Jain temples of Mt Abu and Ranakpur are simply stunning in their intricate stone carving and are an amazing salute to this gentlest of religions.

Romance
The Lake Palace in Udaipur is a showy film star where you can experience the romance in situ or from afar while enjoying the view from one of Udaipur's rooftop restaurants.

p176

Northern Rajasthan (Shekhawati)

Havelis ✓✓✓
Murals ✓✓✓
Rural life ✓

Havelis
The extraordinary *havelis* of Shekhawati are both an anomalous display of wealth in an arid corner and an amazing canvas portraying the changing life of India.

Murals
Inside and outside the *havelis* of Shekhawati are murals depicting the ancient Hindu texts, the everyday life of the residents and fanciful European devices.

Rural Life
Shekhawati is one of the least visited regions in Rajasthan and it's also one of the best places in India to experience and learn from the local culture still so deeply rooted in tradition and the land.

p229

Jaisalmer, Jodhpur & Western Rajasthan

Deserts ✓✓✓
Forts ✓✓✓
Camels ✓✓✓

Desert
The sweeping, sand-dune vistas around Jaisalmer's Sam sand dunes are picture-perfect for your Arabian Nights fantasy.

Forts
Just when you think you have seen them all, up pops Mehrangarh, the hulking giant of a fortress that broods over Jodhpur. And looking like a set from a Indiana Jones film, Jaisalmer's golden-sandstone citadel leaves you feeling like a movie star.

Camels
Not only can you take an overnight camel safari into the desert from either Jaisalmer or Bikaner, you can also do a crash-course in 'camel-ology' at Bikaner's National Research Centre on Camels.

p252

Look out for these icons:

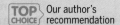 Our author's recommendation

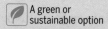 A green or sustainable option

See the Index for a full list of destinations covered in this book.

On the Road

Delhi

Best Places to Eat

» Saravana Bhavan (p71)

» Bukhara (p72)

» Indian Accent (p74)

» Monsoon (p72)

» Olive (p74)

» Gunpowder (p73)

» Rajdhani (p71)

Best Places to Stay

» Shanti Home (p67)

» Devna (p68)

» Bnineteen (p68)

» Cottage Yes Please (p65)

Why Go?

Medieval mayhem, the New India, stately maiden aunt: give it a chance and this schizophrenic capital could capture your heart. Yes, it's aggravating, polluted and hectic, but hey – nobody's perfect.

Like a subcontinental Rome, India's capital is punctuated by vestiges of lost empires: ancient forts freckle the suburbs; Old Delhi was once the capital of Islamic India; the British built New Delhi, with its exaggerated avenues; and even-newer Delhi features utopian malls linked by potholed roads. These disparate, codependent elements are all now gloriously intertwined via the new metro system.

There are also magnificent museums, temples, mosques, and a busy cultural scene – and shopaholics, you are home: all the riches of India twinkle in Delhi's emporiums.

Prepare yourself to tuck into some of the subcontinent's finest food, including the famous *Dilli-ka-Chaat* (Delhi street food) – which, rather like the city itself, jumbles up every flavour in one bite.

When to Go

Delhi has an extreme climate, with hot summers and cold winters. It's at its best from October to March, when the weather is bright and sunny but not too hot. May to August are the months to avoid, when it's hot and humid, and the monsoon season, with rains starting in June and at their heaviest from July to September, is worth avoiding if you can.

Top Tips

» Ensure your taxi or autorickshaw driver has taken you to the hotel/shop you requested, as some try to offload passengers at places where they receive commission.

» Decline offers from taxi or auto drivers to take you to hotels/shops of their choice.

» Avoid chatty young men who hang around touristy spots, some of whom claim humbly to be students wanting to improve their English.

» Don't believe the helpful chaps who try to direct you to a 'tourist office' around Connaught Place. There is only one Government of India tourist office, at 88 Janpath.

» Carry small denominations (below ₹50) as drivers often have a lack of change.

» Ignore touts who surreptitiously dirty your shoe and offer to clean it at a price.

DON'T MISS

One of Delhi's most mystical and atmospheric experiences is to hear *qawwali* singers and musicians perform devotional songs at the Hazrat Nizam-ud-din Dargah (p51). This is a beautiful Islamic holy shrine, where song performances take place after sunset prayers on Thursday. The air is thick with incense and the shrine thronged with pilgrims.

Delhi's Top Festivals

» To check dates contact India Tourism Delhi (p80).

» Delhi celebrates **Diwali** and Dussehra (Durga Puja) with particular verve.

» **Republic Day** (26 January, Rajpath, p53) Incorporates a spectacular military parade.

» **Beating of the Retreat** (29 January, Rajpath, p53) The closing of the Republic Day celebrations is marked by the Beating of the Retreat – more military pageantry. Tickets are essential for both events and are available at India Tourism Delhi.

» **Independence Day** (15 August, Red Fort, p44) India celebrates its Independence from Britain in 1947 and the prime minister addresses the nation from the Red Fort ramparts.

» **Qutb Festival** (October/November, Qutb Minar, p84) Held over several days, featuring Sufi singing and classical dance performances.

» **Delhi International Arts Festival** (DIAF, December) Three weeks of exhibitions, performing arts, films, literature and culinary events at Delhi-wide venues.

MAIN POINTS OF ENTRY

Indira Gandhi International Airport, New Delhi train station, Old Delhi train station, and the Inter State Bus Terminal (ISBT).

Fast Facts

» **Population** 12.8 million

» **Area** 1483 sq km

» **Area code** ☏011

» **Main languages** Hindi and English

» **Sleeping price indicators** $ below ₹1000, $$ ₹1000 to ₹5000, $$$ above ₹5000

Planning Your Trip

» Book accommodation ahead at http://hotels.lonelyplanet.com

» Call your hotel to confirm the day before you arrive

» Book train tickets for longer journeys at least a week ahead on www.indianrail.gov.in

Resources

» Delhi Tourism (http://delhitourism.nic.in/delhi tourism/index.jsp) lists government-rated home-stays and recommended tourist agencies.

» A free AA map is available in many places but, for street-by-street detail, Delhi newsstands sell the excellent 245-page *Eicher City Map* (₹340).

Delhi Highlights

1 Experience the sometime splendour of the **Red Fort** (p44), a sandstone queen bee overlooking the Old Delhi hive

2 See the great Mughal tomb that inspired the Taj Mahal, **Humayun's Tomb** (p49)

3 Explore the greenery-surrounded **Qutb Minar** (p84), in a Delhi suburb.

4 Hear qawwali singers at **Hazrat Nizam-ud-din Dargah** (p51)

5 Sample delicious **Dilli-ka-Chaat** (p69), Delhi's famous street food

6 Take an early-morning ride around Old Delhi with **DelhiByCycle** (p62), ending at **Karim's** (p69)

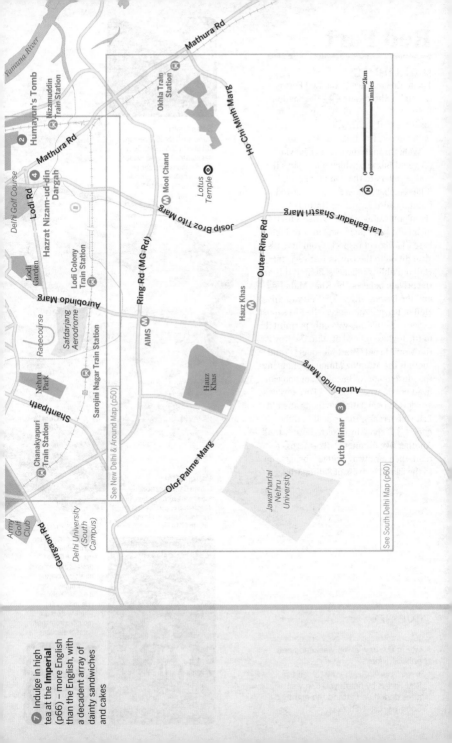

7 Indulge in high tea at the **Imperial** (p66) – more English than the English, with a decadent array of dainty sandwiches and cakes

Red Fort

HIGHLIGHTS

The main entrance to the Red Fort is through Lahore Gate **1** – the bastion in front of it was built by Aurangzeb for increased security. You can still see bullet marks from 1857 on the gate.

Walk through the Chatta Chowk (Covered Bazaar), which once sold silks and jewellery to the nobility; beyond it lies Naubat Khana **2**, a russet-red building, also known as Hathi Pol (Elephant Gate) because visitors used to dismount from their elephants or horses here as a sign of respect. From here it's straight on to the Diwan-i-Am **3**, the Hall of Public Audiences. Behind this are the private palaces, the Khas Mahal **4** and the Diwan-i-Khas **5**. Entry to this Hall of Private Audiences, the fort's most expensive building, was only permitted to the highest official of state. Nearby is the Moti Masjid (Pearl Mosque) **6** and south is the Mumtaz Mahal **7**, housing the Museum of Archaeology, or you can head north, where the Red Fort gardens are dotted by palatial pavilions and old British barracks. Here you'll find the *baoli* **8**, a spookily deserted water tank. Another five minutes' walk – across a road, then a railway bridge – brings you to the island fortress of Salimgarh **9**.

Salimgarh
Salimgarh is the 16th-century fort built by Salim Shah Sur. It was constructed on an island of the Yamuna River and only recently opened to the public. It is still partly used by the Indian army.

Chatta Chowk

Lahore Gate
Lahore Gate is particularly significant, as it was here that Jawaharlal raised the first tricolour flag of independent India in 1947.

Naubat Khana
The Naubat Khana (Drum House) is carved in floral designs and featured musicians playing in the upper gallery. It housed Hathi Pol (Elephant Gate), where visitors dismounted from their horse or elephant.

Baoli
The Red Fort step well is seldom visited and is a hauntingly deserted place, even more so when you consider its chambers were used as cells by the British from August 1942.

Moti Masjid
The Moti Masjid (Pearl Mosque) was built by Aurangzeb in 1662 for his personal use. The domes were originally covered in copper, but the copper was removed and sold by the British.

Diwan-i-Khas
This was the most expensive building in the fort, consisting of white marble decorated with inlay work of cornelian and other stones. The screens overlooking what was once the river (now the ring road) were filled with coloured glass.

Baidon Pavilion

Zafar Mahal

Hammam

Rang Mahal

Mumtaz Mahal

5

6

4

3

2

7

Pit Stop
To refuel, head to Paratha Gali Wali, a food-stall-lined lane off Chandni Chowk noted for its many varieties of freshly made *paratha* (traditional flat bread).

← NORTH

Delhi Gate

Diwan-i-Am
These red sandstone columns were once covered in shell plaster, as polished and smooth as ivory, and in hot weather heavy red curtains were hung around the columns to block out the sun. It's believed the panels behind the marble throne were created by Florentine jeweller Austin de Bordeaux.

Khas Mahal
Most spectacular in the Emperor's private apartments is a beautiful marble screen at the northern end of the rooms; the 'Scales of Justice' are carved above it, suspended over a crescent, surrounded by stars and clouds.

DELHI IN...

Two Days

Acclimatise gently at tranquil sites, such as the **National Museum** (p52), **Gandhi Smriti** (p55) and **Humayun's Tomb** (p49). In the evening head to **Hazrat Nizam-ud-din Dargah** (p51) to hear the Sufis sing *qawwalis*.

On day two, ramble around Old Delhi's **Red Fort** (p44), then scoff *jalebis* (fried sweet 'squiggles'), launch into the old city's action-packed **bazaars** (p77) and visit the mighty **Jama Masjid** (p48). Afterwards, grab an autorickshaw south to **Connaught Place** (p57) for a bite to **eat** (p71) and to explore the hassle-free, treasure-trove **government emporiums** (p77).

Four Days

Follow the itinerary above, then on the third day wander around **Qutb Minar** (p84) and **Mehrauli** (p85) before indulging in some quiet meditation at the **Bahai House of Worship** (p57). In the evening, watch the mesmerising **Dances of India** (p76), then kick back at a **bar** (p74).

On day four, wonder at the glories in the laid-back **Crafts Museum** (p52) and nearby **Purana Qila** (p55). Then head to **Hauz Khas** (p59) to wander around the forgotten tank and mausoleum, and browse in its boutiques.

History

Delhi hasn't always been India's capital but, as a gateway city, it has long played a pivotal role. It was built on the plains near a fording point on the Yamuna River, and on the route between western and Central Asia and Southeast Asia. It's believed to be the site of the fabled city of Indraprastha, which featured in the Mahabharata more than 3000 years ago, but historical evidence suggests that the area has been settled for a mere 2500 years.

At least eight known cities have been founded here. The first four cities of Delhi were to the south, around the area where the Qutb Minar now stands. The fifth Delhi, Firozabad, was at Firoz Shah Kotla, while Emperor Sher Shah created the sixth at Purana Qila (both in present-day New Delhi). The Mughal emperor, Shah Jahan, constructed the seventh Delhi in the 17th century; his Shahjahanabad roughly corresponds to Old Delhi today. In 1911, the British announced the shifting of their capital from Kolkata (Calcutta) and proceeded to build New Delhi, which was inaugurated in 1931. Only 16 years later, the British were out, and Delhi became the capital of an independent India.

Since Independence, the capital has prospered. The downside of this boom is chronic overcrowding, housing shortages, pollution, traffic congestion, and ever more extreme contrasts between rich and poor.

⊙ Sights

Most sights in Delhi are easily accessible via metro. Note that many places are closed on Monday.

OLD DELHI

Medieval-seeming Old Delhi is a crazy hubbub that bombards the senses. Set aside at least half a day to do this fascinating area justice. All of the following attractions feature on Map p46.

Red Fort (Lal Qila) FORT
(Indian/foreigner ₹10/250, video ₹25, combined museum ticket ₹5; ⊙9am-6pm Tue-Sun; ⓂChandni Chowk) This massive fort is a sandstone shadow of its former self; but it's the best place in Delhi to imagine the Mughal city's sometime splendour. It dates from the peak of the dynasty's power, a time of unparalleled pomp: of eunuchs, ceremonial elephants, palanquins, and buildings lined with precious stones.

The walls of the fort extend for 2km and vary in height from 18m on the river side to 33m on the city side. Shah Jahan constructed the fort between 1638 and 1648, but never completely moved his capital from Agra to his new city of Shahjahanabad, because he was deposed and imprisoned in Agra Fort by his son Aurangzeb.

Mughal reign from Delhi was short; Aurangzeb was the first and last great Mughal emperor to rule from here. Subsequent rulers, sapped by civil war, were unable to maintain the fort properly, and slums within the walls were thronged with impoverished imperial descendants. By the 19th century it was already much dilapidated. Following the 1857 First War of Independence, the British cleared all but the most important buildings to make way for ugly barracks and army offices.

The 10m-deep moat, which has been dry since 1857, was originally crossed on creaky wooden drawbridges, replaced with stone bridges in 1811.

Since Independence many landmark political speeches have taken place at the fort, and every year on Independence Day (15 August) it hosts the prime minister's address to the nation.

Lahore Gate

The fort's main gate is so named because it faces towards Lahore, now in Pakistan. The gate is a potent symbol of modern India: during the fight for Independence, there was a nationalist aspiration to see the Indian flag flying over the gate – a dream that became reality in 1947.

You enter the fort through here and immediately find yourself in the vaulted arcade known as the **Chatta Chowk** (Covered Bazaar). The tourist-trap arcade once sold rather more exclusive items to the royal household – silks, jewellery and gold.

The arcade leads to the **Naubat Khana** (Drum House), where musicians used to perform. There's an **Indian War Memorial Museum** upstairs, full of fearsome weaponry and phallic shells.

Diwan-i-Am

In the **Hall of Public Audiences** the emperor would hear disputes from his subjects. Many of the precious stones set above the emperor's throne were looted following the First War of Independence. The hall was restored following a directive by Lord Curzon, the viceroy of India between 1898 and 1905.

Diwan-i-Khas

The white marble **Hall of Private Audiences** was the luxurious chamber where the emperor would hold private meetings. The centrepiece was once the magnificent solid-gold and jewel-studded Peacock Throne, looted from India by Persia's Nadir Shah in 1739. In 1760 the Marathas removed the hall's silver ceiling.

Royal Baths

Next to the Diwan-i-Khas are the hammams (baths) – three large rooms surmounted by domes, with a fountain in the centre – one of which was set up as a sauna. The floors were once inlaid with more pietra dura and the rooms were illuminated through stained-glass roof panels.

Shahi Burj

This modest, three-storey, octagonal tower to the northeastern edge of the fort was once Shah Jahan's private working area. From here, cooling water, known as the *nahr-i-bihisht* (river of paradise), used to flow south through the Royal Baths, the Diwan-i-Khas, the Khas Mahal and on to the Rang Mahal.

Moti Masjid

The small, enclosed, marble **Pearl Mosque** is next to the baths. Its outer walls are oriented exactly in symmetry with the rest of the fort, while the inner walls are slightly askew, so that the mosque is correctly orientated to Mecca.

Other Features

The **Khas Mahal**, south of the Diwan-i-Khas, was the emperor's private palace. It was divided into rooms for worship, sleeping and living, with carved walls and painted ceilings.

The **Rang Mahal** (Palace of Colour), further south again, took its name from its vividly painted interior, now long gone. This was the residence of the emperor's chief wife and is where he dined. On the floor in the centre there's an exquisitely carved marble lotus; the water flowing along the channel from the Shahi Burj would end up here.

Relics from the Mughal era are displayed at the **Museum of Archaeology** in the **Mumtaz Mahal**, once the women's quarters, still further south along the eastern wall. In one of the British-built barracks there's also the interesting **Museum of India's Struggle for Freedom**, with some dramatic life-size dioramas,

It's worth seeking out the deserted **baoli** (step well). A short walk away is **Salimgarh** (☉10am-5pm) built by Salim Shah Suri in 1546. Few visitors make it over here to see the ruined mosque and broad, much restored walls – it's still partly occupied by the Indian army and was only opened to the public in 2008.

The old walled city of **Shahjahanabad** stretches west from the Red Fort. It was at one time surrounded by a sturdy defensive wall, only fragments of which now exist. The **Kashmiri Gate**, to the north, was the scene of desperate fighting when the British retook Delhi during the 1857 First War of Independence.

DELHI

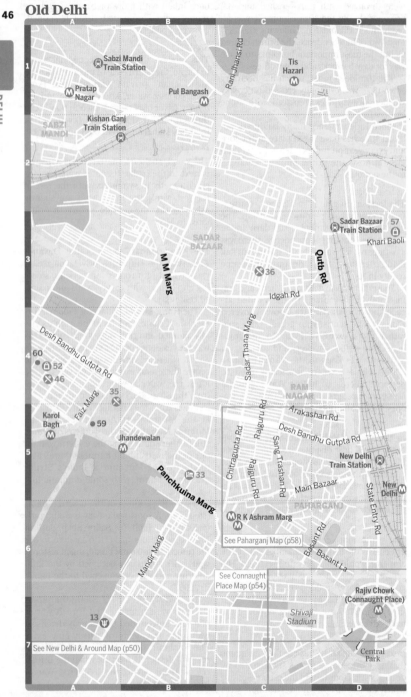

Sabzi Mandi Train Station

Pratap Nagar

Pul Bangash

Ram Jhansi Rd

Tis Hazari

Kishan Ganj Train Station

SABZI MANDI

SADAR BAZAAR

M M Marg

Qutb Rd

Sadar Bazaar Train Station 57

Khari Baoli

⊗ 36

Idgah Rd

Sadar Thana Marg

Desh Bandhu Gutpta Rd

60
⊕ 52
⊗ 46

Faiz Marg

35 ⊗

RAM NAGAR

Arakashan Rd

Karol Bagh

• 59

Jhandewalan

Chitragupta Rd

Rajguru Rd

Pul Bangash

Sang Trashan Rd

Desh Bandhu Gutpta Rd

New Delhi Train Station

State Entry Rd

New Delhi

33

Panchkuina Marg

Main Bazaar

PAHARGANJ

R K Ashram Marg

See Paharganj Map (p58)

Mandir Marg

Basant Rd

Basant La

See Connaught Place Map (p54)

Rajiv Chowk (Connaught Place)

Shivaji Stadium

13

See New Delhi & Around Map (p50)

Central Park

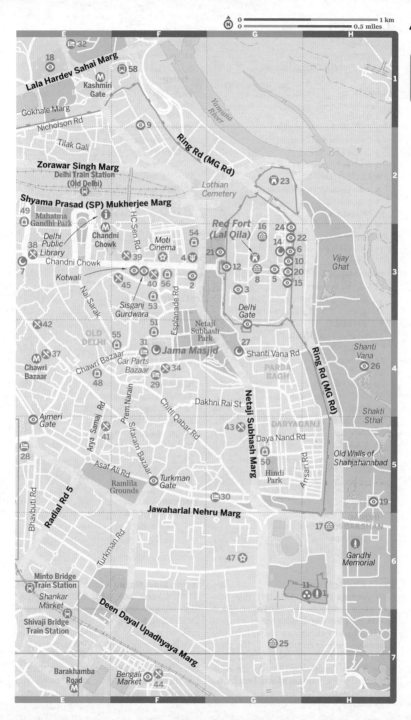

Sound-&-Light Show

Each evening (except Monday) this one-hour **show** (admission ₹60; ⊙in English 7.30pm Nov-Jan, 9pm May-Aug, 8.30pm rest of yr) gives Red Fort history the coloured-spotlight and portentous-voice-over treatment. It's great to see the fort by night, though the history lesson is a tad ponderous. Tickets are available from the fort's **ticket kiosk**. Bring mosquito repellent.

TOP CHOICE   Jama Masjid   MOSQUE

(camera, video each ₹200; tower ₹100; ⊙non-Muslims 8am-½hr before sunset, minaret 9am-5.30pm; Ⓜ Chandni Chowk) India's largest mosque can hold a mind-blowing 25,000 people. Towering over Old Delhi, the 'Friday Mosque' was Shah Jahan's final architectural opus, built between 1644 and 1658. It has three gateways, four angle towers and two minarets standing 40m high, and is constructed of alternating vertical strips of red sandstone and white marble. You can enter from gate 1 or 3.

For an extra charge you can climb the narrow southern minaret (notices say that unaccompanied women are not permitted), up 121 steps, for incredible views. From the top of the minaret, you can see one of the features that architect Edwin Lutyens incorporated into his design of New Delhi – the Jama Masjid, Connaught Place and Sansad Bhavan (Parliament House) are in a direct line.

Visitors should remove their shoes at the top of the stairs. There's no charge to enter the mosque, but you'll have to pay the camera charge whether you want to use your camera or not.

Chandni Chowk   AREA

Old Delhi's backbone is the madcap Chandni Chowk or 'moonlight place', a wide avenue thronged by crowds, hawkers and rickshaws. In the time of Shah Jahan, a canal ran down its centre, lined by peepal and neem trees – at night the waters reflected the moon, hence the name. Tiny bazaar-crammed lanes snake off the broadway like clogged arteries. At the eastern (Red Fort) end of Chandni Chowk, there's the 16th-century **Digambara Jain Temple** (☺5am-noon & 6-9pm) (remove shoes and leather before entering). The fascinating **bird hospital** (donations appreciated; ☺8am-9pm) here was founded in 1939 and is run by the Jains, who believe in the preservation of all life. Only vegetarian birds are admitted, though carnivores are treated as outpatients. The upstairs pigeons' section brings to mind Hitchcock's *The Birds*.

The western end of Chandni Chowk is marked by the mid-17th-century **Fatehpuri Masjid**, named after one of Shah Jahan's wives. It offers a striking tranquility after the craziness of the street. After the 1857 First War of Independence the mosque was sold to a Hindu merchant, who used it as a warehouse, but it was later returned to local Muslims.

There's a CNG shuttle service (small green buses) between Digambara Jain Temple and Fatehpuri Masjid (₹5).

Sunehri Masjid   MOSQUE

South of the Red Fort is the 18th-century Sunehri Masjid. In 1739 Nadir Shah, the Persian invader, stood on its roof and macabrely watched his soldiers conduct a bloody massacre of Delhi's inhabitants.

Raj Ghat   MONUMENT

South of the Red Fort, on the banks of the Yamuna River, a simple square platform of black marble marks the spot where Mahatma Gandhi was cremated following his assassination in 1948. It's inscribed with what are said to have been his final words, 'Hai Ram' (Oh, God), and has a hushed, peaceful atmosphere, set amid tranquil lawns.

Jawaharlal Nehru, the first Indian prime minister, was cremated just to the north, at **Shanti Vana** (Forest of Peace), in 1964. Nehru's daughter, Indira Gandhi, who was assassinated in 1984, and grandsons Sanjay (who died in 1980) and Rajiv (assassinated in 1991) were also cremated in this vicinity.

Nicolson Cemetery   CEMETERY

(9am-5pm) Close to the Kashmiri Gate is this 3-hectare forgotten corner of Delhi. It's named after John Nicolson, who died in 1857 and is buried here amid a sea of British graves that hint at fascinating stories. At the time he was described as the 'Hero of Delhi' but author William Dalrymple calls him an 'imperial psychopath' in *The Last Mughal*. Northwest of here is the British-erected **Mutiny Memorial**, dedicated to the soldiers who died during the First War of Independance. Near the monument is an **Ashoka Pillar**; like the one in Firoz Shah Kotla, it was brought here by Firoz Shah.

National Gandhi Museum   MUSEUM

(☑23311793; admission free; ☺9.30am-5.30pm Tue-Sun) Contains photos and some of Gandhi's belongings.

NEW DELHI & AROUND

All of the attractions in this section feature on Map p50.

TOP CHOICE **Humayun's Tomb**   HISTORIC BUILDING
(Indian/foreigner ₹10/250, video ₹25; ☺dawn-dusk; ⓂJLN Stadium) This tomb is the city's most sublime sight, and the one the Obamas were taken to visit when they were in Delhi. A beautiful example of early Mughal architecture, this tomb was built in the mid-16th century by Haji Begum, the Persian-born senior wife of the second Mughal emperor Humayun. The tomb brought Persian style to Delhi, but the two-tone combination of red sandstone and white marble is entirely local, showing the complementary merging of the different cultures. Various elements in the design of Humayun's Tomb – a squat building with high arched entrances that let in light, topped by a bulbous dome and

DELHI

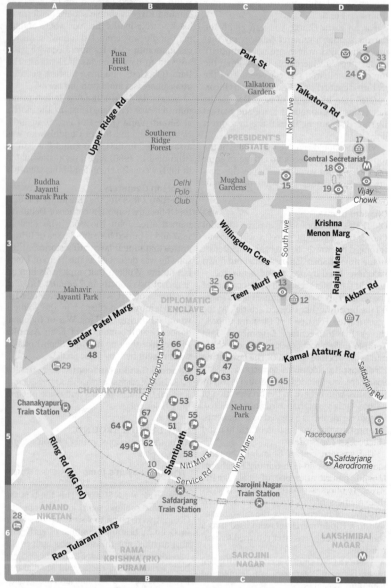

surrounded by 12 hectares of formal gardens – were to be refined in the years that followed to eventually create the magnificence of Agra's Taj Mahal.

Other beautiful tombs dot the complex, including that of the emperor's favourite barber, as well as one belonging to Haji Begum herself and the tomb of Isa Khan – a fine example of Lodi architecture through a gate to the left of the entrance. The magnificent Mughal gardens are a magical place to wander, particularly towards sunset.

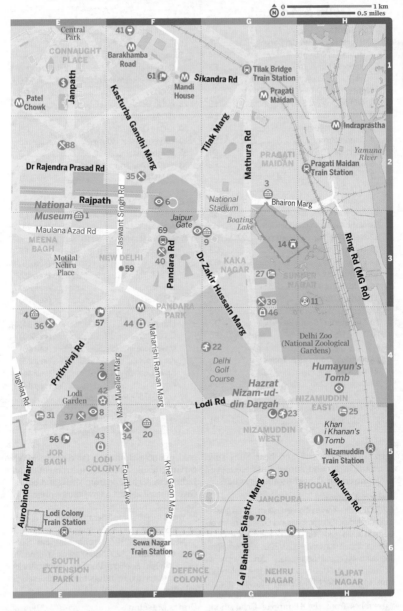

Hazrat Nizam-ud-din Dargah

SACRED SITE

(⊙24hr) Amid a tangle of alleys, and attract-ing hordes of devotees, is the vibrant marble shrine of the Muslim Sufi saint, Nizam-ud-din Chishti. He died in 1325, aged 92, but the mausoleum has been revamped several times, and dates from 1562. Other tombs include the later grave of Jahanara (daugh-ter of Shah Jahan), and the renowned Urdu poet, Amir Khusru. It's one of Delhi's most extraordinary pleasures to experience the

New Delhi & Around

buzz around the site and hear Sufis sing *qawwali* at around sunset, just after evening prayers on Thursdays and feast days.

National Museum   MUSEUM
(☏23019272; www.nationalmuseum india.gov.in; Janpath; Indian ₹10, foreigner incl English, French or German audio guide ₹300, Hindi audio guide ₹150; camera Indian/foreigner ₹20/300; ☉10am-5pm Tue-Sun; ⓂCentral Secretariat) An overview of India's last 5000 years, this is a splendid museum – perfect for a rainy day and not so large that it overwhelms. Exhibits include rare relics from the Harappan Civilisation, including some fascinating mundane items such as tweezers and hairpins from around 2700 BC, Central Asian antiquities including many artefacts from the Silk Route, a mesmerising collection of jewel-bright miniature paintings, exquisite old coins including pure

gold examples from the 1st century, woodcarving, textiles, musical instruments, and Indus jewellery made from shells and bones. Give yourself at least a few hours – preferably half a day – to explore this museum.

You'll need some identification to obtain an audio guide. Video cameras are prohibited.

Next door is the **Archaeological Survey of India** (☏23019108; asi.nic.in; Janpath; ☉9.30am-1pm & 2-6pm Mon-Fri) which stocks publications about India's main archaeological sites.

Crafts Museum   MUSEUM
(☏23371641; Bhairon Marg; admission free; ☉10am-5pm Tue-Sun; ⓂPragati Maidan) This is a tree-shaded treasure trove of a museum. The galleries contain more than 20,000 exhibits from around India, including metalware, woodwork, tribal masks, paintings, terracotta

figurines and richly coloured textiles. The fascinating items display the application of art to everyday life, from village toys to a huge 18th-century wooden Gujarati *jharokha* (elaborate balcony). Artisans demonstrate their skills and sell their products. The onsite **shop** is particularly good. Photography is only allowed with prior permission.

Lodi Garden　　　　　　　　　　　　PARK
(Lodi Rd; ⊙6am-8pm Oct-Mar, 5am-8pm Apr-Sep; ⓂKhan Market) Lodi garden is Delhi's loveliest escape, popular with everyone from power-walking politicians to canoodling couples. The gardens are dotted by the crumbling **tombs** of the Sayyid and Lodi rulers, including the impressive 15th-century **Bara Gumbad**, and inhabited by fluttering butterflies, stalking peacocks and all sorts of birds.

If you're in search of serenity, avoid Sunday – the garden's most social day.

National Gallery of Modern Art　ART GALLERY
(☎23382835; ngmaindia.gov.in; Jaipur House; Indian/foreigner ₹10/150; ⊙10am-5pm Tue-Sun; ⓂKhan Market) This gallery has a fantastic new wing alongside the Maharaja of Jaipur's former place. It includes all the great modern Indian masters, such as the fascinating 'Company Paintings', which were provided by local artists to suit their new British patrons, beautiful works by Amrita Sher-Gil and Nobel Prize–winner Rabindranath Tagore (who started painting aged 67), and stunning pieces by FN Souza and MF Husain. Photography isn't allowed.

Rajpath　　　　　　　　　　　　　　AREA
Rajpath (Kingsway) is the imposing approach to New Delhi. It hosts the huge Republic Day parade every 26 January and the Beating of the Retreat on 29 January.

DELHI

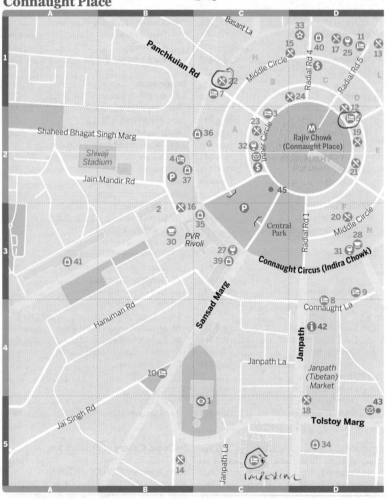

Raj-appointed English architect Edwin Lutyens constructed New Delhi between 1914 and 1931, when the British moved their capital here from Calcutta. His designs were intended to spell out in stone the might of the British empire – but 16 years later, the British were out on their ear. New Delhi became the powerhouse of the new Republic.

At the western end of Rajpath is the official residence of the president of India, the Rashtrapati Bhavan (President's House), built in 1929. Pre-Independence, this 340-room palace was the viceroy's residence. At the time of Mountbatten, India's last viceroy,

the number of servants employed here was staggering. There were 418 gardeners alone, 50 of whom were boys employed to chase away birds. To its west, the Mughal Gardens occupy 130 hectares; it's only open (admission free; photography prohibited) to the public for several days in February/March – for dates contact India Tourism Delhi.

Rashtrapati Bhavan is flanked by the mirror-image, dome-crowned North and South Secretariat buildings, housing government ministries, which have over 1000 rooms between them. The three buildings sit upon a small rise, known as Raisina Hill.

Hotel Palace Heights

ghan ruler Sher Shah during his reign (1538-45), before the emperor Humayun (whom he had previously defeated) regained control of India. The site is thought to be that of ancient Indraprastha

Entering from the south gate you'll see the graceful octagonal, red-sandstone tower, the **Sher Mandal**, later used by Humayun as a library. It was while hurriedly descending the stairs of this tower in 1556 that he slipped and sustained injuries from which he later died. Just beyond it is the 1541 **Qila-i-Kuhran Mosque** (Mosque of Sher Shah), which delicately combines black-and-white marble with the more easily available deep red sandstone.

A popular, picturesque **boating lake** has been created from the former moat, with pedaloes for hire.

Gandhi Smriti   MUSEUM

(☎23012843; 5 Tees January Marg; admission free, camera free, video prohibited; ☿10am-1.30pm & 2-5pm Tue-Sun, closed every 2nd Sat of month; ⓜRacecourse) This poignant memorial is where Mahatma Gandhi was shot dead by a Hindu zealot on 30 January 1948. Concrete footsteps represent Gandhi's final steps and lead to the spot where he died, marked by a small pavilion known as the Martyr's Column.

The impressive indoor museum has photographs, paintings and dioramas depicting scenes from Gandhi's life, including some whizz-bang interactive exhibits.

Gandhi had been staying in the house as a guest, and spent the last 144 days of his life here. In the room he occupied, his meagre possessions are on display, such as his walking stick, spectacles, spinning wheel and chappals (sandals).

Gurdwara Bangla Sahib   SIKH TEMPLE

(Ashoka Rd; ☿4am-9pm; ⓜShivaji Stadium) The Gurdwara Bangla Sahib is an important Sikh shrine and a constant hive of activity. Topped with gold onion domes, it was constructed at the site where the eighth Sikh guru, Harkrishan Dev, spent several months in 1664. This guru dedicated most of his time to helping the destitute and sick and was revered for his healing powers. At the back of the gurdwara (Sikh temple) is a huge tank, surrounded by a graceful colonnade. The water is said to have curative properties. Devotional songs are sung throughout the day.

Safdarjang's Tomb   HISTORIC BUILDING

(Aurobindo Marg; Indian/foreigner ₹5/100, video ₹25; ☿dawn-dusk; ⓜJor Bagh) Built by the

At Rajpath's eastern end is India Gate. This 42m-high stone memorial arch, designed by Lutyens, pays tribute to around 90,000 Indian army soldiers who died in WWI, the Northwest Frontier operations of the same time and the 1919 Anglo-Afghan War.

Sansad Bhavan (Parliament House), a circular, colonnaded structure 171m in diameter, stands at the end of Sansad Marg.

Purana Qila   FORT

(Old Fort; ☎24353178; Mathura Rd; Indian/foreigner ₹5/100, video ₹25; ☿dawn-dusk; ⓜPragati Maidan) With its massive walls and impressive gateways, Purana Qila was built by Af-

Nawab of Avadh for his father, Safdarjang, this grandiose mid-18th-century tomb is one of the last examples of Mughal architecture. It's a fantastical work of overwrought mannerism, which seems reflect the final throes of the great empire.

Indira Gandhi Memorial Museum   MUSEUM
(☏23010094; 1 Safdarjang Rd; admission free; ⊙9.30am-4.45pm Tue-Sun; Ⓜ Racecourse) The former residence of Indira Gandhi is now a fascinating museum, displaying artefacts, photos and newspaper clippings, as well as personal belongings, including the blood-stained sari she was wearing when she was assassinated in 1984. Some of the rooms are preserved as they were, an interesting window into the understated elegance of her life. Another section is devoted to her son Rajiv, also assassinated in 1991 by a suicide bomber. Fragments of the clothes he was wearing and, even more poignantly, his trainers, are

on display. On the way out, you'll pass an enclosed crystal pathway that marks Gandhi's final footsteps before her murder.

Nehru Memorial Museum & Planetarium

MUSEUM

(☏23016734; admission free; ⏰9am-5.15pm Tue-Sun) Teen Murti Bhavan is the former residence of Jawaharlal Nehru (India's first prime minister), and was previously Flagstaff House, home to the British commander-in-chief. Just off Teen Murti Rd, it has been converted into a must-see museum for those interested in the Independence movement. Some rooms have been preserved as Nehru left them, and there's a wealth of photographs, though some contextualisation would come in handy.

In the grounds is a recently renovated **planetarium** (☏23014504; http://nehruplanetarium.org; 45min show ₹50; ⏰in English 11.30am & 3pm).

Tibet House

MUSEUM

(☏24611515; 1 Lodi Rd; admission ₹10; ⏰9.30am-1pm & 2-5.30pm Mon-Fri; Ⓜ JLN Stadium) Tibet House has a small museum displaying ceremonial items, including sacred manuscripts, sculptures and old *thangkas* (Tibetan paintings on cloth). All were brought out of Tibet when the Dalai Lama fled following Chinese occupation. Photography prohibited.

The **bookshop** sells Buddhist books, chanting CDs, prayer flags and *katas* (sacred Tibetan scarves).

National Zoological Gardens

ZOO

(☏24359825; Mathura Rd; Indian/foreigner ₹10/50, video ₹50; ⏰9am-5pm Sat-Thu; Ⓜ Pragati Maidan) Wildly popular with families and couples, this is India's biggest zoo, set in 86 hectares. There are white Bengal tigers, Himalayan black bears, rhinos, wolves, elephants and some spectacular birds.

CONNAUGHT PLACE AREA

New Delhi's colonnaded heart is commercial centre Connaught Place (CP; Map p54), named after George V's uncle who visited in 1921. Its streets radiate from the central circle, divided into blocks and devoted to shops, banks, restaurants, hotels and offices.

Often creating confusion, the outer circle is technically called Connaught Circus (divided into blocks from G to N) and the inner circle Connaught Place (divided into blocks from A to F). There's also a Middle Circle. In 1995 the inner and outer circles were renamed Rajiv Chowk and Indira Chowk respectively, but these names are rarely used.

Touts are especially rampant in Connaught Place.

Jantar Mantar

HISTORIC SITE

(Map p54; Sansad Marg; Indian/foreigner ₹5/100; ⏰9am-dusk; Ⓜ Patel Chowk) The most eccentric of all Delhi's inner-city structures, Jantar Mantar is an odd collection of huge curved terracotta buildings, a giant playground which makes for great photo opps. 'Jantar Mantar' may mean the equivalent to 'abracadabra' in Hindi, but the site was constructed in 1725 for scientific purposes – it's the earliest of Maharaja Jai Singh II's five observatories. It's dominated by a huge sundial and houses other instruments plotting the course of heavenly bodies.

OTHER AREAS

Bahai House of Worship (Lotus Temple)

TEMPLE

(Map p60; ☏26444029; Kalkaji; ⏰9.30am-5.30pm Tue-Sun; Ⓜ Kalkaji Mandir) This extraordinary temple is shaped like the sacred lotus flower and is a wonderful place to seek some otherworldly peace. Designed by Iranian-Canadian architect Fariburz Sahba in 1986, it has 27 immaculate white-marble petals. The Bahai philosophy revolves around universal peace and the elimination of prejudice, and adherents of all faiths are welcome to pray or meditate silently according to their own religion.

Refrain from speaking in the temple; photography inside is prohibited.

Akshardham Temple

TEMPLE

(www.akshardham.com; Noida turning, National Hwy 24; ⏰9am-6pm Tue-Sun Oct-Mar, 10am-7pm Tue-Sun Apr-Sep; Ⓜ Akshardham) The Hindu Swaminarayan Group's controversially ostentatious Akshardham Temple, on Delhi's outskirts, has something of a Disney feel. Inaugurated in 2005, it's made of salmon-coloured sandstone with an interior carved from white marble in giddying detail. It contains around 20,000 carved deities, and reflects traditional Orissan, Gujarati, Mughal and Rajasthani architectural elements. Outside there are 148 carved elephants, each different.

Allow at least half a day to do it justice (weekdays are less crowded) as there's lots to see, including a boat ride through 10,000 years of Indian history, elaborate animatronics telling stories of the life of Swaminarayan, and musical fountains.

DELHI

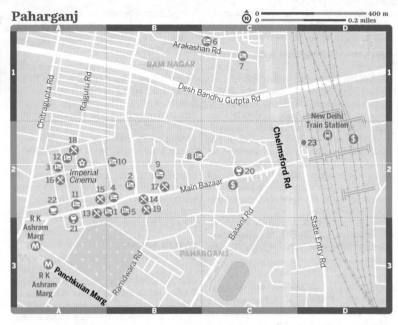

Paharganj

Lakshmi Narayan Temple (Birla Mandir)
TEMPLE

(Map p46; Mandir Marg; ◉6am-9pm; ⓂRK Ashram
Marg) West of Connaught Place, the Orissan-
style Lakshmi Narayan Temple, a rather
overexcited red-and-cream confection, was
erected in 1938 by the wealthy industrialist
BD Birla. It was inaugurated by Gandhi as a
temple for all castes; a sign on the gate says,
'Everyone is Welcome'.

National Rail Museum
MUSEUM

(Map p50; ☏26881816; www.nationalrailmuseum.
org; Chanakyapuri; admission adult/child ₹20/10,
video ₹100;◉9.30am-5pm Tue-Sun Oct-Mar, to 7pm
Apr-Sep) Trainspotters and kids will adore this
museum, with around 30 locomotives and old

carriages. Exhibits include an 1855 steam engine, still in working order, and various oddities including the skull of an elephant that charged a train in 1894, and lost.

There's also the 10-minute **Joy Train** ride (adult/child ₹10/5), and **boating** is also possible (adult/child ₹30/15).

Hauz Khas
AREA

Hauz Khas means 'royal tank', named after a 13th-century reservoir built by Allauddin Khilji. The artificial lake was once the water source for Siri Fort – the second city of Delhi – and now is a beautiful blue-green expanse that feels forgotten by the modern city. Overlooking it are Firoz Shah's 14th-century domed madrasa (religious school) and his tomb (Map p60), which were once covered in brilliantly painted white plaster and topped by gold domes. Some Lodi and Tughlak tombs also dot the area, which whirls with grass-green parakeets and other birds. This is a fascinating, secluded place to explore, and neighbouring Hauz Khas village (Map p60) is one of Delhi's artiest enclaves, filled with upmarket boutiques, quirky bars and curio shops.

Shankar's International Dolls Museum
MUSEUM

(Map p46; ☑23316970; www.childrensbooktrust. com; Nehru House, Bahadur Shah Zafar Marg; adult/child ₹15/5; ☉10am-5.30pm Tue-Sun) From Spanish bullfighting figurines to Indian bridal dolls, this remarkable museum has 6500 dolls from 85 countries.

Coronation Durbar Site
HISTORIC SITE

In a desolate field, north of Old Delhi, stands a lone obelisk. Here, in 1877 and 1903, the great durbars, featuring Indian nobility, paid homage to the British monarch. In 1911, King George V was declared emperor of India here.

Kotla Firoz Shah
HISTORIC SITE

(Map p46; Indian/foreigner ₹5/100, video ₹25; ☉dawn-dusk; Ⓜ Pragati Maidan) Firozabad (the fifth city of Delhi) was built by Firoz Shah in 1354. Its ruins, including a mosque and step well, can be found at Kotla Firoz Shah, off Bahadur Shah Zafar Marg. Visit on a Thursday afternoon when crowds come to pray, light candles and leave bowls of milk to appease Delhi's djinns (invisible spirits or genies) that are reputed to inhabit the kotla. In the fortress/palace is a 13m-high sandstone **Ashoka Pillar** inscribed with Ashoka's edicts (and a later inscription).

Sulabh International Museum of Toilets
MUSEUM

(☑25031518;www.sulabhtoiletmuseum.org;Sulabh Complex, Mahavir Enclave, Palam Dabri Rd; admission free; ☉10am-5pm Mon-Sat) This quirky museum houses toilet-related paraphernalia dating from 2500 BC to modern times. It's not just a curiosity: Sulabh International has done extraordinary work in the field of sanitation, developing pour-flush toilets and bio-gas plants, and educating the children of 'manual scavengers' (whose job is to remove the crap from dry toilets) for other work. A guided tour (free) brings the loos to life.

🏃 Activities

TOP CHOICE Amatrra Spa
SPA

(Map p50; ☑24122921; www.amatrraspa. com; Ashok Hotel, Chanakyapuri; ☉9am-10pm; Ⓜ Racecourse) The most legendarily luxurious of all Delhi's luxury spas, Amatrra is the A-list place to be pampered. There's a cover charge of ₹1000 for nonguests; massages, such as 'Asian Blend', cost from ₹3000, and there are many other treatments, like 'Sparkle Body Scrub' (₹3500).

Delhi Golf Club
GOLFING

(Map p50; ☑24307100; www.delhigolfclub.org; Dr Zakir Hussain Marg; weekdays/weekends US$50/70; ☉sunrise-sunset; Ⓜ Jor Bagh) Dates from 1931 and has beautiful, well-tended fairways; weekends are busy.

Kerala Ayurveda
AYURVEDA

(Map p60; ☑41754888; www.keralaayurveda.biz; E-2 Green Park Extn; ☉8am-8pm; Ⓜ Green Park) For *abhyangam* (oil treatment; ₹1200 for 45 minutes), plus other Ayurvedic therapies, try this place.

Lambency Spa
SPA

(Map p60; ☑40587983; www.chandansparsh.com; M-24 Greater Kailash II; ☉9am-9pm) Here you can have a top-of-the-range manicure and pedicure (₹1000) or one-hour body massage (from ₹1000). Prices don't include tax.

Jaypee Vasant Continental Hotel
SWIMMING

(Map p60; ☑26148800; Basant Lok complex, Vasant Vihar; per person ₹1202) Escape the summer heat at this five-star hotel pool.

Siri Fort Sports Complex
SWIMMING

(Map p60; ☑26496657; day membership Indian/foreigner ₹40/100; ☉Apr-Sep; Ⓜ Green Park) Olympic-sized swimming pool plus a toddler pool.

DELHI

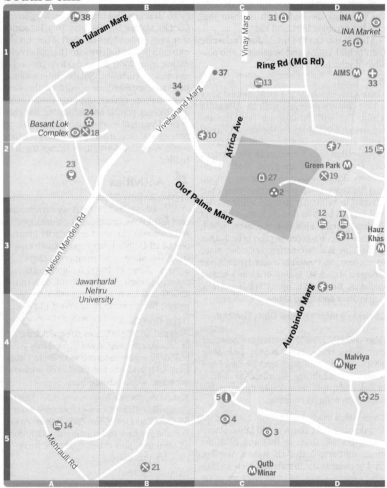

📚 Courses

Tannie Baig COOKING
(☎9899555704; baig.murad@gmail.com; 2hr lesson ₹3200; MHauz Khas) The elegant Tannie, who runs Treetops Guest House in Hauz Khas has written 16 cookery books. A two-hour cooking lesson sounds pricey, but it's a flat rate for up to five people. If you stay at the guesthouse, lessons are half price.

Parul Puri COOKING
(Map p50; ☎9810793322; www.koneone.com; MJangpura) K-One One (p67) runs two-hour classes with a focus on cuisine from

North India regions. The charge is ₹1200 per person; book at least two days in advance.

Central Hindi Directorate LANGUAGE
(☎26103160; hindinideshalaya.nic.in; West Block VII, RK Puram; 60hr course ₹6000) Runs basic Hindi courses (minimum numbers apply) of 60 hours (two hours daily, three lessons per week).

Dhyan Foundation MEDITATION, YOGA
(☎26253374; www.dhyanfoundation.com) Various yoga and meditation options based in South Extension II.

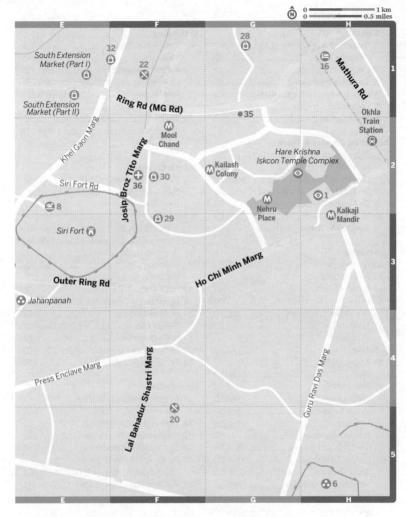

Morarji Desai National Institute of Yoga
MEDITATION, YOGA

(Map p50; ☎23721472; www.yogamdniy.com; 68 Ashoka Rd; ⓂPatel Chowk) Offers one-year diploma courses that include pranayama and hatha yoga as well as meditation.

Sri Aurobindo Ashram MEDITATION, YOGA

(☎26858563; Aurobindo Marg; classes per month ₹500) Yoga and meditation, morning, afternoon and evening, three days a week.

Studio Abhyas MEDITATION, YOGA

(☎26962757, bookings Monica 9810522624; F-27 Green Park) Yoga classes combining *asanas* (fixed body positions) and pranayama,

meditation classes, and Vedic chanting classes (evenings or by appointment).

Tushita Meditation Centre MEDITATION

(☎26513400; 9 Padmini Enclave, Hauz Khas) Tibetan/Buddhist meditation sessions on Monday and Fridays at 6.30pm. Donations are appreciated.

☞ Tours

Delhi is a spread-out city so taking a tour makes sense, although you can feel rushed at some sites. Avoid Monday when many sites are shut. Admission fees and camera/video charges aren't included in tour prices

South Delhi

below, and rates are per person. Book several days in advance as minimum numbers may be required. India Tourism Delhi (p80) can arrange multilingual, government-approved guides (from ₹150/300 per half-/full day).

DelhiByCycle   CYCLING
(☑9811723720; www.delhibycycle.com; ₹1250; ◷6.45-10am) Run by Jack Leenaars, a journalist from the Netherlands, this is a fantastic way to see Delhi. There's the Shah Jahan Tour around the back lanes and bazaars of Old Delhi, and the Raj Tour around

New Delhi. Tours start early to avoid the traffic and the price includes chai and a Mughal breakfast.

Salaam Balaak Trust   WALKING
(Map p58; ☑23584164, 9910099348; www.salaambaalaktrust.com; Gali Chandiwali, Paharganj; suggested donation ₹200; Ⓜ RK Ashram Marg) This charitable organisation offers two-hour 'street walks' with a twist – your guide is a former (Trust-trained) street child, who will show you first-hand what life is like for inner-city homeless kids. The

money goes to the Trust to assist children on the streets.

Hope Project
WALKING

(Map p50; ☑24353006; www.hopeproject india.org; 127 Hazrat Nizamuddin; 90min walk ₹150) Ninety-minute walks around the basti (slum) of Nizamuddin, which surrounds the Dargah, learning about the area. It's a poverty-stricken place, so can be shocking as well as insightful. The walk fee goes towards supporting the Hope Project's work. Wear modest clothing as this is a very traditional area.

Delhi Tourism & Transport Development Corporation
BUS TOURS

(DTTDC; delhitourism.nic.in) Baba Kharak Singh Marg (Map p54; ☑23363607; ◷7am-9pm); international airport (☑25675609; ◷8am-9pm) Bus tours (₹310 AC) of New Delhi (9am to 2pm) and Old Delhi (2.15pm to 5.15pm) . Also runs the new air-conditioned **Hop-on, Hop-off (HOHO) Bus Service** (☑1280; ₹300; ◷every 30 min, 7.30am-8pm Tue-Sun), which passes by all Delhi's major sights. Same-day trips to Agra (₹1100 AC) run three times a week while three-day tours of Agra and Jaipur (₹6350, via rail) operate twice weekly.

Old Delhi Walks
WALKING

(Intach; ☑24641304; www.intachdelhichapter. org; tour ₹50) Intach runs a walking tour (approximately two hours) every month with an expert guide, exploring different areas, such as Chandhi Chowk, Nizamuddin, Hauz Khas, and Mehrauli. Customised tours are also possible. Book ahead.

🛏 Sleeping

It's wise to book in advance, as Delhi's most salubrious places can fill up in a flash, leaving new arrivals easy prey for commission sharks. Most hotels offer pick-up from the airport with advance notice.

Be warned that street din can be diabolical – request a quiet room and keep earplugs handy. Also, room quality in less expensive hotels can vary radically so try to inspect a few rooms first. Delhi's budget bunch tend to offer dreary rooms, bathrooms in need of a good scrub and patchy service. Most backpackers head for hyperactive Paharganj, a touristy pocket near the New Delhi train station that has some of the city's cheapest beds.

Midrange prices have rocketed upwards over recent years, so homestays are becoming an attractive alternative. For details of government-approved places contact India Tourism Delhi, or check www.incredible indianhomes.com and www.mahindrahome stays.com.

Long-term stayers could consider renting a furnished apartment – check ads in the latest *Delhi City Guide, Delhi Diary* and local newspapers. Two good websites are www. speciality-apartments.com and www.delhi escape.net.

Hotels with a minimum tariff of ₹1000 charge 12.5% luxury tax and some also whack on a service charge (5% to 10%). Taxes aren't included in this chapter unless indicated and all rooms have private bathrooms unless otherwise stated. Most hotels have a noon checkout and luggage storage is usually possible (sometimes for a small charge).

It's a good idea to call or email ahead to confirm your booking 24 hours before you arrive.

NORTH DELHI

OLD DELHI

Few foreign tourists stay in teeming Old Delhi – those who do will probably attract a bit of innocuous attention.

Maidens Hotel
HOTEL $$$

(Map p46; ☑23975464; www.maidenshotel.com; Sham Nath Marg; r from ₹15,000; ❄@≋; Ⓜ Civil Lines) Set in a 3.2-hectare garden, Maidens is a graceful wedding cake of a hotel, built in 1903. Lutyens stayed here while supervising the building of New Delhi. The high-ceilinged rooms are traditional and well equipped, and some have good views.

Hotel Bombay Orient
HOTEL $

(Map p46; ☑23242691; s/d ₹400/625; ❄; Ⓜ Chawri Bazaar) Set on the busy bazaar leading from the Jama Masjid's south gate. You'll need to book ahead here. It's one of the old city's best budget bets but, even so, don't expect too much and request one of its newer rooms.

Hotel Broadway
HOTEL $$

(Map p46; ☑43663600; www.hotelbroadwaydelhi .com/; 4/15 Asaf Ali Rd; s/d incl breakfast ₹2495/4495; ❄@; Ⓜ New Delhi) Semiluxurious Broadway, between the old and new cities, has some rooms with views over Old Delhi. Room standards vary (some are sleek and smart), so look at a few. Nos 44 and 46 have been kitschly kitted out by French designer Catherine Lévy, as has the Chor Bizarre restaurant, and there's the atmospheric, if divey, 'Thugs' bar upstairs.

Delhi Metro Map

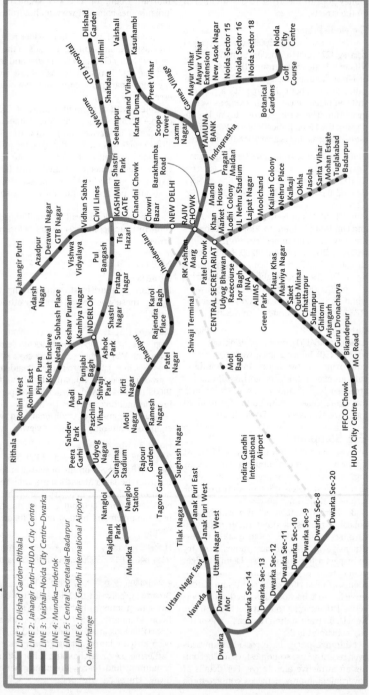

LINE 1: Dilshad Garden–Rithala
LINE 2: Jahangir Putri–HUDA City Centre
LINE 3: Vaishali–Noida City Centre–Dwarka
LINE 4: Mundka–Inderlok
LINE 5: Central Secretariat–Badarpur
LINE 6: Indira Gandhi International Airport
○ Interchange

Hotel New City Palace

HOTEL $

(Map p46; ☑23279548; www.hotelnewcitypalace.in; d ₹400-500, tr ₹600, q ₹700-1300; 🌢; Ⓜ Chawri Bazaar) A palace it's not, but this has an amazing location overlooking the Jama Masjid (some rooms have views over the mosque), snug rooms, bathrooms that could do with a good scrub but are bearable, and friendly reception.

Ginger

HOTEL $$

(Map p46; ☑1800 209 3333; www.gingerhotels.com; Rail Yatri Niwas; r incl tax ₹1300; 🌢@; Ⓜ New Delhi) Offers reasonably smart rooms that are ideal for business travel on the cheap. It is in an ugly building in a desolate-feeling location that's nevertheless a few minutes' walk from New Delhi train station. There's a 24-hour restaurant.

PAHARGANJ AREA

With its bumper-to-bumper budget lodgings, Paharganj – with its seedy reputation for drugs and dodgy characters – isn't everyone's cup of *chai*, though it's certainly got a lively feel. Grot aside, it's walking distance from New Delhi train station and close to the hub of Connaught Place – and it's *the* place to tap into the backpacker grapevine. Paharganj has some of Delhi's cheapest places to sleep, but sun-starved, grimy cells are depressingly common, and hot water erratic.

Despite drastic street-widening measures that forced many businesses to destroy their encroaching facades in preparation for the Commonwealth Games, Main Bazaar remains overwhelmingly congested. Thus, taxi-wallahs may (understandably) refuse to drop you at your hotel's doorstep; however, most are a short walk from the train station. All the following are close to metro stop RK Ashram Marg unless otherwise stated. Note this stop is more convenient for the Main Bazaar than metro stop New Delhi, as from the latter you have to walk all the way through the busy station. The following accommodation features on Map p58.

⬛TOP CHOICE Cottage Yes Please

HOTEL $

(☑23562300; cottageyesplease@yahoo.co.in; 1843 Laxmi Narayan St; d ₹900; 🌢@) Around the corner from Cottage Crown Plaza is this place, its sibling, and one of the best deals in Paharganj, with a range of glitzy, clean rooms, with TVs, fridges, brassware fans and stained glass windows.

Hotel Grand Godwin

HOTEL $$

(☑23546891; www.godwinhotels.com; 8502/41 Arakashan Rd, Ram Nagar; s/d incl breakfast ₹2300/2600; 🌢@🛰; Ⓜ New Delhi) Located

north of Main Bazaar in Ram Nagar, the Grand Godwin is the best midrange choice in this area, with smart rooms, a snazzy lobby, glass-capsule lift and room service. Godwin Deluxe at number 15 is a more upmarket hotel, owned by the same management.

Hotel Amax Inn

HOTEL $

(☑23543813; www.hotelamax.com; 8145/6 Arakashan Rd; s ₹400-450, d ₹550-750, AC s ₹650, d ₹750-850; 🌢🛰; Ⓜ New Delhi) Away from the main bazaar, this chilled place is fantastic value, with nice clean rooms and bathrooms, tucked away in a lane off Arakashan Rd. There's a small roof terrace and wi-fi in reception.

Hotel Namaskar

GUESTHOUSE $

(☑23583456; www.hotelnamaskar.com; 917 Chandiwalan, Main Bazaar; d/tr/q from ₹350/500/600, AC d ₹600; 🌢🛰) This old favourite is run by two amiable brothers. Rooms are spartan – you get what you pay for, but they're usually freshly painted and the colour scheme is bound to tickle you pink. Car hire can be arranged, and wi-fi is available courtesy of the net cafe next door (₹100 per 24 hours).

Cottage Ganga Inn

HOTEL $$

(☑23561516; cottagegangainn@yahoo.co.in; 1562 Bazar Sangtra shan; s/d ₹800/1100; 🌢@🛰) Popular with overlanders, this hotel is tucked away off the Main Bazaar in a courtyard, located next to a nursery school. It is clean, comfortable and a great deal for Paharganj.

Ajay Guest House

GUESTHOUSE $$

(☑23583125; www.anupamhoteliersltd.com; 5084 Main Bazaar; s/d ₹900/1000; 🌢@) Ajay is more promising than it appears from its hallways. Fresh coats of paint mean rooms look bright and snazzy, and some have colourful geometric detailing. Bathrooms are clean and colourfully tiled.

Hotel Rak International

HOTEL $

(☑23562478; hotelrakint@yahoo.co.in; Tooti Chowk, Main Bazaar; s/d ₹450-750, ₹550-850; 🌢) Tucked off the main bazaar and overlooking a messy little courtyard with a temple, the modest rooms at this popular hotel have marble floors, TVs, wardrobes, small dressing tables and...windows!

Vivek Hotel

HOTEL $

(☑46470555; www.vivekhotel.com; Main Bazaar; r ₹600-1000; 🌢@) This multistorey favourite has a good range of rooms – cheaper ones are reasonable and clean and the more expensive even have a small window with a view.

Metropolis Tourist Home HOTEL **$$**
(☏23561794; www.metropolistravels.com; 1634 Main Bazaar; s/d incl tax from ₹1000/1250; ✳@) Rooms (some with tight balconies) here are simple and characterless but come with smooth tiled floors, TVs and fridges. The rooftop restaurant is an added bonus.

Major's Den GUESTHOUSE **$**
(☏23589010; s/d ₹500/600; ✳) In a quietish sidestreet, the friendly Den has no-frills, bearably clean rooms, with cleanish walls; not all have windows.

Hare Krishna Guest House GUESTHOUSE **$**
(☏41541341; 1572 Main Bazaar; r from ₹300) Scuffed but bearable rooms.

Hare Rama Guest House GUESTHOUSE **$**
(☏23561301; Main Bazaar; s/d from ₹300/400; ✳) Grotty but bearable rooms, tucked in behind the bazaar.

MAJNU-KA-TILLA

The antidote for anyone who's got the big-city blues, this mellow enclave (aka Tibetan Colony), a block intercut by narrow lanes, is a long way from the centre, but good for a little Lhasa vibe. It's packed with travel agents, cyber cafes and trinket markets, and you'll rub shoulders with maroon-clad Buddhist monks, curio vendors, local residents and rather a lot of beggars. It's tricky to find though, north of the ISBT (bus station), and its rubbish problem makes Paharganj look tidy. From the centre, take the metro to Vidhan Sabha, then take a rickshaw.

Wongdhen House GUESTHOUSE **$**
(☏23816689; wongdhenhouse@hotmail.com; r ₹575, without bathroom ₹375; ✳) The pick of the Majnu-ka-Tilla bunch has basic but good-sized, clean rooms. The rooftop has views over the Yamuna and the tasty restaurant rustles up everything from banana pancakes to Tibetan noodles (and does room service).

NEW DELHI & AROUND

CONNAUGHT PLACE AREA

CP properties are unbeatably central, but you pay a premium for the location. These listings feature on Map p54 and are close to metro stop Rajiv Chowk.

TOP CHOICE **Imperial** HOTEL **$$$**
(☏23341234; www.theimperialindia.com; Janpath; s/d ₹15,000/17,500; ✳@☎✳) The inimitable, Raj-era Imperial marries Victorian colonial classicism with gilded art deco, houses an impressive collection of 17th- and 18th-century paintings, and has hosted everyone from princesses to pop stars. The high-ceilinged rooms have it all, from French linen and puffy pillows to marble baths and finely crafted furniture. There's a great bar, **1911**, which is perfect for high tea.

Radisson Marina HOTEL **$$$**
(☏43582610; www.hotelpalaceheights.com; 26-28 D-Block; s/d ₹6500/7000; ✳@☎) CP's flashest hotel, the Radisson's update of the old Hotel Marina is nice, with sleek, stylish all-modcon rooms, two restaurants and a cool bar, the **Connaught**.

Park HOTEL **$$$**
(☏23744000; www.theparkhotels.com; 15 Parliament St; s/d from ₹12,000/14,000; ✳@☎✳) Conran-designed, with lots of modern flair, and has a smashing spa, breezily chic restaurant and a great poolside bar.

Hotel Palace Heights HOTEL **$$$**
(☏43582610; www.hotelpalaceheights.com; 26-28 D-Block; s/d ₹6500/7000; ✳@☎) Connaught Place's most accessibly priced boutique hotel has sleek rooms with gleaming white linen, black lampshades and caramel padded headboards. There's an excellent restaurant and 24-hour room service.

Corus HOTEL **$$$**
(☏43652222; www.hotelcorus.com; 49 B-Block; s/d from ₹6000/6500; ✳@) This has clean, swish, compact rooms, with dazzling white sheets. More money buys you a lot more space. But readers report mixed service and occasional problems with hot water. There's an attractive restaurant, **Bonsai**, good for a drink, with outdoor seating in a white-pebbled courtyard.

Hotel Alka HOTEL **$$$**
(☏23344328; www.hotelalka.com; P-Block; s/d from ₹2950/5000; ✳) Alka's cramped standard rooms are overpriced but comfortable, some with wood-panelled walls. More money buys more pizazz, including grrrroovy leopard-skin-themed rooms. There's a good vegetarian restaurant.

Prem Sagar Guest House GUESTHOUSE **$$**
(☏23345263; www.premsagarguesthouse.com; 1st fl, 11 P-Block; s/d from ₹3000/3500; ✳@) This is a reliable choice. The 12 snug rooms aren't flash, but they're clean, with TV, fridge and wardrobe. There's a pot-plant filled outdoor area, and internet in reception.

Ringo Guest House GUESTHOUSE **$**
(☏23310605; ringo_guest_house@yahoo.co.in; 17 Scindia House, Connaught Lane; s/d ₹350/550, without bathroom ₹350/450)

Sunny Guest House GUESTHOUSE $
(☑23312909; sunnyguesthouse1234@hotmail.com;
152 Scindia House, Connaught Lane; s/d ₹400/500,
without bathroom ₹200/350)

WEST OF CONNAUGHT PLACE

If you like home-style lodgings you will love
these hassle-free places but be aware that
they fill up fast – so you should book ahead.

TOP CHOICE **Shanti Home** HOTEL $$$
(☑41573366; www.shantihome.com;
A-1/300 Janakpuri; r incl tax & breakfast from
₹8500; ❄@🛜; ⓜJanak Puri West) Though in an
off-the-radar location in West Delhi, this is
close to the metro station and is a gorgeous
hotel with beautifully decorated rooms and
an excellent rooftop restaurant. Spa treat-
ments are available.

Master Guest House GUESTHOUSE $$
(☑28741089; www.master-guesthouse.com; R-500
New Rajendra Nagar; s/d incl tax & breakfast from
₹2500/3500; ❄@🛜; ⓜRajendra Place) Run by
an obliging couple, this polished suburban
residence is somewhat out of the way, and
has three thoughtfully furnished, characterful rooms with smart, spotless bathrooms.
There's a leafy rooftop terrace.

Bajaj Indian Home Stay GUESTHOUSE $$$
(☑25736509; www.bajajindianhomestay.com;
8A/34 WEA Karol Bagh; s/d/tr incl tax & break-
fast ₹4000/5000/6300; ❄@; ⓜKarol Bagh) It
doesn't feel like a homestay, but this highly
professional place has 10 well-decorated
rooms. The tariff has almost doubled in
recent years, but includes complimentary
tea/coffee, local telephone calls and airport
transfers. There's a rooftop restaurant.

Ess Gee's GUESTHOUSE $$
(☑5725403; www.essgees.net; 12/9 East Patel Na-
gar; d incl breakfast ₹1250; ❄@; ⓜPatel Nagar)
An out-of-the-way, somewhat dowdy guesthouse (no signboard), with shrines in the
hallways, this may bring back fond memories of grandma's place – ask to look at a few
of the rooms as some are better than others.

Yatri House GUESTHOUSE $$
(☑23625563; www.yatrihouse.com; 3/4 Panch-
kuian Marg; s/d from ₹4000/4500; ❄@🛜; ⓜRK
Ashram Marg) Central yet serene, Yatri is less
homey than some of its peers, with spacious
rooms that have flat-screen TVs. It is fronted
by a small garden and backed by a courtyard
with wrought-iron furniture. Price includes
an airport pick-up and drop-off, free inter-
net, local calls, tea and coffee and afternoon
snack. It's only 200m to the metro.

Youth Hostel HOSTEL $
(Map p50; ☑26871969; www.yhaindia.org; 5 Nyaya
Marg, Chanakyapuri; dm/s/d ₹275/450/900, with
AC ₹600/650/1300; ❄@) The dormitory is
good value (YHA membership costs ₹100
per year), pretty clean, basic and centrally
located – it's in the diplomatic enclave.

YWCA Blue Triangle Family Hostel
HOSTEL $$
(Map p50; ☑23360133; www.ywcaofdelhi.org;
Ashoka Rd; dm ₹600, s/d incl tax & breakfast
₹1485/2585; ❄@; ⓜPatel Chowk) Despite
having an institutional vibe and hint
of eau de mothball, this Y (men and
women) is central and has reasonable
rooms.

LODI, DEFENCE COLONY & NIZAMUDDIN

ITC Maurya HOTEL $$$
(Map p50; ☑26112233; www.starwoodhotels.com;
Sardar Patel Marg; s/d ₹13,500/15,000; ❄@🛜🏊)
This is where the Obamas stayed when they
were in town in 2010. In the diplomatic
enclave, it offers all creature comforts, and
excellent service. Luxuriate in high thread
counts and dine at a clutch of sterling res-
taurants, including **Bukhara**.

K-One One GUESTHOUSE $$
(Map p50; ☑43592583; www.parigold.com; K-11
Jangpura Extn; s/d incl breakfast ₹3500/4000;
❄@🛜; ⓜJangpura) Set in a peaceful enclave,
the four rooms are spacious and painted in
jewel-bright hues, with good bathrooms and
LCD TVs, and there's a cool roof terrace dotted by red-painted pots. The owner offers
the Parul Puri cooking lessons.

Colonel's Retreat GUESTHOUSE $$
(Map p50; ☑9999720024; D-418, Defence Colony;
s/d incl breakfast ₹3500/3800; ❄@🛜; ⓜLajpat
Nagar) With four smart, nicely furnished
rooms, this is a bright and well-kept option
in a Delhi suburb. It's handily close to the
metro.

Lutyens Guest House GUESTHOUSE $$$
(Map p50; ☑24625716; www.lutyensguesthouse.
com; 39 Prithviraj Rd; d incl tax & breakfast from
₹8000; ❄@🛜🏊; ⓜRacecourse) This great
rambling house is an atmospheric green
oasis. The garden is great – lawns, flowers
and fluttering parrots – but rooms are basic,
and rates have sky-rocketed in recent years,
and it's now absurdly overpriced. However,
it's a good place to stay with kids.

SOUTH DELHI

TOP CHOICE **Bnineteen** GUESTHOUSE $$$
(Map p50; ☑41825500; www.bnineteen.
com; B-19 Nizamuddin East; d from ₹7500; ❄@) Secluded, and located in fascinating Niza-muddin East, with fabulous views over Humayun's Tomb from the rooftop, this gorgeous place shows an architect's touch. The rooms are spacious and cool, and great for long stayers, with a state-of-the-art shared kitchen on each floor.

Manor HOTEL $$$
(Map p60; ☑26925151; www.themanordelhi.com; 77 Friends Colony (West); d incl breakfast from ₹8500; ❄@) If you're looking for a more intimate alternative to Delhi's opulent five stars, this 16-room boutique hotel is it. Off Mathura Rd, set amid manicured lawns, the renovated bungalow combines contemporary luxury with caramel-hued elegance that seems from another era. The restaurant, **Indian Accent**, is superb, and lush lawns and a sun-warmed terrace complete the picture.

Treetops GUESTHOUSE $$
(Map p60; ☑9899555704; baig.murad@gmail.
com; R-8, Hauz Khas Enclave; d incl breakfast ₹4000; ❄@🛜; Ⓜ Hauz Khas) The elegant home of a hospitable couple, journalist Murad Baig and his wife Tannie, who is a cookery writer and teacher, this has two lovely large rooms opening onto a leafy roof terrace – truly in the treetops. It's minutes from the metro and Tannie gives cookery lessons (see p60). There's a cheaper, single (also en suite) room which occupies the apartment's study (₹2500). Dinner is available (₹300).

Amarya Haveli GUESTHOUSE $$$
(Map p60;☑41759267; www.amaryagroup.com; Hauz Khas Enclave; s/d ₹6500/6900; ❄@; Ⓜ Hauz Khas) The French owners of Amarya Haveli have created a haven in Hauz Khas, a boutique place that is funkily furnished with Indian artefacts, carved furniture and textiles, and has an appealing roof terrace swathed in pink and orange. They also opened in 2010 the even-more-chic **Amarya Villa** (D-179 Defence Colony; Ⓜ Lajpat Nagar), with slightly more expensive rooms (same contact details).

Home Away from Home HOMESTAY $$
(Map p60;☑26560289; permkamte@sify.com; 1st fl, D-8 Gulmohar Park; s/d incl breakfast from ₹2000/2200; ❄; Ⓜ Green Park) This stylish apartment, in a classy suburb, is home

to Mrs Kamte and she keeps the place in a gleaming condition. There are just two rooms, each tasteful, antique-decorated and with small balconies; there's a midnight curfew.

TOP CHOICE **Devna** GUESTHOUSE $$$
(Map p50; ☑24355047; www.newdelhi boutiqueinns.com; 10 Sunder Nagar; d ₹5500; ❄) Fronted by a pretty garden, gloriously pretty Devna is one of Delhi's most charismatic choices, with four curio- and antique-furnished rooms. Those opening onto the terrace upstairs are the best.

AIRPORT AREA

New Delhi Bed & Breakfast HOMESTAY $$
(☑2689 4812; www.newdelhibedandbreakfast.com; C8/8225 Vasant Kunj; s/d ₹3000/3500; @) Renu Dayal's welcoming homestay has two cosy double rooms (one en suite) in her elegant house in a leafy enclave, only 10 minutes' drive from the airport.

Inn at Delhi HOMESTAY $$
(Map p50; ☑24113234; www.innatdelhi.com; s/d ₹3500/4500; ❄@🛜) Between the city and the airport, in a smart area close to the diplomatic enclave, this is a good choice for single women. Your hosts are a professional couple, the rooms are spacious and comfortable and, upstairs, one has an impressive wooden carved bed from Rajasthan.

Chhoti Haveli HOMESTAY $$
(Map p60; ☑2612 4880; http://chhotihaveli.com; A1006, Pocket A, Vasant Kunj; s/d ₹3100/3500; ❄@) Set in a block of low-rise apartments, in a quiet, leafy area near the airport, this well-kept place offers nicely decorated rooms; there are lots of plants, with little touches such as petals adorning the steps.

Radisson Hotel HOTEL $$$
(☑26779191; www.radisson.com/newdelhiin; National Hwy 8; s/d from ₹11,500/12,500; ❄@🛜▦) Radisson's rooms are business-hotel comfortable. But oh, what a joy to lie down on soft linen and orthopaedic beds after a long-haul flight. On site are Chinese, kebab and Italian restaurants.

🍴 Eating

Delhiites love to eat, and visitors will find plenty of delicious options, ranging from ramshackle stalls serving delicious kebabs to top-of-the-range temples of excellence.

Most midrange and all upmarket restaurants charge a service tax of around 10%, while drinks taxes can suck a further 20%

EAT & DUST

Pamela Timms is a Delhiite food writer and blogs at eatanddust.wordpress.com. She can sometimes be persuaded to do food walks in Old Delhi (pamelatimms@gmail.com). Here are some of her top tips.

The Delhi street food I can never resist in the cooler months when Delhi's (particularly Old Delhi's) street food is at its most appealing:

» *Daulat ki chaat,* which is only available in the winter, is a not-too-sweet frothed milk, whisked overnight and, allegedly, set with the morning dew. Vendors bearing huge great platters of it can be seen all over Old Delhi from November to February.

» Roasted and spiced sweet potato *(shakarkandi)* served with slices of star fruit, lime juice and masala is wonderful, available all over Delhi.

» I find it very difficult to walk by the *aloo tikka* vendors. These deep-fried stuffed potato patties a great for filling awkward gaps between meals.

» For possibly the best kebabs in Delhi, head to **Moinuddin** (Map p46; Lal Kuan nr crn Gali Qasimjan; ⓜChawri Bazaar) for melt-in-the-mouth buffalo.

» For a wonderful Korma, chicken and lamb, go to **Ashok and Ashok** (Map p46; 42 Subhas Chowk, Sadar Thana Rd, Sadar Bazaar, Old Delhi; ⓜSadar Bazaar).

» If you have a sweet tooth, stop at the old and famous Jalebiwala (p70). Their deep fried fritters drenched in sugar syrup are about as good as sugar-hits get.

» If *kheer* (rice pudding) is more to your taste, go to **Bade Mian's** (Map p46; Lal Kuan; ⓜChawri Bazaar) shop in Lal Kuan.

» Also near Chawri Bazaar is the legendary **Kuremal ice cream shop** (Map p46; Kucha Pati Ram, off Sitaram Bazaar; ⓜChawri Bazaar) with flavours such as mango, pomegranate and falsa.

(alcoholic) or 12.5% (nonalcoholic) from your moneybelt. Taxes haven't been included in this chapter unless indicated.

Telephone numbers have only been provided for restaurants where reservations are recommended.

NORTH DELHI

OLD DELHI

The following eateries are featured on Map p46.

Karim's   MUGHLAI $
(mains ₹27-110; ⊙7am-midnight) Old Delhi (ⓜChawri Bazaar); Nizamuddin West (168/2 Jha House Basti) Down a lane across from the Jama Masjid's south gate (No 1), legendary Karim's has been delighting Delhi folk with divine Mughlai cuisine since 1913. The chefs prepare brutally good (predominantly nonveg) fare: try the *burrah* (marinated mutton) kebab. There's a newer branch close to Nizamuddin.

Haldiram's   FAST FOOD $$
(mains ₹50-140; ⊙9.30am-10.30pm); Old Delhi (Chandni Chowk; ⓜChandni Chowk); Connaught Place (Map p54; 6 L-Block; ⓜRajiv Chowk)

This clean, bright cafeteria-sweet shop is a handy spot for a top-notch thali (₹156), choley bhature and other morsels, some tasty South Indian cuisine, or *namkin* (savouries) and *mithai* (sweets) on the dash. Try the *soan papadi* (flaky sweet with almond and pistachio).

Chor Bizarre   KASHMIRI $$
(☎23273821; Hotel Broadway, 4/15 Asaf Ali Rd; mains ₹240-500; ⊙7.30-10.30am, noon-3.30pm & 7.30-11.30pm; ⓜNew Delhi) A dimly lit, atmospheric place, filled with eccentric clutter, Chor Bizarre (meaning 'thieves market') offers particularly delicious Kashmiri cuisine. It's popular with tourists and locals

Paratha Wali Gali   STREET FOOD $
(parathas ₹15-35; ⓜChandni Chowk) Head to this foodstall-lined lane off Chandni Chowk for delectable *parathas* (traditional flat bread) fresh off the *tawa* (hotplate). Stuffed varieties include *aloo* (potato), *mooli* (white radish), smashed pappadams and crushed *badam* (almond), all served with a splodge of tangy pickles. Some of the foodstalls have seating.

Jalebiwala
STREET FOOD $

(Dariba Corner, Chandni Chowk; jalebis per kg ₹250; MChandni Chowk) Calories schmalories! Century-old Jalebiwala does Delhi's – if not India's – finest *jalebis* (deep-fried, syrupy squiggles), so pig out and worry about your waistline tomorrow.

Al-Jawahar
MUGHLAI $$

(mains ₹20-120; ⊘7am-midnight; MChawri Bazaar) Next door to Karim's, this offers brighter surroundings for Mughlai cuisine. It serves similar and cheaper, if less legendary, fare (some swear it's even better). You can watch the naan being deftly made at the front of the shop.

Moti Mahal
NORTH INDIAN $$

(☎23273661; 3704 Netaji Subhash Marg, Daryaganj; mains ₹110-250; ⊘noon-midnight) This faded, family-oriented restaurant has been wooing diners with its Indian food for some six decades. It's famed for its butter chicken and dhal Makhani. There's live *qawwali* Wednesday to Monday (8pm–midnight).

Ghantewala
SWEETS $

(Chandni Chowk; mithai per kg from ₹220; MChandni Chowk) Delhi's most famous sweetery, 'the bell ringer' has been churning out *mithai* (Indian sweets) since 1790. Try some *sohan halwa* (ghee-dipped gram flour biscuits).

Bikanerwala
FAST FOOD $

(snacks ₹8-60; ⊘7am-midnight; MChandni Chowk) This bright little canteen offers tasty snacks such as *paratha* (stuffed bread) and *channa bhatura* (spicy chickpeas with fried puffed bread).

PAHARGANJ AREA

Yielding wobbly results, Paharganj's menus are of the mix-it-up variety, serving anything from Israeli to Italian, Mughlai to Mexican. The eateries are nothing fancy but are cheap and abuzz with chattering travellers.

The following places are along, or just off, Main Bazaar (Map p58) and near the RK Ashram Metro Stop.

Sita Ram Dewan Chand
STREET FOOD $

(2246 Chuna Mandi; half/full plate ₹17/30; ⊘8am-6pm) Pran Kohli now runs this place, which his grandfather started over 60 years ago. It's a basic and devoted to just one dish: *chole* (spicy chickpeas) accompanied by delicious, freshly made *paratha* stuffed with spices and paneer.

Tadka
INDIAN $

(4986 Ram Dwara Rd; mains ₹70-85; ⊘noon-11pm) Nothing flash, but one of the best bets in Paharganj: a simple, clean and tasty pure veg restaurant. Try the *saag paneer* (spinach and cottage cheese) and Tadka dhal.

Malhotra
MULTICUISINE $$

(1833 Laxmi Narayan St; mains ₹90-425) Snug, smartish Malhotra offers tasty Indian, continental and Chinese food that keeps it busy with a mix of locals and backpackers.

Sam's Café
MULTICUISINE $$

(Vivek Hotel, 1534-1550 Main Bazaar; mains ₹90-190) On Vivek Hotel's ground floor and (much more atmospheric) rooftop, Sam's does reasonble breakfasts and is a tranquil place to hang; it's usually packed with travellers. The pizzas are a good bet.

Metropolis Restaurant & Bar
MULTICUISINE $$$

(Metropolis Tourist Home, 1634 Main Bazaar; mains ₹225-500) On a rooftop, this crammed, humming travellers' haunt is one of the more upmarket in the area, with an encyclopedic, have-a-go-at-anything menu. It serves alcohol.

Madan Café
CAFE $

(Main Bazaar; mains ₹20-45) Cash crisis? Tuck into a basic thali for just ₹40 at this basic veg cafe; outside tables are ideal for watching the human traffic. Facing is the similar **Khosla Café**.

Kitchen Café
CAFE $

(Hotel Shelton, 5043 Main Bazaar; mains ₹55-150) This cane-furnished, plant-strewn rooftop restaurant is a relaxing place to kill time over the usual world-ranging menu.

KAROL BAGH

Angan
INDIAN $

(Map p46; Chowk Gurudwara Rd; mains ₹60-125; MKarol Bagh) A small but buzzing canteen-style pitstop for Indian and South Indian food, plus yummy snacks (try the *channa bhatura*).

Roshan di Kulfi
ICE CREAM $

(Map p46; Gafal Market, Ajmal Khan Rd; kulfi ₹45; MKarol Bagh) A Delhi institution for its scrumptious *kulfi* (pistachio-, cardamom- or saffron-flavoured frozen milk dessert). Also has good *golgappas* (small fried bread filled with water, tamarind, chilli, chaat masala, potato, onion and chickpeas) and lassi.

CONNAUGHT PLACE AREA

The following eateries appear on Map p54, unless otherwise indicated, and are closest to Metro Rajiv Chowk, unless otherwise stated.

TOP CHOICE **Saravana Bhavan** SOUTH INDIAN $
(mains ₹55-120; ⊘8am-10.30pm) Connaught Place (15 P-Block); Janpath (Map p54; 46 Janpath); Karol Bagh (Map p54; 8/54 Desh Bandhu Gupta Rd; MKarol Bagh) Massively popular, Tamil Saravana has a fast-food feel, but food is by no means junk: dosas, *idlis* and other southern specialities, accompanied by delectable coconut chutneys. Inventive sweets include cucumber-seed *ladoos* (sweet balls). Finish with a South Indian coffee.

Rajdhani INDIAN $$
(1/90 P-Block; thalis from ₹125-249; ⊘noon-3.30pm & 7-11pm) Opposite PVR Rivoli Cinema, this pristine, nicely decorated two-level place serves up excellent-value delicious vegetarian Gujarati and Rajasthani thalis, to grateful local and foreign punters.

Nizam's Kathi Kabab FAST FOOD $$
(5 H-Block; kebabs ₹110-150) This takeaway eatery has some seating and creates masterful kebabs and *kathi* rolls (kebab wrapped in *paratha*). It's always busy with kebab-loving hoards.

Andhra Pradesh Bhawan Canteen
SOUTH INDIAN $
(Map p50; 1 Ashoka Rd; veg thalis ₹80; ⊘noon-3pm; MPatel Chowk) A hallowed bargain: tasty unlimited South Indian thalis at cheap-as-chips prices; nonveg is also available. It's canteen-style, delicious and hugely popular.

Chinese CHINESE $$$
(⌨65398888; 14/15 F-Block; mains ₹300-1200; ⊘lunch & dinner) Popular with Chinese diplomats, here the Hunan chef serves up authentic cuisine, such as Hunan smoked lamb or *gong boa ji ding* (chicken with onion, chilli, peanut and hot garlic sauce) in a wow-factor calligraphy-decorated interior.

United Coffee House MULTICUISINE $$$
(15 E-Block; mains ₹300-400; ⊘10am-midnight) Oozing old-world charm and full of characters that look as elderly as the fixtures and fittings, this classic 1940s restaurant is a splendid spot to slow the pace. It has a long menu covering everything from pizza to *paneer* (cottage cheese). Try the butter chicken. It's great for an afternoon drink too (small Kingfisher ₹165).

Zen CHINESE $$$
(25 B-Block; mains ₹229-400; ⊘11am-11pm) A high-ceilinged place with a dash of old-style glitz – its walls are quilted like a Chanel handbag – this has a venerable Chinese menu, including tasty dishes such as crispy sesame lamb and Szechwan prawns, with a few Japanese and Thai cameos.

Kwality INDIAN $$
(7 Regal bdg; mains ₹200-350; ⊘noon-11pm) Charmingly old-school, with its waiters clad in dark-red jackets, Kwality's speciality is *channa bhatura*, but you might want to try some other hits, such as *malai* kofta or *murgh malai kebab* (chicken and cheese). A Kingfisher beer will set you back a refreshing ₹90.

Véda INDIAN $$$
(⌨41513535; 27 H-Block; mains ₹300-700; ⊘noon-midnight) Head here for atmosphere: fashion designer Rohit Baal created this sumptuous interior – dim red lighting, neo-Murano chandeliers, and twisted gold-a-go-go. Mughlai and North West Frontier specialities are on the menu (try the tandoori grilled lamb chops or the Parsi sea bass). A DJ plays (loudly) in the lounge bar. They also do a mean margharita.

Wenger's BAKERY $
(16 A-Block; cakes/pizza from ₹40/85; ⊘10.45am-7.45pm) Legendary Wenger's has been baking since 1926 when it was opened by a South African expat. It's always buzzing and there's a great array of sweet and savoury treats, including perfect patties.

Sagar Ratna SOUTH INDIAN $
(dishes ₹60-120); Connaught Place (15 K-Block; mains ₹60-120); Defency Colony (Map p60; 18 Defence Colony Market; MLajpat Nagar) Another dosa dreamland, with expertly prepared dosas, *idlis, uttapams* (savoury rice pancakes) and other smashing southern goodies, plus thalis.

Embassy INDIAN $$
(11 D-Block; mains ₹160-380; ⊘10am-11pm) A long-time favourite, gracious and old-fashioned, featuring Indian and continental creations.

Zäffrän MUGHLAI $$$
(mains ₹230-400; ⊘noon-3.30pm & 7pm-midnight); Connaught Place (⌨43582610; Hotel Palace Heights, 26-28 D-Block); Greater Kailash (Map p60; 2 N-Block) An excellent restaurant serving Mughlai cuisine and designed to feel like a bamboo-shuttered terrace.

Kake-da-Hotel
MUGHLAI $$
(☑9136666820; 74 M-Block; mains ₹80-110; ⊘11.30am-midnight) This simple *dhaba* (snack bar) is a basic hole in the wall that's popular with local workers for its butter chicken and other Mughlai Punjabi dishes.

Kerala House
SOUTH INDIAN $
(3 Jantar Mantar Rd; meal ₹30; ⊘1-3pm; Ⓜ Patel Chowk) The staff canteen at Kerala House was, at the time of writing, housed in part of the underground car park, but don't let this put you off. It's open to the public and tasty meals here are a bargain, including unlimited rice, sambar, a couple of veg dishes and pickle.

Tao
PAN-ASIAN $$$
(8 E-Block; mains ₹189-429; ⊘11am-11pm) Sleek and swish, but with something of the feel of an upmarket airport dining option, this is a popular place for its dim sum, Japanese, Thai and Chinese cuisine.

Nirula's
ICE CREAM $
(14 K-Block Connaught Place) Drop into Nirula's for its hot chocolate fudge ice cream, every Delhiite's favourite flavour.

DIPLOMATIC ENCLAVE & CHANAKYAPURI AREA
Bukhara
NORTH INDIAN $$$
(Map p50; ☑26112233; ITC Maurya, Sadar Patel Marg; mains ₹600-800; ⊘lunch & dinner; ❋) Considered Delhi's best restaurant, this rustic place serves Northwest Frontier-style cuisine. Its tandoor and dhal are particularly renowned. Clinton and Obama have eaten here. Reservations are essential (taken between 7pm and 8pm).

Monsoon
INDIAN $$$
(Map p50; ☑23710101; Le Meridien, Janpath; mains around ₹600-1000; ❋; Ⓜ Patel Chowk) With waterfall plate-glass windows, this is a wow-factor restaurant for sampling some creative Indian cuisine. Enjoy beautifully presented, taste-sensation dishes such as *millefeuille* of sole with mint chutney, and sumptuous pistachio *kulfi* to finish off.

Dhaba
PUNJABI $$$
(Map p50; ☑23010211; The Claridges, Chanakyapuri, 12 Aurangzeb Rd; mains ₹400-500; ⊘11.30am-4pm & 7pm-midnight) Claridges does Punjabi highway cuisine, complete with kitsch 'roadside' decor (try the balti meat and fish or chicken tikka).

LODI COLONY & PANDARA MARKET
The eateries below feature on Map p50.

Lodi Garden Restaurant
MEDITERRANEAN $$$
(Lodi Rd; mains ₹395-895; ⊘lunch & dinner; Ⓜ Jor Bagh) Set in an elegant garden shaded by trees hung with lanterns, and with a fountain made out of watering cans, beside Lodi Garden. The menu and clientele are remarkably non-Indian, but it's good for Mediterranean and Lebanese cuisine (think lamb chops with mint and tamarind, and herb-crusted Manali trout). Brunch (₹1399) is available at weekends.

All American Diner
FAST FOOD $$
(India Habitat Centre, Lodi Rd; mains ₹120-270; Ⓜ JLN Stadium) Make like it's 1950s USA and head down to the cherry-red booths and bar stools of the All American, to eat stars-and-stripes classics, from buttermilk pancakes to hot dogs, and work the jukebox. Or try the Habitat's cheap-and-cheerful food court **Eatopia**, with good *chaat,* Chinese and Indian food.

Pandara Market
INDIAN $$$
(Ⓜ Khan Market) This market has a little horseshoe of restaurants popular among night owls – most are open daily from noon to 1am or 2am. Highlights: **Pindi** (mains ₹130-370), serving tasty Mughlai Punjabi food since 1948; **Gulati** (mains ₹140-480), which has a North Indian focus amid the beige and mirrored decor; **Chicken Inn** (mains ₹150-430) flasher than the name suggests, and a popular choice for Indian and Chinese; and **Havemore** (mains ₹160-390), a snug, smartish spot, serving Indian food with a venerable veg selection.

SOUTH DELHI
KHAN & SUNDER NAGAR MARKETS
If you're shopping at the Khan (Ⓜ Khan Market) or Sunder Nagar Markets, there are some great places to top up your tank.

Amici
ITALIAN $$$
(Map p50; Khan Market; mains ₹300-400; ⊘lunch & dinner) This sleek, calm jewel of a cafe serves up splendid pizzas and tasty burgers. It has a soothing biscuit-coloured walls and a palpable sense of style. The only thing missing is a booze licence.

Sidewok
ASIAN FUSION $$$
(Map p50; ☑46068122; Khan Market; mains ₹225-475; ⊘11am-11.30pm) Sleek Sidewok dishes up top-notch Asian cuisine, amid dark slatted wood and Japanese minimalism. Try the delicious Vietnamese spring rolls.

Khan Chacha

MIDDLE EASTERN **$$**

(Map p50; Khan Market; snacks ₹110-160; ⊙noon-11pm) Chacha has gone chi-chi, the prices have doubled, and it has lost something of its original charm in the process. But all is not lost – it still turns out pretty lipsmacking roti-wrapped mutton/chicken/paneer. There is now plentiful seating, set under nail-formed lamps that look like torture implements.

Mamagoto

ASIAN FUSION **$$$**

(Map p50; ☑45166060; 1st fl, Middle Lane, Khan Market; mains ₹325-500; ⊙12.30pm-12.30am) The name means 'to play with food' in Japanese, the decor is prettily kitsch and the food is fun – a meal can span snow peas and green bean salad, lamb sticky rice and date rolls with vanilla ice cream.

Baci

ITALIAN **$$$**

(Map p50; ☑41507445; Sunder Nagar Market; mains ₹360-700; ⊙11am-1am) Reasonable Italian cuisine and good coffee is served up here in grown-up surroundings, either at the informal cafe or in the sleek upstairs restaurant. On Thursday there's live jazz from 8pm. Cocktails are ₹385.

Kitchen

PAN-ASIAN **$$**

(Map p50; ☑41757960; Khan Market; mains ₹269-399) A buzzing, small, backstreet all-rounder, simply and chicly decorated. Kitchen offers tasty dishes such as Thai red curry with rice, yummy *pad thai* and fine fish and chips.

Nathu's

INDIAN **$**

(mains ₹27-105); Sunder Nagar (Map p50; Sunder Nagar Market); Connaught Place (Map p46; 23-25 Bengali Market) Famous sweet shop serving up yummy *chaat* (snacks), *namkin* (savouries) and *mithai* (sweets), plus good thalis (₹130).

Sweets Corner

SWEETS & SNACKS **$**

(Map p50; Sunder Nagar Market; mains ₹16-90) Next door to Nathu's, this is another popular canteen-style eaterie, with a terrace out the front where local families tuck into *chaat*, sweets, South Indian dishes and thalis.

Basil & Thyme

ITALIAN **$$$**

(Map p50; Santushti Enclave; mains ₹375-435;⊙11am-6pm Mon-Sat) A chic yet simple white-washed restaurant that buzzes with expats and locals, here for the reasonable Mediterranean cooking.

[TOP CHOICE] Gunpowder

SOUTH INDIAN **$$** **73**

(Map p60; ☑26535700; 22 Hauz Khas Village; mains ₹80-300; ⊙noon-3pm & 7.30-11pm Tue-Sun; Ⓜ Hauz Khas) You reach this cool place up numerous flights to the 3rd floor. The setting is great: a simple room with wicker chairs that opens onto huge views over the greenery of Hauz Khas. The food is fit to match, with dishes such as Kerala-style vegetable korma, toddy-shop *meen* (fish) curry, and sweet-and-sour pumpkin. Bookings are essential.

Evergreen

INDIAN **$**

(Map p60; S29-30 Green Park Market; mains ₹50-115; ⊙8am-10.30pm; Ⓜ Green Park) Since 1963 Evergreen has been keeping punters happy with its snacks, *chaat* and South Indian dishes. It's a hugely popular, bright, clean two-level place that's perfect for a quick lunch or dinner.

Punjabi by Nature

PUNJABI **$$$**

(Map p60; ☑41516666; Basant Lok complex; mains ₹425-650; ⊙12.30pm-1am) Served against a masculine backdrop featuring murals of turbaned men, this place offers ravishingly delicious Punjabi food. Mop up flavour-packed sauces with *rumali roti* (paper-thin chapatis) or thick garlic naan. Go on, try the vodka *golgappas!*

Arabian Nites

KEBAB **$$**

(Map p60; 59 Basant Lok complex; snacks ₹70-230; ⊙10.30am-11pm) This teeny takeaway (there are a few inside seats) does mighty good chicken shawarma.

Moti Mahal

MUGHLAI **$$**

(Map p60; 30 M-Block; mains ₹140-450; ⊙lunch & dinner Wed-Mon) Smarter than the Old Delhi original and popular with well-off families for its North Indian and Mughlai cooking.

Diva

ITALIAN **$$$**

(Map p60; ☑29215673; M-Block; mains ₹500-950; ⊙lunch & dinner) Chef Ritu Dalmia's *molto chic* Italian restaurant is an intimate space on two levels, with white tablecloths, plate-glass windows, and a wood-fired oven behind glass. Cooking is superlative, imaginative and delicious. *Avanti!*

Smokehouse Grill

MULTICUISINE **$$$**

(Map p60; ☑41435530; 2 VIPPS Center, LSC Masjid Moth; mains around ₹600-800; ⊙7.30pm-1am)

Another uberhip hangout, suffused in minimalist chic, with lots of good, smoked(!) food on the menu. Try the smoked melon mojitos, and leave room for the divine chocolate soufflé. On Friday and Saturday nights there's a DJ playing everything from '80s to Bhangra.

Not Just Parathas NORTH INDIAN $$
(Map p60; 84 M-Block; dishes ₹80-300; ⊙noon-midnight) Yes, this cheery place offers not just *parathas* but, with 120 types on the menu, you've gotta go for the speciality, be they Tawa-fried or roasted tandoori and stuffed with *palak* (spinach), chicken tikka or *aloo gobi* (potato and cauliflower), to name a few.

DEFENCE COLONY & FRIENDS COLONY

TOP CHOICE **Indian Accent** INDIAN $$$
(Map p60; ☑26925151; Manor Hotel, 77 Friends Colony; tasting menu veg/nonveg ₹1875/1975) Overlooking the hotel veranda and lush lawns, this is a remarkable restaurant with inspired creative Indian cuisine. Expect starters such as baked paneer pinwheel and indian coriander pesto, and main dishes such as masala wild mushrooms and water chestnut paper-roast dosai.

Swagath SOUTH INDIAN $$$
(Map p60; Defence Colony Market; mains ₹235-645; ⊙11am-midnight; Ⓜ Lajpat Nagar) Supremely scrumptious Indian fare with a focus on Mangalorean and Chettinad cuisine (especially seafood), this smart six-floor restaurant swarms with well-heeled locals, here for the excellent *dhal-e-Swagath* (lentil curry), delicious *surmai rawas* (fish), butter pepper garlic, butter chicken and similarly satiating dishes.

SAKET & MEHRAULI

Olive MEDITERRANEAN $$$
(Map p60; ☑29574443; One Style Mile, Mehrauli; tasting lunch menu from ₹495, dinner mains from ₹575; ⊙noon-12pm; Ⓜ Qutb Minar) Uberchic, the original Olive has reopened, much to the delight of the Delhi in-crowd. The *haveli* setting, decorated in rustic beach-house chic, with its mismatched antiques, is unlike anywhere else in Delhi. As well as creative Mediterranean dishes, the menu includes pasta and pizzas – as tasty as the clientele.

🍸 Drinking

Whether it's cappuccino and pastries for breakfast, or beer and kebabs for supper, Delhi's cool cafes and buzzing bars deliver.
Most Delhi bars double up as both restaurants and nightclubs. The scene might not be huge, but as the sun goes down, the party starts, particularly from Wednesday to Saturday night. A smart-casual dress code (no shorts, vests or flip-flops) applies at most places.

The fancier bars are overflowing with domestic and foreign booze, but taxes can pack a nasty punch (alcoholic 20%, nonalcoholic 12.5%); taxes aren't included here unless stated. Most bars have two-for-one happy hours from around noon till 8pm or on certain days.

NEW DELHI & AROUND

Latitude CAFE
(Map p50; Khan Market; ⊙11.30am-10.30pm; Ⓜ Khan Market) Above the exclusively priced Good Earth homewares store, this is Khan Market's prettiest cafe, with sparkly chandeliers and handpainted walls. It's a good place for a chi-chi light lunch and to pretend you're not in Delhi.

Café Turtle CAFE
Greater Kailash Part I (Map p60; N-Block); Khan Market (Map p50; 2nd fl, Full Circle Bookstore; ⊙9.30am-9.30pm; Ⓜ Khan Market) This bookish, boho cafe ticks all the boxes when you're in the mood for coffee and gateau (the 'gooey chocolate cake' is a triumph).

Big Chill CAFE
(Map p50; Khan Market; ⊙noon-11.30pm; Ⓜ Khan Market) Khan Market has two film-poster-lined branches of BC, packed with chattering, well-manicured, wholesome folk. The menu is a telephone directory of continental, Indian and other dishes.

Café Oz CAFE
(Map p50; Khan Market; ⊙9am-midnight; Ⓜ Khan Market) A busy Australian cafe, this has reasonable food and Delhi's best coffee, including flat whites.

Indian Coffee House CAFE
(Map p54; Mohan Singh Place; ⊙9am-9pm; Ⓜ Rajiv Chowk) Stuck-in-time Indian Coffee House is down at heel, but serves up basic, cheap snacks and south Indian coffee (₹13!) and has a 2nd-floor terrace.

PAHARGANJ

The following are on Map p58, and close to Metro RK Ashram.

Open Hand Cafe CAFE
(Main Bazaar; ⊙8am-10pm; Ⓜ RK Ashram Marg) Bringing a touch of class to Paharganj, this South African-owned, two-level cafe has a chic, arty feel, sculptural chairs, good coffee and yummy cheesecake.

Gem
BAR

(Main Bazaar) In this dark, wood-panelled dive, a large Kingfisher costs a bargain ₹102 (including tax). Upstairs has more atmosphere. The snacks are good too.

My Bar
BAR

(Main Bazaar; ⊗10am-12.30pm) Another dark and dingy bar where the main charm is the cheap beer (Kingfisher costs ₹72 for 330ml) and the chance to hang out with other backpackers.

Metropolis Restaurant & Bar
BAR

(Metropolis Tourist Home, 1634 Main Bazaar; ⊗7am-11pm) This hotel's rooftop restaurant is a breezier choice than Gem, with al fresco drinking on its terrace and a 330cl Kingfisher for ₹80.

CONNAUGHT PLACE AREA

The following venues are located on Map p54, close to Metro Rajiv Chowk, and most have happy hours during the daytime.

1911
BAR

(Imperial Hotel, Janpath) Named after the year in which Delhi was proclaimed British India's capital, this is the ultimate neocolonial treat. Sip cocktails, while being overlooked by oil-painted Maharajas (drinks ₹650 plus).

Aqua
BAR

(Park Hotel, 15 Parliament St; ⊗11am-1am) A chic poolside bar, this see-and-be-seen place is a perfect bolthole after visiting Jantar Mantar or shopping in Connaught Place. There's seating overlooking the pool, or white-clad, curtained daybeds on which to lounge. A Kingfisher costs ₹225, and you can munch on mezze, kebabs or Lebanese snacks.

Cha Bar
CAFE

(Map p54; Oxford Bookstore, Statesman House, 148 Barakhamba Rd; ⊗10am-7.30pm Mon-Sat, noon-7.30pm Sun; ⓂBarakhamba Rd) After browsing at the Oxford, pop into Cha for a tea with a view (over CP). More than 75 flavours to choose from, and the blueberry muffins are fab too.

@live
LIVE MUSIC

(12 K-Block) Intimate and smart without being formal, @live has a cool gimmick: a live jukebox. The band plays from 8.30pm, and there's a song menu, so you choose the songs from a list including the Bee Gees, Bob Dylan and Sir Cliff. The band mightn't be the most dynamic you've seen, but they're great, and it's a fun night out (food's good too).

Q'BA
BAR

(1st fl, 42 E-Block) Connaught Place's swishest watering hole has a Q-shaped bar, dim lighting, leather chairs and Chesterfield sofas. Upstairs is the fine-dining restaurant (from 7pm) and there's a roof terrace, ideal on sultry evenings.

24/7
BAR

(Lalit Hotel, Maharaja Rajit Singh Marg; ⊗24hr) Every now and again, a 24-hour bar comes in extremely handy. This is at the Lalit hotel, so if you're hankering after a Martini at 5am you can drink it somewhere defiantly unseedy.

Costa
CAFE

(Map p54; L-Block, Connaught Place; ⊗9am-11pm; ⓂRajiv Chowk) Arguably the best of the coffee chains, a dapper downtown cafe with strong coffee, delicate teas, English-toffee milkshakes and good cakes.

Café Coffee Day
CAFE

Connaught Place (Map p54; 11 N-Block, Connaught Place; ⊗9am-11pm; ⓂRajiv Chowk); Khan Market (Map p50; ⓂKhan Market). You know what you're getting at CCD: cappuccinos, Americanised cheery staff and brownies. But sometimes that's what you need. Citywide branches galore.

Pind Balluchi
BAR

(Regal Bldg; ⊗noon-11pm) This location has undergone yet another makeover, and this time emerged as a high-kitsch 'village restaurant' complete with a fake central tree. It still has possibly CP's cheapest beers and cocktails (Kingfisher ₹120, cocktails from ₹120).

Blues
BAR

(18 N-Block) A dark den with reasonably priced beers. The brick walls are plastered with the likes of Jimi Hendrix and other less-recognisable figures. With its cheerily unhip soundtrack (think Sonny and Cher), this is a lively, snob-free zone.

Rodeo
BAR

(12 A-Block) In the mood for saloon doors, tequila, saddle barstools and staff in cowboy hats? Then easygoing Rodeo is for you, partner. Cocktails cost from ₹275, but give the nachos a miss.

SOUTH DELHI

The following drinking venues are on Map p60.

Kunzum Travel Cafe
CAFE

(Map p60; Hauz Khas Village; ⊗11am-7.30pm Tue-Sun; 🕿; ⓂHauz khas) This unique cafe is run by travel authors and photographers and has a pay-what-you-like policy, self-service French-press coffee and tea, and travel books and magazines to browse. You can also BYO drinks and food and put your iPod in the dock!

Love Hotel BAR
(2nd fl, MGF Metropolitan Mall; ☺1pm-1am; Ⓜ Saket) In a mall, but worth seeking out nonetheless: the Love Hotel adjoins **Ai**, an exclusive, popular and chic Japanese restaurant, and occupies a little open terrace. The food is excellent and the atmosphere is best here when there's a party going on – check local listings for what's on. Cocktails cost around ₹400.

Shalom BAR
Greater Kailash I (18 N-Block; ☺noon-1am); Vasant Vihar (4 D-Block) This loungey bar–restaurant, with wooden furniture and whitewashed walls, is one of the doyennes of the Delhi loungebar scene. As well as wine, beers, cocktails (around ₹400) and nightly DJs, there's top-notch Mediterranean fare.

Urban Pind BAR
(4 N-Block, Greater Kailash I; ☺noon-1am) Three-floored, this has cushy flocked sofas, mock-Khajuraho carvings and nightly DJs. Tuesday is Salsa night, with free lessons from 9pm, while expats and diplomats flock on a Thursday for the all-you-can-drink deal.

Red Monkey BAR
(☑24618358; 7 Defence Colony Market; ☺4pm-1am; Ⓜ Lajpat Nagar) A small cosy bar, this is a buzzy if unexciting choice in the Defence Colony. Cocktails cost ₹300-500 and it's worth making it for happy Monday, where it's two-for-one.

☆ Entertainment

To access Delhi's dynamic arts scene, check local listings (see p80). October and March is the 'season', with happenings (often free) nightly.

TLR LIVE MUSIC
(www.tlrcafe.com; Hauz Khas Village; ☺11am-1am; Ⓜ Hauz Khas) Delhi's coolest and most boho hangout, TLR (The Living Room) is in laid-back Hauz Khas Village. It's worth the trek: a 2nd-floor bar with live music, jam sessions and other events from 9pm most evenings. It has a tiny stage complete with a three-piece suite. Meals are also available and cocktails cost from ₹400. If there's something on, book a table or arrive early.

Attic CULTURAL PROGRAM
(Map p54; ☑23746050; www.theatticdelhi.org; 36 Regal bdg; Ⓜ Rajiv Chowk) Small arts space, with regular free classical concerts and talks. There are also explorations of forgotten foods and 'food meditation' (where participants eat in silence and then have a discussion) – these sessions cost ₹100 and should be booked in advance.

Dances of India DANCE
(Map p46; ☑26234689; Parsi Anjuman Hall, Bahadur Shah Zafar Marg; ₹400; ☺6.45pm) A one-hour performance of regional dances that includes Bharata Natyam (Tamil dance), Kathakali, bhangra and Manipuri.

Haze LIVE MUSIC
(8 Basant Lok, Visant Vihar; ☺3pm-midnight) A hip yet unpretentious haunt, this moody, intimate, inexpensive jazz bar has real soul and is *the* place to see live Indian blues and jazz at weekends.

Habitat World CULTURAL PROGRAM
(Map p50; ☑43663333; www.habitatworld.com; India Habitat Centre, Lodi Rd) Check out the Visual Arts Gallery's excellent temporary exhibitions.

India International Centre CULTURAL PROGRAM
(Map p50; ☑24619431; 40 Max Mueller Marg) The IIC holds regular free exhibitions, talks and cultural performances.

PVR Plaza Cinema CINEMA
(Map p54; ☑41516787; H-Block, Connaught Place)

PVR Priya Cinema CINEMA
(Map p60; www.pvrcinemas.com; Basant Lok complex, Vasant Vihar)

PVR Saket (Anupam 4) CINEMA
(Map p60; www.pvrcinemas.com; Saket Community Centre, Saket)

🔒 Shopping

From bamboozling bazaars to *bijoux* boutiques, Delhi is a fantastic place to shop. There's an astounding array of wonderful stuff: handicrafts, textiles, clothing, carpets, jewellery and a kaleidoscope of saris.

Away from the emporiums and other fixed-price shops, put on your haggle hat. Many taxi and autorickshaw drivers earn commissions (via your inflated purchase price) and may not take you to the most reputable stores, either, making it best to decline their shopping suggestions.

For dependable art gallery recommendations (many of which sell exhibits), check *First City* and *Time Out*.

Old Delhi's **bazaars** (Map p46; MChandni Chowk) are a headspinning assault on the senses: an aromatic muddle of flowers, urine, incense, chai, fumes and frying food. They're busiest (and best avoided) on Monday and Friday and during other afternoons. Come at around 11.30am when most shops have opened and the jostling is bearable.

For silver jewellery (some gold) head for **Dariba Kalan**, near the Sisganj Gurdwara. Nearby **Kinari Bazaar** (literally 'trimmings market') is famous for *zari* (gold-thread weaving) and *zardozi* (gold embroidery), and is the place to head for your bridal trousseau. The **cloth market** sells swathes of uncut material and linen, while electrical gadgets are the speciality of **Lajpat Rai Market**. **Chowri Bazaar** is the wholesale paper and greeting-card market. Nearby, **Nai Sarak** deals in wholesale stationery, books and saris.

Near the Fatehpuri Masjid, on Khari Baoli, is the nose-numbing **Spice Market**, ablaze with powdery piles of scarlet-red chilli powder and burnt-orange turmeric, as well as pickles, tea and nuts. As it's a wholesale market, spices here rarely come hermetically sealed – for these, go to Roopak's in Karol Bagh.

The **Daryaganj Book Market**, north of Delhi Gate, is a bookworm's delight (Sunday afternoons).

NORTH DELHI

Chandni Chowk   CLOTHING
(Map p46; Old Delhi; ⊙Mon-Sat; MChandni Chowk) Pure pandemonium, this is the old city's famed shopping strip, with endless haphazard traffic, stores selling a mishmash of saris, Nehru suits, glittering shoes and electrical goods. There are roadside tailors and locksmiths, hawkers selling birdseed, labourers catching a snooze amid the chaos and half-dead dogs everywhere you look. Some stores open from around 10am to 7pm, others from noon to 9pm.

New Gramophone House   MUSIC STORE
(Map p46; ☑23271524; Pleasure Garden Market; ⊙10am-9pm Mon-Sat; MChandni Chowk) Opposite Moti Cinema, this is a 1st-floor wonderland of vintage Bollywood records (₹50 to ₹200) and even older gramophones.

Main Bazaar   MARKET
(Map p58; Paharganj; ⊙around 10am-9pm Tue-Sun; MRK Ashram Marg) The backpacker-oriented spine of Paharganj is the perfect place to pick up bargains in the form of T-shirts, bags, costume jewellery, essential oils, incense and more. Although the Main Bazaar is officially closed on Monday, many of the shops remain open during the tourist season.

Karol Bagh Market   MARKET
(Map p46; ⊙around 10am-7pm Tue-Sun; MKarol Bagh) This brash middle-class market shimmers with all things sparkly, from dressy *lehanga choli* (skirt-and-blouse sets) to princess-style shoes. Get spice-happy at

Roopak's (6/9 Ajmal Khan Rd), two neighbouring shops with similar spices (around ₹60 to ₹100 per 100g and well packed).

CONNAUGHT PLACE

Central Cottage Industries Emporium
HANDICRAFTS
(Map p54; ☑23326790; Janpath; MRajiv Chowk) This government-run, fixed-price multilevel Aladdin's cave of India-wide handicrafts is a great place to shop: woodcarvings, silverware, jewellery, pottery, papier mâché, brassware, textiles (including shawls), beauty products and heaps more.

State Emporiums   HANDICRAFTS
(Map p54; Baba Kharak Singh Marg; ⊙11am-7pm Mon-Sat; MRajiv Chowk) These neighbouring state government emporiums showcase products from different states, from Rajasthan to Bihar. Set aside several hours for these fabulous shops.

Shop   CLOTHING & HOMEWARES
(Map p54; 10 Regal Bldg, Sansad Marg; ⊙9.30am-7pm Mon-Sat; MRajiv Chowk) There are lovely homewares and clothes (including children's clothes) from all over India in this chic boutique with reasonable fixed prices.

🖉 Khadi Gramodyog Bhawan
HANDICRAFTS
(Map p54; Regal Bldg, Sansad Marg; ⊙10.30am-7.15pm Mon-Sat; MRajiv Chowk) Best known for its excellent *khadi* (homespun cloth) clothing, including good-value shawls, but also worth a visit for its handmade paper, incense, spices, henna and lovely natural soaps.

Oxford Bookstore (Statesman House)

BOOKSTORE

(Map p54; 14 G-Block, Connaught Place; 🕙10am-9.30pm Mon-Sat, 11am-9.30pm Sun; MRajiv Chowk) A fantastic bookshop where you could spend hours. It also sells some good gifts, such as handmade paper notebooks. Attached is the **Cha Bar**.

People Tree

HANDICRAFTS

(Map p54; Regal Bldg, Sansad Marg; 🕙10.30am-7pm Mon-Sat; MRajiv Chowk) The blink-and-you'll-miss-it People Tree sells cool, etching-style or embroidered T-shirts, many featuring Indian gods, as well as skirts, dresses, shirts (for men and women), shoulder bags, costume jewellery and books.

Soma

HOMEWARES

(Map p54; 1st fl, 44 K-Block, Connaught Place; 🕙10am-8pm; MRajiv Chowk) Situated opposite PVR Plaza Cinema, 1st-floor Soma stocks brilliant block-printed textiles at reasonable prices: anything from scarves to pyjamas, cushion covers to children's clothing.

Marques & Co

MUSIC STORE

(Map p54; 14 G-Block, Connaught Place; 🕙10.30am-1.30pm & 2-6.30pm Mon-Sat; MRajiv Chowk) This vintage music shop (since 1918) houses polished guitars (from ₹3000), tablas (from ₹6000) and harmonicas (from ₹300) in stuck-in-time glass cabinets. Sheet music is also available.

Janpath Market

MARKET

(Map p54; Janpath; 🕙10.30am-7.30pm Mon-Sat; MRajiv Chowk) Aka the Tibetan Market, this touristy strip sells the usual trinkets: shimmering mirrorwork textiles, colourful shawls, brass oms, and dangly earrings and trinkets galore. It has some good finds if you rummage through the junk. Haggle hard.

Rikhi Ram

MUSIC STORE

(☎23327685; www.rikhiram.com; 8A G-Block, Connaught Place; 🕙11.30am-8pm Mon-Sat; MRajiv Chowk) A beautiful old shop, selling professional classic and electric sitars, tablas and more.

M Ram & Sons

CLOTHING

(Map p54; ☎23416558; 21 E-Block, Connaught Place; 🕙10am-8pm Mon-Sat; MRajiv Chowk) Men's suits from ₹4000 (excluding material), ladies long skirts from ₹500 (excluding material). Tailoring is possible in 24 hours.

SOUTH DELHI

Khan Market

MARKET

(Map p50; 🕙around 10.30am-8pm Mon-Sat; MKhan Market) Favoured by expats and Delhi's elite, the boutiques in this enclave are devoted to fashion, books, homewares, and gourmet groceries. For handmade paperware check out **Anand Stationers**. For a fantastic range of English-language fiction and nonfiction head to **Full Circle Bookstore** and **Bahri Sons**. There's a TARDIS-like branch of **Fabindia** (p79), **Anokhi**, wow-factor homewares store **Good Earth** (featuring London-style prices) and the excellent **Silverline**, which does attractive, reasonable silver and gold jewellery.

Dilli Haat

HANDICRAFTS

(Map p60; Aurobindo Marg; admission ₹15; 🕙10.30am-10pm; MINA) Located opposite the colourful INA Market, this open-air food-and-crafts market sells regional handicrafts; bargain hard. Tasty on-site food stalls cook up regionally diverse cuisine. Avoid the busy weekends.

Hauz Khas Village

ANTIQUES & CLOTHING

(Map p60; 🕙11am-7pm Mon-Sat; MHauz Khas) This arty little enclave is packed with designer Indian-clothing boutiques, art galleries and furniture shops. It's a great place to find superb old Bollywood posters. Try Country Collection for antique and new furniture (they'll post overseas), and Cotton Curios for handprinted *kameez* (women's tunics) and soft furnishings.

C Lal & Sons

HANDICRAFTS

(Map p50; 9/172 Jor Bagh Market; 🕙10.30am-7.30pm; MJor Bagh) After sightseeing at Safdarjang's tomb, drop into kindly Mr Lal's 'curiosity shop'. Much loved by Delhi-based diplomats for its dazzling Christmas-tree decorations, it also sells handicrafts such as papier mâché and carvings.

Timeless

BOOKSTORE

(Map p60; ☎24693257; 46 Housing Society, Part I) Hidden in a back lane (ask around), Timeless has a devoted following for its quality coffee-table books, from Indian textiles to architecture.

Sarojini Nagar Market

CLOTHING

(Map p60; 🕙around 11am-8pm Tue-Sun; MINA) Rummage here for good-value Western-style clothes (seek out the lanes lined exclusively with clothing stalls) that have been dumped here either because they were an export surplus or from a cancelled line. Check for faults. Bargain hard.

Sunder Nagar Market
HANDICRAFTS, TEA

(Map p50; ⊙around 10.30am-7.30pm Mon-Sat) Just south of Purana Qila, this genteel enclave specialises in Indian and Nepali handicrafts and 'antiques' (most are replicas). There are two outstanding teashops here: **Regalia Tea House** (⊙10am-7.30pm Mon-Sat, 11am-5pm Sun); and its neighbour **Mittal Tea House** (⊙10am-7.30pm Mon-Sat, 10am-4.30pm Sun). They stock similar products and offer complimentary tea tastings. There's plenty on offer, from fragrant Kashmiri kahwa (green tea with cardamom; ₹110 per 100g) to the finest of teas, Vintage Musk (₹700 per 100g) and Royal Muscatel (₹600 per 100g). The white tea (₹600/350 per 100g organic/nonorganic) is said to contain more antioxidants than green tea, while dragon balls (₹35-80 each) are a visual thrill when brewed.

Santushti Shopping Complex
HOMEWARES, CLOTHING

(Map p50; Santushti Enclave; ⊙10am-7pm Mon-Sat) This enclave across from the Ashok hotel is an unusually relaxing, if expensive, place to browse and shop, with stores such as **Anokhi**, **Good Earth** and **Shyam Ahuja** (which sells carpets), housed in appealing little pavilions in a landscaped area.

M-Block & N-Block Markets
MARKET

(Map p60; Greater Kailash I; ⊙Wed-Mon) This two-part upmarket shopping enclave is perhaps best known for the awesome mothership of **Fabindia**. Also worth checking out is the clothes store **Anokhi** (N-Block) and the big branch of the lovely **Full Circle Bookstore**, complete with a Café Turtle.

Fabindia
CLOTHING, HOMEWARES

GKI (Map p60; www.fabindia.com; 7 N-Block Market; ⊙10am to 7.30pm); Khan Market (Map p50; Above shop 20 & 21; ⓜKhan Market); Connaught Place (Map p54; Upper Ground fl, 28 B-Block; ⓜRajiv Chowk) Readymade clothes that won't look odd back home, plus great tablecloths, cushion covers, curtains and other homewares.

Nalli Silk Sarees
CLOTHING

Greater Kailash (Map p60; ☑24629926; Greater Kailash II; ⊙10am-8.30pm); Connaught Place (Map p54; 7/90 P-Block; ⓜRajiv Chowk) This multistorey sari emporium is a kaleidoscope of silk varieties, specialising in those from South India. Prices range from ₹1000 to ₹30,000.

Lajpat Nagar Central Market
MARKET

(Map p60; ⊙around 11am-8pm Tue-Sun; ⓜLajpat Nagar) This market attracts bargain-hunting locals on the prowl for household goods, clothing and jewellery. Look out for the local *mehndiwallahs,* who paint beautiful henna designs.

Delhi Musical Stores
MUSIC STORE

(Map p46; ☑23276909; www.indianmusical instruments.com; 1070 Paiwalan, Old Delhi; ⊙10am-6.30pm Mon-Sat; ⓜPatel Chowk) Opposite Jama Masjid's Gate No 3. Check the website for details.

OCM Suitings
CLOTHING

(Map p50; ☑24618937; Khan Market; ⊙11am-8pm Mon-Sat; ⓜKhan Market) Men's wool suits from ₹9000 to ₹22,000 (including material); ankle-length skirts from ₹500 (excluding material). Suits take around 7 to 10 days.

ℹ Information
Dangers & Annoyances

HOTEL TOUTS Taxi-wallahs at the international airport frequently act as touts. These sneaky drivers will try to persuade you that your hotel is full, poor value, overbooked, dangerous, burned down or closed, or even that there are riots in Delhi. Their intention is to take you to a hotel where they'll get some commission. Some will even 'kindly' take you to a 'tourist office' where a colleague will phone your hotel on your behalf, and corroborate the driver's story. In reality, of course, he's talking to his mate in the next room. Alternatively, the driver may claim that he's lost and stop at a travel agency for directions. The agent supposedly dials your hotel and informs you that your room is double-booked, and 'helpfully' finds you another hotel where he'll get commission and you get a high room rate.

Tell persistent taxi drivers that you've paid for your hotel in advance, have recently confirmed the booking, or have friends/relatives waiting for you there. If they continue, ask that they stop the car so that you can write down the registration plate number. Just to be sure, call or email to confirm your hotel booking, if possible, 24 hours before check-in.

TRAVEL AGENT TOUTS Be cautious with travel agencies, as many travellers every year report being overcharged and underwhelmed by unscrupulous agents. To avoid grief, ask for traveller recommendations, or ask for a list of recommended agents from the India Tourist office (88 Janpath). *Think twice before parting with your money.* Choose agents who are members of accredited associations such as the Travel Agents Association of India and the Indian Association of Tour Operators.

Be especially careful if booking a multistop trip out of Delhi. Lonely Planet often gets letters from travellers who've paid upfront and then found out there are extra expenses, they've been overcharged, or the accommodation is terrible. Given the number of letters we've received from unhappy travellers, it's also best not to book tours to Kashmir from Delhi.

TRAIN STATION TOUTS These touts are at their worst at New Delhi train station. Here they may try to prevent you reaching the upstairs International Tourist Bureau and divert you to a local (over-priced and often unreliable) travel agency. Make the assumption that the office is *never* closed (outside the official opening hours; see p81) and has not shifted. It's still in its regular place on the 1st floor, close to the Paharganj side of the station.

Other swindlers may insist that your ticket needs to be stamped or checked (for a hefty fee) before it is considered valid. Some may try to convince wait-listed passengers that there is a charge to check their reservation status – don't fall for it.

For more info on Scams & Touts, see p344.

Internet Access

Internet cafes are mushrooming, with centres in Khan Market, Paharganj and Connaught Place, among others, usually charging around ₹35 per hour, ₹5 to print a page and ₹25 to scan/write a CD. Reviewed places with wi-fi are indicated with 🛜.

Media

To check out what's on, grab *Delhi Diary* (₹10). Fab monthly magazine *First City* (₹50) has comprehensive listings/reviews, ranging from theatre to so-now bars, while *Time Out Delhi* (₹40) is a hip take on the city. Publications are available at newsstands and bookshops.

Medical Services

Pharmacies are ubiquitous in most markets.

All India Institute of Medical Sciences (Aiims; Map p60; ☏26588500; www.aiims.edu; Ansari Nagar; Ⓜ AIIMS)

Apollo Hospital (☏26925858; Mathura Rd, Sarita Vihar)

Dr Ram Manohar Lohia Hospital (Map p50; ☏23365525; Baba Kharak Singh Marg)

East West Medical Centre (Map p60; ☏24690429; www.eastwestrescue.com; B-28 Greater Kailash Part I) Opposite N-Block Market; this is one of the easier options if you have to make an insurance claim.

Money

There are ATMs almost everywhere you look in Delhi. Many travel agents and money changers, including Thomas Cook, can do international money transfers.

Baluja Forex (Map p58; ☏41541523; 4596 Main Bazaar, Paharganj; ⊙9am-7.30pm) Does cash advances on MasterCard and Visa.

Central Bank of India (Map p50; ☏26110101; Ashok Hotel, Chanakyapuri; ⊙24hr)

Thomas Cook International airport (☏25653439; ⊙24hr); Janpath (Map p50; ☏23342171; Hotel Janpath, Janpath; ⊙9.30am-7pm Mon-Sat)

Post & Telephone

Delhi has tons of telephone kiosks where you can make cheap local, interstate and international calls.

DHL (Map p54; ☏23737587; Mercantile Bldg, ground fl Tolstoy Marg; ⊙8am-8pm Mon-Sat) Organises international air freight.

Post office Connaught Place (Map p54; 6 A-Block; ⊙8am-8pm Mon-Sat); New Delhi main post office (Map p50; ☏23364111; Baba Kharak Singh Marg; ⊙10am-1pm & 1.30-4pm Mon-Sat) Poste restante available at the main post office; ensure mail is addressed to GPO, New Delhi – 110001.

Tourist Information

Beware Delhi's many dodgy travel agencies and 'tourist information centres'. Do *not* be fooled – the only official tourist information centre is India Tourism Delhi. Touts may (falsely) claim to be associated with this office.

For Indian regional tourist offices' contact details ask at India Tourism Delhi, or dial directory enquiries on ☏197.

India Tourism Delhi (Government of India; Map p54; ☏23320008/5; www.incredible india.org; 88 Janpath; ⊙9am-6pm Mon-Fri, to 2pm Sat) Gives tourist-related advice as well as a free Delhi map and brochures. Has a list of recommended agencies and bed & breakfasts. Their special branch investigates tourism-related complaints.

🛈 Getting There & Away

Delhi is a major international gateway. It's also a centre for domestic travel, with extensive bus, rail and air connections. Delhi's airport can be prone to thick fog in December and January (often disrupting airline schedules), making it wise not to book back-to-back flights during this period.

Air

International and domestic flights all leave from and arrive at the airport's gleaming new Terminal 3. For flight inquiries, call the **international airport** (☏0124-3376000; www.newdelhi airport.in). At the new Terminal 3 there are 14 'nap & go' rooms with wi-fi, a desk, TV and bed (₹315/hr).

PUBLIC BUSES

Apart from public buses, there are comfortable private bus services (including sleepers), leaving from central locations, but their schedules vary (enquire at travel agencies or your hotel). Example routes are Delhi to Jammu (₹500, 15 hours) and McLeon Ganj (₹650, 14 hours). Himachal Pradesh Tourism Development Corporation (HPTDC) also runs a bus for Dharamsala from Connaught Place. There are buses to Agra, but the train is much easier and quicker.

DESTINATION	ONE-WAY FARE (₹)	DURATION (HR)	DEPARTURES
Amritsar	500-665 (B)	10	hourly 5.30am-9.30pm
Chandigarh	180/345-515 (A/B)	5	every 30min 6am-1.50am
Dehra Dun	179/278-460 (A/B)	7	hourly 5am-11pm
Dharamsala	395/500-780 (A/B)	12	hourly 4.30am-11pm
Kullu	490/830-1050 (A/B)	13	9am
Manali	490/830-1050 (A/B)	15	hourly 1-10pm
Shimla	310/580-860	10	hourly 5am-10.30pm

A – ordinary, B – deluxe AC

For comprehensive details of domestic air routes, see *Excel's Timetable of Air Services Within India* (₹55), available at newsstands. When making reservations request the most direct (quickest) route. Note that airline prices fluctuate and website bookings with some carriers can be markedly cheaper.

DOMESTIC ARRIVALS & DEPARTURES
Check-in at the airport for domestic flights is one hour before departure.

DOMESTIC AIRLINES The **Air India office** (3 Safdarjung Airport; ☉9.30am-5.30pm) is in South Delhi. To confirm flights dial ☎1407.

Other domestic airlines:

Jagson Airlines (Map p54; ☎23721593; Vandana Bldg, 11 Tolstoy Marg)

Kingfisher Airlines (Map p54; ☎23730238; 42 N-Block, Connaught Place)

INTERNATIONAL ARRIVALS The arrivals hall has 24-hour money-exchange facilities, ATM, prepaid taxi and car-hire counters, a tourist information counter, cafes and bookshops.

INTERNATIONAL DEPARTURES At the check-in counter, ensure you collect tags to attach to hand luggage (mandatory to clear security later).

Bus

Bikaner House (Map p50; ☎23383469; Pandara Rd), near India Gate, operates good state-run buses. These are the best buses for Jaipur (super deluxe/Volvo ₹325/625, six hours, hourly); Udaipur (₹750, 15 hours, one daily); Ajmer (₹400, nine hours, three daily); and Jodhpur (₹500, 11 hours, one daily).

Delhi's main bus station is the **Inter State Bus Terminal** (ISBT; Map p46; ☎23860290;

Kashmiri Gate; ☉24hr), north of the (Old) Delhi train station. It has a 24-hour left-luggage facility (₹14 per bag). This station is chaotic so arrive at least 30 minutes ahead of your departure time. State-government bus companies (and their counters) at the ISBT include the following (timetables are online):

Delhi Transport Corporation
(☎23865181; dtc.nic.in; Counter 34)

Haryana Roadways
(☎23861262; hartrans.gov.in; Counter 35)

Himachal Roadways (☎23868694; Counter 40)

Punjab Roadways (☎23867842; www.punjabroadways.gov.in; Counter 37)

Rajasthan Roadways
(☎23386658, 23864470; Counter 36)

Uttar Pradesh Roadways
(☎23868709; Counter 33)

Train

For foreigners, it's easiest to make ticket bookings at the helpful **International Tourist Bureau** (Map p58; ☎23405156; 1st fl, New Delhi train station; ☉8am-8pm Mon-Sat, to 2pm Sun). Do *not* believe anyone – including porters – who tells you it has shifted, closed or burnt down and don't let anyone stop you from going to the 1st floor of the *main* building for bookings. When making reservations here, if you are paying in rupees you may have to provide back-up money-exchange certificates (or ATM receipts), so take these with you just in case. You can also pay in travellers cheques: in Thomas Cook US dollars, euros or pounds sterling, Amex US dollars and euros, and US dollars in Barclays cheques. Any change is given in rupees. Bring your passport.

When you arrive, complete a reservation form, then wait to check availability at the Tourism Counter in the office. You can then queue to pay for the ticket at one of the other counters.

There are two main stations in Delhi – (Old) Delhi train station (Map p46) in Old Delhi, and New Delhi train station (Map p46) at Paharganj; make sure you know which station serves your destination (New Delhi train station is closer to Connaught Place). If you're departing from the Delhi train station, allow adequate time to meander through Old Delhi's snail-paced traffic.

There's also the Nizamuddin train station (Map p50), south of Sunder Nagar, where various trains (usually for south-bound destinations) start or finish.

Railway porters should charge around ₹30 per bag.

There are many more destinations and trains than those listed in the boxed text, p83 – check the Indian Railways Website (www.indianrail.gov.in) consult *Trains at a Glance* (₹45), available at most newsstands, or ask tourist office staff.

Getting Around

The metro system has transformed getting around the city, making it incredibly easy to whizz out to places that were once a long traffic-hampered struggle to reach. Most of Delhi's main sights lie close to a metro station. Local buses get horrendously crowded so the metro, autorickshaws and taxis are desirable alternatives. Keep small change handy for fares.

To/From the Airport

Many international flights arrive at ghastly hours, so it pays to book a hotel in advance and notify it of your arrival time.

PRE-ARRANGED PICK-UPS If you arrange an airport pick-up through a travel agency or hotel, it's more expensive than a prepaid taxi from the airport due to the airport parking fee (up to ₹140) and ₹80 charge for the person collecting you to enter the airport arrivals hall. Sometimes drivers are barred from arrivals for security reasons, in which case most will wait outside Gates 4–6.

METRO The new high-speed metro line is the best way to get to/from the airport, and runs between New Delhi train station and Dwarka Sector 21, via Shivaji Stadium, Dhaula Kuan NH8 (Mahipalpur station) and Indira Gandhi International station (Terminal 3). Trains operate every 10 minutes from 5am to 1am.

BUS Air-conditioned deluxe buses run to the airport about every 40 minutes from ISBT Kashmere Gate, via the Red Fort, LNJP Hospital, New Delhi Station Gate 2, Connaught Place, Parliament Street and Ashoka Rd (₹50). There are several other routes, one of which goes via Saket and Vasant Kunj; another calls at Hauz Khas and Vasant Vihar.

TAXI There is a **Delhi Traffic Police Prepaid Taxi counter** (☑ helpline 23010101; www.delhitrafficpolice.nic.in) inside the arrivals building. It costs about ₹310 to Connaught Place, plus a 25% surcharge between 11pm and 5am.

You'll be given a voucher with the destination on it – insist that the driver honours it. Never surrender your voucher until you get to your destination; without that docket the driver won't get paid.

You can also book a prepaid taxi at the **Megacabs** counter inside the arrivals building at both the international and domestic airports. It costs around ₹600 to the centre, but you get a cleaner, car with air-con, and you can pay by credit card.

Car

HIRING A CAR & DRIVER Numerous operators offer chauffeur-driven cars. The following companies get positive reports from travellers. Each has an eight-hour, 80km limit per day. All offer tours beyond Delhi (including Rajasthan) but higher charges apply for these. The rates below are only for travel within Delhi. Beware of frauds/touts claiming association with these companies or insisting their offices have closed.

Kumar Tourist Taxi Service (Map p54; ☑ 23415930; kumartaxi@rediffmail.com; 14/1 K-Block, Connaught Place; non-AC/AC per day ₹800/900; ☺ 9am-9pm) Near the York Hotel. Tiny office run by two brothers, Bittoo and Titoo. Their rates are among Delhi's lowest.

Metropole Tourist Service (Map p50; ☑ 24310313; www.metrovista.co.in; 224 Defence Colony Flyover Market; non-AC car per day from ₹850; ☺ 7am-7pm) Under the Defence Flyover Bridge (on the Jangpura side).

Cycle-Rickshaw & Bicycle

Cycle-rickshaws are still in use in parts of Old Delhi, though they have been banned in Chandni Chowk to reduce congestion. Let's hope they're not banned in other areas, as they're the best way to get around Old Delhi – the drivers are wizards at weaving through the crowds. Tips are appreciated for this gruelling work.

Cycle-rickshaws are also banned from the Connaught Place area and New Delhi, but they're handy for commuting between Connaught Place and Paharganj (about ₹30).

The largest range of new and secondhand bicycles for sale can be found at **Jhandewalan Cycle Market** (Map p46).

Metro

Delhi's marvellous metro (Map p64) has efficient services with arrival/departure announcements in Hindi and English. Two carriages on each train are designated women-only – look for the pink signs on the platform. The trains can get very busy, particularly at peak commuting times (around 9-10am and 5-6pm).

DESTINA-TION	TRAIN NO & NAME	FARE (₹)	DURA-TION (HR)	FREQUENCY	DEPAR-TURES & TRAIN STATION
Agra	12280 *Taj Exp*	75/263 (A)	3	1 daily	7.10am HN
	12002A *Bhopal Shatabdi*	370/700 (B)	2	1 daily	6.15am ND
Amritsar	12013 *Shatabdi Exp*	645/1200 (B)	5½	1 daily	4.30pm ND
	12029/12031 *Swarna/Amritsar Shatabdi*	600/1145 (B)	5½	1 daily	7.20am ND
Bengaluru	12430 *Bangalore Rajdhani*	2100/2740/4580 (C)	34	4 weekly	8.50pm HN
Chennai	12434 *Chennai Rajdhani*	2075/2700/4500 (C)	28	2 weekly	4pm HN
	12622 *Tamil Nadu Exp*	528/1429/1960/3322 (D)	33	1 daily	10.30pm ND
Goa (Madgaon)	12432 *Trivndrm Rajdhani*	2035/2615/4370 (C)	25½	2 weekly	11am HN
Haridwar	12017 *Dehradun Shatabdi*	435/825 (B)	4½	1 daily	6.50am ND
Jaipur	12958 *ADI SJ Rajdani*	605/775/1285 (C)	5	6 weekly	7.55pm ND
	12916 *Ashram Exp*	175/434/581/969 (D)	5¾	1 daily	3pm OD
	12015 *Shatabdi Exp*	465/885 (B)	4¾	6 weekly	6.05am ND
Khajuraho	12448 *Nizamud-din-Khajuraho Exp*	269/802 (E)	10¼	3 weekly	8.15pm HN
Lucknow	12004 *Lko Swran Shatabdi*	700/1360 (B)	6¼	1 daily	6.15am ND
Mumbai	12952 *Mumbai Rajdhani*	1495/1975/3305 (C)	16	1 daily	4.30pm ND
	12954 *Ag Kranti Rajdani Exp*	1495/1975/3305 (C)	17¼	1 daily	4.55pm HN
Udaipur	12963 *Mewar Exp*	320/801/1087/1821 (D)	12	1 daily	7.05pm HN
Varanasi	12560 *Shivganga Exp*	320/806/1095/1805 (D)	13	1 daily	6.45pm ND

Train stations: ND – New Delhi, OD – Old Delhi, HN – Hazrat Nizamuddin

Fares: A – 2nd class/chair car; B – chair car/1st-class AC; C – 3AC/2AC/1st-class AC; D – sleeper/3AC/2AC/1st-class AC; E – sleeper/3AC

Tokens (₹8 to ₹30) are sold at metro stations; there are also one-/three-day (₹70/200) 'tourist cards' for unlimited short-distance travel; or a Smart Card (₹50, refundable when you return it), which can be recharged for amounts from ₹50 to ₹800 – fares are 10% cheaper than paying by token.

For the latest developments (plus route maps) see www.delhimetrorail.com or call ☏ 23417910.

AUTORICKSHAW RATES

To gauge fares vis-à-vis distances, the following list shows one-way (official) rates departing from Janpath's pre-paid autorickshaw booth. Taxis charge around double.

DESTINATION	COST (₹)
Bahai House of Worship	100
Humayun's Tomb	50
Karol Bagh	50
Old Delhi train station	50
Paharganj	30
Purana Qila	30
Red Fort	50
Defence Colony	65

Motorcycle

For motorcycle rental details, see p366.

Radiocab

If you have a local mobile number, you can call a radiocab. These air-conditioned cars are clean, efficient, and use reliable meters. They charge ₹20 per km. After calling the operator, you'll receive a text with your driver's registration number, then another to confirm arrival time (book 20 to 30 minutes in advance). You can also book online.

Some companies:

Easycabs (✆43434343; www.easycabs.com)
Megacabs (✆41414141; www.megacabs.com)
Quickcabs (✆45333333; www.quickcabs.in)

Taxi & Autorickshaw

All taxis and autorickshaws have meters but they are often 'not working' or drivers refuse to use them (so they can overcharge). If the meter isn't an option, agree on a fare before setting off. If the driver won't agree, look for one who will. From 11pm to 5am there's a 25% surcharge for autorickshaws and taxis.

Otherwise, to avoid shenanigans, catch an autorickshaw from a prepaid booth:

Janpath (Map p54; 88 Janpath; ⊙11am-8.30pm) Outside the India Tourism Delhi office.
New Delhi train station car park (Map p58; ⊙24hr)
Palika Bazaar's Gate No 2 (Map p54; Connaught Place; ⊙11am-7pm)

GREATER DELHI

TOP CHOICE **Qutb Minar**   HISTORIC SITE
(Map p60; ✆26643856; Indian/foreigner ₹10/250, video ₹25; ⊙sunrise-sunset; MQutb Minar) The beautiful religious buildings of the Qutb Minar complex form one of Delhi's most spectacular sights. They date from the onset of Islamic rule in India, and tell of tumultuous rises and falls in stone. Today on Delhi's outskirts, once these constructions formed the heart of the Muslim city.

The Qutb Minar itself is a mighty, awesome tower of victory, which closely resembles similar Afghan towers, and was also used as a minaret. Muslim sultan Qutb-ud-din began its construction in 1193, immediately after the defeat of the last Hindu kingdom in Delhi. It's nearly 73m high and tapers from a 15m-diameter base to a mere 2.5m at the top.

The tower has five distinct storeys, each marked by a projecting balcony. The first three storeys are made of red sandstone, the 4th and 5th storeys are of marble and sandstone. Qutb-ud-din built only to the 1st storey. His successors completed it and then, in 1326 it was struck by lightning. In 1368, Firoz Shah rebuilt the top storeys and added a cupola. An earthquake brought the cupola crashing down in 1803 – it was replaced with another in 1829, which was later removed.

There's a **Decorative Light Show** (Indian/foreigner ₹20/250; ⊙6.30-8pm) nightly. The Qutb Festival takes place here every October/November.

Be warned that Qutb Minar gets crowded on weekends.

Quwwat-ul-Islam Masjid
At the foot of the Qutb Minar stands the first mosque to be built in India, known as the Might of Islam Mosque. Also constructed in 1193, with various additions over the centuries, this building symbolises in stone the ascendance of one religious power over another. The original mosque was built on the foundations of a Hindu temple, and an inscription over the east gate states that it was built with materials obtained from demolishing '27 idolatrous temples' – it's possible to see many Hindu and Jain elements in the decoration.

Altamish, Qutb-ud-din's son-in-law, surrounded the original mosque with a cloistered court between 1210 and 1220.

Iron Pillar

This 7m-high pillar stands in the courtyard of the mosque and it was here a long time prior to the mosque's construction. A six-line Sanskrit inscription indicates that it was initially erected outside a Vishnu temple, possibly in Bihar, and was raised in memory of Chandragupta II, who ruled from AD 375 to 413.

What the inscription does not tell is how it was made, for the iron in the pillar is of exceptional purity. Scientists have never discovered how the iron, which has not rusted after some 2000 years, could be cast using the technology of the time.

Alai Minar

When Ala-ud-din made his additions to the mosque he also conceived a far more ambitious construction program. He aimed to build a second tower of victory, exactly like the Qutb Minar, but twice as high! By the time of his death the tower had reached 27m and no one was willing to continue his over-ambitious project. The incomplete tower, a solid stack of rubble, stands to the north of the Qutb Minar and the mosque.

Other Features

Ala-ud-din's exquisite **Alai Darwaza** gateway is the main entrance to the whole complex. It was built of red sandstone in 1310 and is just southwest of the Qutb Minar. The **tomb of Imam Zamin** is beside the gateway, while the **tomb of Altamish**, who died in 1235, is by the northwestern corner of the mosque. The largely ruined **madrasa of Ala-ud-din** stands at the rear of the complex.

There are some **summer palaces** in the area and also the **tombs** of the last kings of Delhi, who succeeded the Mughals. An empty space between two of the tombs was intended for the last king of Delhi, who died in exile in Yangon, Burma (Myanmar), in 1862, following his implication in the 1857 First War of Independence.

Tughlaqabad FORT

(Map p60; Indian/foreigner ₹5/100, video ₹25; ☺8.30am-5.30pm; MTughlaqabad) Crumbling Tughlaqabad was the third city of Delhi. This mammoth, battered-looking stronghold, with 6.5km of walls and 13 gateways, was built by Ghiyas-ud-din Tughlaq. Its construc-tion was said to have sparked a quarrel with the saint Nizam-ud-din: when the Tughlaq ruler refused the workers whom Nizam-ud-din wanted for work on his shrine, the saint cursed the king, warning that his city would be inhabited only by shepherds. Later, this was indeed the case.

Later, when Ghiyas-ud-din was returning from a military campaign, Nizam-ud-din again prophesised doom for him, telling his followers, 'Delhi is a long way off'. And it was: the king was killed on his way towards Delhi in 1325.

The metro runs to Tughlaqabad.

Mehrauli Archaeological Park HISTORIC PARK

(Map p60; admission free; ☺dawn-dusk; MQutb Minar) There's an entrance a few hundred metres to the left of that to Qutb Minar as you face it – walk down a narrow road which leads into the park. It's a rambling forest, once a hunting ground for the Mughals, then a favoured spot of colonial officers. It's dotted by extraordinary monuments, and has an undiscovered feel. The major monuments include **Jamali Kamali** (sunrise-sunset), a mosque, alongside which lies a small building containing two tombs: that of Jamali, a sufi saint, and Kamali, his unknown male friend, obviously important enough to be buried alongside him. Ask the caretaker to unlock the building to see the well-preserved painting within. A short walk from here is the dizzying **Rajon ki Baoli**, a majestic 16th-century step-well with an Escheresque sweeping flight of steps.

Garden of the 5 Senses PARK

(Map p60; admission ₹15; ☺8am-9pm; MSaket) This relaxing garden, an 8-hectare landscaped park inaugurated in 2003, is filled with intriguing contemporary sculptures, formal gardens and features such as wind chimes and lily ponds. Its discreet corners make it a favourite of canoodling couples. There are several upmarket restaurants and bars close to Gate 3.

ℹ️ Getting There & Away

The metro extends to Qutb Minar, but the entrance is a couple of kilometres away along busy, broad roads from the station, so catch a rickshaw (₹30).

Agra & the Taj Mahal

Best Places to Eat

» Hotel Sheela (p94)
» Tourists Rest House (p96)
» Hotel Kamal (p94)
» Shanti Lodge (p94)
» Oberoi Amar Vilas (p95)

Best Places to Stay

» Lakshmi Vilas (p98)
» Joney's Place (p97)
» Dasaprakash (p98)
» Vedic (p99)
» Taj Cafe (p97)

Why Go?

Obviously you're here for the Taj Mahal, and quite right too. Simply put, it's the most beautiful building in the world and it's almost impossible to see it without feeling awestruck.

But Agra, with its long and rich history, boasts plenty more besides. For 130 years this was the centre of India's great Mughal empire, and its legacy lives on in beautiful artwork, mouth-watering cuisine and, of course, magnificent architecture. The Taj is one of three places here that have been awarded World Heritage status, with the immense Agra Fort and the eerie ruined city of Fatehpur Sikri making up a superb trio of top-draw sights.

Surprisingly, given its tourism clout, Agra is also a city of dusty streets, where squeaky cycle-rickshaws overtake slow-moving camels, where monkeys steal your snacks and where you're well advised to keep an eye out for runaway water buffalo. It all adds to the adventure.

When to Go

September and October are arguably the best months in which to visit Agra. Most of the monsoon rains are over and the summer temperatures have cooled, but it's not too chilly yet in the evenings.

The winter months, from November to February, are very popular because daytime temperatures are at their most comfortable, but the big sights can get overcrowded and evenings are pretty nippy. Spring (March to April) isn't bad either, as that evening chill has mostly disappeared but the raging-hot mid-summer temperatures have yet to materialise.

Agra

☎ 0562 / POP 1,321,410

The magical allure of the Taj Mahal draws tourists to Agra like moths to a wondrous flame. And despite the hype, it's every bit as good as you've heard. But the Taj is not a stand-alone attraction. The legacy of the Mughal empire has left a magnificent fort and a liberal sprinkling of fascinating tombs and mausoleums. There's also fun to be had in the bustling *chowks* (marketplaces), some of which border on the chaotic.

The downside comes in the form of hordes of rickshaw-wallahs, touts, unofficial guides and souvenir vendors, whose persistence can be infuriating at times.

Many tourists choose to visit Agra on a whistle-stop day trip from Delhi. This is a shame. There is much more of interest here than can be seen in that time. In fact, you can enjoy several days' sightseeing with side trips to the superb ruined city of Fatehpur

DON'T MISS

THE TAJ MAHAL BROUGHT TO LIFE

For more inspiration, check out our information-packed 3-D illustration of the world's most beautiful building (p14), a brand new feature for this edition.

Sikri and the Hindu pilgrimage centre of Mathura.

Agra sits on a large bend in the holy Yamuna River. The fort and the Taj, 2km apart, both overlook the river on different parts of the bend. The main train and bus stations are a few kilometres southwest.

The labourers and artisans who toiled on the Taj set up home immediately south of the mausoleum, creating the congested network of alleys known as Taj Ganj, now a popular area for budget travellers.

AGRA & THE TAJ MAHAL AGRA

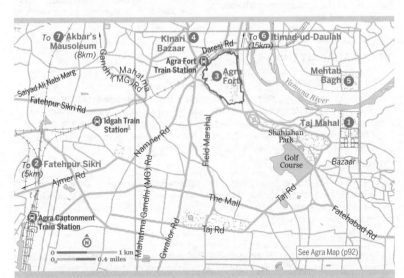

Agra Highlights

❶ Get up bright and early to visit the **Taj Mahal** minus the crowds, before returning at the end of the day for that oh-so-romantic sunset view

❷ Explore the abandoned city of **Fatehpur Sikri**

❸ Gawp at the immensity of the mammoth red

sandstone walls that surround **Agra Fort**

❹ Join the throngs at **Kinari Bazaar**, one of India's most hectic markets

❺ Hire a rickshaw for the day and take in a tour of Agra's Mughal gardens, starting with **Mehtab Bagh**

❻ Cross the Yamuna River to **Itimad-ud-Daulah**, an exquisite marble tomb nicknamed the Baby Taj

❼ Take a trip to the suburbs to see **Akbar's Mausoleum**, the beautiful resting place of the greatest Mughal emperor of them all

History

In 1501 Sultan Sikander Lodi established his capital here, but the city fell into Mughal hands in 1526, when Emperor Babur defeated the last Lodi sultan at Panipat. Agra reached the peak of its magnificence between the mid-16th and mid-17th centuries during the reigns of Akbar, Jehangir and Shah Jahan. During this period the fort, the Taj Mahal and other major mausoleums were built. In 1638 Shah Jahan built a new city in Delhi, and his son Aurangzeb moved the capital there 10 years later.

In 1761 Agra fell to the Jats, a warrior class who looted its monuments, including the Taj Mahal. The Marathas took over in 1770, but were replaced by the British in 1803. Following the First War of Independence of 1857, the British shifted the administration of the province to Allahabad. Deprived of its administrative role, Agra developed as a centre for heavy industry, quickly becoming famous for its chemicals industry and air pollution, before the Taj and tourism became a major source of income.

◉ Sights & Activities

The entrance fee for Agra's five main sights – the Taj, the Fort, Fatehpur Sikri, Akbar's Tomb and Itimad-ud-Daulah – is made up of charges from two different bodies, the Archaeological Survey of India (ASI) and the Agra Development Association (ADA). Of the ₹750 ticket for the Taj Mahal, ₹500 is a special ADA ticket, which gives you small savings on the other four sights if visited in the same day. You'll save ₹50 at Agra Fort and ₹10 each at Fatehpur Sikri, Akbar's Tomb and Itimad-ud-Daulah. You can buy this ₹500 ADA ticket at any of the five sights. Just say you intend to visit the Taj later that day.

All the other sights in Agra are either free or have ASI tickets only, which aren't affected by the ADA one-day offer.

Admission to all sights is free for children under 15.

Taj Mahal   HISTORIC BUILDING
(Map p96; Indian/foreigner ₹20/750, video ₹25; ☉dawn-dusk Sat-Thu) Rabindranath Tagore described it as 'a teardrop on the cheek of eternity', Rudyard Kipling as 'the embodi-

---

TAJ MAHAL MYTHS

The Taj is a Hindu temple

The well-publicised theory that the Taj was in fact a Shiva temple built in the 12th century and only later converted into Mumtaz Mahal's famous mausoleum was developed by Purushottam Nagesh Oak. In 2000 India's Supreme Court dismissed his petition to have the sealed basement rooms of the Taj opened to prove his theory. Oak also claims that the Kaaba, Stonehenge and the Papacy all have Hindu origins.

The Black Taj Mahal

The story goes that Shah Jahan planned to build a negative image of the Taj Mahal in black marble on the opposite side of the river as his own mausoleum, and that work began before he was imprisoned by his son Aurangzeb in Agra Fort. Extensive excavations at Mehtab Bagh have found no trace of any such construction.

Craftsmen Mutilations

Legend has it that, on completion of the Taj, Shah Jahan ordered that the hands of the project's craftsmen be chopped off, to prevent them from ever building anything as beautiful again. Some even say he went so far as to have their eyes gouged out. Thankfully, no historical evidence supports either story.

Sinking Taj

Some experts believe there is evidence to show that the Taj is slowly tilting towards and sinking into the riverbed due to the changing nature of the soil beside an increasingly dry Yamuna River. The Archaeological Survey of India has dismissed any marginal change in the elevation of the building as statistically insignificant, adding that it has not detected any structural damage at its base in the seven decades since its first scientific study of the Taj was carried out, in 1941.

ment of all things pure', while its creator, Emperor Shah Jahan, said it made 'the sun and the moon shed tears from their eyes'. Every year, tourists numbering more than twice the population of Agra pass through its gates to catch a once-in-a-lifetime glimpse of what is widely considered the most beautiful building in the world. Few leave disappointed.

The Taj was built by Shah Jahan as a memorial for his third wife, Mumtaz Mahal, who died giving birth to their 14th child in 1631. The death of Mumtaz left the emperor so heartbroken that his hair is said to have turned grey virtually overnight. Construction of the Taj began the following year and, although the main building is thought to have been built in eight years, the whole complex was not completed until 1653. Not long after it was finished Shah Jahan was overthrown by his son Aurangzeb and imprisoned in Agra Fort where, for the rest of his days, he could only gaze out at his creation through a window. Following his death in 1666, Shah Jahan was buried here alongside Mumtaz.

In total, some 20,000 people from India and Central Asia worked on the building. Specialists were brought in from as far away as Europe to produce the exquisite marble screens and pietra dura (marble inlay work) made with thousands of semiprecious stones.

The Taj was designated a World Heritage Site in 1983 and looks as immaculate today as when it was first constructed – though it underwent a huge restoration project in the early 20th century. In 2002, having been gradually discoloured by city pollution, it was spruced up with an ancient face-pack recipe known as *multani mitti* – a blend of soil, cereal, milk and lime once used by Indian women to beautify their skin. Now only nonpolluting vehicles are allowed within a couple of hundred metres of the building.

Entry & Information

Note: the Taj is closed every Friday to anyone not attending prayers at the mosque.

The Taj can be accessed through the west, south and east gates. Tour groups tend to enter through the east and west gates. Independent travellers tend to use the south gate, which is nearest to Taj Ganj, the main area for budget accommodation, and generally has shorter queues than the west gate. The east gate has the shortest queues of the lot, but this is because the ticket office

ℹ **BEST TIMES TO SEE THE TAJ**

The Taj is arguably at its most atmospheric at **sunrise**. This is certainly the most comfortable time to visit, with far fewer crowds. **Sunset** is another magical viewing time. You can also view the Taj for five nights around **full moon**. Entry numbers are limited, though, and tickets must be bought a day in advance from the **Archaeological Survey of India office** (Map p92; ☎2227263; www.asi.nic.in; 22 The Mall; Indian/foreigner ₹510/750). See its website for details. Note, this office is known as the Taj Mahal Office by some rickshaw riders.

One final word of advice; whatever you do, don't plan your trip around seeing the Taj on a Friday, as the whole complex is closed to anyone not attending Friday prayers at the mosque inside the Taj grounds.

is inconveniently located 1km walk away at Shilpgram, a dire government-run tourist center. There are separate queues for men and women at all three gates.

There are strict rules about what you can and cannot take into the Taj grounds. Free cloakrooms are provided near each ticket office, but to give you some advance warning, items you *can* take in include: cameras, mobile phones, water bottles, small bags, books and small torches. Items you *cannot* take in include: food, large bags, cigarettes, lighters, matches, mobile phone chargers, laptops and loose batteries.

If you want to leave stuff in the cloakrooms, don't forget to visit them first, to avoid queuing twice.

All foreign visitors receive a small bottle of water and some disposable shoe covers with their ticket. Help the environment by saying no to the disposable shoe covers and walking barefoot around the mausoleum instead, just as the locals do.

If you keep your Taj ticket you get small entry-fee reductions when visiting Agra Fort, Fatehpur Sikri, Akbar's Tomb or the Itimad-ud-Daulah on the same day.

From the south gate, entry to the inner compound is through a very impressive, 30m red sandstone **gateway** on the south

DON'T MISS

TAJ MUSEUM

Within the Taj complex, on the western side of the gardens, is the small but excellent **Taj Museum** (admission ₹5; ⊙10am-5pm Sat-Thu), housing a number of original Mughal miniature paintings, including a pair of 17th-century ivory portraits of Emperor Shah Jahan and his beloved wife Mumtaz Mahal. You also find here some very well preserved gold and silver coins dating from the same period, plus architectural drawings of the Taj and some nifty celadon plates, said to split into pieces or change colour if the food served on them contains poison.

side of the forecourt, which is inscribed with verses from the Quran.

Inside the Grounds

Once inside, the **ornamental gardens** are set out along classical Mughal *charbagh* (formal Persian garden) lines – a square quartered by watercourses, with an ornamental marble plinth at its centre. When the fountains are not flowing, the Taj is beautifully reflected in the water.

The Taj Mahal itself stands on a raised marble platform at the northern end of the ornamental gardens, with its back to the Yamuna River. Its raised position means that the backdrop is only sky – a masterstroke of design. Purely decorative 40m-high white **minarets** grace each corner of the platform. After more than three centuries they are not quite perpendicular, but they may have been designed to lean slightly outwards so that in the event of an earthquake they would fall away from the precious Taj. The red sandstone **mosque** to the west is an important gathering place for Agra's Muslims. The identical building to the east, the **jawab**, was built for symmetry.

The central Taj structure is made of semitranslucent white marble, carved with flowers and inlaid with thousands of semiprecious stones in beautiful patterns. A perfect exercise in symmetry, the four identical faces of the Taj feature impressive vaulted arches embellished with pietra dura scrollwork and quotations from the Quran in a style of calligraphy using inlaid jasper. The whole structure is topped off by four small domes surrounding the famous bulbous central dome.

Directly below the main dome is the **Cenotaph of Mumtaz Mahal**, an elaborate false tomb surrounded by an exquisite perforated marble screen inlaid with dozens of different types of semiprecious stones. Beside it, offsetting the symmetry of the Taj, is the **Cenotaph of Shah Jahan**, who was interred here with little ceremony by his usurping son Aurangzeb in 1666. Light is admitted into the central chamber by finely cut marble screens. The real tombs of Mumtaz Mahal and Shah Jahan are in a locked basement room below the main chamber and cannot be viewed.

Agra Fort   FORT

(Map p92; Indian/foreigner ₹20/300, video ₹25; ⊙dawn-dusk) With the Taj Mahal overshadowing it, one can easily forget that Agra has one of the finest Mughal forts in India. By visiting the fort and Taj on the same day you get a ₹50 reduction in ticket price. Construction of the massive red-sandstone fort, on the bank of the Yamuna River, was begun by Emperor Akbar in 1565. Further additions were made, particularly by his grandson Shah Jahan, using his favourite building material – white marble. The fort was built primarily as a military structure, but Shah Jahan transformed it into a palace, and later it became his gilded prison for eight years after his son Aurangzeb seized power in 1658.

The ear-shaped fort's colossal double walls rise over 20m in height and measure 2.5km in circumference. The Yamuna River originally flowed along the straight eastern edge of the fort, and the emperors had their own bathing ghats here. It contains a maze of buildings, forming a city within a city, including vast underground sections, though many of the structures were destroyed over the years by Nadir Shah, the Marathas, the Jats and finally the British, who used the fort as a garrison. Even today, much of the fort is used by the military and so is off-limits to the general public.

The **Amar Singh Gate** to the south is the sole entry point to the fort these days and where you buy your entrance ticket. Its dogleg design was meant to confuse attackers who made it past the first line of defence – the crocodile-infested moat.

A path leads straight from here up to the large **Moti Masjid** (Pearl Mosque), which is always closed. To your right, just before you reach Moti Masjid, is the large open **Diwan-i-Am** (Hall of Public Audiences), which was

Inside the Taj grounds

You may have to pay ₹750 for the privilege, but it's only when you're inside the grounds themselves that you can really get up close and personal with the world's most beautiful building. Don't miss inspecting the marble inlay work (pietra dura) inside the *pishtaqs* (large arched recesses) on the four outer walls. And don't forget to bring a small torch with you so that you can shine it on similar pietra dura work inside the dark central chamber of the mausoleum. Note the translucency of both the white marble and the semi-precious stones inlaid into it.

From Mehtab Bagh

Tourists are no longer allowed to wander freely along the riverbank on the opposite side of the Yamuna River, but you can still enjoy a view of the back of the Taj from the 16th-century Mughal park Mehtab Bagh, with the river flowing between you and the mausoleum. A path leading down to the river beside the park offers the same view for free, albeit from a more restricted angle.

Looking up from the south bank of the river

This is a great place to be for sunset. Take the path that hugs the outside of the Taj's eastern wall and walk all the way down to the small temple beside the river. You should be able to find boat hands down here willing to row you out onto the water for an even more romantic view. Expect to pay them around ₹100 per boat. For safety reasons, it's best not to wander down here on your own for sunset.

On a rooftop cafe in Taj Ganj

Perfect for sunrise shots, there are some wonderful photos to be had from the numerous rooftop cafes in Taj Ganj. We think the cafe on Saniya Palace Hotel is the pick of the bunch, with its plant-filled design and great position, but many of them are good. And all offer the bonus of being able to view the Taj with the added comfort of an early-morning cup of coffee.

From Agra Fort

With a decent zoom lens you can capture some fabulous images of the Taj from Agra Fort, especially if you're willing to get up at the crack of dawn to see the sun rising from behind it. The best places to picture it from are probably Musamman Burj and Khas Mahal, the octagonal tower and palace where Shah Jahan was imprisoned for eight years until his death.

used by Shah Jahan for domestic government business, and features a throne room where the emperor listened to petitioners. In front of it is the small and rather incongruous **grave of John Colvin**, a lieutenant-governor of the northwest provinces who died of an illness in the fort during the 1857 First War of Independence.

A tiny staircase just to the left of the Diwan-i-Am throne leads up to a large courtyard. To your left, is the tiny but exquisite Nagina Masjid (Gem Mosque), built in 1635 by Shah Jahan for the ladies of the court. Down below was the **Ladies' bazaar**, where the court ladies bought goods.

On the far side of the large courtyard, along the eastern wall of the fort, is **Diwan-i-Khas** (Hall of Private Audiences), which was reserved for important dignitaries or foreign representatives. The hall once housed Shah Jahan's legendary Peacock Throne, which was inset with precious stones including the famous Koh-i-noor diamond. The throne was taken to Delhi by Aurangzeb, then to Iran in 1739 by Nadir Shah and dismantled after his assassination in 1747. Overlooking the river and the distant Taj Mahal is **Takhti-i-Jehangir**, a huge slab of black rock with an inscription around the edge. The throne that stood here was made for Jehangir when he was Prince Salim.

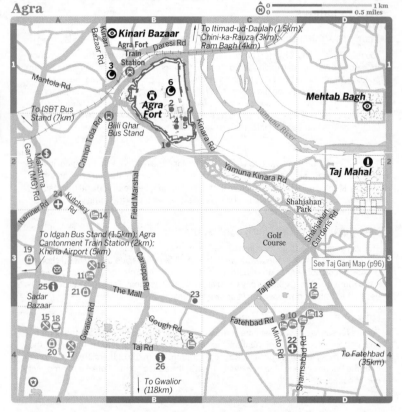

Off to your right from here (as you face the river) is **Shish Mahal** (Mirror Palace), with walls inlaid with tiny mirrors. At the time of research it had been closed for a while due to restoration, although you could peek through cracks in the doors at the sparkling mirrors inside.

Further along the eastern edge of the fort you'll find **Musamman Burj** and **Khas Mahal**, the wonderful white-marble octagonal tower and palace where Shah Jahan was imprisoned for eight years until his death in 1666, and from where he could gaze out at the Taj Mahal, the tomb of his wife. When he died, Shah Jahan's body was taken from here by boat to the Taj. The now closed **Mina Masjid**, set back slightly from the eastern edge, was his private mosque.

The large courtyard here is **Anguri Bagh**, a garden that has been brought back to life in recent years. In the courtyard is an innocuous-looking entrance – now locked – that leads down a flight of stairs into a two-storey labyrinth of underground rooms and passageways where Akbar used to keep his 500-strong harem.

Continuing south, the huge red-sandstone **Jehangir's Palace** was probably built by Akbar for his son Jehangir. It blends Indian and Central Asian architectural styles, a reminder of the Mughals' Afghani cultural roots. In front of the palace is **Hauz-i-Jehangir**, a huge bowl carved out of a single block of stone, which was used for bathing. Walking past this brings you back to the main path to Amar Singh Gate.

You can walk here from Taj Ganj, or it's ₹20-30 in a cycle-rickshaw.

Akbar's Mausoleum   HISTORIC BUILDING
(Indian/foreigner ₹10/110, video ₹25; ◷dawn-dusk) This outstanding sandstone and marble tomb commemorates the greatest of the Mughal emperors. The huge courtyard is entered through a stunning gateway. It has

AGRA & THE TAJ MAHAL AGRA

three-storey minarets at each corner and is built of red sandstone strikingly inlaid with white-marble geometric patterns.

The mausoleum is at Sikandra, 10km northwest of Agra Fort. Buses (₹20, 45 minutes) heading to Mathura from Biili Ghar bus stand go past the mausoleum.

Itimad-ud-Daulah   HISTORIC BUILDING

(off Map p92; Indian/foreigner ₹10/110, video ₹25; ⊙dawn-dusk) Nicknamed the Baby Taj, the exquisite tomb of Mizra Ghiyas Beg should not be missed. This Persian nobleman was Mumtaz Mahal's grandfather and Emperor Jehangir's *wazir* (chief minister). His daughter Nur Jahan, who married Jehangir, built the tomb between 1622 and 1628 in a style similar to the tomb she built for Jehangir near Lahore in Pakistan.

It doesn't have the same awesome beauty as the Taj, but it's arguably more delicate in appearance thanks to its particularly finely carved *jali* (marble lattice screens). This was the first Mughal structure built completely from marble, the first to make extensive use of pietra dura and the first tomb to be built on the banks of the Yamuna, which until then had been a sequence of beautiful pleasure gardens.

You can combine a trip here with Chini-ka-Rauza, Mehtab Bagh and Ram Bagh, all on the east bank. A cycle-rickshaw covering all four should cost about ₹200 return from the Taj, including waiting time. An autorickshaw (auto) will be at least double.

Chini-ka-Rauza   HISTORIC BUILDING

(off Map p92; ⊙dawn-dusk) This Persian-style riverside tomb of Afzal Khan, a poet who served as Shah Jahan's chief minister, was built between 1628 and 1639. Rarely visited, it is hidden away down a shady avenue of trees on the east bank of the Yamuna. Bright blue tiles, which once covered the whole mausoleum, can still be seen on part of the exterior, while the interior is painted in floral designs.

Mehtab Bagh   PARK

(Map p92; Indian/foreigner ₹5/100; ⊙dawn-dusk) This park, originally built by Emperor Babur as the last in a series of 11 parks on the

Yamuna's east bank, long before the Taj was conceived, fell into disrepair until it was little more than a huge mound of sand. To protect the Taj from the erosive effects of the sand blown across the river, the park was reconstructed in recent years and is now one the best places from which to view the great mausoleum. The gardens in the Taj are perfectly aligned with the ones here, and the view of the Taj from the fountain directly in front of the entrance gate is a special one.

It used to be possible to sneak down the side of this park to the riverbank and view the Taj for free in a peaceful, natural ambience of buffaloes and wading birds. You can still reach the riverbank, but guards and a barbed-wire fence prevent you walking freely along the water's edge.

Jama Masjid   MOSQUE
(Map p92; Jama Masjid Rd) This fine mosque, built in the Kinari Bazaar by Shah Jahan's daughter in 1648, and once connected to Agra Fort, features striking marble patterning on its domes.

Kinari Bazaar   MARKET
(Map p92; ☺dawn-late) The narrow streets behind Jama Masjid are a crazy maze of overcrowded lanes bursting with colourful markets. There are a number of different bazaars here, each specialising in different wares, but the area is generally known as Kinari Bazaar as many of the lanes fan out from Kinari Bazaar Rd. You'll find clothing, shoes, fabrics, jewellery, spices, marble work, snack stalls and what seems like 20 million other people. Amazingly, there is somehow room for buffaloes and even the odd working elephant to squeeze their way through the crowds. Even if you're not buying anything, just walking the streets is an experience in itself. Don't forget to look up from time to time at the old wooden balconies above some of the shop fronts. As with all crowded markets, take extra care of your belongings here.

Swimming Pools   SWIMMING
Hotels allowing nonguests to use their pools include Atithi (₹300), Yamuna View (₹350), Park Plaza (₹350), Amar (₹400) – with slide! – and Clarks Shiraz (₹500).

🖝 Tours

UP Tourism   COACH TOURS
(incl entry fees Indian/foreigner ₹400/1700); Agra Cantonment train station (off Map p92; ☎2421204; ☺7am-10pm); Taj Rd (Map p92; ☎2226431;

agrauptourism@gmail.com; 64 Taj Rd; ☺10.30am-5pm Mon-Sat) UP Tourism runs daily coach tours that leave Agra Cantonment train station at 10.30am, after picking up passengers arriving from Delhi on the *Taj Express*. The tour includes the Taj Mahal, Agra Fort and Fatehpur Sikri with a 1¼-hour stop in each place. Tours return to the station so that day trippers can catch the *Taj Express* back to Delhi at 6.55pm. Contact either of the UP Tourism offices to book a seat, or just turn up at the train station tourist office at 9.45am to sign up for that day.

🛏 Sleeping

The main place for budget accommodation is the bustling area of Taj Ganj, immediately south of the Taj, while there's a high concentration of midrange hotels further south, along Fatehabad Rd. Sadar Bazaar, an area boasting good-quality restaurants, offers another option.

Ask at the UP Tourism office for the latest list of recommended homestays. The quality of accommodation in the homestays here is generally pretty good, but locations are rarely central. Prices range from ₹2000 to ₹4000 per room.

TAJ GANJ AREA

TOP CHOICE Hotel Sheela   HOTEL $
(Map p96; ☎2331194; www.hotelsheela agra.com; Taj East Gate Rd; d ₹400-600, with AC ₹800; ❄@) If you're not fussed about looking at the Taj Mahal 24 hours a day, this superb budget option could be just the ticket. Rooms are simple (no TVs here), but spotless and come with towel, soap and loo roll – a nice touch for a cheapie. Best of all they're set around a beautifully landscaped garden with singing birds, plenty of shade and a pleasant restaurant area. Book ahead.

Hotel Kamal   HOTEL $$
(Map p96; ☎2330126; hotelkamal@hotmail.com; Taj South Gate; d ₹600, with AC ₹1000; ❄) The smartest of the hotels in Taj Ganj proper, Kamal has very clean, comfortable rooms with nice touches such as framed photos of the Taj on the walls and rugs on the tiled floors. Some rooms also have sofas. The rooftop restaurant has a decent Taj view, albeit slightly obscured by a tree.

Shanti Lodge   HOTEL $
(Map p96; ☎2231973; shantilodge2000@yahoo.co.in; Taj South Gate; r ₹200-1200; ❄@) There's a huge mixed bag of rooms at this Taj Ganj old-timer; some shoddy, with dodgy bath-

rooms; some much smarter and cleaner. The ones round the back in the newer block are worth asking for, but check a few rooms before you commit. The rooftop restaurant here has one of the best views of the Taj.

Saniya Palace Hotel
HOTEL $

(Map p96; ☑3270199; saniyapalaceemailid@gmail.com; Taj South Gate; d ₹400, without bathroom ₹200, with AC ₹800) Set back from the main strip down a tiny alleyway, this place has more character than its rivals, with marble floors and Mughal-style framed carpets hung on the walls. The rooms (apart from the cramped bathroomless cheapies) are clean and big enough, although the bathrooms in the non-AC rooms are minuscule. The very pleasant, plant-filled rooftop restaurant has a fabulous view of the Taj.

Hotel Sidhartha
HOTEL $

(Map p96; ☑2230901; www.hotelsidhartha.com; Taj West Gate; d ₹400, with AC ₹800; ❋@) First opened its doors in 1986 and still going strong. The 18 very smart double rooms are bright and clean and are set around a small, leafy courtyard, which has an OK restaurant. Hot water is available for all the rooms but only the AC ones have hot-water showers.

Oberoi Amar Vilas
HOTEL $$$

(off Map p96; ☑2231515; www.oberoihotels.com; Taj East Gate Rd; d ₹35,000-40,500, ste ₹75,000-261,000; ❋@❋) If money is no object, look no further. By far the best hotel in Agra, this place oozes style and luxury. Elegant interior design is suffused with Mughal themes, a composition carried over into the exterior fountain courtyard and swimming pool, both of which are set in a delightful water garden. All rooms (and even some bathtubs) have wonderful views of the Taj, as do the two excellent restaurants and classy cocktail bar, all of which are open to nonguests.

Taj Plaza
HOTEL $$

(off Map p96; ☑2232515; www.hoteltajplaza.com; Taj East Gate Rd; s/d ₹800/1200, with AC ₹2000/3000, ❋@) This former good-quality budget hotel has been stretched into a mid-range price bracket in recent years. You won't be disappointed if you stay here – rooms are clean and have TV, and some come with Taj views – but you won't write home about it. Still, it's a whole lot closer to the Taj than most hotels in the same price range.

FATEHABAD ROAD AREA

Howard Park Plaza
HOTEL $$$

(Map p92; ☑4048600; www.sarovarhotels.com; Fatehabad Rd; s/d/ste ₹6000/7000/12,000; ❋@❋❋) Rooms in this very welcoming hotel are decked out in elegant dark-wood furniture and stylish decorative tiling. Bathrooms are a little on the compact side for this price, but still very smart. There's an unusual splash-shaped pool out the back, a small gym and a spa offering a whole range of ayurvedic treatments. Wi-fi-enabled throughout.

Hotel Amar
HOTEL $$$

(Map p92; ☑4008402; www.hotelamar.com; Fatehabad Rd; s ₹3000-4500, d ₹3400-4500, ste ₹6000-8000; ❋❋❋) Smart rooms come with big TV, wi-fi and clean bathrooms, but the real treat here is the pool area, complete with a lush green lawn and a 3.5m-tall water slide.

Amar Yatri Niwas
HOTEL $$

(Map p92; ☑2233030; www.amaryatriniwas.com; Fatehabad Rd; s ₹1500-2500, d ₹1800-2800; ❋@❋) Sandwiched between a Costa Coffee and a Pizza Hut (but don't let that put you off), this place has had a recent makeover so that even the standard rooms are now smart and clean, and come with modern furnishings and bright bathrooms. Be warned; wi-fi is chargeable at the ludicrous rate of ₹100 per hour!

Mansingh Palace
HOTEL $$$

(Map p92; ☑2331771; www.mansinghhotels.com; Fatehabad Rd; s/d from ₹7000/8000; ❋@❋) The service isn't up to scratch for the quality of this hotel, but if you can put up with the grumpy staff on reception you'll find plush rooms inside a complex crammed with Mughal design themes and exotic furnishings. The garden has an interestingly shaped pool and outdoor BBQ area. There's a gym and the quality **Sheesh Mahal** restaurant has live *ghazals* (Urdu songs) nightly.

Hotel Atithi
HOTEL $$

(Map p92; ☑2330878; www.hotelatithiagra.com; Fatehabad Rd; s ₹2400-2900, d ₹2900-3800; ❋@❋) Simple but comfortable rooms are a decent size, while the white-tiled bathrooms are clean, if a little old-fashioned. Guests can use the lovely public swimming pool next door for free.

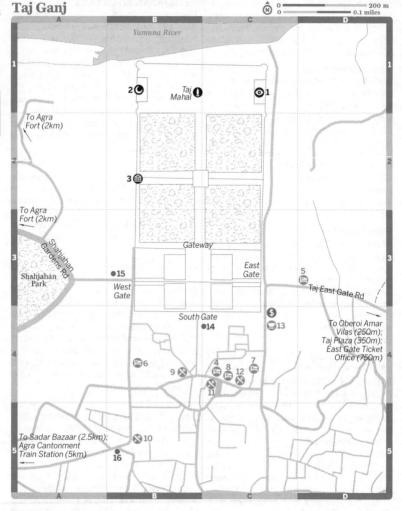

Yamuna River

To Agra Fort (2km)

Taj Mahal

To Agra Fort (2km)

Gateway

Shahjahan Gardens Rd

Shahjahan Park

West Gate

East Gate

South Gate

Taj East Gate Rd

To Oberoi Amar Vilas (250m); Taj Plaza (350m); East Gate Ticket Office (750m)

To Sadar Bazaar (2.5km); Agra Cantonment Train Station (5km)

AGRA & THE TAJ MAHAL

SADAR BAZAAR AREA

Tourists Rest House HOTEL $
(Map p92; ☑2463961; dontworrychickencurry@hotmail.com; Kutchery Rd; d ₹250-550, with AC ₹750; ✺@) Very clean rooms of varying sizes come with tiled floors, TV and hot water and are set around a peaceful plant-filled, palm-shaded courtyard restaurant. Owners speak English and French and are very helpful. Phone ahead for a free pick-up. Otherwise, it's ₹30 in a cycle-rickshaw from the train station.

Clarks Shiraz Hotel HOTEL $$$
(Map p92; ☑2226121; www.hotelclarksshiraz.com; 54 Taj Rd; s/d from ₹6500/7000; ✺@🛜🏊) One of

Agra's original five-star hotels has seen some recent renovation. The standard doubles are still nothing special, but marble-floored deluxe versions are excellent and all bathrooms have been retiled so are spotless. There are two very good restaurants, three bars, a gym, a shaded garden pool area and ayurvedic massages. Some rooms have distant Taj views.

Hotel Yamuna View HOTEL $$
(Map p92; ☑2462990; www.hotelyamunaview agra.com; 6B The Mall; s/d from ₹4800/5500; ✺@🛜🏊) A pool in the garden, a water feature in the grand sunken lobby, a plush Chinese restaurant and some spacious rooms

Taj Ganj

with gleaming bathrooms make this friendly hotel in a quiet part of Sadar Bazaar worth the splurge. It also has a 24-hour cafe. The free wi-fi is in the lobby only.

✗ Eating

Dalmoth is Agra's famous version of *namkin* (spicy nibbles). *Peitha* is a square sweet made from pumpkin and glucose that is flavoured with rosewater, coconut or saffron. You can buy it all over Agra. From October to March look out for *gajak,* a slightly spicy sesame-seed biscuit strip.

TAJ GANJ AREA

This lively area directly south of the Taj has plenty of budget rooftop restaurants, where menus appear to be carbon copies of one another. None are licensed but most will find you a beer if you ask nicely and drink discreetly.

Joney's Place   MULTICUISINE $
(Map p96; mains ₹40-90; ◷5am-10.30pm) Open at the crack of dawn, this pocket-sized,

brightly painted, travellers' institution whipped up its first creamy lassi in 1978 and continues to please despite having to cook its meals in what must be the smallest restaurant kitchen in Agra. Everything they do here is good, but the cheese and tomato 'jayfelles' (toasted sandwich), the banana lassi and the *malai* kofta get consistently good reviews.

Taj Cafe   MULTICUISINE $
(Map p96; mains ₹45-90; ◷6.30am-11pm) Up a flight of steps and overlooking Taj Ganj's busy street scene, this friendly, family-run restaurant is a nice choice if you're not fussed about Taj views. There's a good choice of breakfasts, thalis (₹70-120) and pizza (₹130-170), and the lassis here are even better than at Joney's Place.

Saniya Palace Hotel   MULTICUISINE $$
(Map p96; mains ₹70-200; ◷6am-11pm) With cute tablecloths, dozens of potted plants and a bamboo pergola for shade, this is the most pleasant rooftop restaurant in Taj Ganj. It also has the best rooftop view of the Taj bar none. Again, it's the usual mix of Western dishes and Western-friendly Indian dishes on offer, including set breakfasts, pizza and pancakes.

Esphahan   NORTH INDIAN $$$
(off Map p96; ☏2231515; Oberoi Amar Vilas hotel; Taj East Gate Rd; mains ₹1000-1400; ◷dinner) Agra's best hotel has now opened the doors of its top-notch Indian restaurant to non-guests. There are only two sittings each evening, at 7pm and 9.30pm, so booking a table is essential. The menu is small but exquisite, specialising in Mughlai cuisine with unusual offerings such as quail curry. We couldn't afford the ₹2500 thali, but it's bound to be extraordinarily good.

Hotel Sheela   MULTICUISINE $$
(Map p96; mains ₹60-200; ◷7am-10pm) Actually the menu here is a bit limited compared to others in Taj Ganj, meaning this isn't the best spot for an evening meal. It's fine for breakfast or a lunchtime snack, though – and, let's face it, no one comes here specifically for the food. They come for the wonderfully peaceful garden retreat that makes it hard to believe you're 100m from one of the biggest tourist attractions in the world.

Shanti Lodge Restaurant   MULTICUISINE $$
(Map p96; mains ₹50-150; ◷6.30am-10.30pm) The rooftop Taj view here is superb so this is a great place for breakfast or a sunset

TAKE A BREAK: FIVE RELAXING RETREATS

Touts, vendors and rickshaw-wallahs can be pretty draining in Agra, particularly around the big sights. Here are some ideas for how to escape their attentions.

Garden Retreat

Wandering around any of the half-ruined Mughal gardens of Agra can make a pleasant change from the noisy, bustling city streets. Try Mehtab Bagh or Ram Bagh. In summer, it's best to visit in the cool of the morning. Alternatively, sit in the shade of the wonderfully peaceful garden restaurant at Hotel Sheela, just a stone's throw from the Taj Mahal's east gate.

Rooftop Retreat

You'll be almost physically dragged off the street by over-keen owners trying to ensure you choose theirs, but once you're actually sitting down at a rooftop cafe in Taj Ganj you'll have all the peace and quiet you could wish for, plus fabulous views of the Taj. Saniya Palace Hotel is our favourite.

Rickshaw Retreat

Find a cycle-rickshaw with a deep, comfy, padded seat, agree to pay the rider ₹100–200 for a half-day tour of the city then sit back and watch Agra roll past you. The beauty of this retreat is that rickshaw riders don't bother tourists who are already in a rickshaw.

Poolside Retreat

For a total escape, pack your swimmers and head to one of Agra's more expensive hotels for a day by the pool. Fees for nonguests are typically ₹300–500.

Coffee Break

For a quick break, slip inside Cafe Coffee Day by the east gate of the Taj. Yes, it's a chain and, yes, it's relatively expensive, but it has AC and it's the only place in Taj Ganj that sells proper fresh coffee.

beer. There's some shade for hot afternoons, although it's not as comfortable as nearby Saniya Palace. The only let-down is the menu, which, although not bad, lacks innovation. Banana pancakes, anyone?

Yash Cafe MULTICUISINE **$**
(Map p96; mains ₹30-130) This chilled-out 1st-floor cafe has wicker chairs, sports channels on TV, DVDs shown in the evening and a good range of meals, from good-value set breakfasts to thali (₹55) and pizza (₹80–150). It also offers a shower and storage space (₹50 for both) to day visitors.

Shankar Restaurant INDIAN **$**
(Map p96; mains ₹25-50; ⏰9am-10pm) Those who are bored with the multicuisine Western-friendly tourist restaurants in Taj Ganj, and are after something a bit more down to earth, should head round the corner to the *dhaba* (snack bars) near the autorickshaw stand. Most are little more than shacks serving up simple Indian dishes. Shankar is as basic as any, but is friendly and has an English menu.

SADAR BAZAAR

This area offers better quality restaurants and makes a nice change from the please-all, multicuisine offerings in Taj Ganj.

TOP CHOICE **Lakshmi Vilas** SOUTH INDIAN **$**
(Map p92; Taj Rd; meals ₹40-90;✱) This no-nonsense, plainly decorated, nonsmoking restaurant is *the* place in Agra to come for affordable South Indian fare. Treats include *idli* (spongy, round, fermented rice cake), *vada* (doughnut-shaped, deep-fried lentil savoury), *uttapam* (thick, savoury rice pancake) and more than 20 varieties of dosa (large savoury crepe), including a family special that is 1.2m long! The thali meal (₹88), served noon–3.30pm and 7–10.30pm, is very good indeed.

Dasaprakash SOUTH INDIAN **$$**
(Map p92; ☑2363535, 1 Gwalior Rd; meals ₹90-150; ⏰11am-10.45pm; ✱) Highly recommended by locals for consistently good South Indian vegetarian food, Dasaprakash whips up spectacular unlimited thalis (₹100–225),

dosa and a few token continental dishes. The ice-cream desserts (₹90–125), which take up a whole page of the two-page menu, are another speciality. Comfortable booth seating and wood-lattice screens make for intimate dining.

Vedic
NORTH INDIAN **$$**
(Map p92; ☑2250041, 1 Gwalior Rd; meals ₹140-200; ⊘11.30am-11pm; ✳) This classy new restaurant with modern decor but a traditional ambience has a mouth-wateringly good North Indian veg menu, with paneer (unfermented cheese) dishes featuring highly. The paneer tikka masala is particularly good. There's also a range of delicious vegetarian kebabs.

Mughal Room
NORTH INDIAN **$$$**
(Map p92; ☑2226121; 54 Taj Rd; mains ₹295-950; ⊘lunch & dinner) The best of four eating options at Clarks Shiraz Hotel, this top-floor restaurant serves up sumptuous Mughlai cuisine with a distant view of the Taj and Agra Fort. Remember, though, you won't be able to see either at night. There's also live classical music here every evening.

Tourists Rest House
MULTICUISINE **$**
(Map p92; ☑2363961; Kutchery Rd; meals ₹45-80) The courtyard garden restaurant here is often full of chattering travellers enjoying the candle-lit atmosphere around the small fountain, and the all-veg menu is decent.

Brijwasi
SWEETS **$**
(Map p92; Sadar Bazaar; sweets from ₹220/kg, meals ₹75-120; ⊘8am-10.30pm; ✳) Mouth-watering selection of traditional Indian sweets, nuts and biscuits on the ground floor, with a decent-value Indian restaurant upstairs.

♟ Drinking & Entertainment

A night out in Agra tends to revolve around sitting at a rooftop restaurant with a couple of bottles of beer. None of the restaurants in Taj Ganj are licensed, but they can find alcohol for you if you ask nicely, and don't mind if you bring your own drinks, as long as you're discreet. You can catch live Indian classical music and *ghazals* at restaurants in several of Agra's top-end hotels, most of which also have bars, albeit of the rather soulless variety.

Cafe Coffee Day
CAFE
(Map p96; ⊘6am-8pm) This AC-cooled branch of the popular cafe chain is the closest place to the Taj selling proper coffee (from ₹39). Also does cakes and snacks. There's another branch in Sadar Bazaar (Map p92).

Amar Vilas Bar
BAR
(off Map p96; Oberoi Amar Vilas hotel, Taj East Gate Rd; ⊘noon-midnight) For a beer (₹300) or cocktail (₹500) in sheer opulence, look no further than the bar at Agra's best hotel. A terrace opens out to views of the Taj.

🔒 Shopping

Agra is well known for its marble items inlaid with coloured stones, similar to the pietra dura work on the Taj. Sadar Bazaar, the old town and the area around the Taj are full of emporiums. Taj Mahal models are all made of alabaster rather than marble. Very cheap ones are made of soapstone, which scratches easily.

Other popular buys include rugs, leather and gemstones, though the latter are imported from Rajasthan and are cheaper in Jaipur.

STAYING AHEAD OF THE SCAMS

As well as the usual commission rackets and ever-present gem import scam (see p344), some specific methods to relieve Agra tourists of their hard-earned include:

» When taking an auto- or cycle-rickshaw to the Taj Mahal, make sure you are clear about which gate you want to go to when negotiating the price. Otherwise, almost without fail, riders will take you to the roundabout at the south end of Shahjahan Gardens Rd – where expensive tongas (horse-drawn carriage) or camels wait to take tour groups to the west gate – and claim that's where they thought you meant. Autos cannot go right up to the Taj because of pollution rules, but they can get a lot closer than this.

» Lots of 'marble' souvenirs are actually alabaster, or even just soapstone. The mini Taj Mahals are always alabaster because they are too intricate to carve quickly in marble.

Subhash Emporium   HANDICRAFTS
(Map p92; 2850749; 18/1 Gwalior Rd) This expensive but honest marble-carving shop has been knocking up quality pieces for more than 35 years. Watch artisans at work in the entranceway before delving into the stock out the back. Small marble boxes start at about ₹500.

Kinari Bazaar   MARKET
(Map p92; dawn-late) This is just one market of many in a crowded tangle of streets in the old town, selling everything from textiles and handicrafts to fruit and produce.

Subhash Bazaar   MARKET
Skirts the northern edge of Agra's Jama Masjid and is particularly good for silks and saris.

Khadi Gramodyog   CLOTHING
(Map p92; 2421481; MG Rd; 10.30am-7pm) Stocks simple, good-quality men's Indian clothing made from the homespun *khadi* fabric famously recommended by Mahatma Gandhi. No English sign: on Mahatma Gandhi (MG) Rd, look for the *khadi* logo of hands clasped around a mud hut.

Modern Book Depot   BOOKS
(Map p92; 2225695; Sadar Bazaar; 10.30am-9.30pm, closed Tue) Great selection of novels, plus Lonely Planet guides, at this 60-year-old establishment.

Information

Taj Ganj is riddled with **internet cafes** (per hr ₹20-40). Many have webcams for Skype use, and some let you use your own laptop. Some also have CD-burning facilities for **digital photography** (per disc ₹50-100).

Emergency
Tourist police (2421204; Agra Cantonment train station; 24hr) The guys in sky-blue uniforms are based just outside the train station, but it's easier to go through the tourism office inside where they often hang out.

Medical Services
Amit Jaggi Memorial Hospital (Map p92; 2230515; www.ajmh.in; Vibhav Nagar, off Minto Rd) Private hospital recommended by readers.

District Hospital (Map p92; 2466099; Mahatma Gandhi (MG) Rd) Government-run local hospital.

Money
ATMs are all over the city. There's only one close to the Taj, though; just by the east gate.

State Bank of India (10am-4pm Mon-Fri, to 1pm Sat) Changes cash and travellers cheques.

Post
Main post office (Map p92; The Mall; 10am-5pm Mon-Sat, Sunday Speed Post only) Has a handy 'facilitation office' for foreigners.

Tourist Information
Government of India Tourism (Map p92; 2226378; www.incredibleindia.org; 191 The Mall; 10am-5.30pm Mon-Fri, to 2pm Sat) Very helpful branch; has brochures on local and India-wide attractions and can arrange guides (half-/full day ₹500/700).

UP Tourism Agra Cantonment train station (off Map p92; 2421204; 7am-10pm); Taj Rd (Map p92; 2226431; agrauptourism@gmail.com; 64 Taj Rd; 10.30am-5pm Mon-Sat) The friendly train station branch has round-the-clock help and advice, and is the place to contact the tourist police. Either branch can arrange guides (half/full day ₹600/750).

DELHI–AGRA TRAINS (DAY TRIPPERS)

TRIP	TRAIN NO & NAME	FARE (₹)	DURATION (HR)	DEPARTURES
New Delhi–Agra	12002 *Shatabdi Exp*	370/700*	2	6.15am (except Fri)
Agra–New Delhi	12001 *Shatabdi Exp*	400/745*	2	8.30pm (except Fri)
Hazrat Nizamuddin–Agra	12280 *Taj Exp*	75/263**	3	7.10am
Agra–Hazrat Nizamuddin	12279 *Taj Exp*	75/263**	3	6.55pm

*chair/1AC; **2nd/chair

MORE HANDY TRAINS FROM AGRA

DESTINATION	TRAIN NO & NAME	FARE (₹)	DURATION (HR)	DEPARTURES
Gorakhpur*	19037/19039 Avadh Exp	249/672/920	15½	10pm
Jaipur*	14853/14863 Marudhar Exp	135/349/474	5	6.15am (except Thu)
Khajuraho	12448 UP SMPRK KRNTI	207/526**	8	11.20pm (Tue, Fri, Sun)
Kolkata (Howrah)	13008 UA Toofan Exp	394/1079**	31	12.40pm
Lucknow	13238/13240 MTJ PNBE Exp	161/422/574	6½	11.30pm
Mumbai (CST)	12138 Punjab Mail	410/1098/1501	23	8.55am
Varanasi	13238/13240 MTJ PNBE Exp	262/707/969	12	11.30pm

Fares are sleeper/3AC/2AC; *leaves from Agra Fort station; **sleeper/3AC only

Getting There & Away

Air

Kingfisher Airlines (☎2400693; www.flyking fisher.com; airport; ◷10am-5pm) has one daily flight to Delhi (from ₹2000, one hour, 3pm). Agra's Kheria airport is in Indian Air Force territory so you won't get in without your name being on the list of those who have booked flights for that day. You'll have to purchase your ticket online or over the phone.

Bus

Some services from **Idgah Bus Stand** (off Map p92):

Delhi non-AC/AC ₹149/226, five hours, frequent, 24 hours (non-AC)/6am–6pm (AC)

Fatehpur Sikri ₹27, one hour, every 30 minutes, 6am–5pm

Gwalior ₹82, three hours, frequent, 5am–1am

Jhansi ₹141, six hours, four daily: 5am, 6am, 7am and 11.30am

Jaipur ₹159, six hours, frequent, 6am–1am

Services from **ISBT Bus Stand** (off map p92) include **Dehra Dun** (seat/sleeper ₹512/574, 11 hours, at 8pm and 8.30pm, both AC).

Biili Ghar Bus Stand (Map p92) serves **Mathura** (₹42, 90 minutes, every 30 minutes, 6am–7pm).

Shared autos (₹10) run between Idgah and Biili Ghar bus stands. To get to ISBT, take the AC public bus from Agra Cant train station to Dayalbagh (₹20) but get off at Baghwan Talkies (₹15), from where shared autos (₹5) can take you to ISBT.

Train

Train is easily the quickest way to travel to/ from Delhi, Varanasi, Jaipur and Khajuraho. Most trains leave from **Agra Cantonment (Cant) train station** (off Map p92; ☎2421204), although some go from **Agra Fort station** (Map p92).

Express trains are well set up for day trippers to/from Delhi, but trains run to Delhi all day. If you can't reserve a seat, just buy a 'general ticket' for the next train (about ₹60), find a seat in Sleeper class then upgrade when the ticket collector comes along. Most of the time, he won't even make you pay any more.

For Orchha, catch one of the many daily trains to Jhansi (sleeper ₹150, 3hr), then take a shared auto to the bus stand (₹5) from where shared autos run all day to Orchha (₹10).

ⓘ Getting Around

Autorickshaw

Agra's green-and-yellow autorickshaws run on CNG (compressed natural gas) rather than petrol, and so are less environmentally destructive. Just outside Agra Cantonment train station is the **prepaid autorickshaw booth** (◷24hr), which gives you a good guide for haggling elsewhere. Note, autos aren't allowed to go to Fatehpur Sikri. Sample prices: Fatehabad Rd ₹50; ISBT bus stand ₹80; Sadar Bazaar ₹40; Sikandra ₹80; Taj Mahal ₹50; half-day (four-hour) tour ₹200; full-day (10-hour) tour ₹400.

Cycle-Rickshaw

Prices from the **Taj Mahal** include: Agra Cantonment train station ₹40-50; Agra Fort ₹20; Biili Ghar bus stand ₹30; Fatehabad Rd ₹20; Kinari Bazaar ₹30; Sadar Bazaar ₹30; haf-day tour ₹150–200.

Taxi

Outside Agra Cantonment train station the **prepaid taxi booth** (⊘24hr) gives a good idea of what taxis should cost. Prices include: Delhi ₹2500; Fatehabad Rd ₹150; Sadar Bazaar ₹70; Taj Mahal ₹150; half-day (four-hour) tour ₹450; full-day (eight-hour) tour ₹650.

Around Agra

FATEHPUR SIKRI

☑ 05613 / POP 28,750

This magnificent fortified ancient city, 40km west of Agra, was the short-lived capital of the Mughal empire between 1571 and 1585, during the reign of Emperor Akbar. Akbar visited the village of Sikri to consult the Sufi saint Shaikh Salim Chishti, who predicted the birth of an heir to the Mughal throne. When the prophecy came true, Akbar built his new capital here, including a stunning mosque – still in use today – and three palaces for each of his favourite wives, one a Hindu, one a Muslim and one a Christian. The city was an Indo-Islamic masterpiece, but erected in an area that suffered from water shortages and so was abandoned shortly after Akbar's death.

It's easy to visit this World Heritage Site as a day trip from Agra, but there are a couple of decent places to stay, and the colourful bazaar in the village of Fatehpur, just below the ruins, as well as the small village of Sikri, a few kilometres north, are worth exploring. Also, the red sandstone palace walls are at their most atmospheric, and photogenic, at sunset.

The bus stand is at the eastern end of the bazaar. Walking another 1km northeast will bring you to Agra Gate and the junction with the main Agra–Jaipur road, from where you can catch buses.

◉ Sights

The palace buildings lie beside the Jama Masjid mosque. Both sit on top of a ridge that runs between the small villages of Fatehpur and Sikri. Official guides, hired from the ticket office, will show you around for ₹125. There are other ruins scattered all over this area, all of which can be viewed for free. Colourful Fatehpur Bazaar also deserves some of your time.

Jama Masjid   MOSQUE

This beautiful, immense mosque was completed in 1571 and contains elements of Persian and Indian design. The main entrance, at the top of a flight of stone steps, is through the spectacular 54m-high **Buland Darwaza** (Victory Gate), built to commemorate Akbar's military victory in Gujarat.

Inside the courtyard of the mosque is the stunning white-marble **tomb of Shaikh Salim Chishti**, which was completed in 1581 and is entered through a door made of ebony. Inside it are brightly coloured flower murals while the canopy is decorated with mother-of-pearl shell. Just as Akbar came to the saint four centuries ago hoping for a son, childless women visit his tomb today and tie a thread to the *jali,* which are among the finest in India. To the right of the tomb lie the gravestones of family members of Shaikh Salim Chishti and nearby is the entrance to an underground tunnel (barred by a locked gate) that reputedly goes all the way to Agra Fort! Behind the entrance to the tunnel, on the far wall, are three holes, part of the ancient ventilation system. You can still feel the rush of cool air forcing its way through them. Just east of Shaikh Salim Chisti's tomb is the red sandstone **tomb of Islam Khan**, the final resting place of Shaikh Salim Chisti's grandson and one-time governor of Bengal.

On the east wall of the courtyard is a smaller entrance to the mosque – the **Shahi Darwaza** (King's Gate), which leads to the palace complex.

Palaces & Pavilions   PALACES

(Indian/foreigner ₹20/260, video ₹25; ⊘dawn-dusk) The first of the palace buildings you enter from the south is the largest, the **Palace of Jodh Bai**, and the one-time home of Akbar's Hindu wife, said to be his favourite. Set around an enormous courtyard, it blends traditional Indian columns, Islamic cupolas and turquoise Persian roof tiles.

Just outside, to the left of Jodh Bai's former kitchen, is the **Palace of the Christian Wife**. This was used by Akbar's Goan wife Mariam, who gave birth to Jehangir here in 1569. Like many of the buildings in the palace complex, it contains elements of different religions, as befitted Akbar's tolerant religious beliefs. The domed ceiling is Islamic in style, while remnants of a wall painting of the Hindu god Shiva can also be found.

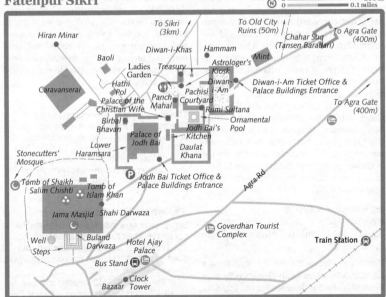

Continuing anticlockwise will bring you to the **Ornamental Pool**. Here, singers and musicians would perform on the platform above the water while Akbar watched from the pavilion in his private quarters, known as **Daulat Khana** (Abode of Fortune). Behind the pavilion is the **Khwabgah** (Dream House), a sleeping area with a huge stone bunk bed. Nowadays the only sleeping done here is by bats, hanging from the ceiling. The small room in the far corner is full of them!

Heading north from the Ornamental Pool brings you to the most intricately carved structure in the whole complex, the tiny but elegant **Rumi Sultana**, the palace built for Akbar's Turkish Muslim wife.

Just past Rumi Sultana is **Pachisi Courtyard** where Akbar is said to have played the game *pachisi* (an ancient version of ludo) using slave girls as pieces.

From here you can step down into **Diwan-i-Am** (Hall of Public Audiences), a large courtyard (which is now a garden) where Akbar dispensed justice by orchestrating public executions, said to have been carried out by elephants trampling convicted criminals to death.

The **Diwan-i-Khas** (Hall of Private Audiences), found at the northern end of the Pachisi Courtyard, looks nothing special from the outside, but the interior is dominated by a magnificently carved stone central column. This pillar flares to create a flat-topped plinth linked to the four corners of the room by narrow stone bridges. From this plinth Akbar is believed to have debated with scholars and ministers who stood at the ends of the four bridges.

Next to Diwan-i-Khas is the **Treasury**, which houses secret stone safes in some corners (one has been left with its stone lid open for visitors to see). Sea monsters carved on the ceiling struts were there to protect the fabulous wealth once stored here. The so-called **Astrologer's Kiosk** in front has roof supports carved in a serpentine Jain style.

On one corner of the **Ladies Garden** is the impressive **Panch Mahal**, a pavilion whose five storeys decrease in size until the top one consists of only a tiny kiosk. The lower floor has 84 columns, all different.

Walking past the Palace of the Christian Wife once more will take you west to **Birbal Bhavan**, ornately carved inside and out, and thought to have been the living quarters of one of Akbar's most senior ministers. The **Lower Haramsara**, just to the south, housed the royal stables.

Plenty of ruins are scattered behind the whole complex, including the **Caravanse-rai**, a vast courtyard surrounded by rooms where visiting merchants stayed, and the bizarre 21m-tall **Hiran Minar**, a tower decorated with hundreds of stone representations of elephant tusks, which is said to be the place where Akbar's favourite execution elephant died. Badly defaced carvings of elephants still guard **Hathi Pol** (Elephant Gate), while the remains of the small **Stonecutters' Mosque** and a **hammam** (bath) are also a short stroll away. Other unnamed ruins can be explored north of what is known as the **Mint** but is thought to have in fact been stables, including some in the interesting village of Sikri to the north.

🛏 Sleeping & Eating

Fatehpur Sikri's culinary speciality is *khataie,* the biscuits you can see piled high in the bazaar.

Hotel Ajay Palace GUESTHOUSE **$**
(☏282950; Agra Rd; d ₹200) This friendly family guesthouse has three simple but tidy double rooms with marble floors and sit-down flush toilets. It's also a very popular lunch stop (mains ₹30–70). Sit on the rooftop at the large, elongated marble table and enjoy a view of the village streets with the Jama Masjid towering above. Nonguests can store luggage (₹10) here while they visit the ruins.

Goverdhan Tourist Complex HOTEL **$**
(☏282643; www.hotelfatehpursikriviews.com; Agra Rd; d ₹400, with AC ₹700; ❋@⎙) Brightly painted, spotless rooms set around a very well-kept garden. There's communal balcony and terrace seating, free internet and wi-fi, and the restaurant is decent (meals ₹50 to ₹120).

❶ Information

Take no notice of anyone who gets on the Fatehpur Sikri–Agra bus before the final stop at Idgah bus stand, telling you that you have arrived at the city centre or the Taj Mahal. You haven't. You're still a long rickshaw ride away, and the person who is trying to tease you off the bus early is – surprise surprise – a rickshaw driver.

❶ Getting There & Away

Buses run to Agra's Idgah Bus Stand from the bazaar every half hour, from 6am to 5.30pm. If you miss those, walk to Agra Gate and wave down a Jaipur–Agra bus on the main road. They run regularly, day and night.

For Bharatpur (₹15, 40 minutes) or Jaipur (₹140, 4½ hours), wave down a westbound bus from Agra Gate.

Trains for Agra Fort Station (₹6, one to two hours) leave Fatehpur Sikri at 4.53am, 10.28am, 2.10pm (to Agra Cantonment station), 3.56pm and 8.17pm. Just buy a 'general' ticket at the station and pile in.

Jaipur

AREA: 65 SQ KM / POPULATION: 3.21 MILLION / TELEPHONE CODE: 0141

Best Places to Eat

» Niro's (p126)

» LMB (p128)

» Dāsaprakash (p127)

» Peacock Rooftop Restaurant (p126)

Best Places to Stay

» Rambagh Palace (p125)

» Hotel Pearl Palace (p120)

» Madhuban (p122)

» Hotel Bissau Palace (p123)

Why Go?

Jaipur, Rajasthan's capital, is an enthralling historical city and the gateway to India's most flamboyant state.

The city's colourful, chaotic streets ebb and flow with a heady brew of old and new. Careering buses dodge dawdling camels, leisurely cycle-rickshaws frustrate swarms of motorbikes, and everywhere buzzing autorickshaws watch for easy prey. In the midst of this mayhem, the splendours of Jaipur's majestic past are islands of relative calm evoking a different pace and another world. At the city's heart, the City Palace continues to house the former royal family; the Jantar Mantar, the royal observatory, maintains a heavenly aspect; and the honeycomb Hawa Mahal gazes on the bazaar below. And just out of sight, in the arid hill country surrounding the city, is the fairy-tale grandeur of Amber Fort.

When to Go

Jaipur is a year-round destination but in the height of summer, as temperatures soar, personal comfort is compromised. Spring and autumn days are still warm to hot, while winter days are very pleasant and the nights can be decidedly cool. Jaipur celebrates its own special festivals, as well as numerous state-wide and national festivals, with vigour and flair. It's worth visiting for any of these to catch the build-up, the dressing up and a few processions.

History

*Je na dekkhyo Jaipario to kal main
akar kaai kario?*

If one has not seen Jaipur, what is the
point of having been born?

Jaipur is named after its founder, the great
warrior–astronomer Jai Singh II (1688–
1744), who came to power at age 11 after the
death of his father, Maharaja Bishan Singh.
The maharaja had been assured by astrologers that the boy would achieve great things
in his lifetime, and young Jai (meaning 'victory') received the best education in the arts,
sciences, philosophy and military affairs.

Jai Singh could trace his lineage back to
the Rajput clan of Kachhwahas, who consolidated their power in the 12th century. Their
capital was at Amber (pronounced amer),
about 11km northeast of present-day Jaipur,
where they built the impressive Amber Fort

(p136). The Kachhwahas had a talent for
war and alliances of convenience, so their
dominion spread, eventually encompassing
a large area abutting the kingdoms of Mewar (in the Udaipur region) and Marwar (in
the Jodhpur region).

It's said that at 15 years of age, the prodi-
gal Jai Singh – already king for four years –
met the Mughal emperor Aurangzeb. When
the emperor grasped the lad's hand, the
youth retorted that, as the emperor had extended the traditional gesture of protection
offered by a bridegroom to his new wife by
taking his hand, it was incumbent on Aurangzeb to protect the young ruler and his
kingdom in a similar fashion. Luckily Aurangzeb was impressed rather than peeved
by such precocious behaviour, and conferred
on Jai Singh the title 'Sawai', meaning 'one
and a quarter', a title that was proudly borne
by all of Jai Singh's descendants – there is

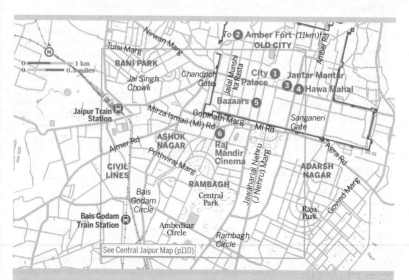

Jaipur Highlights

❶ Marvel at the maharaja
high-life in the opulent **City
Palace** (p108)

❷ Explore the imposing
Amber Fort (p136), a mighty
Rajput citadel rising from
the rocks 11km from Jaipur

❸ Follow your stars among
the outsized astronomical
and astrological

instruments at the **Jantar
Mantar** (p111)

❹ Hide like the harem in
the **Hawa Mahal** (p114), the
Palace of the Winds, a
multiwindowed honeycomb
built for the women of the
court

❺ Barter and bargain with
the wily shopkeepers in the

colourful **bazaars** (p129) of
the Old City

❻ Catch a Bollywood
blockbuster at the
marshmallow-pink **Raj
Mandir Cinema** (p129)

❼ Join the party and the
painted pachyderms at one
of Jaipur's vibrant **festivals**
(p107)

Jaipur celebrates several unique festivals, as well as numerous statewide and national festivals. For more information on festivals, see p24.

» **Jaipur Heritage International Festival** (Jan; www.jaipurfestival.org) In celebration of Jaipur's heritage, this festival aims to revive and conserve the regional culture and traditions. Performances are held throughout the Old City, in atmospheric venues from forts to temples.

» **Jaipur Literature Festival** (Jan; www.jaipurliteraturefestival.org) Featuring international and Indian authors and a program of talks, films, debates and theatre. See the website for exact dates.

» **Elephant Festival** (Mar) Takes place the day before Holi. Elephants painted in amazing patterns and dressed in ribbons and jewellery (spot the females by their jangling anklets) lumber through the streets. Pachyderm craziness includes matches of elephant polo at Chaughan Stadium in the Old City, elephant races, and a tug-of-war between elephants and humans.

» **Gangaur** (Mar/Apr) Rajasthan's most important festival, especially for women, celebrates the love between Gan (Shiva) and his consort Gauri (Parvati). It commences on the day following Holi and is celebrated with particular fervour in Jaipur. An elaborately garbed image of the goddess is carried on a palanquin from the Tripolia Gate, at the City Palace, through the streets of the Old City. The traditional dish to eat in Jaipur at this time is *ghewar,* a kind of sweet.

» **Teej** (Jul/Aug) This is the swing festival, and heralds the onset of the monsoon month, Shravan. It's celebrated across Rajasthan in honour of the marriage of Gan and Gauri, but is at its best in Jaipur.

still a quarter-sized flag flying above the full-sized version over the City Palace today.

Jai Singh did, however, severely peeve Aurangzeb's successor, Bahadur Shah, who came to power following Aurangzeb's death in 1707. Bahadur Shah's accession was contested by his younger brother, Azam Shah, and Jai Singh backed the wrong Shah. Bahadur responded by demanding his removal from Amber Fort, and installing Jai Singh's younger brother, Vijay, in his place. Jai Singh was unimpressed and eventually succeeded in dislodging his brother. Soliciting the support of other large Rajput states, Jai Singh formed a strong front against the Mughal ruler and eventually clawed his way back.

The kingdom grew wealthier and wealthier, and this, plus the need to accommodate the burgeoning population and a paucity of water at the old capital at Amber, prompted the maharaja in 1727 to commence work on a new city – Jaipur.

Northern India's first planned city, it was a collaborative effort using his vision and the impressive expertise of his chief architect, Vidyadhar Bhattacharya. Jai Singh's grounding in the sciences is reflected in the precise symmetry of the new city. The small villages that lay in the vicinity were incorporated into the new city, which was dissected by wide boulevards flanked by stalls of equal size that formed nine *mohallas* (rectangles) of varying size.

The city wasn't just an aesthetic triumph; its stout walls protected its inhabitants from would-be invaders, encouraging merchants and artisans to flock here, further serving to enhance the city's growth and prosperity. Jai Singh's interest in the arts, sciences and religion fostered their development, and the royal court became a booming centre of intellectual and artistic endeavour.

Following Jai Singh's death in 1744, power struggles between his many offspring laid the kingdom open to invasion by neighbouring Rajput kingdoms, which appropriated large tracts of territory. The kingdom maintained good relations with the British Raj, although the British gradually undermined the independence of the state, exercising increasing control over its administration.

During the first war of independence, the Indian Uprising of 1857, Maharaja Ram Singh conspicuously helped the British and, in so doing, raised his status with the imperial power. In 1876 Maharaja Ram Singh had the entire Old City painted pink (traditionally the colour of hospitality) to welcome the Prince of Wales (later King Edward VII). Today all residents of the Old City are compelled by law to preserve the pink facade. Maharaja Ram Singh also built Ramgarh Lake to supply water to the burgeoning city.

During the 19th and 20th centuries, the spacious and carefully planned city burst from its city walls and began to sprawl outwards, with no notion of the controlled planning at its conception.

In 1922 Man Singh II, Jaipur's last maharaja, took the throne on the death of his adoptive father, Maharaja Madho Singh II. Following Independence in 1947, the status of the princely state changed forever. In March 1949 Jaipur merged with the Rajput states of Jodhpur, Jaisalmer and Bikaner, becoming the Greater Rajasthan Union. Jaipur was honoured above the other former states when the title *rajpramukh,* meaning 'head of state', was conferred on Man Singh II, who was invested with administrative supervision of the new province. The title was later revoked, and Man Singh II was posted as Indian ambassador to Spain. In 1949 Jaipur became the capital of the state of Rajasthan.

Since 1950 the population has exploded from 300,000 to over three million, and it shows: unplanned urban sprawl has disfigured what was once one of India's most beautiful cities. Such massive growth breeds its own problems; overcrowding, pollution and traffic are the most obvious. The city is prosperous and attracts plenty of investment as a commercial, business and tourist centre.

⊙ Sights

The sights in and around Jaipur are well and truly on the tourist trail, but you can avoid the majority of the busloads of tourists (and the long queues) by visiting the City Palace and Jantar Mantar in the morning and Amber Fort in the afternoon. Consider buying a **composite ticket** (Indian/foreigner ₹50/300), which gives you entry to Amber Fort, Central Museum, Jantar Mantar, Hawa Mahal and Narhargarh and is valid for two days from time of purchase.

OLD CITY (PINK CITY)

The bustling Old City, often referred to as the Pink City for obvious reasons, was laid out by Jai Singh and his talented architect, Vidyadhar, according to strict principles of town planning set down in the *Shilpa Shastra,* an ancient Hindu treatise on architecture. At the centre of the grid is the City Pal-

ace complex, containing the palace itself, the administrative quarters, the Jantar Mantar (Jai Singh's remarkable observatory) and the *zenana mahals* (women's palaces). The Old City is partially encircled by a crenellated wall punctuated at intervals by grand gateways. The major gates are Chandpol (*pol* means 'gate'), Ajmer Gate and Sanganeri Gate.

Avenues divide the Pink City into neat rectangles, each specialising in certain crafts, as ordained in the *Shilpa Shastra.* The main bazaars in the Old City include Johari Bazaar, Tripolia Bazaar, Bapu Bazaar and Chandpol Bazaar – see the walking tour (p118) or Shopping (p129) for more details of these bazaars.

City Palace   PALACE

(Indian/foreigner incl camera & audio guide ₹75/300, video camera ₹200, Chandra Mahal tour ₹2500; ⊙9.30am-5pm) A complex of courtyards, gardens and buildings, the impressive City Palace is right in the centre of the Old City. The outer wall was built by Jai Singh, but within it the palace has been enlarged and adapted over the centuries. There are palace buildings from different eras, some dating from the early 20th century. Despite the gradual development, the whole is a striking blend of Rajasthani and Mughal architecture.

The Kachhwaha Rajputs were patrons of the arts and took pride in their collection of valuable artefacts. For a long time there was a private museum here, for viewing by visiting dignitaries, and in 1959 this became a public museum under Man Singh II. His successor, Maharaja Bhawani Singh, took a keen interest in its development and enlarged the museum substantially.

The price of admission also gets you in to Jaigarh Fort (see p138), a long climb above Amber Fort. This is valid for two days.

Mubarak Mahal

Entering through Virendra Pol, you'll see the Mubarak Mahal (Welcome Palace), built in the late 19th century for Maharaja Madho Singh II as a reception centre for visiting dignitaries. Its multiarched and colonnaded construction was cooked up in an Islamic, Rajput and European stylistic stew by the architect Sir Swinton Jacob. It now forms part of the **Maharaja Sawai Mansingh II Museum**, containing a collection of royal costumes and superb shawls, including Kashmiri *pashmina.* One remarkable exhibit is Sawai Madho Singh I's capacious

Holding pride of place in the pink Diwan-i-Khas pavilion are two enormous silver *gangaja-lis* (urns), 1.6m tall and each weighing about 345kg. They were made for Maharaja Madho Singh II, a devout Hindu, so that he could take sufficient holy Ganges water to England for bathing when he visited for Edward VII's coronation in 1902. These enormous vessels each have a capacity of over 4000L, and have been listed in the *Guinness Book of World Records* as the largest sterling-silver objects in the world. They were beaten into shape from silver sheets – each made from 14,000 melted silver coins – without any soldering.

clothing. It's said he was a cuddly 2m tall, 1.2m wide and 250kg. Guides will take great delight in telling you how much he supposedly ate for breakfast and that he had 108 wives. Appropriate for such an excessive figure.

Also on display here is Maharaja Pratap Singh's more diminutive wedding dress – a red-and-gold piece with a massively pleated skirt dating from 1790. There are also several dresses with exquisite gold embroidery, dating from the 19th century, which were worn by royalty around Diwali.

Rajendra Pol

North of the Mubarak Mahal is the grand Rajendra Pol, flanked by carved elephants with lotus flowers in their mouths – symbolising royalty – that date from 1931. The gate has brass doors and walls embedded with precious and semiprecious stones.

Diwan-i-Khas (Sarvatobhadra)

Set between the Armoury and the Diwan-i-Am art gallery is an open courtyard known in Sanskrit as Sarvatobhadra. At its centre is a pink-and-white, marble-paved gallery that was used as the Diwan-i-Khas (Hall of Private Audience), where the maharajas would consult their ministers. Here you can see the two enormous silver vessels.

Diwan-i-Am

Within the lavish Diwan-i-Am (Hall of Public Audience) is the **art gallery**. Its great array of exhibits includes a touching collection of illustrated manuscripts showing everything from scenes of daily life to tales of the gods. The hall still has its beautifully preserved painted ceiling, with its barely faded, original semiprecious-stone colours, and an enormous crystal chandelier.

Exhibits include a copy of the entire Bhagavad Gita handwritten in tiny script, and miniature copies of other holy Hindu scriptures, which were small enough to be easily hidden in the event that Mughal zealot Aurangzeb tried to destroy the sacred texts. There are Persian translations of the Ramayana and Mahabharata; the latter was made especially for Akbar, and has illustrations by the greatest Mughal painters. Some beautiful Sanskrit books are also on display, as are early manuscripts on palm leaf, and particularly fine miniature paintings from the Rajasthani, Mughal and Persian schools depicting religious themes. On the walls are some beautiful carpets, made in Lahore in the 17th century and probably bought to decorate the new fort–palace at Amber.

The Armoury

The Anand Mahal Sileg Khana – the Maharani's Palace – houses the Armoury, which has one of the best collections of weapons in the country.

Fearsome daggers are arranged over the entrance to say 'Welcome'. Many of the ceremonial weapons are elegantly engraved and inlaid belying their grisly purpose. They include two-bladed steel daggers that, at the flick of a catch, become scissors inside their victims; walking-stick swords; swords with pistols attached to their blades; and beautiful crystal-, ivory- and silver-handled daggers. Some pieces have a history attached to them, such as a sword inscribed for Shah Jahan, and a sword encrusted with rubies and emeralds that was presented by Queen Victoria to Maharaja Ram Singh, ruler of Jaipur from 1835 to 1880. Gun-lovers fear not, there is a fine array, including a gun the size of a small cannon for use on camel back; and double-barrelled pistols, which held bullets made of lead, dipped in poison and packed with gunpowder.

If weaponry isn't your bag, however cunningly vicious and finely engraved, the 19th-century mirrored and gold-inlaid ceiling, decorated with a gorgeous floral pattern and women in various moods, is well worth a gaze.

JAIPUR SIGHTS

JAIPUR

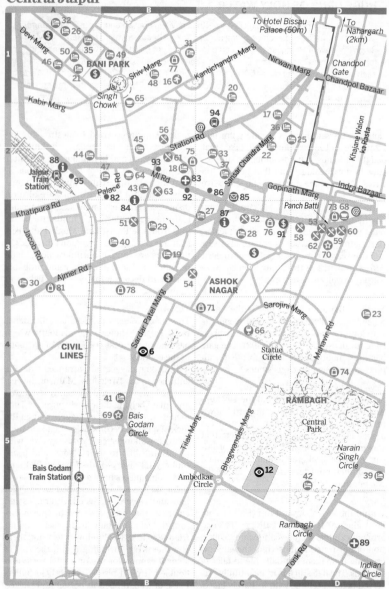

Bagghi-Khana – The Carriage Museum

This museum houses a ramshackle collection of carriages and palanquins, featuring special covered versions for palace women, with the purpose of maintaining purdah (the custom among some Muslims and Hindus of keeping women hidden from men outside their own family). It's interesting also to see 19th-century European cabs adapted to Indian conditions, such as the small Victoria *bagghi* (carriage) given to the maharaja by the Prince of Wales in 1876 (the same year

Pitam Niwas Chowk & Chandra Mahal

Located towards the palace's inner courtyard is Pitam Niwas Chowk. Here four glorious gates represent the seasons. The **Peacock Gate** depicts autumn, with zigzagging patterns and peacock motifs – around the doorway are five beautiful repeated peacock bas reliefs in all their feathered glory. The **Lotus Gate**, signifying summer, is just as splendid, and is covered in repeated flower and petal patterns. The **Green Gate** (or Leheriya, literally 'waves') representing spring is more subdued, but still beautiful with its simple green design, and winter is embodied by the **Rose Gate**, again with repeated flower patterns, but less colourful than the autumn or summer gates.

Beyond this *chowk* (square) is the private palace, the Chandra Mahal, which is still the residence of the descendants of the royal family and where you can take a 45-minute guided **tour** (₹2500) of select areas. Flying above the building, you can see the one-and-a-quarter flags that signify the presence of the maharaja. If he is away, the queen's flag will fly in its place.

Govind Devji Temple

This early 18th-century Krishna temple is part of the City Palace complex, though outside the walls. It's decorated with a mixture of European and Indian designs – the chandeliers are European, the paintings Indian. The ceiling is decorated in gold. A popular place of worship, it's set in gardens and was situated so that the maharaja could see the deity from his palace. The deity is unveiled seven times daily for *aarti* (worshipping ritual).

Jantar Mantar HISTORIC SITE
(Indian/foreigner ₹ 20/100 incl audio guide, optional guide Hindi/English ₹200/250; ⏰9am-4.30pm)
Adjacent to the City Palace is Jantar Mantar, an observatory begun by Jai Singh in 1728, which resembles a collection of bizarre sculptures. The name is derived from the Sanskrit *yanta mantr* meaning 'instrument of calculation', and in 2010 it was added to India's list of World Heritage Sites.

Jai Singh liked astronomy even more than he liked war and town planning. Before constructing the observatory he sent scholars abroad to study foreign constructions. He built five observatories in total, and this is the largest and best preserved (it was restored in 1901). Others are in Delhi, Varanasi and Ujjain. No traces of the fifth, the Mathura observatory, remain.

Jaipur was painted pink). An unusual piece is the *mahadol* – a palanquin with a single bamboo bar – usually used by priests and carried by bearers. Also on display here is the Thakurji ka Rath, a chariot used for carrying the state religious icon on special occasions.

Central Jaipur

Each construction within Jantar Mantar has a specific purpose, for example, measuring the positions of the stars, altitude and azimuth, and calculating eclipses. Paying for the half-hour to one-hour guide is worthwhile if you wish to learn how each fascinating instrument works and have questions.

Brihat Samrat Yantra

The most striking instrument is the Brihat Samrat Yantra (King of the Instruments) sundial, a massive edifice with a staircase running to the top. It has a 27m-high gnomonic arm set at an angle of 27 degrees – the same as the latitude of Jaipur. The shadow this casts moves up to 4m in an hour, and aids in the calculation of local and meridian time and various attributes of the heavenly bodies, including declination (the angular distance of a heavenly body from the celestial equator) and altitude. It's still used by astrologers and is the focus of a gathering during the full moon in June or July, when it purportedly helps predict local monsoon rains, and subsequent success or failure of crops.

JAIPUR

Laghu Samrat Yantra

If you tour the *yantras* in a clockwise direction, to the left as you enter the compound is the Laghu Samrat Yantra, a small sundial of red sandstone and white marble, inclined at 27 degrees. It does not measure as precisely as the Brihat Samrat Yantra, but does calculate the declination of celestial bodies, and the shadow cast by its gnomon enables local time (which differs from 10 to 40 minutes from Indian Standard Time) to be determined. On either side are two quadrants and local time can be determined by the shadow cast on each quadrant (one for the morning, one for the afternoon). Nearby is the **Dhruva Darshak Yantra**, used to find the location of the Pole Star and the 12 zodiac signs.

Narivalaya Yantra

The large circular object nearby, known as the Narivalaya Yantra, is actually two small sundials. The two faces of the instrument represent the northern and southern hemispheres, and enable calculation of the time within a minute's accuracy.

Yantra Raj

Two large disks suspended from the wooden beams nearby comprise the Yantra Raj, a multipurpose instrument that, among other things, can help determine the positions of constellations and calculate the date of the Hindu calendar. A telescope is at the centre. The similar-looking **Unnatansha Yantra** lies in the northeastern corner of the observatory complex. This metal ring is divided into four segments by horizontal and vertical lines. A hole where these lines intersect, in the centre of the instrument, aids in the calculation of the altitude of celestial bodies. Nearby is **Dakhinovrith Bhitti Yantra**, which serves a similar function to the Unnatansha Yantra.

Rashi Yantras

West of the Brihat Samrat Yantra, near the southern wall of the observatory, you come to a cluster of 12 yellow instruments, the Rashi Yantras. Each *rashi* (individual instrument) represents one of the 12 zodiac signs. The gradient of each *rashi* differs in accordance with the particular sign represented and its position in relation to the ecliptic.

Jai Prakash Yantra

The Jai Prakash Yantra, resembling two huge slotted bowls, was the last instrument installed at the observatory and was invented by Jai Singh, after whom it was named. The instrument is used in celestial observations, but can also verify the calculations determined by other instruments at the observatory. Each of the two cavities is divided into six marble slabs, which are marked with minutes and seconds and with signs of the zodiac. The metal ring suspended in the centre represents the sun, and calculations can be made from the shadow cast by it on the marble slabs. This instrument may be used to calculate auspicious days for weddings, business negotiations and so on.

Kapali Yantra

The two other sunken concave structures in the western section of the observatory compound comprise the Kapali Yantra. The eastern Kapali Yantra is inscribed with lines to which astronomers refer in their deliberations, and is used for graphical analysis. The western Kapali Yantra is used to determine the position of a celestial body. Between the two bowls stands the **Chakra Yantra**, a pair of metal wheels, which can revolve parallel to the earth's axis, and can be fitted with a brass tube in order to calculate the declination of celestial bodies.

Ram Yantras

Two other impressive instruments are the Ram Yantras, which look like miniature coliseums made of 12 upright slabs and 12 horizontal slabs. They are used in the calculation of the altitude and azimuth of celestial bodies. Between them is another circular instrument, the **Digansha Yantra**, with a pillar in the middle and two outer circles. It's used for calculating azimuths, particularly of the sun. It can also be used to determine the time of sunrise and sunset.

Hawa Mahal   HISTORIC BUILDING
(Palace of the Winds; Indian/foreigner incl camera ₹10/50, audio guide Hindi/English ₹80/110, guide ₹200; ⊙9am-5pm) Jaipur's most distinctive landmark, the Hawa Mahal is an extraordinary, fairy-tale, pink sandstone, delicately honeycombed hive that rises a dizzying five storeys. It was constructed in 1799 by Maharaja Sawai Pratap Singh to enable ladies of the royal household to watch the life and processions of the city. Inside it's barely a building at all, only around one room deep, with narrow, delicately scalloped walkways. It's still a great place for people-watching from behind the small shutters. The top offers stunning views over Jantar Mantar and the City Palace one way, and over Siredeori Bazaar the other. The palace was built by Pratap Singh and is part of the City Palace complex.

There's also a small **museum** (⊙9am-4.30pm Sat-Thu), with miniature paintings and some rich relics, such as ceremonial armour, which help evoke the royal past.

Entrance to the Hawa Mahal is from the back of the complex. To get here, return to the intersection on your left as you face the Hawa Mahal, turn right and then take the first right again through an archway.

Shree Sanjay Sharma Museum   MUSEUM
(Thatheron ka Rasta; admission ₹100, photography prohibited; ⊙10am-5pm) This museum is a fascinating jumble of precious objects gathered by the parents of Shree Sanjay Sharma (who died as a boy) in his memory. It includes rare manuscripts and Indian art from around the country. There's a set of 18th-century paintings of yoga postures, elaborate locks, shoes, drawings of temple architecture, beautiful royal games, 19th-century paper cut-outs, illustrated alchemy books and much more.

The original museum is signposted (though not all that clearly) off Chaura Rasta, while a new museum under construction on Amber Rd, opposite the Jal Mahal, will eventually house the museum's decorative items.

DON'T MISS

ISWARI MINAR SWARGA SAL

(Heaven-Piercing Minaret; Indian/foreigner ₹5/10, camera ₹10; ⊙9am-4.30pm) Piercing the skyline near the City Palace is the unusual Iswari Minar Swarga Sal, just west of Tripolia Gate. The minaret was erected by Jai Singh's son Iswari, who later ignominiously killed himself by snakebite (in the Chandra Mahal) rather than face the advancing Maratha army – 21 wives and concubines then did the necessary noble thing and committed *jauhar* (ritual mass suicide by immolation) on his funeral pyre. You can spiral to the top of the minaret for excellent views over the Old City. The entrance is around the back of the row of shops fronting Chandpol Bazaar – take the alley 50m west of the minaret along Chandpol Bazaar or go via the Atishpol entrance to the City Palace compound, 150m east of the minaret.

NEW CITY

By the mid-19th century it became obvious that the well-planned city was bulging at the seams. During the reign of Maharaja Ram Singh (1835–80) the seams ruptured and the city burst out beyond its walls. Civic facilities, such as a postal system and piped water, were introduced. This period gave rise to a part of town very different from the bazaars of the Old City, with wide boulevards, landscaped grounds and florid buildings. The maharaja commissioned the landscaping of the Ram Niwas Public Gardens, on Jawaharlal Nehru (J Nehru) Rd, and the uproarious splendour of Albert Hall, built in honour of the Prince of Wales' 1876 visit, which now houses the Central Museum.

These civic improvements were continued by Jaipur's last maharaja, Man Singh II, who is credited with the university, the Secretariat, residential colonies, schools, hospitals and colleges. Unfortunately the city has further developed wildly outwards, in an unplanned urban sprawl.

Central Museum   MUSEUM
(Albert Hall; Indian/foreigner ₹20/150, audio guide Hindi/English ₹80/110; ⊙9.30am-5pm) The museum is housed in the spectacularly florid Albert Hall, south of the old city. It was designed by Sir Swinton Jacob, and combines elements of English and North Indian architecture. It was known as the pride of the new Jaipur when it opened in 1887. The grand old building hosts an eclectic array of tribal dress, clay models of yogis in various positions, dioramas, puppets, sculptures, miniature paintings, carpets, musical instruments and even an Egyptian mummy.

SRC Museum of Indology   MUSEUM
(Prachyavidya Path, 24 Gangwell Park; Indian/foreigner incl guide ₹20/40; ⊙8am-6pm) This ram-shackle, dusty treasure trove is an extraordinary private collection. It contains folk-art objects and other pieces – there's everything from a manuscript written by Aurangzeb and a 200-year-old mirrorwork swing from Bikaner to a glass bed (for a short queen). The museum is signposted off J Nehru Rd, south of the Central Museum.

Philatelic Bureau & Museum   MUSEUM
(Main Post Office; MI Rd; admission free; ⊙10am-5pm Mon-Sat) At the rear of the main post office, this interesting little museum has historical stamps, telegrams and artefacts, including brass belt buckles and badges for Mail Runners and Packers. Even the Mail Peon could wear a badge with pride. With wild animals and dacoits to deal with, little wonder the postmen were armed with swords, spears and pistols.

Birla Lakshmi Narayan Temple   HINDU TEMPLE
(J Nehru Rd; admission free; ⊙6am-noon & 3-8.30pm) This splendid, modern marble edifice lies at the foot of Moti Dungri Fort. The wealthy industrialist Birla, born in Palani, Rajasthan, bought the land on which the temple now stands from the maharaja for a token ₹1. Stained-glass windows depict scenes from Hindu scriptures. Ganesh, the protector of households, is above the lintel, and the fine quality of the marble is evident when you enter the temple and look back at the entrance – Ganesh can be made out *through* the marble, which is almost transparent. The images of Lakshmi and Narayan were carved from one piece of marble. Many of the deities of the Hindu pantheon are depicted inside the temple, and on the outside walls historic figures from other religions are shown, including Socrates, Zarathustra, Christ, Buddha and Confucius.

Ganesh Temple   HINDU TEMPLE

(J Nehru Rd; photography prohibited; ☺5am-9pm Thu-Tue, 5am-11pm Wed) If you don't like crowds avoid the temple on Wednesdays (the auspicious day), when there are throngs of devotees. You can buy *ladoos* (sweet balls made from gram flour) to offer to Ganesh from the sweet stalls outside the temple.

Zoo   ZOO

(Indian/foreigner ₹15/150, camera ₹40; ☺9am-5pm) Opposite Albert Hall, one of the oldest in India, and housing the usual motley array of disconsolate animals.

Modern Art Gallery   ART GALLERY

(admission free; ☺10am-5pm Mon-Sat) An old theatre houses this gallery, on the 1st floor of the Ravindra Manch building, a very peaceful place with some striking contemporary work.

Moti Dungri   FORT

To the south, looming above J Nehru Rd, is this small, romantic fort. It has served as a prison, but today remains in the possession of the former royal family, and entry is prohibited.

CITY EDGE

Surrounding the city are several historic sites including forts, temples, palaces and gardens. Some of these can be visited on the way to Amber Fort (see p136).

Nahargarh   HISTORIC BUILDING

(Tiger Fort; ☎5148044; Indian/foreigner ₹10/30; ☺10am-5pm) Built in 1734 and extended in 1868, sturdy Nahargarh overlooks the city from a sheer ridge to the north. An 8km-long road runs up through the hills from Jaipur, or the fort can be reached along a zigzagging 2km-long footpath, which starts northwest of the Old City. The views are glorious – it's a great sunset spot, and there's a restaurant that's perfect for a beer. The story goes that the fort was named after Nahar Singh, a dead prince whose restless spirit was disrupting construction. Whatever was built in the day crumbled in the night. He agreed to leave on condition that the fort was named for him.

The fort was built in 1734 by Jai Singh to increase the Amber defences, and was adapted in 1868 to its present form by Maharaja Ram Singh, to house the maharaja's numerous wives. You can visit the **Madhavendra Bhawan**, which has the nine apartments of Maharaja Ram Singh's nine other

halves, with a separate suite for the king himself. There are bathrooms, toilets, boudoirs and kitchens.

Doors and windows had coloured panes, of which a few remain. Some of the boudoirs retain Belgian mirrors, and all are decorated with floral and bird motifs.

The rooms are linked by a maze of corridors – used so that the king could visit any queen without the others' knowledge.

You can even stay at the fort (see p125).

Royal Gaitor   HISTORIC SITE

(Gatore ki Chhatryan; Indian/foreigner ₹20/30; ☺9am-5pm) The royal cenotaphs, just outside the city walls, beneath Nahargarh, are an appropriately restful place to visit and feel remarkably undiscovered. The stone monuments are beautifully and intricately carved. Maharajas Pratap Singh, Madho Singh II and Jai Singh II, among others, are honoured here. Jai Singh II has the most impressive marble cenotaph, with a dome supported by 20 carved pillars.

The **cenotaphs of the maharanis of Jaipur** (Maharani ki Chhatri; Amber Rd; Indian/foreigner ₹20/30; ☺9am-5pm) are also worth a visit. They lie between Jaipur and Amber, opposite the Holiday Inn.

Jal Mahal   HISTORIC BUILDING

(Water Palace; ☺closed to public) Near the cenotaphs of the maharanis of Jaipur, on Amber Rd, is the red-sandstone Jal Mahal, built in 1799 by Madho Singh as a summer resort for the royal family – they used to base duck-hunting parties here. It's accessed via a causeway at the rear and is beautifully situated in the watery expanse of Man Sagar, whose water level varies seasonally. Suffering from subsidence, much of the palace is waterlogged, although it is undergoing redevelopment for tourism.

Sisodia Rani Palace Garden   HISTORIC SITE

Six kilometres from the city, on Agra Rd (leave by the Ghat Gate), are a pair of formal gardens that are enjoyable to wander around and take in a breath of fresh air. The first, grand formal **terraced gardens** (Indian/foreigner ₹5/10; ☺8am-5pm), with fountains and statuary, were built in the 18th century for Maharaja Jai Singh's second wife, a Sisodian princess. They're overlooked by the **Sisodia Rani Palace** (☺closed to public), whose outer walls are decorated with murals depicting hunting scenes and the Krishna legend.

The second park of similar formal gardens, **Vidyadharji-ka-Bagh**, is nearby but currently closed to the public. Regular local buses leave from Ghat Gate for the Sisodia Rani Palace (₹8). An autorickshaw will cost around ₹280 return from the city centre to visit both.

Galta & Surya Mandir   HINDU TEMPLE

Perched between the cliff faces of a rocky valley, Galta is a desolate, if evocative, place. It is also known as the Monkey Temple and you will find hundreds of monkeys living here – bold and aggressive macaques and more graceful and tolerable langurs. You can purchase peanuts at the gate to feed to them, but be prepared to be mobbed by teeth-barring primates.

The temple houses a number of sacred tanks, into which some daring souls jump from the adjacent cliffs. The water is claimed to be 'several elephants deep' and fed from a spring that falls through the mouth of a sculpted cow.

There are some original frescoes in reasonable condition in a chamber at the end of the bottom pool, including those depicting athletic feats, the maharaja playing polo, and the exploits of Krishna and the *gopis* (milkmaids).

On the ridge above Galta is the Surya Mandir (Temple of the Sun God), which rises 100m above Jaipur and can be seen from the eastern side of the city. A 2.5km-long walking trail climbs up to the temple from Suraj Pol, or you can walk up from the Galta side. There are hazy views over the humming city.

🏃 Activities

Several hotels will let you use their pool for a daily fee. Try the pools at the Raj Mahal Palace (p125; admission ₹270), the Mansingh Hotel (p121; admission ₹225) and the Narain Niwas Palace Hotel (p125; admission ₹150).

Yoga Sadhana Ashram   YOGA

(Bapu Nagar; ⊙Wed-Mon) Nestled among trees off University Rd (near Rajasthan University). Classes incorporate breathing exercises, yoga asanas (poses) and exercise. Most of the classes are in Hindi, but some English is spoken in the 7.30am to 9.30am class.

Rajasthan Astrological Council & Research Institute   ASTROLOGY

(☑2613338; Chandani Chowk, Tripolia Gate; ⊙consultations 9am-8pm) Dr Vinod Shastri is the medal-laden general secretary who will read your palm or prepare a computerised horoscope if you have your exact time and place of birth. Prices for basic readings and predictions start at around ₹600 and quickly enter the stratosphere from there. Dr Shastri can be found in his shop near the City Palace. Though he should know when you're arriving, it's best to make an appointment.

Kerala Ayurveda Kendra   AYURVEDA

(☑5106743; www.keralaayurvedakendra.com; F-30 Jamnalal Bajaj Marg; ⊙8am-noon & 4-8pm) Is Jaipur making your nerves jangle? Get help through ayurvedic massage and therapy. Treatments include *sirodhara* (₹1500), where medicated oil is streamed steadily over your forehead for 1½ hours to reduce stress, tone the brain and help with sleep disorders. Massages (male masseur for male clients and female for female clients) cost from ₹500 for 55 minutes. It offers free transport to/from your hotel.

Madhavanand Girls College   YOGA

(☑2200317; C19 Behari Marg, Bani Park) Alternatively you could try the casual classes held next door to the Madhuban guesthouse. There are free daily classes, in Hindi and in English, from 6am to 7am.

Chakrapania Ayurveda   AYURVEDA

(☑2624003; www.chakrapaniayurveda.com; 8 Diamond Hill, Tulsi Circle, Shanti Path; ⊙9am-2pm & 3-7pm Mon-Sat, 9am-1pm Sun) Here you can get your body type analysed before having it massaged and you can have 30 to 45 minutes of *sirodhara* for ₹600.

Charak Ayurveda   AYURVEDA

(☑2205628; www.charakayurveda.com; E-7 Kanti Chandra Rd, Bani Park; ⊙9am-2pm & 3-7pm Mon-Sat, 9am-1pm Sun) A full range of ayurvedic treatments are available. General body massages start at ₹500.

Rambagh Golf Club   GOLF

(Bhawan Singh Marg; ⊙6am-6.30pm) Near the Rambagh Palace, this golf club has a scenic 18-hole course that was once part of the polo grounds. There are caddie charges and a small green fee; equipment is available for hire.

✏ Courses

Rajasthan Astrological Council & Research Institute   ASTROLOGY

(☑2613338; Chandani Chowk, Tripolia Gate; ⊙consultations 9am-8pm) Dr Vinod Shastri offers lessons in astrology. The charge is ₹3000 per person (minimum of five people) for 15 one-hour lectures, given over a period of five days. More advanced lessons are also available.

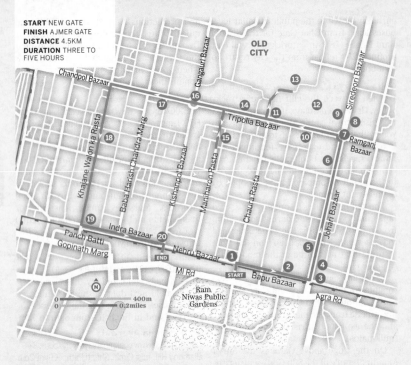

START NEW GATE
FINISH AJMER GATE
DISTANCE 4.5KM
DURATION THREE TO
FIVE HOURS

Walking Tour
Pink City

❯ Entering the old city from ❶ **New Gate**, turn right into ❷ **Bapu Bazaar**, inside the city wall. Brightly coloured bolts of fabric, *jootis* (traditional shoes) and aromatic perfumes make the street a favourite destination for Jaipur's women. At the end of Bapu Bazaar you'll come to ❸ **Sanganeri Gate**. Turn left into ❹ **Johari Bazaar**, the jewellery market, where you will find jewellers, goldsmiths and artisans doing highly glazed *meenakari* (enamelling), a speciality of Jaipur.

Continuing north you'll pass the famous ❺ **LMB Hotel**, and the ❻ **Jama Masjid**, with its tall minarets, and the bustling ❼ **Badi Chaupar**. Be very careful crossing the road here. To the north is ❽ **Siredeori Bazaar**, also known as Hawa Mahal Bazaar. The name is derived from the spectacular ❾ **Hawa Mahal**, a short distance to the north. Turning left on ❿ **Tripolia Bazaar**, you will see a lane leading to the entrance to the Hawa Mahal. A few hundred metres west is the ⓫ **Tripolia Gate**. This is the main entrance to the ⓬ **Jantar Mantar** and ⓭ **City Palace**, but only the maharaja's family may enter here. The public entrance is via the less ostentatious Atishpol (Stable Gate), a little further along.

After visiting the City Palace complex, head back to Tripolia Bazaar and resume your walk west past ⓮ **Iswari Minar Swarga Sal**, which is well worth the climb for the view. Cross the bazaar at the minaret and head west. The next lane on the left is ⓯ **Maniharon ka Rasta**, the best place to buy colourful lac (resin) bangles.

Back on Tripolia Bazaar, continue west to cross ⓰ **Choti Chaupar** to ⓱ **Chandpol Bazaar** until you reach a traffic light. Turn left into ⓲ **Khajane Walon ka Rasta**, where you'll find marble and stoneware carvers at work. Continue south until you reach a broad road, just inside the city wall, ⓳ **Indra Bazaar**. Follow the road east towards ⓴ **Ajmer Gate**, which marks the end of this tour.

Sakshi

BLOCK PRINTING

(☎2731862; Laxmi Colony; ⊙shop 8.30am-8.30pm, factory 9am-6pm) You can do block-printing courses in nearby Sanganer village, around 16km south of Jaipur. Here you can do basic block-printing or blue-pottery courses (eight hours per day). You can also do two- to three-month courses. Costs depend on numbers of students; contact Sakshi for more details.

Kripal Kumbh

BLUE POTTERY

(☎2201127; B18A Shiv Marg, Bani Park) Free lessons in blue pottery (although it's not possible during the monsoon, from late June to mid-September). Advance bookings are essential.

Dhamma Thali Vipassana Meditation Centre

MEDITATION

(☎2680220; www.thali.dhamma.org) *Vipassana* is one of India's oldest forms of meditation. The aim of this form is to achieve peace of mind and a contented and useful life through a process of mental purification and self-examination. Located in beautiful surrounds, this centre runs courses (for a donation) in meditation for both beginners and more advanced students throughout the year. Courses are usually for 10 days, throughout which you must observe 'noble silence' – no communication with others. This serene meditation centre is tucked away in the hilly countryside near Galta, about 12km (by road) east of the city centre. Accommodation is in single rooms (some with private bathroom) and vegetarian meals are available. Courses are offered in Hindi, English, German, French, Spanish, Japanese, Hebrew, Italian, Korean, Portuguese, Mandarin and Burmese. Bookings are essential.

Maharaja Sawai Mansingh Sangeet Mahavidyalaya

MUSIC & DANCE

(☎2611397; www.sangeetmahavidyalaya.org; Chandni Chowk, City Palace) Lessons in music and dance are available behind Tripolia Gate. The sign is in Hindi – ask locals to point you in the right direction. Tuition is given in traditional Indian instruments, such as tabla, sitar and flute. It costs from ₹500 per month in a small group for regular students. There is also tuition in *kathak*, the classical Indian dance. Classical Indian vocal tuition can also be undertaken. For details contact the school principal, Mr Shekhawat.

☞ Tours

Approved guides for local sightseeing can be hired through the **RTDC Tourist Reception Centre** (☎5155137; www.rajasthantourism.gov.in; Room 21; former RTDC Tourist Hotel; ⊙9.30am-6pm Mon-Fri). A half-day tour (four hours) costs ₹350. A full-day tour (eight hours) is ₹450. An extra fee of ₹100 to ₹150 for both tours is levied for guides speaking French, German, Italian, Japanese or Spanish.

RTDC

SIGHTSEEING

(☎22020778; tours@rtdc.in; RTDC Tourist Information Bureau, Platform 1, Jaipur Railway Station; ⊙8am-6.30pm Mon-Sat) Offers half-/full-day tours of Jaipur and its surrounds for ₹150/200. The full-day tours (9am to 6pm) take in all the major sights (including Amber Fort), with a lunch break at Nahargarh. The lunch break can be as late as 3pm, so have a big breakfast. Rushed half-day tours are confined to the city limits (8am to 1pm, 11.30am to 4.30pm and 1.30pm to 6.30pm) – some travellers recommend these, as you avoid the long lunch break. Fees don't include admission charges. The **Pink City by Night tour** (₹250) departs at 6.30pm, explores several well-known sights, and includes dinner at Naharagarh Fort. Tours depart from Jaipur railway station; the company also picks up and takes bookings from the RTDC Hotel Teej, RTDC Hotel Gangaur and the Tourist Information Bureau at the main bus station.

🛏 Sleeping

Prepare yourself to be besieged by autorickshaw and taxi drivers when you arrive by train or bus. If you refuse to go to their choice of hotel, many will either snub you or will double the fare. Some rickshaw drivers will openly declare their financial interest, which at least is honest.

To avoid this annoyance, go straight to the prepaid autorickshaw and taxi stands at the bus and train stations. Even better, many hotels will pick you up if you ring ahead.

From May to September, most midrange and top-end hotels offer bargain rates, dropping prices by 25% to 50%.

All of the rooms listed here have private bathrooms unless otherwise indicated. Prices quoted for midrange and top-end options exclude luxury taxes (officially 8% and applicable to rooms with rates over ₹1000).

A recommended alternative to the hotels is the homestay programme run by **Jaipur Pride** (www.pridehomestay.com; r incl breakfast

₹1800-5000). There are about 40 homes participating in the project divided into three price categories. All are comfortable, friendly and offer an unsurpassed way to get under the skin of the city.

Jaipur has an impressive selection of luxury hotels, the best of which are the converted palaces of the maharajas and the *havelis* of lesser nobles.

AROUND MI ROAD

TOP CHOICE **Hotel Pearl Palace**   HOTEL $
(2373700, 9414236323; www.hotelpearl palace.com; Hari Kishan Somani Marg, Hathroi Fort; dm ₹175, r ₹350-1200; ⊛@☎) The delightful Pearl Palace continues to raise the bar for budget digs. There's quite a range of rooms to choose from – small, large, shared bath, private bath, some balconied, some with AC or fan cooled, and all are spotless. Congenial hosts Mr and Mrs Singh offer all manner of services including free pick-up (8am to 11pm only), money-changing and travel services, and the hotel boasts one of Jaipur's best restaurants, the Peacock Rooftop Restaurant (p126). Rightfully popular; advance booking is highly recommended.

Pearl Palace Heritage   HOTEL $$
(2375242; 9829404055; www.pearlpalace heritage.com; 54 Gopal Bari, lane 2; r ₹1500-1800; ⊛@☎) The second hotel for the successful Pearl Palace team is a midrange hotel with several special characteristics and great attention to detail. Stone carvings adorn the halls and each room re-creates an individual cultural theme such as a village hut, a sandstone fort, or a mirror-lined palace boudoir. Modern luxuries and facilities have been carefully integrated into the traditional designs, and a pool and restaurant are planned.

Atithi Guest House   GUESTHOUSE $
(2378679; atithijaipur@hotmail.com; 1 Park House Scheme Rd; s ₹650-1100, d ₹750-1200; ⊛@☎) This well-presented guesthouse, situated between MI and Station Rds, offers strikingly clean, simple rooms dotted around a quiet courtyard. Atithi Guest House is central but peaceful, and the service is friendly and helpful. The rooms without airconditioning have fans, air coolers and cool tiled floors. There's a spotless kitchen and restaurant (for guests only) and you can also enjoy dinner on the very pleasant rooftop terrace. Rickshaw drivers don't like this place because the owner won't pay commission.

Hotel Arya Niwas   HOTEL $$
(4073456; Sansar Chandra Marg; www.arya niwas.com; s from ₹900, s/d with AC from ₹1800/1150; ⊛@☎) Just off Sansar Chandra Marg, behind a high-rise tower, this is a very popular travellers' haunt with a travel desk, bookshop and yoga lessons. For a hotel of 92 rooms it is very well run, though its size means it is not as personal as smaller guesthouses. The spotless rooms vary in layout and size so check out a few. There's an extensive terrace facing a soothing expanse of lawn for relaxing. The self-service vegetarian restaurant doesn't serve beer (so bring your own).

Sheraton Rajputana Hotel   HOTEL $$$
(5100100; www.itcwelcomgroup.in; Palace Rd; r incl breakfast from ₹7500; ⊛@☎) Ritzy and comfortable and staffed to the hilt, this grand hotel is a high-walled oasis in an otherwise scruffy part of town near the railway station. There is an enormous pool, a select shopping arcade and several plush dining options. The rack rates are heavily discounted if the hotel isn't full, particularly April to September.

Alsisar Haveli   HERITAGE HOTEL $$
(2368290; www.alsisar.com; Sansar Chandra Marg; s/d from ₹3400/4300; ⊛☎) Another genuine heritage hotel that has emerged from a gracious 19th-century mansion. Alsisar Haveli is set in beautiful green gardens, and boasts a lovely swimming pool and a wonderful dining room. Its bedrooms don't disappoint either, with elegant Rajput arches and antique furnishings. This is a winning choice, though again a little impersonal, perhaps because it hosts many tour groups.

Dera Rawatsar   HOTEL $$
(2200770; www.derarawatsar.com; D194, Vijay Path; r ₹2800-3800, ste ₹4500; ⊛@☎) Situated off the main drag and close to the bus station, this quiet hotel is managed by three generations of women of a gracious Bikaner noble family. The hotel has a varying range of lovely decorated rooms, sunny courtyards, and home-style Indian meals. It is an excellent choice for solo female travellers.

Hotel Diggi Palace   HERITAGE HOTEL $$
(2373091; www.hoteldiggipalace.com; off Sawai Ram Singh Rd; s/d incl breakfast ₹2200/2500; ⊛@) About 1km south of Ajmeri Gate, this former splendid residence of the *thakur* (nobleman) of Diggi is surrounded by shaded lawns. Once a budget hotel, the more ex-

pensive rooms are substantially better than the cheaper options. The tariff includes all taxes and breakfast, and there's free pick-up from the bus and train stations. The management also prides itself on using organic produce from the hotel's own gardens and farms in the restaurant.

Nana-ki-Haveli HERITAGE HOTEL **$$**
(✆2615502; www.nanakihaveli.com; Fateh Tiba, Moti Dungri Marg; r ₹1800-3000; ✻) Found off Moti Dungri Marg is this tucked-away, tranquil place with attractive, comfortable rooms decorated with traditional flourishes (discreet wall painting, wooden furniture). It's hosted by a lovely family and is a good choice for solo female travellers. It's fronted by a relaxing lawn and offers home-style cooking and discounted rooms in summer.

Karni Niwas HOTEL **$**
(✆2365433; www.hotelkarniniwas.com; C5 Motilal Atal Marg; s ₹600-1100, d ₹650-1200; ✻@🖣) Tucked behind Hotel Neelam, this friendly hotel has clean, cool and comfortable rooms, often with balconies. There is no restaurant, but there are relaxing plant-decked terraces to enjoy room service on. And being so central, restaurants aren't far away. The owner shuns commissions for rickshaw drivers, and free pick-up from the train or bus station is available.

Jwala Niketan GUESTHOUSE **$**
(✆5108303; www.jwala-niketan.com; C6 Motilal Atal Marg; s ₹150-650, d ₹200-800; ✻) This quiet yet centrally located guesthouse (behind the large Hotel Neelam) has a range of good-value, clean but very basic pastel-toned rooms. The host family lives on the premises and the atmosphere is decidedly noncommercial – almost monastic – though the rooms do have TVs. There is no restaurant, but meals can be delivered to your room from the nearby cheap and multicuisine Mohan Restaurant or you can sample the family's vegetarian fare.

Mansingh Hotel HOTEL **$$$**
(✆2378771; www.mansinghhotels.com; Sansar Chandra Marg; s/d from ₹7500/8500; ✻@✻) Located just off Sansar Chandra Marg, the Mansingh is a very central and well-appointed business-class hotel. It has comfortable though run-of-the-mill rooms, a coffee-shop beside the pool and a rooftop bar and restaurant. Right next door is the similarly priced sister hotel, **Mansingh Towers**.

Hotel Om Tower HOTEL **$$$**
(✆4046666; www.hotelomtower.com; Church Rd, off MI Rd; s/d incl breakfast from ₹6500/7000; ✻@✻🖣) Resembling a piece of mislaid space junk, this tower, though modest by world standards, is a Jaipur landmark. Rooms are modern business bland, comfortable but hardly inspiring, and the bathrooms are space-capsule tiny. At least the views get better the higher you go. The pure-vegetarian revolving restaurant (see p127) has a certain appeal.

Mandawa Haveli HERITAGE HOTEL **$$**
(✆2374130; www.mandawahotels.com; Sansar Chandra Marg; s/d from ₹4000/4500; ✻✻) Mandawa Haveli is another lovely heritage hotel, though if you are expecting bright Shekhawati murals you will be disappointed. Mandawa Haveli's rooms are spacious and elegantly, if simply, furnished. Some boast beautiful double baths set under Rajput arches. The private swimming pool and alfresco dining area get good marks.

RTDC Hotel Swagatam HOTEL **$$**
(✆2200595; Station Rd; s/d incl breakfast ₹950/1100, with AC ₹1200/1500; ✻) One of the closest digs to the train station (100m), this government-run hotel has helpful and friendly management and a neatly clipped lawn. On the downside, the laneway leading to the hotel from Station Rd is rather grotty. Rooms are drab and well worn, but spacious, clean and acceptable.

Devi Niwas GUESTHOUSE **$**
(✆2363727; singh_kd@hotmail.com; Dhuleshwar Bagh, Sadar Patel Marg, C-Scheme; s/d ₹350/500, d with AC & TV ₹700; ✻) This guesthouse is a genuine family affair in a pale-yellow building nestled in the middle-class C-scheme. It has a homier feel than most with the extended family living downstairs. There are just seven basic rooms and happy guests have left their compliments on the walls. Food is home-cooked and there's a small garden.

Hotel Luna Rosa HOTEL **$**
(✆2372855; hotellunarosa@airtelmail.in; off Sansar Chandra Marg; r ₹900-1400; ✻@✻) This welcoming small hotel is found by continuing down the small lane past Hotel Arya Niwas. Rooms are clean and neat with a soft bed, TV and tea- and coffee-making facilities. The free internet is a bonus, while the downside is the lack of natural light owing to the building's cheek-by-jowl positioning and its design.

Krishna Palace HOTEL $

(☏2201395; www.krishnapalace.com; E26 Durga Marg, Bani Park; r ₹550-1250; ❄@☎) Krishna Palace is an overly managed hotel with some boisterous staff; however, there are some quiet corners and a relaxing lawn to retreat to with a book. It's convenient to the train station (free pick up) and the generally spacious rooms are maintained to an adequate standard.

Hotel Anuraag Villa HOTEL $

(☏2201679; www.anuraagvilla.com; D249 Devi Marg; s ₹600-1850, d ₹790-1850; ❄@☎) This quiet and comfortable option has no-fuss, spacious rooms (there are three grades) and an extensive lawn where you find some quiet respite from the hassles of sightseeing. It has a recommended restaurant with its kitchen on view, and efficient, helpful staff.

RTDC Hotel Gangaur HOTEL $$

(☏2371641; www.rtdc.in; Sanjay Marg; s/d incl breakfast from ₹1500/1800; ❄) This, another RTDC option, is just off MI Rd and can be recognised by a crazy-paving exterior and small lawn. Rooms are what you'd expect for a government-run hotel – drab but spacious and functional. The hotel's restaurants aren't bad, serving South Indian, Chinese, North Indian and continental food, and there's a helpful travel desk.

RTDC Hotel Teej HOTEL $$

(☏2203199; www.rajasthantourism.gov.in; Collectorate Rd; s/d ₹990/1300, with AC ₹1500/1800; ❄) Located opposite the Moti Mahal Cinema, Hotel Teej is set in a pleasant garden, and is marginally better than the average RTDC hotel. The unexciting rooms are spacious, with high ceilings and TVs, while the dour restaurant has a multicuisine menu.

Evergreen Guest House HOTEL $

(☏2361284; www.hotelevergreen.net; Chameliwala Market; s/d ₹300/350; @) This backpacker stalwart was morphing into the midrange Hotel Palms (same owners) at the time of research. The small section of 20 backpacker rooms remaining is accessed just off MI Rd, in the backpacking ghetto of Chameliwala Market. Even the management were a little unsure of the future of the remaining budget rooms, which are unadorned and basic. The cheap terrace restaurant and internet cafe is the saving grace.

Chirmi Palace Hotel HERITAGE HOTEL $$

(☏2365063; www.chirmi.com; Dhuleshwar Bagh, Sardar Patel Marg; s/d from ₹1000/1200, de-

luxe ₹1800/2000, ste ₹2800; ❄@☎) Set in a 150-year-old *haveli,* Chirmi Palace is run by a traditional Rajput family. Rooms are atmospheric with high ceilings and make up in character what they lack in luxury. There are only three (smallish) rooms at the cheaper tariff, so booking is essential. The dining room is ornate while the pool is a summeronly affair and not very private.

Hotel Palms HOTEL $$

(☏4047786; www.palmsthehotel.com; Ashok Marg, C-Scheme; r from ₹2800; ❄@☎) With a grand front door facing Ashok Marg, this 'newlooking' hotel features the rather ordinarily renovated rooms of erstwhile backpacker hangout Evergreen Guest House. There's a shady garden courtyard and small roof-top swimming pool, but it can all get a bit rowdy when the 95 rooms fill up with families with young children.

Retiring rooms RAILWAY RETIRING ROOM $

(Male-only dm ₹70, s without bathroom ₹150, s/d ₹225/450, r with AC ₹750-1000; ❄) Located upstairs at the train station and very handy if you're catching an early-morning train. Rooms are well worn but surprisingly neat and clean. Make reservations on the inquiries number (☏131).

BANI PARK

The Bani Park area is relatively peaceful (away from the main roads), about 2km west of the old city (northwest of MI Rd).

TOP CHOICE **Madhuban** HERITAGE HOTEL $$

(☏2200033; www.madhuban.net; D237 Behari Marg, Bani Park; s ₹1700-2300, d ₹1900-3600; ❄@☎) Madhuban is an elegant, heritage hotel and guesthouse run by the convivial Dicky and his family. It features a range of bright, spotless, antique-furnished rooms including a suite with a Jacuzzi. Most guests gravitate quickly to the peaceful lawn where they can drink tea, read a newspaper over breakfast, watch a puppet show at night or just pat the dog. The brightly frescoed restaurant features a small, focused menu and sits beside the petite courtyard pool, which is lit in the evening. Money-changing and travel services are available as is free pickup from the bus or train station. The family once ruled Patan (p155), 115km northeast of Jaipur, and you can stay at the former royal palace.

Umaid Bhawan HERITAGE HOTEL $$

(☏2206426; www.umaidbhawan.com; Kali Das Marg, via Bank Rd, Bani Park; s ₹1400-2400, d

₹1600-2800, ste ₹4000; 🕸@🖾) This mock-heritage hotel, behind the Collectorate in a quiet cul-de-sac, is extravagantly decorated in traditional style. The cascading stairways and numerous private balconies have you feeling you have entered a miniature Rajasthani painting. Rooms are stately, full of marble and carved furniture and the rooftop restaurant is wonderful. Free pick-up is available from the train or bus station and all taxes and breakfast are included in the tariff.

Shahpura House   HERITAGE HOTEL **$$**
(☏2203069; www.shahpurahouse.com; D257 Devi Marg, Bani Park; s/d from ₹3000/3500, ste from ₹4500; 🕸@🛜🖾) Elaborately built and decorated in traditional style, this heritage hotel offers immaculate rooms, some with balconies, featuring murals, coloured-glass lamps, flat-screen TVs, and even ceilings covered in small mirrors (in the suites). This rambling palace boasts a durbar hall with huge chandelier and a cosy cocktail bar. There's an inviting swimming pool and an elegant rooftop terrace that stages cultural shows.

Jas Vilas   HOTEL **$$**
(☏2204638; www.jasvilas.com; C9 Sawai Jai Singh Hwy, Bani Park; s/d ₹3500/3800; 🕸@🛜🖾) This small but impressive hotel was built in 1950 and is still run by the same charming family. It offers 11 spacious rooms, most of which face the large sparkling pool set in a romantic courtyard. Three garden-facing rooms are wheelchair accessible. In addition to the relaxing courtyard and lawn, there is a cosy dining room and management will help with all onward travel planning.

Hotel Meghniwas   HOTEL **$$**
(☏4060100; www.meghniwas.com; C9 Sawai Jai Singh Hwy; standard/deluxe r ₹3000/3800, ste ₹4200; 🕸@🖾) In a building erected by Brigadier Singh in 1950 and run by his gracious descendants, this very welcoming hotel has comfortable and spotless rooms, with traditional carved-wood furniture and leafy outlooks. The standard rooms are good, but the suite does not measure up to expectations. There's a first-rate restaurant and an inviting pool set in a pleasant lawn area.

Jaipur Inn   HOTEL **$$**
(☏2201121; www.jaipurinn.com; B17 Shiv Marg, Bani Park; r ₹1250-3000, 🕸@🛜) Once a budget travellers' favourite, with a vast range of accommodation, this hotel has shrunk and now offers a mishmash of varying rooms. Some have balconies and you should inspect a few rooms before settling in. Plus points include the helpful manager and several common areas where travellers can make a coffee, pick-up wi-fi, or grab a meal. There's also free pick-up from the train or bus station and a rooftop restaurant.

Tara Niwas   GUESTHOUSE **$$**
(☏2203762; www.aryaniwas.com; B-22-B Shiv Marg; s/d from ₹1150/1600, s/d per month from ₹22,000/28,000; 🕸@🛜) Run by the people behind Hotel Arya Niwas, Tara Niwas offers well-furnished apartments suitable for longer stays. Some rooms have attached kitchenettes, and there's also a cafe and dining room and a business centre.

Umaid Mahal   HOTEL **$$**
(☏206426; www.umaidmahal.com; C-20, B/2 Behari Marg, Bani Park; s ₹1600-3000, d ₹1800-3500; 🕸@🛜) This extravagantly decorated hotel is run by the same family behind the popular Umaid Bhawan. It may not be a castle but it has plenty of front. Rooms are spacious, elaborate, and regal, and downstairs is a pool, bar and restaurant. Smokers have their own zenana-style screened balconies. Breakfast and pick-up from the train or bus station are complimentary.

OLD CITY

Hotel Bissau Palace   HERITAGE HOTEL **$$**
(☏2304391; www.bissaupalace.com; outside Chandpol; r from ₹3000-6000; 🕸@🛜🖾) This is a worthy choice if you want to stay in a palace on a budget. It's actually just outside the city walls, less than 10 minutes walk from Chandpol (a gateway to the Old City) where there is a very earthy produce market. The hotel has oodles of heritage atmosphere, with lots of antique furnishings and mementos, such as moustached photos and hunting paraphernalia. It feels a bit run down, however, and could do with a lick of paint. There's a swimming pool, a handsome wood-panelled library, and three restaurants (the one on the rooftop offering splendid views is for guests only).

Raj Palace   HERITAGE HOTEL **$$$**
(☏2634077-9; www.rajpalace.com; Chomu Haveli, Zorawar Singh Gate, Amber Rd; r US$350-450, ste from US$750; 🕸@🖾) A former royal home, Raj Palace was built by Thakur Mohan Singhji of Chaumoo, then prime minister. The stunning, award-winning hotel, just north of the city wall on Amber Rd, overlooks a splendid courtyard and has a range of individual and atmospheric rooms featuring

splendid decoration and luxurious furnishings. There's also disabled access, excellent restaurants, and a four-storey suite (the Maharaja's Pavillion) featuring a gold-leaf decorated room plus a private lift and pool.

Samode Haveli
HERITAGE HOTEL $$$

(☎2632370; www.samode.com; Gangapol; s/d incl breakfast from €190/215/198, ste from €250; ✳@❄) Tucked away in the northeast corner of the old city is this charming 200-year-old building, once the town house of the *rawal* (nobleman) of Samode, Jaipur's prime minister. The suites are astonishingly decorative, covered in twinkling mirrorwork, ornate paintings, tiny alcoves and soaring arches. Rooms have large beds and most have private terraces. The standard rooms are more ordinary but still manage to charm. The pool with its bar is a veritable oasis. The tariff is much reduced from May to September.

Saba Haveli
HERITAGE HOTEL $$$

(☎/fax 2630521; www.sabahaveli.co.in; Gangapol; s/d incl breakfast ₹5500/6500; ✳) In the northeastern part of the town, Saba Haveli is an authentic, friendly hotel positioned among a warren of narrow streets. Here the rooms have been kept to the old size, which is to say very large, with modern bathrooms attached. Enjoy lunch or dinner on the terrace, in the garden or the decorated dining room. In the low season (May to September) you'll get a hefty discount.

LMB Hotel
HOTEL $$

(☎2565844; www.hotellmb.com; Johari Bazaar; s/d from ₹2325/2525; ✳) Situated in the old city above the renowned vegetarian restaurant of the same name (see p128), this hotel offers a prime vantage point from where you can check out the mayhem of the Old City bazaars. Rooms are generally large, bright and clean, though possibly overpriced. Check out a few rooms (including the plumbing) before settling in.

Hotel Kailash
HOTEL $

(☎2577372; Johari Bazaar; s/d ₹500/575, without bathroom ₹330/360) This hotel, opposite the Jama Masjid, is one of the few budget digs within the old city. Kailash is right in the

---

THE RANI OF RAMBAGH

The life story of the late Gayatri Devi, the celebrated maharani of Jaipur, is an allegory of 20th-century Rajasthan, capturing the state's ambivalence towards its transition from princely rule to part of post-Independence, democratic India.

In her heyday, Gayatri Devi was an icon of royal glamour, adored by gossip columnists and dubbed one of the most beautiful women in the world by *Vogue* magazine. She was born in 1919, a princess from the small state of Cooch Behar (now in West Bengal). At the age of 19 she fell in love with Man Singh II, the last maharaja of Jaipur. Although Man Singh already had two wives, they were married in 1939 and settled down to the life of luxury enjoyed by Indian royalty of the time. There were polo matches, hunting jaunts, dinner parties and summers in England.

Man Singh converted his former hunting lodge, 3km southwest of the old city, into the magnificent Rambagh Palace for Gayatri Devi. Today the palace is surrounded by Jaipur's sprawling suburbs, but it was once a secluded retreat. Here the couple entertained some of the world's rich and famous, including Eleanor Roosevelt and Jackie Kennedy. In 1958 it became the first former palace in Rajasthan to be converted into a hotel.

By this time, however, the Man Singhs were adjusting to their new role in post-Independence India. Rajasthan's ancestral rulers had been stripped of their powers, but many were still held in high regard by a large proportion of their former subjects. Banking on this support, Gayatri Devi, like many other royals, decided to enter politics. She stood against the Congress Party in the national elections in 1962 and enjoyed a stunning victory. In the 1967 and 1971 elections she retained her seat.

Indira Gandhi's Congress Party, however, was quick to act against the royals who were successfully challenging its hold on power. The privileges that the maharajas were promised following Independence (notably the privy purses paid to the royals from public funds) were abolished and investigations into their financial affairs were mounted. In the early 1970s Gayatri Devi was convicted of tax offences and served five months in Delhi's notorious Tihar Jail. On her release she penned her fascinating autobiography, *A Princess Remembers*. Gayatri Devi passed away in her beloved Jaipur on 17 July 2009.

thick of it. It's nothing fancy. Enter through a narrow stairway to the undersized rooms, which are basic and stuffy despite the central air-cooling. The cheapest rooms are little more than windowless cells and the shared bathrooms can be challenging, but the bigger doubles with attached bath are adequate. Rooms at the back are quieter and management is buoyantly friendly and welcoming.

RAMBAGH ENVIRONS

Rambagh Palace   HERITAGE HOTEL $$$
(☎2211919; www.tajhotels.com; Bhawan Singh Marg; r from ₹27,500; ❀@≋) This splendid palace was once the Jaipur pad of Maharaja Man Singh II and, until recently, his glamorous wife Gayatri Devi. Veiled in 19 hectares of gardens, the hotel has fantastic views across the immaculate lawns. More expensive rooms are naturally the most sumptuous. Nonguests can join in the magnificence by dining in the lavish restaurants or drinking tea on the gracious veranda. At least treat yourself to a drink at the spiffing Polo Bar (p128).

Raj Mahal Palace   HERITAGE HOTEL $$
(☎4143000; www.royalfamilyjaipur.com; Sadar Patel Marg; s/d ₹4000/4400, superior ₹5000/5500, ste ₹7500; ❀@≋) In the south of the city, this place is a more modest, relaxed (and a bit dog-eared) edifice than the Rambagh Palace. The superior rooms boast cool marble floors and small patches of lawn to the front. Standard rooms are still good, though much less appealing. The suites are cavernous and impersonal. Built in 1729 by Jai Singh, it was also once the British Residency, and temporary home of Maharaja Man Singh II while his residence, Rambagh Palace, was converted into a luxury hotel. Nonguests can use the excellent pool for ₹270.

Narain Niwas Palace Hotel HERITAGE HOTEL $$
(☎2561291; www.hotelnarainniwas.com; Narain Singh Rd; s/d incl breakfast from ₹4000/4500; ste from ₹8100; ❀@≋) In Kanota Bagh, just south of the city, this genuine heritage hotel has a wonderful ramshackle splendour. There's a lavish dining room with liveried staff, an old-fashioned veranda on which to drink tea, and antiques galore. The high-ceilinged rooms are varyingly atmospheric and the bathrooms also vary greatly – so inspect before committing. You will find a large secluded pool, heavenly spa and sprawling gardens complete with peacocks out the back.

Jai Mahal Palace Hotel   HERITAGE HOTEL $$$
(☎2223636; www.tajhotels.com; Jacob Rd; r from ₹16,000, ste from ₹30,000; ❀❀@≋) Located south of the train station, this impressive hotel is set in 7 hectares of beautifully manicured gardens, which most of the swish rooms overlook. The 18th-century building was once the residence of Jaipur's prime minister and is now run as a hotel by the Taj Group. Tastefully furnished standard rooms are very comfortable and enhanced by miniature paintings. The suites are conservative and refined, with some exquisite antiques. There's a gorgeous circular pool set in the gardens.

Raj Vilas   HOTEL $$$
(☎2680101; www.oberoihotels.com; Goner Rd; r & luxury tents from ₹30,500, villas from ₹150,000; ❀@≋) About 8km from the city centre is Jaipur's most sophisticated and expensive hotel. It has 71 luxurious rooms, yet a boutique feel and attentive, unobtrusive service. Its terracotta domes are set in more than 32 shady orchard- and fountain-filled acres. Immaculate rooms, with sunken baths, are subtly decorated. Each of the three villas has its own pool. Guests ride around in golf buggies. Check the website for special offers.

Chokhi Dhani   HOTEL $$$
(☎2225001; www.chokhidhani.com; Tonk Rd; d/ste incl breakfast ₹8000/9000; ❀≋) This is a mock-traditional Rajasthani village, 20km from Jaipur, with wonderful restaurants and entertainment in the evenings (see p129). Accommodation is in traditional-style mud huts with nontraditional interiors. These are well appointed, with a bedroom and sitting room decorated with mirrorwork. There are also eight big rooms in a *haveli*. Additional features are the commodious pool and spacious grounds. It's extremely popular with middle-class Indian families.

Nahargarh   HERITAGE HOTEL $$
(Tiger Fort; ☎5148044; d ₹2500; ❀) Nahargarh is a potentially romantic choice set high above the old city. There's only one double room, in one of the fort's parapets behind the restaurant (Café Durga) – the views from the bed are unparalleled.

Holiday Inn   HOTEL $$$
(☎2672000; www.holidayinnjaipur.com; r incl breakfast from ₹5000; ❀@≋) One kilometre north of the city on Amber Rd, this impressive, traditional-style building offers the usual comfortable Holiday Inn standards, and is good value if you ask for a discount.

JAIPUR SLEEPING

Hotel Clarks Amer   HOTEL $$$
(☑2550616; www.hotelclarks.com; r from ₹10,500; ✳@☻) About 8km south of the city, this 200-room hotel is welcoming and plush, and has everything you need for a very comfortable stay.

Trident   HOTEL $$$
(☑2670101; www.tridenthotels.com; Amber Rd; s/d from ₹10,000/10,500; ✳@☻) About 5km north of the city on the road to Amber Fort, the Trident is a slick and very well-managed international-class hotel. The well-appointed rooms offer balconies with lingering views of the Jal Mahal situated opposite. Disabled access.

✗ Eating

Despite its size, Jaipur doesn't have a huge array of quality restaurants in the city centre. Apart from hotel restaurants (which are often the best option), there are a few traveller-friendly stalwarts. As elsewhere in Rajasthan, many vegetarian restaurants don't serve beer.

AROUND MI ROAD

TOP CHOICE Niro's   INDIAN $$
(☑2374493; MI Rd; mains ₹110-350; ◷10am-11pm) Established in 1949, Niro's is a long-standing favourite in MI Rd that continues to shine. Escape the chaos of the street by ducking into its cool, clean, mirror-ceiling sanctum to savour veg and nonveg Indian cuisine. Classic Chinese and Continental food are available but the Indian menu is definitely the pick. Try the delectable *bhuna gosht* (lamb) but remind them not to tone it down for delicate Western palates if you like it spicy.

Four Seasons   VEGETARIAN $$
(☑2373700; D43A Subhas Marg; mains ₹100-210; ◷noon-3.30pm & 6.30-11pm) Four Seasons is one of Jaipur's best vegetarian restaurants and being pure vegetarian there's no alcohol. It's a vastly popular place on two levels, with a glass wall to the kitchens. There's a great range of dishes on offer, including tasty Rajasthani specialities, dosas and a selection of pizzas. Try a thali or the speciality *rawa masala dosa* (South Indian ground rice and semolina pancake with coconut, onions, carrots and green chillies).

Little Italy   ITALIAN $$
(☑4022444; 3rd fl, KK Square, C-11, Prithviraj Marg; mains ₹165-200; ◷noon-3.30pm & 6.30-11pm) Easily the best Italian restaurant in town,

Little Italy is part of a small national chain that offers excellent vegetarian pasta, risotto and wood-fired pizzas in cool, contemporary surroundings. The menu is extensive and includes some Mexican items and first-rate Italian desserts. There is a lounge bar attached so you can accompany your vegetarian dining with wine or beer.

Moti Mahal Delux   NORTH INDIAN $$
(☑4017733; MI Rd; mains Rs140-300; ◷11am-4pm & 7-11pm) The famous Delhi restaurant now has franchises all over India delivering its world-famous butter chicken to the masses. The tantalising menu features a vast range of veg and nonveg, including seafood and succulent tandoori dishes. Snuggle into a comfortable booth and enjoy the ambience, spicy food and, last but not least, a delicious *pista kulfi* (pistachio-flavoured sweet similar to ice cream). Beer and wine available.

Reds   INDIAN $$$
(☑4007710; 5th fl, Mall 21, Bhagwandas Marg; mains ₹275-600; ◷11am-11pm) Decked out in red-and-black sofas and overlooking the Raj Mandir cinema, Reds is a smart-casual restaurant with draught beer, great views and good service. The Indian (and some Chinese) cuisine is excellent and there are special beer and food deals before 7pm. Speciality of the house is *shahi gilawat ka kebab*, a lamb kebab blessed with 36 aromatic and digestive spices that was created for the nawab of Lucknow. Don't take the stairs – they don't reach the 5th floor – use the lift.

Peacock Rooftop Restaurant   MULTICUISINE $$
(☑2373700; Hotel Pearl Palace, Hari Kishan Somani Marg, Hathroi Fort; mains ₹35-120; ◷7am-11pm) This multi-level rooftop restaurant at the popular Hotel Pearl Palace (p120) gets rave reviews for its excellent and inexpensive cuisine (Indian, Chinese and Continental) and relaxed ambience. The mouth-watering food, attentive service, whimsical furnishings and romantic view towards Hathroi Fort make this a first-rate restaurant and the economical prices all the more unbelievable. There are great value thalis as well as pizzas and Western breakfasts for homesick travellers.

Sheesha   NORTH INDIAN $$$
(☑4033668; 5th fl (rooftop), City Pearl Bldg, Sanjay Marg; mains ₹200-500; ◷7-11.30pm) Sheesha is a sophisticated rooftop restaurant for couples and family groups, with a retractable awning should the weather gods intervene.

The emphasis is on the tandoor ovens smoking away behind a glass panel. Carnivores will be in heaven (think mutton Punjabi and *Murg kadai Peshwari*) and vegetarians are well catered for. Seating is on several terraces with dim lighting provided by coloured lights and the moon. Yes, you can puff on an after-dinner sheesha.

Dãsaprakash
SOUTH INDIAN $$
(☎2371313; Kamal Mansions, MI Rd; mains ₹90-200; ☺11am-11pm) Part of a renowned chain, Dãsaprakash specialises in South Indian cuisine including thalis and several versions of *dosa* and *idli* (rice cake). Afterwards you can choose from a wonderful selection of cold drinks and over-the-top ice cream sundaes.

Surya Mahal
SOUTH INDIAN $$
(☎2362811; MI Rd; mains ₹90-170; ☺8am-11pm) Near Panch Batti is this popular option specialising in South Indian vegetarian food; try the delicious *masala dosa* and the tasty *dhal makhani* (black lentils and red kidney beans). There are also Chinese and Italian dishes, and good ice creams, sundaes and cool drinks.

OM Revolving Restaurant
VEGETARIAN $$
(☎4046629; Church Rd; mains ₹160-325; ☺noon-4pm & 7-11pm) Add Om to your list of revolving restaurants. This rocket-inspired landmark boasts a showy, emphatically vegetarian (no alcohol or eggs) revolving restaurant at 56m. It spins at a cracking pace and, despite the odd bump and shudder, it's an amazing way to see the city. The menu of Indian, Continental and Chinese features several Rajasthani specialities – try the thalis (₹200 to ₹440). If you are lucky you will orbit past the centrally located stage featuring live *ghazal* singing.

Handi Restaurant
NORTH INDIAN $$
(☎2364839; MI Rd; mains ₹140-300; ☺noon-3.30pm & 6.30-11pm) Handi has been satisfying customers for years. It's opposite the main post office, tucked at the back of the Maya Mansions, offering scrumptious tandoori and barbecued dishes and rich Mughlai curries. In the evenings it sets up a smoky kebab stall at the entrance to the restaurant. Good vegetarian items are also available. No beer.

Natraj
VEGETARIAN $$
(☎2375804; MI Rd; mains ₹85-200; ☺9am-11pm) Not far from Panch Batti is this classy vegetarian place, which has an extensive menu featuring North Indian, Continental and Chinese cuisine. Diners are blown away by the potato-encased vegetable bomb curry. There's a good selection of thalis and South Indian food – the *dosa paper masala* is delicious – as well as Indian sweets.

Copper Chimney
INDIAN $$
(☎2372275; Maya Mansions, MI Rd; mains ₹100-220; ☺noon-3pm & 6.30-11pm) Copper Chimney is casual, almost elegant and definitely welcoming, with the requisite waiter army and a fridge of cold beer. It offers excellent veg and nonveg Indian cuisine, including aromatic Rajasthani specials. There is also Continental and Chinese food and a small selection of Indian wine, but the curry-and-beer combos are hard to beat. Take a seat behind the front window to watch the mayhem of MI Rd or settle further back under the rollicking horse mural.

Rawat Kachori
FAST FOOD $
(Station Rd; kachori ₹40, lassis ₹25) For great Indian sweets (₹10 or ₹120 to ₹300 per kg) and famous *kachori* (potato masala in fried pastry case), head to this exceedingly popular place. A delicious milk crown should fill you up for the afternoon.

Hotel Kanji
SWEETS $
(Station Rd; sweets per kg ₹120-340) Across the road from Rawat Kachori, Kanji also has a fabulous array of sweets.

Chocolate Boutique
SWEETS $
(68 Gopal Bari Rd; cakes ₹25-250; ☺10.30am-8.30pm Mon-Sat) This tiny shop of tempting treats has a small range of fresh cakes, brownies, tarts and pies, as well as quality homemade chocolates, which you can buy separately (Rs10 to Rs12 each) or gift-boxed.

Bake Hut
BAKERY $
(Arvind Marg, off MI Rd; cakes ₹25-100; ☺9am-10pm Mon-Sat) An extremely busy bakery that does a roaring trade in sweet cakes and various breads. It's attached to the back of the Surya Mahal restaurant.

Jal Mahal
SWEETS $
(MI Rd; ice creams ₹12-110; ☺10am-midnight) This packed little takeaway ice-cream parlour has some inventive concoctions, from the earthquake to the after ate.

Baskin Robbins
SWEETS $
(Sanjay Marg; ice creams ₹20-150; ☺noon-11.30pm) Tucked into the edge of the Hotel Gangaur's compound is this pint-sized ice-cream pit stop.

TOP CHOICE **LMB** VEGETARIAN $$

(☎2560845; Johari Bazaar; mains ₹95-190; ⊙11.30am-3.30pm & 7-11pm) Laxmi Misthan Bhandar, LMB to you and me, is a *sattvik* (pure vegetarian) restaurant in the Old City that's been going strong since 1954. A welcoming AC refuge from frenzied Johari Bazaar, LMB is also an institution with its singular decor, attentive waiters and extensive sweet counter. Travellers like to chalk up at least one meal here. The menu opens with a warning from Krishna about people who like *tamasic* (putrid and polluted food), which gets you into the *sattvik* mood. Try the Rajasthan thali followed by the signature kulfa, a fusion of kulfi and falooda with dry fruits and saffron.

Mohan VEGETARIAN $

(144-5 Nehru Bazaar; mains ₹25-90; ⊙9am-10pm) The tiny Mohan is a few steps down from the pavement on the corner of the street, and is easy to miss. It's basic, cheap and a bit grubby, but the thalis, curries (half-plate and full plate) and snacks are freshly cooked and very popular.

Ganesh Restaurant VEGETARIAN $

(☎2312380; Nehru Bazaar; mains ₹50-90; ⊙9.30am-11pm) This pocket-sized outdoor restaurant is in a fantastic location on the top of the old city wall near New Gate. The cook is in a pit on one side of the wall, so you can check out your pure vegetarian food being cooked. If you're looking for a local eatery with fresh tasty food, such as paneer butter masala, you'll love it. There's an easy-to-miss signpost, but no doubt a stallholder will show you the narrow stairway.

🍷 Drinking

Many bars around town tend to be oppressive, all-male affairs; however, most upper-end hotel bars are good for casual drinking.

TOP CHOICE **Lassiwala** LASSI

(MI Rd; ⊙7.30am till sold out) This famous, much-imitated institution, opposite Niro's, is a simple place that whips up fabulous, creamy lassis at ₹14/28 for a small/jumbo clay cup. Get there early to avoid disappointment! Will the real Lassiwala please stand up? It's the one that says 'Shop 312' and 'Since 1944', directly next to the alleyway. Imitators spread to the right as you face it.

Indian Coffee House CAFE

(MI Rd; coffee ₹11-15; ⊙8am-9.30pm) Set back from the street, down an alley, this traditional coffee house (a venerable co-op–owned institution) offers a very pleasant cup of filtered coffee in very relaxed surroundings. Aficionados of Indian Coffee Houses will not be disappointed by the fan-cooled ambience. Inexpensive samosas, pakoras and *dosas* grace the snack menu.

Reds BAR

(☎4007710; 5th fl, Mall 21, Bhagwandas Marg; ⊙11am-midnight Sun-Fri, 11am-1.30pm Sat) Overlooking the Raj Mandir cinema and MI Rd with views to Tiger Fort, slick Reds is a great place to kick back with a drink or take a meal (see p126). Drop into one of the low-slung, red-and-black couches with a beer (bottled or draught), cocktail or mocktail and enjoy the sound system. Things usually heat up on Saturday and Sunday when the dance floor is cleared and the DJs pump out a mix of Hindipop and techno.

Henry's the Pub BAR

(Park Prime Hotel, C-59 Prithviraj Marg; ⊙noon-11.45pm) With coloured glass, dark wood and studded leather this English pub wannabe has local Golden Peacock on tap and a small selection of international beer (OK, all they had was Corona). You will also find Australian wine and a full array of Indian spirits. Meals are also available.

Polo Bar BAR

(Rambagh Palace Hotel, Bhawan Singh Rd; ⊙noon-midnight) A spiffing watering hole adorned with polo memorabilia and arched, scalloped windows framing the neatly clipped lawns. A bottle of beer costs ₹350 to ₹450 and cocktails around ₹450.

Café Coffee Day CAFE

(Country Inn Hotel, MI Rd; coffee ₹50-90) The franchise that successfully delivers espresso to coffee addicts, as well as the occasional iced concoction and muffin, has several branches in Jaipur. In addition to this one, sniff out the brews at Paris Point on Sawai Jai Singh Hwy (aka Collectorate Rd), and near the exit point at Amber Fort.

Steam BAR

(Rambagh Palace Hotel, Bhawan Singh Rd; ⊙7pm-midnight Wed-Mon) The Rambagh's lounge bar is a relaxed and stylish haven with a steam engine and a DJ. Sip a cocktail, sample a pizza and lighten your wallet.

☆ Entertainment

Jaipur isn't a big late-night party town, although many of its hotels put on some sort of evening music, dance or puppet show. English-language films are occasionally screened at some cinemas in Jaipur – check the cinemas and local press for details.

Raj Mandir Cinema CINEMA
(☑2379372; Baghwandas Marg; admission ₹50-110; ⊙reservations 10am-6pm, screenings 12.30pm, 3.30pm, 6.30pm & 9.30pm) Just off MI Rd, Raj Mandir is *the* place to go to see a Hindi film in India. This opulent cinema looks like a huge pink cream cake, with a meringue auditorium and a foyer somewhere between a temple and Disneyland. It's a tourist attraction in its own right and is usually full, despite its immense size. Bookings can be made one hour to seven days in advance at window Nos 7 and 8 – this is your best chance of securing a seat, although you can forget it in the early days of a new release. Alternatively, sharpen your elbows and join the queue when the current booking office opens 45 minutes before curtain up. Avoid the cheapest tickets, which seat you very close to the screen.

Chokhi Dhani THEME PARK
(☑2225001; Tonk Rd; adult/child aged 3-9 incl dinner ₹350/200) Chokhi Dhani means 'special village' and this mock Rajasthani village, 20km south of Jaipur, lives up to its name. As well as the restaurants, where you can enjoy an oily Rajasthani thali, there is a bevy of traditional entertainment. You can wander around and watch traditional tribal dancers setting fire to their hats, children balancing on poles and dancers dressed in lion costumes lurking in a wood. You can also take elephant or camel rides. Children will adore it. It's hugely popular with middle-class Indian families. A return taxi from Jaipur, including waiting time, will cost about ₹600.

Polo ground SPORTS
(Ambedkar Circle, Bhawan Singh Marg) Maharaja Man Singh II indulged his passion for polo by building an enormous polo ground next to Rambagh Palace, which is still a polo-match hub today. A ticket to a match also gets you into the lounge, which is adorned with historic photos and memorabilia. The polo season extends over winter, with the most important matches played during January and March – contact the **Rajasthan Polo Club** (☑2385380) for ticket details.

During Jaipur's Elephant Festival in March (see p107) you can watch elephant polo matches at the Chaughan Stadium in the Old City. Contact the **RTDC Tourist Reception Centre** (☑5155137; www.rajasthan tourism.gov.in; Room 21; former RTDC Tourist Hotel; ⊙9.30am-6pm Mon-Fri) for details.

Inox Cinema CINEMA
(☑2379372; www.inoxmovies.com; Crystal Palm complex, Bais Godam Circle; admission from ₹160) A modern three-screen multiplex with the latest Bollywood blockbusters and Hollywood offerings.

Shopping

Jaipur is a shopper's paradise. You'll have to bargain hard, though – shops have seen too many cash-rich, time-poor tourists. Shops around major tourist centres, such as the City Palace and Hawa Mahal, tend to be pricier. Also commercial buyers come here from all over the world to stock up on the amazing range of jewellery, gems, artefacts and crafts that come from all over Rajasthan.

Most of the larger shops can pack and send your parcels home for you – although it may be slightly cheaper if you do it yourself (see p133), it's generally not worth the hassle.

The city is still loosely divided into traditional artisans' quarters. The Pink City Walking Tour (p118) will take you through some of these.

SHOPPING FOR GEMS

Jaipur is famous for precious and semiprecious stones. There are many shops offering bargain prices, but you do need to know your gems. The main gem-dealing area is around the Muslim area of Pahar Ganj, in the southeast of the old city. Here you can see stones being cut and polished in workshops tucked off narrow backstreets.

There is a **gem-testing laboratory** (www.gtjaipur.info; ⊙10am-5.15pm Mon-Sat) in the Rajasthan Chamber Bhawan on MI Rd. Deposit gems before noon and receive an authenticity certificate on the same day between 4.30pm and 5.15pm. Certification charges start at ₹550 for a single stone.

THE ART OF HAGGLING

Haggling is a must in most parts of India. Shopkeepers in tourist hubs like Jaipur are accustomed to travellers who have lots of money and little time to spend it. It's not unusual to be charged at least double or even triple the 'real' price.

So how do you know if you're being overcharged and need to strike back with some serious haggling? Well, you're safe in government emporiums, cooperatives and modern shopping complexes, where the prices are usually fixed. But in most other shops that cater primarily to tourists, be prepared to don your haggling hat. The kind of places that usually fall into this category include handicraft, carpet, painting, souvenir and clothing shops.

The first 'rule' to haggling is never to show too much interest in the item you want to buy. Secondly, don't buy the first item that takes your fancy. Wander around and price things, but don't make it obvious. Otherwise if you return to the first shop the vendor will know it's because they are the cheapest.

Decide how much you would be happy paying and then express a casual interest in buying. If you have absolutely no idea of what something should really cost, start by slashing the price by half (even more if you're feeling bold). This is usually completely unacceptable to the vendor but it works as a good starting point to haggle for a happy compromise. You'll find that many shopkeepers lower their so-called final price if you proceed to head out of the shop saying you'll 'think about it'.

Haggling is a way of life in India, but it should never turn ugly. Keep in mind exactly how much a rupee is worth in your home currency so you don't lose perspective, and if a vendor seems to be charging an unreasonably high price and is unwilling to negotiate, simply look elsewhere.

Bapu Bazaar is lined with saris and fabrics, and is a good place to buy trinkets. Johari Bazaar (⊘closed part of Sun) and **Siredeori Bazaar** are where many jewellery shops are concentrated, selling gold, silver and highly glazed enamelwork known as *meenakari*, a Jaipur speciality. You may also find better deals for fabrics with the cotton merchants of Johari Bazaar.

Kishanpol Bazaar is famous for textiles, particularly *bandhani* (tie-dye). **Nehru Bazaar** also sells fabric, as well as *jootis,* trinkets and perfume. MI Rd is another good place to buy *jootis*. The best place for bangles is Maniharon ka Rasta, near the Shree Sanjay Sharma Museum.

Plenty of factories and showrooms are strung along the length of Amber Rd, between Zorawar Singh Gate and the Holiday Inn, to catch the tourist traffic. Here you'll find huge emporiums selling block prints, blue pottery, carpets and antiques; but these shops are used to busloads swinging in to blow their cash, so you'll need to wear your bargaining hat.

Rickshaw-wallahs, hotels and travel agents will be getting a hefty cut from any shop they steer you towards. Stay clear of friendly young men on the street trying to steer you to their uncle's/brother's/cousin's shop – commission is the name of their game too. Many unwary visitors get talked into buying things for resale at inflated prices, especially gems. Beware of these get-rich-quick scams.

Kripal Kumbh
HANDICRAFTS
(☎2201127; B18A Shiv Marg, Bani Park; ⊘10am-6pm) This is a showroom in a private home and a great place to buy Jaipur's famous blue pottery produced by the late Mr Kripal Singh, his family and his students. The renowned, multi-award-winning potter was an accomplished artist and there are some stunningly beautiful artworks for sale. Ceramics go for anything from ₹30 (for a paperweight) to ₹25,000 (for a large vase). Touts may take you elsewhere, so make sure that you are taken to the right place (near the Jaipur Inn).

Rajasthali
HANDICRAFTS
(MI Rd; ⊘11am-7.30pm Mon-Sat) The state-government emporium, opposite Ajmeri Gate, is packed with quality Rajasthani artefacts and crafts, including enamelwork, embroidery, pottery, woodwork, jewellery, colourful puppets, block-printed sheets, cute miniatures, brassware, mirror work and more, but it has an air of torpor that doesn't make shopping much fun. The best reason

to visit is to scout out prices, before launching into the bazaar. Items can be cheaper at the markets, after haggling, and you'll find more choice.

Juneja Art Gallery
CONTEMPORARY ART

(www.artchill.com; 6-7 Laksmi Complex, MI Rd; ☺10am-6.30pm Mon-Sat) This gallery, tucked in behind the brash Birdhichand Ghanshyamdas jewellery store, has some striking pieces of contemporary art by Rajasthani artists (₹500 to ₹50,000). There are regular shows of contemporary artists changing almost weekly. It has a sister gallery, Artchill, at Amber Fort featuring works for sale as well as a display of masterworks.

Himalaya
HEALTH PRODUCTS

(MI Rd; ☺10am-8pm Mon-Sat) For ayurvedic preparations, try this place located just near Panch Batti, which exports internationally, and has been selling herbal remedies and beauty products for over 70 years. There are even treatments for your pet. The shampoos, moisturisers and beauty products are reasonable buys.

Music N Sports
MUSIC STORE

(73 Chaura Rasta; ☺10.30am-8pm Mon-Sat) This store sells a range of musical instruments, including sitars, tablas, hand cymbals, bamboo flutes, dancing bells on ankle cuffs and harmoniums. The helpful staff can recommend music teachers.

Mojari
CLOTHING

(Shiv Heera Marg; ☺11am-6pm Mon-Sat) Calling all foot fetishists! This shop sells fabulous footwear for around ₹700 a pair. Named after the traditional decorated shoes of Rajasthan, Mojari is a UN-supported project that helps rural leatherworkers, traditionally among the poorest members of society. There is a wide variety of footwear available, including embroidered, appliquéd and open-toed shoes, mules and sandals. There are also shoes featuring creative stitching, unusual cuts and decoration with bells, beads and sequins. The products meet export quality, but are based on traditional leatherwork skills and design. Mojari also sells a small collection of covetable leather and felt bags.

Anokhi
CLOTHING

(www.anokhi.com; 2nd fl, KK Square, C-11, Prithviraj Marg; ☺9.30am-8pm Mon-Sat, 11am-7pm Sun) Anokhi is a classy, upmarket boutique that's well worth visiting – there's a wonderful little cafe on the premises and an excellent bookshop in the same building. Anokhi sells stunning high-quality textiles, such as block-printed fabrics, tablecloths, bed covers, cosmetic bags and scarves, as well as a range of well-designed, beautifully made clothing that combines Indian and Western influences. The pieces are produced just outside Jaipur at an unusually ethical factory, built on the grounds of an organic farm.

Soma
CLOTHING

(5 Jacob Rd, Civil Lines; ☺10am-8pm Mon-Sat, 10am-6pm Sun) This is a chic boutique, which sells first-rate textiles, including

ℹ GEM SCAMS – A WARNING

If you believe any stories about buying anything in India to sell at a profit elsewhere, you'll simply be proving (once again) that old adage about separating fools from their money. Precious stones are favourites for this game. Merchants will tell you that you can sell the items back home for several times the purchase price, and will even give you the (often imaginary) addresses of dealers who will buy them. You may also be shown written statements from other travellers documenting the money they have made, even photographs of the merchants shaking hands with their so-called business partners overseas. Don't be taken in, it's all a scam. The gems you buy will be worth only a fraction of what you pay. Often the scams involve showing you real stones and then packing up worthless glass beads to give you in their place. Don't let greed cloud your judgment.

These scams can be elaborate productions and can begin when touts strike up conversations in excellent English while you're waiting for a bus or eating in a restaurant, until you develop a friendly relationship with them. It might be several hours (or even days if they know where you hang out and can arrange to see you again) before any mention is made of reselling items.

Tip: beware of anyone who wants to become your best friend in areas that see a lot of tourists, eg hotel and shopping strips and transport hubs.

bright, fresh block prints and lots of unique furnishings, as well as some lovely children's clothes. Other textile and furnishing shops can be found in the immediate neighbourhood.

Silver Shop JEWELLERY
(Hotel Pearl Palace, Hari Kishan Somani Marg, Hathroi Fort; ☺6-10pm) A trusted jewellery shop backed by the hotel management that hosts the store, and offering a money-back guarantee on all items. Find it under the peacock canopy in the hotel's Peacock Rooftop Restaurant.

Jodhpur Tailors CLOTHING
(www.jodhpurtailors.com; 9 Ksheer Sagar Hotel, Motilal Atal Rd; ☺9am-8.30pm Mon-Sat, 9am-5pm Sun) You can have a beautiful pair of jodhpurs (₹2500) made in preparation for your visit to the Blue City. Or you can just go for a made-to-measure suit (₹7000 to ₹15000) or shirt (₹700 to ₹900).

Fabindia CLOTHING
(☏5115991; www.fabindia.com; B-4E Prithviraj Marg; ☺11am-8pm) A great place to coordinate colours with reams of rich fabrics plus furniture and home accessories. As well, you can find organically certified garments, beauty products and condiments. Located opposite Central Park gate number four.

Charmica CLOTHING
(MI Rd; ☺10am-8pm Mon-Sat) Opposite Natraj restaurant, this small shop is the place for well-made but pricey *jootis*.

PM Allahbuksh & Son ANTIQUES
(MI Rd; ☺10am-6pm Mon-Sat) A treasure trove of dusty antiques in a long-standing store, a few steps west of the Indian Coffee House.

❶ Information

Dangers & Annoyances
Travellers have reported problems with commission merchants in Jaipur. The town is notorious for gem scams – don't get involved in any get-rich-quick export schemes. So common they even have their own terminology, these *lapkas* (crooked touts) are involved in *dabbabazi* (the business of scamming tourists). They're particularly annoying around the City Palace, at train and bus stations, and at Amber Fort. Usually they'll leave you alone if you steadfastly ignore them, but if this doesn't work, you can report them to the tourist police (Tourism Assistance Force) stationed at these places. Often simply threatening to report them is enough to do the

trick. For more information, see Gem Scams – A Warning, p131.

Internet Access
Many places provide internet access, including most hotels and guesthouses. However fast or slow, it'll set you back about ₹25 per hour.

Dhoom Cyber Café (MI Rd; per hr ₹25) Enter through an arch into a quiet courtyard just off the main drag.

Mewar Cyber Café & Communication (Station Rd; per hr ₹25; ☺8am-11pm) Near the main bus station.

Media
Jaipur Vision and *Jaipur City Guide* are two useful, inexpensive booklets available at bookshops and some hotel lobbies (where they are free). They feature up-to-date listings, maps, local adverts and features. The redoubtable Mr Singh at the Hotel Pearl Palace publishes his free *Jaipur for Aliens* guide, which is a handy traveller survival kit with everything from bus timetables to butter chicken recipes.

Medical Services
Most hotels can arrange a doctor on site. At **Galundia Clinic** (☏2361040, 9829061040; dagalundia@doctor.com; MI Rd), **Dr Chandra Sen** (☏9829061040) is on 24-hour call.

Good hospitals include:

Santokba Durlabhji Hospital (☏2566251; Bhawan Singh Marg)

Sawai Mansingh Hospital (☏2560291; Sawai Ram Singh Rd)

Money
There are plenty of places to change money, including numerous hotels, and masses of ATMs, most of which accept foreign cards, including **HDFC** (Ashoka Marg & Sawai Jai Singh Hwy), **HSBC** (Sardar Patel Marg), **ICICI** (ground fl, Ganpati Plaza, MI Rd), **IDBI** (Sawai Jai Singh Hwy), **State Bank of India** (Hotel Om Tower), and **Standard Chartered** (Bhagwat Bhavan, MI Rd), which are open 24 hours.

Thomas Cook (☏2360940; Jaipur Towers MI Rd; ☺9.30am-6pm Mon-Sat) Changes cash and travellers cheques.

Photography
Photo labs, including those listed here, sell lithium batteries, memory sticks and compact flash cards, and will save your digital photos onto CD for around ₹100.

Goyal Colour Lab (☏2360147; MI Rd; ☺10.30am-8.30pm Mon-Sat, 10am-4pm Sun)

Sentosa Colour Lab (☏2388748; Ganpati Plaza, MI Rd; ☺10am-8.30pm Mon-Sat)

Post

DHL Express (☎2361159; www.dhl.co.in; G8 Geeta Enclave, Vinobha Rd; ⊙10am-8pm) This reliable international courier also has a small and friendly office (but dealing in cash payments only) beside the Standard Chartered bank on MI Rd. To get to the head office, take the alley beside the small office for about 50m to the Geeta Enclave building. Ensure that you ask to pay customs charges for the destination country upfront.

Main post office (☎2368740; MI Rd; ⊙8am-7.45pm Mon-Fri, 10am-5.45pm Sat) A cost-effective and efficient institution (though you will inevitably get a little frustrated with the back-and-forth) . Parcels need to be wrapped according to the rules, so stand back and watch the parcel-packing wallah (10am to 4pm Monday to Saturday) in the foyer, who will pack, stitch and wax seal your parcels for a reasonable fee.

Telephone

There are numerous public call offices (PCOs) scattered around Jaipur, which are usually cheaper than the hotels for long-distance calls. The international reverse-charges operator can be reached on ☎186.

Tourist Information

The Tourism Assistance Force (police) is stationed at the railway and bus stations, the airport and at Jaipur's major tourist sights.

Foreigners' Regional Registration Office (FRRO; ☎2618508; City Palace Complex; ⊙10am-5pm Mon-Sat) Any applications for visa extensions should be lodged at the FRRO at least one week before the visa expires. It is somewhat hard to find behind the Hawa Mahal, so ask around. The likelihood you'll get an extension on a tourist visa is slight – see p357 for more details.

Government of India Tourist Office (GITO; ☎2372200; Khasa Kothi Circle; ⊙9am-6pm Mon-Fri) Inside the Hotel Khasa Kothi compound (go through the arch and look to the left). Provides brochures on places all over India.

RTDC Central Reservations Office (☎2202586; former RTDC Tourist Hotel, MI Rd; ⊙9.30am-5pm Mon-Fri) Handles bookings for RTDC hotels around Rajasthan, accommodation in the RTDC tourist village during the Pushkar Camel Fair (see p144) and reservations for the *Palace on Wheels* and Royal Rajasthan on Wheels trains (see p368).

RTDC Tourist Reception Centre Main branch (☎5155137; www.rajasthantourism. gov.in; Room 21, former RTDC Tourist Hotel; ⊙9.30am-6pm Mon-Fri); Airport (☎2722647); Amber Fort (☎2530264); Jaipur train station

(☎2200778; platform 1; ⊙24hr); main bus station (☎5064102; platform 3; ⊙10am-5pm Mon-Fri) Has maps and brochures on Jaipur and Rajasthan.

Travel Agencies

There are plenty of travel agencies that can tailor local sightseeing trips, though your hotel can probably organise the same trips for a competitive price. For a half-day tour it costs around ₹700/900 for a non-AC/AC car with driver; a full day costs ₹1200/1800. You can hire guides for about ₹800 per day. See p134 for rates on longer trips. The following agencies can arrange cars and jeep or camel safaris, make hotel reservations and book air tickets.

Crown Tours (☎2363310; Palace Rd) Opposite the Sheraton Rajputana Hotel.

Rajasthan Travel Service (☎2389408; www. rajasthantravelservice.com; ground fl, Ganpati Plaza, MI Rd)

Getting There & Away

Air

It's possible to arrange flights to Europe, the USA and other places, such as Dubai, all via Delhi. It's best to compare ticket prices from travel agencies with what the airlines supply directly and through their websites – the latter is where you will usually find the best price.

Offices of domestic airlines:

Air India/Indian Airlines (☎2743500; www. indian-airlines.nic.in; Nehru Place, Tonk Rd)

IndiGo (☎2743500; www.goindigo.in; Airport)

Jet Airways (☎5112225; www.jetairways.com; Room 112, Jaipur Tower, MI Rd; ⊙9.30am-6pm Mon-Sat)

Kingfisher Airlines (☎4030372; www.flyking fisher.com; Usha Plaza, MI Rd; ⊙9.30am-5.30pm Mon-Sat, 10am-3pm Sun)

Bus

Rajasthan State Road Transport Corporation (RSRTC aka Rajasthan Roadways) buses all leave from the **main bus station** (Station Rd), picking up passengers at Narain Singh Circle (you can also buy tickets here). There is a left- luggage office at the main bus station (₹10 per bag for 24 hours), as well as a prepaid autorickshaw stand.

Deluxe or private buses are far preferable to RSRTC Blue Line or Star Line or local buses, which stop in small villages and can be crowded bone-rattlers with questionable safety. Deluxe buses all leave from Platform 3, tucked away in the right-hand corner of the bus station; seats may be booked in advance from the **reservation office** (☎5116032) within the main bus station.

For long journeys, the RSRTC Volvo and Gold Line buses are easily the most comfortable and safe AC services. Even the cheaper RSRTC Silver

DOMESTIC FLIGHTS FROM JAIPUR

There are plenty of domestic flights from Jaipur, mostly run by Indian Airlines, Kingfisher Airlines and Jet Airways, who offer similar prices. Other airlines serving Jaipur include IndiGo and SpiceJet. Fares and schedules vary widely and these are just indicative fares at the time of research.

DESTINATION	FARE (₹)	DURATION (HR)
Ahmedabad	110	1hr
Delhi	55	40min
Jodhpur	100	40min
Kolkata (Calcutta)	145	2hr
Mumbai (Bombay)	70	1½hr
Udaipur	110	1¾hr

Line services get good reviews. The RSRTC Gray Line is a sleeper service. Private companies also provide sleeper buses over long distances – they are usually cheaper, but not as reliable when it comes to schedules and safe drivers. There is a cluster of private offices on Motilal Atal Rd, near the Polo Victory Cinema.

There are regular buses that travel to many destinations, including those outlined in the table (p135). Numerous private agencies also operate direct services to these cities.

Car

There are no car-hire operators offering self-drive cars in Rajasthan. You'll have to hire a car in Delhi if you're crazy enough to try this.

You can arrange car and driver hire directly with the driver at the taxi stand at the train station. Usually the drivers need only a day's notice for a long trip. A much easier way to do this is to utilise the services provided by your hotel. Most hotels will be able to contact drivers (with cars) who are known to the hotel. These drivers value the work they obtain through the hotels and that provides you with greater security and service standards. A reasonable price is non-AC/AC ₹7/8 per kilometre, with a 250km minimum per day and an overnight charge of ₹150 per night. See p364 for more information. Rates with the RTDC at the time of writing are from ₹6.25/7.25 per kilometre (₹150 overnight charge) for a non-AC/AC Ambassador, with the usual 250km minimum per day.

Motorcycle

You can hire, buy or fix a Royal Enfield Bullet (and lesser motorbikes) at **Rajasthan Auto Centre** (☑2568074; www.royalenfieldsaleem. com; Sanjay Bazaar, Sanganeri Gate), the cleanest little motorcycle workshop in India. To hire a 350cc Bullet costs ₹500 per day (including helmet) within Jaipur.

Train

The efficient **railway reservation office** (☑135; ⊙8am-2pm & 2.15-8pm Mon-Sat, 8am-2pm Sun) is to your left as you enter Jaipur train station. It's open for advance reservations only (more than five hours before departure). Join the queue for 'Freedom Fighters and Foreign Tourists' (counter 769). See p134 for routes and fares.

For same-day travel, buy your ticket at the northern end of the train station on **Platform 1, window 10** (⊙closed 6-6.30am, 2-2.30pm & 10-10.30pm). The railway inquiries number is ☑131.

Station facilities on Platform 1 include an RTDC tourist information bureau, Tourism Assistance Force (police), a cloakroom for left luggage (₹10 per bag per 24 hours), retiring rooms (p122), restaurants and AC waiting rooms for those with 1st class and 2AC train tickets.

There's a prepaid autorickshaw stand and local taxis at the road entrance to the train station.

Getting Around
To/From the Airport

There are no bus services from the airport, which is 12km southeast of the city. An autorickshaw/taxi costs at least ₹200/350 for the 15km journey into the city centre, or there's a prepaid taxi booth inside the terminal.

Autorickshaw

There are prepaid autorickshaw stands at the bus and train stations. Rates are fixed by the government, so there's no need to haggle. In other cases be prepared to bargain hard.

If you want to hire an autorickshaw for local sightseeing, it should cost about ₹200/400 for a half/full day (including a visit to Amber but not Nahargarh); be prepared to bargain. This price is per rickshaw, not per person, and don't let drivers tell you otherwise. Make sure you fix a price before setting off to avoid a scene later.

Cycle-Rickshaw

You can do your bit for the environment by flagging down a lean-limbed cycle-rickshaw rider. Though it can be uncomfortable watching someone pedalling hard to transport you, this *is* how they make a living. A short trip costs about ₹30.

Taxi

There are unmetered taxis available, which will require negotiating a fare, or you can try **Mericar** (☑4188888; www.mericar.in; flagfall incl 3km ₹50, afterwards per km ₹11, 25% night surcharge 10pm-5am). It's a 24-hour service and taxis can hired for sightseeing for four-/six-/eight-hour blocks costing ₹550/850/1050.

AROUND JAIPUR

Jaipur's environs take in some fascinating historical sites and interesting towns and villages that make great day trips. A comprehensive network of local buses and the ease of finding a taxi or autorickshaw makes getting to these regions simple (if not always comfortable). It's also possible to join a tour run by the RTDC that includes a commentary on the various places visited. See p119 for more details.

Amber

The formidable, magnificent, honey-hued fort–palace of Amber (pronounced Amer), an ethereal example of Rajput architecture, rises from a rocky mountainside about 11km northeast of Jaipur. Amber was the former capital of Jaipur state.

Amber was built by the Kachhwaha Rajputs, who hailed from Gwalior, in present-day Madhya Pradesh, where they reigned for over 800 years. They were adept at diplomacy through marriage, and it was a marital alliance between a Kachhwaha prince, Taj Karan, and a Rajput princess that resulted in the granting of the region of Dausa to the prince by the princess' father.

Taj Karan's descendants eyed the hill-top on which Amber Fort was later built, recognising its virtue as a potential military stronghold. The site was eventually prised from its original inhabitants, the Susawat Minas, and the Minas were granted guardianship of the Kachhwahas' treasury in perpetuity.

The Kachhwahas, despite being devout Hindus belonging to the Kshatriya (warrior) caste, realised the convenience of aligning

BUSES FROM JAIPUR

DESTINATION	FARE (₹)	DURATION (HR)	FREQUENCY
Agra	195, AC 370	5½	11 daily
Ajmer	110, AC 200	2½	13 daily
Bharatpur	128*	4½	5 daily
Bikaner	190	8	hourly
Bundi	160, AC 220	5	5 daily
Chittorgarh	210, AC 335	7	6 daily
Delhi	325, AC 425-600	5½	at least hourly
Jaisalmer	430	15	daily
Jhunjhunu	140	5	half-hourly
Jodhpur	240, AC 350	7	every 2 hours
Kota	255, AC 370	5	hourly
Mt Abu	AC 531	13	daily
Nawalgarh	95	4	hourly
Pushkar	120	3	daily (direct)
Sawai Madhopur	110	6	2 daily
Udaipur	300, AC 605	10	6 daily

* To take an AC bus to Bharatpur, you must pay the full Agra fare on an Agra-bound bus and alight at Bharatpur.

MAJOR TRAINS FROM JAIPUR

DESTINATION	TRAIN NO & NAME	FARE (₹)	DURATION (HR)	DEPARTURE
Agra	12308 *Jodhpur–Howrah Exp*	160/385/515 (A)	4¾	2.10am
	12966 *Udaipur–Gwalior Exp*	90/305/385/515/840 (B)	4¼	6.10am
Ahmedabad	12958 *Ahmedabad SJ Rajdhani Exp*	890/1215/2055 (C)	9½	12.35am
	12916 *Ahmedabad Ashram Exp*	280/730/990/1650 (D)	11	8.45pm
Ajmer	12015 *Ajmer Shatabdi*	270/530 (E)	2	10.40pm (Thu-Tue)
	19708 *Aravalli Exp*	120/245/330 (A)	2½	8.30am
	12195 *Intercity Exp*	65/222 (F)	2	9.40am
	09622 *Intercity Exp*	65/222 (F)	2	2.15pm
Bikaner	12468 *Intercity Exp*	115 (G)	7	3.45pm
Delhi	12016 *Shatabdi*	535/1015 (D)	5	5.50pm (Thu-Tue)
	14060 *Jaisalmer–Delhi Exp*	90/155/410/550 (H)	6	5am
	12413 *Jaipur–Delhi Exp*	100/175/440/590/970 (I)	5	4.30pm
Jaisalmer	14059 *Delhi–Jaisalmer Exp*	145/255/680/930/1555 (I)	13	11.55pm
Jodhpur	12465 *Ranthambhore Exp*	100/180/355/450 (J)	5½	5pm
	14059 *Delhi–Jaisalmer Exp*	90/160/415/565/940 (I)	5½	11.55pm
Sawai Madhopur	12956 *Jaipur–Mumbai Exp*	140/275/355/585 (D)	2	2.10pm
	12466 *Intercity Exp*	65/140/225/275 (J)	2¼	10.55am
Udaipur	12965 *Jaipur–Udaipur Exp*	125/215/435/545/735/1230 (K)	9½	10.25pm

Fares: A – sleeper/3AC/2AC, B – 2nd class/AC Chair/3AC/2AC/1AC, C – 3AC/2AC/1AC, D – sleeper, 3AC, 2AC, 1AC, E – AC Chair/1AC, F – 2nd class/AC chair, G – 2nd class, H – 2nd class/sleeper/3AC/2AC, I – 2nd class/sleeper/3AC/2AC/1AC, J – 2nd class/sleeper/AC Chair/3AC, K – 2nd Class/sleeper/AC Chair/3AC/2AC/1AC.

themselves with the powerful Mughal empire. They paid homage at the Mughal court, cemented the relationship with marital alliances and defended the Mughals in their various skirmishes. For these actions they were handsomely rewarded. With war booty they financed construction of the fort–palace at Amber, which was begun in 1592 by Maharaja Man Singh, the Rajput commander of Akbar's army. The fort was later extended and completed by the Jai Singhs before the move to Jaipur on the plains below.

⊙ Sights

Amber Fort HISTORIC SITE

(Indian/foreigner ₹25/200, guide ₹200, audio guide Hindi/English/various European/various Asian ₹100/150/200/250; ⊙8am-6pm, last entry 5.30pm) This magnificent fort is more of a palace, built from pale yellow and pink sandstone and white marble, and divided into four main sections, each with its own courtyard.

You can trudge up to the fort from the road in about 10 minutes (cold drinks are available at the top). A seat in a jeep up to the fort costs ₹200 return. Riding up on elephant back (₹900 per two passengers; ⊘8-11am & 3.30-5.30pm) is very popular, however. Elephants return empty and once an individual elephant has done five trips it is rested for the rest of the day. In the mornings, when most of the tour buses arrive, the queue for elephants is very long and you must be prepared to wait in the full blaze of the sun.

If you walk or ride an elephant you will enter Amber Fort through **Suraj Pol** (Sun Gate), which leads to the **Jaleb Chowk** (Main Courtyard), where returning armies would display their war booty to the populace – women could view this area from the veiled windows of the palace. The ticket office is directly across the courtyard from Suraj Pol. If you arrive by car you will enter through **Chand Pol** (Moon Gate) on the opposite side of Jaleb Chowk. Hiring a guide or grabbing an audio guide is highly recommended as there are very few signs and many blind alleys.

From Jaleb Chowk, an imposing stairway leads up to the main palace, but first it's worth taking the steps just to the right, which lead to the small **Siladevi Temple** (photography prohibited; ⊘6am-noon & 4-8pm). Every day from the 16th century until 1980 (when the government banned the practice), a goat was sacrificed here. It's a beautiful temple, entered through gorgeous silver doors featuring repoussé (raised relief) work. Before the image (an incarnation of Kali) lie two silver lions. According to tradition, Maharaja Man Singh prayed to the goddess for victory in a battle with the ruler of Bengal. The goddess came to the maharaja in a dream advising that if he won the battle he should retrieve her image, which was lying at the bottom of the sea. After vanquishing his foes, the maharaja recovered the statue and installed it in the temple as Sila Devi (*sila* means 'slab' – the image is carved from one piece of stone). Above the lintel of the temple is the usual image of Ganesh, this one carved from a single piece of coral.

Heading back to the main stairway will take you up to the second courtyard and the **Diwan-i-Am** (Hall of Public Audience), which has a double row of columns, each topped by a capital in the shape of an elephant, and latticed galleries above. Here the maharaja held audience and received petitions of his subjects.

The maharaja's apartments are located around the third courtyard – you enter through the fabulous **Ganesh Pol**, decorated with mosaics and sculptures. The **Jai Mandir** (Hall of Victory) is noted for its inlaid panels and multi-mirrored ceiling. Patterns made with coloured foil and paint are covered in glass. At night this would have been candlelit and the mass of convex mirrors would have glittered brightly like stars. Regrettably, much of the decoration was allowed to deteriorate, but restoration of varying quality proceeds. Carved marble relief panels around the hall are fascinatingly delicate and quirky, depicting cartoon-like insects and sinuous flowers.

Opposite the Jai Mandir is the **Sukh Niwas** (Hall of Pleasure), with an ivory-inlaid sandalwood door and a channel that once carried cooling water right through the room. Not a single drop of water was wasted, with the overflow passing through conduits to the gardens. From the Jai Mandir you can enjoy fine views from the palace ramparts over picturesque **Maota Lake** below. The lake, at the foot of the hillside, reflects the fort's terraces and ramparts, but it often dries up in the winter months.

The **zenana** (women's quarters) surrounds the fourth courtyard. The rooms were designed so that the maharaja could embark on his nocturnal visits to his wives' and concubines' respective chambers without the others knowing, as the chambers are independent but open onto a common corridor.

The **Amber Sound & Light Show** (English/Hindi ₹200/100; ⊘English 6.30pm, Hindi 7.30pm) is held at the Kesar Kiyari complex at Maota Lake at the foot of Amber Fort.

For refreshments, there are cool drinks available in the Jaleb Chowk. There's also a **Café Coffee Day,** near the exit, as well as the expensive **1135 Restaurant** (mains ₹475-1150; ⊘10am-11pm) above Chand Pol (Jaleb Chowk).

Anokhi Museum of Hand Printing MUSEUM (Anokhi Haveli, Kheri Gate; child/adult ₹15/30, camera/video ₹50/150; ⊘10.30am-4.30pm Tue-Sat, 11am-4.30pm Sun, closed 1 May-15 Jul) Just beyond Amber Fort, in Amber town, is this interesting museum that documents the art of hand-block printing and runs hands-on demonstrations. Of course there's a cafe and gift shop. From the museum you can walk around the ancient town to the restored **Panna Meena Baori** (stepwell), and the fascinating **Jagat Siromani Temple** (known locally as the Meera Temple, if you are asking for directions).

ⓘ Getting There & Away

There are frequent (crowded) buses to Amber from near the Hawa Mahal in Jaipur (₹10, 25 minutes). An autorickshaw/taxi will cost at least ₹150/550 for the return trip. RTDC city tours (see p119) include Amber Fort.

En route to Amber you can squeeze in visits to Royal Gaitor (p116), the Jal Mahal (p116) and the cenotaphs of the maharanis of Jaipur (p116).

A good option is to hire a taxi from the stand near Jaipur train station – a round trip covering Amber Fort, Jaigarh and Nahagarh will cost around ₹900, including waiting time (maximum five people). Try to arrive at Nahagarh in time for a sunset beer overlooking the city.

Jaigarh

A scrubby green hill – Cheel ka Teela (Mound of Eagles) – rising above Amber, is topped by the imposing fortress of Jaigarh (Indian/foreigner ₹25/75, camera or video ₹50, car ₹50, Hindi/English guide ₹150/200; ⊙9am-5pm). This massive fort was planned by Jai Singh I, but what you see today dates from the reign of Jai Singh II. It was only opened to the public in mid-1983 and hence has remained very much intact. Punctuated by whimsically hatted lookout towers, the fort was never captured and is a splendid example of grand 18th-century defences, without the palatial frills that are found in many other Rajput forts. It has water reservoirs, residential areas, a puppet theatre and the world's largest wheeled cannon, Jaya Vana.

During the Mughal empire Jaipur produced many weapons for the Mughal and Rajput rulers. This most spectacular example was made in the fort foundry, which was constructed in Mughal times. The huge cannon dates from 1720, has a barrel around 6m long, is made from a mix of eight different metals and weighs 50 tonnes. To fire it requires 100kg of gunpowder, and it has a range of 30km. It's debatable how many times this great device was used.

A sophisticated network of drainage channels feed three large tanks that used to provide water for all the soldiers, residents and livestock living in the fort. The largest tank has a capacity for 22.8 million litres of water. The fort served as the treasury of the Kachhwahas, and for a long time people were convinced that at least part of the royal treasure was still secreted in this large water tank. The Indian government even searched it to check, but found nothing.

Within the fort is an **armoury** and **museum**, with the essential deadly weapons collection and some royal knick-knacks, including interesting photographs, maps of Jaigarh, spittoons and circular 18th-century playing cards. The structure also contains various open halls, including the **Shubhat Niwas** (Meeting Hall of Warriors), which has some weather-beaten sedan chairs and drums lying about.

The fort is a steep uphill walk (about 1km) from Amber and offers great views from the Diwa Burj watchtower.

Admission is free if you have a ticket to Jaipur's City Palace that is less than two days old. Vehicles can drive up to the fort, though your taxi driver will expect an extra 'hill fee' of ₹100. There are cool drinks and snacks for sale inside the fort.

Sanganer & Bagru

The large village of Sanganer is 16km south of Jaipur, and has a ruined palace, a group of Jain temples with fine carvings (to which entry is restricted) and two ruined tripolias (triple gateways). The main reason to visit, however, is to see its handmade paper and block-printing shops, workshops and factories (most shops can be found on or just off the main drag, Stadium Rd), where you can see the products being made by hand.

Best of all in Sanganer is walking down to the riverbank to see the brightly coloured fabrics drying in the sun. Though more and more of Sanganer's cloth is screen-printed, the time-honoured block printers of Sanganer are famous for their small floral prints, and the cloth produced here was traditionally used by the royal court. Traditional papermakers were also brought to the court at Amber in the 16th century, but moved to Sanganer in the late 18th century due to water shortages.

Salim's Paper (☑2730222; www.handmadepaper.com; Gramodyog Rd; ⊙9am-5pm) is the largest handmade paper factory in India and claims to be one of the biggest in the world. It's well set up for visitors: you can take a free tour to see the paper production process. Significantly, the paper is not made from trees, but from scrap pieces of fabric, and often decorated with petals or glitter. You'll recognise lots of styles and designs, as the paper is exported all over the world. The 300 or so employees produce 40,000 sheets a day. There's also a beautiful range of tree-free paper products for sale in the showroom – great (and light) gifts for friends back home.

Another huge handmade paper manufacturer is **AL Paper House** (☎2731706; www.alpaperhouse.com; ☺9am-5pm), near the tempo stand. This factory is also open to visitors.

For block-printed fabrics and blue pottery, there are a number of shops, including **Sakshi** (☎2731862; Laxmi Colony; ☺shop 8.30am-8.30pm, factory 9am-6pm). You can see the block-printing workshop here, and even try your hand at block printing. It also runs courses in block printing and blue pottery (see p119). There's a tremendous range of blue pottery and natural-dye, block-printed fabrics for sale.

About 20km west of Sanganer is the little village of **Bagru**, also known for its block printing, particularly of colourful designs featuring circular motifs. You won't see as much here as in Sanganer, but it's more off the beaten track. The fabric is dyed with natural colours here and the printers' quarter – full of small family businesses – is a hive of activity.

❶ Getting There & Away

Local buses leave from the Ajmeri Gate in Jaipur for Sanganer every few minutes (₹10, one hour). To Bagru, there are daily buses from Sanganer (₹26, 1½ hours).

Samode

☎01423

The small village of Samode is spectacularly set among rugged hills, about 40km north of Jaipur. The only real reason to visit is if you are staying at **Samode Palace** (admission ₹500). The steep admission cost can be offset with a meal or accommodation purchase once inside. If you want to be precise, it's not a palace, as it was owned by a nobleman rather than a ruler, but it's certainly palatial enough to get away with the title. Like Samode Haveli in Jaipur, this building was owned by the *rawal* (nobleman) of Samode, and today it's run by his descendants.

Mainly dating from the 19th century, it's a fantastic building nestling between the Aravalli hills and built on three levels, each with its own courtyard. The highlight is the exquisite Diwan-i-Khas, which is covered with original paintings and mirrorwork.

Above the palace is the overgrown Samode Fort – ask around and you'll find someone to let you in – where there are great views from the ramparts. This is also good walking country, with paths heading off into the countryside. Beneath the palace is a small village, where locals sell block-printed cloth and glass bangles.

🛏 Sleeping & Eating

Samode Bagh　　　　BOUTIQUE HOTEL **$$$**
(☎240235; www.samode.com; s/d ₹7000/8000; ✴[@☄]) Also part of the Samode group, this luxurious tented accommodation (featuring private modern bathrooms) is a wonderful retreat. It's set in 8 peaceful hectares of land, surrounded by formal gardens and near a 150-year-old pavilion. Samode Bagh is 4km from Samode Palace. You can book through Samode Haveli in Jaipur.

Samode Palace　　　　HERITAGE HOTEL **$$$**
(☎/fax 240014/23; www.samode.com; s/d from ₹14,000/15,000; ✴@☄) Largely extended in the 19th century, this magnificent palace is a gloriously grand hotel decorated in no-holds-barred Rajput splendour, with a great courtyard swimming pool plus an infinity pool. The suites are particularly atmospheric and the room tariff includes breakfast. The ₹500 palace admission fee for nonguests is deducted when you purchase a meal (à la carte ₹350 to ₹700, buffet ₹1200). You can book through Samode Haveli in Jaipur. There are discounts from May to September and you should check the website for special offers.

❶ Getting There & Away

There are a few direct buses to Samode from the main bus station in Jaipur (₹35, 1½ hours), or you can hire a taxi for around ₹1000 return.

Ramgarh

☎01426

This green oasis, about 35km northeast of Jaipur, has a pretty, though much shrunken lake, the **Jamwa Ramgarh Wildlife Sanctuary**. The area around here has been scarred by mines – all are now closed as the area is protected. Leopards, hyenas, antelopes and wild boars once roamed the area, as the trophy-laden walls of Ramgarh Lodge testify, but loss of habitat, lack of water and hunting have, understandably, driven the wildlife away. The scenery, with lush palms, huge banyans, remote villages, and small temples set into craggy rock, make it worth a visit to explore and walk in the area. There's a picturesque **polo ground** and the **Jamwa Maa Di Mandir**, an ancient Durga temple.

📖 Sleeping

RTDC Jheel Tourist Village
HOTEL $$

(☎01426-214084; s/d ₹875/1040) This peaceful resort offers simple accommodation in small round huts that would benefit from a lick of paint. The gardens are well kept with colonially trim lawns, and the views across to the remains of the lake are lovely. An extra bed costs ₹325. There's a small dining area with veg thalis. Boating on Ramgarh Lake can be arranged when the water level is high enough. The hotel can also arrange jeep and camel safaris through the park.

Gateway Hotel Ramgarh Lodge
HERITAGE HOTEL $$$

(☎2552217; www.tajhotels.com; s/d incl breakfast & dinner ₹8000/9000; ❇@☒) A one-time royal hunting lodge overlooking Ramgarh Lake, this place is spectacular, and recently renovated. Inside the lodge are masses of glass-eyed stuffed beasts. Billiards, squash and tennis are available, as well as boating when the lake's water level is high enough. The pool (check it's full) has a great setting, and the most expensive rooms have fabulous views. Jeep safaris to the park can be arranged.

Buses travel between Jaipur (from the main bus station) and Ramgarh (₹15, one hour).

Abhaneri

About 95km from Jaipur on Agra Rd, this remote village surrounded by rolling wheat fields is the unlikely location of one of Rajasthan's most awe-inspiring step-wells, the Chand Baori (admission free; ⊙sunrise-sunset).

With around 11 visible levels of zigzagging steps, this 10th-century water tank is an incredible, geometric sight, 20m deep. Flanking the *baori* is a small, crumbling palace, where the royals used to picnic and bathe in private rooms (water was brought up by oxen) – it's now inhabited by pigeons and bats. Next door is the Harshat Mata Temple, also dating from the 10th century, which was damaged by Muslim invaders, but retains some beautiful deep-relief sculptures in warm-orange sandstone. Both are thought to have been built by King Chand, ruler of Abhaneri and a Rajput from the Chahamana dynasty.

From Jaipur, catch a bus to Sikandra (₹45, 1½ hours), from where you can hop into a crowded share taxi (₹5) for the 5km trip to Gular. From Gular catch a passenger jeep or minibus to Abhaneri (another 5km and ₹5). If you have your own transport, this is a worthwhile stop between Jaipur and Bharatpur or Agra.

Balaji

The Hindu exorcism temple of Balaji, about 102km from Jaipur, is about 3km off the Jaipur–Agra road. People bring their loved ones who are suffering from possession here to have bad spirits exorcised through prayer and rituals. Most exorcisms take place on Tuesday and Saturday. At these times the only people who can get inside the temple are the holy men and the possessed – services are relayed to the crowds outside on crackly video screens.

If you wait until the service has finished, you will be able to look inside the temple. Remove your shoes and you may want to cover your head with a scarf as a mark of respect. No photography is permitted inside.

From the main bus station in Jaipur there are numerous buses to Balaji (local/express ₹32/50, 2½/two hours).

Sambhar Salt Lake

The country's largest salt lake, around 60km west of Jaipur, Sambhar Salt Lake's vast 230-sq-km wetland expanse once attracted flamingos, cranes, pelicans and many other waterfowl. According to myth, Sambhar is believed to have been given to local people by the goddess Shakambari some 2500 years ago. Her shrine, Mata Pahari, juts into the lake west of Jhapok. The people are certainly making good use of the lake – around 80 sq km of it is used for salt farming. On the eastern end, the lake is divided by a 5km-long stone dam. East of the dam are salt-evaporation ponds where salt has been farmed for the past thousand years.

Sambhar was designated as a Ramsar site (recognised wetland of international importance) in 1990, because it is a key wintering area for birds that migrate from northern Asia, some from as far as Siberia.

Usually the water depth fluctuates from a few centimetres during the dry season to about 3m after the monsoon. The specialised algae and bacteria growing in the lake provide striking water colours and support the lake ecology that, in turn, sustains the migrating waterfowl.

Eastern Rajasthan

Includes »

Best Places to Eat

» Sixth Sense (p168)

» Out of the Blue (p168)

» Sunset Café (p168)

» Sheesh Mahal (p159)

Best Places to Stay

» Khem Villas (p173)

» Inn Seventh Heaven (p165)

» Birder's Inn (p145)

» Hotel Tiger Safari Resort (p173)

» Patan Mahal (p155)

Why Go?

The cities and sites of eastern Rajasthan are easily accessible from Jaipur and the other axes of the 'Golden Triangle', Agra and Delhi. For immersion in history, see Alwar and Deeg's evocative palaces, and magnificent forts at Bharatpur and Ranthambhore.

Wildlife enthusiasts will relish opportunities at the national parks of Ranthambhore, Sariska Tiger Reserve and Keoladeo Ghana. Tiger-spotting is unsurpassed at Ranthambhore, which has provided the tigers to repopulate Sariska. India's premier bird sanctuary, Keoladeo Ghana, hosts an astonishing population of resident and migratory birds in a picturesque wetland setting.

Travellers of all description are drawn to Pushkar, a pale blue town that hosts an extravagant, internationally renowned camel fair. While Pushkar is a Hindu pilgrimage and a legendary travellers' halt to chill and shop, nearby Ajmer hosts the extraordinary dargah (shrine or place of burial of a Muslim saint) of Khwaja Muin-ud-din Chishti, India's most important Muslim pilgrimage site.

When to Go

Wildlife enthusiasts need to note that Ranthambhore National Park is closed during the monsoon from July through to September. The migration and breeding cycles of Keoladeo Ghana's bird population varies from species to species, but novice birdwatchers will be amazed by the feathery show from September to December. As elsewhere in Rajasthan, temperatures soar during summer, while spring and autumn days are still quite warm, and winter days are very pleasant, even cool. For information on regional festivals, such as the famous Pushkar Camel Fair, see p144. For festivals celebrated statewide and nationwide, see p24.

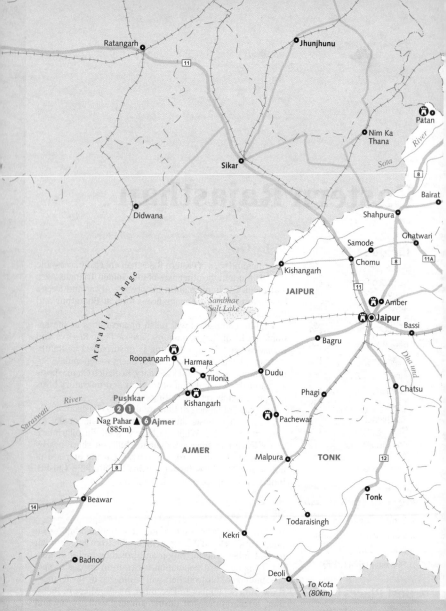

Eastern Rajasthan Highlights

① Relax in the pastel-hued pilgrimage town of **Pushkar** (p162), with its sacred ghats and enchanting lake

② Mingle with camels, converse with cameleers

and catch the circus at the amazing **Pushkar Camel Fair** (p144)

③ Spot a striped feline in the lush jungle and explore a magical cliff-top fortress

at **Ranthambhore National Park** (p171)

④ Observe abundant wildlife and explore temples, forts and a ghost city in and around **Sariska Tiger Reserve** (p152)

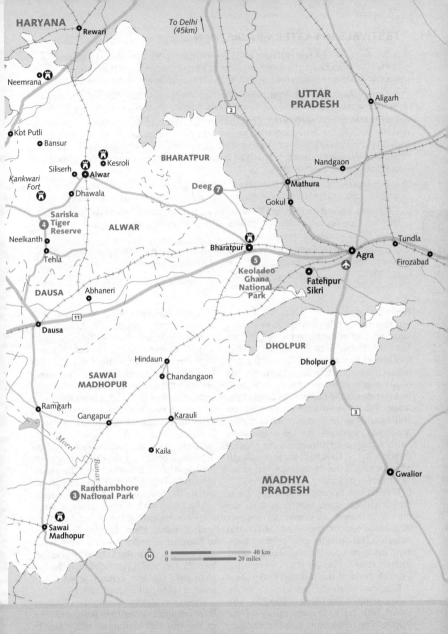

5 Cycle in peace while twitching for birds in the World Heritage–listed **Keoladeo Ghana National Park** (p148)

6 Merge with masses of pilgrims at India's most revered Muslim shrine – the **dargah of Khwaja Muin-ud-din Chishti** (p157) in Ajmer

7 Explore the whimsical palace of the extraordinary Suraj Mahl found in the ancient fiefdom of **Deeg** (p150)

» **Brij Festival** (2-4 Feb; Bharatpur, p145) The Brij takes place over several days prior to Holi (so expect a bit of premature colour to be splashed around). It's known for the *rasalila* dance, which acts out the story of the love between Krishna and Radha.

» **Alwar Utsav** (Feb/Mar; Alwar, p149) A tourist carnival showcasing cultural activities with a procession, traditional music and dance, a flower show and craft displays.

» **Shri Mahavirji Fair** (Mar/Apr; Chandangaon, p171) This huge Jain fair is held in honour of Mahavir, the 24th and last of the Jain *tirthankars* (great teachers), at the village of Chandangaon in Sawai Madhopur district. Thousands of Jains congregate on the banks of the Gambhir River, to which an image of Mahavir is carried on a golden palanquin (carried enclosed seat).

» **The Urs** (Ajmer, p155) This anniversary of Sufi saint Khwaja Muin-ud-din Chishti's death signals a huge Muslim pilgrimage to Ajmer. It follows the Islamic calendar.

» **Ganesh Chaturthi** (Aug/Sep; Ranthambhore, p171) Celebrated nationwide, Ganesh's birthday is particularly popular at Ranthambhore, which holds one of Rajasthan's most important Ganesh temples.

» **Pushkar Camel Fair** (Oct/Nov; Pushkar, p144) Eastern Rajasthan hosts one of India's greatest festivals: a surreal, mass gathering of tribespeople, camels, horses, tourists and touts.

History

Alwar is perhaps Rajasthan's most ancient kingdom, part of the Matsya kingdom since 1500 BC. It has been much coveted and fought over, owing to its position on the strategic southwestern frontier of Delhi. The city of Alwar is believed to have been founded by a member of the Kachhwaha family from Amber, but it saw ownership pass from one raiding army to the next over the centuries. Alwar was eventually granted to Sawai Jai Singh of Jaipur by Aurangzeb, the Mughal emperor, but he took back his generous gift when he visited the city and saw the strategic virtues of its forts.

In 1803 the British invested the Alwar *thakur* (Hindu caste, noblemen) with the title of maharaja as thanks for support in a battle against the Marathas (central Indians). This friendly alliance was shortlived, however, since the maharaja of Alwar strongly resented British interference when a British Resident was installed in the city.

Bharatpur is another ancient city of the region, traditionally home of the Jats, who settled here before the emergence of the Rajputs. The relationship between the Jats, tillers of the soil, and the warrior Rajputs was, at best, uneasy. Marital alliances helped to reduce the friction, but they continually tussled over territory. The differences were only overcome when both groups turned to face the mutual threat posed by the Mughals.

It was Jat leader Suraj Mahl who built Deeg's beautiful palace and gardens, and commenced work on the Bharatpur fort, which was completed in the late 18th century after nearly 60 years of toil. This was time well spent, as the British unsuccessfully besieged the fort for around six months, finally conceding defeat after substantial losses. The rulers of Bharatpur were the first to enter into an agreement with the East India Company.

The huge fort at Ranthambhore, founded in the 10th century by the Chauhan Rajputs, predates that at Bharatpur by many centuries, and is believed to be one of Rajasthan's oldest. The Mughal Emperor Akbar negotiated a treaty with Surjana Hada, a Bundi ruler who bought the fort of Ranthambhore from Jhunjhar Khan, and the fort passed to Jagannatha, under whose leadership the Jain religion flourished. Later, Aurangzeb took the fort, and it remained with the Mughals until the 18th century, when it was granted to the maharaja of Jaipur.

Ajmer was also founded by the Chauhans three centuries earlier than Ranthambhore. In the late 12th century it was taken by Mohammed of Ghori and remained a possession of the sultanate of Delhi until the 14th century. Another strategic jewel, it was fought over by various neighbouring states through subsequent centuries, but was mostly under Mughal rule. It was one of the few places in Rajasthan to be directly controlled by the British, from 1818.

After Independence in 1947, Alwar was merged with the other princely states of Bharatpur, Karauli and Dholpur, forming the United State of Matsya, a name that reflected the fact that these states comprised the ancient Matsya kingdom. In 1949 Matsya was merged with the state of Rajasthan.

Bharatpur

📞05644 / POP 263,800

Bharatpur is famous for its Unesco–listed Keoladeo Ghana National Park (p148), a wetland and significant bird sanctuary. Apart from the park, Bharatpur has a few historical vestiges, though it would not be worth making the journey for these alone. The town is dusty, noisy and not particularly visitor friendly. Bharatpur hosts the boisterous and colourful Brij Festival (p144) just prior to Holi celebrations.

Keoladeo Ghana National Park lies 3km to the south of Bharatpur's centre.

◎ Sights

Lohagarh   HISTORIC BUILDING
Lohagarh, the early-18th-century Iron Fort, was so named because of its sturdy defences. Today still impressive, though also forlorn and derelict, it occupies the entire small artificial island in the town centre. The main entrance is the **Austdhatu (Eight-Metal) Gate** – apparently the spikes on the gate are made of eight different metals. The fort also has three much-decayed palaces within its precincts.

Maharaja Suraj Mahl, constructor of the fort and founder of Bharatpur, built two towers, the **Jawahar Burj** and the **Fateh Burj**, within the ramparts to commemorate his victories over the Mughals and the British. The Jawahar Burj viewing point is a short walk to the northeast of the museum along a steep path that starts opposite the large water tank. It was from here that the maharajas surveyed their city. It's a peaceful, evocative place capturing the cool breezes in a series of pavilions. The ceiling of one of the pavilions features badly deteriorating frescoes with hundreds of tiny scenes of daily life, elephants and chariots.

One of the palaces, centred on a tranquil courtyard, houses a seemingly forgotten **museum** (admission ₹10, free Mon, camera/ video ₹10/20, no photography inside museum;

⊘10am-4.30pm Sat-Thu). Downstairs is a Jain sculpture gallery that includes some beautiful 7th- to 10th-century sculpture, and most spectacularly, the palace's original *hammam* (bathhouse), which retains some fine carvings and frescoes. Upstairs, dusty cabinets contain royal toys, weapons – such as miniature cannons, some creepy animal trophies, and portraits and old photographs of the maharajas of Bharatpur. It's worth clambering up onto the roof for views across the city and other bird-inhabited palaces.

Ganga Temple   HINDU TEMPLE
Not far from the Lohiya Gate is this exquisite red sandstone two-storey temple dedicated to the goddess Ganga, with elaborately carved stone terraces. Construction started in 1845 during the rule of Maharaja Balwant Singh, but it was not finished until 1937, five generations later, during the reign of Maharaja Brijendra Sawai.

🛏 Sleeping & Eating

Don't be pressured by touts at Bharatpur train or bus stations. Most hotels can also can arrange guides and offer binocular and bike hire. Guests usually eat in the hotel they are staying at and most places offer a thali (all-you-can-eat meal) for between ₹80 and ₹180. All of the following options are within easy walking distance of the national park entrance, except for Shagun Guest House.

TOP⟩ **Birder's Inn**   HOTEL $$
CHOICE (📞227346; www.birdersinn.com; Bird Sanctuary Rd; s/d incl breakfast from ₹1600/2100; ❄@🛜🐾) The Birder's Inn is rightly the most popular base for exploring the park. The atmospheric stone and thatch-roof restaurant is a great place for a meal and to compare birdwatching stories. The rooms are airy, spacious, nicely decorated, have LCD TVs and are set far back from the road in well-tended gardens. The in-house naturalist welcomes guests and conducts tours. The hotel can arrange pick-up from Delhi airport and other taxi services.

Hotel Sunbird   HOTEL $$
(📞225701; www.hotelsunbird.com; Bird Sanctuary Rd; s/d from ₹1700/2000, cottages ₹2200/2500; ❄) Another well-run and popular place next door to Birder's Inn. Rooms are clean and comfortable and there's an appealing garden bar and restaurant with a good range of tasty dishes and cold beer. Packed lunches and guided tours for the park are available.

EASTERN RAJASTHAN

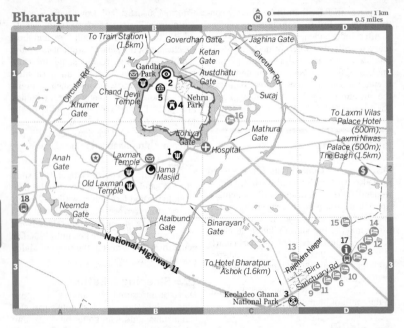

Bharatpur

Kiran Guest House   GUESTHOUSE **$**

(☏223845; www.kiranguesthouse.com; 364 Rajendra Nagar; r ₹150-300, with AC ₹750; ❋) Managed by eager-to-please brothers, this guesthouse delivers great value with seven simple, spacious, clean rooms and a pleasant rooftop where you can eat tasty home cooking. It's on a quiet road not far from the park. Nature guiding and free pick-up from the Bharatpur train and bus stations are offered.

Hotel Bharatpur Ashok   HOTEL **$$**

(☏222722; www.theashokgroup.com; s/d ₹2700/3000; ❋@) This lodge, run by the Indian Tourism Development Corporation (ITDC), is 1km inside the park and 8km from the Bharatpur train station. It's looking a little faded, and service is typically lax. However, the comfortable, quiet rooms have balconies with swing seats and there's a bar downstairs. The multicuisine restaurant's handy if you want something to eat while within the park (nonguests are welcome).

Laxmi Vilas Palace Hotel   HOTEL $$

(☏223523; www.laxmivilas.com; Kakaji-ki-Kothi, Old Agra Rd; s/d/ste ₹4400/4800/6100; ❄@☰) This exquisite heritage hotel, about equidistant between the national park and the town centre, was once owned by the younger son of Maharaja Jaswant Singh. Arched ceilings and heavy old furniture make for atmospheric rooms, set around a courtyard. A new 'palace', **Laxmi Niwas Palace**, with another 20 rooms for the same tariff, has been constructed next door. This place is a busy lunch stop for tour groups travelling between Jaipur and Agra.

The Bagh   HOTEL $$$

(☏225415; www.thebagh.com; Old Agra Rd; s/d from ₹6000/7500; ❄@☰) A picturesque hotel 2km from town, the Bagh has 23 elegant rooms spread out in separate pavilions nestled in a former royal orchard. All rooms boast cool marble floors, antique furnishings and wonderful bathrooms. Decor is traditional but the cool, clean lines have a contemporary feel. The 4-hectare garden is over 200 years old and has masses of birds if you're feeling too lazy to go to the park.

Royal Guest House   HOTEL $

(☏9414315457; www.royalguesthousebharatpur. com; r ₹250-750; ❄@) The ultrakeen management, who live on the premises, also do moneychanging and run an internet cafe here. The rooms are all very clean and fresh, and the rooftop restaurant is cosy. Guests can use a kitchen for self-catering, and have free access to the internet.

Falcon Guest House   HOTEL $

(☏223815; falconguesthouse@hotmail.com; Gori Shankur Colony; r ₹300-1600; ❄@) The Falcon may well be the pick of a bunch of hotels all in a row and all owned by the same extended family. It is a well-kept, snug place to stay, run by the affable Mrs Rajni Singh. Her husband, Tej, is an ornithologist and he's happy to answer any bird-related questions. There is a range of comfortable, good-sized rooms, and as many tariffs: more money gets you a softer mattress and private balcony. Flavoursome home-cooked food is served in the garden restaurant.

Spoonbill Hotel & Restaurant   HOTEL $

(☏223571; www.hotelspoonbill.com; Gori Shankur Colony; s ₹150-600, d ₹200-700; mains ₹30-150; ❄) The original Spoonbill has a variety of different rooms – all good-value and clean, if a bit worn. The place is run by a businesslike retired major and his son who also conducts

birdwatching tours. The hotel has excellent food, with curd from the family cow and Rajasthani delicacies, such as *churma* (sugar, cheese and dried fruit fried in butter), the royal dish of Rajasthan. There's often a campfire in winter.

Jungle Lodge   HOTEL $

(☏225622; www.junglelodge.dk; Gori Shankur Colony; r ₹200-400, with AC summer only ₹600; ❄@) Surrounded by an overgrown garden, the simple rooms, which could do with more ventilation, face onto a shady verandah. The more private and brighter rooms are upstairs. The owner is a naturalist, and home-cooked meals are available.

New Spoonbill Hotel & Restaurant
   HOTEL $

(☏223571; www.hotelspoonbill.com; Gori Shankur Colony; r ₹300-600; ❄@) Not to be confused with the Spoonbill Hotel & Restaurant, this place has simple but smart rooms, each with a small terrace. The larger rooms are great, with lots of windows. The dining room looks onto the garden.

Hotel Pratap Palace   HOTEL $

(☏225093; www.hotelpratappalace.net; Bird Sanctuary Rd; s/d ₹550/650, deluxe ₹950/1150, with AC ₹1400/1550; ❄@☰) This grand looking hotel offers spacious but faded rooms. The standard of upkeep at all tariff levels is variable, so look at a few rooms. The pool (if clean) is available for nonguests for ₹100 per person.

Hotel Pelican   HOTEL $

(☏224221; Bird Sanctuary Rd; r ₹150-450) This funky little hotel with old car windscreens for windows has an overgrown garden and modest room rates. There's a variety of rooms: from a pokey little cheapie with a shared bathroom to a couple of good-value doubles with attached bathroom, fans and TV.

Evergreen Guest House   HOTEL $

(☏225917; Gori Shankur Colony; s/d ₹200/300) This is a very basic option, with just two rooms. Nevertheless it is a good cheapie that satisfies customers with the option of rooftop or garden dining and home cooking. The owner also offers classes in Indian cooking.

Shagun Guest House   GUESTHOUSE $

(☏9828687488; rajeevshagun@hotmail.com; s/d ₹120/150, r without bathroom ₹100) It doesn't get much more basic than this. Down a lane inside Mathura Gate, you will find yourself well off the tourist trail with a little tree-shaded courtyard and friendly locals keen for a chat. The affable owner is knowledgeable about the national park and conducts village tours.

❶ Information

Main post office (☺10am-1pm & 2-5pm Mon-Sat) Near Gandhi Park.

Perch Forex (New Civil Lines; ☺5am-11pm) Cash travellers cheques, get credit-card advances or change money here.

Royal Forex (New Civil Lines; ☺6am-10pm;@) Moneychanger that has expanded into the hotel and internet cafe business (per hour ₹40).

Tourist Reception Centre (☎222542; ☺9.30am-6pm Mon-Fri) About 700m from the park entrance; sells maps of Bharatpur (₹10).

❶ Getting There & Away

Bus

There are regular buses to various places, including Agra (₹55, 1½ hours), Fatehpur Sikri (₹30, one hour), Jaipur (₹110, 4½ hours), Deeg (₹25, one hour) and Alwar (₹60, four hours). Buses leave from the main bus station, but also drop off and pick up passengers at the bus stop at the crossroads by the Tourist Reception Centre.

Train

The 19023/4 *Janata Express* leaves New Delhi (sleeper ₹120) at 1.05pm and arrives in Bharatpur at 5.30pm. It leaves Bharatpur at 8.10am, arriving in the capital at 12.50pm. The 12925/6 *Paschim Express* leaves New Delhi (sleeper/3AC/2AC/1AC ₹140/315/410/675) at 4.55pm and arrives in Bharatpur at 7.40pm. It leaves Bharatpur at 6.15am, arriving in the capital at 10.55pm.

There are several trains daily to Sawai Madhopur (sleeper/3AC/2AC/1AC ₹140/325/425/700) including the 12094 *Golden Temple Mail*, which departs at 10.40am and arrives at Sawai Madhopur at 1.05pm and then continues to Kota and Mumbai (Bombay).

To Agra (2nd class/sleeper/ AC chair/3AC/2AC/1AC ₹47/140/195/240/310/505), the 12966 *Udaipur-Gwalior Express* departs at 9.05am, arriving at Agra Cantt at 10.15am.

❶ Getting Around

An auto- or cycle-rickshaw from the bus station to the tourist office and most of the hotels should cost around ₹30 (₹35 from the train station). An excellent way to zip around is by hiring a bicycle, which can be done at many of the hotels or at the park entrance – see p149 for further details.

Keoladeo Ghana National Park

This famous bird sanctuary and **national park** (Indian/foreigner ₹55/400, video ₹400; ☺6am-6pm Apr-Sep, 6.30am-5pm Oct-Mar) has long been recognised as one of the world's most important bird breeding and feeding grounds. In a good monsoon season over one-third of the park can be submerged, hosting over 360 species within its 29 sq km. The marshland patchwork is a wintering area for aquatic birds, including visitors from Afghanistan, Turkmenistan, China and Siberia.

In recent years, however, poor monsoons and less water has meant fewer birds. In 2003 the Panchana Dam on the Gambhir River became operational and the park ceased to receive its usual monsoon water. In 2004 the park appealed for a higher allocation of water from the dam, but came up against fierce opposition from landholders. In 2007 the park was mostly dry and thousands of cattle grazed the grasslands that occupied the former wetlands. In early 2008 it was announced that floodwaters from the Yamuna River via the Govardhan drain would be piped to the park. In early 2011 this project was still being discussed but had not materialised. In the meantime, healthier monsoon seasons and an increased allocation from Panchana Dam has restored much of the wetlands and the bird population.

History

Keoladeo originated as a royal hunting reserve in the 1850s. Before then Maharaja Suraj Mahl, the founder of Bharatpur, built the Ajun Bund on the Gambhir River, converting a low-lying swamp into a reservoir. During the late 1800s further earthworks increased the water capacity and a network of canals and sluice gates diverted monsoon run-off into a series of impoundments. In doing so, a wetland ecosystem was created which, albeit artificial, was the perfect habitat for an astonishing variety of birds (as well as turtles, pythons and fish). It was named Keoladeo (one of Shiva's many incarnations) after the small temple that is located in the park.

Keoladeo continued to supply the maharajas' tables with fresh game until as late as 1965. A large tablet near the small temple in the park records that 12 November 1938 was a particularly bad day to be a duck – 4273 were shot by the then viceroy of India, Lord Linlithgow, and his party.

The post-Independence period was one of great turmoil. Local communities were keen to divert the canals, which feed the swamplands, for irrigation and to convert the wetlands into crops. Although this tension still exists, the conservationists won the day, and in 1956 the region was made a sanctuary, although hunting was not prohibited until 1972. In 1982 Keoladeo was declared a national park and in 1985 it was listed as a World Heritage Site.

Visiting the Park

The best time to visit is from October to February, when you will see many migratory birds.

Admission entitles you to one entrance per day; if you want to spend the day inside the park, carry plenty of drinking water, as birdwatching is thirsty work. There is a **bookshop** and a snack bar near the second checkpoint. You can also get a bite to eat at the **Hotel Bharatpur Ashok** (see p146) inside the park.

One narrow road (no motorised vehicles are permitted past checkpoint 2) runs through the park, and countless embankments thread their way between the shallow wetlands.

Hiring an experienced ornithologist guide will cost ₹100 per hour for up to five people and ₹120 per hour for more than six people. Guides can be hired at the park entrance. Many hotels are run by qualified guides or will arrange guides for you, who charge the same rate. All registered guides provide a good service, but you may find a guide who speaks better English by arranging one through your hotel. If you want a guide who speaks another language, it's also best to enquire at your hotel.

Only the government-authorised cycle-rickshaws (recognisable by the yellow license plate) are allowed to travel beyond checkpoint 2. You don't pay an admission fee for the drivers, but they charge ₹70 per hour. Some are very knowledgeable. However, these cycle-rickshaws can only travel along the park's larger tracks.

An excellent way to see the park is by hiring a bike/mountain bike (₹25/40 per six hours) at the park entrance. Having a bike is a wonderfully quiet way to travel, and allows you to avoid bottlenecks and take in the serenity on your own. You get a map with your entrance ticket.

See p145 for places to stay near the park.

Alwar

♪ 0144 / POP 313,300

Alwar has a rambling palace with an above-average museum packed with royal booty, testifying to its former importance as capital of a Rajput state. Alwar is perhaps the oldest of the Rajasthani kingdoms, forming part of the Matsya territories of Viratnagar in 1500 BC. It became known again in the 18th century under Pratap Singh, who pushed back the rulers of Jaipur to the south and the Jats of Bharatpur to the east, and who successfully resisted the Marathas. It was one of the first Rajput states to ally itself with the fledgling British empire, although British interference in Alwar's internal affairs meant that this partnership was not always amicable.

Not many tourists come here, so there is a refreshing lack of hustle, and you will find some colourful bazaars, leafy avenues as well as the remarkable palace. It is also the nearest town to **Sariska Tiger Reserve**, where you'll find a grand hunting lodge that is another relic of Alwar's royal past.

The city palace and museum are found in the northwest of the city, a steep 1km north of the bus stand. There's a collection of budget hotels a short distance to the east of the bus stand. The train station is on the eastern edge of town, and the main post office is about midway between it and the bus stand. Usually quiet, Alwar comes to life during the annual three-day festival of Alwar Utsav (p144).

◉ Sights

Bala Qila HISTORIC BUILDING

This imposing fort stands 300m above the city, its fortifications hugging the steep incline. Predating the time of Pratap Singh, it's one of the few forts in Rajasthan built before the rise of the Mughals, who used it as a base for attacking Ranthambhore. Babur and Akbar have stayed overnight here, and Prince Salim (later Emperor Jehangir) was exiled in Salim Mahal for three years. Now in ruins, unfortunately, the fort houses a radio transmitter station and parts can only be visited with permission from the superintendent of police. However, this is easy to get: just ask at the superintendent's office in the City Palace Complex. You can walk up to the fort entrance or take a rickshaw (it's a very steep couple of kilometres by foot and 7km by rickshaw).

SURAJ MAHL'S PALACE, DEEG

Deeg is a small, rarely visited, dusty tumult of a town. At its centre stands an incongruously glorious palace edged by stately formal gardens. **Suraj Mahl's Palace** (Indian/foreigner ₹5/100; ☺9.30am-5.30pm Sat-Thu) is one of India's most beautiful and carefully proportioned palace complexes. Pick up a map and brochure at the entrance and note that photography is not permitted in some of the *bhavans* (buildings).

Built in a mixture of Rajput and Mughal architectural styles, the 18th-century **Gopal Bhavan** is fronted by imposing arches to take full advantage of the early-morning light. Downstairs is a lower storey that becomes submerged during the monsoon as the water level of the adjacent tank, **Gopal Sagar**, rises. It was used by the maharajas until the early 1950s, and contains many original furnishings, including faded sofas, huge *punkas* (cloth fans) that are over 200 years old, chaise longues, a stuffed tiger, elephant-foot stands, and fine porcelain from China and France. In an upstairs room at the rear of the palace is an Indian-style marble dining table – a stretched oval-shaped affair raised just 20cm off the ground. Guests sat around the edge, and the centre was the serving area. In the maharaja's bedroom is an enormous, 3.6m by 2.4m wooden bed with silver legs.

Two large tanks lie alongside the palace, the aforementioned Gopal Sagar to the east and **Rup Sagar** to the west. The well-maintained gardens and flowerbeds, watered by the tanks, continue the extravagant theme with over 2000 fountains. Many of these fountains are in working order and coloured waters pour forth during the monsoon festival in August.

The **Keshav Bhavan** (Summer or Monsoon Pavilion) is a single-storey edifice with five arches along each side. Tiny jets spray water from the archways and metal balls rumble around in a water channel imitating monsoon thunder. Deeg's massive walls (which are up to 28m high) and 12 vast bastions, some with their cannons still in place, are also worth exploring. You can walk up to the top of the walls from the palace.

Other bhavans (in various states of renovation) include the marble **Suraj Bhavan**, reputedly taken from Delhi and reassembled here, the **Kishan Bhavan** and, along the north side of the palace grounds, the **Nand Bhavan**.

Deeg is about 36km north of Bharatpur, and is an easy day trip (and there's nowhere good to stay) from Bharatpur or Alwar by car. All the roads to Deeg are rough and the buses crowded. Frequent buses run to and from Alwar (₹45, 2½ hours) and Bharatpur (₹25, one hour).

City Palace Complex HISTORIC BUILDING

Below the fort sprawls the colourful and convoluted City Palace, or Vinay Vilas Mahal, with massive gates and a tank reflecting a symmetrical series of ghats and pavilions. Today most of the complex is occupied by government offices, overflowing with piles of dusty papers and soiled by pigeons and splatters of *paan* (a mixture of betel nut and leaves for chewing).

Hidden within the City Palace is the excellent **Alwar Museum** (Indian/foreigner ₹5/50; ☺10am-5pm Tue-Sun). Its eclectic exhibits evoke the extravagance of the maharajas' lifestyle: stunning weapons, stuffed Scottish pheasants, royal ivory slippers, erotic miniatures, royal vestments, a solid silver table, and stone sculptures, such as an 11th-century sculpture of Vishnu. There are also some striking 'widescreen' paintings of Imperial processions. Somewhat difficult to find in the Kafkaesque tangle of government offices, it's on the top floor of the palace, up a ramp from the main courtyard. However, there are plenty of people around to point you in the right direction and from there you can follow the signs.

Cenotaph of Maharaja Bakhtawar Singh
HISTORIC BUILDING

This double-storey edifice, resting on a platform of sandstone, was built in 1815 by Maharaja Vinay Singh in memory of his father. To gain access to the cenotaph, take the steps on the far left when facing the palace. The cenotaph is also known as the Chhatri of Moosi Rani, after one of the mistresses of Bakhtawar Singh who performed *sati* (self-immolation) on his funeral pyre – after this act she was promoted to wifely status. Every day several women can be seen paying homage to the maharani by pouring holy water over raised sculpted footprints of the deceased royal couple. You will discover fine carving on the interior of the cenotaph (shoes should be removed), but unfortunately the paintings on the ceiling have almost disappeared. The cenotaph is located alongside a beautiful tank, which is lined by a row of ghats and temples.

🛏 Sleeping

As not many tourists stop here, Alwar's hotels are mostly aimed at budget business travellers and are not particularly good value. Contact the **Tourist Reception Centre** (☏2347348; Nehru Rd; ☺10am-5pm Mon-Sat) for details about the houses involved in the Paying Guest House Scheme (₹400 to ₹1500).

TOP CHOICE **Alwar Hotel** HOTEL $$

(☏2700012; www.alwarhotel.com; 26 Manu Rd; s/d incl breakfast ₹1750/2500, ste ₹2850; ❄@☎) Set back from the road in a neatly manicured garden, this well-run hotel has spacious, comfortable rooms. This is easily the best option in town, and staff can be helpful with general information and sightseeing advice. Tours to Sariska and visits to sporting and swimming clubs can be arranged. The Alwar Hotel also boasts one of the town's better multicuisine restaurants, **Angeethi**.

Hotel Aravali HOTEL $
(☏2332883; www.hotelaravali.co.in; Nehru Rd; s/d from ₹450/500, with AC from ₹850/950; ❄@❄) This is also one of the town's better choices, but nevertheless is a bit like *Fawlty Towers* without the humour. Its room options stretch to midrange and there's a summer-only pool. Rowdy guests can be a problem – if the hotel isn't full, request a quiet room. To reach the hotel, turn left out of the train station and it's about 100m down the road.

RTDC Hotel Meenal HOTEL $$
(☏2347352; Topsingh Circle; s/d ₹1000/1100, with AC ₹1200/1300; ❄) This is a respectable option with bland and tidy rooms typical of the chain. It is located about 1km south of town, so it's quiet and leafy, though it's a long way from the action.

🍴 Eating

Prem Pavitra Bhojnalaya INDIAN $
(☏2700925; Old Bus Stand; mains ₹40-70; ☺10am-10pm; ❄) Alwar's renowned restaurant has been going since 1957. It is in the heart of the old town and serves fresh, tasty pure veg food – try the delicious *aloo parathas* (bread stuffed with spicy potato) and *palak paneer* (unfermented cheese cubes

in spinach purée). The servings are big and half-serves are available. You have to pay 10% extra to eat in the air-conditioned section – but it is worth it. Do finish off with the special *kheer* (creamy rice pudding).

Angeethi MULTICUISINE $
(Alwar Hotel, Manu Rd; mains ₹50-100; ☺Tue-Sun; ❄) Alwar Hotel's restaurant serves first-rate Indian, Continental and Chinese food; the South Indian selection is particularly good. It's slightly gloomy in the restaurant but you can eat in the pleasant gardens.

Thali House – New South Indian Café
SOUTH INDIAN $
(mains ₹40-80; ☺9am-10pm) This dimly lit place, opposite the Gopal Cinema, has a shuffling, half-hearted atmosphere, but it's popular with families and offers cheap, excellent South Indian dishes, such as delicious *masala dosa* (curried vegetables inside a crisp pancake) and good value thalis.

Inderlok Restaurant VEGETARIAN $
(Company Bagh Rd; mains ₹110-140; ☺noon-3pm & 7-11pm) This main road restaurant has lots of palatable veg and unusual *paneer* choices. There's a typically hushed and low-lit ambience in the AC room, which is plain and functional. It's popular for business-lunch deals and with courting couples.

Tija CAFE $
(Nangli Circle; ☺10am-10pm) This small cafe is a town favourite and a meeting point for teenagers. Grab a coffee (hot/cold ₹20/25) or one of the excellent lassis (₹20).

ℹ Information

ICICI ATM Next door to the State Bank of Bikaner & Jaipur.

Merharwal's Internet Cyber Zoné (1 Company Bagh Rd; per hr ₹40; ☺7am-10pm) Opposite Inderlok restaurant.

State Bank of Bikaner & Jaipur (Company Bagh Rd) Near the bus stand. Changes travellers cheques and major currencies and has an ATM.

Tourist Reception Centre (☏2347348; Nehru Rd; ☺10am-5pm Mon-Sat) Located near the train station, this helpful centre has a map of Alwar and information on homestays.

ℹ Getting There & Away

Bus

From Alwar there are numerous buses to Sariska (₹21, 1½ hours, half-hourly 5.15am to 8.30pm), which go on to Jaipur (₹80, four hours). There are also frequent (bumpy) services to Bharatpur

(₹50, four hours) for Keoladeo Ghana National Park, and Deeg (₹45, 2½ hours). Buses to Delhi take two different routes (₹95, via Tijara/Ramgarh four/five hours, half-hourly).

Car

A return taxi to Sariska Tiger Reserve (including a stop at Siliserh) will cost you around ₹1150.

Train

The 2015/6 *Shatabdi Express* passes through Alwar. It departs for Ajmer (AC chair/1st class ₹435/830, four hours) at 8.39am and stops at Jaipur (₹320/605) at 10.45am. For Delhi, it departs at 7.30pm (₹335/640, 2½ hours). The 2461 *Mandore Express* to Jodhpur (2AC/3AC ₹793/578, 10½ hours) departs Alwar at 9.45pm.

❶ Getting Around

An autorickshaw/taxi from the train station to the town centre should cost about ₹40/125. You can hire bicycles near the train station (₹70 per day).

Around Alwar

SILISERH
☎0144

For a breath of fresh air, this former royal retreat, 20km southwest of Alwar (off the road to Sariska Tiger Reserve), is one of the state's lesser known secrets. Uninhabited forested hills encircle a 10.5 sq km lake, and perched above the lake is the erstwhile hunting lodge – a cream-coloured confection with cupolas, balconies and courtyards. It was built by the Alwar Maharaja Vinay Singh in 1845, and is now the government-run RTDC Hotel Lake Palace. Apart from the **Lake Palace** (admission ₹30) there's not much else here except for some touristy waterborne activities and cheap restaurants. You can get a water view by hiring a decidedly unseaworthy **paddleboat** (per 30min ₹90), or putt-putting around on a **motorboat** (per 15min ₹450).

The **RTDC Hotel Lake Palace** (☎2886322; s/d ₹990/1250, with AC ₹1850/2200, ste ₹3150/3500; ❅), within the palace, has wonderful lake views and a relaxed atmosphere, but you will have to put up with the erratic cleanliness and service, the very ordinary food and the evening crowds of daytrippers. The admission charge can be offset by buying a meal at the restaurant. Breakfast is complimentary Monday to Thursday, while higher room rates apply on Friday to Sunday when lunch or dinner is included.

A taxi from Alwar to Siliserh and back will cost you about ₹600.

KESROLI
☎01468

This pleasant small town, 12km from Alwar, has a rambling 14th-century fort (with seven turrets) – now a hotel – still keeping a watch over bucolic agricultural scenery. The fort ramparts offer splendid views across the fields, where the hard-working villagers make splashes of colour.

The fairy-tale hotel **Hill Fort Kesroli** (☎289352; www.neemranahotels.com; r ₹2500-6750) is an authentic stone fortress perching on a rocky knoll that would set any kid's imagination flying. It is a bit haphazard, with mysterious passageways, changing floor levels and 21 very different, character-loaded rooms. It's an isolated, self-sufficient place set in tranquil countryside, with bike rides and car excursions available to break any self-imposed siege. Breakfast is complimentary, lunch is ₹400 and dinner costs ₹550.

Many guests will be from small tour groups, but plenty of independent travellers rest their weary feet here for a couple of stress-free days. From Alwar you can take a taxi or an autorickshaw to the fort.

Sariska Tiger Reserve
☎0144

Enclosed within the dramatic, shadowy folds of the Aravallis, the **Sariska Tiger Reserve** (Indian/foreigner ₹60/450, vehicle ₹250; ⊙ticket sales 7am-3.30pm Oct-Mar, 6.30am-4pm Apr-Sep, park closes at sunset) is a tangle of remnant semideciduous jungle and craggy canyons sheltering streams and lush greenery. It covers 866 sq km (including a core area of 498 sq km), and is home to peacocks, monkeys, majestic sambars, nilgai, chital, wild boars and jackals.

Although Project Tiger has been in charge of the sanctuary since 1979, there has been a dramatic failure in tiger protection. In 2004 there were an estimated 18 tigers in Sariska; however, this was called into question after an investigation by the WWF. That report prompted the federal government to investigate what has happened to the tigers of this reserve.

Sariska is in any case a fascinating sanctuary. Unlike most national parks, it opens year-round, although the best time to spot wildlife is November to March, and you'll see most wildlife in the evening. During July and August your chance of spotting wildlife is minimal, as the animals move on to high-

Sariska Tiger Reserve has taken centre stage in one of India's most publicised wildlife dramas. It wasn't until 2005 that it was revealed that the tiger population here had been eliminated.

An enquiry into the crisis recommended fundamental management changes before tigers should be reintroduced to the reserve. Extra funding was proposed to cover relocation of villages within the park as well as increasing the protection force. While poaching is the most likely cause of the extinction of the last of Sariska's tigers, a WWF report highlighted the issues of widespread woodcutting and grazing within park boundaries and the low morale among park staff. Action on the recommendations has been slow and incomplete, despite extensive media coverage and a high level of concern in India.

Nevertheless, tigers from Ranthambhore National Park were moved by helicopter to Sariska. The first pair were air-lifted in 2008. By 2010 five tigers had been transferred, however in November 2010 the male of the original pair was found dead in suspicious circumstances. Later it was confirmed that it had been poisoned. Authorities pointed the finger at local villagers who are not supportive of the reintroduction. The underlying problem – the inevitable battle between India's poorest and ever-expanding village populace with rare and phenomenally valuable wildlife on their doorstep – remains largely unresolved despite official plans to relocate and reimburse villagers.

Only time will tell if this reintroduction is successful – another big concern is that the reintroduced tigers are all closely related – but, as things stand, Sariska remains a sad indictment of tiger conservation in India, from the top government officials down to the underpaid forest guard.

er ground, and the park is open primarily for temple pilgrimage rather than wildlife viewing.

Proposals to stop private car access and to end the free access to pilgrims visiting the Hanuman temple often get press coverage, but to date there has been no further action taken.

◉ Sights

Besides wildlife, Sariska has some fantastic sights within the reserve or around its peripheries, which are well worth seeking out. If you take a longer tour, you can ask to visit one or more of these. A couple of them are also accessible by public bus.

Kankwari Fort   HISTORIC BUILDING

Deep inside the sanctuary, this imposing small jungle fort, 22km away from Sariska, offers amazing views over the plains of the national park, dotted with red mud-brick villages. This is the inaccessible place that Aurangzeb chose to imprison his brother, Dara Shikoh, Shah Jahan's chosen heir to the Mughal throne, for several years before he was beheaded. A four- to five-hour **jeep safari** (one to five passengers plus guide) to Kankwari Fort from the Forest Reception Office near the reserve entrance costs ₹1600, plus guide fee (₹150).

Hanuman Temple   HINDU TEMPLE

You can visit a small Hanuman temple, deep in the park. Its recumbent idol, adapted from a rock, is painted orange and is shaded by silver parasols. People give offerings of incense and receive tiny parcels of holy ash. From the temple there is a pleasant walk, for over a kilometre to **Pandu pol**, a gaping natural arch. The rough trail follows an ephemeral stream beneath sheer ravine walls, which merge at the 'gateway'. There is a deep green pool below the arch and the track becomes a steep, slippery climb, best left alone.

Neelkantheshwar Temple   HISTORIC BUILDING

Around 35km from Sariska is an 8th-century temple complex, up a dramatically winding road that allows fantastic views. It sits on a small plateau ringed by low hills where the old defensive wall is still visible. It's said that the temples remained preserved because bees chased Aurangzeb away when he tried to attack them. The **main temple** (photography prohibited) is dedicated to Shiva. The small pod-like shrines outside the temple are priests' graves. A little bit further away, through a tangle of vegetation (ask locals to point out the right path), is a **Jain temple** built from orange-red sandstone, with a huge stone statue of the 23rd *tirthankar* (teacher) known locally as Nogaza.

Bhangarh

HISTORIC SITE

Around 55km from Sariska, beyond the inner park sanctuary and out in open countryside, is this deserted, well-preserved, notoriously haunted city. It was founded in 1631 by Madho Singh, and had 10,000 dwellings, but was suddenly deserted about 300 years ago for reasons that remain mysterious. The favoured explanation is that a magician who loved the queen found his love unrequited and cursed the city. The buildings today, in their wonderful setting of unspoilt countryside, are largely restored, which gives a remarkable sense of the city and its town planning. Temples and *chhatris* (cenotaphs, literally 'umbrellas') dot the surrounding area.

After you enter the main gate, there is a **haveli**, once a grand house, to the right. Beyond it, you can walk through the market area's well-defined and ordered bazaars up to the ruined, evocative palace for striking views. Within the complex are two well-preserved, ornate **Shiva temples**. One has its lingam (phallic image of Shiva) still intact, and lies alongside a green-shaded tank.

Bhangarh can be reached by a bus that runs twice daily through the sanctuary (₹35) to nearby Golaka village. Check what time the bus returns, otherwise you risk getting stranded.

⌒ Tours

Private cars, including taxis, are limited to sealed roads. The best way to visit the park is by 4WD gypsy (open-topped, takes five passengers), which can explore off the main tracks. Gypsy safaris start at the park entrance and you'll be quoted ₹1050 for three hours, or ₹3200 for a full day. They can take up to five people. Guides are available (₹150 for three hours).

Bookings can be made at the **Forest Reception Office** (☏2841333; Jaipur Rd), directly opposite the Hotel Sariska Palace, which is where buses will drop you.

🛏 Sleeping & Eating

TOP CHOICE **Alwar Bagh**　　HOTEL **$$**
(☏2885231; www.alwarbagh.com; r & tent ₹2800, ste ₹3500; breakfast/lunch/dinner ₹150/350/350; ❋❋) This is a very peaceful option located in the village of Dhawala, between Alwar (14km) and Sariska (19km). It can arrange pick-up and drop-off from Alwar and can also arrange safaris of Sariska. The bright heritage-style hotel boasts traditional styling, spotless rooms and romantic

tents, an organic orchard, a garden restaurant and a gorgeous swimming pool.

RTDC Hotel Tiger Den　　HOTEL **$$**
(☏2841342; s/d incl breakfast & lunch or dinner; ₹1290/1850, with AC ₹2150/2800; ❋) Hotel Tiger Den is a quasi-Soviet block, backed by a rambling garden. Accommodation and meals are drab, but the rooms have balconies and occupy a pleasant setting close to the reserve entrance. Bring a mosquito net or repellent.

Sariska Tiger Heaven　　HOTEL **$$**
(☏224815; www.sariskatigerheaven.com; s/d with full board ₹3500/4000, with AC ₹4000/5000; ❋❋) This is an isolated place about 3km west of the bus stop at Thanagazi village and free pick-up is on offer. Rooms are set in stone-and-tile cottages and have big beds and windowed alcoves. It's a tranquil, if overpriced, place to stay. Staff can arrange jeeps and guides to the park and pick-up from Jaipur (₹1200).

Hotel Sariska Palace　　HERITAGE HOTEL **$$$**
(☏9214451327; www.thesariskapalace.in; r incl breakfast ₹7000, ste from ₹13,500, mains ₹350-500; ❋❋) Near the park entrance is this imposing former hunting lodge of the maharajas of Alwar. There's a driveway leading from opposite the Forest Reception Office. Rooms have LCD TVs, soaring ceilings and soft mattresses. Those in the annexe by the swimming pool have newer interiors and good views. The Fusion Restaurant here serves expensive Indian and Continental dishes and guests can help themselves to the buffet. Entry is ₹500, which is redeemable against accommodation or meals. It's set in 20 hectares, and it's possible to take short horse and camel rides around the grounds.

Amanbagh　　HOTEL **$$$**
(☏065-68873337; www.amanresorts.com; r from US$700; ❋@❋❋) Set 10km from Bhangarh and isolated among the folds of the Aravalli range, is this vastly opulent hotel. It's a lush walled compound that was once a site for the hunting camps of the maharaja of Alwar. The splendid rooms have domed ceilings and huge baths – it's like walking into a movie set – and the most expensive have a private pool.

ⓘ Getting There & Away

Sariska is 35km from Alwar, a convenient town from which to approach the reserve. There are frequent (and crowded) buses from Alwar (₹21, one to 1½ hours, at least hourly) and on to Jaipur (₹75). Buses stop in front of the Forest Reception Office.

Patan

☑ 01574

Patan is a small village in a corner of Rajasthan – it's a wonderful place to stay with a fascinating story to tell. Patan is a 23km detour off the Delhi–Jaipur National Hwy 8 at Kot Puli, which is 100km from Jaipur and 160km from Delhi. Patan's place in history was sealed when one of Rajasthan's epic battles (yes, there were many) took place here in 1790. On one side were the Rajputs, loosely affiliated with the Mughal armies, and on the other side, the well-trained Maratha armies who enjoyed the services of French mercenary, General Benoite de Boigne. The French general won the day and the Rajputs lost more than men and pride. Patan itself was looted for three days and to this day the old town remains largely abandoned within its crumbling walls.

Patan remains the homeland of the Tanwar Rajputs, and the palace, which was built after the battle, has been beautifully restored into a peaceful and luxurious retreat by the descendants of the royal family. **Patan Mahal** (☑282311 or Jaipur ☑0141-2200033; www .patanmahal.com; s/d incl breakfast ₹4500/5000; ste ₹6000; ❈@≋), is owned and managed by Rao Digvijay Singh, who has for many years run the Madhuban, a hotel in Jaipur. The palace rooms have been painstakingly restored and decorated and the organic gardens supply the kitchen. This is a relaxing retreat where you won't be distracted by TV – you can laze in a luxurious marble pool or trek up to the battle-scarred ruins of the first palace and even to the fort, to see the handiwork of de Boigne's cannon. Alternatively, you can quietly read a book in the garden or venture into the village and watch the women making *lac* (resin) bangles.

Neemrana

☑ 01494

This town lies about 75km north of Alwar on the main Delhi–Jaipur Hwy, a short distance to the south of the Haryana border. The reason to visit is the magnificent **fortress palace** (nonguest admission ₹500 for 2hr visit; ☺9am-4pm), 2km away from Neemrana village. The entrance fee can be offset against accommodation, a meal (only from 50% of meal cost), or a ride on the flying fox. Dating from 1464, it was from here that the Rajput

Maharaja Prithviraj Chauhan III reigned, and it's now one of Rajasthan's oldest luxury hotels.

The magnificent **Neemrana Fort Palace** (☑246007; www.neemranahotels.com; s/d/ste from ₹2500/3500/9000; ❈@≋) surmounts a fortified rugged plateau. The fort rises an amazing 10 levels, set in 25 acres among the folds of the Aravalli Hills. Unfortunately the plains below the fort are rapidly being swallowed by belching industries. Hotel rooms are decorated in a mixture of Rajput and colonial styles, and are massively varied – you should try to get one with a balcony or terrace. The fort layout is fascinatingly complex, with hidden courtyards and terraces, and corridors that resemble mazes.

For those who want to add a bit of adrenalin to their visit, **Flying Fox** (www.flyingfox. asia; adult/child ₹1330/1660; ☺9am-4pm, closed Jun) have a two-hour circuit of five zip lines flying back and forth above the fort's bastions. Equipment and safety standards are very good and you are given a brief training session before you start. Flying Fox has a desk above Aranya Terrace inside the fort. There are decent discounts for booking online at least one day before.

❶ Getting There & Away

Buses on the main Delhi to Jaipur route generally stop at Behror, 14km from Neemrana (from where it's a further 2km to the hotel). A taxi from Behror to the hotel will cost about ₹350.

Ajmer

☑ 0145 / POP 557,000

Ajmer is a bustling chaotic city around 130km southwest of Jaipur. It surrounds the tranquil lake of Ana Sagar, and is itself ringed by the rugged Aravalli hills. Ajmer is Rajasthan's most important site in terms of Islamic history and heritage. It contains one of India's most important Muslim pilgrimage centres – the shrine of Khwaja Muin-ud-din Chishti, a venerated Sufi saint who founded the Chishtiya order, the prime Sufi order in India today. As well as some superb examples of early Muslim architecture, Ajmer is also a significant centre for the Jain religion, possessing an amazing golden Jain temple. However, most travellers just use Ajmer as a stepping stone to nearby Pushkar, a supremely sacred town to Hindus and a former hippy hangout. With Ajmer's combination of high-voltage crowds, commerce and

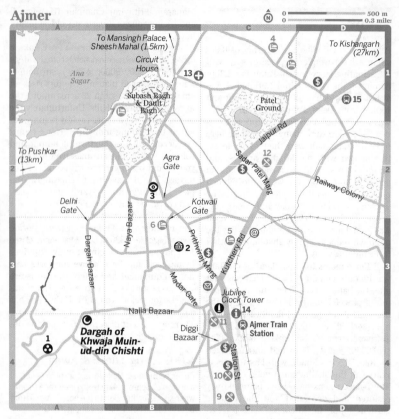

traffic, most travellers choose to stay in laid-back Pushkar, and visit on a day trip.

Ajmer gets very busy during Ramadan, and the anniversary of the saint's death – The Urs (see p144).

History

Ajmer once had considerable strategic importance. Located on the major trade route between Delhi and the ports of Gujarat, it was fought over for centuries. Its significance was such that its rulers, from the time of the Turks until the East India Company, tried to keep Ajmer under direct control.

The city was founded in the 7th century by Ajaipal Chauhan, who constructed a hill fort and named the place Ajaimeru (Invincible Hill). Ajmer was ruled by the Chauhans until the late 12th century, when Prithviraj Chauhan lost it to Mohammed of Ghori. It became part of the sultanate in Delhi and remained

so until 1326. Ajmer then entered a tumultuous period when it was continually fought over by surrounding states, including the sultans of Delhi and Gujarat, and the rulers of Mewar (Udaipur) and Marwar (Jaipur).

Later in its history, Ajmer became a favourite residence of the great Mughals. One of the first contacts between the Mughals and the British occurred in Ajmer when Emperor Jehangir (who lived here for three years) met Sir Thomas Roe in 1616.

In 1659 Aurangzeb battled and won here against his brother Dara Shikoh, changing the course of succession and signalling the end of the Mughal empire.

The city was subsequently taken by the Scindias and, in 1818, was handed over to the British, becoming one of the few places in Rajasthan controlled directly by the British rather than being part of a princely state. The British set up Mayo College here in 1875, a prestigious school in an overexcited building, exclusively for the Indian nobility. Today it's open to all boys (whose parents can afford the fees). Other monuments that stand as reminders of Ajmer's colonial past are the Edward Memorial Hall, Ajmer Club and Jubilee Clock Tower.

◉ Sights

Ana Sagar
LAKE

This large lake, created in the 12th century by damming the River Luni, is set against the blue-grey hills that are reflected on its oily surface. On its bank are two green parks, the **Subash Bagh** and **Dault Bagh**, containing a series of marble pavilions erected in 1637 by Shah Jahan. There are good views towards Ajmer from the hill beside the Dault Bagh, particularly at sunset. It's a popular place for an evening stroll, though you may get quite a lot of attention. Pedalos and motorboats can be hired from the Fun N Joy Boat Club.

Dargah of Khwaja Muin-ud-din Chishti
SUFI SHRINE

(www.dargahajmer.com; ⏰5am-9pm winter, 4am-9pm summer) This is the tomb of a Sufi saint, Khwaja Muin-ud-din Chishti, who came to Ajmer from Persia in 1192 and died here in 1236. The tomb gained its significance during the time of the Mughals – many emperors added to the buildings here. Construction of the shrine was completed by Humayun, and the gate was added by the Nizam of Hyderabad. Akbar used to make the pilgrimage to the dargah from Agra every year.

You have to cover your head in certain parts of the shrine, so remember to take a scarf or cap, although there are plenty for sale at the colourful bazaar leading to the dargah, along with floral offerings and delicious toffees.

Following a fatal bomb blast in October 2007, security is extremely tight, adding to the usual bottleneck of pilgrims at the entrance. The first gate is the **Nizam Gate**, built in 1915 up some steps to protect it from the rains. The green-and-white mosque, **Akbari Masjid**, on the right was constructed by Akbar in 1571 and is now Moiniua Usmania Darul-Uloom, an Arabic and Persian School for religious education. The second gate was built by Shah Jahan, and is often called the **Nakkarkhana** because it has two large *nakkharas* (drums) fixed above it. In an inner court there is another mosque, built by Shah Jahan. Of white marble, it has 11 arches and a Persian inscription running the full length of the building.

The third gate, **Buland Darwaza**, dates from the 16th century. It's tall – about 28m high – and whitewashed, and leads into the dargah courtyard. Flanking the entrance of the courtyard are the *degs* (large iron cauldrons), one donated by Akbar in 1567, the other by Jehangir in 1631, for offerings for the poor.

The saint's tomb has a marble dome, and the tomb inside is surrounded by a silver platform. Pilgrims believe that the saint's spirit will intercede on their behalf in matters of illness, business or personal problems, so the notes and holy string attached to the railings around are thanks or requests.

THE INCLUSIVE SAINT

Born in eastern Persia sometime in 1138 or 1139, Khwaja Muin-ud-din Chishti was orphaned in his early teens and lived on the proceeds of his ancestral orchards. According to legend, a holy man passed his garden and when Khwaja rushed out to greet him, the holy man gave him some food that enlightened him. Khwaja then renounced all worldly goods, became a *fakir* (Muslim holy man) and began to wander in search of knowledge. He visited Samarkand and Bukhara, great centres of Islamic learning, and absorbed all he could from great Central Asian Sufis – theirs was an Islam with an emphasis on devotion, mysticism and miracles. He then settled in Baghdad, and later made a pilgrimage to Medina for the hajj, where he heard a divine voice telling him to go to Hindustan. Now in his 50s, he wandered to India, arriving in Ajmer in 1192, where he settled on a hill by Ana Sagar. His beliefs and life of meditation and fasting – it's said he only ate one *chapati* (unleavened bread) every eight days – brought him great renown, and people flocked to him to hear his teachings. Even Mohammed of Ghori took time off raiding temples to pay his respects to the holy man.

His preachings were notably generous and inclusive. He spoke to Hindus as much as to Muslims, emphasising that theirs were different approaches along the same path. Hindus could relate to many aspects of Sufism (for example, holy men renouncing everything except their faith bears considerable resemblance to Hindu practice). He preached against discrimination and differentiation between believers of different faiths.

In 1236 he died, aged 97, and was buried in his simple brick cell, now covered by its elaborate shrine. In tribute to his teachings and beliefs, it is regarded as a holy place by people of many different faiths.

At the entrance, *khadims* (Muslim holy servants or mosque attendants) wielding donation books will ask you for cash. It's likely you'll be asked for more money again, where you might be blessed with the edge of the tomb blanket. If you don't want to give, just be firm about it or give a small amount.

Despite the hustle, it's a fascinating shrine with a sense of profound significance. It's good to visit in the evening, when it's decorated in twinkling lights and there are *qawwali* singers, who sing verses in praise of the Prophet and saints.

Pilgrims and Sufis come from all over the world on the anniversary of the saint's death, the Urs, in the seventh month of the lunar calendar, Jyaistha. The saint retired to his cloister for a long meditation, and when it was opened six days later he was dead, hence the festival lasts six days. It's an interesting time, but the crowds can be suffocating. Many pilgrims also come here in the month of Ramadan.

Adhai-din-ka-Jhonpra　　　HISTORIC SITE
Beyond the dargah, on the town outskirts, are the extraordinary ruins of the Adhai-din-ka-Jhonpra (Two-and-a-Half-Day Building) mosque. According to legend, construction took 2½ days. Others say it was named after a festival lasting 2½ days. It was built as a Sanskrit college, but in 1198 Mohammed of Ghori seized Ajmer and converted the building into a mosque by adding a seven-arched wall covered with Islamic calligraphy in front of the pillared hall.

Although in need of restoration, it's an exquisite piece of architecture, with soaring domes, pillars and a beautiful arched screen, largely built from pieces of Jain and Hindu temples.

Taragarh　　　FORT
(Star Fort; admission free; ☉sunrise to sunset) About 3km and a steep 1½-hour climb beyond the Adhai-din-ka-Jhonpra mosque, the ancient Taragarh commands a superb view over the city (accessible by car). Built by Ajaipal Chauhan, the town's founder, it saw lots of military action during Mughal times and was later used as a British sanatorium.

Nasiyan (Red) Temple　　　JAIN TEMPLE
(Prithviraj Marg; admission ₹10; ☉8am-4.30pm) This marvellous Jain temple was built in 1865. It's also known as the Golden Temple, due to its amazing display – its double-storey temple hall is filled with a huge golden diorama depicting the Jain concept of the ancient world, with 13 continents and oceans, the intricate golden city of Ayodhya, flying peacock and elephant gondolas, and gilded elephants with many tusks. The hall

is decorated with gold, silver and precious stones. It's unlike any other temple in Rajasthan and is worth a visit. Children will love the imaginative display.

Akbar's Palace   MUSEUM

Not far from the main post office, Akbar built this imposing building in 1570 – partly as a pleasure retreat, but mainly to keep an eye on pesky local chiefs. This is just part of the original impressive fortifications. It saw life as an arms magazine during the British rule, and is still known locally as the 'Magazine'. It houses the underwhelming **government museum** (Indian/foreigner ₹5/50; ⊙9.45am-5.15pm Tue-Sun), with a small collection of old weapons, miniature paintings, ancient rock inscriptions and stone sculptures that date back to the 8th century.

🛏 Sleeping

You'll be accosted by autorickshaw drivers the minute you step off the bus or train and it's usually a far better idea to hop on a bus and stay in nearby Pushkar. The **Tourist Reception Centre** (p160) has details about Ajmer's Paying Guest House Scheme, which gives you the opportunity to stay with an Indian family.

Haveli Heritage Inn   HOTEL $

(☏2621607; www.haveliheritageinn.com; Kutchery Rd; r ₹650-1850; ❇) Set in a 140-year-old *haveli*, this is a welcoming city-centre oasis and arguably Ajmer's best budget choice. The high-ceilinged rooms are spacious, simply decorated, air-cooled and set well back from the busy road. There's a pleasant, grassy courtyard and the hotel is infused with a family atmosphere, complete with home-cooked meals.

Badnor House   GUESTHOUSE $$

(☏2627579; www.badnorhouse.com; Civil Lines; d incl breakfast ₹2500, ste ₹2800; ❇) This guesthouse provides an excellent opportunity to stay with a delightful family. The down-to-earth hospitality includes three new heritage-style doubles and an older-style, spacious and comfortable self-contained suite with a private courtyard.

Mansingh Palace   HOTEL $$$

(☏2425956; www.mansinghhotels.com; Circular Rd; s/d from ₹4600/5400, ste ₹9000; ❇@❇) This modern place, on the shores of Ana Sagar, is rather out of the way, but has attractive and comfortable rooms, some with views and balconies. The hotel has a shady garden, a bar and a good restaurant, the **Sheesh Mahal**.

RTDC Hotel Khadim   HOTEL $$

(☏2627490; Civil Lines; s/d from ₹990/1200, with AC ₹1500/1800; ❇) This RTDC option is welcoming and is convenient to the bus station. It has a decent restaurant and bar and well-maintained rooms set in quiet grounds. The bright, air-conditioned rooms have soft beds.

Hotel Merwara Estate   HERITAGE HOTEL $$$

(☏2420691; www.merwaraestate.com; Dault Bagh; s/d from ₹6000/7000, ste ₹10000; ❇@❇) Overlooking Ana Sagar and Dault Bagh is this enormous heritage property, part of which was constructed in 1887 for the British High Commissioner. Rooms are high-ceilinged affairs, some with enormous windows and fine views. However, the echoing corridors and vast, dusty spaces are not particularly cosy. There's a vegetarian multi-cuisine restaurant and coffee shop. Note that it is a popular wedding venue.

Hotel Ajmeru   HOTEL $

(☏2431103; Khailand Market; s/d from ₹500/600, with AC ₹900/1100; ❇) This hotel with a veg restaurant and small tidy rooms can be found just past the narrow Kotwali Gate off Prithviraj Marg. It's convenient to the railway station, Jain Temple and Dargah.

🍴 Eating

Sheesh Mahal   MULTICUISINE $$

(Circular Rd; mains ₹150-350; ⊙noon-3pm & 7-10.30pm) This upmarket restaurant, located in Ajmer's top hotel, the Mansingh Palace, offers Indian, Continental and Chinese dishes as well as a buffet when the tour groups pass through. The service is slick and the food is very good; it also boasts a bar.

Honeydew   MULTICUISINE $$

(☏2622498; Station Rd; mains ₹90-290; ⊙9am-11pm) The Honeydew offers a great selection of veg and nonveg Indian, Chinese and Continental food in a pleasant, clean, relaxed, but overly dim, atmosphere. It has long been one of Ajmer's best, and is the restaurant of choice for Mayo College students' midterm treat. The ice cream, milkshakes and floats will keep you cool.

Mango Masala   VEGETARIAN $$

(☏2422100; Sadar Patel Marg; mains ₹50-170; ⊙11am-11pm) With dim, bar-like lighting and nursery school decor, this no-alcohol veg restaurant is where Ajmer's teens hang out. There's an imaginative menu of pizzas, Chinese, and North and South Indian vegetarian food. There are also cakes, ice cream, ice-cream sodas and mocktails.

Bhola Hotel Restaurant
VEGETARIAN $

(2432844; Agra Gate, Prithviraj Marg; mains ₹30-130; ⊙11am-10pm) This cheap hotel has a gloomy but surprisingly appealing, good-value vegetarian restaurant at the top of a seedy staircase. Tasty thalis cost ₹70.

Madina Hotel
NORTH INDIAN $

(Station Rd; mains ₹30-100; ⊙9am-11pm) Handy if you're waiting for a train (it's opposite the station), this simple, open-to-the-street eatery cooks up cheap veg and nonveg fare, with specialities such as chicken Mughlai and *rumali roti* (huge paper-thin chapati).

Elite
VEGETARIAN $

(2429544; Station Rd; mains ₹50-105; ⊙11am-11pm) Elite has a welcoming ambience attracting families to feast on the town's best value thali (₹66), as well as South Indian and tandoori vegetarian dishes.

ℹ Information

Bank of Baroda (Prithviraj Marg) Changes travellers cheques and does credit-card advances.

Bank of Baroda ATM (Station Rd) By the entrance to Honeydew restaurant.

HDFC ATM (Sadar Patel Marg)

JLN Hospital (2625500; Daulat Bagh)

Main post office (Prithviraj Marg; ⊙10am-1pm & 1.30-6pm Mon-Sat) Less than 500m from the train station.

Satguru's Internet (60-61 Kutchery Rd; per hr ₹20; ⊙9am-10pm)

State Bank of India (Civil Lines) Changes travellers cheques and foreign currency and has an ATM.

Tourist Reception Centre RTDC Hotel Khadim (2627426; ⊙9am-6pm Mon-Fri); train station (⊙9am-6pm)

ℹ Getting There & Away

The main bus stand is to the northeast, and the train station (and many hotels) are to the east of the Dargah of Khwaja Muin-ud-din Chishti.

Bus

There are frequent RSRTC buses of various grades and comfort leaving from the busy main bus stand to destinations listed in the table. Fares quoted are for express and/or AC services either Gold Line or Volvo. The inquiry number is 2429398.

In addition, there are numerous private buses to these destinations – many companies have offices on Kutchery Rd. If you book your ticket to one of these destinations through an agency in Pushkar, they should provide a free transfer to Ajmer to start your journey.

DESTINATION	FARE (₹)	DURATION (HR)
Agra	232	10
Ahmedabad	311	13
Bharatpur	195	8
Bikaner	155	8
Bundi	110	5
Chittorgarh	115	5
Delhi	265/570 AC	9
Indore	250	12
Jaipur	110/200 AC	2½
Jaisalmer	315	10
Jodhpur	125/300 AC	6
Kishangarh	20	15
Pushkar	10	½
Udaipur	170/200 AC	8

Train

There are no tourist quotas for many Ajmer trains, so book early. Use the services of an agent or go to booth 5 at the train station's **reservations office** (⊙8am-2pm & 2.15-8pm Mon-Sat, 8am-2pm Sun).

Ajmer is a busy station on the Delhi–Jaipur–Ahmedabad–Mumbai line. The 12016/5 *Shatabdi Express* runs between Ajmer and Delhi (AC chair/1st class ₹645/1200, four hours) via Jaipur (₹300/575). It leaves Delhi at 6.05am and arrives in Ajmer at 12.45pm. Going the other way, the train leaves Ajmer at 3.50pm, arriving in Jaipur at 5.35am and in Delhi at 10.45pm. There's also the 12957 *Rajdhani Express* to Delhi (3AC/2AC/1AC, ₹660/880/1480, seven hours), which leaves Ajmer at 12.40am.

The 19105/6 *Delhi-Ahmedabad Mail* departs from Ajmer at 8.45pm and arrives in Delhi (sleeper/3AC/2AC/1AC ₹200/525/725/1200) at 5.20am. Heading for Gujarat, the train leaves Ajmer at 7.30am and arrives in Ahmedabad (₹227/608/832/1385) at 6.40pm.

The 12195/6 *Ajmer Agra Fort City Express* leaves at 2.50pm, arriving in Agra Fort (2nd class/AC chair ₹111/393) at 9.30pm via Jaipur (₹65/222, 4.55pm).

The 12992 *Ajmer Udaipur City Express* leaves at 4.15pm, arriving in Udaipur (2nd class/AC chair ₹100/347) at 9.30pm via Chittorgarh (₹75/263, 7.15pm).

ℹ Getting Around

There are plenty of autorickshaws (anywhere in town should cost around ₹30), as well as cheaper cycle-rickshaws.

Around Ajmer

KISHANGARH
☎ 01463 / POP 153,600

Kishangarh is 27km northeast of Ajmer and was founded in the early 17th century by Kishan Singh, a Rathore prince. Since the 18th century the town of Kishangarh has been associated with one of India's most famous schools of miniature painting. Among its renowned works is the *Bani Thani* painting by Kishangarh master Nihal Chand – a sensual, graceful portrayal of Krishna's consort, Radha, depicted with exaggeratedly slanting, almond-shaped eyes – you'll see this reprinted all over Rajasthan. Today local artists are trying to revive this magnificent school of painting by making copies of the originals on surfaces such as wood, stone and cloth (the originals were done on paper). Kishangarh is also famous for painted wooden furniture.

Kishangarh town is divided into the charming old city and the less-charming new part, which is mainly commercial. Pollution is steadily increasing, along with the growing number of dusty marble factories and textile mills.

🛏 Sleeping

Phool Mahal Palace HERITAGE HOTEL **$$**
(☎247405; www.royalkishangarh.com; s/d ₹3200/3700; ❄) This romantic heritage building on the shores of Gundalao Lake was built in 1870 as a 'monsoon palace'. The lake fills after the monsoon rains and the palace, with its looming backdrop of Kishangarh Fort, is very picturesque. Nevertheless the waters have taken their toll and the rambling hotel is rather musty and insect-prone. Fresh frescoes brighten the rooms.

Roopangarh Fort HERITAGE HOTEL **$$**
(☎220444; www.royalkishangarh.com; s/d ₹3300/3800, ste ₹5500; ❄) About 25km out of town, Roopangarh Fort has been converted into an evocative hotel. Roopangarh was the capital of this province for about 100 years and was never conquered, despite being repeatedly attacked by its neighbouring states. The fort was founded in 1653 by Maharaja Roop Singh. Rooms are large, and decorated with lots of traditional furniture. The road to the fort passes through a timeless village, where it seems life has been the same for centuries. The hotel can arrange village tours, birdwatching, and camel, horse or jeep safaris, and if you stay here you can view the maharaja's private collection of miniatures. The fort itself is well endowed with fine paintings. The hotel will arrange a taxi (₹900) from Kishangarh railway station.

ⓘ Getting There & Away

Frequent daily buses (₹20) go between Ajmer and Kishangarh. Trains from Ajmer include the 12413 *Ajmer-Jammu Express* which departs Ajmer at 2.10pm and arrives in Kishangarh (2nd class/sleeper/3AC/2AC/1AC ₹42/140/240/309/502) at 2.40pm before moving on to Jaipur. Going the other way, the 19708 *Aravalli Express* departs Jaipur at 8.30am arriving in Kishangarh (sleeper/3AC/2AC ₹120/235/293) at 10.07am before moving on to Ajmer.

161

WORTH A TRIP

BAREFOOT COLLEGE

In Tilonia village, located about 25km northeast of Kishangarh and 7km off the Ajmer to Jaipur road, is the inspiring **Barefoot College** (☎01463-288205; www.barefootcollege.org). This NGO is run by and for villagers, and uses their skills for development work in the area to address problems of water supply, housing, education, health and employment. Part of the complex is devoted to an impressive showroom where goods made by villagers are on sale – it's a fantastic place to pick up high-quality, reasonably priced souvenirs, including everything from textiles to furniture and leather goods. Other great gifts include bell *totas* (colourful strings of toy birds), painted ceramic bowls and wooden toys. All proceeds go towards maintaining and developing rural projects.

The entire complex is solar powered, and Barefoot has been instrumental in bringing solar power to many communities. It's even pulled women out of *purdah* (seclusion) to teach them how to become solar-power engineers. Other major projects are the installation of hand pumps and the implementation of rainwater harvesting projects.

The easiest way to get to Tilonia is to hire a taxi from Ajmer, Pushkar or Kishangarh. From Ajmer you could take a Harmara-bound bus (₹28) and ask to be dropped off at Tilonia. There are also local buses from Kishangarh (₹15). The Barefoot College centre is about 1km from the bus stop.

PACHEWAR
📞 01437

This little village, about 90km east of Ajmer, has a lake that attracts migratory birds in winter. It has an imposing fort, once ruled by the Khangarot Rajputs. Thakur Anoop Singh Khangarot captured the fort of Ranthambhore from the Marathas and annexed it to his family allies in Jaipur. To reward him, Maharaja Sawai Madho Singh I of Jaipur granted him the Pachewar territory in 1758.

Pachewar Garh (📞28756, in Jaipur 0141-2601007; www.pachewargarhfort.com; s/d ₹4000/4500, ste ₹5500; ❀@☎) is the impressive 300-year-old fort. The spacious rooms are furnished with antiques, and some are splendidly decorated with frescoes. The hotel can also arrange village safaris.

Pushkar
📞 0145 / POP 14,789

Pushkar has a magnetism all of its own, and is quite unlike anywhere else in Rajasthan. It's a prominent Hindu pilgrimage town and devout Hindus should visit at least once in their lifetime. The town curls around a holy lake, said to have appeared when Brahma dropped a lotus flower. It also has one of the world's few Brahma temples. With 52 bathing ghats and 400 milky-blue temples, the town literally hums with regular *pujas* (prayers) generating an episodic soundtrack of chanting, drums and gongs, and devotional songs.

Besides pilgrims, travellers have long discovered Pushkar's charms, and small, budget hotels outnumber the temples and *dharamsalas* (pilgrims guesthouses). Many visitors reach here and grind to a satisfied halt, experimenting variously with spirituality, *bhang* (marijuana) and facial hair. Time can slip by very easily in Pushkar.

The result is a muddle of religious and tourist scenes. The main street is one long bazaar, selling anything to tickle a traveller's fancy, from hippy-chic tie-dye to didgeridoos. Despite the commercialism and banana pancakes, the town remains enchantingly small and authentically mystic. You can help preserve the spiritual balance by respecting tradition and dressing appropriately and abiding by local restrictions (no alcohol, meat or eggs, and no public displays of affection).

Pushkar is world famous for its spectacular camel fair (p144), which takes place here in the Hindu lunar month of Kartika (October/November). If you're anywhere nearby at the time, you'd be crazy to miss it.

During this period the town is jam-packed with tribal people from all over Raja-

Pushkar

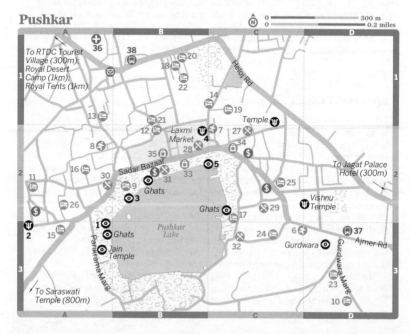

sthan, pilgrims from all over India, and film-makers and tourists from all over the world. And there are plenty of camels and other livestock (it's best to arrive a few days before the official start to see serious trading).

Pushkar is only 11km from Ajmer but separated from it by Nag Pahar, the Snake Mountain.

◉ Sights

Temples HINDU TEMPLES

Pushkar boasts hundreds of temples, though few are particularly ancient, as they were mostly desecrated by Aurangzeb and subsequently rebuilt.

Brahma Temple

Most famous is the Brahma Temple, said to be one of the few such temples in the world as a result of a curse by Brahma's consort, Saraswati. The temple is marked by a red spire, and over the entrance gateway is the *hans* (goose symbol) of Brahma. Inside, the floor and walls are engraved with dedications to the dead.

Saraswati Temple

The one-hour trek up to the hilltop Saraswati Temple overlooking the lake is best made before dawn (to beat the heat and capture the best light), though the views are fantastic at any time of day.

Pap Mochani (Gayatri) Temple

The sunrise views over town from the closer Pap Mochani (Gayatri) Temple, reached by a track behind the Marwar bus stand, are also well worth the 30-minute climb.

Shiva temples

About 8km southwest of the town (past the turn-off to Saraswati) is a collection of Shiva temples near Ajaypal, which make a great trip by motorbike (or bike if you're fit and start early in the day), through barren hills and quiet villages. Be warned: the track is hilly and rocky. Another Shiva temple is about 8km north of Pushkar, tucked down inside a cave, which would make for a good excursion.

Pushkar

DREAMER OF THE UNIVERSE

According to one Indian saying, GOD stands for Generation, Operation, Destruction, and the Hindu trinity of Brahma, Vishnu and Shiva are respectively responsible for these three tasks. Of the three, Brahma, the Creator, is the most mysterious. Unlike Vishnu and Shiva, he is rarely worshipped, although reality itself is Brahma's dream. Each of his lifetimes spans 311,040,000,000,000 human years and corresponds to a great cycle of the universe, at the end of which it is destroyed by Shiva. Then Brahma is reborn to dream it all again.

Brahma is usually depicted with four bearded faces facing the four directions, and four hands, each holding one of the four books of the *Vedas* (Books of Knowledge). His vehicle is the swan and his consort is Saraswati, the Goddess of Education.

According to legend, the sacred lake of Pushkar sprang up at the spot where Brahma dropped a lotus flower from the sky. Pushkar takes its name from this incident – *push* means 'flower' and *kar* means 'hand'. Brahma had planned to perform a *yagna* (self-mortification) at the lake on a full-moon night, a ceremony that required the presence of his consort. But Saraswati was late. Irritated, Brahma quickly married a convenient milk-maid named Gayatri, and when Saraswati arrived she discovered Gayatri seated in her own honoured place beside Brahma. Saraswati was understandably furious and vowed that Brahma would be forgotten by the people of the earth. It was a profound curse and the gods pleaded with her to reconsider. Finally she relented, decreeing that he could be worshipped, but only in Pushkar. Since then, the Brahma temple at Pushkar has re-mained one of the only temples in the world dedicated to Brahma and allegedly the only one in India. Meanwhile, Saraswati and Gayatri receive their *puja*s at separate temples, at opposite ends of the town.

Ghats
BATHING GHATS

Fifty-two bathing ghats surround the lake, where pilgrims bathe in the sacred waters. If you wish to join them, do it with respect. Remember, this is a holy place: remove your shoes and don't smoke, kid around or take photographs.

Some ghats have particular importance: Vishnu appeared at **Varah Ghat** in the form of a boar, Brahma bathed at **Brahma Ghat**, and Gandhi's ashes were sprinkled at **Gandhi Ghat** (formerly Gau Ghat).

🏃 Activities

The following hotels allow nonguests use of their swimming pools: Jagat Palace Hotel (₹300 per person), Hotel Navaratan Palace (₹100) and Green Park Resort (₹30).

Shannu's Riding School
HORSE RIDING

(☑2772043; http://shannus.weebly.comm; Panch Kund Marg; ride/lessons per hr ₹350) Long-time Pushkar resident Marc can organise riding lessons and horse safaris on his graceful Marwari steeds. On top of that you can also stay here, nice and close to the horses.

Dr NS Mathur
REFLEXOLOGY

(☑2622777, 9828103031; Ajmer Rd; ⊙10.30am-6.30pm) Provides back, hand and foot reflexology (from ₹250), which will most certainly take your mind off any pains you might have had. The doctor also teaches reiki and his daughter teaches yoga and provides beauty treatments.

Roshi Hiralal Verma
REIKI, YOGA

For reiki, yoga and shiatsu, Roshi is based at the Ambika Guesthouse. Costs depend on the duration and nature of your session.

✍ Courses

Saraswati Music School
MUSIC

(☑2773124; Mainon Ka Chowk) Teaches classi-cal *tabla* (drums), flute, singing and *kathak* (classical dance). For music, contact Birju on ☑9828297784, who's been playing for around 20 years, and charges from ₹350 for two hours. He often conducts evening performances (7pm to 8pm), and also sells instruments. For dance contact Hemant on ☑9829333548.

Cooking Bahar
COOKING

(☑2773124; www.cookingbahar.com; Mainon Ka Chowk) Part of the Saraswati Music School family, Deepa conducts three-hour cooking classes that cover three vegetarian courses.

Dr NS Mathur
REIKI

(☑2622777; 9828103031; Ajmer Rd; ⊙10.30am-6.30pm) Reflexologist Dr NS Mathur is also a teacher of reiki (I/II/III ₹1500/3000/10,000).

☞ Tours

Plenty of people in Pushkar offer **camel safaris** (around ₹175 per hour), which are a good way to explore the starkly beautiful landscape – a mixture of desert and the rocky hills – around town. These safaris are far removed from the camel-crazy hype of Jaisalmer; it's an entirely different experience to safaris in the west of the state. Don't expect iconic sweeping dunes – this is more of a chance to have a rural ramble and visit some little-known spots. It's best to ask your hotel, a travel agent or other travellers to recommend somebody who organises good trips. Most organisers are happy to tailor-make a safari and they have good suggestions about places of interest in and around Pushkar.

For longer camel treks, Pushkar makes a convenient starting point. Trips start at around ₹700 per day, and head out to Jodhpur (six to seven days) and Jaisalmer (10 to 12 days). See p291 for general details about camel treks. Numerous operators line Panch Kund Marg.

For **horse safaris** check out Shannv's Riding School.

🛏 Sleeping

Owing to Pushkar's status among backpackers, there are far more budget options than midrange, though many have a selection of midrange-priced rooms. Most hotels are basic, clean, whitewashed and well run, though few are legally registered businesses. There are a couple of choice upmarket options here, too.

At the time of the camel fair, prices multiply up to five times and it's essential to book several weeks, even months ahead.

TOP CHOICE Inn Seventh Heaven

BOUTIQUE HOTEL **$$**

(☏5105455; www.inn-seventh-heaven.com; Chotti Basti; r ₹550-2400; ❄@) You enter this lovingly converted *haveli* through heavy wooden doors into an incense-perfumed courtyard, centred with a marble fountain. There are just a dozen individually decorated rooms situated on three levels, all with traditionally crafted furniture and comfortable beds. All the rooms have their own character and vary in size from the downstairs budget rooms to the spacious 'Asana' suite. On the roof you'll find the excellent **Sixth Sense** restaurant as well as sofas and swing chairs for relaxing with a book. Early booking (two-night minimum, no credit cards) is recommended.

Dia

B&B **$$**

(☏5105455; www.inn-seventh-heaven.com/Dia.html; Panch Kund Marg; r incl breakfast ₹2400; ❄@❄) This beautifully designed bed and breakfast by the folks at Seventh Heaven has just four very private, very serene doubles a short walk out of town. The rooms are straight out of a design magazine and will have you swooning (and extending your booking). You can choose to dine here in the cosy rooftop restaurant or head to the Sixth Sense restaurant at Inn Seventh Heaven.

Hotel Pushkar Palace

HOTEL **$$$**

(☏2773001; www.hotelpushkarpalace.com; s/d from ₹4225/5150, ste ₹10,850; ❄@❄) Once belonging to the maharaja of Kishangarh, the top-end Hotel Pushkar Palace boasts a romantic lakeside setting. The rooms have carved wooden furniture and beds, and the suites look directly out onto the lake. There is also a pleasant outdoor dining area overlooking the lake.

Jagat Palace Hotel

HOTEL **$$**

(☏2772953; www.hotelpushkarpalace.com; Ajmer Rd; s/d ₹3575/4225; ❄@❄) This is a lovely heritage-style hotel in new but traditional-style buildings resembling a palace. It's in a quiet spot on the town's outskirts and offers romantic bedrooms with carved wooden furniture and lovely bathrooms. Balconies overlook large, lush gardens and a gorgeous, secluded pool (₹300 for nonguests) with mountain views. There are tempting packages including meals and low-season discounts.

Hotel Everest

HOTEL **$**

(☏2773417; www.pushkarhoteleverest.com; r ₹200-600, with AC ₹850; ❄@) This welcoming budget hotel is secreted in the quiet laneways north of Sadar Bazaarand is convenient to the bazaar and the mela ground. It is run by a friendly father-and-son team who can't do too much for their appreciative guests. The rooms are variable in size, colourful and spotless and the beds are comfortable. The roof is a pleasant retreat for meals or just relaxing with a book.

Ananta Spa & Resort

HOTEL **$$$**

(☏3054000; www.anantaindia.in; Ajmer Rd; r incl breakfast ₹5000-6000; ❄@❄) The arrival of Ananta, an (almost) five-star resort sprawling on 9 acres in the rugged ranges 4km outside Pushkar's city limits, heralds a new era in pilgrimages to this holy town. Lucky pilgrims zip from reception to the

PUSHKAR CAMEL FAIR

Come the month of Kartika, the eighth lunar month of the Hindu calendar and one of the holiest, Thar camel drivers spruce up their ships of the desert and start the long walk to Pushkar in time for Kartik Purnima (Full Moon). Each year around 200,000 people converge here, bringing with them some 50,000 camels, horses and cattle. The place becomes an extraordinary swirl of colour, sound and movement, thronged with musicians, mystics, tourists, traders, animals, devotees and camera crews.

Trading begins a week before the official fair (a good time to arrive to see the serious business), but by the time the RTDC mela (fair) starts, business takes a back seat and the bizarre sidelines (snake charmers, children balancing on poles etc) jostle onto centre stage. Even the cultural programme is bizarre, with events such as moustache contests, turban-tying contests and seeing how many people can balance on a camel.

It's hard to believe, but this seething mass is all just a sideshow. Kartik Purnima is when Hindu pilgrims come to bathe in Pushkar's sacred waters. The religious event builds in tandem with the camel fair in a wild, magical crescendo of incense, chanting and processions to dousing day, the last night of the fair, when thousands of devotees wash away their sins and set candles afloat on the holy lake.

Although fantastical, mystical and a one-off, it must be said that it's also crowded, touristy, noisy (light sleepers should bring earplugs) and tacky. Those affected by dust and/or animal hair should bring appropriate medication. However, it's a grand epic, and not to be missed if you're anywhere within camel-spitting distance.

It usually takes place in October or November and because dates can change the following are indicative only: 2–10 November 2011, 20–28 November 2012, 9–17 November 2013 and 1–8 November 2014.

Balinese style cottages on golf buggies. Rooms are spacious and fully appointed but most guests will be at the luscious pool, spa, games room, restaurant, lounge or bar.

Pushkar Resorts HOTEL $$$
(☎2772944; www.sewara.com; Motisar Marg, Village Gandhera; r from ₹3950, ste ₹7450; ❄❂) This sprawling resort, about 5km out of town, is set in an orchard and has a lovely pool shaded by palms. Other activities include an indulgent spa and camel rides. There are four clusters each of 10 renovated and comfortable cottages set in a trimmed lawn. Apart from the serenity, one aspect of this resort's popularity is that it is outside the city limits and so has meat, eggs and alcohol on the menu.

Hotel Shannu's Ranch Inn BOUTIQUE HOTEL $
(☎2772043; http://shannus.weebly.com; Panch Kund Marg; r ₹600, ste ₹1200) Especially for horse lovers but not exclusively so, this relaxed, family-run hotel is just a short walk from the lake. There is a large garden compound featuring the family home, separate guest accommodation and, of course, the stables housing Marc's beloved Marwari horses. There are usually a couple of friendly dogs wandering around too. The large suites easily accommodate a family of five.

Hotel Kanhaia Haveli HOTEL $
(☎2772146; http://pushkarhotelkanhaia.com; Chotti Basti; r with bathroom ₹200-1200, s/d without bathroom ₹150/200; ❄@) With a vast range of rooms from budget digs to AC suites you are sure to find a room and price that suits. As you spend more dosh the rooms get bigger and lighter, with more windows and even balconies. All rooms have cable TVs, while AC rooms start at ₹750. There are excellent views from the multicuisine rooftop restaurant.

Bharatpur Palace HOTEL $
(☎2772320; bharatpurpalace_pushkar@yahoo.co.in; r ₹200-800; ❄) This rambling old building occupies one of the best spots in Pushkar, on the upper levels adjacent to Ghandi Ghat. It features aesthetic blue-washed simplicity: bare as bones rooms with unsurpassed views of the holy lake. Respect for bathing pilgrims is paramount for intended guests. Room 1 is the most romantic place to wake up: it's surrounded on three sides by the lake. Rooms 9, 12, 13 and 16 are also good. There's a variety of rooms with or without bathrooms, running hot water and AC.

Sun-n-Moon HOTEL $
(☎2772883; r ₹400) With a neohippy vibe, the Sun-n-Moon has a lovely, serene courtyard

surrounding a bodhi tree and a small shrine. It's a very quiet and relaxing place to stay, with clean, inexpensive rooms and excellent food.

Shri Shyam Krishna Guesthouse
GUESTHOUSE $

(☎2772461; skguesthouse@yahoo.com; Sadar Bazaar; s/d ₹300/500, without bathroom ₹200/300) Housed in a lovely old blue-washed building with lawns and gardens, this guesthouse has ashram austerity and genuinely friendly management. Some of the cheaper rooms are cell-like, though all share the simple, authentic ambience. The outdoor kitchen and garden seating are a good setting for a relaxing meal of hearty vegetarian fare.

Hotel Navaratan Palace
HOTEL $

(☎2772145; www.pushkarnavaratanpalace.co.in; s/d from ₹300/400, with AC from ₹600/700; ❋❋) Located close to the Brahma Temple, this hotel has a lovely enclosed garden with a fabulous pool (₹100 for nonguests), children's playground and pet tortoises. The rooms are clean, small and crammed with carved wooden furniture.

Pushkar Inn's Hotel
HOTEL $

(☎2772010; hotelpushkarinns@yahoo.com; Pushkar Lake; s/d ₹650/700, r with AC ₹1200; ❋) A charming little hotel comprising a row of clean and bright rooms, backed by a garden and orchard. The rooms catch the breeze from the lake and that is mostly a positive, though some wafts are less than holy. The best rooms have lake views.

Hotel New Park
HOTEL $$

(☎2772464; www.newparkpushkar.com; Panch Kund Marg; s/d ₹1050/1200; ❋@❋) This quiet hotel is blissfully rural, located among fields of red roses, but still an easy walk to/from the lake. Smart, modern rooms with TVs and balconies overlook an inviting pool, gardens and a backdrop of hills.

Hotel Kishan Palace
HOTEL $$

(☎2773056; www.kishanpalacepushkar.com; Panch Kund Marg; s/d from ₹800/1200, ste ₹4500; ❋@) A welcoming, brightly coloured hotel with abundant potted plants and a range of well-appointed rooms. The blue-domed rooftop terrace is very communal, with guests mingling, munching and watching the satellite TV.

Green Park Resort
HOTEL $$

(☎2773532;www.greenparkpushkar.com;Gurdwara Marg; s/d ₹800/1200; ❋❋) This welcoming place has 18 spiffy rooms all with marble floors, comfy beds and satellite TV. The swimming pool is big and inviting (₹30 for nonguests) and there's a relaxing rooftop restaurant. It's only a 10-minute stroll to town along a shady country lane.

Hotel Paramount Palace
HOTEL $

(☎2772428; hotelparamountpalace@hotmail.com; Bari Basti; r ₹200-1000) Perched on the highest point in town overlooking an old temple, this welcoming hotel has excellent views over the town and lake (and lots of stairs). The rooms vary widely. The best rooms (106, 108, 109) have lovely balconies, stained glass windows and are good value; smaller rooms can be dingy. There's a dizzyingly magical rooftop terrace.

Milkman Guesthouse
GUESTHOUSE $

(☎2773452; vinodmilkman@hotmail.com; Mali Mohalla; r ₹200-700, without bathroom ₹100; ❋@❋) Milkman is a cosy guesthouse in a backstreet location with a relaxing rooftop retreat featuring the Ooh-la-la Café and a lawn with high-altitude tortoises. The rooms are all brightly decorated with paintings. Some of the cheaper rooms are small and doorways are low, though the bright colours, cleanliness and friendly family atmosphere keep this place cheerful.

RTDC Hotel Sarovar
HOTEL $$

(☎2772040; s/d without bathroom ₹375/650, with lake view ₹900/1100, with AC ₹1650/1800; ❋❋) This hotel is set in spacious grounds and has a great position along the eastern shore of the lake. It has a lot more character than most RTDC places, with colonnades, arches and domes, and a swimming pool.

Hotel White House
GUESTHOUSE $

(☎2772147; www.pushkarwhitehouse.com; r ₹250-650, with AC ₹650-1350; ❋@) This place is indeed white, with spotless rooms, though some rooms are decidedly on the small side and the stairwells are narrow and steep. There is good traveller fare and fine views from the plant-filled rooftop restaurant. It is efficiently run by a tenacious businesslike mother-and-son team. Yoga is offered.

New Rituraj Palace
HOTEL $

(☎2772875; Gurdwara Marg; s/d ₹100/150) This place, tucked away behind an untidy garden, is a peaceful nook with homestyle meals and very basic rooms in line with the tariff. At camel fair time tents are erected and the place gets very crammed/communal.

Maharaja Guesthouse HOTEL $
(☎2773527; Mali Mohalla; s ₹100, d ₹250-450)
Managed by the family at nearby Milkman Guesthouse. Simple, clean rooms in a tucked-away spot with a restful rooftop.

Mayur Guest House GUESTHOUSE $
(☎2772302; www.mayurguesthouse.com; Holi ka Chowk; r ₹200-700, s without bathroom ₹100)
A pleasant blue-washed place, with neat, unspectacular rooms around a tiny leafy courtyard. Upstairs rooms have balconies and there's a cheerful welcome and more views from the rooftop.

Hotel Akash HOTEL $
(☎2772498; filterboy21@yahoo.com; d ₹400, s/d without bath ₹120/140) A simple budget place with keen young management and an overly relaxed vibe. Rooms are basic fan-cooled affairs that open out to a balcony restaurant good for spying on the street below.

Hotel Diamond HOTEL $
(☎9829206787; Holi ka Chowk; r ₹300, s without bathroom ₹150-200) In a quiet part of town, Diamond has tiny cell-like rooms around a small tranquil courtyard. The better rooms with attached bathrooms are upstairs.

TOURIST VILLAGE
During the camel fair, the RTDC and many private operators set up a sea of luxury tents near the fairground. It can get rather cold at night, so bring something warm. A torch (flashlight) may also be useful. You're advised to book ahead. The following all have private bathrooms.

RTDC Tourist Village LUXURY TENTS $$
(☎2772074; s/d huts from ₹4500/5000, s/d tents from ₹6000/6500; ✿) This option has various permanent huts and semipermanent tents that are usually booked out by tour groups well in advance. Full payment must be received two months in advance. Rates include all meals.

Royal Tents LUXURY TENTS $$$
(www.jodhpurheritage.com; tents s/d ₹14,500/16,500; ✿) Owned by the former royal family of Jodhpur, these are probably the most luxurious tents you'll ever come across. They all have comfy beds, verandas and deck chairs, and running hot and cold water. Note that meals cost extra.

Royal Desert Camp LUXURY TENTS $$$
(☎2772001; www.hotelpushkarpalace.com; tents s/d ₹10,000/11,500; ✿) Further away from the

fairground than Royal Tents, but another super luxurious option run by owners of Jagat Palace Hotel and Hotel Pushkar Palace. Again, note that meals are extra.

✖ Eating

Pushkar has plenty of atmospheric eateries with lake views and menus reflecting backpacker tastes and preferences. Strict vegetarianism, forbidding even eggs, limits the range of ingredients, but the cooks usually make up for this with imagination and by using fresh ingredients.

TOP CHOICE Sixth Sense MULTICUISINE $
(Inn Seventh Heaven, Chotti Basti; mains ₹50-180; ☻8.30am-4pm, 6-10pm) This chilled rooftop restaurant is a great place to head even if you didn't score a room in its popular hotel. The Indian seasonal vegetables and rice, vegetable sizzlers, pasta and pizzas are all excellent, as are the filter coffee and fresh juice blends. Its ambience is immediately relaxing and the pulley apparatus that delivers the delicious food from the ground-floor kitchen is enthralling. Save room for the desserts, such as the excellent homemade tarts.

Little Italy ITALIAN $
(Panchkund Marg; mains ₹80-200; ☻10am-11pm) This superb garden restaurant has excellent thin-crust, wood-fired pizzas and imported pasta with tasty sauces. As well as homemade pesto and gnocchi, there are some Indian and Israeli dishes and freshly ground Keralan coffee.

Sunset Café MULTICUISINE $
(mains ₹75-200; ☻7.30am-midnight) Right on the eastern ghats, this cafe has sublime lake views. It offers the usual traveller menu, including curries, pizza and pasta, plus there's a German bakery serving reasonable cakes. The lakeshore setting is perfect at sunset and gathers a crowd.

Out of the Blue MULTICUISINE $
(mains ₹50-180; ☻8am-11pm) Distinctly a deeper shade of blue in this sky-blue town, Out of the Blue is a new addition to the horde of lakeview restaurants. Let's hope the standard of food, cleanliness and service, which raises the bar in this part of town, continues. The menu ranges from noodles and *momos* (Tibetan dumplings) to pizza, pasta and pancakes. A nice touch is the espresso coffee, which can also be enjoyed at street level.

Honey & Spice
MULTICUISINE $

(Laxmi Market off Sadar Bazaar; mains ₹75-120; ⊘7am-7pm) Run by a friendly man who is a mine of information, this tiny breakfast and lunch place has delicious South Indian coffee and homemade banana cake. Soups and hearty vegetable stews served with brown rice are thoroughly healthy.

Sun-n-Moon
MULTICUISINE $

(⊘2772883; Bari Basti; mains ₹40-180; ⊘7.30am-11pm) This neohippy haunt attracts all kinds for its Italian menu, including pizzas, pasta and apple pie, and for its friendly, super-relaxed atmosphere. The shady courtyard is home to a bodhi tree and a shrine. Breakfast includes lassis and masala chai, while for the homesick there are hash browns and hot chocolate.

Raju Terrace Garden Restaurant
MULTICUISINE $

(Sadar Bazaar; mains ₹40-90; ⊘10am-10pm) This relaxed rooftop restaurant serves lots of dishes for the homesick (for example, shepherd's pie, pizza and baked potatoes) and rather tame Indian food. It's on a pleasant terrace that's filled with pot plants and fairy lights and has great views of the lake. Note the service can be super slow.

Om Shiva
MULTICUISINE $

(⊘5105045; mains ₹70-150; ⊘7.30am-late) Another traveller stalwart, Om Shiva continues to satisfy with its ₹80 buffet. Wood-fired pizzas and espresso coffee are new additions to the try-anything menu.

Baba Restaurant
MULTICUISINE $

(⊘2772858; mains ₹60-120; ⊘8am-10pm) Not to be confused with Sai Baba, Baba Restaurant is tucked away, east of Sadar Bazaar, and open to the street. It offers up good pizzas and Israeli food and a chilled-out atmosphere.

🛍 Shopping

Pushkar's Sadar Bazaar is lined with enchanting little shops and is a good place for picking up gifts. Many of the vibrant textiles come from the Barmer district south of Jaisalmer. There's plenty of silver and beaded jewellery catering to foreign tastes, and some old tribal pieces, too. Coloured glass lamps are another appealing buy (you can ponder trying to get them home intact) as are embroidered and mirrored wall hangings. The range of Indian-music CDs makes this market an excellent place for sampling local tunes.

Pushkar is also good for getting clothes made. One reliable place with reasonable prices is **Navjyoti Tailors** (Sadar Bazaar). Also recommended is **Maloo Enterprises** (Varah Ghat Chowk), opposite the old post office. **Khadi Gramodhyog** (Sadar Bazaar) sells traditional hand-weaves – mainly men's shirts, scarves and shawls.

As Pushkar is touristy, you'll have to haggle. Ignore 'last-price' quotes that aren't negotiable – take your time and visit a few shops.

❶ Information

Cash and travellers cheques may be changed at places along Sadar Bazaar Rd, but check the commission and/or the rate. Numerous places offer internet services for ₹25 per hour.

Hospital (⊘2772029) North of the post office.

Post office (off Heloj Rd,⊘9.30am-5pm) Near the Marwar bus stand.

Punjab National Bank ATM (Sadar Bazaar; ⊘9.30am-5pm Mon-Fri, to 4pm Sat) ATM inside branch accepts Cirrus and MasterCard but not Visa cards. There's a second ATM near the SBBJ ATM (north of the Brahma temple).

State Bank of Bikaner & Jaipur (SBBJ; Sadar Bazaar; ⊘10am-4pm Mon-Fri, to 12.30pm Sat) Changes travellers cheques and cash. The SBBJ ATM accepts international cards.

Thomas Cook (Sadar Bazaar; ⊘9.30am-6.30pm Mon-Sat) Changes cash and travellers cheques and also provides train and flight ticketing.

Tourist Reception Centre (⊘2772040; ⊘10am-5pm) In the grounds of RTDC Hotel Sarovar; staff will give out a free map.

Dangers & Annoyances

Priests – some genuine, some not – will approach you near the ghats and offer to do a *puja* (prayer) for which you'll receive a 'Pushkar passport' (a red ribbon around your wrist). Others may proffer flowers (to avoid trouble, don't take any flowers you are offered). Some of these priests genuinely live off the donations of others and this is a tradition that goes back centuries. Others can be pushy and aggressive. Walk away if you feel bullied and agree on a price before taking a ribbon or flowers.

Flowers are offered at the Brahma Temple, where there are simple donation boxes. Here you can offer flowers and sacred sweets for the happiness of your friends, family and everyone you've ever known – and still have change for a masala chai.

During the camel fair, Pushkar is besieged by pickpockets working the crowded bazaars. You can avoid the razor gang by not using thin-walled daypacks and by carrying your daypack in front of you. Fortunately, there is very little motorised traffic in the main bazaar, making it a pleasurable place to explore at leisure – though watch out for stray motorbikes.

① Getting There & Away

Frequent buses to/from Ajmer (₹8, 30 minutes) stop on the road heading eastwards out of town; other buses leave from the Marwar bus stand to the north.

Local travel agencies sell tickets for private buses – you should shop around. These buses generally leave from Ajmer, but the agencies should provide you with free connecting transport. Those that leave from Pushkar usually stop for an hour or more in Ajmer anyway. Be warned that some buses (particularly those via Jodhpur) don't go all the way; in spite of promises, they'll involve a change of bus *and* an extra fare. Some destinations and fares from Pushkar:

DESTINATION	FARE (₹)	DURATION (HR)
Ajmer	express/local 8/7	1/2
Bundi	117	6
Delhi	ordinary/sleeper 200/300	10½
Jaipur	120	4
Jaisalmer	ordinary/sleeper 240/340	10½
Jodhpur	120	5

The post office will book train tickets for services out of Ajmer for about ₹15 commission. For around ₹50 private agencies do the same, including transfer to Ajmer. See p160 for details of trains from Ajmer.

When entering Pushkar by car there is a toll of ₹35. (Buses also pay a toll which is included in your ticket.)

① Getting Around

There are no autorickshaws, but it's a breeze to get around on foot. Another good option is to hire a bicycle (₹30 per day) or a motorbike (₹200 to ₹250 per day, helmet ₹30 per day). Try **Shree Ganpati Motorbike Hire** (☑2772830; Brahma Rd) whose bikes have an all-Rajasthan tourist permit. A *wallah* can carry your luggage on a thela (hand-drawn cart) to/from the bus stand for around ₹30.

Tonk

☑01432 / POP 172,500

This town, 95km south of Jaipur, on the way to Ranthambhore National Park, was built in the mid-17th century. The colourful bazaar and the beautifully painted mosque are worth a look, though the town is regularly the focus of Hindu–Muslim tension and is very much off the tourist trail.

The town of Tonk was originally ruled by a tribe of Afghani Pathans, and their prosperous Muslim descendants have left a legacy of fine mansions, a testament to the wealth they accumulated when they ruled as *nawabs* (Muslim ruling prince or landowner) from this region. Tonk also served as an important administrative centre during the era of the Raj, and the British have left behind colonial buildings.

Worth seeking out is the early-19th-century **Sunehri Kothi** (Najar Bagh Rd), which is decorated with exquisite coloured Belgium glass, inlay work and gilding. However it is all much in decay with amateurish renovation attempts. You must sign in at the small office opposite the entrance and the guide will expect a tip. A contrasting but equally beautiful sight is the imposing **Jama Masjid**, Rajasthan's finest mosque. Delicately frescoed inside and out with interlocking patterns, ferns and flowers, and sinuous gold decoration. This important place of worship was begun in 1246 by the first nawab of Tonk, Nawab Amir Khan, and completed by his son in 1298.

At the **Arabic & Persian Research Institute** (☺10am-5pm Mon-Fri) a rare collection of old Arabic and Persian manuscripts and books is housed, dating from the 12th to the 17th century.

About 22km out of town, off the Ranthambhore Rd, is a huge elephant carved out of a single block of stone. This is **Hathi Bhata**, carved in 1200 – the date is given in script on the elephant's right ear. Beside the elephant are 64 plate-sized depressions in the rock. This is where worshippers sit and eat at festival times. The flickering firelight from the open kitchen must make the *hathi* an impressive sight.

① Getting There & Away

Many local buses from Jaipur's main bus stand pass through Tonk (₹52, 2½ hours) en route to Kota. There are also numerous buses between Tonk and Sawai Madhopur for Ranthambhore National Park (₹69, two hours).

Ranthambhore National Park

☎07462

This famous national park, open from October to June, is the best place to spot wild tigers in Rajasthan. Comprising 1334 sq km of wild jungle scrub hemmed in by rocky ridges, at its centre is the amazing 10th-century Ranthambore Fort. Scattered around the fort are ancient temples and mosques, hunting pavilions, crocodile-filled lakes and vine covered *chhatris*. The park was a maharajas' hunting ground until 1970 – a curious 15 years after it had become a sanctuary.

Project Tiger has been in charge of the tiger population since 1979, but the project's difficulties were thrown into sharp relief when government officials were implicated in poaching in 2005. Getting an accurate figure on the number of tigers comes down to who you believe – the park probably has around 32 tigers, after the relocation of five tigers to Sariska Tiger Reserve (see p153).

Seeing a tiger is partly a matter of luck; you should plan on two or three safaris to improve your chances. But remember there's plenty of other wildlife to see, including more than 300 species of birds. Other animals inhabiting Ranthambore include the endangered caracal, also a member of the cat family, the leopard and the jungle cat; several members of the dog family, such as hyenas, foxes and jackals; the sloth bear; and varieties of deer, including the *chital* (spotted deer) and the sambar, India's largest deer. There are also two species of antelope: the *chinkara* (Indian gazelle) and the *nilgai* (antelope). However, the park is also worth visiting for its scenery, particularly if you walk up to the fort.

Aside from during August's Ganesh mela (fair), traffic into the park is restricted to organised safaris. Still, the remaining tigers are so used to being observed that they're not scared away by jeeps and canters (open-topped trucks seating 20) and appear to be intrigued by visitors.

It's 10km from the town of Sawai Madhopur to the first gate and another 3km to the main gate and Ranthambore Fort. Accommodation is stretched out along the road from the town to the park. The train station is in the heart of Sawai Madhopur, just south of the main bazaar. A large and colourful Jain festival, the Shri Mahavirji Fair (p144) is celebrated in the village of Chandangaon, within the Sawai Madhopur district.

◉ Sights

Ranthambore Fort   HISTORIC SITE

(admission free; ⊙6am-6pm) In the heart of the national park, this ancient fort is believed to have been built by the Chauhan Rajputs in the 10th century, only a few years before the invasion by Mohammed of Ghori. According to tradition, the fort was erected over the site at which two princes were engaged in a boar hunt. The boar eluded the princes and dived into a lake. Not to be thwarted, the princes prayed to Shiva to bring back the boar. Shiva deigned to do this, on condition that the princes build a fort in his honour at the spot.

However, it is ever-popular Ganesh who rules the roost at the fort, and a **temple** to him overlooks its southern ramparts – often busy with pilgrims. The temple hosts the annual Ganesha Chaturthi festival (see p144). Traditionally, when a marriage is to take place, invitations are forwarded to Ganesh before any other guests. The temple at the fort receives hundreds of letters each week addressed to the elephant god. There are two other Hindu temples inside the fort: the others are dedicated to Shiva and Ramlalaji. All three date from the 12th and 13th centuries and are constructed with impressive blocks of red Karauli stone.

From a distance, the fort is almost indiscernible on its hilltop perch – as you get closer, it seems almost as if it is growing out of the rock. It covers an area of 4.5 sq km, and affords peerless views from the disintegrating walls of the **Badal Mahal** (Palace of the Clouds), on its northern side. The ramparts stretch for more than 7km, and seven enormous gateways are still intact.

DEATH OR DISHONOUR

Ranthambhore Fort is believed to be the site of the first *jauhar* (ritual mass suicide by immolation) in Rajput history. In the early 14th century the fort's ruler, Hammir Deva, was engaged in a protracted battle with the Muslims. Although Hammir repulsed the Muslim forces, the women who were installed in the fort for their safety heard that he had succumbed on the battlefield. Preferring death to dishonour, they committed mass suicide. When confronted with the grisly news, the victorious Hammir beheaded himself before the image of Shiva in the temple at the fort.

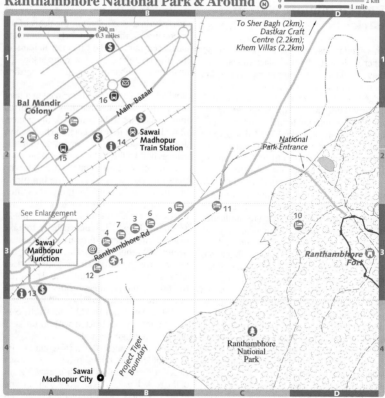

🏃 Activities

The only way to travel into the core of the park is by **safari** (Indian/foreigner per person in gypsy ₹500/890, in canter ₹425/812; video camera ₹400). The canter and jeep gypsy vehicles are open-topped. If you've ever been on safari in Africa you might be thinking this is risky, but the tigers appear unconcerned by garrulous tourists toting cameras only metres away from where they're lying. No-one has been mauled or eaten – yet!

Safaris take place in the early morning and late afternoon. The mornings can be very chilly in the open vehicles, so bring some warm clothes. The best option is to travel by jeep gypsy. You still have a good chance of seeing a tiger from the canter, though sometimes other passengers can be rowdy. Guides will lead you into one of five core zones or three buffer zones.

Safaris take three hours. In October canters and gypsies leave at 6.30am and 2.30pm; from November to January they leave at 7am and 2pm; from February to March they leave at 6.30am and 2.30pm; from April to May they leave at 6am and 3pm; from May to June they leave at 6am and 3.30pm.

Be aware that the rules for booking safaris (and prices) are prone to change. Seats in gypsies and canters can be reserved on the official website (www.rajasthanwildlife.in). If you book online you will need to pay the balance at the **Forest Office** (Ranthambhore Rd; ⊙5.30am-7am & noon-2pm) on the day of the safari or risk being cancelled. Cancelled seats are subsequently made available for direct booking. A single gypsy and five canters are also kept for direct booking at the Forest Office. Demand often outstrips supply during holiday seasons. Direct bookings on the day of the safari are best done through your hotel, which will send someone down to the Forest Office to obtain your ticket and naturally this will incur a small fee. This is the easiest way to do it, even though there is a dedicated window for foreigners at the Forest Office. If you do decide to do it yourself, be prepared for plenty of jostling and confusion.

🛏 Sleeping

Budget travellers may find the cheapest lodgings in Sawai Madhopur itself, but it isn't a particularly inspiring place to stay. All of the places on Ranthambhore Rd can help with safari bookings, though some are better at this than others. Some hotels may close when the park is closed.

RANTHAMBHORE ROAD

TOP CHOICE Khem Villas BOUTIQUE HOTEL $$$
(☎252099;www.khemvillas.com;Ranthambhore Rd; s/d incl all meals & taxes ₹8000/9500, tents ₹10,600/14,000, cottage ₹14,000/17,000; ❄) This splendid option has been created by the Singh Rathore family – the patriarch Fateh Singh Rathore is lauded as the driving force behind the conservation of the tiger at Ranthambhore. His son Goverdhan, and his daughter-in-law Usha, run this impressive ecolodge set in 22 acres of organic farmland and reafforested land. The accommodation ranges from rooms in the colonial-style bungalow to luxury tents to sumptuous stone cottages. Privacy is guaranteed – you can even bathe under the stars. Join the tiger talk at sunset drinks while the jungle sounds switch from the day shift to the night shift.

Hotel Tiger Safari Resort HOTEL $$
(☎221137; www.tigersafariresort.com; d incl breakfast ₹1280-1600; ❄@☲) This is one of the best options for those on a budget, where the

helpful management is adept at organising safaris, wake-up calls and early breakfasts before the morning safari. They can also organise pick-up and drop-off from the train station and sightseeing trips to the fort. The spacious doubles and so-called 'cottages' (larger rooms with bigger bathrooms) face a well-kept garden and small pool. And there's a very good multicuisine restaurant.

Hotel Ranthambhore Regency HOTEL $$$
(☎221176; www.ranthambhor.com; r ₹5500, s/d incl meals from US$135/165; ❄@☲) This is a very professional place that caters to tour groups but can still provide a good service to independent travellers. It has immaculate, well-appointed rooms (think marble floors, flat-screen TVs etc), which would rate as suites in most hotels. The central garden is a virtual oasis and the impressive pool is very inviting. There is also a bar and a spa.

Sher Bagh BOUTIQUE HOTEL $$$
(☎252120; www.sherbagh.com; luxury tent incl all meals & taxes ₹25,000; ☉Oct-Apr) A tented camp: here luxurious tents – based on the design for the maharaja of Jodhpur last century – are set on manicured lawns in an isolated woodland near the park. Each of the 12 tents has a verandah and gorgeous ensuite bathrooms with sunken marble showers.

Vivanta Sawai Madhopur Lodge
HERITAGE HOTEL $$$
(☎220541; www.vivantabytaj.com; r incl meals & tax from ₹9,500, ste ₹13,000; ❄@☲) This lodge, situated 3km from the train station, once belonged to the maharaja of Jaipur. The curvy art deco space has delightful suites refurbished with period flare. The luxury ex-

tends to the 4.5 hectares of trimmed gardens with a pool (₹400 for nonguests) and tennis court. The bar boasts half a tiger and a billiard table. The marble-adorned standard rooms are in bungalows with regal colonnaded verandas.

Hotel Aditya Resort HOTEL $
(☎9414728468; www.adityaresort.com; r ₹400, without bathroom ₹250, with AC ₹750; ❄) This friendly place represents good value for money. There are just six simple, unadorned rooms and a cute rooftop restaurant. The keen young staff will help organise safari bookings.

Hotel Ankur Resort HOTEL $$
(☎220792; www.hotelankurresort.com; r incl breakfast ₹1500, cottages ₹2000; ❄@☀) Ankur Resort is another hotel that is good at organising safaris, wake-up calls and early breakfasts for tiger spotters. Standard rooms are clean and comfortable with TVs, if fairly unadorned. The cottages boast better beds and a settee overlooking the surrounding gardens with its inviting pool.

Ranthambhore Forest Resort HOTEL $$$
(☎221120; www.ranthambhorforestresort.com; s/d incl all meals ₹5000/6000; ❄@☀) This well-appointed hotel is run by the well-known WelcomHeritage group and provides no-fuss service and comfortable rooms. Not surprisingly, it is frequented by bus groups. The rooms are grouped into villas in the gardens where guests will find the sparkling pool.

RTDC Castle Jhoomar Baori HOTEL $$$
(☎220495; www.rtdc.in; s/d incl breakfast ₹3300/4300, ste ₹6000; ❄) A former royal hunting lodge with a stunning hilltop setting, about 7km from the train station (you can spot it from the train). The multi-chamber rooms are loaded with character, although they're a bit shabby in true RTDC style. Open-rooftop areas add appeal.

RTDC Vinayak Hotel HOTEL $$
(☎221333; www.rtdc.in; s/d ₹1900/2800, tent ₹1700/2600, with AC ₹2600/3500; ❄) This RTDC complex is close to the park entrance and, although institutional in atmosphere, has bright and spacious rooms that are generally better than typical RTDC rooms. The tents on concrete bases are less appealing. There's a nice lawn area and a campfire is lit in the winter.

SAWAI MADHOPUR
Sawai Madhopur has gritty, cheap options convenient to the train station, but these are not always convenient when it comes to getting assistance with safari bookings.

Ganesh Ranthambhore HOTEL $$
(☎220230; 58 Bal Mandir Colony, Civil Lines; r without/with AC ₹1500/1800; ❄) On the western side of the overpass, this business-traveller hotel has basic but clean rooms. Rack rates are expensive but 30% discount is readily offered.

Rajeev Resort HOTEL $
(☎221413; 16 Indira Colony, Civil Lines; s/d ₹300/400) Rajeev Resort has decent fan-cooled rooms with TV, phone and running hot water. Cheap and simple set meals are available.

Hotel Chinkara HOTEL $
(☎222642; 13 Indira Colony, Civil Lines; r from ₹300) This place is quiet, with basic, dusty, rooms.

🛍 Shopping

Dastkar Craft Centre HANDICRAFTS
(Ranthambhore Rd; ⊙10am-8pm) This workshop and outlet located beyond the park entrance, near Khem Villas, is well worth a visit. The organisation helps to empower low-caste village women, who gain regular income through selling their textile and embroidery work. Many attractive handicrafts are on sale, including saris, scarves, bags and bedspreads. There is another outlet about 3km from the train station. Beware of imitators.

Ranthambhore School of Art
HANDICRAFTS
(Ranthambhore Rd) This place aims to promote conservation through art, and sells signature photo-realistic wildlife watercolours and prints with 20% of the proceeds going towards conservation.

ℹ Information

Bank of Baroda ATM (Bazariya Market) 200m northwest of the train station.

Post Office (Sawai Madhoper) 400m northeast of the train station.

Project Tiger office (☎223402; Ranthambhore Rd) The office is 500m from the train station. Don't expect much in the way of information.

State Bank of Bikaner & Jaipur (SBBJ) The place to change cash or travellers cheques, also with an ATM. There's another ATM east of the entrance in the train station building and one on Hamir Circle near the start of Ranthambhore Rd.

Tiger Track (☎222790; Ranthambhore Rd; per hr ₹60; ☉7am-10.30pm) Near Ankur Resort Hotel. Offers internet access and a good range of books.

Tourist Reception Centre (☎220808; Train Station; ☉9.30am-6pm Mon-Fri) This friendly office has a good, although not to scale, map of Sawai Madhopur and the park.

❶ Getting There & Away

Bus

Firstly, trains are preferable on all routes. Buses to Jaipur (₹110, six hours, four daily) via Tonk (₹44), and to Kota (₹86, five hours) via Bundi (₹74, 3½ hours) leave from the Bundi bus stand near the petrol station close to the overpass. Travelling to Bharatpur by bus invariably involves a change in Dausa (on the Jaipur–Bharatpur road). Buses to Jaipur (₹85, six hours) via Dausa (₹65, five hours), leave from the roundabout near the main post office. The inquiries number is ☎2451020.

Train

At Sawai Madhopur train station there's a computerised **reservation office** (☉8am-8pm Mon-Sat, to 2pm Sun).

The 12956 *Jaipur-Mumbai Express* departs Jaipur at 2.10pm, arriving at Sawai Madhopur (sleeper/3AC/2AC/1AC ₹140/275/355/585) at 4pm. Going the other way (No. 12955) it departs Sawai Madhopur at 10.45am arriving at Jaipur at 12.50pm. The 12466 *Intercity Express* leaves Jaipur at 10.55am, arriving at Sawai Madhopur (2nd class/sleeper/AC chair/3AC ₹65/140/225/275) at 1.15pm. Going the other way, the 12465 *Ranthambhore Express* departs Sawai Madhopur at 2.40pm and reaches Jaipur at 4.40pm.

The 12903 *Golden Temple Mail* leaves Sawai Madhopur at 12.30pm, stopping at Bharatpur (sleeper/3AC/2AC/1AC ₹140/322/424/699) at 3pm and continuing to arrive at Delhi (₹187/469/628/1051) at 6.30pm. From Delhi (No 12904), it leaves at 7.40am, stopping at Bharatpur at 10.40am and arriving at 1pm. It then departs at 1.05pm and arrives at Kota (₹140/265/323/526) at 2.25pm. Another convenient train to Kota is the 19037/8 *Avadh Express*. It leaves Sawai Madhopur at 9.10am and arrives in Kota (sleeper/3AC/2AC ₹120/235/293) on Monday, Wednesday, Friday and Saturday at 10.50am. Going the other way, it departs from Sawai Madhopur at 4.20pm, arriving in Agra (₹130/335/454) at 9.50pm on Tuesday, Wednesday, Friday and Sunday.

❶ Getting Around

Bicycle hire is available in the main bazaar (around ₹30 per day). Autorickshaws are available at the train station; the journey to Ranthambhore Rd will cost around ₹40.

Karauli

☎07464 / POP 66,200

Karauli was founded in 1348 and is the home of Shri Madan Mohanji, the deity of Lord Krishna, and has some important Krishna temples attracting many pilgrims. Around 23km from Karauli is the massively popular temple of Kaila Devi – during the Navratri celebrations in March/April and September/October, thousands of devotees flood the town en route to the temple (see p144).

Completely off the tourist trail, the area is also famous for its red-sandstone quarries and for its lac bangles. Nearby is the rugged **Kaila Devi Game Sanctuary** (25km away), which adjoins the buffer zone of Ranthambhore National Park.

The mainly 17th-century **old city palace** (Indian/foreigner ₹50/100; ☉sunrise-sunset) was constructed over different periods; the oldest part has existed for 600 years. Occupied by the Karauli royal family until around the 1950s, the palace is run-down and worn, but very atmospheric with great views from the roof. It's worth tipping the guard to get them to guide you. There's a **Krishna temple** (☉5-11.30am & 4-8pm) in the compound.

Around 40km from town, along a pot-holed road, is a tragically ruined fort, **Timangarh**. Built around 1100 and reconstructed in 1244, this once mighty fort overlooks a lake filled with water lilies. It was deserted 300 years ago, but was destroyed by looters over the last 50 years. You'll need to hire a taxi to get here, and one that can manage the track.

Bhanwar Vilas Palace (☎20024, 2290763; www.karauli.com; s/d from ₹3025/3575, ste ₹6050; ✱✿) , owned by Maharaja Krishna Chandra Pal, is closer to a large country manor than a palace. A back-in-time place, it features a billiard room, shady verandahs, rambling grounds and classic cars in the garages. Rooms are comfortable here and at the neighbouring Bhumendra Vilas. Excursions to nearby points of interest, including the old city palace, can be organised.

The town is 182km southeast of Jaipur, situated between Bharatpur (110km) and Sawai Madhopur (104km). There are buses running between Jaipur and Karauli (₹75, five hours).

The nearest train stations are Gangapur (31km) and Hindaun (30km), both on the main Delhi–Mumbai (Bombay) line.

Udaipur & Southern Rajasthan

Why Go?

Udaipur is one of India's most magical cities, a bastion of Rajasthani tradition, with its creamy-white palaces beside a shimmering lake, rambling old *havelis* (traditional mansions) and romantic luxury hotels that pull in honeymooners and more than a few wedding parties. Elsewhere in southern Rajasthan you'll clamber around mighty forts full of heroic and tragic legends, visit exquisitely carved Hindu and Jain temples, wander through medieval streets and markets in tangled old town centres, and, if your budget allows it, indulge in the luxuries of quaint palace-hotels. You can shop endlessly for a vast range of colourful artisanry, and get right off the beaten track exploring a host of wildlife sanctuaries from the wild, forested hills of Kumbhalgarh to the grasslands of Sorsan. And if the heat gets too much, skip away to the cooler heights of Mt Abu, Rajasthan's only hill station.

Best Places to Eat

» Ambrai (p210)
» Paantya Restaurant (p210)
» 1559 AD (p210)

Best Places to Stay

» Haveli Braj Bhushanjee (p183)
» Taj Lake Palace (p209)
» Udaivilas (p209)

When to Go

The best time to come to the south, like everywhere else in Rajasthan, is the winter months, November to March, for the main reason that the temperatures are temperate then. Indeed it can get cold in December and January. The winter months also see the bulk of the region's outstanding festivals, and are the best time for visiting the area's wildlife sanctuaries. The monsoon period, July to September, doesn't scorch like May and June, but its heat is steamy.

There's a flurry of colourful festivals in the south, while statewide and nationwide festivals (see p24) are also celebrated with plenty of enthusiasm.

» **Baneshwar Fair** (Baneshwar, Jan/Feb) This large event, honouring both Lord Shiva and Vishnu (worshipped as Mavji) is celebrated by thousands of Bhil tribal people, the fair site lying at the confluence of the Mahi and Som Rivers. Festivities include acrobatic and cultural programmes, and a silver image of Mavji is paraded through the village on horseback and doused in the river.

» **Holi** (Udaipur; Feb/Mar) Udaipur is the place to be for this joyful festival, which marks the beginning of spring. The Udaipur royal family hosts an elaborate function at the City Palace, with an evening horse procession, a band, and local nobility in traditional attire. After performing an ancient religious ceremony, the royal family lights a huge sacred fire, Holika Dahan, signifying the triumph of good over evil.

» **Gangaur** (Mt Abu; Mar/Apr) Gangaur, celebrated across Rajasthan, has some interesting adaptations in this region. Essentially a festival for women, it's dedicated to the goddess Gauri (Parvati). The Garasia tribes of the Mt Abu region celebrate for an entire month, with an image of Gauri carried aloft from village to village. In Bundi, Kota and Jhalawar, unmarried girls collect poppies from the fields and make them into wreaths for the goddess; in Nathdwara the Gangaur procession lasts for seven days, the goddess dressed differently each day.

» **Mewar Festival** (Udaipur; Mar/Apr) Udaipur's colourful take on Gangaur, this festival also celebrates spring. People in traditional costumes sing and dance in a lively procession to Gangaur Ghat on Lake Pichola. There are also free cultural programmes.

» **Summer Festival** (Mt Abu; May/Jun) Mt Abu registers the coolest temperatures in the state at this scorching time of the year; the festival includes classical and traditional folk-music programmes, as well as boat races on Nakki Lake and fireworks.

» **Kajli Teej** (Bundi; Aug/Sep) The traditional Rajasthani festival of Kajli Teej, marking the onset of the monsoon, is celebrated somewhat differently in Bundi where it's observed on the third day of the month of Bhadra. The celebrations are a good chance to see local artists perform.

» **Bundi Utsav** (Bundi; Oct/Nov) This cultural festival showcases the colourful traditions of the region with a procession, classical raga performances, magic and fireworks.

» **Dussehra** (Kota; Oct/Nov) Kota is the place to be for this festival, when enormous effigies, some around 20m high, are filled with crackers and set alight. The festival – an India-wide celebration – celebrates the story of Rama's victory over Ravana.

» **Ghans Bheru Festival** (Bharodia, Oct/Nov) Held on the day after Diwali in the village of Bharodia, about 10km northwest of Bundi, this colourful festival, almost unknown to tourists, honours the Hindu god Ghans Bheru. Thousands of villagers converge on Bharodia to celebrate a prosperous harvest.

» **Chandrabhaga Fair** (Jhalrapatan, Oct/Nov) This huge cattle fair takes place on the banks of the holy Chandrabhaga River near Jhalrapatan. Includes livestock trading and folk music, song and dance, while pilgrims bathe in a sacred part of the river known as Chandrawati.

History

The kingdom of Mewar (the area encompassing Udaipur, Chittorgarh and Kumbhalgarh) has dominated the history of the south, which is splattered with bloodshed and vast doses of valour.

Chittorgarh, Mewar's former capital, was sacked by invaders from Delhi or Gujarat three times between 1303 and 1568, each defeat ending in immense carnage, with its impossibly noble Rajputs (the ruling warrior caste) reliably choosing death before dishonour. While the men died in battle, the women committed *jauhar* (collective self-sacrifice), throwing themselves into the flames of huge pyres. After the third attack, Mewar's ruler,

Udaipur & Southern Rajasthan Highlights

❶ Roam the vast fort of **Chittorgarh** (p192), an island in the sky dotted with exquisitely beautiful buildings

❷ Indulge in the romance of **Udaipur** (p197), with its gorgeous lake vistas, fascinating shops and labyrinthine palace

❸ Soak up the medieval atmosphere of endearing **Bundi** (p180), a small, blue-painted town overlooked by a ramshackle fort and magical palace

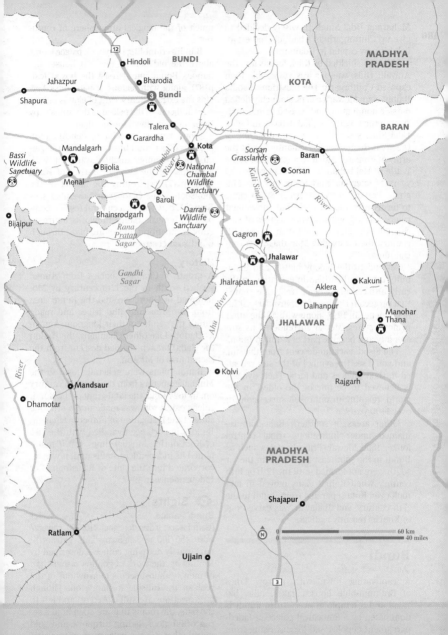

MADHYA
PRADESH

BUNDI

Hindoli

Jahazpur

Bharodia

Shapura

KOTA

3 **Bundi**

BARAN

Talera

Garardha

*Bassi
Wildlife
Sanctuary*

Mandalgarh

Kota

*Sorsan
Grasslands*

Baran

Bijolia

Sorsan

Menal

Chambal River

*National
Chambal
Wildlife
Sanctuary*

Kali Sindh

Parvan

River

Bijaipur

Bhainsrodgarh

Baroli

*Darrah
Wildlife
Sanctuary*

*Rana
Pratap
Sagar*

Gagron

Ahu River

Jhalawar

*Gandhi
Sagar*

Jhalrapatan

Aklera

Kakuni

Dalhanpur

Manohar
Thana

JHALAWAR

Mandsaur

Kolvi

Rajgarh

Dhamotar

**MADHYA
PRADESH**

Shajapur

Ratlam

0   60 km
0   40 miles

Ujjain

3

4 Explore the mighty fort of
Kumbhalgarh (p216) and hike
across the forested hills of the
neighbouring **Kumbhalgarh
Wildlife Sanctuary** (p217).

5 Trek around the forests,
lakes, temples and superb
panoramas of **Mt Abu** (p225)

6 Enjoy a **horse ride** around
the hills, villages and lakes
near Udaipur (p203)

7 Admire the sublimely
delicate carving in the Jain
temples at **Mt Abu** (p223) and
Ranakpur (p217)

Maharana Udai Singh II, wisely decided to give up Chittorgarh as a bad job and establish his new capital in Udaipur.

Udaipur, shielded by thick forests and the Aravalli Hills, was far less vulnerable than exposed Chittorgarh. The illustrious Sisodia Rajput clan, Mewar's rulers, staunchly defied outside domination and refused to intermarry with the mighty Mughal dynasty in Delhi. Udai Singh's son, Maharana Pratap, one of the great Rajput heroes, gallantly fought the army of Emperor Akbar to a stalemate at the Battle of Haldighati in 1576, then waged 20 years of guerrilla warfare against the Mughals. Pratap's successor Amar Singh came to terms with the Mughals, but subsequent rulers resisted, with varying degrees of success, first the Mughals and then, in the 18th century, the rampaging Marathas from central India.

An end to the bloody battles and instability came with British intervention in the early 19th century, when a treaty was signed that protected Udaipur from invaders. At Independence in 1947, along with all the other princely states, Mewar surrendered its sovereignty and became part of a united India.

The Sisodias claim descent from the sun, and you'll see the symbol of the sun repeated in their palaces and forts. Their dynasty is believed to be one of the oldest in the world, reigning in unbroken succession for over 1400 years.

Other areas of southern Rajasthan remained under indigenous tribal control longer than Mewar. Princely states such as Bundi in the southeast and Vagad in the far south were not formed until the 12th or 13th century when Rajput clans moved in and took over. Kota separated from Bundi in the 17th century, and Jhalawar was carved out of Kota as recently as 1838.

Bundi

📞0747 / POP 88,312

A captivating town with narrow lanes of Brahmin-blue houses, lakes, hills, bazaars and a temple at every turn, Bundi is dominated by a fantastical palace of faded-parchment cupolas and loggias rising from the hillside above the town. Though popular with travellers, Bundi attracts nothing like the tourist crowds of cities like Jaipur or Udaipur, nor are its streets choked with noisy, polluting vehicles or dense throngs of people. Few places in Rajasthan retain so much of the magical atmosphere of centuries past.

Bundi's crumbling storybook palace looms above the old part of town. It houses the famous Bundi murals (see the boxed text, p187), along with legions of bats; dusk heralds the extraordinary sight of clouds of bats streaming out of the palace as this still-sleepy town quietens down for the night.

From January to March, delicate pink poppies fill surrounding fields. A visit in August or September might reward you with a glimpse of the cheerful festival of **Kajli Teej** (p177), celebrating the arrival of the monsoon, while October or November sees **Bundi Utsav** (p177), a cultural festival complete with music, dance, fireworks, a turban-tying competition and more, blaze through Bundi's quiet streets.

History

A group of Chauhan nobles from Ajmer, pushed south in the 12th century by Mohammed of Ghori, wrested the Bundi area from the Mina and Bhil tribes and made Bundi the capital of their kingdom, known as Hadoti. Like other Chauhans, the Hadoti (or Hada) branch claimed descent from the sacred fires of Mt Abu.

Bundi rulers were generally loyal to the Mughal emperors from the late 16th century on. In 1624 Kota, the land grant of the Bundi ruler's eldest son, was made into a separate state at the instigation of Emperor Jehangir. Bundi's importance dwindled with the rise of Kota during Mughal times, but it maintained its independent status until it was incorporated into the state of Rajasthan after Independence in 1947.

⊙ Sights

Bundi Palace PALACE

(Garh Palace; Indian/foreigner ₹10/100, camera/video ₹50/100; ⊘8am-5pm) This extraordinary, partly decaying edifice – described by Kipling as 'the work of goblins rather than of men' – almost seems to grow out of the rock of the hillside it stands on. Though large sections are still closed up and left to the bats, the rooms that are open hold a series of fabulous, fading turquoise-and-gold murals that are the palace's chief treasure. Knowledgeable guides (₹250) hang around the ticket office to illuminate your visit. The palace was constructed in the reign of Rao Raja Ratan Ji Heruled (Ratan Singh; 1607–31) and added to by his successors.

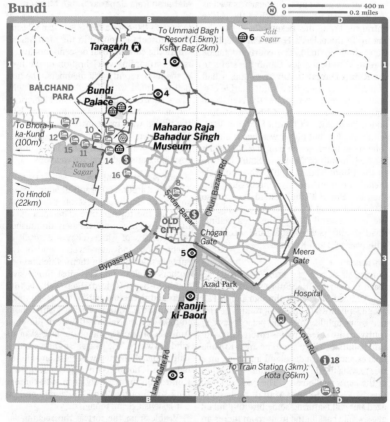

Bundi

If you are going up to Taragarh as well as the palace, get tickets for both at the palace entrance. From the ticket office you zig-zag up to the palace's **Hathi Pol** (Elephant Gate), built in 1620. The courtyard inside here used to be stables. Climb the stairs to the **Ratan Daulat** or Diwan-e-Aam, a hall of public audience with a white marble coronation throne, overlooking the courtyard. You then pass into the **Chhatra Mahal**, added by Rao Raja Chhatra Shabji in 1644, with some fine but rather weathered murals (one room features one painting of Krishna for each month of the year). Stairs lead up to the **Phool Mahal** (1607) whose murals include an immense royal procession, and then the **Badal Mahal** (Cloud Palace, also 1607), with Bundi's very best murals, including a wonderful Chinese-inspired ceiling, divided into petal shapes and decorated with peacocks and Krishnas.

Chitrasala   PALACE
(Ummed Mahal; admission free; ☺dawn-dusk) To reach this small 18th-century palace built by Rao Ummed Singh, exit through Bundi Palace's Elephant Gate and walk round the corner going uphill. Above the palace's garden courtyard are several rooms covered in beautiful paintings. There are some great Krishna images, including a detail of him sitting up a tree playing the flute after stealing the clothes of the *gopis* (milkmaids). The back room to the right is the **Sheesh Mahal**, badly damaged but still featuring some beautiful inlaid glass, while back in the front room there's an image of 18th-century Bundi itself.

Taragarh   FORT
(Star Fort; Indian/foreigner ₹10/100, camera/video ₹50/100; ☺8am-5pm) The ramshackle, partly overgrown Taragarh fort, on the hilltop above the palace, is great to ramble around – but take a stick to battle the overgrown vegetation, help the knees on the steep climb, and provide confidence when surrounded by testosterone-charged macaques. The fort was originally built by Rao Bav Singh in 1354.

Take the path up behind the Chitrasala, then head 250m east along the inside of the ramparts and then 300m left up the steep stone ramp which starts just before the **Dudha Mahal**, a small disused building.

The views from the top are magical. Inside the ramparts are three deep *baoris* carved out of solid rock and the **Bhim Burj**, the largest of the great bastions (currently occupied by the police and off limits).

Maharao Raja Bahadur Singh Museum
                                                MUSEUM
(admission ₹50, camera ₹50; ☺9am-1pm & 2-5pm) This museum is housed in the Moti Mahal, where the current royal descendants live. It is an extraordinary celebration of the lives of the more recent royal members. The first hall is stuffed with stuffed wildlife, chiefly tigers shot by Indian, British and American luminaries. Most visitors are dumbstruck by the tigress with two cubs – all shot by 'Mr Milton Reynolds, inventor of the ballpoint pen, in 1953 at Bhimlat'. Other halls contain royal portraits and arrays of weapons.

Baoris & Water Tanks   NOTABLE BUILDINGS
Bundi has around 60 beautiful *baoris* (stepwells; see the boxed text on p185), some right in the town centre. The majesty of many of them is unfortunately diminished by their lack of water today – a result of declining groundwater levels – and by the rubbish that collects in them which no one bothers to clean up. The most impressive, **Raniji-ki-Baori** (Queen's Step-Well), is 46m deep and decorated with sinuous carvings, including the avatars of Lord Vishnu. Built in 1699 by Rani Nathawati, wife of Rao Raja Anirudh Singh, it's one of the largest of its kind anywhere. The **Nagar Sagar Kund** is a pair of matching step-wells just outside the old city's Chogan Gate. The **Dhabhai-ka-Kund** is an impressively deep 19th-century tank south of the Raniji-ki-Baori – and on our last visit clean, though dry.

Visible from the fort is the rectangular artificial lake **Nawal Sagar**, which tends to dry up if the monsoon is poor. At its centre is a temple to Varuna, the Aryan god of water.

Opposite the **Abhaynath Temple**, one of Bundi's oldest Shiva temples, west of Nawal Sagar, is the 16th-century tank **Bhora-ji-ka-Kund**, which attracts a variety of bird life after a good monsoon, including kingfishers.

Jait Sagar   LAKE
Round the far side of the Taragarh hill, about 2km from the centre of town, this picturesque, 1.5km-long lake is flanked by hills and strewn with pretty lotus flowers during the monsoon and winter months. At its near end, the **Sukh Mahal** (admission free; ☺10am-5pm) is a small summer palace surrounded by terraced gardens where Rudyard Kipling once stayed and wrote part of *Kim*.

Just past the east end of the lake is the atmospheric, partly overgrown **Kshar Bag** (Indian/foreigner/camera ₹20/50/50; ☺9am-5pm), with the cenotaphs of 66 Bundi rulers and queens. Some have terrific, intricate carvings, especially of elephants and horses. The caretaker will probably show you round and detail the rulers' names, dates and number of wives – 17th-century ruler Maharaja Satru Sele apparently had 64 queens but even more are carved on his cenotaph. Fork right just after Kshar Bag to reach **Shikar Burj**, a small former royal hunting lodge (once there were tigers, deer and boars here) next to a water tank. It's a popular place for a picnic.

It's nice to visit Jait Sagar by bicycle and with a bike or autorickshaw you could combine it with other sights further out of town.

Old City   AREA
It's great to explore the ancient winding streets, gateways and bazaars of the old city, as well as the more touristic Balchand Para area below the palace. Bundi has more than 200 temples, and the market area just outside the Chogan Gate, around Nagar Sagar Kund, is the most vibrant area of town.

84-Pillared Cenotaph   HISTORIC BUILDING
Towards the southern edge of town, this cenotaph, set in gardens just off the Kota road, is particularly stunning when lit up at night. It was built to honour the son of a maharaja's ayah (nurse) about 600 years ago. To find it turn west off Kota Rd 800m south of the tourist office and go 80m.

🖝 Tours

OP 'Kukki' Sharma (☑9828404527; bundirock paintings@gmail.com; 43 New Colony) is a passionate amateur archaeologist who has discovered around 70 prehistoric rock painting sites in a lifetime's exploring around Bundi. His trips (half/whole day ₹500/1000, plus vehicle costs) also get you out into the villages and countryside, which he knows like the back of his hand. You can visit his collection of finds and select sites from his laptop at his house (about 300m south of the tourist office) beforehand.

🛏 Sleeping & Eating

Most accommodation clusters in the Balchand Para area beneath the palace. Guesthouses and hotels provide the main eating options and many of them happily serve nonguests as well as guests. Most places will pick you up from the train station or bus stand if you call ahead. Bundi was once a dry town, so it's not a place for evening revelry; however, a cold beer can usually be arranged. Mosquitoes can be a nuisance

in places near Nawal Sagar: keep repellent handy.

TOP CHOICE **Haveli Braj Bhushanjee**
HERITAGE HOTEL **$$**
(☑2442322; www.kiplingsbundi.com; r ₹500-4500, AC from ₹1200; ✳📶) This rambling, authentic, 200-year-old *haveli* is run by the very helpful and knowledgeable Braj Bhushanjee family, descendants of the former prime ministers of Bundi. It's an enchanting place with original stone interiors (plenty of low doorways), splendid rooftop views, beautiful, well-preserved murals, and all sorts of other historic and valuable artefacts. The terrific range of accommodation includes some lovely, recently modernised rooms that are still in traditional style. It's a fascinating living museum where you can really get a feel for Bundi's heritage.

Hotel Bundi Haveli   BOUTIQUE HOTEL **$$**
(☑2447861; http://hotelbundihaveli.com; r ₹1000-2500, ste ₹4000; ✳) The exquisitely renovated Bundi Haveli certainly leads the pack in terms of up-to-date style and sophistication. White walls, stone floors, colour highlights and framed artefacts are coupled with modern plumbing and electricity. Yes, it is very comfortable and relaxed and there's a lovely rooftop dining area boasting palace views and an extensive, mainly Indian menu (mains ₹90 to ₹250).

Haveli Katkoun   GUESTHOUSE **$**
(☑2444311; http://havelikatkoun.free.fr; s from ₹350, d ₹500-1800; ✳) Just outside the town's west gate, Katkoun is a completely revamped *haveli*. It boasts large, spotless rooms offering superb views of the lake or palace and has a good courtyard restaurant (mains ₹65 to ₹200).

Kasera Heritage View   HERITAGE HOTEL **$$**
(☑2444679; www.kaseraheritageview.com; s/d ₹800/1000, AC from ₹1500/1800; ✳) Another revamped *haveli*, Kasera has an incongruously modern lobby but offers a range of slightly more authentic rooms. The welcome is friendly, it's all cheerfully decorated, the rooftop restaurant has great views, and discounts of 40% to 50% are frequently offered. The owners' fancy sister haveli, **Kasera Paradise**, just below the palace, has the same contact details and very similar rates.

RN Haveli   GUESTHOUSE **$**
(☑2443278, 9784486854; rnhavelibundi@yahoo.co.in; Rawle ka Chowk; r ₹300-400, without bathroom ₹150-200, AC ₹1000-1200; ✳) This is an

old, rambling house with a grassy garden, recently decorated rooms and delectable, home-cooked, vegetarian meals (mains ₹60 to ₹80). Run by a dynamic mother-and-two-daughters team, it's a place where solo female travellers will feel comfortable at once.

Hadee Rani Guest House GUESTHOUSE **$**
(☎2442903; hadeeranipg@yahoo.com; Sadar Bazar; s ₹150-700, d ₹200-800) A friendly, enthusiastic family runs this three-centuries-old *haveli* with rooms of varied sizes up and down its staircases. It has a very good multicuisine restaurant (mains ₹50 to ₹200, thali ₹100 or ₹180).

Ishwari Niwas HERITAGE HOTEL **$$**
(☎2442414; www.ishwariniwas.com; 1 Civil Lines; r ₹600, AC ₹800-1500, incl breakfast; ✳@) This is a family-run hotel with royal associations in a graceful 100-year-old building set around an oddly decorated courtyard. It has spacious rooms with murals, and an interesting dining hall (heads, skins and old maps), but is inconveniently situated 1km south of the old city.

Bundi Vilas HERITAGE HOTEL **$$**
(☎5120694; www.bundivilas.com; r incl breakfast ₹2500-3000; ✳@) This 300-year-old *haveli* has been tastefully renovated with Jaisalmer sandstone, earth-toned walls and deft interior design. Rooms are medium-sized, except for two larger ones next to the restaurant.

Ummaid Bagh Resort HOTEL **$$**
(☎2447066; www.hadotiholidayresorts.com; Jait Sagar Rd; tent s/d incl breakfast ₹2000/2500; ✳) This lakeside tent hotel is a nice option if you fancy staying 3km from Bundi centre. There's a tree hide for watching Jait Sagar's birds (best from November to February).

Shivam Tourist Guest House GUESTHOUSE **$**
(☎2447892, 9214911113; www.shivam-bundi.co.in; r ₹250-800; ✳) Rooms are good and clean, if a trifle Spartan. The energetic, talkative hosts offer good veg meals on the rooftop, plus classes in cooking, henna design and Hindi.

Haveli Uma Megh GUESTHOUSE **$**
(☎2442191; haveliumamegh@yahoo.com; r ₹200-600) Has plenty of dilapidated charm, with wall paintings, alcoves and a lakeside garden for candlelit dinners (mains ₹40 to ₹60, thali ₹80 to ₹200). The pricier rooms are spacious.

Lake View Paying Guest House
GUESTHOUSE **$**
(☎2442326; lakeviewbundi@yahoo.com; r ₹200-450) Overseen by a kindly family, this guesthouse has some rooms with lake views and stained-glass windows. The nice little lakeside garden restaurant does multicuisine dishes for ₹50 to ₹100.

Haveli Parishan GUESTHOUSE **$**
(☎9829774218; r ₹200-400) A popular little cheapie with keen owners offering cooking classes and multicuisine meals.

Information

There's an Axis Bank ATM on Sadar Bazar and a State Bank ATM west of Azad Park.

Ayurvedic Hospital (☎2443708; ⊘9am-1pm & 4-6pm Mon-Sat, 9-11am Sun) Opposite Haveli Braj Bhushanjee, this charitable hospital prescribes natural plant-based remedies. There are medicines for all sorts of ailments, from upset tummies to arthritis, and many of them are free. There's also a conventional government hospital opposite the bus stand.

Front Page Cyber Cafe (Balchand Para; internet per hr ₹40; ⊘8am-10pm) One of the less expensive places to check your email.

Roshan Tour & Travel (⊘8am-5pm) Will exchange currency and travellers cheques; about 300m south of the palace.

Tourist office (☎2443697; Kota Rd; ⊘9.30am-6pm Mon-Fri) This very helpful office has bus and train schedules and offers free maps and helpful advice on most practical questions you can toss at it.

ⓘ Getting There & Away

Bus

Bus journeys to and from Bundi are bone-rattlers, although the recently-made four-lane Hwy 76 which you hit about halfway to Chittorgarh has improved journeys in that direction. 'Express' government buses from the bus stand run to Kota (₹24, one hour, every 15 minutes), Chittorgarh (₹100, four hours, two evening buses), Udaipur (₹175, six hours, two evening buses), Ajmer (₹111, four hours, half-hourly), Jaipur (₹120, five hours, half-hourly), Sawai Madhopur (₹60, 4½ hours, four daily), Jodhpur (₹160, 10 hours, three daily), Delhi (₹270, 11 hours, three daily) and Indore (₹175, 12 hours, 8am and 11am). For Pushkar, change buses at Ajmer. There are also buses to Bijolia (₹30, 1½ hours) and Menal (₹35, two hours) at 9am and 3pm.

Private sleeper buses with similar seat prices to government buses launch around 10pm for Chittorgarh, Udaipur, Ajmer and Delhi (one each), but they are for thrill-seekers only.

Step-wells, or *baoris* as they are also known, are widespread throughout Rajasthan. In the south you will find not only the famous wells at Bundi but also step-wells at smaller, more out-of-the-way locations such as within the remote fort at Kumbhalgarh and in quiet, pastoral Narlai.

Building a step-well is lauded in Hindu scriptures as an act of great merit, the wealthy having built wells to gain kudos and good karma. There are several other terms used to describe these wells, including *kund*, which generally refers to a structural lake/tank, and *vapi, vav* or *wav*, a water supply accessed via a series of steps.

In addition to their essential function as a water supply in arid areas, step-wells were frequently attached to temples and shrines, enabling devotees to bathe and purify themselves. Many formed part of a larger complex that included accommodation for travellers along caravan routes. The more elaborate *baoris* have intricate pillars, steps built in artistic configurations, and rooms, corridors, galleries and platforms cut into the various levels. Their spiritual and life-giving properties, and their pivotal role in daily life, meant that many were adorned with carvings of gods and goddesses, especially Ganesh, Hanuman, Durga and Mahishasura. The presence of these wells served to transform the everyday necessity of collecting water into a social occasion, and women would dress to impress in their finest outfits just to go out for the day's supply.

Train

The station is 4km south of the old city; trains are fewer but smoother and sometimes quicker than buses. The 12963 *Mewar Express* departs at 2.04am for Chittorgarh (sleeper/3AC/2AC/1AC ₹150/288/371/608, 2¾ hours) and Udaipur (₹167/399/527/874, 5¼ hours). In the other direction the 12964 *Mewar Express* leaves at 10.50pm for Delhi's Nizamuddin station (₹242/609/817/1375, 7¾ hours), stopping at Kota, Sawai Madhopur and Bharatpur en route. Two other trains go to Chittorgarh: the 59812 *Haldighati Passenger* at 7.20am (sleeper ₹90, 3¼ hours), and the 29020 *Dehradun Express* at 9.38am (sleeper/2AC/1AC ₹130/341/558, 3¼ hours). Eastbound, the 59811 *Haldighati Passenger* at 5.50pm heads to Sawai Madhopur (sleeper ₹90, 5½ hours) and Agra (₹119, 12 hours); the 29019 *Nimach-Kota Express* at 5.21pm heads to Kota, Sawai Madhopur (sleeper/2AC/1AC ₹130/362/593, four hours), Bharatpur and Delhi Nizamuddin (₹202/787/1325, 12 hours).

ⓘ Getting Around

Bicycles are an ideal way to get around this area. They are available at many guesthouses for around ₹30 or ₹40 per day. You can also hire motorbikes for ₹200 to ₹300 per day.

An autorickshaw to the train station costs ₹50 to ₹70 by day and ₹100 to ₹120 by night; a half-day trip out to Akoda and Rameshwar is around ₹250.

You can rent taxis for ₹700 to ₹1200 per day through your accommodation.

Around Bundi

With a bicycle, motorbike, autorickshaw or taxi you can make some lovely excursions from Bundi. Around 6km north are **Akoda**, a merchants' village, and **Thikarda**, which has various potteries. About 20km north are a Shiva cave temple and a waterfall at **Rameshwar**. Twenty-two kilometres towards Jaipur is **Hindoli**, home to a huge lake and a ruined hilltop fort. If you're in Bundi on the day after Diwali (October or November), head 10km northwest to the small village of **Bharodia**, off the Jaipur road, to witness the spectacular **Ghans Bheru** festival (p177).

Southwest of Bundi off the Chittorgarh road are two of the best of dozens of prehistoric rock painting sites in the area. **Garardha**, south of the road and about 33km from Bundi, has about 30 caves with paintings between 2000 and 20,000 years old, flanking a river. There's a curious depiction of a man riding a huge bird, as well as some hunting scenes. **Bhimlat** has 13 shelters with paintings in a jungle-clad gorge 37km from town and north of the road. The paintings, from 5000 to 12,000 years old, include human and animal figures. There's also a 50m waterfall here. It's best to visit these places with a local guide: OP 'Kukki' Sharma (p183) is recommended.

Further towards Chittorgarh are a few places worth stopping at if you're travelling by taxi between Bundi and Chittorgarh. **Bijolia**, 52km from Bundi, was once a famous pilgrimage centre with 100 temples built in the 11th to 13th centuries. Most of these were destroyed by Mughal invaders, and today only three are left standing. One of them, **Hajaresvara Mahadeva**, is devoted to Shiva, with delicate carving and a high lingam (phallic symbol) surrounded by lots of small linga.

Menal (⊗dawn-dusk), 19km beyond Bijolia, is a temple complex built way back in the Gupta period (4th to 6th centuries AD). The main **Shiva temple**, still in good condition, has a wealth of carvings of Shiva, Parvati, animals, dancers, musicians and sexual positions on its exterior. Outside the temple compound the Menal River tumbles over a 100m cliff, forming a spectacular waterfall when enough water is released from a dam upstream. When the water is low, you can cross the river above the fall to reach two more temples and the crumbling **Rutirani Palace**, said to have been a retreat of Prithviraj Chauhan, the 12th-century ruler from Ajmer who also held Delhi for a while. Eight kilometres past Menal, you can turn right at Ladpura to detour 9km to **Mandalgarh**, one of many forts built by Rana Kumbha, the 15th-century ruler of the Mewar kingdom (the others include Kumbhalgarh and parts of Chittorgarh). The vast, sprawling ruins afford good views.

Kota

📞0744 / POP 695,899

Historically a city of strategic importance, Kota still boasts a huge army base but its contemporary guise is that of a modern industrial centre. It also has a spectacular palace with an excellent museum and lovely murals, and Rajasthan's only permanent river, the Chambal, runs through the town, offering opportunities for scenic boat trips. Kota is famous, too, for its exquisite *kota doria* saris, prized wedding apparel which attract shoppers from all over India. They are woven of cotton or silk in an assortment of colours, many with delicate golden-thread designs, in the nearby village of Kaithoon.

You can easily visit Kota as a day trip from Bundi or see its sights in a few hours when making a transport connection. Kota is strung out along the east bank of the Chambal River, with the train station near the north end of town and Kishore Sagar lake roughly in the middle, 5km from the station. South of Kishore Sagar is an area of narrow, winding streets and crowded commercial areas within the old city walls. The fort and its palace sit near the river here, with the Kota Barrage dam just to their west.

History

Building of the city began in 1264 after the Hadoti Chauhans defeated and beheaded Koteya, a Bhil chieftain who gave the city his name. The foundation stone of the fort was laid, rather gruesomely, on the very spot he lost his head. Kota separated from the Bundi princedom in 1624 when Rao Madho Singh, a son of the ruler of Bundi, was made ruler of Kota by the Mughal emperor Jehangir. Kota subsequently became a larger and more powerful city and state than Bundi. Chemical and engineering plants and a large thermal power station are mainstays of its industrial economy today. It's also a renowned centre for university-entrance coaching courses in medicine and engineering.

⊙ Sights & Activities

City Palace & Fort
PALACE, FORT

The fort and the palace within it make up one of the largest such complexes in Rajasthan. This was the royal residence and centre of power, housing the Kota princedom's treasury, courts, arsenal, armed forces and state offices. Some of its buildings are now used as schools. The **City Palace** (Indian/foreigner ₹10/100, camera/video ₹50/100; ⊗10am-4.30pm Sat-Thu), entered through a gateway topped by rampant elephants, contains the excellent **Rao Madho Singh Museum** where you'll find all the stuff necessary for a respectable Raj existence – silver furniture, an old-fashioned ice cream maker and ingenious, beautiful weapons. The oldest part of the palace dates from 1624. Downstairs is an elegant durbar (royal audience) hall with beautiful mirror work, while the elegant, small-scale apartments upstairs dance with exquisite, beautifully preserved paintings, particularly the hunting scenes for which Kota is renowned.

After visiting the museum it's worth exploring the rest of the complex to appreciate how magnificent it must have been in its heyday. The **fort ramparts** are some of the highest in Rajasthan, with three-level fortifications, six double gates and 25 towers. Unfortunately, a lot of it is falling into disrepair and the gardens are no more, but there are some excellent views over the old city and the Chambal and less-inspiring views of the thermal power station across the river.

Some of Rajasthan's finest miniature and mural painting was produced around Bundi and Kota, the ruling Hada Rajputs being keen artistic patrons. The style combined the dominant features of folk painting – intense colour and bold forms – with the Mughals' concern with naturalism.

The Bundi and Kota schools were initially similar, but developed markedly different styles, though both usually have a background of thick foliage, cloudy skies and scenes lit by the setting sun. When architecture appears it is depicted in loving detail. The willowy women sport round faces, large petal-shaped eyes and small noses – forerunners of Bollywood pin-ups.

The Bundi school is notable for its blue hues, with a palette of turquoise and azure unlike anything seen elsewhere. Bundi Palace in particular hosts some wonderful examples.

In Kota you'll notice a penchant for hunting scenes with fauna and dense foliage – vivid, detailed portrayals of hunting expeditions in Kota's once thickly wooded surrounds. Kota City Palace has some of the best-preserved wall paintings in the state.

Boat Trips   BOATING

A lovely hiatus from the city is a Chambal River boat trip. The river upstream of Kota is part of the Darrah National Park and once you escape the city it's beautiful, with lush vegetation and craggy cliffs on either side. It's an opportunity to spot birds, gharials (those thin-snouted, fish-eating crocodiles), muggers (those keep-your-limbs-inside-the-boat crocodiles) and possibly sloth bears. A 20-minute jaunt costs ₹40 per person; longer trips for up to six people are ₹1000 an hour. Boats start from **Chambal Gardens** (Indian/foreigner ₹2/5), 1.5km south of the fort on the river's east bank, and normally operate from 10.30am to sunset.

Chhattar Bilas Gardens   GARDEN

Also just north of Kishore Sagar, next to the Tourist Reception Centre, these gardens contain the **Kshar Bagh**, a collection of overgrown but impressive royal cenotaphs interspersed with carved elephants.

Kishore Sagar   LAKE

This picturesque artificial lake was constructed in 1346. In the middle, on a small island amid palm trees, is the enchanting little tangerine palace of **Jagmandir**. Built in 1740 by one of the maharanis of Kota, it's a sight that seems to mock the frantic streets on either side of the lake. The palace, sadly, is closed to the public.

Brij Vilas Bhavan Museum   MUSEUM

(Indian/foreigner/foreign student ₹5/50/25; ☺10am-5pm Tue-Sun) Just north of Kishore Sagar, this small, run-down government museum has a collection of 9th- to 12th-century stone idols and other sculptural fragments

(mainly from Baroli and Jhalawar), as well as some miniature paintings.

★ Festivals & Events

If you happen to hit Kota in October or November, check whether your visit coincides with the city's huge **Dussehra Mela**, during which massive effigies are built then spectacularly set aflame (p177). Thousands of pilgrims descend on the city in the month of Kartika (October/November) for **Kashavrai Patan**. See the Tourist Reception Centre for festival programs.

🛏 Sleeping & Eating

Budget accommodation in Kota is lacklustre, but the city is well served for more expensive heritage hotels (where it's always worth asking for a discount). All the hotels listed here, except Palkiya Haveli, are in the northern half of town between Kishore Sagar and the train station.

Most of these hotels have good restaurants, or you can graze at the early-evening snack stalls outside the main post office just along the street from Hotel Phul Plaza.

TOP CHOICE **Palkiya Haveli**   HERITAGE HOTEL **$$**
(☎2387497; www.alsisar.com; palkiya haveli@yahoo.com; Mokha Para; s/d ₹1800/2300, ste ₹2600; ☀) This is an exquisite *haveli* that has been in the same family for 200 years. Set in a deliciously peaceful corner of the old city, about 800m east of the City Palace, it's a lovely, relaxing place to stay, with welcoming hosts, a high-walled garden and a courtyard with a graceful neem tree. There are impressive murals and appealing heritage rooms, and the food is top notch.

Brijraj Bhawan Palace Hotel

HERITAGE HOTEL **$$**

(☎2450529; brijraj@dil.in; off Collectorate Circle, Civil Lines; s/d ₹2500/3550, ste ₹3700/4600; ❈) High above the Chambal River, this charismatic hotel has drawn exclusive guests since 1830. It was built to house the British Residency and is named after the current Maharao of Kota, Brijraj Singh (who still lives here and runs the hotel). The enormous, classically presented rooms, admittedly not refurbished very recently, open onto lofty verandas and terraces overlooking the river. Queen Mary chose No 4 for a snooze in 1911. There are well-maintained gardens, a croquet lawn and an intimate dining room (for guests only), which, unlike those in most palaces, is homy rather than grand.

Sukhdham Kothi

HERITAGE HOTEL **$$**

(☎2320081; www.sukhdhamkothi.com; Civil Lines; s/d ₹3000/3250; ❈) Sukhdham Kothi is atmospheric, comfortable and family-run. It's 140 years old and was once the home of the British Resident's surgeon. The old-fashioned rooms have solid 1930s furniture and big bathrooms with tubs. Some open onto balconies overlooking the pretty gardens. The hotel has a nice Indian restaurant and is hung with interesting old photos and maps.

Umed Bhawan Palace

HERITAGE HOTEL **$$**

(☎2325262; www.welcomheritagehotels.com; off Station Rd; s/d ₹3500/4000, ste from ₹4500/5000; ❈@) Surrounded by sprawling gardens, this grand stone palace is stuffily Edwardian and lacks the sparkle and intimacy of Sukhdham Kothi or the Brijraj Bhawan Palace. Still, it's fancy and comfortable, with voluminous rooms, a restaurant, bar and billiard room.

Hotel Navrang

HOTEL **$**

(☎2323294; Collectorate Circle, Civil Lines; s/d ₹450/550, AC ₹750/950; ❈) Better than the exterior suggests, the Navrang's rooms are worn but good-sized, comfortable and arranged around a modern internal courtyard. It's about halfway between the train station and Kishore Sagar. The attached **New South Indian Restaurant** (mains ₹50-90; ☺9am-11pm) is OK, if slow.

Hotel Phul Plaza

HOTEL **$**

(☎2329351; Civil Lines; s/d from ₹375/475, AC from ₹600/800; ❈) Next door to Hotel Navrang, Phul Plaza is a no-nonsense business hotel with unspectacular but clean air-conditioned rooms. The not-yet-modernized rooms without aircon are grungy. There are two restaurants, one of which doubles as a bar.

Hotel Shree Anand

HOTEL **$**

(☎2462473; s/d ₹200/350, AC ₹400/700; ❈) Along the street opposite the train station, this pink hotel is useful if you're catching an early-morning train. The cells are tiny and dingy but all feature attached bathrooms.

🛍 Shopping

For *kota doria* saris head to Bharu Gali, a small street in the Rampura Bazar area just west of Kishore Sagar. Prices can range from around ₹300 to ₹20,000. Or you can hunt them down at source in **Kaithoon**, 9km southeast of Kota (₹10, 30 minutes by bus from Aruvam Circle, Sabzi Bazar; ₹150 return in a rickshaw). **Hamid Bihari** (Kota Saree Wala, Kaithoon; ☺10am-7pm), opposite Taileyan Mandirwhich near Kaithoon police station, sells exquisite pieces, which you can see being woven upstairs.

ℹ Information

There are numerous ATMs, including HDFC and ICICI, outside Hotel Phul Plaza, and HDFC and SBBJ at the train station.

Inter Net Cafe (internet per hr ₹15; ☺9am-9pm) Facing Nayapura Park, 800m north of Kishore Sagar.

Tourist Reception Centre (☎2327695; RTDC Hotel Chambal; ☺9.30am-6pm Mon-Sat) About 250m north of Kishore Sagar.

ℹ Getting There & Away

Bus

The bus stand is east of the Bundi Rd river bridge, 1km north of Kishore Sagar. 'Express' government buses go to Ajmer (₹133, six hours, half-hourly), Bundi (₹24, one hour, every 15 minutes), Chittorgarh (₹120, four hours, five daily), Jaipur (₹149, six hours, half-hourly), Jodhpur (₹225, 10 hours, six daily), Udaipur (₹195, seven hours, nine daily), Jhalawar (₹52, 2½ hours, half-hourly) and Delhi (₹224, 12 hours, eight daily). There's an AC deluxe bus to Jaipur (₹255, five hours) at 2.30pm, and a Volvo AC bus to Jaipur (₹370, five hours) and Delhi (₹900, 11 hours) at 11pm.

Train

Kota is on the main Mumbai–Delhi train route via Sawai Madhopur, so there are plenty of trains to choose from (see the table, p189), though departure times are not always convenient.

ℹ Getting Around

Minibuses link the train station and bus stand (₹6). An autorickshaw should cost ₹30 for this journey; there's a prepay place at the station.

DESTINATION	TRAIN NUMBER & NAME	FARE (₹)	DURATION (HR)	DEPARTURE
Agra	19037/19039 Avadh Exp	174/445/601 (A)	7¼	2.50pm
Chittorgarh	59812 Haldighati Pass	90 (B)	4	6.30am
	29020 Dehradun Exp	130/395/650 (C)	3¼	9am
Delhi (Nizamuddin)	12903 Golden Temple Mail	230/576/770/1294 (E)	7¼	11.12am
	12964 Mewar Exp	230/576/770/1294 (E)	6½	11.55pm
Jaipur	12181 Dayodaya Exp	163/390/512 (A)	4	8am
	12955 Mumbai–Jaipur Exp	163/390/512/852 (E)	4	8.52am
Mumbai	12904 Golden Temple Mail	349/913/1237/2078 (E)	15	2.35pm
Sawai Madhopur	12059 Shatabdi	87/240 (D)	1¼	6am
	12903 Golden Temple Mail	150/280/338/551 (E)	1¼	11.12am
Udaipur	12963 Mewar Exp	179/433/573/955 (E)	6	1.25am

Fares: A – sleeper/3AC/2AC; B – sleeper; C – sleeper/2AC/1AC; D – 2nd class/AC chair; E – sleeper/3AC/2AC/1AC.

Around Kota

WILDLIFE SANCTUARIES

The thickly forested, wildly beautiful, 250-sq-km **Darrah Wildlife Sanctuary** (Indian/foreigner ₹20/160, car ₹130, camera/video free/₹400; ◷10am-5pm) is about 50km south of Kota, accessed from the Jhalawar road. Once a royal hunting ground, its wildlife includes spotted deer, sloth bears, sambars, leopards and antelopes. The sanctuary is sometimes closed during the monsoon (usually from early July to mid-September). You need permission to visit from the local forest ranger, or contact the **District Forest Office** (☏0744-2321263; Chhattar Bilas Gardens) near the Kota Tourist Reception Centre. If all else fails, ask at the Tourist Reception Centre itself, where they should be able to provide you with information and guide costs. Darrah Sanctuary and two other sanctuaries along the Chambal River were declared Darrah National Park in 2004, and there is talk of relocating tigers from Ranthambore here.

About 50km east of Kota are the **Sorsan Grasslands**, a 35-sq-km bird sanctuary where the scrubby vegetation and numerous small water bodies harbour an amazing variety of birds, as well as animals such as blackbuck and chinkara. Sorsan is rich with insects during the monsoon season, which attracts plenty of birds, including orioles, quails, partridges, robins, weavers, and waterfowl such as bar-headed and greylag geese, common pochards, teals and pintails. Flocks of migrants, such as warblers, flycatchers, larks, starlings and rosy pastors, winter here between October and March. Sadly the Indian bustard is reportedly no longer found here. To get to Sorsan turn south at Palaita on Hwy 76 and head 8km to Amalsara village at the northern end of the sanctuary.

You can hire a jeep with a driver to reach these parks from Kota for around ₹10 per km. Ask at the tourist reception centre for details.

BAROLI

The **Baroli Temples** (⊙10am-5pm), in a peaceful rural area 45km southwest of Kota, are one of Rajasthan's oldest temple complexes. Many of these 9th- to 12th-century temples were vandalised by the armies of Mughal emperor Aurangzeb, but much remains. The main edifice is the **Ghateshvara Temple**, which features a hall of impressive columns and a finely carved *sikhara* (temple spire) with figures including a dancing Shiva, Vishnu and Brahma. Beneath the spire is a fat Shiva lingam looking like an upturned pot *(ghata)*, hence the temple name. **Trimurti**, a ruined temple to the southwest, contains a three-headed Shiva. Between the Ghateshvara and Trimurti, the **Mahishasuramardini Temple** is dedicated to the demon-slaying goddess Durga. North of the Ghateshvara you'll find a red-headed Ganesh and a step-well dedicated to Hanuman.

Many of the sculptures from the temples are displayed in the Brij Vilas Bhavan Museum in Kota.

Three kilometres beyond Baroli, the town of Rawatbhata sits beneath the massive **Rana Pratap Sagar Dam**, one of four dams on the Chambal River. The **Rajasthan Atomic Power Station**, one of six nuclear power plants in India, stands beside the reservoir, southeast of Rawatbhata.

There are buses to Baroli (₹22, 1¾ hours) and Rawatbhata roughly hourly from Kota's Central Bus Stand.

Jhalawar

⏺07432 / POP 48,049

Jhalawar is a quiet, sprawling town 84km south of Kota that sees few visitors but has some charming sights in the surrounding area, part of their appeal being that they are so seldom visited.

Jhalawar was once the capital of a small princely state created in 1838 by Zalim Singh, the charismatic regent of Kota. Singh signed a treaty with the British on behalf of the young Kota prince, and in return received Jhalawar for his descendants to rule in their own right.

The town is siutaued at the centre of an opium-producing region, evidence of which you'll see during winter, when the fields are carpeted with picturesque pink and white poppies.

⦿ Sights

Ghar Palace   PALACE

(admission free; ⊙10am-5pm Mon-Sat) Inside the walled fort in the town centre, this sprawling cream-and-terracotta palace was built by Maharaja Madan Singh in 1838. It currently houses courts and a warren of dusty government offices filled with piles of ledgers, but the offices are in gradual process of being moved elsewhere so that the palace can be spruced up for tourism. Try, nevertheless, to get a look at the former **District Rural Development Authority offices**, a set of rooms around a courtyard filled with Ramayana and Krishna murals and paintings of poets; the former **Superintendent of Police's office**, with portraits of Jhalawar rulers and lovely flower-pattern murals; and the **Aina Mahal**, a sadly dilapidated mirror hall.

Also inside the palace is the **Bhawani Natyashala**, a Parsi theatre built in 1921 and modelled on Western opera houses, with a unique design including special underground constructions that allowed horses and carriages onto the stage.

Government Museum   MUSEUM

(admission ₹5; ⊙10am-5pm Tue-Sun) Just outside the fort's east gate, this small museum has a curious collection comprising 8th-century sculptures, gold coins, weapons, old paintings, a handwritten copy of the Quran and a leopard-skin coat.

🛏 Sleeping & Eating

Attracting only a smattering of tourists, Jhalawar has limited and uninspiring accommodation.

Hotel Dwarika   HOTEL $$

(⏺232626; Hospital Rd; s/d ₹500/600, AC ₹1000/1100; ❄) The best of the bunch, this hotel has rooms that are rectangular, grey and brown and all almost exactly the same, but they're clean and have comfy beds. Checkout is 24 hours and the small restaurant does a great *aloo paratha* for breakfast. Hot water is by bucket except in winter. It's beside the main highway running through the west side of town.

RTDC Hotel Chandrawati   HOTEL $$

(⏺234023; Jhalrapatan Rd; dm ₹100, s/d ₹725/900, AC ₹900/1100; ❄) A pleasant enough place at the south end of town, with bare rooms around a leafy courtyard. All have TV and bathroom. There's a passable restaurant (mains ₹30 to ₹40) too.

DON'T MISS

GAGRON FORT

Don't miss a trip to this spectacular **fort** (◷dawn-dusk), 7km north of Jhalawar. Almost 1km long, it's set high above the confluence of the Kalisindh and Ahu Rivers and has big, big views, as the rivers surround the building on three sides, while on the fourth is a deep moat. Though not as famous as the forts at Chittorgarh, Jodhpur and Jaisalmer, the huge fort occupies a prominent place in the annals of Rajput chivalry and has been fought over for centuries. It was established in the 8th century, changed hands many times, and was the site of a huge *jauhar* in 1443. Later, it was conquered by the Mughal emperor Akbar.

For the best view of the fort itself, head to Changari, the little village on the outcrop opposite its east end.

In the small village of Gagron at the fort's west end is the **shrine of Mitthesha**, a Sufi saint, constructed in 1423. The gate to the shrine was built by Akbar in 1580 and the place is the scene of a colourful fair during the Islamic month of Muharram.

An autorickshaw from Jhalawar should cost around ₹100 return.

Purvaj Hotel　　　　　　　　　　HOTEL $
(☑231355; Mangalpura Gantaghar; r ₹300-500) This simple, extremely run-down, 200-year-old *haveli* is next to the Central Bank of India near the clock tower. Rooms are basic, but have private bathrooms, and the building at least has character, with Brahmin-blue paint inside and good views from the roof. Solo female travellers might prefer to stay elsewhere since the area can feel a bit deserted at night and in the early morning.

Rupali Dhani　　　　　　　　　　INDIAN $
(Hospital Rd; mains ₹40-60; ◷9am-11pm) Opposite Hotel Dwarika, this is a friendly garden restaurant dishing up tasty veg fare including a few South Indian and Chinese options.

Information

There's an Axis Bank ATM on Hospital Rd 250m north of Hotel Dwarika, and an SBBJ ATM in the Ghar Palace building.

Tourist office (☑230081; ◷9.30am-6pm Mon-Fri) A very helpful if underutilised office, next to the RTDC Hotel Chandrawati.

Getting There & Away

The potholed road from Kota has to be one of the worst 'national highways' in India. Buses to Kota (₹52, 2½ hours) leave every half-hour from the bus stand, 1km southeast of the fort.

Around Jhalawar

JHALRAPATAN

Seven kilometres south of Jhalawar, the walled town of Jhalrapatan (City of Temple Bells) once had more than 100 temples. Far fewer remain now, but the huge 11th-century **Surya Temple** (◷7am-noon & 5-10pm), in the busy heart of town, is the pride of the region. The carving on the high, red-stone *sikhara* is very intricate, almost organic, and the spacious, high-ceilinged space beneath it contains magnificent sculptures. The idol of Padam Nath (an incarnation of the sun god Surya) worshipped here today dates from the 19th century, the previous gold one having apparently disappeared during the 1857 Indian Uprising. Also here are the 11th-century **Shantinath Jain Temple** – colourful, brightly painted and restored with intricately carved statues, an inlaid black-and-white marble floor, and two huge stone elephants – and the **Sheetaleshvara Temple**, a fine example of Gupta architecture. If you are visiting during October or November, you should look out for the huge **Chandrabhaga Fair** (p177), a lively cattle fair that consumes the town.

One kilometre east of the town centre, the enchanting, peaceful, 7th-century **Chandrabhaga Temple** is set in well-kept gardens on the banks of the holy Chandrabhaga River. Ghats along the riverbank neighbour some hidden-away erotic carvings.

Frequent buses run to Jhalrapatan (₹27, 15 minutes) from Jhalawar bus stand. An autorickshaw will cost around ₹100 for a return trip.

Chittorgarh (Chittor)

☑01472 / POP 96,028

Chittorgarh, the *garh* (fort) at Chittor, is the greatest in Rajasthan, and is well worth reshuffling an itinerary to explore. It rises from

ℹ CHITTORGARH – WHERE TO SLEEP?

The modern town of Chittor below the fort's west side is an ordinary place, and its accommodation options are ordinary too. The best places to stay in the area are two heritage hotels in villages to the east (see p196). Alternatively you can visit Chittorgarh as a long day-trip from Udaipur or as a half-day stopover between Udaipur and Bundi.

the plains like a huge rock island, nearly 6km long and surrounded on all sides by 150m-plus cliffs. Wandering around the plateau on top is like being on an island in the sky, or a gigantic boat, dotted with a collection of sublimely beautiful stone buildings. Chittorgarh's history epitomises Rajput romanticism, chivalry and tragedy, and it holds a special place in the hearts of many Rajputs. Three times Chittorgarh was under attack from a more powerful enemy; each time, its people chose death before dishonour, performing *jauhar*. The men donned saffron martyrs' robes and rode out from the fort to certain death, while the women and children immolated themselves on huge funeral pyres.

History

Chittor is mentioned in the Mahabharata: Bhima, one of the Pandava heroes, struck the ground here so hard that water gushed out to form a large reservoir. Bappa Rawal, an early king of Mewar, is believed to have established himself and his Guhilot dynasty here in AD 743. Over the following six centuries the Guhilots and their successors, the Sisodias, held Chittor on and off between occupations by the rulers of Gujarat and Malwa (western Madhya Pradesh). The first of Chittor's three great disasters occurred in 1303 when the Delhi sultan Ala-ud-din Khilji besieged the fort – according to legend, in order to capture the beautiful Padmini, the wife of the Mewar king, Ratan Singh. When defeat was inevitable, the men rode out to die and the Rajput noblewomen, including Padmini, committed *jauhar*. The fort was recaptured in 1326 by Hamir Singh, from a junior branch of the Mewar ruling family. Under Rana Kumbha (1433–68), a poet and musician as well as a military leader who surrounded his kingdom with 30 forts, Chit-

torgarh reached its cultural peak and Mewar attained its territorial zenith.

The arrival of the Mughals in northern India in the 1520s spelled the beginning of the end for Chittorgarh, but it was a siege by Bahadur Shah, the sultan of Gujarat, in 1535, that precipitated the second great *jauhar,* in which, it's thought, 13,000 Rajput women and 32,000 Rajput warriors died.

The final sacking of Chittor came just 33 years later, in 1568, when the Mughal emperor Akbar took the fort. Once again, the odds were overwhelming, and again the women performed *jauhar,* while 8000 orange-robed warriors rode out to certain death. On this occasion, Rana Udai Singh II fled to Udaipur, where he established a new capital for Mewar. In 1616, Jehangir returned Chittor to the Rajputs. There was no attempt at re-settlement, though it was restored in 1905.

◎ Sights

TOP CHOICE **Chittorgarh Fort**   FORT

(Indian/foreigner ₹5/100; ◎dawn-dusk) A zigzag ascent of more than 1km leads through six outer gateways to the main gate on the western side, the **Ram Pole** (the former back entrance). On the climb you pass two **chhatris**, domed memorials, between the second and third gates. These mark the spots where Jaimal and Kalla, heroes of the 1568 siege, fell during the struggle against Akbar. Jaimal had already been fatally wounded but was carried out by Kalla to fight on to the death.

Inside Ram Pole is a village of perhaps 4000 people that occupies a small northwestern part of the fort. (Turn right here for the ticket office). The rest of the plateau is deserted except for the wonderful palaces, towers and temples that remain from its heyday, with the addition of a few more recent temples. A loop road runs around the plateau, which has a deer park at the southern end.

There is a **Sound & Light Show** (Indian/foreigner ₹75/200; ◎dusk) at the Rana Kumbha Palace. The commentary is in English on days when the Palace on Wheels and Royal Rajasthan on Wheels tourist trains hit Chittor (Tuesday and Friday at time of writing).

Rana Kumbha Palace

Past the ticket office, you arrive almost immediately at this ruined palace group, which takes its name from the 15th-century ruler who renovated and added to earlier palaces

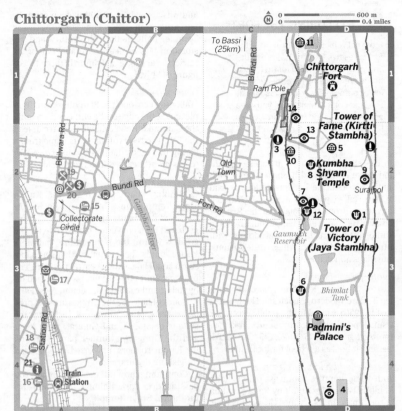

Chittorgarh (Chittor)

EXPLORING THE FORT

A typical vehicular exploration of the fort takes two to three hours. Guides charging around ₹350 for up to four hours are available for either walking or autorickshaw tours, usually at the ticket office. Make sure you get a government guide (they carry a guide licence).

on this site. The complex includes elephant and horse stables and a Shiva temple. Padmini's *sati* (suicide by immolation) is said to have taken place in a now-blocked cellar. Across from the palace is the **Sringar Chowri Temple**, a Jain temple built by Rana Kumbha's treasurer in 1448 and adorned with attractive, intricate carvings of elephants, musicians and deities.

Fateh Prakash Palace

East of the Rana Kumbha Palace, this palace is more modern (Maharana Fateh Singh died in 1930). Closed to the public except for a small, poorly labelled **museum** (Indian/foreigner/foreign student ₹5/50/25; ⊙9.45am-5.15pm Tue-Sun), it houses a school for local children.

Meera & Kumbha Shyam Temples

Both these temples southeast of the Rana Kumbha Palace were built by Rana Kumbha in the ornate Indo-Aryan style, with classic, tall *sikharas* (spires). The Meera Temple, the smaller of the two, is now associated with the mystic-poetess Meerabai, a 16th-century Mewar royal who was poisoned by her brother-in-law but survived due to the blessings of Krishna. The Kumbha Shyam Temple is dedicated to Vishnu and its carved panels illustrate 15th-century Mewar life.

Tower of Victory

The glorious Tower of Victory (Jaya Stambha), symbol of Chittorgarh, was erected by Rana Kumbha in the 1440s, probably to commemorate a victory over Mahmud Khilji of Malwa. Dedicated to Vishnu, it rises 37m in nine exquisitely carved storeys, and you can climb the 157 narrow stairs (the interior is also carved) to the 8th floor, from which there's a good view of the area. Hindu sculptures adorn the outside; its dome was damaged by lightning and repaired during the 19th century.

Below the tower, to the southwest, is the **Mahasati** area where there are many *sati* stones – this was the royal cremation ground

and was also where 13,000 women committed *jauhar* in 1535. The **Samidheshwar Temple**, built in the 6th century and restored in 1427, is nearby. Notable among its intricate carving is a Trimurti (three-faced) figure of Shiva.

Gaumukh Reservoir

Walk down beyond the Samidheshwar Temple and at the edge of the cliff is a deep tank, the Gaumukh Reservoir, where you can feed the fish. The reservoir takes its name from a spring that feeds the tank from a *gaumukh* (cow's mouth) carved into the cliffside.

Padmini's Palace

Continuing south, you reach the **Kalika Mata Temple**, an 8th-century sun temple damaged during the first sacking of Chittorgarh and then converted to a temple for the goddess Kali in the 14th century. Padmini's Palace stands about 250m further south, beside a small lake with a central pavilion. The bronze gates to this pavilion were carried off by Akbar and can now be seen in Agra Fort.

South of here are the **Bhaksi**, a small prison where captured invaders, including the sultans of Malwa and Gujarat, were kept; and the **Chogan**, a former parade ground for Rajput soldiers, now used as a helipad for visiting dignitaries.

Continuing around the loop road, you pass the deer park, Bhimlat Tank and **Adhbudhnath Shiva Temple**.

Surajpol & Tower of Fame

Surajpol, on the fort's east side, was the main gate and offers fantastic views across the empty plains. Opposite is the **Neelkanth Mahadev Jain Temple**. A little further north, the 24m-high Tower of Fame (Kirtti Stambha) is older (dating from 1301) and smaller than the Tower of Victory. Built by a Jain merchant, the tower is dedicated to Adinath, the first Jain *tirthankar* (one of the 24 revered Jain teachers) and is decorated with naked figures of various other *tirthankars,* indicating that it is a monument of the Digambara (sky-clad) order. A narrow stairway leads up the seven storeys to the top. Next door is a 14th-century Jain temple.

Ratan Singh Palace

While Padmini's Palace was the summer abode of the Chittorgarh royals, the winter palace takes the name of her husband, Ratan Singh I (or possibly of Ratan Singh II, who ruled briefly in the 16th century). It overlooks a small lake and, although run down, is an interesting place to explore.

📥 Sleeping & Eating

A handful of new business hotels near the train station have improved the accommodation picture a bit. Fortunately most hotels have their own restaurants: other eateries are very ordinary.

Hotel Pratap Palace   HOTEL $$

(📞240099; www.hotelpratappalacechittaurgarh.com; r ₹800-1000, AC s ₹1250-2500, d ₹1550-3000; ❄@) This is Chittorgagh's best option, with a wide range of rooms, a convenient location and travel-savvy staff. The more expensive rooms have window seats and leafy outlooks. There's a garden-side multicuisine restaurant too – drop in for lunch and they may let you stash your luggage while you visit the fort.

Hotel Nandan Palace   HOTEL $$

(📞243314; hotel.nandanpalace2@gmail.com; Station Rd; s/d from ₹1900/2200; ❄@) New in 2010, this is a step up from other options near the train station, a business hotel with good-sized, all-AC rooms in shades of orange and apricot, a lift and an Indian restaurant (mains ₹60 to ₹100). Discounts are often available.

Hotel Shree Ji   HOTEL $$

(📞249131; Station Rd; s/d from ₹1200/1400; ❄) Another decent business hotel, 300m from the train station, with bright, all-AC rooms and free morning tea and newspaper! The restaurant serves an ₹80 thali in the evening.

Hotel Amber Plaza   HOTEL $

(📞248862; 32 Kidwai Nagar; r without/with AC ₹500/900; ❄) Down a quietish street near the bus stand, this has quite comfy, medium-sized rooms with bright decorations (eg large posters of Versailles) and a restaurant.

DEATH BEFORE DISHONOUR

History has been kept alive by bards and folk songs in Rajasthan, and thus historical fact often merges with myth. This is the story told of the first sacking of Chittorgarh.

By the turn of the 14th century, much of North India had been conquered by the Sultans of Delhi. However, the *rana* (king) of Chittorgarh, Ratan Singh, like many Rajput rulers, had managed to resist the invaders.

The jewel of the kingdom was Padmini, Ratan Singh's wife. Although she never left the zenana (women's quarters) uncovered, word had spread of her beauty, and Padmini was admired far beyond the sturdy walls of the fortress. The rumours aroused the curiosity of Delhi sultan, Ala-ud-din Khilji, and he decided to confirm them for himself.

In 1303 Ala-ud-din massed his armies around Chittorgarh and sent word to Ratan Singh that he wanted to meet Padmini. Knowing his forces were no match for the sultan's armies, the *rana* reluctantly agreed, but set a number of conditions. The sultan was required to enter the fort unarmed; once inside, Ala-ud-din was not permitted to meet Padmini in person, but was only able to gaze upon her reflection in a mirror, while she sat well out of his reach inside a pavilion built (just to be sure) in the middle of a lotus pool.

But this glimpse was enough. Ala-ud-din was mesmerised and resolved to possess her at any cost. As Ratan Singh escorted him to the gate, Ala-ud-din gave an order to his forces lying in wait. The *rana* of Chittorgarh was taken hostage and the ransom demanded for his return was Padmini herself.

The court was thrown into panic, until Padmini came up with a plan. She sent word that she agreed to Ala-ud-din's terms and soon a long train of 150 beautiful curtained palanquins, befitting great ladies of the court in purdah (the custom of keeping women in seclusion), trundled slowly out of the fort. The palanquins were Chittor's Trojan Horse – as soon as they had made their way into the sultan's camp, four armed Rajput warriors leapt out of each palanquin and rescued their leader.

The furious Ala-ud-din laid siege to the fort, patiently waiting as the Rajputs slowly starved. It was clear the sultan could not be defeated, but the Rajputs couldn't consider the dishonour of surrender. Instead, a funeral pyre was lit in an underground tunnel. Padmini and all the ladies of the court put on their wedding saris and threw themselves into the fire as their husbands watched. The men then donned saffron robes, smeared sacred ashes on their foreheads and rode out of the fort to certain death.

Although it's clear that Ala-ud-din Khilji did lay siege to Chittorgarh in 1303, and that the Rajput women indeed committed the horrific act of *jauhar,* it's also rumoured that the beautiful Padmini may have been invented by a 16th-century bard.

Hotel Chetak
HOTEL **$**

(☑241589; Station Rd; s/d from ₹500/650, AC ₹1100/1500; ❄) The pick of the cheaper train station lodgings, Chetak has run-of-the-mill rooms with TVs and hot water, and a veg restaurant with North and South Indian and Chinese.

Hotel Vinayak Palace
INDIAN, CHINESE **$**

(Collectorate Circle; mains ₹40-75) Vinayak serves up North Indian veg dishes as well as Chinese and South Indian food. It's in a gloomy basement, but enlivened by its popularity and sweets counter.

The **samosa & kachori stand** near Collectorate Circle does a mean potato samosa for ₹10, and there are handy coffee and tea stands across the street.

❶ Information

You can access an ATM and change money at the **SBBJ** (Bhilwara Rd), and there's an ATM at **SBI** (Bundi Rd).

Mahavir Cyber Cafe (Collectorate Circle; internet per hr ₹25; ⊙8am-10pm)

Tourist Reception Centre (☑241089; Station Rd; ⊙10am-1.30pm & 2-5pm Mon-Sat) Friendly and helpful, with a town map and brochure to give out.

❶ Getting There & Away

Bus

'Express' services from the bus stand head to Delhi (₹354, 14 hours, two daily), Ajmer (₹120, four hours, frequent), Jaipur (₹180 to ₹192, seven hours, 19 daily), Udaipur (₹72, 2½ hours, half-hourly), Bundi (₹100, four hours, 10am) and Kota (₹120, four hours, eight daily), among other places. There are also a few 'deluxe' services to Jaipur (₹225).

Train

At least six daily trains head to Udaipur including the 12963 *Mewar Express* at 7.20am (sleeper/3AC/2AC/1AC ₹150/280/344/561, 2¼ hours) and the 12992 *Ajmer-Udaipur Express* at 7.35pm (2nd class/AC chair ₹70/223, two hours). For Bundi there are four daily trains including the 12964 *Mewar Express* at 8.50pm (sleeper/3AC/2AC/1AC ₹150/288/371/608, two hours) and the 29019 *Nimach-Kota Express* at 2.55pm (sleeper/2AC/1AC ₹130/341/558, 2½ hours).

The 12966 *Udaipur-Gwalior Super Express* leaves Chittorgarh at 12.35am and arrives in Jaipur (2nd class/sleeper/AC chair/3AC/2AC/1AC ₹112/191/376/467/619/1036) at 6am. There are also six or more trains daily to Ajmer.

❶ Getting Around

It's about 6km from the train station to the fort (4km from the bus stand), and a further 9km to make a full loop around the fort (7km if you don't go south of Padmini's Palace). Autorickshaws charge around ₹200 from the bus or train station to go around the fort and come back (including waiting time). You'll have to haggle, and make sure it's clear that you're going to visit the sights and have time to look around. A fort tour by car from Hotel Pratap Palace is ₹350.

Around Chittorgarh (Chittor)

A couple of heritage hotels in villages east of Chittorgarh provide much more attractive accommodation than the dingy Chittor options.

BASSI

About 25km northeast of Chittorgarh, just off Hwy 76, the lively and friendly village of Bassi is famous for its woodcarvers, who create brilliantly coloured religious pieces (see p197). **Bassi Fort Palace** (☑01472-225321; www.bassifortpalace.com; s/d incl breakfast ₹2000/2200) is a glorious 450-year-old meringue of a place on the slope beneath the shell of Bassi's fort. It's a peaceful spot with 18 lovely rooms sporting attractive murals and antique furnishings including bedside lamps made from chain-mail helmets. In case you need a spot of luck, ask a favour of the tree in the courtyard known as kalp vraksha, which is said to grant wishes. A pool was under construction on our visit, and jeep safaris to Bassi Wildlife Sanctuary, a haunt of leopards, antelopes and many birds about 5km northeast, are on offer for ₹400 per person (three hours).

BIJAIPUR

The village of Bijaipur, 16km south of Bassi, is home to the adorable **Castle Bijaipur** (☑01472-276351; www.castlebijaipur.com; r incl breakfast from ₹2500; ❄☀), a fantastically set 16th-century palace apparently plucked from the whimsy of Udaipur and dropped into this rural retreat. It's a great place to settle down with a good book, compose a fairy-tale fantasy or just laze around. Rooms are romantic and luxurious, and there is a pleasant garden courtyard and an airy restaurant serving Rajasthani food. Reservations should be made through the website or Chittorgarh's Hotel Pratap Palace. The owners can arrange transfer from Chittorgarh as

The artisans of Bassi are famous for their amazing folding boxes known as kaavads. Carved from mango wood, these portable temples – usually painted in traffic-stopping reds or yellows – are made of a number of hinged doors that open outwards, each one covered in colourful pictures that illustrate the great Indian epics. They were the tools of professional bards, known as Kavadia Bhatts, who traditionally travelled from village to village chanting the tales of the Mahabharata. As the stories unfolded, so did the boxes. At the climax of the tale, the last door opened to reveal the supreme deities – usually Rama, Lakshmana and Sita or Krishna. Today, you can buy these magical boxes from artisans around Bassi's Nala Bazar. In deference to the passing tourist trade, they now turn out minature versions for as little as ₹200, and even produce kaavads on innovative themes such as the story of Jesus.

well as horse and jeep safaris, birdwatching, cooking classes, massage and yoga.

❶ Getting There & Away

Buses to Bassi (₹13, 30 minutes) leave Chittorgarh's Bus Stand about every half-hour. A taxi from Bassi to Bijaipur costs around ₹100.

Udaipur

📞 0294 / POP 389.317

Beside shimmering Lake Pichola, with the ochre and purple ridges of the wooded Aravalli Hills stretching away in every direction, Udaipur has a romance of setting unmatched in Rajasthan and arguably in all India. Fantastical palaces, temples, *havelis* and countless narrow, crooked, colourful streets add the human counterpoint to the city's natural charms. If Jaipur is the pink city and Jodhpur the blue, Udaipur is the city of cream, rose and honeysuckle hues. The huge, cupola-crowned City Palace lines the eastern shore of Lake Pichola, with its balconies gazing out at Udaipur's other famous landmark, the Lake Palace – a fairy-tale confection that seems to float on the lake's waters, gleaming by day and spotlit by night. Eastward, away from the lake shore, extends a tangled inner city of lanes lined with homes, temples, shops and businesses that is fascinating to explore.

It's tag of 'the most romantic spot on the continent of India' was first applied in 1829 by Colonel James Tod, the East India Company's first Political Agent in the region. Today the romance is wearing ever so slightly thin as Udaipur strains to exploit it for tourist rupees. In the parts of the city nearest the lake, almost every building is a hotel, shop, restaurant, travel agent – or all four rolled into one. Ever-taller hotels compete for the best view, too many mediocre restaurants serve up near-identical menus, and noisy, dirty traffic clogs some of the streets that were made for people and donkeys.

Take a step back from the hustle, however, and Udaipur still has its magic, not just in its marvellous palaces and monuments, but in its matchless setting. Allow yourself a few days to enjoy the tranquillity of boat rides on the lake, the bustle of its ancient bazaars, its lively arts scene, the quaint old-world feel of its better hotels, its scattering of genuinely good restaurants, its endless tempting shops and some lovely countryside to explore on wheels, feet or horseback.

The old city is bound by the meagre remains of a city wall, with the train station and bus stand both just outside the city wall to the southeast. Udaipur's aesthetically challenging urban sprawl ranges out beyond.

History

Udaipur was founded in 1568 by Maharana Udai Singh II following the final sacking of Chittorgarh by the Mughal emperor Akbar. According to legend, Udai Singh had found the site of his new capital some years earlier, after coming across a holy man meditating on a hill near Lake Pichola, who advised the maharana to establish his capital on that very spot. Since the site is surrounded by forests, lakes and the protective Aravalli Hills, the old man's advice was sound: the new capital of Mewar had a much less vulnerable location than Chittorgarh.

Mewar still had to contend with repeated invasions by the Mughals and, later, the Marathas, until British intervention in the early 19th century. This resulted in a treaty that protected Udaipur from invaders while allowing Mewar's rulers to remain effectively

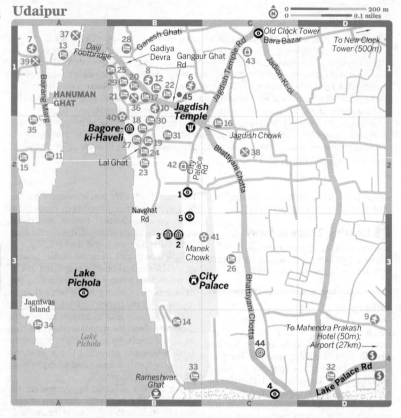

all-powerful in internal affairs. The ex-royal family remains influential and in recent decades has been the driving force behind the rise of Udaipur as a tourist destination. Today it runs a number of Rajasthan's most luxurious hotels.

◉ Sights

Lake Pichola   LAKE
Limpid and large, Lake Pichola reflects the cool grey-blue mountains on its rippling mirror-like surface. It was enlarged by Maharana Udai Singh II, following his foundation of the city, by flooding Picholi village, which gave the lake its name. The lake is now 4km long and 3km wide, but remains shallow and dries up in severe droughts, when you can walk to Jagniwas and Jagmandir, its two major islands, and camels and buffalo graze around the exposed foundations of the seemingly shipwrecked Lake Palace.

The lake is allegedly home to a handful of crocodiles, believed to reside near uninhabited sections of the shore (making it an unappealing option for swimming and wading); occasionally, the waters get choked up with water hyacinths.

The City Palace complex, including the gardens at its south end, extends nearly 1km along the lake's eastern shore. South of the palace gardens are a smaller, separate lake, Dudh Talai, and the Sunset Point garden. To the palace's north, you can reach the lakeside through the narrow old-city streets at two or three bathing and dhobi (laundry) ghats, or cross to the western shore by the pretty Daiji footbridge.

Boat rides (adult/child 30min ₹200/100, 1hr ₹300/150, sunset ₹500/250; ◑10am-5pm) leave roughly hourly from Rameshwar Ghat in the City Palace gardens. Note that you also have to pay ₹25 to enter the City Palace complex. The one-hour trips (including sunset trips) make a stop at Jagmandir Island.

Jagniwas Island

The world-famous Lake Palace hotel island of Jagniwas is about 15,000 sq metres in size, entirely covered by the opulent palace built by Maharana Jagat Singh II in 1754. Once the royal summer palace, it was greatly extended and converted into the Lake Palace hotel in the 1960s by Maharana Bhagwat Singh, and is now in the hands of the

Indian-owned Taj hotel group. One of the world's top luxury hotels, with gleaming courtyards, lotus ponds and a pool shaded by a mango tree, it has been largely responsible for putting Udaipur on the international tourist map. You may also remember it from that classic Bond movie, *Octopussy*, along with the Shiv Niwas Palace and the Monsoon Palace. The Taj Lake Palace doesn't welcome casual visitors: the only time non-guests might be able to experience its magic is during the quietest seasons (eg May and June) when the hotel sometimes accepts outside reservations for lunch or dinner.

Jagmandir Island

The palace on Jagmandir Island, about 800m south of Jagniwas, was built by Maharana Karan Singh in 1620, added to by his successor Maharana Jagat Singh, and then changed very little until the last few years when it was partly converted into another (small) hotel. When lit up at night it has more romantic sparkle to it than the Lake Palace. It's said that the Mughal emperor Shah Jahan (then Prince Khurram) derived some of his inspiration for the Taj Mahal from this palace after staying here in 1623 and 1624 while leading a revolt against his father, Jehangir. European women and children were sheltered here by Maharana Swaroop Singh during the 1857 First War of Independence (Indian Uprising). With its entrance flanked by a row of enormous stone elephants, the island has an ornate 17th-century tower, the Gol Mahal, carved from bluestone and containing a small exhibit on Jagmandir's history, plus a garden and lovely views across the lake. As well as the seven hotel rooms, the island has a restaurant, bar and spa, which are open to visitors. The one-hour boat trips from Rameshwar Ghat call here, or you can get a boat direct to the island (adult/child ₹300/150 return) from the same jetty.

TOP CHOICE City Palace PALACE
(www.eternalmewar.in; adult/child ₹25/15, not charged if visiting City Palace Museum; ☺7am-11pm) Surmounted by balconies, towers and cupolas towering over the lake, the imposing City Palace is Rajasthan's largest palace, with a facade 244m long and 30.4m high. Construction was begun by Maharana Udai Singh II, the city's founder, and it later became a conglomeration of structures (including 11 separate smaller palaces) built and extended by various maharanas, though it still manages to retain a surprising uniformity of design. There are fine views over the lake and the city from the palace's upper terraces.

You can enter the complex at the **Badi Pol** (Great Gate; 1615) at the top of City Palace Rd at the palace's north end, or at the **Sheetla Mata Gate** on Lake Palace Rd. Tickets for the City Palace Museum are sold at both entrances. At Badi Pol you can rent an audio guide in English, French, German or Spanish for ₹250, or hire a human guide for ₹150 for up to five people.

The complex also contains the Shiv Niwas Palace and Fateh Prakash Palace Hotels, and a jetty from which boat trips can be taken around the lake.

Inside the Badi Pol, eight **arches** on the left commemorate the eight times maharanas were weighed here and their weight in gold or silver distributed to the lucky locals. You then pass through the three-arched **Tripolia Gate** (1711) into a large courtyard, **Manek Chowk**, with a number of pricey handicraft shops and the main palace buildings towering on the right. Spot the large tiger-catching cage, which worked rather like an oversized mousetrap, and the smaller one for leopards.

City Palace Museum

(adult/child ₹50/30, camera or video ₹200; ☺9.30am-5.30pm, last entry 4.30pm) The main part of the palace is open as the City Palace Museum, with rooms extravagantly decorated with mirrors, tiles and paintings and housing a large, varied collection of artefacts. It gives a good sense of Mewar history and the aristocratic lifestyle of its rulers. It's entered from **Ganesh Chowk**, which you reach from Manek Chowk through an entrance hall displaying the very lengthy Mewar royal family tree (to the right is an armoury section sporting old weapons, including a lethal two-pronged sword). Ganesh Chowk also contains the **Chhota Darikhana**, with sculptures from the temple ruins at the early Mewar capital of Nagda (21km north of Udaipur) and the entrance to the Government Museum.

The City Palace Museum begins with the **Rai Angan** (Royal Courtyard), the very spot where Udai Singh met the sage who told him to build a city here. Rooms along one side contain historical paintings including several of the Battle of Haldighati. As you move through the palace, highlight spots include the **Baadi Mahal** (1699) where a pretty central garden gives fine views over the city. **Kishan (Krishna) Vilas** has a remarkable collection of miniatures (no photography

DURBAR GLITZ

Many palaces in India have a durbar hall (royal reception hall). Usually the grandest room in the place, with a respectable amount of chandeliers and gilt overlay, the durbar hall was dressed to impress – it was used by Indian rulers for official occasions, such as state banquets, and to hold meetings.

The restored Durbar Hall in the City Palace complex is one of India's most impressive, vast and lavish, with some of the country's biggest chandeliers. The walls display royal weapons and striking portraits of former maharanas of Mewar – a most distinguished-looking lot, who come from what is believed to be the oldest ruling dynasty in the world, spanning 76 generations.

The foundation stone of the hall was laid in 1909 by Lord Minto, the viceroy of India, during the reign of Maharana Fateh Singh, and it was originally named Minto Hall. The upper level of this high-ceilinged hall is surrounded by viewing galleries, where ladies of the palace could watch in veiled seclusion what was happening below. Nowadays, these are the Crystal Gallery.

The Durbar Hall is included in visits to the Crystal Gallery and you will also see it if you go to the Gallery Restaurant. The hall still has the capacity to hold hundreds of people and can even be hired for conferences or social gatherings.

permitted) from the time of Maharana Bhim Singh (r 1778–1828). The story goes that Bhim Singh's daughter Krishna Kumari drank a fatal cup of poison here to solve the dilemma of rival princely suitors from Jaipur and Jodhpur who were both threatening to invade Mewar if she didn't marry them. The **Moti Mahal** (Palace of Pearls) has beautiful 19th-century mirror work. The 18th-century **Pritam Niwas** served as the private apartment of Maharana Bhupal Singh, who signed the Instrument of Accession joining Mewar to the Indian Union in 1948. Exhibits include this disabled maharana's wheeled armchair. The **Surya Choupad** boasts a huge, ornamental sun – the symbol of the sun-descended Mewar dynasty – and opens into **Mor Chowk** (Peacock Courtyard) with its lovely mosaics of peacocks, the favourite Rajasthani bird. The **Manek Mahal** (Ruby Palace) at the far end of Mor Chowk contains exquisite 19th-century glass and mirror work. The south end of the museum comprises the **Zenana Mahal**, the royal ladies' quarters built in the 17th century. It now contains a long picture gallery with lots of royal hunting scenes, showing far more dead tigers than Rajasthan now has live ones. The Zenana Mahal's central courtyard, **Laxmi Chowk**, contains a beautiful white pavilion and a stable of howdahs, palanquins and other people carriers.

Crystal Gallery & Durbar Hall
(adult/child incl audio guide & drink ₹500/300; ☉9am-7pm) South of the City Palace Muse-

um, the Crystal Gallery houses rare crystal that Maharana Sajjan Singh ordered from F&C Osler & Co in England in 1877. The maharana died before it arrived, and all the items stayed forgotten and packed up in boxes for 110 years. The extraordinary, extravagant collection includes crystal chairs, sofas, tables and even beds. There's an exquisite antique jewel-studded carpet that has to be seen to be believed. The rather hefty admission fee also includes entry to the grand **Durbar Hall** and tea or a soft drink in the Gallery Restaurant adjoining the Durbar Hall or on the Fateh Prakash Palace Hotel's Sunset Terrace. Tickets are available at the city palace gates or the Crystal Gallery entrance. No photography is permitted.

Government Museum
(admission free; ☉10am-5pm Tue-Sun) Entered from Ganesh Chowk, this has a splendid collection of jewel-like miniature paintings of the Mewar school and a turban that belonged to Shah Jahan, creator of the Taj Mahal. Stranger exhibits include a stuffed monkey holding a lamp. There are also regal maharana portraits in profile, documenting Mewar's rulers along with the changing fashions of the moustache.

Jagdish Temple   HINDU TEMPLE
(☉5.30am-2pm & 4-10pm) Entered by a steep, elephant-flanked flight of steps 150m north of the City Palace's Badi Pol entrance, this busy Indo-Aryan temple was built by Maharana Jagat Singh in 1651. The wonderfully

carved main structure enshrines a black stone image of Vishnu as Jagannath, Lord of the Universe; there's a brass image of the Garuda (Vishnu's man-bird vehicle) in a shrine facing the main structure. You can donate money, which is used to feed the hungry, beside the northwest corner shrine.

Bagore-ki-Haveli
NOTABLE BUILDING

(admission ₹30; ◷10am-5pm) This gracious 18th-century *haveli*, set on the water's edge in the Gangaur Ghat area, was built by a Mewar prime minister and has since been carefully restored. There are 138 rooms set around courtyards. Some rooms are arranged to evoke the period during which the house was inhabited, while others house cultural displays, including – intriguingly enough – the world's biggest turban. The *haveli* also houses an interesting art gallery, featuring contemporary and folk art, and an eclectic selection of world-famous monuments lovingly carved out of polystyrene. The upper courtyard makes an atmospheric setting for the fabulous nightly **Dharohar performances** of Rajasthani dance (see p211).

Sajjan Garh (Monsoon Palace)
PALACE

Perched on top of a distant mountain like a fairy-tale castle, this melancholy, neglected late 19th-century palace was constructed by Maharana Sajjan Singh. Originally an astronomical centre, it became a monsoon palace and hunting lodge. Now government owned, it's in a sadly dilapidated state but visitors stream up here for the marvellous views, particularly at sunset. It's 5km west of the old city as the crow flies, about 9km by the winding road. The building itself is empty except for some perfunctory natural history displays. At the foot of the hill you enter the 5-sq-km **Sajjan Garh Wildlife Sanctuary** (Indian/foreigner ₹10/80, car ₹60, camera/video free/₹200). A good way to visit is with the daily sunset excursion in **taxi No RJ-27-TA 2108** (☏9784400120; per person ₹200), a minivan, which leaves Udaipur's Gangaur Ghat at 5pm daily; the charge does not include the sanctuary fees. Autorickshaws charge ₹200 including waiting time for a round trip to the sanctuary gate, which they are not allowed to pass. Taxis ferry people the final 4km up to the palace for ₹100 per person.

Vintage & Classic Car Collection
MUSEUM

(Garden Hotel, Garden Rd; admission ₹150, incl lunch or dinner ₹250; ◷9am-9pm) The maharanas' car collection makes a fascinating diversion, for what it tells about their elite lifestyle and for the vintage vehicles themselves. Housed within the former state garage are 22 splendid vehicles, including a seven-seat 1938 Cadillac complete with purdah system, the beautiful 1934 Rolls-Royce Phantom used in *Octopussy* and the Cadillac convertible that whisked Queen Elizabeth II to the airport in 1961. If you enjoy a vegetarian thali, the combined museum-and-meal ticket is a very good option (lunch 11.30am to 3pm, dinner 7.30pm to 10pm). The museum is situated 1km east of the City Palace, just opposite Sajjan Niwas Gardens.

Sunset Point & Machla Magra
VIEWPOINT, CABLE CAR

The small **Sunset Point park** (admission ₹5) has dazzling views over Lake Pichola, Jagmandir Island and off toward the Monsoon Palace. A musical fountain plays each evening (drought permitting). It's about 1.5km south from the Rangniwas Palace Hotel on Lake Palace Rd. Opposite the park is the lower station of the **Ropeway** (☏6508755; round-trip adult/child ₹66/33; ◷9am-9pm), a cable car which swings over to Machla Magra hill where the views are even more expansive. Atop Machla Magra are a **Karni Mata Temple** and the sparse remains of the Eklingarh Fort. You can also walk up by a zigzag path from the park on the east side of pretty Dudh Talai lake, which you pass en route to Sunset Point.

Fateh Sagar
LAKE

One kilometre north of Lake Pichola, this lake – which also dries up if the monsoon has been poor – is ringed by hills and is a popular local hang-out. Overlooked by a number of hills, it was originally constructed in 1678 by Maharana Jai Singh but reconstructed by Maharana Fateh Singh in 1888 after heavy rains destroyed the dam. A pleasant drive winds along the east bank, where you can take boat or camel rides. In the middle of the lake is **Nehru Park**, a garden island. An autorickshaw from the old city costs ₹35 (one way).

Moti Magri
PARK

(Pearl Hill; adult/child ₹25/15, autorickshaw/scooter ₹10/5, camera/video ₹15/30; ◷7.30am-7pm) This hill park overlooking Fateh Sagar is topped by a statue of the Rajput hero Maharana Pratap and his beloved horse Chetak, who defied the Mughals together (see Haldighati, p215, for more about this noble quadruped).

It takes about 20 minutes to walk up the road to the top. You can stop off at the **Hall of Heroes** which contains 20 large paintings on Mewar history and models of Chittorgarh and the Haldighati battlefield.

Saheliyon-ki-Bari
GARDEN

(Garden of the Maids of Honour; admission ₹5; ☺8am-7pm) In the north of the city, the Saheliyon-ki-Bari was built by Sangram Singh II in 1710. This small, quaint ornamental garden was laid out for the enjoyment of 48 women attendants who came as part of a princess's dowry and has beautiful, well-maintained fountains (water shortages permitting), kiosks, marble elephants and a delightful lotus pool.

Bhartiya Lok Kala Museum
MUSEUM

(☎2529296; Indian/foreigner ₹20/35, camera/video ₹10/50; ☺9am-5.30pm) This private folk-art museum, with an uncannily Dalek-like entrance tower, exhibits dresses, tribal jewellery, turbans, dolls, masks, musical instruments, paintings and – its high point – puppets. Diverting one-hour **puppet shows** (Indian/foreigner ₹30/50), a good reason to visit if you're travelling with children, are staged at 6pm. It's 300m north of Chetak Circle in the north of the city.

Ahar
HISTORIC BUILDINGS, MUSEUM

About 3km east of the old city, at Ahar, is Udaipur's **royal cremation ground** (admission free; ☺6am-6pm), with 372 cenotaphs of maharanas and queens of Mewar forming a spectacular city of snowy domes built over 400 years. Nineteen maharanas were cremated here, and the most striking cenotaph is that of Maharana Sangram Singh (r 1710–34). The newest, erected in 2004, is that of Udaipur's last maharana, Bhagwat Singh (r 1955–84), father of the current head of the ex-ruling household. The security guard will probably show you round (a tip is in order). The beautiful **Ayad Jain Temple**, 300m back towards Udaipur, is also well worth a look while you are here.

Ahar was also the site of ancient settlement that predated Udaipur by 3½ millennia. Just 150m along the road from the cremation ground, the **Ahar Government Museum** (Indian/foreigner/foreign student ₹5/50/25; ☺9.45am-5.15pm Tue-Sun) contains copper and pottery objects more than 3300 years old, plus sculptures of Hindu gods and Jain *tirthankars* from the 8th to 16th centuries AD.

A return trip by autorickshaw should cost around ₹80, including waiting time.

Shilpgram
CRAFTS

(☎2431304; www.shilpgram.org; Indian/foreigner ₹20/30, camera ₹30; ☺11am-7pm) A crafts village 3km west of Fateh Sagar lake, Shilpgram was inaugurated by Rajiv Gandhi in 1989. Set in dusty, rolling countryside, it's contrived but remains interesting. There are 26 traditional village houses from Rajasthan, Gujarat, Goa and Maharashtra, some with glittering mirrored interiors, and craft exhibits. Best, though, are the excellent demonstrations by traditional dancers and artisans, with groups ready to perform as you approach (you'll be expected to proffer a tip if you stay to watch). Outside the tourist season, however, Shilpgram can be almost deserted of artisans, performers and visitors. The best time to come is during the mela (fair) in the last 10 days of December: it's a fantastic spectacle, often with hundreds upon hundreds of artisans and performers from all over India in attendance.

Shilpi Restaurant (mains ₹60-130; ☺11.30am-10.30pm), next door to Shilpgram, is a pleasant open-air place serving veg and nonveg Indian, Continental and Chinese food. It also has a **swimming pool** (admission ₹100; ☺11am-8pm).

Some people walk or cycle out to Shilpgram; a return autorickshaw trip (including a 30-minute stop) from the old city will cost ₹250.

Activities

See p198 for information about boat rides on Lake Pichola.

Horse Riding

The wooded hills, villages and lakes around Udaipur make lovely riding country. Several operators offer horse rides from a couple of hours to multiday safaris – usually on Rajasthan's celebrated medium-sized Marwari horses, which are known for their intelligence, stamina and cute inward-curved ears. Expect to pay about ₹900 for a half-day ride, including lunch or snacks and transport to/from your hotel.

Krishna Ranch
HORSE RIDING

(☎9828059505; www.krishnaranch.com) Situated in beautiful countryside near Badi village, 7km northwest of Udaipur, and run by the owners of Kumbha Palace guesthouse; experienced owner-guide Dinesh Jain leads most trips himself. There are also attractive **cottages** (s/d incl 3 meals ₹1200/2000, per person incl day's riding/trekking ₹2200/1900) at the ranch.

HELPING UDAIPUR'S STREET ANIMALS

Cows, sacred to Hindus, enjoy many privileges in India. But the no-slaughter ethic can mean that some cows end their lives in misery. Once a cow reaches the end of her milk-producing life, owners may simply turn her out on the streets to graze on rubbish, which can lead to death by starvation or stomach problems as many kilos of plastic accumulate in the cow's digestive system.

Such animals are among those given succour by animal refuge **Animal Aid Unlimited** (☎9950531639, 9829596637; www.animalaidunlimited.com) in Badi village, 7km northwest of Udaipur. Founded in 2002 by Americans Erika Abrams, Jim Myers and their daughter Claire, Animal Aid Unlimited now has a full-time staff of over 30, treating 250 animals each day.

Animal Aid Unlimited has also administered 20,000 rabies injections to street dogs, and treats and sterilises injured dogs. It provides injured donkeys with comfortable conditions to live out their lives, answers more than 3000 emergency rescue calls a year, and does a lot of animal-welfare educational work. A visit to the spacious refuge at Badi village – around ₹250 round-trip by autorickshaw, including waiting time – is a heartwarming experience.

The refuge welcomes volunteers and visitors: make contact in advance to fix a time between 9am and 5pm any day. Volunteers need no special qualifications; help with giving animals affection, stimulation, play and walks, and sometimes holding them during treatments, is invaluable. Volunteers are encouraged to stay long enough to learn the routines and develop relationships with individual animals. You can also help by making a donation; see the website for details.

Call Animal Aid Unlimited if you see an injured or ill street animal in Udaipur.

Princess Trails
HORSE RIDING

(☎3096909, 9829042012; www.princesstrails.com; city office Boheda Haveli, Kalaji Goraji) An Indian-German operation offering extended horse safaris and half-day nature rides.

Pratap Country Inn
HORSE RIDING

(☎2583138; www.horseridingindia.in; Titaradi village, Jaisamand Rd) Run by the pioneer of horse safaris in Rajasthan, Maharaja Narendra Singh, this inn about 7km south of town organises day or part-day rides and long-distance safaris.

Massage

Ayurvedic Body Care
AYURVEDA

(☎2413816; www.ayurvedicbodycare.com; 39 Lal Ghat; ◎10.30am-9pm) A small and popular old-city operation offering ayurvedic massage at reasonable prices, including a 15-minute head or back massage (₹250) and a 45-minute full-body massage (₹750). It also has ayurvedic products such as oils, moisturisers, shampoos and soaps for sale.

Panghat Spa
AYURVEDA

(☎2528026; treatments from ₹1500; ◎8am-8pm) This luxurious spa at the Shiv Niwas Palace and Jagmandir Island Palace Hotels offers a big range of ayurvedic massages and therapies. The Jagmandir spa has a lovely setting around lawns with elephant sculptures, plus a sauna, while the Shiv Niwas branch also does aromatherapy and beauty treatments.

Walking

Exploring the surrounding countryside and villages on foot is a fantastic way to see rural and tribal life while taking in some beautiful scenery.

Mountain Ridge
WALKING

(☎3291478, 9602192902; www.mountainridge.in; Sisarma; half-day trek per person ₹650) This British-run homestay 6km west of town has pioneered country walking around Udaipur. The trips, with local tribal guides, include morning pick-up in Udaipur, lunch and a ride back to town afterwards. A hearty breakfast will also be included if you like.

Krishna Ranch
WALKING

(☎9828059505; www.krishnaranch.com; Badi village; full day trek per person ₹1200) Day hikes (15km) including lunch are offered by this riding ranch. Routes cover Sajjan Garh Wildlife Sanctuary and the Badi Talai area.

Hot-Air Ballooning

Sky Waltz
HOT-AIR BALLOONING

(☎9717295801; www.skywaltz.com; Indian ₹8000-12,000, foreigner US$200-300; ◎Nov-Mar) The fearless can float high above Udaipur's lakes on these one-hour flights with professional British and American pilots.

🍴 Courses

Cooking

Spice Box COOKING
(📞2424713; www.spicebox.co.in; 38 Lal Ghat; 2-3hr class ₹750) Shakti Singh, from this spice, tea, oils and incense shop, offered Udaipur's original cooking classes and they are still recommended. The recipes are all vegetarian but the curries are also good with additional meat.

Queen Cafe COOKING
(📞2430875; 14 Bajrang Marg; 2/4hr class ₹900/1400) The four-hour introductory class with Meenu, composer of many of this little eatery's delicious dishes, encompasses a grand 14 veg items. Meenu also teaches Hindi and henna painting and does ayurvedic massage; she may be moving to separate premises nearby at 9 Bhrampole Marg, but Queen Cafe will direct you.

Shashi Cooking Classes COOKING
(📞9929303511; www.shashicookingclasses. blogspot.com; Sunrise Restaurant, 18 Gangaur Ghat Rd; 4hr class ₹500) Readers rave about Shashi's high-spirited classes (maximum four students), teaching many fundamental Indian dishes.

Noble Indian Cooking Classes COOKING
(📞94142342737; nicc_indyat@yahoo.co.in; Nani Gali, Jagdish Chowk) Ruchi and Swati, and proud mum Rajni, run these popular classes where you can tackle anything from a chapati (₹150 per person) to an eight-course extravaganza (₹1000).

Hotel Krishna Niwas COOKING
(📞2420163; www.hotelkrishnaniwas.com; 35 Lal Ghat; North/South Indian class incl meal ₹850/1250) Sushma runs 2½-hour classes in a bright, purpose-built kitchen.

Music

Prem Musical Instruments MUSIC
(📞2430599; 28 Gadiya Devra; per hr ₹200) Rajesh Prajapati (Bablu) is a successful local musician who gives sitar, tabla and flute lessons. He also sells and repairs those instruments and can arrange performances.

Prajapati Musical Instruments MUSIC
(📞2430599, 9928353167; 16 Bajrang Marg) Suresh Prajapati, Bablu's elder brother, is one of Udaipur's top musicians. He too has a music shop and gives recommended sitar, tabla and flute classes.

Painting

Hotel Krishna Niwas PAINTING
(📞2420163; www.hotelkrishnaniwas.com; 35 Lal Ghat; 2hr class ₹600) Jairaj Soni is a renowned artist who teaches miniature and classical painting.

Ashoka Arts PAINTING
(Hotel Gangaur Palace, Gadiya Devra; per hr ₹150) Here you can learn the basics of classic miniature painting.

Yoga

Astang Yoga Ashram YOGA
(📞2524872; Raiba House, Inside Chandpol) A friendly hatha yoga centre with 1½-hour classes at 8am and 5pm. The teacher has over 20 years' experience. Pay by donation. It's 150m north of the east side of Daiji Bridge.

Tours

City tours (per person excl admission charges ₹140) run by the Rajasthan Tourism Development Corporation (RTDC) leave at 8.30am from the RTDC Hotel Kajri by Shastri Circle (400m northeast of Delhi Gate), and take in the main sights in 4½ hours. There are also five-hour **excursions** (per person excl admission charges ₹200) to Haldighati, Nathdwara and Eklingji Temple at 2pm. Contact the Tourist Reception Centre for more information.

🎆 Festivals & Events

If you're in Udaipur in February or March, you might be lucky enough to experience the festival of **Holi**, Udaipur-style, when the town comes alive in a riot of colour (p177). Holi is followed in March or April by the procession-heavy **Mewar Festival** (p177) – Udaipur's own version of the springtime Gangaur festival.

🛏 Sleeping

Accommodation clusters where most people want to stay – close to the lake, especially on its eastern side, in and near the narrow street Lal Ghat. This area is a tangle of streets and lanes (some quiet, some busy and noisy), close to the City Palace and Jagdish Temple. It's Udaipur's tourist epicentre and the streets are strung not just with lodgings but also with tourist-oriented eateries and shops whose owners will be doing their best to tempt you in.

Directly across the water from Lal Ghat, Hanuman Ghat has a slightly more local

ⓘ ARRIVING IN UDAIPUR

Udaipur has its share of autorickshaw drivers who will want to take you to a guesthouse or hotel where they can expect a nice commission. If a driver tells you the place you want has burnt down or suddenly closed, insist on seeing for yourself. To bypass rapacious rickshaw drivers altogether, use the prepaid autorickshaw stands outside the train and bus stations (if they are operating). Some unscrupulous drivers may still try to take you to the hotel of *their* choice, but remember: they don't get reimbursed until you hand over the receipt at the end of your journey.

If you're heading for the Lal Ghat area to find accommodation, you can avoid discussions about individual lodgings by taking a rickshaw to the nearby Jagdish Temple, which should cost ₹30. If you do have any complaints about rickshaw drivers, taxis (note their registration numbers) or hotels, contact the police or the Tourist Reception Centre.

vibe and often better views, though you're certainly not out of the touristic zone.

Discounts are often available outside the peak tourist seasons.

LAL GHAT AREA

Many budget and midrange lodgings cluster here, with a particular concentration along the relatively peaceful Lal Ghat.

Jagat Niwas Palace Hotel HERITAGE HOTEL **$$**
(☑2420133; www.jagatniwaspalace.com; 23-25 Lal Ghat; r ₹1750-3950, ste ₹6350; ✳@☎) This leading midrange hotel set in two converted lakeside *havelis* takes the location cake. The lake-view rooms are charming, with carved wooden furniture, cushioned window seats and pretty prints. Non-lake-facing rooms are almost as comfortable and attractive, and considerably cheaper. The building is full of character with lots of attractive sitting areas, terraces and courtyards, and it makes the most of its position with a picture-perfect rooftop restaurant.

Jaiwana Haveli HOTEL **$$**
(☑2411103; www.jaiwanahaveli.com; 14 Lal Ghat; s/d ₹1890/1990; ✳@☎) Professionally run by two helpful, efficient brothers, this smart

midrange option has spotless, unfussy rooms with good beds, some decorated with attractive block-printed fabrics. Book corner room 11, 21 or 31 for views. The rooftop restaurant has great lake views and presentable Indian food (mains ₹160 to ₹300).

Poonam Haveli HOTEL **$$**
(☑2410303; www.hotelpoonamhaveli.com; 39 Lal Ghat; r ₹800-1600, ste ₹2000; ✳@☎) A fairly modern place decked out in traditional style, friendly Poonam has 16 spacious, spotlessly clean rooms with big beds and spare but tasteful decor, plus pleasant sitting areas. None of the rooms enjoy lake views, but the rooftop restaurant does, and boasts 'real Italian' pizzas among the usual Indian and traveller fare.

Nukkad Guest House GUESTHOUSE **$**
(☑2411403; nukkad_raju@yahoo.com; 56 Ganesh Ghati; r ₹300-500, s/d without bathroom ₹100/200; @) Always busy with travellers, Nukkad has a relaxed atmosphere and a sociable, breezy, upstairs restaurant with very good Indian and international dishes (mains ₹60 to ₹85). Your hosts Raju and Kala are most helpful and you can join afternoon cooking classes and morning yoga sessions without stepping outside the door. Rooms are simple, fancooled, very clean and good value; there's plenty of hot water and many rooms have cushioned window seats.

Mewar Haveli HOTEL **$$**
(☑2521140; www.mewarhaveli.com; 34-35 Lal Ghat; r ₹990-1620; ✳@☎) Mewar is a good midranger with excellent staff who oversee sunfilled rooms with good beds. It has a nice, clean, fresh feel, with bright fabrics and wall paintings. All rooms are AC and most have lake views. There's a restaurant too.

Pratap Bhawan Paying Guest House
GUESTHOUSE **$**
(☑2560566; 12 Lal Ghat; r ₹500-800) A curving marble staircase leads up from the wide lobby to large, sparkling-clean rooms with good, big bathrooms and, in many cases, cushioned window seats. Recently taken over by friendly new management, this place will probably get even better. The roof terrace is nice for sitting out at night.

Hotel Minerwa HOTEL **$**
(☑2523471; www.hotelminerwaudaipur.com; 5/13 Gadiya Devra; r ₹300-700, AC ₹900; ✳@☎) A good-value, new-on-the-scene budget bet with clean rooms that is proving pretty popular. Rooms improve in size, decor and views as

you go up the price scale: a few have lake glimpses. The pleasant, well-priced, two-level roof restaurant has a floor-cushion zone.

Hotel Baba Palace   HOTEL $$

(☎2427126; www.hotelbabapalace.com; Jagdish Chowk; s ₹950, d ₹1400-2800; ✳🛜) This slick hotel has spotless, fresh rooms with decent beds behind solid doors, and offers free train station or airport pick-ups. It's eye to eye with Jagdish Temple so many of them have interesting views; all rooms have AC and TVs. On top there's the first-rate Mayur Rooftop Cafe.

Hotel Lake Ghat Palace   HOTEL $$

(☎2521636; http://lakeghatpalace.com; 23/165 Lal Ghat; s ₹600-800, d ₹500-1900; ✳🛜) Some of the smart, biggish rooms at this travellers' hot spot have views, others have balconies, and all are decorated with stained glass. The rooms are set around a small atrium, about six stories high and hung with plants; there are splendid views from the roof and a good multicuisine restaurant (mains ₹60 to ₹120).

Jheel Palace Guest House   GUESTHOUSE $$

(☎2421352; www.jheelguesthouse.com; 56 Gangaur Ghat; r ₹1800-2800; ✳) Right on the lake edge (when the lake is full), Jheel Palace has three nice rooms with little balconies and four-poster beds, and three more ordinary ones. All are AC. Staff are accommodating and hands-off, and there's a good Brahmin pure veg rooftop restaurant (no beer).

Hotel Krishna Niwas   HOTEL $$

(☎2420163; www.hotelkrishnaniwas.com; 35 Lal Ghat; d ₹1350-1650; ✳@) Run by an artist family, Krishna Niwas has smart, clean, all AC rooms; those with views are smaller, and some come with balconies. There are splendid views from the rooftop, and a decent restaurant. Or you can eat your own cooking after taking a lesson here.

Lalghat Guest House   GUESTHOUSE $

(☎2525301; lalghat@hotmail.com; 33 Lal Ghat; dm ₹100, r ₹400-1500; ✳@) This mellow guesthouse by the lake was one of the first to open in Udaipur, and it's still a sound choice, with an amazing variety of older and newer rooms. Accommodation ranges from a spruce, nonsmoking dorm (with curtained-off beds and lockers under the mattresses) to the best room, which sports a stone wall, a big bed, a big mirror and AC. Most rooms have lake views and those in the older part of the building generally have more character. There's a small kitchen for self-caterers.

Kankarwa Haveli   HERITAGE HOTEL $$

(☎2411457; www.kankarwahaveli.com; 26 Lal Ghat; s ₹1100-1650, d ₹1250-2200; ✳@🛜) This is one of Udaipur's few hotels that are genuine old *havelis* (as opposed to old *havelis* that have been gutted and rebuilt, or new buildings made to look like old *havelis*, or places that simply stick 'Haveli' on the end of their name). It's right by the lake, and the whitewashed rooms, set around a courtyard, have a lovely simplicity with splashes of colour. The pricier ones look right onto Lake Pichola; the cheapest lack AC.

Hotel Gangaur Palace   HERITAGE HOTEL $

(☎2422303; www.ashokahaveli.com; Gadiya Devra; s ₹400-2000, d ₹500-2500; ✳) This elaborate, faded *haveli* is set around a stone-pillared courtyard, with a wide assortment of rooms on several floors. It's gradually moving upmarket and rooms range from windowless with flaking paint to bright and recently decorated with lake views. Many have wall paintings and window seats. The hotel also boasts an in-house palm reader, an art shop, an art school, the good Cafe Namaste and a rooftop restaurant serving the same fare as the cafe as well as multicuisine dishes.

Hotel Pichola Haveli   HOTEL $$

(☎2413653; info@picholahaveli.com; 64 Gangaur Ghat; s/d ₹1200/1500; ✳@🛜) A sound choice with medium-sized heritage-style rooms, friendly and helpful management, and a quiet location. Lake Pichola, across the street, is visible from some rooms and the pleasant rooftop restaurant.

Anjani Hotel   HOTEL $$

(☎2421770; www.anjanihotel.com; 77 Gangaur Ghat Rd; r ₹1350-2700; ✳@🏊) A well-run hotel with rooms in traditional-style decor, varying widely in size and comfort. The top-floor rooms have fantastic city views. Other features include a pool and rooftop restaurant.

Old Jheel Guest House   GUESTHOUSE $

(☎2421352; www.jheelguesthouse.com; 56 Gangaur Ghat; r ₹400-600) Across the street from Jheel Palace, the original Jheel establishment has simple but clean and well-sized rooms. Those up at the top are brighter.

Hotel Udai Niwas   HOTEL $

(☎5120789; www.hoteludainiwas.com; Gangaur Ghat Rd; r ₹500-1500; ✳@) A friendly place with clean and brightly decorated, if not huge, rooms, and more natural light as you move up this very tall building (it's at least eight floors).

HANUMAN GHAT AREA

Amet Haveli HERITAGE HOTEL **$$$**
(☏2431085; www.amethaveliudaipur.com; s/d/ste ₹4000/5000/6000; ✳@☎☀) This 350-year-old heritage building on the lake shore has delightful rooms with cushioned window seats and coloured glass with little shutters. They're set around a pretty little courtyard and pond. Splurge on one with a balcony or giant bathtub. One of Udaipur's most romantic restaurants, Ambrai, is part of the hotel.

Dream Heaven GUESTHOUSE **$**
(☏2431038; www.dreamheaven.co.in; Hanuman Ghat; r ₹150-600; ✳) A deservedly popular place to come to a halt, with clean rooms featuring wall hangings and paintings. Bathrooms are smallish, though some rooms have a decent balcony and/or views. The food at the rooftop restaurant (dishes ₹40 to ₹90), which overlooks the lake and shows Udaipur at its best, is fresh, tasty and highly recommended – the perfect place to chill out on a pile of cushions.

Udai Kothi HOTEL **$$$**
(☏2432810; www.udaikothi.com; Hanuman Ghat; r ₹4000-10,000; ✳@☎☀) A bit like a five-storey wedding cake, Udai Kothi is a glittery, modern building with lots of traditional touches – cupolas, interesting art and fabrics, window seats in some rooms, marble bathrooms and carved-wood doors in others, and thoughtful touches such as bowls of floating flowers. Rooms are pretty, individually designed and well equipped. It's a work in progress: one new suite has its own heated pool and 360-degree view. The apex is the roof terrace, where you can dine well and swim in Udaipur's *only* rooftop pool (nonguests ₹300).

Hibiscus Guest house GUESTHOUSE **$$**
(☏2803490; www.hibiscusinudaipur.com; 190 Naga Nagri; r ₹800-1000, AC ₹1200-2500; ✳)
A friendly, family-run house with a walled garden in a quiet setting. The well-sized rooms have pretty Rajasthani decor, and the roof provides nice lake views. Meals are available.

LAKE PALACE ROAD AREA

TOP CHOICE **Mahendra Prakash Hotel** HOTEL **$$**
(☏2419811; www.hotelmahendraprakash.com; r ₹1400-3000; ✳@☎☀) Spacious gardens, spick-and-span rooms well furnished in traditional style, a cheery atmosphere and friendly staff are the name of the game

at the very well-run Mahendra Prakash. There's a fabulous pool (nonguests ₹100), a decent restaurant and a lawn with tortoises. Rooms at the top have private balconies and City Palace views.

Kumbha Palace GUESTHOUSE **$**
(☏2422702, 9828059505; www.hotelkumbhapalace.com; 104 Bhattiyani Chotta; r ₹300-450, AC ₹900; ✳@) This excellent place run by a Dutch-Indian couple is tucked up a quiet lane off busy Bhattiyani Chotta and is backed by a lovely lush lawn. The 10 rooms are simple but comfortable (just one has AC), and the restaurant knows how to satisfy homesick travellers. The owners also run Krishna Ranch, where excellent horse riding and cottage accommodation are on offer.

Rangniwas Palace Hotel HERITAGE HOTEL **$$**
(☏2523890; www.rangniwaspalace.com; Lake Palace Rd; s ₹880-2200, d ₹990-2500, ste s/d ₹3000/3500; ✳☎☀) This 19th-century palace boasts plenty of heritage character and a peaceful central garden with a small pool. The quaint rooms in the older section are the most appealing, while the suites – full of carved wooden furniture and terraces with swing seats – are divine.

CITY PALACE

Shiv Niwas Palace Hotel HERITAGE HOTEL **$$$**
(☏2528016; www.hrhhotels.com; City Palace Complex; r ₹12,000, ste ₹24,000-80,000; ✳@☎☀)
This hotel, in the former palace guest quarters, has opulent common areas like its pool courtyard, bar and lovely lawn garden with a 30m-long royal procession mural. Some of the suites are truly palatial, filled with fountains and silver, but the standard rooms are not great value. Go for a suite, or just for a drink, meal, massage or swim in the gorgeous marble **pool** (nonguests ₹300; ☉9am-6pm). Rates drop dramatically from April to September.

Fateh Prakash Palace Hotel
HERITAGE HOTEL **$$$**
(☏2528016; www.hrhhotels.com; City Palace Complex; r ₹15,000, premier ste ₹31,500; ✳@☎) Built in the early 20th century for royal functions (the Durbar Hall is part of it), the Fateh Prakash has luxurious rooms and gorgeous suites, all comprehensively equipped and almost all looking straight out onto Lake Pichola. Views apart, the general ambience is a little less regal than at the Shiv Niwas.

OTHER AREAS

TOP CHOICE **Taj Lake Palace**   HERITAGE HOTEL **$$$**
(☑2428800; www.tajhotels.com; r ₹37,500-
43,500, ste from ₹150,000; ✳@🌐☀) The icon of
Udaipur, this romantic white-marble palace
seemingly floating on the lake is extraordi-
nary, with open-air courtyards, lotus ponds
and a small, mango-tree-shaded pool. Rooms
are hung with breezy silks and filled with
carved furniture. Some of the cheapest over-
look the lily pond rather than the lake; the
mural-decked suites will make you feel like a
maharaja. Service is superb. Access is by boat
from the hotel's own jetty in the City Palace
gardens. Rates can vary a lot with season and
demand: check the website.

TOP CHOICE **Udaivilas**   HOTEL **$$$**
(☑2433300; www.oberoihotels.com; r
₹35,000-40,500, ste ₹180,00-250,000; ✳@🌐☀)
In lovely grounds running down to the
northwest shore of Lake Pichola, 2km west
of the old city by road, Udaivilas' butter-
sculpture domes are breathtaking. It's a
beautifully designed, luxurious but personal
hotel that doesn't spare the glitz or gold leaf,
and the suites, as well as many rooms, even
come equipped with private or semiprivate
pools. The hotel houses three fine restaurants and a plush spa. You can arrive by land
or by boat from the hotel's own dock below
Sunset Point.

Mountain Ridge   HOMESTAY **$$**
(☑3291478, 9602192902; www.mountainridge.in;
Sisarma; r incl breakfast & dinner ₹1950-3950; ☀)
This country homestay run by a resident
Briton makes a great alternative to the city
noise and hustle, and a good base for explor-
ing the Udaipur countryside. It's a lovely
stone-built house with five spacious rooms
and great views, perched on a hilltop near
Sisarma village, 6km from the city cen-
tre. Guided hikes and birdwatching, yoga,
yummy food and free cooking lessons are all
available here. An autorickshaw/taxi from
town costs around ₹100/300: fork southwest
at the Bheruji Mandir sign just south of Si-
sarma village.

Hotel Rampratap   HOTEL **$$**
(☑2431701; www.hotelrampratap.com; Fateh Sagar
Lake; r ₹2300-4500; ✳@) This delightful hotel appeals for its peaceful location (within
10 minutes' walk of the old city but it feels
a world away), creature comforts (including a herbal massage centre) and friendly
service. Many rooms have a terrific view of
Fateh Sagar through large windows, though

not the standard rooms on the ground floor.
One of the two restaurants sits in a beautiful
lakeside garden.

✗ Eating

Udaipur has scores of sun-kissed rooftop
cafes, many with mesmerising lake views
but often with uninspired multicuisine fare.
Fortunately there's also a healthy number of
places putting a bit more thought into their
food, featuring very fine dining at some of
the top-end hotels. If you like a drink, the
local liquor, *duru* – a heady mixture of saffron, cardamom and aniseed – may appeal.
Otherwise, beer is plentiful.

Some budget restaurants have nightly
screenings of contemporary movies or *Octopussy* – in case you'd forgotten this was
partly filmed in Udaipur.

LAL GHAT AREA

Jagat Niwas Palace Hotel   INDIAN **$$**
(☑2420133; 23-25 Lal Ghat; mains ₹120-300;
☺6.30am-10.30am, noon-3.30pm & 7-10pm) A
wonderful, classy, rooftop restaurant with
superb lake views, delicious Indian cuisine
and good service. Choose from an extensive
selection of rich curries (tempered for West-
ern tastes) – mutton, chicken, fish, veg – as
well as the tandoori classics. There's a tempt-
ing cocktail menu and the beer is icy. It's wise
to book ahead for dinner.

Lotus Cafe   MULTICUISINE **$**
(15 Bhattiyani Chotta; dishes ₹50-120; ☺9am-
10.30pm) This funky little restaurant serves
up fabulous chicken dishes (predominantly
Indian), plus salads, baked potatoes and
plenty of vegetarian fare. It's ideal for meet-
ing and greeting other travellers, with a
mezzanine to loll about on and cool back-
ground sounds.

Cafe Edelweiss   CAFE **$**
(73 Gangaur Ghat Rd; snacks ₹30-80; ☺7am-7pm)
The Savage Garden restaurant folks run this
itsy piece of Europe that appeals to home-
sick and discerning travellers with superb
baked goods and good coffee. If sticky cinna-
mon rolls, squidgy blueberry chocolate cake,
spinach-and-mushroom quiche or apple
strudel don't appeal, give it a miss.

Cafe Namaste   CAFE **$**
(Gadiya Devra; cakes, pies, breakfast dishes ₹20-80;
☺7.30am-9.30pm) A European-themed street-
side cafe at the Gangaur Palace Hotel that
delivers the goods with scrumptious muffins,
apple pies, cinnamon rolls, brownies etc.

209

UDAIPUR & SOUTHERN RAJASTHAN UDAIPUR

DON'T MISS

TOP FIVE UDAIPUR MEALS WITH A VIEW

» **Ambrai** Lake Pichola from water level

» **Jagat Niwas Palace Hotel** Lake Pichola from a rooftop

» **Gallery Restaurant** Lake Pichola from a palace

» **Jasmin** Gaze at Daiji Footbridge

» **Mayur Rooftop Cafe** Eye to eye with Jagdish Temple

And to wash it down there is coffee from a shiny silver espresso machine (₹40 to ₹70) taking pride of place. The noisy street is a minus.

Mayur Rooftop Cafe   MULTICUISINE **$$**
(Hotel Baba Palace, Jagdish Chowk; mains ₹80-210) This rooftop restaurant has a great view of the multihued light show on the Jagdish Temple. You can choose the AC room or the breezy open section. The usual multicuisine themes fill out the menu, while the ₹55 thali is good value.

HANUMAN GHAT AREA

TOP CHOICE Ambrai   NORTH INDIAN **$$**
(☑2431085; Amet Haveli hotel; mains ₹145-325; ◌12.30-3pm & 7.30-10.30pm) The cuisine at this scenic restaurant – at lake-shore level, looking across to Lake Palace Hotel, Lal Ghat and the City Palace – does justice to its fabulous position. Highly atmospheric at night, Ambrai feels like a French park, with its wrought-iron furniture, dusty ground and large shady trees, and there's a terrific bar to complement the dining.

Jasmin   MULTICUISINE **$**
(mains ₹50-80) Very tasty vegetarian dishes are cooked up here in a lovely, quiet, open-air spot looking out on the quaint Daiji footbridge. There are plenty of Indian options, and some original variations on the usual multicuisine theme including Korean and Israeli dishes. The ambience is super-relaxed and service friendly.

Queen Cafe   INDIAN **$**
(14 Bajrang Marg; mains ₹60-75; ◌8am-10pm) This homey little eatery with just a couple of tables serves up fabulous home-style Indian vegetarian dishes. Try the pumpkin curry with mint and coconut, and the Kashmir

pullao with fruit, vegies and coconut. Don't pass on the chocolate desserts either! Happily the cook, Meenu, gives classes too.

Udai Kothi   MULTICUISINE **$$**
(mains ₹125-250) The terrace restaurant set high atop the Udai Kothi hotel has tables and cushioned alcoves around the rooftop pool and is especially romantic in the evening. The service is professional and the food, in our experience, good without being outstanding. There's live sitar and tabla music in the evenings during the winter months.

CITY PALACE

Note that you have to pay ₹25 to enter the City Palace complex if you're not staying in one of its hotels.

Paantya Restaurant   MULTICUISINE **$$$**
(☑2528016; Shiv Niwas Palace Hotel; mains ₹500-1400) Most captivating in the evening, this semiformal restaurant in the ritzy Shiv Niwas Palace has indoor seating, but if the weather's warm enough it's best out in the open-air courtyard by the pool. Indian classical music is performed nightly, and the food is great. For local flavour try the very tasty *laal maas dhungar,* a Rajasthani spiced and smoked mutton dish.

Gallery Restaurant   CONTINENTAL **$$$**
(Durbar Hall; Durbar tea ₹325; ◌9am-6pm) Alongside the splendiferous Durbar Hall, this elegant little restaurant has beguiling views across Lake Pichola. It does snacks and a continental lunch, but the time to come is between 3pm and 5pm when you can indulge in afternoon tea with cakes and the all-important scones, jam and cream.

OTHER AREAS

1559 AD   MULTICUISINE **$$$**
(☑2433559; PP Singhal Marg; mains ₹200-650; ◌11am-11pm) Waiters in embroidered-silk waistcoats serve up lovely Indian, Thai and continental dishes in elegant surroundings at this secluded restaurant near the southeastern side of Fateh Sagar Lake. There are garden tables as well as several different rooms with just a few candlelit tables in each, and Indian classical music in the evenings. Includes a coffee shop with the best coffee we tasted in Udaipur.

Savage Garden   MEDITERRANEAN **$$**
(☑2425440; 22 Inside Chandpol; mains ₹190-320; ◌11am-11pm) Tucked away in the backstreets (but well signposted) near Chandpol, Savage Garden does a winning line in soups, chick-

en and homemade pasta dishes with assorted sauces, though portions aren't huge. There are some Middle Eastern influences too – try the three meze: babaganoush, hummus and tabouli. The setting is atmospheric, in a 250-year-old *haveli* with indigo walls and bowls of flowers, and tables in alcoves or a pleasant courtyard. The bar is slick, with red, white and sparkling Indian wines from Nasik, Maharashtra.

Natraj Hotel   GUJARATI $
(New Bapu Bazaar; thali ₹70; ☺10.30am-3.30pm & 6.15-10.30pm) Famous throughout town for its delicious all-you-can-eat vegetarian Gujarati thalis, this place has been filled to the brim for two decades with devout locals, who arrive to chow down on its huge portions of cheap, fresh food. The thali includes a whopping selection of rice, dhal, roti, pickles and at least five different vegetable dishes. It's a bit hard to find, tucked away in a backstreet 1.5km northeast of the City Palace, but definitely worth the hunt.

Udaivilas   MULTICUISINE $$$
(☑2433300; mains ₹800-1950) Like everything else at the Udaivilas hotel, the restaurants are top class. For a special night out, book a table at the outdoor Chandni restaurant where you can enjoy a traditional music and dance show with your meal. Reservations are obligatory.

Parkview Restaurant   INDIAN $$
(Town Hall Rd; mains ₹70-160; ☺9am-11pm) A celebrated local restaurant (since 1968) with a surprisingly low tourist quota, Parkview does a solid spread of Indian staples in a 90-seater elongated room with fuzzy red seats and well-dressed waiters. It's 1.5km northeast of the City Palace and 400m north of the Surajpol gate.

🍸 Drinking

Most guesthouses have a roof terrace serving up cold Kingfishers with views over the lazy waters of Lake Pichola, but for a real treat try the top-end hotels. Note that you have to pay ₹25 to enter the City Palace complex if you're not staying in one of its hotels.

Panera Bar   BAR
(Shiv Niwas Palace Hotel; Kingfisher or Indian whisky ₹250-275; ☺11.30am-10pm) Sink into plush sofas surrounded by huge mirrors, royal portraits and beautiful paintwork, or sit out by the pool and be served like a maharaja.

Sunset Terrace   BAR
(Fateh Prakash Palace Hotel; ☺7am-10.30pm) On a terrace overlooking Lake Pichola, this is perfect for a sunset gin and tonic. It's also a restaurant, with live music performed every night.

☆ Entertainment

Dharohar   DANCE
(☑2523858; Bagore-ki-Haveli, Gangaur Ghat; admission ₹60, camera ₹50; ☺7pm) The beautiful Bagore-ki-Haveli hosts the best (and most convenient) opportunity to see Rajasthani folk dancing, with nightly shows of colourful, energetic Mewari, Bhil and western Rajasthani dances, by talented performers.

Mewar Sound & Light Show
                              SOUND & LIGHT SHOW
(Manek Chowk, City Palace; lower/upper seating English show ₹150/400, Hindi show ₹100/200; ☺7pm Sep-Feb, 7.30pm Mar-Apr, 8pm May-Aug) Fifteen centuries of intriguing Mewar history are squeezed into one atmospheric hour of commentary and light switching – in English from September to April, in Hindi other months.

🛍 Shopping

Tourist-oriented shops – selling miniature paintings, wood carvings, silver and other jewellery, bangles, traditional shoes, spices, leather-bound handmade-paper notebooks, ornate knives, camel-bone boxes, and a large variety of textiles – line the streets radiating from Jagdish Chowk: City Palace Rd, Gadiya Devra, Bhattiyani Chotta and its continuation Lake Palace Rd. There are more on Bajrang Marg near Hanuman Ghat. Udaipur is known for its local crafts, particularly its miniature paintings in the Rajput-Mughal style, but finding an authentic artist takes a collector's eye. Numerous 'art schools' certainly teach the craft to youngsters, but they also cheaply generate the bulk of the mass-produced miniatures flogged on the streets.

Be prepared to bargain hard in these areas, as most places will probably quote you a ridiculous opening price: as a rule of thumb, aim to pay around 50% of the initial asking price.

The local market area extends east from the old clock tower at the north end of Jagdish Temple Rd, and buzzes loudest in the evening. It's fascinating as much for browsing and soaking up local atmosphere as for buying. Bara Bazar, immediately east of the

KEEPING UDAIPUR GREEN

Slowly, Udaipur's tourist industry is realising that it pays to be green, not only for the future of their city but also to attract eco-conscious travellers.

Shikshantar (☎2451303; www.swaraj.org/shikshantar; 83 Adinath Nagar, Kharol Colony), a community group working for a 'zero waste' Udaipur, has instigated much of the green consciousness in this area. Shikshantar has created a 'green leaf' rating for hotels, based on 20 different criteria, including energy usage and waste management. Check out www.swaraj.org/shikshantar/greenleafintro.htm for ratings. (Also interesting is its 'Ecotourism in Udaipur' video on YouTube.)

Shikshantar works on many fronts, including healthy lifestyles, herbal medicines, urban and organic farming, alternative technologies, zero-waste design and community media. It invites volunteers to work on these issues and also to offer or participate in workshops on them. A good place to make contact is Halchal Saturday Cafe (☺6.30-10pm Sat), at the Shikshantar offices (in the north of the city) – a slow food (healthy, local and organic) cafe where travellers can connect with local artists and activists.

old clock tower, sells silver and gold, while its narrow side street, Maldas St, specialises in saris and fabrics. A little further east, traditional shoes are sold on Mochiwada. Foodstuffs are mainly found around the new clock tower at the east end of the bazaar area – including spice stalls immediately north of the tower and a plethora of fruit and vegetables in the Mandi Market, about 200m north of the tower.

Numerous shops clustered around Lal Ghat purvey and exchange guidebooks, nonfiction and fiction about Rajasthan and India, in English and other languages.

Rajasthali HANDICRAFTS
Chetak Circle (26 Chetak Circle; ☺10.30am-7.30pm Mon-Sat); old city (City Palace Rd; ☺10am-6.30pm) This government fixed-price emporium is worth dropping into to gauge handicraft prices. The branch at Chetak Circle, 1km north of the old clock tower, has a pretty representative range of Rajasthan crafts.

Sadhna HANDICRAFTS
(www.sadhna.org; Jagdish Temple Rd; ☺10am-7pm) This is the crafts outlet for Seva Mandir, a long-established NGO working with rural and tribal people (see p358). The small shop sells attractive fixed-price textiles; profits go to the artisans and towards community development work.

ℹ Information

Emergency
Police (☎2414600, 100) There are police posts at Surajpol, Hatipol and Delhi Gate, three of the gates in the old-city wall.

Internet Access
You can surf the internet at plenty of places, particularly around Lal Ghat, for ₹30 per hour. Many places double as travel agencies, bookshops, art shops etc.

BA Photo N Book Store (69 Durga Sadan; ☺10am-11pm)

Lake City (Lal Ghat; ☺9am-11pm)

Mewar International (35 Lal Ghat; ☺9am-11pm)

Shiv Goraksha (5 Gadiya Devra; ☺8am-10pm)

Shreeji Tours & Travels (Gadiya Devra; ☺8.30am-10pm)

Maps & Guides
Udaipur Maps & Information, produced by Piers Helsen from Mountain Ridge, is a mini-guide as well as an incredibly accurate map. For even more detail, Piers has also published *Udaipur for All* and *Rural Udaipur for Hikers & Bikers*.

Medical Services
GBH American Hospital (☎3056000; www.gbhamericanhospital.com; 101 Kothi Bagh, Bhatt Ji Ki Bari, Meera Girls College Rd) Modern, reader-recommended private hospital with 24-hour emergency service, about 2km northeast of the old city.

Maharana Bhopal Hospital (☎2528811; Hospital Rd) Government-run general hospital near Chetak Circle, about 1.5km north of the old city.

Money
There are lots of ATMs, including Axis Bank and State Bank ATMs on City Palace Rd near Jagdish Temple; HDFC, ICICI and State Bank ATMs near the bus stand; and two ATMs outside the train station. Places to change currency and travellers cheques include the following:

Centrum (Lake Palace Rd; ⏱9.30am-6pm Mon-Fri, 9.30am-3pm Sat)

Sai Tours & Travels (168 City Palace Rd; ⏱8am-9pm)

Thomas Cook (Lake Palace Rd; ⏱9.30am-6pm Mon-Sat)

Post

DHL (1 Town Hall Rd; ⏱10am-7pm Mon-Sat) Has a free collection service within Udaipur.

Main post office (Chetak Circle; ⏱10am-1pm & 1.30-6pm Mon-Sat) North of the old city.

Post office (City Palace Rd; ⏱9.30am-1pm & 2-5.30pm Mon-Sat) Beside the City Palace's Badi Pol ticket office, 1.5km northeast of the City Palace.

Tourist Information

Apart from the Tourist Reception Centre listed below, smaller tourist information counters operate erratically at the train station and airport.

Tourist Reception Centre (☎2411535; Fateh Memorial Bldg; ⏱10am-5pm Mon-Sat) Not situated in the most convenient position, 1.5km east of the Jagdish Temple (although only about 500m from the bus stand), this place dishes out a limited amount of brochures and information.

Websites

Two useful sites, with tourist and cultural information and news, are **Discover Udaipur** (www.discoverudaipur.com) and **Udaipur Plus** (www.udaipurplus.com). **Eternal Mewar** (www.eternalmewar.in) is great for detail on the area's history, monuments and culture.

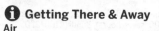

ⓘ Getting There & Away

Air

Air India (☎2410999; www.airindia.com; 222/16 Mumal Towers, Saheli Rd) flies to Mumbai daily and to Delhi via Jodhpur also daily.

Jet Airways (☎2561105; www.jetairways.com; Blue Circle Business Centre, Madhuban) flies direct to Delhi daily, and to Mumbai once or twice daily.

Kingfisher Airlines (☎1800 2093030; www.flykingfisher.com; 4/73 Chetak Circle) has daily flights to Delhi, Mumbai and Jaipur, with the Jaipur flight continuing to Jodhpur from about October to March. It's strongly advisable to make flight bookings well in advance during the busy tourist season. If you can't book online, Udaipur has dozens of travel agencies eager to help you.

Bus

Frequent **Rajasthan State Road Transport Corporation** (RSRTC) buses travel from the main bus stand near the Udaipol gate to other Rajasthani cities, as well as Delhi, Agra and Ahmedabad. If you use these buses, take an express or one of the infrequent deluxe services, as the ordinary buses take an incredibly long time and can be very uncomfortable. The best RSRTC buses are the air-conditioned Volvo services, which run once a day on just a few routes. For long-distance travel it's best to book ahead.

Private buses, mostly leaving from Station Rd a little south of the main bus stand, operate

RSRTC BUSES FROM UDAIPUR

DESTINATION	FARE (EXPRESS/DELUXE/ VOLVO, ₹)	APPROXIMATE DURATION (HR)	FREQUENCY
Agra	415/456/-	14	2 daily
Ahmedabad	157/170/390	5	hourly, 4am-11pm
Ajmer	161/201/-	7	every 30 minutes
Bundi	160/-/-	6	4 daily, 4.30-9.30am
Chittorgarh	70/81/-	2½	every 30 minutes, 5.30am-11.30pm
Delhi	406/456/1207	15	4
Jaipur	235/285/685	9	hourly
Jodhpur	145/160/400	6-8	10 daily
Kota	170/204/-	7	every 30 minutes, 5am-9.30am
Mt Abu	127/-/-	4	about every 30 minutes, 5am-4pm

to destinations including Kota (seat/sleeper ₹150/200, seven hours), Bundi (₹160/220, seven hours), Jaipur (₹180/280, seven to eight hours), Jodhpur (₹180/250, five to eight hours), Agra (₹300/400, 13 hours), Delhi (₹450/800, 12 hours), Ahmedabad (₹160/260, five hours), Mumbai (₹400/600, 15 hours) and Mt Abu (seat ₹150, four hours). AC buses costing around 50% more are available to Jaipur, Delhi, Ahmedabad and Mumbai; Mumbai even has some Volvo AC services (seat/sleeper around ₹1200/1500). You can get tickets from plenty of travel agencies, hotels and guesthouses, though you may find commission charges are lower at the ticket offices near the departure area.

Taxi

Most hotels, guesthouses and travel agencies can organise you a car and driver to just about anywhere you want. A typical round-trip day outing in a non-AC car costs around ₹800 to Eklingji and Nagda, ₹1400 to Chittorgarh, and also ₹1400 to Ranakpur and Kumbhalgarh. One-way trips to Mt Abu, Ahmedabad, Bundi via Chittorgarh, or Jodhpur via Kumbhalgarh and Ranakpur are around ₹2500 (this includes a charge for the driver's trip back to Udaipur). You may need to negotiate a little.

Train

The computerised main **ticket office** (⊙8am-8pm Mon-Sat, 8am-2pm Sun) at the station has a window for foreign tourists and other special categories of passenger.

12964 *Mewar Express* departs Udaipur at 6.15pm and arrives in Delhi's Nizamuddin station (sleeper/3AC/2AC/1AC ₹315/816/1102/1846) at 6.30am, via Chittorgarh, Bundi, Kota, Sawai Madhopur and Bharatpur.

12982 *Chetak Express* departs Udaipur at 5.20pm Monday, Wednesday, Friday and Sunday, reaching Delhi Sarai Rohilla station (sleeper/3AC/2AC ₹297/766/1033) at 5.30am, via Chittorgarh and Ajmer.

12966 *Udaipur-Gwalior Super Express* departs Udaipur at 10.20pm and arrives in Gwalior (sleeper/3AC/2AC/1AC ₹324/844/1142/1915) at 12.45pm, via Chittorgarh, Ajmer, Jaipur (₹224/559/747/1255, 7½ hours) and Bharatpur.

12991 *Udaipur-Ajmer Express* departs at 6.15am and arrives in Ajmer (2nd class/AC chair ₹109/362) at 11.40am, via Chittorgarh (₹70/223, two hours).

52927 *Udaipur-Ahmedabad Passenger* departs Udaipur at 9.35am, arriving in Dungarpur (sleeper ₹90) at 2.05pm and Ahmedabad (₹107) at 9.05pm. The 19943 *Udaipur-Ahmedabad Express* at 7.25pm reaches Dungarpur (sleeper/2AC ₹130/314) at 10.56pm and Ahmedabad (₹162/554) at 4.25am.

🅐 Getting Around

To/From the Airport

The airport is 25km east of town, about 900m south of Hwy 76 to Chittorgarh. A prepaid taxi to the Lal Ghat area costs ₹400. Hotels mostly charge ₹450 to ₹500 for airport transfers.

Autorickshaw

These are unmetered, so you should agree on a fare before setting off – the normal fare anywhere in town is around ₹30. You will usually have to go through the rigmarole of haggling, walking away etc to get this fare. Some drivers ask tourists for ₹100, ₹150 and other absurdities. It costs around ₹300 to hire an autorickshaw for a day of local sightseeing.

The commission system is in place, so tenaciously pursue your first choice of accommodation.

Bicycle & Motorcycle

A cheap and environmentally friendly way to buzz around is by bike; many guesthouses can arrange bikes to rent, costing around ₹50 per day. Scooters and motorbikes, meanwhile, are great for exploring the surrounding countryside. **Heera Cycle Store** (⊙7.30am-9pm), just off Gangaur Ghat Rd, hires out bicycles/mountain bikes/mopeds/scooters/motorbikes/Bullets for ₹50/100/200/350/350/450 per day (with a deposit of US$50/100/200/300/400/500); you must show your passport and driver's licence.

North of Udaipur

EKLINGJI & NAGDA

In the village of Kailashpuri – only 22km and a short bus ride north of Udaipur – the fascinating **Eklingji Temple Complex** (⊙4.15-6.45am, 10.30am-1.30pm & 5.15-7.45pm), with its 108 temples, attracts lots of pilgrims but few tourists. The main temple's present form dates from the 15th-century rule of Maharana Raimal, although it was originally built in the 8th century, according to legend, by the early Mewar king Bappa Rawal. Constructed from sandstone and marble, it has an elaborately pillared hall under a large pyramidal roof and features a four-faced, black-marble image of Eklingji, an incarnation of Shiva and the family deity of the Mewar royal family. Note that opening hours change quite regularly, so you might have to wait an hour or two if you arrive at the wrong time. Avoid the temple on Monday (an auspicious day for devotees), as it can get very crowded; the current head of Mewar's ex-ruling family pays a private visit to the temple on Monday evening. Guides are available at the temple; bank on paying around ₹100 to engage their services. Photography is not permitted.

About 1km back towards Udaipur then 1km to the west, **Nagda** was an early Mewar capital, established in the 7th century. It was ruined by the invader Altamash in the 1220s but still has a few temples worth seeing. The 10th-century **Saas Bahu Temples** (☉8am-6pm) – the name meaning 'mother-in-law daughter-in-law' – are dedicated to Vishnu and feature fine, intricate carvings, including a number of erotic figures. The **Jain temple of Adbudji** remains very fine, despite damage at the hands of the Mughals, and contains a 15th-century black-marble idol of *tirthankar* Shanti Nath. There are also some small temples submerged in the nearby lake; after a poor monsoon they're completely exposed.

🛏 Sleeping

Devi Garh   HERITAGE HOTEL $$$
(☎02953-289211; Delwara; www.deviresorts.in; ste incl breakfast & airport transfers from ₹19,000; ✹@🛜🏊) Think of every conceivable 21st-century luxury, all parcelled up within a gorgeous 18th-century palace, and you've pretty much got Devi Garh, which towers over the village of Delwara, 5km north of Kailashpuri on Hwy 8. The pool, the spa, you name it, they've thought of it, and they do it impeccably. Rooms are beautifully minimalist but luxurious, with white marble furniture, terrazzo floors and mirror inlay; the food is outstanding (if inevitably pricey); and the gliding staff will cater to your every sybaritic whim.

❶ Getting There & Away

Local buses leave Udaipur bus stand for Kailashpuri (₹15, 30 minutes) every half-hour from 5am to 10pm. You can reach Nagda by bicycle from Kailashpuri where there's a bike-hire shop; a day's rental should cost around ₹40.

NATHDWARA
☎02953

The 18th-century **Shri Nathji Temple** (☉5-5.30am, 7-7.30am, 9-9.30am, 11.15-11.45am, 3.45-4.15pm, 4.30-5.30pm & 6.30-7pm) stands at Nathdwara, 48km north of Udaipur by Hwy 8. Like Eklingji, it's another place that draws many pilgrims but sees few tourists; photography is not permitted. The shrine has special significance for Vaishnavites (followers of Vishnu, of whom Shri Nathji is an incarnation). The black-stone Shri Nathji image housed in the temple was brought here

from Mathura in 1669 to protect it from the destructive impulses of the Mughal ruler Aurangzeb. According to legend, the getaway vehicle, a wagon, sank into the ground up to the axles as it was passing through Nathdwara. The priests realised that this was a sign from Krishna that the image did not want to travel any further; accordingly, the Shri Nathji Temple was built on the spot.

Attendants treat the black-stone image like a delicate child, waking it up in the morning, washing it, dressing it, offering it specially prepared meals and putting it to sleep, all at precise times through the day – the temple opens and closes around the image's daily routine. It gets very crowded during the first afternoon session, when Krishna gets up after a siesta, and attracts many thousands of devotees for festivals such as Janmastami (August or September) and Annakoot (November). Note that opening times can vary by 15 minutes either way.

Nathdwara is also well known for its *pichwai* paintings, which were produced after the image of Krishna was brought to the town in the 17th century. These bright screen paintings, with their rather static images, were usually created on handspun fabric and intended to be hung behind the idol – they usually show Shri Nathji decked out in different outfits. Inferior reproductions are created for the tourist market.

🛏 Sleeping & Eating
Nathdwara has plenty of hotels; most of the best ones are on Hwy 8.

Garden View Hotel   HOTEL $$
(☎232285; www.gardenviewhotel.com; r ₹2300-2700; ✹@) About 300m north of the central bus stand, the pinkish-coloured Garden View has decent, comfortable rooms in dull brown and white tones, plus a multicuisine restaurant and large lawn.

Shrinath Inn   HOTEL $$
(☎9214252777; www.hotelshrinathinn.com; s/d ₹750/950, AC from ₹1200/1500; ✹) This modern and functional hotel, 200m north of the bus stand, has fairly bright rooms, most with balconies.

❶ Getting There & Away
Buses run every half-hour from Udaipur bus stand to Nathdwara (₹25, one hour).

HALDIGHATI
This battlefield site, 40km north of Udaipur, is where Maharana Pratap defied the superior Mughal forces of Akbar in 1576. The site

is marked by a small *chhatri* that commemorates the warrior's horse, Chetak. Although badly wounded and exhausted after a set-to with the Mughal commander and his elephant, this loyal steed carried Maharana Pratap to safety before dying with his head in his master's lap. Apart from a **museum** (admission ₹20; ⊙7am-7pm), with dioramas on the Pratap story, there's not much else to see, but the historic site attracts many Indian visitors. The town of Haldighati can be reached by bus from Nathdwara (₹14, 30 minutes); the battle site is 2km southeast.

KUMBHALGARH
☑02954

About 80km north of Udaipur, **Kumbhalgarh** (Indian/foreigner ₹5/100; ⊙9am-6pm) is a fantastic, remote fort, fulfilling romantic expectations and vividly summoning up the chivalrous, warlike Rajput era. One of the many forts built by Rana Kumbha (r 1433–68), under whom Mewar reached its greatest extents, the isolated fort is perched 1100m above sea level, with endless views melting into blue distance. The journey to the fort, along twisting roads through the Aravalli Hills, is a highlight in itself.

Kumbhalgarh was the most important Mewar fort after Chittorgarh, and the rulers, sensibly, used to retreat here in times of danger. Not surprisingly, Kumbhalgarh was only taken once in its entire history. Even then, it took the combined armies of Amber, Marwar and Mughal emperor Akbar to breach its strong defences, and they only managed to hang on to it for two days.

The fort's thick walls stretch about 36km; they're wide enough in some places for eight horses to ride abreast and it's possible to walk right round the circuit (allow two days). They enclose around 360 intact and ruined temples, some of which date back to the Mauryan period in the 2nd century BC, as well as palaces, gardens, step-wells and 700 cannon bunkers. The complex was renovated in the 19th century by Maharana Fateh Singh. It's worth taking a leisurely walk in the large compound, which has some interesting ruins and temples and is usually very peaceful.

According to legend it was here that the young Maharana Udai Singh II was brought for safety by his nurse Panna Dhai after an assassination attempt. Kumbhalgarh was also the birthplace of Udai Singh II's famed warrior son Maharana Pratap.

If you stay near Kumbhalgarh, you can walk a few kilometres from your hotel to the fort, a dramatic way to approach it. It costs ₹15 to park a car outside the entrance.

The large and rugged Kumbhalgarh Wildlife Sanctuary can be visited from Kumbhalgarh and most accommodation here can organise jeep, horse or walking trips in the sanctuary, although on balance Ranakpur (p217) is marginally better set up as a base for this.

🛌 Sleeping & Eating

Aodhi   HOTEL $$$
(☑242341; www.eternalmewar.in; r ₹6000, ste ₹7000, meals ₹400-1000; ❀@☎❀) Just under 2km from the fort is this luxurious and

---

THE ULTIMATE SACRIFICE

A Mewar royal servant named Panna Dhai has been immortalised for the most extraordinary loyalty to the royal family that you could possibly imagine.

In 1535 Udai Singh II was just a boy when his father, Rana Vikramaditya, was assassinated by an ambitious regent named Banbir. Banbir then determined also to eliminate the young heir to the throne – Udai Singh himself. One night, Banbir managed to break into the prince's bedroom at Chittorgarh, planning to kill the boy.

Udai Singh's devoted nurse, Panna Dhai, was, however, one step ahead of him. She had placed, as a precaution, her own son Chandan in the prince's bed. When Banbir demanded to know which child was the prince, Panna Dhai pointed to her own son. Banbir whipped out his sword and slaughtered the child.

Panna Dhai then hid the real prince in a basket and fled to the fort at Kumbhalgarh. She told the nobles and people of Mewar what had happened, and the prince was soon crowned, ensuring the unbroken lineage of Mewar's Sisodia dynasty.

The current head of the Mewar ex-ruling family has ensured the memory of Panna Dhai lives on with a special award at the annual Maharana Mewar Foundation Awards ceremony. The Panna Dhai Award is given to an individual who 'ventures beyond the call of duty and sets an example in society of permanent value through sacrifice'.

blissfully tranquil hotel with an inviting pool, rambling gardens and winter camp-fires. The spacious rooms, in stone buildings, all boast their own palm-thatched terraces, balconies or pavilions, assorted wildlife and botanical art and photos. Non-guests can dine in the restaurant – where good standard Indian fare is the pick of the options on offer – or have a drink in the cosy Chowpal Bar. Room rates plummet from April to September.

Kumbhal Castle
HOTEL $$

(☎242171; www.thekumbhalcastle.com; Fort Rd; s/d ₹2000/2400, super deluxe ₹2500/2900, meals ₹250-500; ✵✵) The modern Kumbhal Castle, 2km from the fort, has plain but pleasant white rooms featuring curly iron beds, bright bedspreads and window seats, shared balconies and good views. The 'super deluxe' rooms are considerably bigger and worth considering for the few hundred extra rupees.

Karni Palace Hotel
HOTEL $$

(☎242033; www.karnipalace.com; Bus Stand Rd, Kelwara; s/d ₹500/750, AC ₹800/1200, ste ₹1500/2000; ✵) In the town of Kelwara, 7km south of Kumbhalgarh, this hotel backs onto lovely cornfields. Rooms are clean and adequately comfortable, with bathtubs in the bathrooms and balconies overlooking the main street, and there's a rooftop restaurant.

❶ Getting There & Away
Buses leave Udaipur bus stand at 5.15am, 8.15am and 2.30pm for Kelwara (₹50, three hours), 7km south of the fort, from where you can continue by autorickshaw or jeep. Hiring a taxi from Udaipur means you can visit both Ranakpur and Kumbhalgarh in a day: the round-trip costs around ₹1400 (or ₹1600 with AC).

RANAKPUR
☎02934

In a remote setting at the foot of a steep wooded escarpment of the Aravalli Hills, **Ranakpur** (camera/video ₹50/150; ☺Jains 6am-7pm, non-Jains noon-5pm) is one of India's biggest and most important Jain temple complexes. It's 75km northwest of Udaipur, and 12km west of Kumbhalgarh as the crow flies (but 50km by road, via Saira). The main temple, the **Chaumukha Mandir** (Four-Faced Temple), is dedicated to Adinath, the first Jain *tirthankar* (depicted in the many Buddha-like images in the temple), and was built in the 15th century in milk-white marble. An incredible feat of Jain devotion,

this is a complicated series of 29 halls, 80 domes and 1444 individually engraved pillars. The interior is completely covered in knotted, lovingly wrought carving, and has a marvellously calming sense of space and harmony. Shoes, cigarettes and all leather articles must be left at the entrance; menstruating women are asked not to enter.

Also exquisitely carved and well worth inspecting are two other Jain temples, dedicated to **Neminath** (22nd *tirthankar*) and **Parasnath** (23rd *tirthankar*), both within the complex, and a nearby **Sun Temple**. About 1km from the main complex is the **Amba Mata Temple**.

Ranakpur makes a convenient stop between Udaipur and Jodhpur. For those with time, it's also a great place to kick back for a few days. You can visit Kumbhalgarh from here and Ranakpur also makes a great base for exploring the hilly, densely forested **Kumbhalgarh Wildlife Sanctuary** (Indian/foreigner ₹20/160, jeep or car ₹130, camera/video free/₹400, guide per day ₹200; ☺dawn-dusk), which extends over some 600 sq km to the northeast and southwest. The sanctuary is criss-crossed by a number of tracks, making for good jeep or horse safaris or walks. It's known for its leopards and wolves although the chances of spotting antelopes, gazelles, deer and sloth bears are higher. You will certainly see some of the sanctuary's 200-plus bird species. The scarcity of waterholes between March and June makes this the best time to see animals; early morning and late afternoon are the best times of day. Also within the sanctuary are a number of temples including the **Parshuram Shiva Temple** in a cave, and the 10th-century **Muchala Mahavir Jain Temple** flanked by two mighty elephants, with walls richly carved with warriors, horses and chariot-mounted gods.

Some of the best safaris and treks are offered (to guests and nonguests) by Shivika Lake Hotel; the knowledgeable host family here has been guiding visitors in the sanctuary for over two decades. Options include three-hour jeep safaris (per person ₹650), a three-hour forest and lake walk (₹300), a six-to-seven-hour round-trip walk leading to Parshuram Shiva Temple (₹450), a one-way hike to Kumbhalgarh (about five hours; ₹650), and a two-night camping trip, with one jeep safari included, for ₹3500 (all prices are per person, with a two-person minimum and park fees included).

🛏 Sleeping & Eating

There are about 10 places to stay on and just off Hwy 32 within a few kilometres of the Ranakpur temple.

Shivika Lake Hotel   HOTEL **$$**
(☑285078; www.shivikalakehotel.com; r ₹600-1600, tent ₹1200; 🕸@🕸) Two kilometres north of the temple, Shivika is a welcoming, rustic and family-run hotel that provides free pick-ups and drops at the bus stop near the temple. You can stay in clean, cosy rooms amid leafy gardens, or safari-style tents. Two of the tents have prime positions beside beautiful Nal-wania Lake on the edge of the property. Due to the presence of a few crocodiles, the lake is not safe for swimming, but there's a swimming pool right beside it and some meals are served here too (mains ₹70 to ₹160, thali ₹170, buffet lunch about ₹300).

Aranyawas   HOTEL **$$**
(☑02956-293029; www.aranyawas.com; r incl breakfast ₹3500; 🕸@🕸) In beautifully secluded, tree-shaded grounds just off Hwy 32, 12km south of the temple, Aranyawas has 28 attractive rooms in stone-built cottages. They are not fancy but neat and tasteful, with pine furnishings and, in most cases, balconies overlooking a small river and hills. There's a large pool surrounded by broad, stone-paved terraces, and the inside-and-outside restaurant (mains ₹150 to ₹250, buffet lunch/dinner ₹300/350) is a lovely place to stop for an Indian meal even if you're not staying here.

Ranakpur Hill Resort   HOTEL **$$**
(☑286411; www.ranakpurhillresort.com; Ranakpur Rd; s ₹2000-3500, d ₹2500-4000, s/d tent ₹2000/2500; 🕸@🕸) This is a well-run hotel with a nice pool in grassy gardens, around which are ranged the attractive, all-AC rooms sporting marble floors, stained glass, floral wall paintings and touches of mirrorwork. There are also five large tents with fans and big bathrooms, plus a good multicuisine restaurant (lunch or dinner ₹350). It's 3.5km north of the temple along Hwy 32.

Maharani Bagh Orchard Retreat   HOTEL **$$$**
(☑285105; www.jodhanaheritage.com; s/d ₹4500/5500; 🕸@🕸) Maharani Bagh (Queen's Garden) is set in lush 5-sq-km grounds with many mango and sandalwood trees and its own 1.5km walking trail. Accommodation is in colourful, comfortable, spacious cottages with verandas and traditional Rajasthani decor. There's a beautiful pool, a garden restaurant, and volleyball and table tennis if you have energy to burn. It's down a short lane from Hwy 32, 4km north of the temple.

❶ Getting There & Away

Buses to Ranakpur leave roughly hourly from the bus stand in Udaipur (₹70, three hours), and 10 times daily from the central bus stand in Jodhpur (₹109, four to five hours). The stop in Ranakpur is outside the temple, so you should either ask to be dropped at your accommodation or arrange for a pick-up on arrival. Buses from Ranakpur to both Udaipur and Jodhpur leave every one to two hours; the best services are the expresses, at around 7am, 2pm, 4pm and 6pm to both destinations.

A taxi day-trip from Udaipur to Ranakpur, Kumbhalgarh and back costs around ₹1400 (₹1600 with AC).

NARLAI
☑02934

Quiet yet spectacular, the village of Narlai, on an appallingly surfaced back-country road 30km north of Ranakpur, has a beautiful heritage hotel that makes a nice, if expensive, base for exploring the attractions of the countryside between Udaipur and Jodhpur. Opposite the Rawla Narlai hotel is a mammoth granite rock that's dotted with caves and temples; the village is also home to an 1100-year-old *baori* and several old temples, and offers lots of opportunities for quiet walks.

Rawla Narlai (☑260443; www.rawlanarlai.com; r ₹9000-20,000; 🕸@🕸) was once a hunting lodge of the royal family of Jodhpur. It's a beautifully maintained place, with 26 appealing, antique-furnished rooms. Many of these are decorated with frescoes, stained glass and hanging baubles, and open onto balconies and porches that face the huge granite outcrop opposite. Sumptuous Indian dinners can be eaten poolside, or, if you're in the mood, beside the secluded *baori* which will be lit with flickering oil lamps for the occasion. Horse and jeep safaris and village tours are on offer.

Some private buses running between Udaipur and Jodhpur stop at Narlai, about four hours from each.

South of Udaipur

BAMBORA
☑0294

In gently rolling countryside about 55km southeast of Udaipur, the sleepy village of Bambora has a dramatic 250-year-old fort that was converted in the 1990s from a derelict ruin into an impressive hotel. The 10th-century **Ambika Mata Temple** at Jagat, 28km west of the town, is dedicated to Digpal, a form of the goddess Durga, and is one of those dubbed the 'Khajuraho of...' (in this case Rajasthan) for its erotic carvings.

Karni Fort (☏9982984041, 9414136157; www.karnihotels.com; s/d/ste ₹3850/5300/6700; ❋ ❋) sits on the hill that rises over Bambora and is a place to come if you'd like to immerse yourself in the Rajasthani countryside for a couple of days. Inside the fort walls the main building occupies the hilltop like a grand country house. All rooms are light, bright and colourfully decorated; the best come with stunning panoramic views. There's a good Rajasthani restaurant, an old underground 'secret' passageway, and an alluring marble swimming pool with four water-spurting marble elephant. A central pavilion is set in the hilly garden. Staff are extremely helpful and tribal-area horse safaris, village walks, massage, birdwatching and croquet are all on offer.

JAISAMAND LAKE
☏0294

This large (88-sq-km) artificial lake was created when Maharana Jai Singh had the Gomti River dammed back in the 17th century. It's rich in bird life especially in winter. There are beautiful marble *chhatris* and carved elephants along the 330m-long embankment on the western shore just above Jaisamand village, 50km southeast of Udaipur. The **Jaisamand Wildlife Sanctuary** (Indian/foreigner ₹20/160, jeep or car ₹130, camera/video free/₹400, guide per day ₹200; ☺8am-5pm) stretches along the shoreline here and away to the northwest. Composed mainly of grassy hills with a medium tree covering, it harbours some sloth bears, leopards and chinkara gazelles, though it isn't well set up for visitors, with no information or guides available on the spot. Two old royal country palaces on hilltops are worth a look if you have a vehicle: the Hawa Mahal to the right from the embankment, and the small Ruti Rani Mahal, opposite.

Jaisamand Island Resort (☏02906-234723; www.jaisamand.com; s/d ₹3500/4500, ste between ₹4500/5500; ❋ @ ❋) is a modernish hotel in a wonderful setting on one of the lake's 11 islands, but while the pool (when full) and terraced gardens are lovely, the spacious rooms are generally rather tired and/or musty. Jeep trips into the sanctuary, boating, birdwatching and camel rides are on offer. Discounts can make it reasonable value.

Boats from the embankment cross to the hotel for ₹200 per person round-trip. They're also available for lake tours.

Buses run from Udaipur bus stand to Jaisamand village (₹30, 1½ hours) about every 30 minutes.

SITAMATA WILDLIFE SANCTUARY
If you want to get away from it all into picturesque countryside and plenty of fresh air, this is a place to visit. About 110km southeast of Udaipur, Sitamata Wildlife Sanctuary covers 423 sq km of mainly deciduous forest, which is known for its ancient teak trees. Wildlife includes a variety of deer, leopards, lynx-like caracals, flying squirrels and pangolins (scaly anteaters). Few tourists make it out this way.

Fort Dhariyawad (☏02950-270050; www.fortdhariyawad.com; r ₹2400-3500; ❋ @) is in the Sitamata sanctuary area, 120km from Udaipur. It's housed in a 16th-century fort founded by Prince Sahasmal, second son of Maharana Pratap, and offers all-round creature comforts, though the beds aren't the most comfy. The restaurant serves tasty Indian food, and meals can be taken in the enchantingly lit gardens. Jeep and horse safaris can be arranged to places of interest in the area.

RISHABDEO
☏02907

The village of Rishabdeo, 66km south of Udaipur, is a significant pilgrimage centre with a magical atmosphere. Its 15th-century **Jain temple** (☺7am-9.30pm) is dedicated to Rishabdeo, a reincarnation of Mahavir, the 24th and last of the Jain *tirthankars,* who founded Jainism around 500 BC. Rishabdeo is also worshipped by Brahmins as a reincarnation of Vishnu and by the area's Bhil tribal people as Kala Baba. Two large, glossy, grey-stone elephants flank the temple's entrance, two darker ones are beyond them, and another huge one is inside. The interior is multipillared and decorated with carvings in white marble. At the centre is a beautiful black-stone image of Rishabdeo.

RTDC Hotel Gavri (☏230145; gavri@rtdc.in; s/d ₹850/950, AC ₹925/1150, incl breakfast; ❋) is about 500m from the temple, beside Hwy 8. The rooms are functional, if thoroughly unspectacular, and meals are available.

Buses to Rishabdeo (₹50, 1½ hours) leave Udaipur bus stand about every 15 minutes.

DUNGARPUR
02964

Attractive Dungarpur, the City of Hills, lies 100km south of Udaipur. Encircling the pretty Gaib Sagar lake, it was founded in the 13th century when Rawal Veer Singh Dev, leader of a minor Rajput clan, took over this area from the Bhils. This southernmost corner of Rajasthan, called Vagad, is set in the Aravalli foothills, with a wild and stony landscape dotted with cacti and hardy trees.

The wonderful, deserted, crumbling royal palace, the **Juna Mahal** (admission ₹150; ☺9am-5pm), was built in stages between the 13th and 18th centuries on a 450m-high rocky peak. It's filled with old frescoes and paintings, and has a seven-storey tower that formed the private residence of the maharawals and maharanis (kings and queens). The fascinating murals include an 18th-century Kamasutra on the maharawal's floor, discreetly cupboarded off in the 20th century. The Aam Khas (queen's quarters) has impressive mirror work, fascinating 19th-century paintings and a wall of embedded willow-pattern plates. Get your ticket to Juna Mahal from Udai Bilas Palace.

Also of interest is the **Rajmata Devandra Kunwar State Museum** (Indian/foreigner ₹5/50; ☺9.45am-5.15pm Tue-Sun), opposite the government hospital. As well as a regional sculpture gallery featuring pieces from the 6th to 17th centuries, this museum boasts large pictures of the Victory Tower at Chittorgarh and Delhi's Qutb Minar made entirely of George VI–era postage stamps!

The multilayered **Deo Somnath Temple**, 25km northeast of town, dates back to the 12th century and is worth a visit for its beautiful, harmonious architecture. An amazing centuries-old banyan tree grows opposite the temple.

🛏 Sleeping & Eating

TOP CHOICE **Udai Bilas Palace** HERITAGE HOTEL $$$
(230808; www.udaibilaspalace.com; s/d ₹4450/5600, ste from ₹6950, breakfast/lunch/dinner ₹350/575/650; ❄☀) Set on the tranquil south shore of Gaib Sagar, this fantastical 19th- and 20th-century palace (with beautifully carved balconies built of *pareva,* Dungarpur's bluestone) is where the Dungarpur royals moved when the Juna Mahal ceased to be habitable. Built around the astonishing Ek Thambia Mahal (One-Pillared Palace), it is now partly converted to a hotel, most of whose rooms have original art deco and 1940s furnishings. An assortment of stuffed beasts observe your progress around the hotel, including in the long dining hall with its Burmese teak ceiling. The gorgeous outdoor pool, overlooked by two large stone elephants, is so designed that it seems to merge with the lake as you swim. Bicycle and boat hire and birdwatching excursions can be organised for guests. Meals take the form of lavish buffets, and a large drinks cabinet is opened up on the lakeside lawn for your predinner aperitif.

Hotel Pratibha Palace HOTEL $
(230775; Sagwara Rd, Shastri Colony; s/d ₹150/300, AC r ₹700; ❄) The best budget hotel in town, 300m east of the bus station. Its tiny rooms are nothing flash but are good and clean, and it has its own restaurant two doors away.

❶ Getting There & Away
Buses to Dungarpur (₹72, three hours) leave Udaipur bus stand about every 15 minutes. Dungarpur is on the Udaipur-Ahmedabad railway: the 52928 *Ahmedabad–Udaipur Passenger* departs Dungarpur at 1.10pm, reaching Udaipur (sleeper ₹90) at 5.45pm; and the 19944 *Ahmedabad–Udaipur Express* departs at 4.16am, arriving in Udaipur (sleeper/2AC ₹130/314) at 8.05am. Southward to Ahmedabad, the 52927 leaves Dungarpur at 2.07pm, and the 19943 at 10.58pm.

BANESHWAR
The Baneshwar group of temples stands at the confluence of two holy rivers, the Mahi and the Som, a 60km drive east of Dungarpur. In January or February the week-long **Baneshwar Fair** (p177) attracts thousands of Bhil tribal people. The fair honours both Baneshwar Mahadev (Shiva) and Vishnu incarnated as the Hindu saint Mavji – the Vishnu temple here is believed to stand on the spot where Mavji meditated. Direct buses run to Baneshwar from Dungarpur and Udaipur during the festival.

Mt Abu
02974 / POP 22,045 / ELEV 1200M

Rajasthan's only hill station sits among green forests on the state's highest mountain at the southwestern end of the Aravalli Range and close to the Gujarat border. Quite unlike anywhere else in Rajasthan, Mt Abu provides Rajasthanis, Gujaratis and a steady flow of foreign tourists with respite from scorching temperatures and arid beige terrain elsewhere. It's a particular hit with

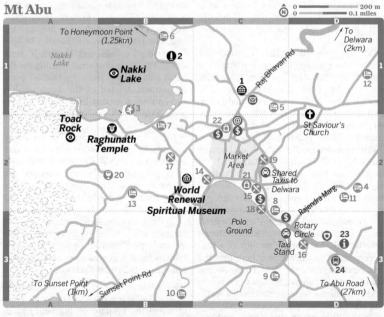

Mt Abu

honeymooners, middle-class families from Gujarat and others from that alcohol-dry state in search of a beverage more potent than lassi.

Mt Abu town sits towards the southwest end of the plateau-like upper part of the mountain, which stretches about 19km from end to end and 6km from east to west. The town is surrounded by the flora- and fauna-rich, 289-sq-km Mt Abu Wildlife Sanctuary which extends over most of the mountain from an altitude of 300m upwards.

The mountain is of great spiritual importance for both Hindus and Jains and has over 80 temples and shrines, most notably the exquisite Jain temples at Delwara, built between 400 and 1000 years ago. According to one legend, Mt Abu is as old as the Himalaya, and named after Arbuda, a mighty serpent who saved Nandi, Shiva's revered bull, from plunging into an abyss. According to another, it was here that the four great Agnivanshi (Fire-Born) Rajput clans – the Chauhans, Solankis, Pramaras and Pratiharas – were created from a seething pit of fire.

In the 19th century the British and several Rajput princes took a liking to Mt Abu's relatively temperate climate and launched its career as a hill station, building summer palaces and country cottages among the folds of the hills near Nakki Lake.

Try to avoid arriving in Diwali (October or November) or the following two weeks, when prices soar and the place is packed. Mt Abu also gets pretty busy from mid-May to mid-June, before the monsoon. This is when the **Summer Festival** hits town, with music, fireworks and boat races (p177). In the cooler months, you will find everyone wrapped up in shawls and hats; pack something woolly to avoid winter chills in poorly heated hotel rooms. If you come in spring, you may come across the local variation of the **Gangaur festival** (p177), celebrated by Garasia tribespeople.

◉ Sights & Activities

Nakki Lake   LAKE
Scenic Nakki Lake, the town's focus, is one of its biggest attractions. It's so named because, according to legend, it was scooped out by a god using his *nakh* (nails). Some Hindus thus consider it a holy lake. Another version of its origins is that it was constructed by the British in the 19th century. It's a pleasant stroll around the perimeter – the lake is

surrounded by hills, parks and strange rock formations. The best known, **Toad Rock**, looks just like a toad about to hop into the lake. The 14th-century **Raghunath Temple** (☉dawn-dusk) stands near the lake's south shore. The lurid nocturnal lighting on the north shore comes from the **Mother India monument**, erected by the Sahara airline and banking company in 2007 for the purpose, local cynics say, of having its name shining out too.

Nakki Lake is the heart of all activity in Mt Abu. At the edge nearest the town centre, there's a carnival of juice and food stalls, ice-cream parlours, balloon vendors and souvenir shops. The honeymoon market is catered for by aphrodisiac vendors, with potions that allegedly 'make big difference'.

To enter into the spirit of things, you can do as the local tourists do and hire a **pedalo** (per person per 30min ₹30), or, for the romantically inclined, a gondola-like **shikara love-boat** (2-person boat per 30min ₹110).

Viewpoints   VIEWPOINTS
Sunset Point is a popular and lovely place to watch the brilliant setting sun, though distinctly unromantic unless being thrust red roses, bags of peanuts or Polaroid cameras gets you into a loving mood. Hordes stroll out here every evening to catch the end of the day, the food stalls and all the usual jolly hill-station entertainment. Another good viewpoint is **Honeymoon Point**. With a guide you can follow the often obscured path to the summit of **Shanti Shikhar**, west of Adhar Devi Temple, where there are panoramic views.

Brahma Kumaris Peace Hall & Museum
                          MEDITATION, MUSEUM
The white-clad people you'll see around town are either armed forces or members of the **Brahma Kumaris World Spiritual University** (www.bkwsu.com, www.brahma kumaris.com), a worldwide organisation whose headquarters are here in Mt Abu. Founded in what's now Pakistan in 1937 by a man known as the Medium, Brahma Kumaris teaches that all religions lead to God and are equally valid, and that the principles of each should be studied. Its aim is the establishment of universal peace through 'the impartation of spiritual knowledge and training of easy raja yoga meditation'. Tens of thousands of followers come to Mt Abu each year for intense meditation or outreach training courses.

DELWARA TEMPLES

These remarkable **Jain temples** (donations welcome; ⊙ Jains 6am-6pm, non-Jains noon-6pm) are Mt Abu's most remarkable attraction and feature some of India's finest temple decoration. They predate the town of Mt Abu by many centuries and were built when this site was just a remote mountain vastness. It's said that the artisans were paid according to the amount of dust they collected, encouraging them to carve ever more intricately. Whatever their inducement, there are two temples here in which the marble work is dizzyingly intense, a collection of delicate milky kaleidoscope patterns, with icing-like carving so fine it looks like you could break it off and eat it.

The older of the two is the **Vimal Vasahi**, on which work began in 1031 and which was financed by a Gujarati chief minister named Vimal. Dedicated to the first *tirthankar*, Adinath, it took 1500 masons and 1200 labourers 14 years to build, and allegedly cost ₹185.3 million. Outside the entrance is the **House of Elephants**, featuring a procession of stone elephants marching to the temple, some of which were damaged long ago by marauding Mughals. Inside, a forest of beautifully carved pillars surrounds the central shrine, which holds an image of Adinath himself. Around the courtyard are 58 cells, each enclosing a cross-legged Buddha-like *tirthankar* – the crucial difference between these statues and those of the Buddha is that their eyes are always open. Cell 23 holds an image of Adinath that has sat in this same place since AD 994.

The **Luna Vasahi Temple** is dedicated to Neminath, the 22nd *tirthankar*, and was built in 1230 by the brothers Tejpal and Vastupal for a mere ₹125.3 million. Like Vimal, the brothers were both Gujarati government ministers. The marble carving here took 2500 workers 15 years to create, and its most notable feature is its intricacy and delicacy, which is so fine that, in places, the marble becomes almost transparent. The many-layered lotus flower that dangles from the centre of the dome is a particularly astonishing piece of work. It's difficult to believe that this huge lace-like filigree started life as a solid block of marble. The temple remains incredibly well preserved, employing several full-time stone masons to maintain the work.

There are three other temples in the enclosure – **Bhimashah Pittalhar** (built between 1315 and 1433), sporting a 4-tonne, five-metal statue of Adinath; **Mahaveerswami** (1582), a small shrine flanked by painted elephants; and the three-storey **Khartar Vasahi**. None, however, competes with the ethereal beauty of Luna Vasahi and Vimal Vasahi.

As at other Jain temples, leather articles (belts as well as shoes) have to be left at the entrance, and menstruating women are asked not to enter. No photography is permitted.

Delwara is about 2.5km north of Mt Abu town centre: you can walk there in less than an hour, or hop aboard a shared taxi (₹5 per person) from up the street opposite Chacha Cafe. A taxi all to yourself should be ₹50, or ₹150 round-trip with one hour's waiting.

For many the teachings are intensely powerful; there are over 800 branches in 130 countries. Brahma Kumaris even has consultative status with the Economic and Social Council of the UN. For others, it gives off a New Age–sect vibe and sceptical Mt Abu locals might try to warn you away. You can find out more for yourself by paying a visit to the university's **Universal Peace Hall** (Om Shanti Bhawan; ⊙ 8am-6pm), just north of Nakki Lake, where free 30-minute tours are available, including an introduction to the Brahma Kumaris philosophy. If you want to take things further, they will give you information on Brahma Kumaris centres in your own country where you can start a free meditation course.

The organisation also runs the **Peace Park** (admission free; ⊙ 8am-6pm), located 8km northeast of town on the road to Guru Shikhar, and the small **World Renewal Spiritual Museum** (admission free; ⊙ 8am-8pm) in the town centre, the entrance of which is labelled 'Gateway to Paradise'. The museum gives an overview of Brahma Kumaris teachings through kitschy dioramas and maxims like 'Man was never a beast nor will he ever become a beast, but he has now become worse than a beast'.

MT ABU PRECAUTIONS

Unless you are in a group, it is very unwise to visit Sunset Point or Honeymoon Point any time other than sunset when lots of people will be around. It is also unwise to walk off the streets alone – for example along some of the paths shown on Tourist Reception Centre maps. Muggings and at least one murder have happened in recent years to people who ignored these precautions, and some paths get quickly overgrown and hard to follow after the monsoon.

Bears sometimes come into town, even to the lake, especially during the monsoon (July and August). If you encounter one, don't panic, but back away calmly.

Government Museum   MUSEUM
(Raj Bhavan Rd; admission ₹3; ⊙10am-5pm Sat-Thu) The highlight of this small, seldom-visited museum is the sculpture gallery, with works from the ancient town of Chandravati, 7km from Mt Abu, dating from the 6th to 12th centuries. Note the sculpture of the snake goddess Vish Kanya breastfeeding a snake – something not to attempt at home. It also features a diorama illustrating local tribal life.

Adhar Devi Temple   HINDU TEMPLE
In the hills just north of town, about 1.5km from Nakki Lake, 360 steps lead up to this 15th-century **Durga temple** (⊙7.45am-6.30pm) located in a natural cleft in the rock. You have to stoop to get through the low entrance to the temple, which is visited by a constant stream of devotees and tourists.

☞ Tours
The RSRTC runs full-day (₹83) and half-day (₹45) bus tours of Mt Abu's main sights, leaving from the bus stand at 9.30am and 1pm respectively (times may vary). Both tours visit Achalgarh, Guru Shikhar and the Delwara Temples and end at Sunset Point. The full-day tour also includes Adhar Devi, the Brahma Kumaris Peace Hall and Honeymoon Point. Admission and camera fees and the ₹20 guide fee are extra. Make reservations at the **enquiries counter** (☑235434) at the main bus stand.

☷ Sleeping
Mt Abu seems to consist mostly of hotels. Room rates can double or worse during the peak seasons – mid-May to mid-June, Diwali and Christmas/New Year – but generous discounts are often available at other times in midrange and top-end places. If you have to come here at Diwali, you'll need to book way ahead and you won't be able to move for crowds. Most hotels have an ungenerous 9am check-out time.

Usually there are touts working the bus and taxi stands. In the low season ignore them, but at peak times they can save you legwork, as they'll know where to find the last available room.

TOP CHOICE Connaught House   HERITAGE HOTEL $$$
(☑238560; www.jodhanaheritage.com; Rajendra Marg; s/d incl breakfast ₹4000/5000; ✳@) Connaught House is a charmingly stuck-in-time colonial bungalow that looks like an English cottage, with lots of sepia photographs, dark wood, angled ceilings and a gorgeous shady garden. It's owned by the descendants of Jodhpur's ruling family and was used by Jodhpur's English chief minister, Sir Donald Field, in the 1930s and '40s. The five rooms in the original 'cottage' have most character – and big colonial-era baths. The other five sit in a newer building with good views from their own verandas.

Shri Ganesh Hotel   HOTEL $
(☑237292; lalit_ganesh@yahoo.co.in; dm ₹150-200, without bathroom ₹100, s ₹300, d ₹400-1200; @) Deservedly the most popular budget spot, Shri Ganesh is well set up for travellers, with an inexpensive cafe, a small internet room and plenty of helpful travel information. Rooms are well used but kept clean. Some have squat toilets and limited hours for hot water; clothes washing is not allowed. Daily forest walks and cooking lessons are on offer. It's fairly central, on the street leading up to Jaipur House.

Hotel Lake Palace   HOTEL $$
(☑237154; http://savshantihotels.com; r ₹2000-2800; ✳☎) Spacious and friendly, Lake Palace has an excellent location, with small lawns overlooking the lake. Rooms are simple, uncluttered, bright and clean. All have AC and some have semiprivate lake-view terrace areas. There are rooftop and garden multicuisine restaurants too.

Getting off the well-worn tourist trail and out into the forests and hills of Mt Abu is a revelation. This is a world of isolated shrines and lakes, weird rock formations, fantastic panoramas, nomadic villagers, orchids, wild fruits, plants used in ayurvedic medicine, sloth bears (which are fairly common), wild boars, langurs, 150 bird species and even the occasional leopard, hyena, jackal and porcupine.

Mt Abu-born Mahendra Dan ('Charles') of **Mt Abu Treks** (☎9414154854; www.mount -abu-treks.blogspot.com; Hotel Lake Palace) is a passionate and knowledgable nature lover who leads excellent tailor-made treks ranging from three or four hours close to Mt Abu (₹300 per person) to overnight treks to nomad villages beyond Guru Shikhar (up to ₹1500 per person including meals). There's a two-person minimum, and on some routes wildlife sanctuary entrance fees (Indian/foreigner ₹20/160) and/or transport costs (minimum ₹250 for a car drop and pick-up) have to be paid too.

Champak, one of the family who run the **Shri Ganesh Hotel** (☎237292, 9414219013) also leads good short treks starting at 9am or 3pm. Routes vary and the level of difficulty depends on the fitness of the group. It's common to spot bears and other wildlife.

A final warning from the locals: it's very unsafe to wander unguided in these hills. Travellers have been mauled by bears, and, even more disturbing, have been mugged (and worse) by other people.

Kishangarh House
HERITAGE HOTEL $$$

(☎238092; www.royalkishangarh.com; Rajendra Marg; s/d cottage room ₹2500/3000, deluxe ₹4000/4500; ✸) The former summer residence of the maharaja of Kishangarh has been successfully converted into a heritage hotel. The deluxe rooms in the main building are big, with extravagantly high ceilings. The cottage rooms at the back are smaller but cosier. There is a delightful sun-filled drawing room and the lovely terraced gardens are devotedly tended.

Honey Dew Paying Guest House
GUESTHOUSE $$

(☎238429; off Raj Bhavan Rd; r ₹1500) Honey Dew sits at the top of the central area, near the post office. Its five rooms are set around a courtyard-like area, and are unostentatious but comfy, clean, well kept and a good size. They're also decorated with a touch of modern art, which makes for a nice change. Meals are available (mains ₹60 to ₹80).

Mushkil Aasan
GUESTHOUSE $$

(☎235150; r ₹1000-1500) A lovely guesthouse nestled in a tranquil vale in the north of town, with nine homely decorated rooms and a small garden above a stream. Home-style Gujarati meals are available, and check-out is a civilised 24 hours.

Palace Hotel
HERITAGE HOTEL $$

(☎235363; www.palacehotelbikanerhouse.com; Bikaner House, Delwara Rd; s/d from ₹5200/5600, ste from ₹6900/7200, incl breakfast; ✸) Out to-

wards the Delwara Temples is this huge hilltop palace, designed by Sir Swinton Jacob in the 1890s as a summer residence for the maharaja of Bikaner. The sprawling grey-and-pink stone building resembles a stately Scottish manor, with tree-shaded gardens, a private lake, two tennis courts and a restaurant. There are 33 massive, formally decorated rooms; the ones in the old wing have the most character – some feel, as does the grand old dining room, very much like you've stepped into a little piece of Britain, or at least the British Raj.

Hotel Samrat International
HOTEL $$

(☎235153; samrat.hotel@yahoo.in; s ₹890-1590, d ₹1890-2390, ste ₹2690-3290; ✸) This hotel has honeymooners in mind and its hotchpotch of rooms ranges from tight-fit doubles to attractive, spacious suites with sheltered balconies overlooking the polo ground. The traffic below is hectic by Mt Abu standards, but tariffs fall by 50% at the drop of a hat outside peak periods.

Hotel Saraswati
HOTEL $

(☎238887; r ₹590-1000; ✸⊛) Saraswati is a reasonably appealing place in a peaceful setting behind the polo ground. Rooms are big enough and in varied states of repair: see a few of the 36 on offer before you decide. Hot water is only available from 7am to 11am. The restaurant serves good Gujarati thalis (₹80).

Kesar Bhawan Palace
HOTEL **$$**

(☎235219; www.kesarpalace.com; Sunset Point Rd; s/d ₹2100/2600, AC ₹2600/2950, ste ₹5000; ❄) This property is perched up among trees and has appealing leafy views and comfortable, rather grand, marble-floored rooms with balconies, but feels a little antiseptic and austere. The suites are on two levels. Check the bathrooms as some are in poor shape for these prices.

Hotel Panghat
HOTEL **$**

(☎238886; r ₹450-500) The rooms are plain and worn, with unheated showers, but the lake is across the street and some rooms overlook it. There's a good rooftop with a swing, and management is friendly and obliging.

✖ Eating

Most holidaymakers here are Gujarati – hence the profusion of veg thali restaurants.

Sankalp
SOUTH INDIAN **$**

(Hotel Maharaja; mains ₹50-120; ◷9am-11pm) A branch of a quality Gujarat-based chain serving up excellent South Indian vegetarian fare. Unusual fillings like pineapple or spinach, cheese and garlic are available for its renowned dosas and *uttapams* (savoury South Indian rice pancake), which come with multiple sauces and condiments. Order *masala papad* (wafer with spicy topping) for a tasty starter.

Kanak Dining Hall
INDIAN **$**

(Gujarati/Punjabi thali ₹90/100; ◷11.30am-3pm & 7-10.30pm) The excellent all-you-can-eat thalis are contenders for Mt Abu's best meals; there's seating indoors in the busy dining hall or outside under a canopy. It's conveniently near the bus stand for the lunch break during the all-day RSRTC tour.

Chacha Cafe
MULTICUISINE **$**

(dishes ₹60-120; ☎) A very neat, bright eatery with red-check tablecloths and welcome AC. The presentable fare ranges over dosas, pizzas, vegetarian burgers, cashew curry and biryanis. It's next to the large Chacha Museum crafts and souvenirs shop.

Sher-e-Punjab Hotel
PUNJABI **$**

(mains ₹60-160) This place in the market area has bargain Punjabi food. There are plenty of regular veg and nonveg curries that won't stretch the budget. You can eat outside or in the clean inner room.

Arbuda
INDIAN **$**

(Arbuda Circle; mains ₹65-90) This big restaurant is set on a sweeping open terrace filled with chrome chairs. It's very popular for its Gujarati, Punjabi and South Indian food, and does fine continental breakfasts and fresh juices.

King's Food
FAST FOOD **$**

(mains ₹45-75; ◷8am-10pm) A busy, open-to-the-street fast-food joint near Nakki Lake. King Food has the usual have-a-go menu, including a range of Chinese, Punjabi and South Indian food, and good lassis, as well as filling breakfasts and nice Indian dinner-sized curries.

♟ Drinking

Most of the more upmarket hotels have bars serving local and imported drinks; the prices are predictably high, but the heritage hotels can justify this with their quaint atmosphere.

Jaipur House
BAR

(shots & cocktails ₹90-200) The terrace at this hotel, formerly the maharaja of Jaipur's summer palace, is a dreamy place for an evening tipple, with divine views over the hills, lake and the town's twinkling lights. (In contrast, the hotel's restaurant has disappointing food and a rather sombre atmosphere.)

Cafe Coffee Day
CAFE

(Hotel Maharaja; coffees, teas & snacks ₹35-100; ◷9am-11.30pm) A branch of the popular caffeine-supply chain. The tea and cakes aren't bad either.

🛍 Shopping

The street leading down to Nakki Lake is lined with bright little shops mostly flogging all sorts of kitsch curios, and there's more of the same around the market area. Chacha Museum (◷10am-8pm) is a larger, fixed-price shop with some crafts and souvenirs worth a browse.

ℹ Information

There are State Bank ATMs on Raj Bhavan Rd, opposite Hotel Samrat International and outside the Tourist Reception Centre, and a Bank of Baroda ATM on Lake Rd.

Main post office (Raj Bhavan Rd; ◷9am-5pm Mon-Sat)

DESTINATION	TRAIN NUMBER & NAME	FARE (₹)	DURATION (HR)	DEPARTURE
Ahmedabad	19106 *Haridwar-Ahmedabad Mail*	134/331/442/732 (A)	5½	1.21pm
	19224 *Jammu Tawi-Ahmedabad Exp*	130/312/415 (B)	4½	11.10am
Bhuj	14311 *Ala Hazrat Exp*	245/644/876 (B)	13	1.35am Wed, Fri, Sat, Sun
	14321 *Bareilly-Bhuj Exp*	197/511/694 (B)	9	1.35am Mon, Tue, Thu
Delhi	19105 *Ahmedabad-Haridwar Mail*	295/786/1072/1796 (A)	15	2.13pm
Jaipur	19105 *Ahmedabad-Haridwar Mail*	204/529/717/1205 (A)	8½	2.13pm
	19707 *Aravalli Exp*	204/529/717 (B)	9	10.02am
Jodhpur	19223 *Ahmedabad-Jammu Tawi Exp*	153/386/519	4¾	3.22pm

Fares: A – sleeper/3AC/2AC/1AC; B – sleeper/3AC/2AC.

Tourist Reception Centre (☏235151; ⊙9.30am-1.30pm & 2-6pm Mon-Fri) Opposite the main bus stand; offers free, not very accurate maps of town, and staff don't seem to know much about the place either.

Union Bank of India (Main Market; ⊙10am-3pm Mon-Fri, 10am-12.30pm Sat) The only bank changing travellers cheques and currency.

Yani-Ya Cyber Zone (Raj Bhavan Rd; internet per hr ₹30; ⊙9am-10pm) There are also a couple of cybercafes down in the market area below here.

 Getting There & Away

Access to Mt Abu is by a dramatic 28km road that winds its way up thickly forested hillsides from the town of Abu Road on Hwy 14, about 140km west of Udaipur. The nearest train station is at Abu Road. Some buses from other cities go all the way up to Mt Abu; others only go as far as Abu Road. Buses (₹22, one hour) run between Abu Road and Mt Abu bus stands roughly hourly in each direction from about 6am to 7pm. A taxi from Abu Road to Mt Abu is ₹300 by day or ₹400 by night: make it clear you want to be taken to your hotel and not just Mt Abu bus stand.

There's a charge of ₹10 for each person (including bus passengers) and car as you enter Mt Abu.

Bus

For many destinations you will find a direct bus faster and more convenient than going down to Abu Road and waiting for a train.

Public buses from the main bus stand go to Udaipur (₹137, 4½ hours, four daily), Jodhpur (₹150, six hours, one daily), Jaisalmer (₹220, 10 hours, one daily), Jaipur (₹480, 11 hours, one AC bus daily) and Ahmedabad (₹130, seven hours, nine daily). Private bus companies, serving similar destinations at usually slightly higher prices, have ticket offices on the street near the bus stand.

Taxi

To hire a jeep or taxi for sightseeing costs about ₹500/900 per half-day/day. Many hotels can arrange a vehicle, or you can hire your own in the town centre.

Train

Abu Road station is on the line between Delhi and Mumbai via Ahmedabad. An autorickshaw from Abu Road train station to Abu Road bus stand costs ₹10. Mt Abu has a **railway reservation centre** (⊙8am-2pm), above the tourist office, with quotas on most of the express trains.

Around Mt Abu

ACHALGARH

The fascinating, atmospheric Shiva temple of **Achaleshwar Mahandeva**, 8km north-east of Mt Abu in Achalgarh (off the road to Guru Shikhar), boasts a number of diverting features, including what's said to be a toe of Shiva, as well as a Nandi bull (Shiva's vehicle) made of five metals. Where the Shiva lingam would normally be there's a deep hole, believed by devotees to extend all the way down to the underworld.

Just outside the temple, beside the car park, three stone buffaloes stand around a tank, while the figure of a king shoots at them with his bow and arrows. A legend tells that the tank was once filled with ghee, but demons, in the form of the buffaloes, arrived from the skies to pollute the holy ghee – until, that is, the king managed to shoot them.

A path leads up to the hilltop group of colourful **Jain temples**, which have fantastic views out over the plains.

The RSRTC tour visits the Shiva temple but doesn't allow time to climb the hill.

GURU SHIKHAR

At the northeast end of the Mt Abu plateau, 17km by the winding road from the town, rises 1722m-high Guru Shikhar, Rajasthan's highest point. A road goes almost all the way to the summit and the **Atri Rishi Temple**, complete with a priest and fantastic, huge views. A popular spot, it's a highlight of the RSRTC tour; if you decide to go it alone, a jeep will cost ₹500 return.

GAUMUKH TEMPLE

Down off the road to Abu Road, 8km south of Mt Abu town, a small stream flows from the mouth of a marble cow, giving the shrine its name (*gaumukh* means 'cow's mouth'). There's also a marble figure of the bull Nandi. Legend tells that the tank here, Agni Kund, was the site of the *yagna* (sacrificial fire) made by the sage Vasishta, from which were born the four Agnivanshi (Fire-Born) Rajput clans. An image of Vasishta is flanked by figures of Rama and Krishna.

To reach the temple you must take a path of 750 steps down into the valley – and then trudge those same 750 steps back up again.

Northern Rajasthan (Shekhawati)

Best Places to Stay

» Apani Dhani (p237)

» Hotel Jamuna Resort (p242)

» Shekhawati Guesthouse (p237)

» Hotel Mandawa Haveli (p249)

Best Places to Eat

» Bungli Restaurant (p250)

» Art Café (p248)

» Shekhawati Guesthouse (p237)

» Narayan Niwas Castle (p245)

Why Go?

Far less visited than other parts of Rajasthan, the Shekhawati region is most famous for its extraordinary painted *havelis* (traditional, ornately decorated residences), highlighted with dazzling, often whimsical murals. Part of the region's appeal and mystique is due to these works of art being found in tiny towns, connected to each other by single-track roads that run through lonely, arid countryside. Today it seems curious that such care, attention and finance was lavished on these out-of-the-way houses, but from the 14th century onwards, Shekhawati's towns were important trading posts on the caravan routes from Gujarati ports.

What makes the artwork on Shekhawati's *havelis* so fascinating is the manner in which their artists combined traditional subjects, such as mythology, religious scenes and images of the family, with contemporary concerns, including brand-new inventions and accounts of current events, many of which these isolated painters rendered straight from their imagination.

When to Go?

Winter is the most pleasant time to visit Shekhawati. Spring and autumn days are still warm and occasionally hot, while summer can be unbearably hot with temperatures climbing into the mid-40s (Celsius) and even higher. Another important consideration is the monsoon, which usually starts around July but can be unpredictable. Although monsoon rains cool the air, they can also make a complete mess of the roads. As well as national festivals, Shekhawati celebrates a few events of its own (see p231).

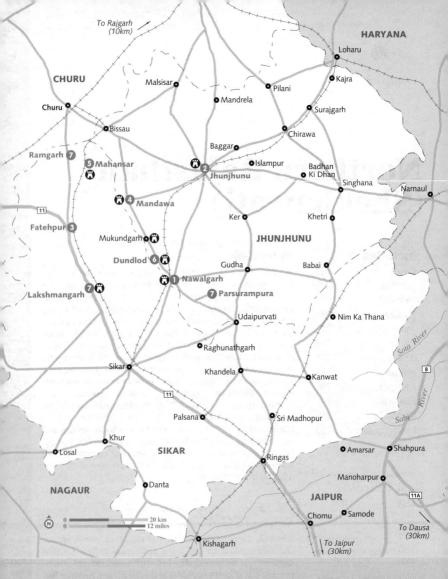

Northern Rajasthan (Shekhawati) Highlights

1 Head out on a heritage walk among the painted *havelis* of **Nawalgarh** (p236)

2 Experience the beautifully proportioned but derelict Khetri Mahal in **Jhunjhunu** (p240)

3 Take time out in the wonderfully restored Haveli Nadine Le Prince in **Fatehpur** (p246)

4 Enjoy the comical murals, good food and bustling bazaar in **Mandawa** (p248), Shekhawati's most visited town

5 Stay in a castle and visit Sone ki Dukan Haveli in sleepy **Mahansar** (p244)

6 Ride a magnificent Marwari horse across the desert from the romantic fort at **Dundlod** (p238)

7 Find your favourite mural in the fading treasures of little-visited desert towns **Ramgarh** (p245), **Parsurampura** (p239) and **Lakshmangarh** (p250)

FESTIVALS IN NORTHERN RAJASTHAN

Shekhawati has a couple of festivals to its name, but also celebrates statewide and nationwide festivals with fervour (see p24).

» **Shekhawati Festival** (www.shekhawatifestival.com; Feb) Promoted by the Rajasthan Tourism Development Corporation (RTDC), the official programme includes safaris, tours of the region, competitions and fireworks, but remains a small and locally flavoured affair.

» **Bissau Festival** (Bissau; Sep/Oct) Ten days before the festival of Dussehra, Bissau hosts dramatic mime performances of the Ramayana. The actors wear locally made costumes and masks, and the performances take place in the bazaar at twilight.

History

A rich but lawless land on the trade route between the ports of the Arabian Sea and the fertile Ganges Valley, this region was, in its early history, dominated by the Shekhawats, with portions (principally Jhunjhunu and Fatehpur) held by the Muslim Kayamkhani nawabs (Muslim ruling princes or landowners). The Shekhawati *thakurs* (noblemen), like other Rajasthani rulers, were once most noted for their penchant for arguing among themselves. Unlike other areas of Rajasthan, the region was never combined into a single principality, but remained a conglomeration of separate, quarrelsome feudal domains.

The name 'Shekhawati' can be traced to a 15th-century Rajput Kachhwaha chieftain by the name of Rao Shekha. As the Mughal empire declined after the death of the emperor Aurangzeb in 1707, his descendants, who had already installed themselves in the area to the east of the Aravalli Hills, encroached to the north and west.

The *thakurs* of the region retained a nominal loyalty to the Rajput states of Amber and Jaipur, which in turn honoured them with the hereditary titles of nobility. The Rajputs, however, never really trusted the *thakurs* – for example, when Jaipur was built in the 18th century, the Shekhawats were offered land *outside* the city walls to build their houses. Despite not being allowed in the inner circle, it was probably exposure to the courts of Jaipur that encouraged the *thakurs* to commission the very first murals to decorate their *havelis*.

By 1732 two of these *thakurs* – Sardul Singh and Shiv Singh – had overthrown the nawabs of Fatehpur and Jhunjhunu and carved out their territories in the region. Their descendants, particularly the sons of Sardul Singh, installed themselves in surrounding villages, filling their pockets with heavy taxes imposed on the poor farmers of the area and duties levied on caravans carrying goods from the ports of Gujarat. But for the merchants travelling on the Shekhawati route, this trail was nevertheless a cheap option – the Rajput states on either side imposed even greater levies and the arid region soon became busy with trade, attracting more and more merchants. The riches, inevitably, also attracted dacoits (bandits), imbuing the area with a distinctly lawless flavour.

The rise of the British Raj could potentially have been a death blow for Shekhawati, since the British ports in Bombay (Mumbai) and Calcutta (Kolkata) were able to handle a far higher volume of trade than those in Gujarat. Moreover, pressure from the British East India Company compelled Jaipur state to reduce its levies, so it was no longer necessary for traders to travel with their goods through Shekhawati. But Shekhawati merchants had received a good grounding in the practices and principles of trade, and were reluctant to relinquish a lucrative source of income.

Towards the end of the 19th century, Shekhawati's men thus emigrated en masse from their desert homes to the thriving trading centres emerging on the ports of the Ganges. Their business acumen was unparalleled, and soon some of the richest merchants residing in Calcutta were those who hailed from the tiny region of Shekhawati. Some of India's wealthiest industrialists of the 20th century, such as the Birlas, were originally Marwaris, as the people of Shekhawati later became known.

🏃 Activities

A number of operators offer camel or horse-riding safaris in the Shekhawati region. These are a relaxing way to see rural life and birdlife, fitting in well with the pace of life

SEEING SHEKHAWATI RESPONSIBLY

Shekhawati is a rural area, still off the beaten track for the majority of tourists, where traditions and customs remain very different from the West. By respecting the local population during your stay, you will contribute to preserving its authenticity, while greatly enhancing your own experience.

Many *havelis* have, for decades, been plundered or left to fade away, and responsible tourism can play a positive role in the preservation of the region's masterpieces, generating the will among locals to preserve and cherish its heritage.

Currently, only a handful of *havelis* are open as museums or specifically for display, and consequently many others are locked up. They are frequently still owned by the family who built them a century or more ago. While the *chowkidar* (caretaker) or tenants are often tolerant of strangers wandering into their front courtyard, be mindful that these are private homes. You may be asked for a little baksheesh to let you in; ₹20 is usually a good price to pay for a glimpse of hidden treasures.

For those visiting Shekhawati, there are several things you can do to reduce your impact.

» Remember that most havelis are private homes and you should ask permission politely before entering or taking photos.

» Local custom dictates that shoes should be removed when entering the inner courtyard of a *haveli*.

» To avoid offence it is advisable to dress yourself in such a way that most part of your body is covered, particularly legs and shoulders.

» On your travels you may find shops filled temptingly with beautiful items ripped from *havelis*. Never purchase these items – by doing so, you will be actively encouraging further desecration.

» Flashes from cameras can damage the paintings. Refrain from using flash photography, even when there may not be an express prohibition on it.

» In many towns, it's easy to get around by bike or on foot, rather than plumping for polluting autorickshaws.

» When on a village tour or camel safari, ensure that your rubbish is carried away and insist on kerosene fires instead of using scarce sources of wood.

» Do not distribute sweets, pens, money (this list is not exhaustive). Never give money in exchange for a photograph. If you wish to give away something, do it via an organization or development project.

» Keep in mind that tourism is also what we leave behind.

outside the towns. In Nawalgarh you have a wide choice of trekking, horse riding, camel safaris or tours by bicycle (p236). In Dundlod experienced riders can go horse riding on fine Marwari horses (p238), or you can take a camel or jeep safari. Camel safaris are on offer at Mahansar's **Narayan Niwas Castle** (☎ 01595-264322) and camel and jeep safaris at Mukundgarh, while you have the choice of camel, jeep or horse trips at Mandawa (p249), or camel, jeep or bicycle trips at Jhunjhunu (p242).

There are also several places where, inspired by all this artwork, you can undertake courses in painting or local crafts (p236). In Jhunjhunu you can also take cooking courses (p242).

Getting Around

The Shekhawati region is crisscrossed by narrow, dusty roads and all towns are served by government or private buses and jam-packed shared jeeps. Buses are crowded, but they are usually more comfortable than the sardine-tin jeeps. Many of the roads are in extremely poor condition, so be prepared for an uncomfortably bumpy journey. Though several towns are served by trains, services are currently slow and unreliable, so bus or jeep is definitely the better bet.

To zip from town to town more speedily and in greater comfort, hire a taxi for the day. The usual rate for a non-AC taxi is ₹5 to ₹7 per kilometre with a minimum charge of 250km per day. Around four or five people can travel in one car, so having a larger group will keep costs down.

Another means of getting around the area is by bicycle – you can hire bikes in most of the major places – but be prepared for a bumpy, dusty ride. The best way to explore the towns themselves is on foot. Some of the larger towns also offer transport in autorickshaws and tongas (two-wheeled horse carriages).

Nawalgarh

☑ 01594 / POP 60,000

Nawalgarh is a small town almost at the very centre of the region, and hence makes a great base for exploring. It boasts several fine *havelis*, a colourful, mostly pedestrianised bazaar and some excellent accommodation options.

The town was founded in 1737 by Nawal Singh, one of the five sons of the Rajput ruler Sardul Singh. The arrival of merchants from Jaipur increased the town's prosperity, and some of India's most successful merchants, such as the wealthy Goenka family (responsible for many *havelis*), hailed from Nawalgarh. The town is built in a depression where a number of rivers terminate; the accumulated silt carried by these rivers was used to make the bricks (some of the best preserved in Shekhawati) for local *havelis*.

Nawalgarh is quite compact, and most of its *havelis* are centrally located and easy to reach on foot. The train station and bus stands are all at the western end of town, while accommodation is concentrated in the north and west.

◉ Sights

Bala Qila Fort   HISTORIC BUILDING
The fort of Bala Qila was founded in 1737, but today its modern additions largely obscure the original building, and it houses a fruit-and-vegetable market and a bank. The **Sheesh Mahal** in the southeastern quarter of the fort, though, is one room that retains mirrorwork and beautiful paintings on its ceiling, depicting map-like street scenes of both Jaipur and Nawalgarh from the mid-19th century. The grand but rather spooky room was once the dressing room of the maharani of Nawalgarh. To find it, climb a small greenish staircase in the southeastern corner of the fort to the 2nd floor. The room is hidden behind a sweet shop, where you will be asked for ₹20 to be allowed through.

MUSEUM
(www.poddarhavelimuseum.org; admission ₹100, camera ₹30; ◷8.30am-6.30pm) Built in 1902 on the eastern side of town, this is one of the region's few buildings to have been thoroughly restored. The paintings are defined in strong colours, as they must have looked when new. Note the trompe l'œil windows on the facade, the fresco subjects (including religious scenes, trains, cars and the British people) and the curious panel that depicts a bull's head from one side and an elephant's head from the other. On the ground floor are several galleries on Rajasthani culture, including examples of different schools of painting, turbans, tablas and polystyrene forts.

Morarka Haveli Museum   MUSEUM
(admission ₹50; ◷8am-7pm) This museum has well-presented original paintings, preserved for decades behind doorways blocked with cement. The inner courtyard hosts some gorgeous Ramayana scenes; look out for the slightly incongruous image of Jesus on the top storey, beneath the eaves in the courtyard's southeast corner.

Bhagton ki Choti Haveli   MUSEUM
(admission ₹50) To the northwest of the Morarka Haveli Museum is Bhagton ki Choti Haveli (aka Bhagat Haveli). On the external west wall is a locomotive and a steamship. Above them, elephant-bodied *gopis* (milkmaids) dance. Adjacent to this, women dance during the Holi festival.

Above the doorway to the inner courtyard is a detailed picture of the marriage of Rukmani, at which Krishna cheated the groom Sisupal of his prospective wife. The walls of the salon resemble marble, painted black with decorative incisions. The inner chamber upstairs contains the family quarters, also elaborately painted. A room on the west side is home to a strange picture of a European man with a cane and pipe and a small dog on his shoulder. Adjacent, a melancholy English woman plays an accordion.

Khedwal Bhavan   HISTORIC BUILDING
West of Baori Gate is the still-inhabited Khedwal Bhavan, which features beautiful mirrorwork above the entrance to the inner courtyard, and fine blue tilework. A locomotive is depicted above the archway, and a frieze along the north wall shows the Teej festival (spot the women on swings). On the west wall is a large locomotive crossing

NORTHERN RAJASTHAN (SHEKHAWATI) NAWALGARH

NORTHERN RAJASTHAN (SHEKHAWATI)

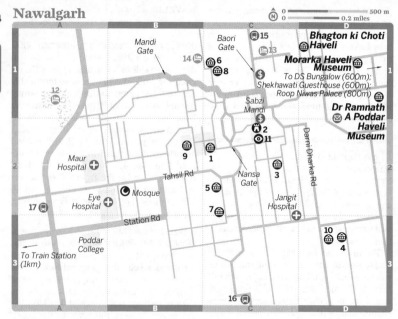

a bridge and underneath are portraits of various English people. On the outside north wall is the story of Dhola Maru (p247), painted in two frames. In the first frame, soldiers chase the fleeing camel-borne lovers. Maru fires arrows at the assailants while Dhola urges the camel on.

Hem Raj Kulwal Haveli   HISTORIC BUILDING
Near the Khedwal Bhavan is the Hem Raj Kulwal Haveli, built in 1931. This *haveli* is empty and locked, but the key is kept at the Koolwal Kothi hotel opposite and you may be allowed entry for the customary baksheesh. Above the entrance are portraits of the Kulwal family, of Mahatma Gandhi and Jawaharlal Nehru, and of a European lady applying make-up. Kaleidoscopic architraves surround the windows, and the outer courtyard features a triumphant train. An ornate silver door adorned with miniature peacocks leads to the inner courtyard, which features paintings depicting mostly religious themes.

Aath Havelis   HISTORIC BUILDING
To the west of Bala Qila is a group of six *havelis*, known as the Aath Havelis, erected around 1900. *Aath* means 'eight', and they were so named because originally eight *havelis* were planned. The paintings are not technically as proficient as some others

in this town, but they illustrate the transition in painting styles over the decades. The front section depicts a steam locomotive and the back section features some monumental pictures of elephants, horses and camels. There are many eclectic, lively subjects to peruse, including barbers, trains and false windows. Many of the murals are in very bad condition.

Morarka Uattara Haveli   HISTORIC BUILDING
(admission ₹50; ☺8am-6.30pm) Another *haveli* owned by the Morarka family, with some fine paintings, including miniatures above the entrance depicting the legends of Krishna (the most celebrated of the Hindu deities). Nowadays it is rented out for weddings and that may help explain its sorry condition.

Hira Lal Sarawgi Haveli   HISTORIC BUILDING
To the southwest of the fort is the Hira Lal Sarawgi Haveli, famous for its different representations of cars. Other entertaining pictures on its external walls include an English couple sitting stiffly on a bench, a tractor with a tip-tray – an exciting new invention – and a woman trying to distract a sadhu (holy man) with an erotic dance.

Parsurampura Haveli   HISTORIC BUILDING
This *haveli* dates from the early 20th century and belongs to a merchant from Parsurampura. Look for the soldier statues on the roof. Demonstrating the change in style that came with the influence of magazines and Western art, the grandiose paintings featuring horses are almost *too* perfect.

THE ARCHITECTURE OF THE HAVELI

The Persian term *haveli* means 'enclosed space', but the architecture of the *haveli* did much more than simply enclose space; it in fact provided a comprehensive system that governed the everyday lives of its inhabitants.

Most *havelis* have a large wooden gate (usually locked) as their main entrance, in which is set a smaller doorway that gives access to the outer courtyard. Often a huge ramp leads from the street to this grand gate, up which a prospective groom would have been able to ascend in appropriate grandeur on horse- or elephant-back. Above the entrance you can usually see one or more small shield-shaped devices called *torans*. These are wrought of wood and silver, and often feature a parrot – the bird of love. In a mock show of conquest, the groom was required to pierce the *toran* with his sword before claiming his bride.

The doorway leads into an outer courtyard known as the *mardana* (men's courtyard). To one side there's usually a *baithak* (salon) in which the merchant of the household could receive his guests. In order to impress visitors, this room was generally the most elaborately crafted and often featured marble or mock-marble walls. Here, you'll frequently see images of Ganesh, god of wealth and good fortune, and this was where the merchant and his guests reclined against bolsters and were fanned by manually operated *punkahs* (cloth fans) as they discussed their business. Opposite the *baithak* is often a stable and coach house called a *nora*.

The outer *mardana* leads into the second, inner women's courtyard, known as the *zenana*, where the women of the household spent the majority of their lives in strict purdah (seclusion). Between the two courtyards there was often a small latticed window, through which they could peep out at male guests. Sometimes, there was also a screened-off balcony, known as the *duchatta*, above the *mardana* for them to spy on proceedings. Entry into the inner courtyard was restricted to women, family members and, occasionally, privileged male guests.

The *zenana* was the main domestic arena – the walls today are often smoke-stained by countless kitchen fires. Rooms off this courtyard served as bedrooms or storerooms, and staircases led to galleries on upper levels, which mostly comprised bedrooms – some of which were roofless, for hot nights. The courtyard arrangement, together with thick walls, provided plenty of shade to cool the inner rooms, a vital necessity in this sun-scorched land. The *haveli* thus provided everything for the women and there was no need for them to venture into the outside world – and in Shekhawati these were spectacularly gilded cages.

In the wealthiest of families, there were far more than two simple courtyards, some *havelis* enclosing as many as eight, with galleries up to six storeys high. This meant plenty of wall space to house the elaborate murals that wealthy Shekhawati merchants were so fond of commissioning.

Dharni Dharka Haveli HISTORIC BUILDING

This *haveli* dates from 1930. There's an ornate painted carving above the arches and there are portraits of Gandhi, Nehru in an automobile, and Krishna and Radha (favourite mistress of Krishna when he lived as a cowherd) on a swing.

Chhauchharia Haveli HISTORIC BUILDING

A short distance south of the fort are a number of interesting buildings, including the Chhauchharia Haveli, behind Jangit Hospital, with paintings dating from the last decade of the 19th century. These include a hot-air balloon being optimistically inflated by passengers blowing vigorously through pipes.

Courses

Apani Dhani (☑222239) and **Ramesh Jangid's Tourist Pension** (☑224060) both arrange lessons and workshops in Hindi, tabla drumming, cooking and local crafts such as *bandhani* (tie-dyeing); tell them exactly what you're interested in and chances are they'll be able to arrange a workshop for you.

Tours

Ramesh Jangid at **Apani Dhani** (☑222239; www.apanidhani.com) and his son Rajesh at **Ramesh Jangid's Tourist Pension** (☑224060; www.touristpension.com) are keen to promote sustainable rural tourism, in part by organising village treks, camel-cart safaris, and informative guided tours. These activities offer an in-depth discovery of the culture and bring revenues to the local community and include workshops introducing local art and crafts, and concerts with a musician from the village.

Guided **walking tours** of Nawalgarh cost ₹350 and take two to three hours. **Treks** start at ₹2050/2000/1750 per person per day for up to two/three/four people. Treks include food, accommodation, transfers and a guide. See www.touristpension.com/exploring_region for further details.

Prices for **jeep tours** to the villages of Shekhawati from Nawalgarh are as follows: a three-hour trip taking in Dundlod and Parsurampura is ₹1900 for up to four people; a five-hour trip taking in Mandawa, Dundlod and Fatehpur is ₹2200 for up to four people;

RAMESH JANGID

Ramesh Jangid founded the NGO Friends of Shekhawati and a local chapter of the Indian National Trust for Art and Cultural Heritage (INTACH) to protect and raise awareness of the famous murals and architectural heritage of Shekhawati. He is also the founder of the eco-sensitive lodge Apani Dhani in Nawalgarh.

Quick Tip

First of all I would recommend people to visit less places, to take time, to discover the selected places thoroughly instead of running or jumping from one town to the other.

Which Towns?

Well, I do not want it to appear like the promotion of my own town, but I feel the two more interesting places to see in Shekhawati are Nawalgarh and the nearby village of Dundlod. Why is it so? In Nawalgarh, as well as Dundlod, some *havelis* have been converted into museums. That means you can enter them without disturbing anyone, you can take your time and visit the whole building. Also, Nawalgarh and Dundlod are still authentic places, if I may say. So far, they have not been affected much by the negative impact of tourism. If you walk in the local market of Nawalgarh, there is no shop for tourists, just shops for things locals need.

Which Havelis?

In Nawalgarh, I would recommend Bhagton ki Choti Haveli, Morarka Haveli Museum and Dr Ramnath A Poddar Haveli Museum. You can enter these three havelis. The first one is in a relatively good original condition, especially inside, and the two others have been restored.

In Dundlod, where the Goenka family was very influential, one can see the Seth Arjun Das Goenka Haveli. The family has displayed some items belonging to them and tried to recreate the lifestyle of the past era.

a seven- to eight-hour trip visiting Mandawa, Mahansar, Ramgarh and Fatehpur is ₹2500.

Roop Niwas Kothi (☏222008; www.royal ridingholidays.com) specialises in high-end **horse and camel excursions**. Camel/horse rides cost ₹500/600 for one hour; for more elaborate overnight excursions, including accommodation in luxury tents, costs start at around US$200 per person per day. It offers themed package rides of a week or more; details can be found on the website.

Sleeping & Eating

TOP CHOICE **Apani Dhani** GUESTHOUSE $$
(☏222239; www.apanidhani.com; s/d from ₹995/1350) This award-winning eco-tourism venture is a delightful and relaxing place. Rooms are in traditional, cosy mud-hut bungalows, enhanced by thatched roofs and comfortable beds, around a bougainvillea-shaded courtyard. The adjoining organic farm supplies delicious ingredients and alternative energy is used wherever possible – there's solar lights, water heaters and compost toilets. It's on the west side of the Jaipur road. Multilingual Ramesh Jangid runs the show and 5% of the room tariff goes to community projects. Tours around the area, via bicycle, car, camel cart or foot, are available.

TOP CHOICE **Ramesh Jangid's Tourist Pension**
GUESTHOUSE $
(☏224060; www.touristpension.com; s/d from ₹400/450) Near the Maur Hospital, this pension is well known, so if you get lost, just ask a local to point you in the right direction. The guesthouse, run by genial Rajesh, Ramesh's son, offers homely, clean accommodation in spacious rooms with big beds. Some rooms have furniture carved by Rajesh's grandfather, and the more expensive rooms also have murals created by visiting artists. Pure veg meals, made with organic ingredients, are available (including a delectable vegetable thali for ₹180). The family also arranges all sorts of tours around Shekhawati.

Shekhawati Guesthouse GUESTHOUSE $
(☏224658; www.shekhawatiguesthouse.com; s/d ₹400/500, cottages s/d ₹ 700/800, r with AC ₹1000; ❄@) This friendly guesthouse is more like a homestay run by a very friendly couple. There are six rooms in the main building plus five atmospheric, thatch-roofed, mud-walled cottages in the garden. The organic garden supplies most of the hotel's produce needs, which can be enjoyed in the lovely outdoor restaurant. The restau-

rant has received awards for its delicious organic food and we heartily recommend the kheer (rice pudding). It's 4km east of the bus stand (₹60 by taxi). Pick-up from the bus or train station can be arranged, as can cooking lessons.

Grand Haveli & Resort HERITAGE HOTEL $$
(☏225301; www.grandhaveli.com; Baori Gate; r from ₹1200, ste ₹2500; ❄) The rooms at this beautifully renovated *haveli* are individual, spacious and very atmospheric, with heritage furnishings. The two-tiered, multicuisine restaurant, **Jharoka**, overlooks a timeless scene of *chhatris* through a large window.

Koolwal Kothi HERITAGE HOTEL $$
(☏225817; www.welcomheritagehotels.com; 40 Government Hospital Rd; s/d ₹3500/4000; ❄@☀) Rooms are either in a garish, early 20th-century *haveli*, or in a recently constructed facsimile next door. The older *haveli* features antique furnishings and dusty authenticity, but the reproduced building has a brighter interior. A spa and pool were under construction when we visited.

DS Bungalow GUESTHOUSE $
(☏9983168916; s ₹350-450, d ₹400-500) Run by a friendly, down-to-earth couple, this simple place with boxy air-cooled rooms is a little out of town on the way to Roop Niwas Palace. It's backed by a garden with a pleasant outdoor mud-walled restaurant. The home cooking is decent; a full veg/nonveg dinner comes in at at ₹250/300.

About 4km east of the town is the rural retreat of the former *thakur* of Nawalgarh, Nawal Singh (1880–1926). Roop Niwas Palace is now occupied by two hotels: the **Roop Niwas Kothi** (☏01594-222008; www.roopniwas kothi.com; s/d/ste Rs2600/2900/4500; ❄@), and **Roop Vilas Palace Hotel** (☏224321; www.roopvilas.com s/d from Rs3000/3500; ❄@☀). Both have a back-to-the-Raj feel, with grand grounds and old-fashioned rooms. Roop Vilas has the brighter, restored rooms, while Roop Niwas is more your dusty Raj. Both organise horse riding.

ⓘ Information

There are several internet cafes around town; they change frequently but all charge ₹30 to 50 per hour. Ask at your hotel if you have any trouble locating one. The **State Bank of Bikaner & Jaipur** (SBBJ; Bala Qila complex) changes currency and travellers cheques, and there's an SBBJ ATM near Baori Gate.

❶ Getting There & Away

Bus

There are RSRTC buses between Nawalgarh and Jaipur (₹85, 3½ hours, every 15 minutes), and several morning services each day to Delhi (₹175, eight hours). There's also a daily deluxe bus to Jaipur departing at 8am (₹120, 3 hours) and several private services, most of which drop you an inconvenient 5km outside Jaipur. Buses for destinations in Shekhawati leave every few minutes, while shared jeeps leave according to demand (₹15 to Sikar, ₹20 to Jhunjhunu). Buses run to Fatehpur (₹30, hourly) and Mandawa (₹20, every 45 minutes).

Train

At the time of research, work was about to commence on converting the line from Delhi to Jaipur via Jhunjhunu, Nawalgarh and Sikar to broad gauge. In the meantime services to/from Nawalgarh are erratic and unreliable. It might be worth checking for up-to-date information at the train station, but generally it's quicker and more convenient to travel here by bus.

Dundlod

📞 01594

Dundlod is a peaceful, back-in-time village lying about 7km north of Nawalgarh. Its small fort was built in 1750 by Keshri Singh, the fifth and youngest son of Sardul Singh. Major additions were made in the early 19th century by his descendant Sheo Singh, who resettled in the region despite attempts on his life by Shyam Singh of Bissau (Shyam Singh also murdered his father and brother in an attempt to claim the region for himself). Members of the wealthy Goenka merchant family also settled here and their prosperity is evident in their richly painted *havelis*.

◉ Sights

Dundlod Fort   HISTORIC BUILDING
(admission ₹20; ☉sunrise-sunset) This fort was built and frequently modified over 200 years, and features a blend of Rajput and Mughal art and architecture. Inside, it combines a mix of European and Rajput decorative elements; the Diwan-i-Khas (Hall of Private Audience) has a mustard-coloured colonnade, stained-glass windows, Louis XIV antiques and a dusty collection of books. Above the Diwan-i-Khas is the *duchatta* (women's gallery) from where the women in purdah could view the proceedings below through net curtains. The zenana opens out onto the reading room of the *thakurani* (noblewoman). This room has a hand-carved wooden writing table, which bears oriental dragon motifs. Parts of the fort have been transformed into a hotel and you can also take horse-riding, camel or jeep tours from here.

Satyanarayan Temple   HINDU TEMPLE
In a small square to the right just before the entrance to Dundlod Fort is Satyanarayan Temple, which was built by Hariram Goenka in 1911. On the temple's west wall is a long frieze, with pictures showing Europeans on sturdy bicycles and in cars, and a long train with telegraph lines above it (all very cutting-edge for the day). The portraits under the eaves show nobles at leisure, reading and sniffing flowers. One fine moustached and turquoise-turbaned fellow has a bird in his hand, while another painting shows a woman admiring herself in a mirror.

Seth Arjun Das Goenka Haveli   MUSEUM
(admission ₹40; ☉8am-7pm) A short distance to the south of Satyanarayan Temple is the stunning restored 1875–85 haveli belonging to the powerful Goenka family. As with all restored havelis, the bright colours are something of a shock after becoming used to the discrete tones of murals faded with age. The interior offers a good illustration of the merchants' lives, beginning with their reception room, cooled by huge punka fans swinging from ropes and all about there are scatterings of everyday life from another era. Look for reminders of the cotton merchant's samples from Calcutta.

☞ Tours

Dundlod Fort   HORSE RIDING
(📞/fax 252519, in Jaipur 0141-2211276; www. dundlod.com) Dundlod Fort has around 60 horses stabled at its Royal Equestrian and Polo Centre – India's largest Marwari horse-breeding centre. They organise upmarket horse safaris for experienced riders only. You can ride for three to 12 days along various routes around Shekhawati or to other areas of Rajasthan such as Pushkar or Nagaur.

🛏 Sleeping

Dundlod Fort   HERITAGE HOTEL $$
(📞/fax 252519, in Jaipur 0141-2211276; www.dundlod .com; s/d/ste from ₹2300/2500/4000; ❄🖥) Still run by the extremely friendly and welcoming family of Dundlod's founder, a descendant of Sardul Singh, the fort has grand and imposing communal areas, but the rooms themselves are rather shabby. The suites are better restored than the rest of the rooms on offer.

Mukundgarh

📞 01594

About 5km north of Dundlod, Mukundgarh is a crafts centre, renowned for its textiles, brass and iron scissors and betel-nut cutters. It's a charming, quiet town with little tourist development and some interesting *havelis,* including Kanoria, Ganriwal and Saraf.

The Saraf Haveli (admission ₹20) is open whenever there's a caretaker around. It was built in 1909, though it took eight years to complete. The main entrance is on an elevated platform almost 2m high. One of the biggest *havelis* in all of Shekhawati, it has eight courtyards, though not all may be open for viewing. Rooms retain old family pictures and punkas, while the paintings in the main courtyard are faded and many have been washed over with green paint.

The impressive Mukundgarh Fort, dating from the 18th century, is the only accommodation in town, although it was closed for extensive renovation at the time of research.

Parsurampura

📞 01594

This sleepy little village, 20km southeast of Nawalgarh, is home to some of Shekhawati's oldest paintings. The Shamji Sharaf Haveli, just south of the bus stand, dates from the end of the 18th century and is decorated with a mixture of Hindu gods and Europeans. Pictures include a grandmother having her hair dressed, a woman spinning yarn and an intriguing image of a European woman in patent-leather shoes carrying a parasol. Above the lintel are some well-preserved portraits and, below, portrayals of Ganesh, Vishnu, Krishna and Radha. Saraswati (wife of Hindu god Brahma) is riding a peacock in the right-hand corner.

Beautiful paintings featuring the lives of the gods ring the interior of the dome of the Chhatri of Thakur Sardul Singh cenotaph, 50m south of the *haveli,* which dates from the mid-18th century. The work here is reminiscent of miniature painting and its antiquity is

SHEKHAWATI'S OUTDOOR GALLERIES

In the 18th and 19th centuries, shrewd Marwari merchants lived frugally and far from home while earning money in India's new commercial centres. They sent the bulk of their vast fortunes back to their families in Shekhawati to construct grand *havelis* (traditional, ornately decorated mansions) to show their neighbours how well they were doing and to compensate their families for their long absences. Merchants competed with one another to build ever more grand edifices – homes, temples, step-wells – which were richly decorated, both inside and out, with painted murals.

The artists responsible for these acres of decoration largely belonged to the caste of *kumhars* (potters) and were both the builders and painters of the *havelis*. Known as *chajeras* (masons), many were commissioned from beyond Shekhawati – particularly from Jaipur, where they had been employed decorating the new capital's palaces – and others flooded in from further afield to offer their skills. Soon, there was a cross-pollination of ideas and techniques, with local artists learning from the new arrivals.

Haveli walls were frequently painted by the *chajeras* from the ground to the eaves. Often the paintings mix depictions of the gods and their lives with everyday scenes featuring modern inventions, such as trains and aeroplanes, even though these artists themselves had never seen them. Hence, Krishna and Radha are seen in flying motorcars and Europeans can be observed inflating hot-air balloons by blowing into them.

These days most of the *havelis* are still owned by descendants of the original families, but not inhabited by their owners, for whom small-town Rajasthan has lost its charm. Many are occupied just by a single *chowkidar* (caretaker), while others may be home to a local family. Though they are pale reflections of the time when they accommodated the large households of the Marwari merchant families, they remain a fascinating testament to the changing times in which they were created. Only a few *havelis* have been restored; many more lie derelict, crumbling slowly away.

For a full rundown on the history, people, towns and buildings of the area, try tracking down a copy of *The Painted Towns of Shekhawati* by Ilay Cooper, which can be picked up at bookshops in the region or Jaipur. Another good book, available locally, is *Shekhawati: Painted Townships* by Kishore Singh.

evident in the use of muted, natural pigments. Images include those of the *thakur* and his five sons, graphic battle scenes from the Ramayana, and the love story of Dhola Maru (p247), a common Romeo-and-Juliet–style theme employed by the painters of Shekhawati. To visit the cenotaph you must obtain the key from a caretaker (never far away).

Also to be found in Parsurampura is the small **Gopinathji Mandir**, on the left just before you leave the village on the road to Nawalgarh. The temple was built by Sardul Singh in 1742 and it's believed that the same artist responsible for the paintings on the Chhatri of Thakur Sardul Singh executed the paintings here.

There are numerous buses to Parsurampura from Nawalgarh (₹12, one hour).

Jhunjhunu

🖉 01592 / POP 131,000

Shekhawati's most important commercial centre has a different atmosphere from the smaller towns, with lots of traffic, concrete and hustle and bustle as befits the district headquarters. Though it's is not the most exciting or inspiring of Shekhawati destinations, it does have a few appealing *havelis* and a colourful bazaar.

Jhunjhunu was founded by the Kayamkhani nawabs in the middle of the 15th century, and remained under their control until it was taken by the Rajput ruler Sardul Singh in 1730. It was here that the British based their Shekhawati Brigade, a troop formed in the 1830s to try to halt the activities of the dacoits, local petty rulers who had discovered that an easy way to become wealthy was to pinch other people's money.

Jhunjhunu has numerous impressive *chhatris,* as well as some remnants of forts and a palace. Unfortunately, though, many of the fine frescoes that once adorned the town's architecture have been whitewashed out of existence. The town is also notorious for its Rani Sati Temple – dedicated to a young bride who burned to death on her husband's funeral pyre in 1595.

◉ Sights

Rani Sati Temple   HINDU TEMPLE
(admission free, ☺4am-10pm) In the northeast corner of town is the enormous, multistorey Rani Sati Temple, notorious and hugely popular for commemorating an act of *sati* (self-immolation) by a merchant's wife in 1595. Rani Sati Temple has long been embroiled in

a national debate about *sati*, especially after the 19-year-old widow Roop Kanwar committed *sati* in the nearby Sikar district in 1987. It's fronted by two courtyards, around which 300 rooms offer shelter to pilgrims. The main hall is made of marble with elaborate silver repoussé work before the inner sanctum. (Photography is permitted.)

There's a tile-and-mirror mosaic on the ceiling of the *mandapa* (pillared pavilion) depicting Rani Sati, with Ganesh, Shiva and Durga (the Inaccessible; a form of Devi, Shiva's wife) watching over her. A relief frieze on the north wall shows her story. Her husband is killed by the nawab's army; Rani Sati mounts the funeral pyre and is consumed by flames while Durga sends her power to withstand the pain. In the next panel Rani commands a chariot driver to place her ashes on a horse and to build a temple over the spot where the horse halts. Rani Sati is the patron goddess of the merchant class, and the temple apparently receives the second-highest number of donations of any temple in India.

Khetri Mahal   HISTORIC BUILDING
(admission ₹20) A series of small laneways at the western end of Nehru Bazaar (a short rickshaw drive north of the bus station) leads to the imposing Khetri Mahal, a small palace dating from around 1770 and once one of Shekhawati's most sophisticated and beautiful buildings. It's believed to have been built by Bhopal Singh, Sardul Singh's grandson, who founded Khetri. Unfortunately, it now has a desolate, forlorn atmosphere, but the architecture remains a superb open-sided collection of intricate arches and columns.

The various levels of the palace are connected by a series of ramps (big enough to accommodate small horses) along which the *thakur* could be pulled. There are good views over the town from here, stretching across to the old Muslim quarter, Pirzada Mahalla, and its mosques.

HAVELIS
Modi Havelis   HISTORIC BUILDING
The Modi Havelis face each other and house some of Jhunjhunu's best murals and woodcarving. The *haveli* on the eastern side has a painting of a woman in a blue sari sitting before a gramophone; a frieze depicts a train, alongside which soldiers race on horses. The spaces between the brackets above show the Krishna legends. Part of the *haveli* facade on the eastern side of the road has been painted over. The *haveli* on the western side has

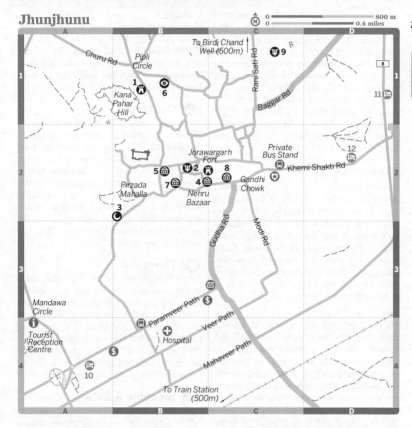

some comical pictures, featuring some remarkable facial expressions and moustaches.

Kaniram Narsinghdas Tibrewala Haveli
HISTORIC BUILDING

A short distance away from the Modi Havelis, fronted by a vegetable market, is this closed *haveli*. On the west wall of the first courtyard is a frieze depicting two trains approaching each other: one is a passenger train, the other is a goods train filled with livestock, and both look like they have come straight from the artist's imagination.

Mohanlal Ishwardas Modi Haveli
HISTORIC BUILDING

On the north side of Nehru Bazaar is Mohanlal Ishwardas Modi Haveli, which dates from 1896. A train runs merrily across the front facade. Above the entrance to the outer courtyard are scenes from the life of Krishna. On

Jhunjhunu

◉ Sights

⌂ Sleeping

a smaller, adjacent arch are British imperial figures, including monarchs and robed judges. Facing them are Indian rulers, including maharajas and nawabs.

Around the archway, between the inner and outer courtyards, there are some glass-covered portrait miniatures, along with some fine mirror-and-glass tilework. The inner courtyard shows the hierarchy of the universe, with deities in the upper frieze, humans in the middle band, and animal and floral motifs below.

OTHER ATTRACTIONS

Bihariji Temple   HINDU TEMPLE
A short distance northwest of Jorawargarh Fort is the Bihariji Temple, which dates from approximately 1776 and is dedicated to Krishna. It has some fine, though worn, murals. On the inside of the dome, Krishna and the *gopis* are rendered in natural pigments – their circular dance, called the *rasalila*, suits the form of the dome and so is a popular theme here.

Birdi Chand Well   HISTORIC SITE
On the northwest side of town, about 1km from Nehru Bazaar, is Birdi Chand Well, surmounted by four imposing minarets (two minarets generally symbolise the presence of a step-well), which are covered in fading paintings. As water is such a precious commodity in the desert, wells were sacred, and it's common to see a temple at a well – there's a small one here devoted to Hanuman (the Hindu monkey god).

Mertani Baori   HISTORIC SITE
The Mertani Baori, to the northwest of the fort, is Shekhawati's most impressive step-well, named after the woman who commissioned it, Mertani, the widow of Sardul Singh. Built in 1783, it has since been restored and is about 30m deep, with sulphuric waters said to cure skin diseases. An English official reported in 1930, however, that the water here was so poisonous that anyone who drank it died a couple of hours later.

Dargah of Kamaruddin Shah   HISTORIC SITE
To the south of Kana Pahar Hill is the Dargah of Kamaruddin Shah, a complex consisting of a madrasa (Islamic college), a mosque and a *mehfilkhana* (concert hall in which religious songs are sung). Fragments of paintings depicting floral motifs remain around the courtyard (although many have been whitewashed).

Badalgarh   HISTORIC BUILDING
Northwest of Khetri Mahal, Badalgarh (originally called Fazalgarh after its constructor, Nawab Fazal Khan) is a mighty 16th-century fort, dating from the period of the nawabs. It belongs to the Dundlod family and is closed to the public, awaiting renovation.

Courses

If you are interested in tuition in traditional Shekhawati painting, contact Laxmi Kant Jangid at the Hotel Jamuna Resort or Hotel Shiv Shekhawati. Laxmi also runs hands-on cookery courses at Hotel Jamuna Resort; these cost around ₹300 per person. One-day decorative art workshops are also available, and cover henna painting, textiles (including *bandhani* – tie-dyeing) and fresco painting; the Jamuna Resort also offers free morning yoga classes.

Tours

Laxmi Kant Jangid (of the Hotel Shiv Shekhawati and Hotel Jamuna Resort) is a knowledgeable, government-approved guide. He provides guided tours around Jhunjhunu and can arrange car tours of surrounding towns. Half-/full-day excursions by car in the area cost ₹1000/1500 per person. Multiday camel safaris and bicycle trips around the region can also be arranged.

Sleeping & Eating

Hotel Jamuna Resort   HOTEL $$
(☏512696; www.hoteljamunaresort.com; s/d from ₹1500/2000, d with AC from ₹1200; ❄@☰) Perched upon a hill overlooking the town and operated by Laxmi Kant Jangid (who also runs Hotel Shiv Shekhawati), Hotel Jamuna Resort has everything that you need. The rooms in the older wing are either vibrantly painted with murals or decorated with traditional mirrorwork, while the rooms in the newer wing are modern and airy. There's an inviting pool (₹50 for nonguests) set in the serene garden and purpose-built kitchens set up for cooking courses.

Hotel Shiv Shekhawati   HOTEL $
(☏232651; www.shivshekhawati.com; Khemi Shakti Rd; s/d from ₹600/800; ❄@) East of the centre, Shiv Shekhawati is the best budget option with plain but squeaky-clean rooms. It's 600m from the private bus stand in a quiet area on the eastern edge of town. The affable owner, Laxmi Kant Jangid (usually

found at Hotel Jamuna Resort), is a wealth of knowledge on the villages of Shekhawati and tours can be organised here.

Hotel Fresco Palace HOTEL **$$**
(☎325233; Off Paramveer Path; s/d from ₹950/2100⌘) One of a pair of hotels south-west of the RSRTC bus stand. It's tucked away down a laneway, with clean colour-ful rooms, some with leafy outlooks, and a small restaurant. Like its neighbour, it seems overpriced for what is on offer.

ⓘ Information

SBBJ ATM (Paramveer Path) This ATM accepts international cards, or one of the many others in Ghandi Chowk.

UAE Exchange (Paramveer Path) Money exchange and Western Union office.

Tourist Reception Centre (☎232909; ⊗10am-5pm Mon-Fri) Out of the centre at the Churu Bypass Rd, Mandawa Circle. The office has helpful, cheery staff, but all they can provide are a few brochures and a basic map of the town and region.

ⓘ Getting There & Away

Bus

Regular buses run between Jhunjhunu and Jaipur (₹80, four hours), Churu (₹30, 1½ hours) and Bissau (₹25, 1½ hours). Numerous buses go to Mandawa (₹15, one hour), Nawalgarh (₹20, one hour) and Baggar (₹8, 40 minutes).

Buses leave for Delhi from 5am (₹140, seven hours, hourly). There are also buses to Bikaner (₹105, five hours). A private bus stand on Khemi Shakti Rd runs a number of similar services.

Train

At the time of research, work was due to com-mence on converting the line from Delhi to Jai-pur via Jhunjhunu, Nawalgarh and Sikar to broad gauge. In the meantime services to/from Nawal-garh are erratic and unreliable. Ask for updates at the train station, but generally it's quicker and more convenient to travel here by bus.

ⓘ Getting Around

For local sightseeing, you'll pay about ₹50 per hour for an autorickshaw. A rickshaw from the train or bus station to the Hotel Shiv Shekhawati costs about ₹30.

THE COLOURS OF SHEKHAWATI

Shekhawati's colourful paintings are a vivid response to its incredibly parched and arid landscape, serving at once to educate, entertain and depict the concerns of the day.

Originally the colours used in the murals were all ochre based, the colour obtained from the urine of cows fed on mango leaves – a practice discontinued after it was deemed cruel. Other colours were obtained from stones and minerals: copper, lead, gold, indigo and lapis lazuli were all used. In the 1860s, artificial pigments were introduced from Ger-many, and colours began to change from subtle natural tones to brasher artificial hues.

To create fresco images, artists engaged in a painstaking process: first, the wall was covered in several layers of plaster (with clay often gathered from ant hills), to which were added various ingredients such as lime and hessian. The final layer was lime dust mixed with buttermilk and jaggery (coarse brown sugar made from the sap of the date palm). The painters worked on the plaster while it was still wet, which accounts for the brilliance of the colours. Once completed, the works were polished with agate and rubbed with dry coconut to seal them; some were also set with semi-precious stones. After the turn of the 20th century, the artists instead began to paint on dry plaster, allow-ing greater intricacy but losing the original urgency.

The early paintings are strongly influenced by Mughal decoration, with floral ara-besques and geometric designs (according to the dictates of Islam, the Mughals never created a representation of an animal or human). The Rajput royal courts were the next major influence; scenes from Hindu mythology were prevalent – usually featuring Krish-na and Rama (seventh incarnation of Vishnu).

With the arrival of Europeans, walls were embellished with paintings of the new tech-nological marvels to which the Shekhawati merchants had been exposed in centres such as Calcutta. Pictures of trains, planes, telephones, gramophones and bicycles featured, often painted direct from the artist's imagination.

The paintings of Shekhawati are thus an extraordinary synthesis of Eastern and West-ern influences, the cultural collision perfectly illustrated in paintings showing Krishna playing a gramophone for Radha, or the two of them flying off in a Rolls Royce.

Baggar

📞01592

This small, peaceful village, 15km northeast of Jhunjhunu, has few *havelis*, but the main reason to stay here is its great hotel.

Piramal Haveli (📞01592-221220; www. neemranahotels.com; r ₹1500-2000) has just eight rooms so advance bookings are essential. This is a gorgeous, colonial-style 1920s house – somewhere between Tuscan villa and Rajasthani mansion – built by a merchant who traded in opium, cotton and silver in Bombay. The house is appointed with original furniture and kitsch paintings featuring gods in motorcars. The *haveli* serves up terrific vegetarian thalis for lunch/dinner (₹250/300); afterwards, sip a strong drink on the porch and enjoy a peaceful game of backgammon.

Bissau

📞01595 / POP 21,500

Pint-sized Bissau lies about 32km northwest of Jhunjhunu. Founded in 1746 by Keshri Singh, the last of Sardul Singh's sons, it has one of Shekhawati's fiercest histories. The town prospered under Keshri, but fell into brigandry during the rule of his grandson Shyam Singh. It is said that the merchants of Bissau, who had been encouraged to set up in the town by Keshri, packed up and left when Shyam extracted vast sums of money from them. The *thakur* then resorted to a life of crime, embarking on raids with dacoits to neighbouring regions. The British called on the Shekhawati Brigade to restore order in the anarchic town, but by the time the expedition was mounted Shyam Singh had expired and his heir, Hammir Singh, had driven out the brigands and encouraged the merchants to return. The British were impressed by the town's prosperity and left without a single shot being fired. Look out for the Bissau Festival (p231), which hits the town for ten days annually, in either September or October, when locals perform scenes from the Ramayana.

◎ Sights

Chhatri of Hammir Singh   HISTORIC SITE
On the facade of the Chhatri of Hammir Singh (1875), near the private bus stand, you can see British folk in fancy carriages, including one carriage shaped like a lion and another like a hybrid lion–elephant. The *chhatri* is now

multipurpose, being both a primary school, with lessons held under the dome and even in the sandy courtyard, and a storage place for fodder.

Haveli of Girdarilal Sigtia   HISTORIC BUILDING
Walking north from the bus stand, take the first right and on the left-hand side at the next intersection is the Haveli of Girdarilal Sigtia. The paintings on the external walls have been destroyed, but the rooms retain some vibrant murals. A room in the northeast corner of the *haveli* shows Shiva (with the unusual addition of a moustache) with the Ganges flowing from his hair. Note the orange handprints on the outer courtyard wall; these are a custom peculiar to Shekhawati, signifying the birth of a male child.

Motiram Jasraj Sigtia Haveli
   HISTORIC BUILDING
On the opposite side of this lane is the Motiram Jasraj Sigtia Haveli, now a junior school. On the north wall, Krishna has stolen the *gopis'* clothes; the maidens have been modestly covered by the artist in the coils of snakes, although one reptile can be seen slinkily emerging from between a *gopi's* legs.

❶ Getting There & Away

There are daily buses from Bissau to Jhunjhunu (₹20, 1½ hours) every 30 minutes and to Mahansar (₹6, 20 minutes) and Mandawa (₹20, 1½ hours).

Mahansar

📞01595

The quaint, slow-moving and untouristed village of Mahansar is a dusty place with rural charm set in the middle of vast tracts of arid field and sand. It was founded by Nawal Singh in 1768, and the town prospered for several decades, with gemlike *havelis* financed by the wealthy Poddar clan, until one of the Poddars lost his livelihood when two shiploads of opium sank without a trace. The town is nowadays famous for homemade liquor, known as *daru,* which resembles Greek ouzo; imbibe with care as it's extremely potent.

◎ Sights

Sone ki Dukan Haveli   HISTORIC BUILDING
(admission ₹100; ◷7am-5pm) The name of this glorious *haveli* means 'gold shop', due to the striking paintings, which use a shim-

mering amount of gold leaf – unusual for Shekhawati. The scenes from the Ramayana in the southern section of the ceiling in the first chamber are particularly intense, with their glorious quantities of gold leaf. The lower walls are richly adorned with floral and bird motifs, a fantasy of butterflies, fruit-laden trees and flowers. On the north side of the ceiling, the life of Krishna is portrayed. If it's locked up, enquire at neighbouring shops.

Raghunath Mandir   HINDU TEMPLE

A short distance southwest of Sone ki Dukan Haveli is the Raghunath Mandir, a mid-19th-century temple that resembles a *haveli* in its architecture. It has fine floral arabesques beneath the arches around the courtyard and a grand façade. There are good views across the small town from the *chhatri*-ringed upper floor.

Sahaj Ram Poddar Chhatri   HISTORIC BUILDING

About 10 minutes' walk from the bus stand, past the fort on the right-hand side of Ramgarh Rd, is the Sahaj Ram Poddar Chhatri. Some archways have been bricked in, but there are still some well-preserved paintings on the lower walls of this well-proportioned and attractive building.

🛏 Sleeping & Eating

Narayan Niwas Castle   HERITAGE HOTEL $$

(☑01595-264322; r ₹1200-1800) Located in the old fort, about 100m north of the bus stand, Narayan Niwas Castle is the only place to stay in Mahansar (although a separate hotel is being developed in the same fort). This is a proper creaky Rajasthani castle dating from 1768 that feels evocatively uncommercial. Rooms are dusty but characterful, some (including rooms 1 and 5) with antique furniture and paintings covering the walls. Bathrooms are basic affairs. It's run by the *thakur* of Mahansar and his wife and mother. The food is sumptuous and a few glasses of the castle's own liquor before bedtime will be sure to have you seeing ghosts of Rajputs flitting by.

ⓘ Getting There & Away

Regular bus services go between Mahansar and Ramgarh (₹8), Churu (₹10), the closest railway station, Fatehpur (₹15) and Bissau (₹6). Change at Bissau for buses to Jhunjhunu (₹20). A rickshaw from Churu railway station to the castle is about ₹150.

Ramgarh

Sixteen kilometres south of Churu and 20km north of Fatehpur is Ramgarh, which was founded by a disaffected group from the wealthy Poddar family in 1791, and has the biggest concentration of painted *havelis* in the region. The Poddars defected from nearby Churu in a fit of pique after the local *thakur* imposed an extortionate wool levy. They set about building extravagant homes for themselves, and Ramgarh thus has a splendid, albeit uncared-for and faded, artistic legacy. It prospered until the late 19th century, but remains pretty snoozy today.

The town is easy to explore on foot. The bus stand is at the western edge of town; in the northern section of town, about 600m from the bus stand, there's a concentration of *havelis*, as well as the main Shani Mandir temple and the Ganga Temple.

◉ Sights

Ram Gopal Poddar Chhatri   HISTORIC BUILDING

The imposing Ram Gopal Poddar Chhatri, to the south of the bus stand, was built in 1872. The main dome of the *chhatri* is surrounded by a series of smaller domes; on the west side of the main dome's outer rim, one of the projecting braces bears a picture of a naked woman stepping into her *lenga* (skirt), while another woman shields her from a man's gaze with the hem of her skirt. The drum of the main dome is brightly painted and has well-preserved paintings in blues and reds depicting the battle from the Ramayana. Unfortunately, the *chhatri* is in a sorry state. To enter the compound, you will probably need to find the caretaker, who'll ask for about ₹20.

Ganga Temple   HINDU TEMPLE

A short distance north of the town wall, on the east side of the road, is the Ganga Temple. It was built by one of the Poddar clan in 1845, and is an imposing building with large elephant murals on its facade, with plenty of images of the local favourite, Krishna. The right side of the facade is deteriorating and the foundations are crumbling. The temple only opens for morning and evening *puja* (prayers).

Shani Mandir   HINDU TEMPLE

The spectacular yet tiny Shani Mandir (Saturn Temple) was built in 1840 and, despite a crude exterior, has a richly ornamented interior, completely covered in fantastic mirrorwork. In the chamber before the inner sanctum are some fine murals worked in gold. Subjects include Krishna and Radha and events from the Mahabharata.

Poddar Havelis HISTORIC BUILDINGS

Heading back to the main Churu Gate, continue past the gate for about 50m, then turn left to reach a group of Poddar havelis. Popular motifs include soldiers, trains and an unusual design, peculiar to Ramgarh, of three fish arranged in a circle. One *haveli* has a painting of women carrying water in pitchers, and there's a novel portrayal of the Dhola Maru legend (p247) on the west wall of another: while Maru fires at the advancing assailants, Dhola nonchalantly smokes a hookah.

🛌 Sleeping & Eating

Ramgarh Fresco Hotel HERITAGE HOTEL **$$**
(☑01571-240595; www.ramgarhfresco.com; Subhash Chowk; r ₹1600/2000; ✴@) This new hotel boasts several colourfully decorated rooms in a lovingly restored haveli. The hotel can organise sightseeing and cultural shows. Traditional Indian cuisine and continental meals are available. Prior booking is recommended.

ℹ️ Getting There & Away

There are buses to Nawalgarh (₹30, 2½ hours), Bissau (₹8, 45 minutes), Fatehpur (₹15, 45 minutes) and Mandawa (₹25, 1½ hours) from the bus station at the western edge of town. For other destinations, change at Fatehpur or Mandawa.

Fatehpur

☑01571 / POP 89,000

The scruffy, workaday small town of Fatehpur is chock-full of wonderful but slowly disintegrating *havelis* on either side of its main street. Though many are in a state of disrepair, it's hoped that the restoration of Haveli Nadine Le Prince, now a wonderful gallery and cultural centre, will help rescue the area's other beautiful buildings by refocusing attention on the area.

Established in 1451 as a capital for Muslim nawabs, Fatehpur was their stronghold for centuries before it was taken over by the Shekhawati Rajputs in the 18th century. Curiously, it was even ruled by an Irish sailor-turned-mercenary, George Thomas, in 1799, before he lost it to the maharaja of Jaipur. The wealth of the merchant community,

which included the Poddar, Choudhari and Ganeriwala families, is illustrated by the town's grandiose *havelis, chhatris,* wells and temples.

👁️ Sights

Haveli Nadine Le Prince MUSEUM
(☑233024; www.cultural-centre.com; adult/child ₹100/50; ⊙10am-7pm) Without doubt the main sight in town is the Haveli Nadine Le Prince, an 1802 *haveli* that has been brightly restored to its former glory.

French artist Nadine Le Prince spent three years having the *haveli* restored (after it had lain empty for nearly 40 years), and turned it into a gallery and cultural centre. Inside, the grand hall retains the original woodcarving and has a ceiling lined with real gold. Charming features include a couple's winter room with specially designed steep steps to deter children, and niches for musicians in the dining room.

There's a gallery displaying art by French artists working here, as well as a tribal art gallery, which shows some beautiful work by local artists. Its **Art Café** is a cool retreat from a hot day and serves tasty snacks, and you can stay here too (see p248).

Chauhan Well HISTORIC SITE

Just south of this *haveli* is the small Chauhan Well, which dates from the early 18th century and was built by the Rajput wife of a Muslim nawab. There's some painting around the windows and a couple of the pavilions, and the minarets retain fragments of geometric and floral designs.

Jagannath Singhania Haveli
HISTORIC BUILDING

West from the Haveli Nadine Le Prince is the Jagannath Singhania Haveli, dating from 1855. It has a fantastic ornately painted interior, but is often locked. There are some interesting paintings on its facade, including that of Krishna and Radha framed by four elephants, and, above this, some British men with guns.

Geori Shankar Haveli HISTORIC BUILDING

Further south from Jagannath Singhania Haveli is the Geori Shankar Haveli, an atmospheric and still-inhabited ruin with fine mirror mosaics on the ceiling of the antechamber, religious paintings in the outer courtyard, and elephant statues on the roof. You'll probably be asked for a donation to enter.

One of the most popular paintings to be seen on the walls of Shekhawati's *havelis* depicts the legend of Dhola Maru, India's own, happier answer to *Romeo and Juliet*.

Princess Maru hailed from Pugal, near Bikaner, while Dhola was a young prince from Gwalior. When Maru was two years old, there was a terrible drought in her homeland, so her father, the maharaja, shifted to Gwalior, where his friend, Dhola's father, ruled. He remained there for three years, returning to Pugal when he learned that the drought was over. But before he left, as a token of friendship between the two rulers, a marriage alliance was contracted between their children, Maru and Dhola. After 20 years, however, the promise was forgotten and Princess Maru was contracted to marry someone else.

Wedding plans would have proceeded as normal, except that a bard, who'd travelled from Pugal to Gwalior, sang at the royal court of the childhood marriage of Dhola and Maru. In this way Dhola came to hear of the beautiful and virtuous Maru, with whom he immediately, sight unseen, fell in love and resolved to meet. Of course, when Maru laid eyes on him she returned his affections and they decided to elope at once.

Her betrothed, Umra, heard of their flight and gave chase with the help of his brother, Sumra. They pursued the camel-borne lovers on horseback as the brave Maru fired at them with arrows, though this proved of little use against the brothers, who were armed with guns. Nevertheless, they were able to elude the brothers, taking shelter in a forest where Dhola was promptly bitten by a snake and succumbed on the spot. Maru, thus thwarted by death, wept so loudly for her lost lover that her lamentations were heard by Shiva and Gauri who, luckily, were walking nearby. Gauri beseeched Shiva to restore the dead Dhola to life and thus the loving couple was reunited.

Mahavir Prasad Goenka Haveli
HISTORIC BUILDING

On the same road as the Geori Shankar Haveli is the Mahavir Prasad Goenka Haveli, which was built in 1885 and is considered by some to have some of the best paintings in Shekhawati. The rooms on the 1st floor are most dazzling: stepping into one is like entering a jewellery box – it glimmers with mirrorwork, colour and gold. One of the rooms shows elaborate Krishna illustrations. Unfortunately, the *haveli* is often locked, though you can usually enter the first courtyard.

Jagannath Singhania Chhatri   HISTORIC SITE

On the east side of the Churu–Sikar road (enter via a gateway behind the *chhatri*), Jagannath Singhania Chhatri has well-tended gardens. The imposing building houses relatively few paintings, some that appear to be unfinished. There's a small Shiva shrine here at which villagers still pay homage. Opposite is the small, still-used Singhania well.

Baori
HISTORIC SITE

Near the private bus stand is a large *baori* (step-well), built by Sheikh Mohammed of Nagaur in 1614, which for centuries provoked legends of bandits hiding in its depths. There's a path to the *baori* from a lane opposite the private bus stand. Unfortunately, the *baori* is in a shocking state of disrepair – even dangerous (don't get too close to the edges) – and appears to be a rubbish dump. It was obviously a great feat to dig to this depth, and around the sides there's a series of arched galleries, mostly collapsed. On the south side, a *haveli* has half fallen into the well and its courtyard paintings are exposed. The minarets of the *baori* stand as sad testament to its former grandeur.

Harikrishnan Das Saraogi Haveli
HISTORIC BUILDING

Diagonally opposite the *baori,* on the south side of the private bus stand, the Harikrishnan Das Saraogi Haveli features a colourful facade with iron lacework on the upper verandas and shops at street level, and a painted outer courtyard. Spot the woman smoking a hookah and, in the inner courtyard, a camel-drawn cart juxtaposed with a motorcar.

Vishnunath Keria Haveli   HISTORIC BUILDING

Adjacent, to the south, is the Vishnunath Keria Haveli. The outer courtyard has some wonderful pictures on either side of the inner courtyard door that show the marriage of religion and technology. Radha and Krishna can be seen in strange gondola-like flying contraptions, one with an animal's head, the other with the front part of a vintage car, and both featuring angel-like wings. On the north wall of the outer courtyard is a portrait of King George and Queen Victoria. On the southern external wall, pictures include Queen Victoria, a train, a holy man and Krishna playing a gramophone to Radha.

🛏 Sleeping & Eating

Haveli Cultural Centre Guest House & Art Café   BOUTIQUE HOTEL $$
(☑233024; www.cultural-centre.com; r from ₹800; dishes ₹50-150) The beautifully restored Haveli Nadine Le Prince (p246) has opened up its artist residence rooms to travellers. Several traditional-style rooms overlook the central courtyard. Tariff is room only, with breakfast ₹150 and dinner ₹300. To just visit the Art Café you'll have to pay to get into the *haveli,* but this is a good option for a light lunch. It's a cosy place with low tables, serving food such as omelettes, toast and rum-blazed bananas, as well as Indian snacks.

RTDC Hotel Haveli   HOTEL $$
(☑230293; s/d from ₹625/900, with AC ₹900/1200; mains ₹ 40-75; ❈) About 500m south of the RSRTC bus stand on the Churu–Sikar road. Rooms are spacious though dim and well worn, and the hotel manager is friendly and helpful. There's the requisite gloomy RTDC dining hall serving reasonable food.

Rendezvous   RESTAURANT $$
(☑9829493938; thali ₹150) This small family-run restaurant, a short stroll north of the Haveli Nadine Le Prince, prepares a great veg thali. You can even enquire about long-term stays with the family.

ℹ Getting There & Around

At the private bus stand, on the Churu–Sikar road, buses leave for Jhunjhunu (₹25, one hour), Mandawa (₹20, one hour), Churu (₹25, one hour), Ramgarh (₹15, 45 minutes) and Sikar (₹30, one hour). From the RSRTC bus stand, which is further south down this road, buses leave for Jaipur (₹80, 3½ hours, every 15 minutes), Delhi (₹170, seven hours, six daily) and Bikaner (₹115, 3½ hours, hourly).

Mandawa

☑01592 / POP 20,717

Once a quiet little market town, Mandawa is now Shekhawati's most frequented destination on the tourist trail. As such, you can expect more hassle from would-be guides and souvenir vendors than elsewhere in the region, though compared to some of Rajasthan's most visited destinations, it's still fairly relaxed. The gorgeous painted *havelis,* moreover, make up for any misgivings.

Settled in the 18th century and fortified by the dominant merchant families, the town's fort was built by Sardul Singh's youngest son in 1760, though inhabited much later, and has some fine frescoes in what is nowadays an upmarket hotel.

◉ Sights

Binsidhar Newatia Haveli   HISTORIC BUILDING
This *haveli* on the northern side of the Fatehpur–Jhunjhunu road houses the State Bank of Bikaner & Jaipur. Its interior paintings have been whitewashed, but there are fantastically entertaining paintings on the external eastern wall (accessible through a metal fence beside the bank). These include a European woman in a car driven by a chauffeur; a man on a bicycle; the Wright brothers evoking much excitement in their aeroplane as women in saris point with astonishment; a boy using a telephone; a strongman hauling along a car; and a bird-man flying in a winged device. The paintings date from the 1920s.

Hanuman Prasad Goenka Haveli
                                          HISTORIC BUILDING
Several *havelis* to the northwest of the bank belong to the wealthy Goenka family. Among them is the Hanuman Prasad Goenka Haveli, which has a composite picture that shows either Indra (the most important Vedic god) on an elephant or Shiva on his bull, depending on which way you look at it.

Goenka Double Haveli   HISTORIC BUILDING
Across the road from the Hanuman Prasad Goenka Haveli, this Geonka-owned *haveli* has two entrance gates and monumental pictures, including of elephants and horses, on the facade.

Murmuria Haveli   HISTORIC BUILDING
The Murmuria Haveli dates back to the 1930s, and here you can see how European art was beginning to influence local artists. From the sandy courtyard in front of this *haveli,* you can get a good view of the southern external wall of the adjacent double *haveli:* it features a long frieze depicting a train, with a crow flying above the engine and much activity at the railway crossing. Nehru is depicted on horseback holding the Indian flag. Above the arches on the south side of the courtyard are two paintings of gondolas on the canals of Venice.

Harlalka Well
HISTORIC BUILDING

A road leads south from the Murmuria Haveli; after 50m, take a detour to the right to see the impressive Harlalka Well, marked by four pillars and its old camel ramp. It is unfenced and very deep – take care!

Jhunjhunwala Haveli
HISTORIC BUILDING

(admission ₹50; ⊙dawn to dusk) Near the Harlalka Well, the Jhunjhunwala Haveli has an impressive gold leaf-painted room to the right of the main courtyard.

Mohan Lal Saraf Haveli
HISTORIC BUILDING

(admission ₹50; ⊙dawn to dusk) About 50m southeast is the Mohan Lal Saraf Haveli. On the south wall, a maharaja is depicted grooming his bushy moustache. There's fine mirror- and mosaic-work around the door to the inner courtyard, and Surya, the sun god, can be seen over the lintel.

Lakshminarayan Ladia Haveli
HISTORIC BUILDING

Further south on the same street as Mohan Lal Saraf Haveli is the Lakshminarayan Ladia Haveli. The west wall features a faded picture of a man enjoying a hookah, and a good procession frieze. Other pictures include that of Rama slaying Ravana (demon king of Lanka, now Sri Lanka).

Gulab Rai Ladia Haveli
HISTORIC BUILDING

Unfortunately, many of the erotic images in the Gulab Rai Ladia Haveli, a short distance to the east, have been systematically defaced by prudish souls. In the last pair of brackets on the first half of the southern wall, a woman is seen giving birth, attended by maidservants. There's an erotic image in the fifth niche from the end on this wall, but don't draw too much attention to it, or it may suffer the same fate as the other erotic art.

Chokhani Double Haveli
HISTORIC BUILDING

(admission ₹50; ⊙dawn to dusk) About 50m south past Gulab Rai Ladia Haveli is the grand Chokhani Double Haveli, dating from 1910 and so called because it was built in two adjoining wings for the families of two brothers. The paintings inside include floral arabesques and peacocks above the archways, as well as the Krishna legends and some mournful British soldiers.

🏃 Activities

You can organise camel and horse rides at the Hotel Castle Mandawa or the Mandawa Desert Resort. A one-hour camel ride costs ₹500 and a half/full-day trip is ₹800/1100.

Both places can also organise horse and jeep safaris on request.

Another possibility is the Hotel Heritage Mandawa, which organises half-/full-day camel rides and longer safaris, as well as jeep hire or guide hire for around the same prices. The Hotel Shekhawati also offers camel rides, along with jeep and horse tours, at good prices.

🛏 Sleeping & Eating

Hotel Shekhawati
HOTEL $

(☎9314698079; www.hotelshekwati.com; r ₹350-1800; ❄️❖@) Near Mukundgarh Rd, the real budget choice in town is run by a retired bank manager and his son (who's also a registered tourist guide). Bright, comically bawdy murals painted by artistic former guests give the rooms a splash of colour. Tasty meals are served on the peaceful rooftop, and competitively priced camel, horse and jeep tours can also be arranged.

Hotel Mandawa Haveli
HERITAGE HOTEL $$

(☎223088; www.hotelmandawa.com; s/d/ste from 1450/1950/4250;❄️) Close to Sonathia Gate and Subhash Chowk, this hotel is set in a glorious, restored 19th-century *haveli* with rooms surrounding a painted courtyard. The cheapest rooms are small, so it's worth splashing out on a suite, filled with arches, window seats and countless small windows. There's a rooftop restaurant serving good food; it's especially romantic at dinner time, when the lights of the town twinkle below. A set dinner will set you back ₹450.

Hotel Heritage Mandawa
HERITAGE HOTEL $$

(☎223742; www.hotelheritagemandawa.com; r ₹1700-2700, ste ₹4700;❄️) South of the Subhash Chowk is this gracious old *haveli*. Somewhat dark rooms with often clashing interiors are set around tranquil courtyards; the suites have small upstairs areas either for the bed or the bathroom. Rooms are highly variable in airiness and layout so check a few. Nightly music performances and puppet shows are held in the little garden.

Hotel Castle Mandawa
HERITAGE HOTEL $$$

(☎223124; www.castlemandawa.com; s/d from ₹4000/4500; ❄️@❖) Mandawa's large upmarket hotel in the town's converted fort attempts a slightly twee medieval atmosphere but is still a swish and generally comfortable choice. Some rooms are far better appointed than others (the best are the suites in the tower, with four-poster and swing beds), so check a few before you settle in. The gardens

WORTH A TRIP

TAL CHHAPAR WILDLIFE SANCTUARY

This little-known, small grassland **sanctuary** (Indian/foreigner ₹10/80, vehicle ₹200; ⊘) lies about 215km northwest of Jaipur and 95km southwest of Churu. It covers 70 sq km of ponds, sand, scrub and salt flats, and has healthy populations of blackbuck, elegant antelopes with long spiralling horns, as well as fast, graceful chinkaras (Indian gazelles), wolves and smaller mammals such as desert foxes. The sanctuary lies on the migration route of a number of bird species, most notably harriers, which descend here during September. Other wintering birds include various species of eagle (tawny, imperial, short-toed, steppe) and the demoiselle crane. Throughout the year there are populations of crested larks, ring and brown doves and skylarks.

It's best to visit the sanctuary with your own transport as a day trip from Shekhawati, Bikaner or Jaipur. There's a **forest resthouse** (☎01562-250938; r ₹300) near the sanctuary entrance at Chhapar offering basic double rooms.

and grounds boast restaurants, coffee shops, large pool and ayurvedic spa.

Mandawa Desert Resort HOTEL $$
(☎223151; in Jaipur 0141-2371194; www.mandawa hotels.com; rooms s/d ₹3500/4000, cottages s/d ₹5000/6000; ✿@☂) A top-end resort run by Castle Mandawa, this is laid out in the style of a Rajasthani village and is situated 1km south of town. The spacious rooms, in mud-walled huts decorated with twinkling mirrorwork, are a lot plusher than your average village home and have big bathrooms. It's in a very pretty spot but it all feels a bit contrived.

Bungli Restaurant INDIAN $$
(☎9413546937; Goenka Chowk; mains Rs70-250; ⊘6am-11pm) A popular outdoor travellers' eatery near the Bikaner bus stand, Bungli serves piping-hot tandoori and cold beer. The food is cooked fresh by a chef who hails from Hotel Castle Mandawa. Early risers can have an Indian breakfast and yoga class for a total of ₹375.

Monica Rooftop Restaurant INDIAN $$
(☎224178; Goenka Chowk; mains Rs90-250; ⊘7.30am-10.30pm) This delightful rooftop restaurant, in between the fort gate and main bazaar, serves tasty meals.

❶ Information

Gayatri Art Gallery (⊘8am-8pm) Provides internet for ₹60 per hour. Also changes cash and travellers cheques.

State Bank of Bikaner & Jaipur (⊘10am-4pm Mon-Fri, to 1pm Sat) In Binsidhar Newatia Haveli; changes cash only.

❶ Getting There & Away

There are buses to Nawalgarh (₹20, 45 minutes), Fatehpur (₹20, one hour), Bissau (₹18, 1½ hours) and Ramgarh (₹25, 1½ hours). Direct buses also run to Jaipur (₹90, four hours) – change at Fatehpur – and Bikaner (₹80, 3½ hours). A taxi between Mandawa and Fatehpur costs ₹400 (one way), or you can take a crammed share jeep for ₹15.

Lakshmangarh

☎01573 / POP 47,288

Off the tourist track, 20km south of Fatehpur, is this unusual town, laid out in an easy-to-explore grid pattern, with a main north–south-oriented bazaar dissected at intervals by three busy *chaupars* (town squares formed by the intersection of major roads).

The most imposing building here is the small fortress, which looms over the township to its west, built by Lakshman Singh, raja (king) of Sikar, in the early 19th century after the prosperous town was besieged by Kan Singh Saledhi.

◉ Sights

Fort HISTORIC BUILDING
About 50m north of the bus stand through the busy bazaar, a wide cobblestone path wends its way up to the eastern side of the fort. A sign warns that the fort is private property, but there's a good view from the top of the ramp before you get to the main entrance. From here you can see the layout of the double Char Chowk Haveli, below and to the northeast. Head for this point when you descend the ramp.

Char Chowk Haveli
HISTORIC BUILDING

Beneath the eaves on the northern external wall of this *haveli,* you'll find a picture of a bird standing on an elephant and with another elephant in its beak. The large paintings on the facade of the northern *haveli,* meanwhile, have mostly faded, and the paintings in the outer downstairs courtyard are covered by blue wash. The murals in the inner courtyard, however, are well preserved, and the walls and ceiling of a small upstairs room on the east side of the northern *haveli* are completely covered with paintings. It has some explicit erotic images, but it's ill-lit. No-one lives in the *haveli,* but the caretaker will open it for you and will bring out a torch to show you the erotic murals for some baksheesh.

In the same building, a room in the northwest corner retains floral swirls and motifs on the ceiling with scenes from the Krishna legends interspersed with inlaid mirrors. The black-and-white rectangular designs on the lower walls create a marbled effect. The front facade is disintegrating at the lower levels, with the plaster crumbling and the bricks exposed. The southern *haveli* is still inhabited.

Radhi Murlimanohar Temple
HINDU TEMPLE

About 50m east of Char Chowk Haveli is the large Radhi Murlimanohar Temple (1845), which retains a few paintings beneath the eaves and some sculptures of deities around the external walls.

Chetram Sanganeeria Haveli
HISTORIC BUILDING

If you take the road east from the Radhi Murlimanohar Temple, on the corner of the second laneway on the right is the Chetram Sanganeeria Haveli. The lower paintings on the west wall are badly damaged; the plaster has peeled away and concrete rendering has been applied. But you can still spot a woman on a swing suspended from a tree, a man dancing on a pole while balancing some knives, and folks enjoying a ride on a Ferris wheel.

Rathi Haveli
HISTORIC BUILDING

On the northeast corner of the clock tower square is the Rathi Family Haveli. On the west wall, a European woman in a smart red frock sews on a treadle machine. The European influence is much in evidence here, with painted roses and a Grecian column effect. On the south side of this *haveli* are ostentatious flourishes and the British Crown flanked by unicorns. On the east side are some blue-eyed British soldiers and a railway station.

On the west side of the *haveli* there's a busy set of chai stalls – a good place to sit down and admire these extraordinarily over-the-top paintings.

🛈 Getting There & Away

There are many buses to/from Sikar (₹19), Fatehpur (₹15) and Nawalgarh (₹19).

Jaisalmer, Jodhpur & Western Rajasthan

Best Places to Eat

» Indique (p264)
» Nirvana (p264)
» Desert Boy's Dhani (p286)
» Jaisal Italy (p286)

Best Places to Stay

» Rohet Garh (p269)
» Hotel Killa Bhawan (p285)
» Singhvi's Haveli (p261)
» Devi Bhawan (p263)
» Desert Moon (p283)
» Badal House (p292)

Why Go?

The west is a different Rajasthan, with the romance of desert cities and camel caravans. Most of the region is covered by the Thar Desert, which also extends into Punjab, Gujarat and Pakistan. The Thar is the world's most populous arid zone, mostly covered by scrub vegetation, with plentiful villages eking out a living from their animals and maintaining a richly colourful desert culture. Three atmospheric old cities form the focus of most travels here, each with a majestic fort at its heart. Proud Jodhpur is a halfway house between the relatively urbane cities of eastern Rajasthan and the state's wild west. Bikaner and above all Jaisalmer are romantically isolated desert towns and the main starting points for renowned desert safaris. These adventures need careful organising, but you won't quickly forget nights sleeping under the desert stars or your camel's rhythmic rambling progress across the landscape.

When to Go

The west consists largely of desert, so the best months to come are October to February, when the weather is at its most moderate for camel safaris and just about everything else. It even gets chilly at night in December and January, but that's easier to deal with than the searing heat of mid-April to mid-July, when daytime temperatures normally top 40°C. The monsoon brings a small drop in temperatures in late July and August. Jodhpur has a slightly less extreme climate than Jaisalmer and Bikaner.

History

In Hindu mythology, Rama, hero of the Ramayana, enraged at the sea god who policed the straits between India and Sri Lanka, resolved to fire a destructive arrow into the sea. In the nick of time the sea god appeased him. Rama switched his aim, firing his arrow into the northwest and creating the Thar Desert of western Rajasthan.

Legends aside, the region's early history is hazy. Aryan tribes from Afghanistan or Central Asia seem to have moved into the region from about 1500 BC, and in the 4th century BC the Mauryan empire spread across northern India from its capital at present-day Patna, in Bihar. Subsequent centuries saw a bit of pass the parcel until the Rathore Rajputs, who hailed from Kannauj, east of Agra, came out on top. The Rathores originally settled at Pali, southeast of present-day Jodhpur, shifting to Mandore in 1381. In 1459 Rao Jodha, the Rathore leader, moved the capital about 9km to the south and founded the city of Jodhpur. The Rathores' kingdom, Marwar, grew to be the largest in Rajputana and the third largest in India, after Kashmir and Hyderabad.

Jaisalmer, the second of the west's major kingdoms, was founded by the Bhati Rajputs in 1156, after their capital at nearby Lodhruva had proved indefensible. Jaisalmer enjoyed its heyday during the 16th to 18th centuries, when it was a stop on important international caravan routes.

The third major city and kingdom, Bikaner, was founded by one of the sons of Jodhpur's founder Rao Jodha, and like Jaisalmer it flourished as a caravan trade centre from the 16th to 18th centuries.

The desert kingdoms retained their autonomy for 1½ years after Independence in 1947, before their princes were finally persuaded to unite their territories with India. The forces stationed near the India–Pakistan border today underscore the area's high strategic importance.

Jodhpur

☏ 0291 / POP 846,400

Mighty Mehrangarh, the muscular fort that towers over the Blue City of Jodhpur, is a magnificent spectacle and an architectural masterpiece. Around Mehrangarh's feet, the old city, a jumble of Brahmin-blue cubes,

---

FESTIVALS IN WESTERN RAJASTHAN

Western Rajasthan's colourful festivals, often featuring camels, splash colour against the desert. For details of statewide and nationwide festivals, see p24.

» **Bikaner Camel Festival** (Dec/Jan; Bikaner, p292) Witness decorated camels and best-breed competitions, camels dancing to drum beats, and camel tugs-of-war, processions and races.

» **Jaisalmer Desert Festival** (Jan/Feb; Jaisalmer, p275) Touristy festival with camel races, camel polo, folk music, snake charmers, turban-tying contests and the famous Mr Desert competition. Many events take place at the Sam sand dunes.

» **Nagaur Fair** (Jan/Feb; Nagaur, p270) A several-days-long cattle and camel fair – more about trading and more authentic than most. Plenty of song, dance, camel fashion and trinket traders.

» **Karni Mata Fair** (Mar/Apr & Sep/Oct; Deshnok, p302) Devotees throng to the Karni Mata Temple, where rats are worshipped as the reincarnations of local people. The spring fair is the bigger one.

» **Ramdevra Fair** (Aug/Sep; Ramdevra, p273) Ramdev Mandir is the focus of this festival, celebrated by Hindus and Muslims to commemorate Ramdev, a saint who helped the downtrodden. Female performers with small cymbals attached to their costumes dance the *terahtal* (a traditional dance) while balancing pitchers of water on their heads.

» **Marwar Festival** (Sep/Oct; Jodhpur, p253) Celebrates the rich cultural legacy of Marwar (Jodhpur), with events in evocative settings including Mehrangarh fortress.

» **Kapil Muni Mela** (Oct/Nov; Kolayat, p301) A kind of mini-Pushkar, with fewer camels but lots of sadhus and very few tourists. As in Pushkar, devotees take a dip in the holy lake at the full moon.

Western Rajasthan Highlights

1 Listen to the Blue City's secrets from the soaring ramparts of Jodhpur's magnificent fortress, **Mehrangarh** (p257)

2 Discover the secrets of ancient **Jaisalmer Fort** (p278) – the world's biggest sandcastle

3 Climb aboard for a **camel safari** from Jaisalmer (p291), Khuri (p292) or Bikaner (p297) – the best way to experience the Rajasthan desert, and you get to sleep under the stars

4 Enjoy a great Indian meal on one of Jodhpur's scenic **rooftop restaurants** (p264), gazing up at mighty Mehrangarh

5 Marvel at the overworked stone carving of the lavish **havelis of Jaisalmer** (p280) – delicate yet powerful symbols of wealth

6 Spot a white rat at Deshnok's **Karni Mata Temple** (see p302), where holy rodents run riot, gnawing sweets, slurping milk and scampering over your feet

7 Admire the surprising splendour of Bikaner's **Junagarh** (p293), one of the few Rajasthan forts not built on a hill

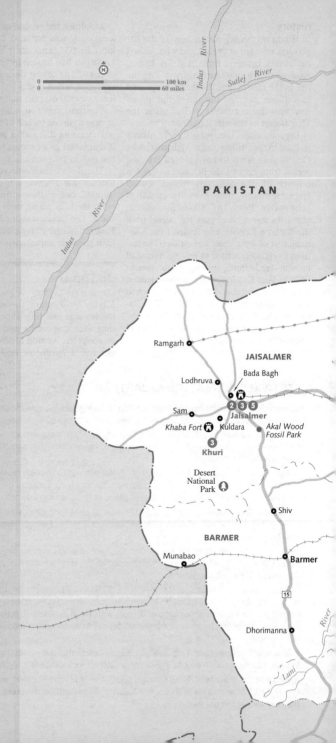

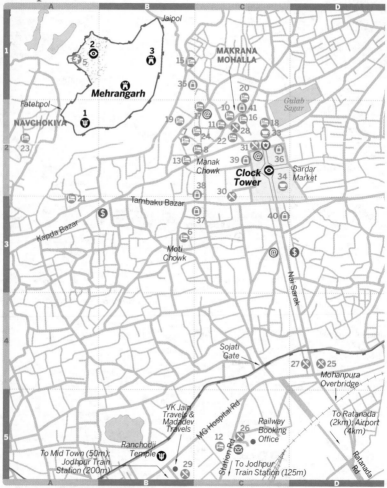

stretches out to the 10km-long, 16th-century city wall. The 'Blue City' really is blue! Inside is a tangle of winding, glittering, medieval streets, which never seem to lead where you expect them to, scented by incense, roses and sewers, with shops and bazaars selling everything from trumpets and temple decorations to snuff and saris. Traditionally, blue signified the home of a Brahmin, but non-Brahmins have got in on the act, too. As well as glowing with a mysterious light, the blue tint is thought to repel insects.

Modern Jodhpur stretches well beyond the city walls, but it's the immediacy and

buzz of the old Blue City and the larger-than-life fort that capture travellers' imaginations. The old city has something like 100 guesthouses, most of which scramble for your custom within half a kilometre of Sardar Market and its landmark clock tower. This crowded, hectic zone is also Jodhpur's main tourist shopping and eating area, and it often seems you can't speak to anyone without them trying to sell you something. Areas of the old city further west, such as Navchokiya, are just as atmospheric, with far less hustling.

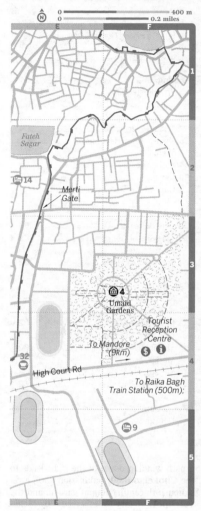

Fateh
Sagar

📖14

Merti
Gate

🏛4
Umaid
Gardens

Tourist
Reception
Centre

To Mandore
(9km)

32

High Court Rd

To Raika Bagh
Train Station (500m);

📷9

pered to such a degree that they managed to oust the Pratiharas of Mandore, 9km north of present-day Jodhpur.

By 1459 it became evident that more secure headquarters were required. The rocky ridge 9km south of Mandore was an obvious choice for the new city of Jodhpur. The Rathores greatly enhanced the natural fortifications afforded by its steep flanks by erecting a fortress of staggering proportions, Mehrangarh.

Founded by Rao Jodha, from whom it takes its name, Jodhpur lay on the vital trade route between Delhi and Gujarat. The Rathore kingdom grew on the profits of opium, sandalwood, dates and copper, and controlled a large area that became cheerily known as Marwar (the Land of Death) due to its harsh topography and climate. It stretched as far west as what's now the India–Pakistan border area, and bordered with Mewar (Udaipur) in the south, Jaisalmer in the northwest, Bikaner in the north and Jaipur and Ajmer in the east.

A war for independence from the Mughals and struggles for succession dominated the 17th and 18th centuries. However, the 19th century saw the commencement of competent rule by Sir Pratap Singh (of jodhpurs riding pants fame), followed by Maharaja Umaid Singh. Thus Jodhpur – Rajasthan's largest kingdom – was reasonably stable when it came to Independence in 1947.

⊙ Sights & Activities

TOP CHOICE Mehrangarh FORT

(www.mehrangarh.org; museum admission adult/senior & student incl camera & audio guide ₹300/250, video ₹200; ⊙9am-5.30pm) Rising perpendicular and impregnable from a rocky hill that itself stands 120m above Jodhpur's skyline, Mehrangarh is one of the most magnificent forts in India. The battlements are 6m to 36m high and as the building materials were chiselled from the rock on which the fort stands, the structure merges with its base. Still run by the Jodhpur royal family, Mehrangarh is chock-full of history and legend. One story tells that to secure a propitious future for the fort, its founder Rao Jodha had a man named Rajiya Bambi buried alive in its foundations; in exchange the Rathores have looked after Rajiya's family ever since.

Mehrangarh's main entrance, at the northeast gate, Jaipol, is a 300m walk up from Hill View Guest House in the old city.

South of the old city, the newer parts of Jodhpur are less hectic, with broader, much less crowded streets. The city as a whole is cleaner than it used to be since shops were banned from giving out plastic bags in 2010.

History

Driven from their homeland of Kannauj by Afghans serving Mohammed of Ghori, the Rathores fled west to the region around Pali, 70km southeast of Jodhpur. An expedient marriage between the Rathore Siahaji and the sister of a local prince enabled the Rathores to take root in the region. They pros-

Alternatively you can take a winding 5km autorickshaw ride (around ₹80). Cast off your audio-tour prejudices, as the one included with the museum ticket here (in multiple languages and requiring a deposit of passport, credit/debit card or ₹2000) covers the whole fort and is a terrific, entertaining mix of history, information and royal reminiscences.

The **Jaipol** was built by Maharaja Man Singh in 1808 following his defeat of invading forces from Jaipur. Inside here are the ticket office (tickets are needed only for the museum), and a lift (₹20) that whisks disabled or weary travellers up to the museum near the top of the fort.

Past the ticket office, the 16th-century **Dodh Kangra Pol** was an external gate before the Jaipol was built, and still bears the scars of 1808 cannonball hits. Through here,

a path winding down to the right leads to the **Chokelao Bagh** (admission ₹30), a restored 18th-century Rajput garden, and the **Fatehpol** (Victory Gate), erected by Maharaja Ajit Singh to commemorate his defeat of the Mughals. The main route heads up to the left, through the 16th-century **Imritiapol** and then the **Loha Pol**, the fort's original entrance, with iron spikes to deter enemy elephants. Just inside the gate are two sets of small handprints, the *sati* (self-immolation) marks of royal widows who threw themselves on their maharajas' funeral pyres – the last to do so were widows of Maharaja Man Singh in 1843.

Past Loha Pol you'll find a cafe and the Surajpol gate, which gives access to the museum. Once you've visited the museum, continue up to the panoramic **ramparts**, which are lined with impressive antique artillery. The sounds of the city below come floating up as from a separate world. At the southwest end, the **Chamunda Devi Temple**, dedicated to the goddess Durga in her wrathful aspect, is normally a lovely, peaceful place to sit in the window alcoves overlooking the city below. However, thousands of devotees mass at the temple for Navratri (Festival of Nine Nights) in October, and in 2008 over 240 people were killed in a stampede here.

Museum

This beautiful network of stone-latticed courtyards and halls, formerly the fort's palace, is a superb example of Rajput architecture, so finely carved that it often looks more like sandalwood than sandstone. Its splendid collection of royal trappings shows off the wealth and power of Marwar's rulers.

The galleries around **Shringar Chowk** (Anointment Courtyard) display India's best collection of elephant howdahs and Jodhpur's royal palanquin collection. Some of the howdahs feature exquisite repoussé (raised relief) silverwork. Some of the palanquins are covered for women in purdah (seclusion). Apparently one of these sent the British media into a frenzy during a Jodhpur royal trip to the UK – one photographer managed to catch a picture of the hidden queen's ankle, but there was such an outcry that all the newspapers in which it was printed had to be recalled. The palanquin presented to Jaswant Singh I in 1657 by Emperor Shah Jahan is exquisitely worked in silver and gold, and has a natty little parasol to beat the heat.

One of the two galleries off **Daulat Khana Chowk** displays textiles, paintings, manuscripts, headgear and the curved sword of the Mughal emperor Akbar, plus some wonderful ephemera, such as ladies' ivory-inlaid dumb-bells. The other gallery is the armoury, whose daggers, armour, rifles, spears, swords and axes are all works of art.

Upstairs are a **gallery of miniature paintings** from the sophisticated Marwar school and the beautiful 18th-century **Phul Mahal** (Flower Palace), which was used for music, poetry and dance performances. The Phul Mahal has a ceiling of gold filigree and mirrors, and 19th-century wall paintings depicting the 36 moods of classical ragas as well as royal portraits. The artist took 10 years to create the paintings using a curious concoction of gold leaf, glue and cow's urine.

Takhat Vilas was the bedchamber of Maharaja Takhat Singh (r 1843–73), who had just 30 maharanis and numerous concubines. Its beautiful ceiling is covered with Christmas baubles. You then enter the extensive zenana (women's quarters), whose lovely latticed windows (from which the women could watch the goings-on in the courtyards) are said to feature over 250 different designs. Here you'll find the **Cradle Gallery**, exhibiting the elaborate cradles of infant princes, and the 17th-century **Moti Mahal** (Pearl Palace), which was the palace's main durbar hall for official meetings and receptions, with gorgeously colourful stained glass (women could listen in from secret balconies above the alcoves). The lovely courtyard outside, Moti Mahal Chowk, is also home to the office of SL Sharma, the fort's long-time resident **palm reader** (normal/detailed reading ₹250/350). Remove nail polish if you intend to get a reading, as nails are used to ascertain your state of health.

Flying Fox

(www.flyingfox.asia; 1/6 zips ₹330/1330; ⊙9am-4pm) This two-hour circuit of six zip lines flies back and forth over walls, bastions and lakes on the north side of Mehrangarh. A brief training session is given before you start and safety standards are good: 'awesome' is the verdict of most who dare. Flying Fox has a desk near the main ticket office and its starting point is in the Chokelao Bagh.

Jaswant Thada　　　　　　HISTORIC BUILDING
(Indian/foreigner ₹15/30, camera/video ₹25/50; ⊙9am-5pm) This milky-white marble memorial to Maharaja Jaswant Singh II, sitting above a small lake 1km northeast of Mehrangarh, is an array of whimsical domes. It's a welcome, peaceful spot after the hubbub of the city, and the views across to the fort and over the city are superb. Built in 1899, the cenotaph has some beautiful *jalis* (carved marble lattice screens) and is hung with portraits of Rathore rulers going back to the 13th century. Look out for the memorial to a peacock that flew into a funeral pyre.

Clock Tower & Markets　　　　LANDMARK
The century-old clock tower is an old city landmark surrounded by the vibrant sounds, sights and smells of Sardar Market, which is marked by triple gateways at its north and south ends. The narrow, winding lanes of the old city spread out in all directions from here. Westward, you plunge into the

JODHPUR'S JODHPURS

A fashion staple for self-respecting horsey people all around the world, jodhpurs are riding breeches – usually of a pale cream colour – that are loose above the knee and tapered from knee to ankle. It's said that Sir Pratap Singh, a legendary Jodhpur statesman, soldier and horseman, originally designed the breeches for the Jodhpur Lancers. When he led the Jodhpur polo team on a tour to England in 1897, the design caught on in London and then spread around the world.

old city's commercial heart, with crowded alleys and bazaars selling vegetables, spices, sweets, silver and handicrafts.

Sardar Government Museum   MUSEUM
(Indian/foreigner ₹5/50; ☺9.45am-5.15pm Tue-Sun) In the Umaid Gardens park, the Sardar Government Museum feels charmingly frozen somewhere in the 19th century. The ill-labelled exhibits in dusty cabinets include weapons and 6th- to 10th-century sculptures, as well as the obligatory moth-eaten stuffed animals.

There's also a desultory **zoo** (Indian/foreigner ₹8/50; ☺8am-noon & 3-6pm Wed-Mon) in the park.

Umaid Bhawan Palace   PALACE
Take a rickshaw or taxi to this hill-top palace 3km southeast of the old city, sometimes called the Chittar Palace because local Chittar sandstone was used to build it. Building began in 1929 and the 365-room edifice was designed by the British architect Henry Lanchester for Maharaja Umaid Singh. It took over 3000 workers 15 years to complete, at a cost of around ₹11 million. The building is mortarless, and incorporates 100 wagon loads of Makrana marble and Burmese teak in the interior. The impressive central dome sits 30m above the sky-blue inner dome. It was built surprisingly close to Independence, after which the maharajas and their grand extravagances became a thing of the past. Apparently the construction of this over-the-top palace began as a royal job-creation programme during a time of severe drought.

Umaid Singh died in 1947, four years after the palace was completed; the current royal incumbent, Gaj Singh II (known as Bapji), still

lives in part of the building. Most of the rest has been turned into a suitably grand hotel.

Most interesting in the **museum** (Indian/foreigner ₹15/50; ☺9am-5pm) are the photos showing the elegant art deco design of the palace interior. The museum also has beautifully crafted weapons; an array of stuffed leopards; an enormous banner presented by Queen Victoria to Maharaja Jaswant Singh II in 1877; and a fantastic clock collection, including specimens shaped like windmills and lighthouses. Attendants will ensure that you don't stray into the hotel, but you can peer at the soaring domed central hall. Alternatively, you can visit the hotel to eat at one of its restaurants. Look out for some of the maharaja's highly polished classic cars displayed on the lawn in front of the museum.

☞ Tours

Most guesthouses and hotels can lay on city tours by autorickshaw (half-day/day around ₹350/700) or taxi (around ₹500/1000). If you prefer to organise your own taxi, there's a stand outside the main train station.

Further afield, tours to Bishnoi and craft-making villages south of Jodhpur are popular (see p268). Another option is the town of Osian to the north.

★ Festivals & Events

In September or October Jodhpur hosts the colourful **Marwar Festival**, which includes polo and a camel tattoo. It coincides with the **Rajasthan International Folk Festival** (www.jodhpurfolkfestival.org), five days of traditional and innovative music by Indian and international artists.

🛏 Sleeping

Jodhpur has a lot more budget choices than midrange options. However, the quality of accommodation in all categories is, overall, good. Budget accommodation clusters in the old city, mostly concentrated within half a kilometre of the clock tower. Most guesthouses have a range of rooms at different prices, often with some AC rooms available. Many midrange and top-end options are found outside the old city, especially in the Ratanada area (about 2km south), and on Circuit House Rd (1km southeast).

The Tourist Reception Centre has an up-to-date list of paying guesthouses in and around the city – some 60 participants with prices ranging from ₹100 to ₹1200 per night. This is an excellent way to get under the skin of this city, which, with pollution, noise and activity, can seem as formidable to new visitors as Mehrangarh was to invading armies.

OLD CITY

TOP CHOICE **Singhvi's Haveli** GUESTHOUSE $
(☏2624293; www.singhvihaveli.com; Ramdevji-ka-Chowk, Navchokiya; r ₹300-1800; ❄@🛜)
This red-sandstone, family-run, 500-odd-year-old *haveli* is an understated gem. It's in Navchokiya, one of the most atmospheric yet least touristy parts of the old city, beneath the western end of Mehrangarh (which you can enter by the Fatehpol gate). Run by a friendly Jain family, Singhvi's has 13 individual rooms, ranging from the simple to the magnificent Maharani Suite with 10 windows and a fort view. The relaxing and romantic vegetarian restaurant is decorated with sari curtains and floor cushions.

Krishna Prakash Heritage Haveli
HERITAGE HOTEL $$
(☏2633448; www.kpheritage.com; Nayabas, Killikhana; s/d standard ₹850/1050, deluxe incl breakfast ₹1550/1750, ste incl breakfast ₹2450-3500; ❄🛁)
This multilevel heritage hotel right under the fort walls is a good-value and peaceful choice. It has prettily painted furniture and murals, and rooms are well proportioned; the deluxe ones are a bit more spruced up, generally bigger, and set on the upper floors, so airier. There's an undercover swimming pool and a relaxing terrace restaurant. Free bus and train station pickups are offered.

Pal Haveli HERITAGE HOTEL $$
(☏3293328; www.palhaveli.com; Gulab Sagar; r incl breakfast ₹2500-4000; ❄@) This stunning *haveli*, the best and most attractive in the old city, was built by the Thakur of Pal in 1847. There are 21 charming, spacious rooms, mostly large and elaborately decorated in traditional heritage style, surrounding a cool central courtyard. The family still live here and can show you their small museum. Three restaurants serve excellent food and the rooftop Indique boasts unbeatable views.

Raas BOUTIQUE HOTEL $$$
(☏2636455; www.raasjodhpur.com; Tunvarji-ka-Jhalra, Makrana Mohalla; incl breakfast r ₹15,000-18,000, ste ₹26,000; ❄🛜🛁) Developed from a 19th-century city mansion, Jodhpur's first contemporary-style boutique hotel is a splendid retreat of clean, uncluttered style, hidden behind a big castle-like gateway. If you fancy a change from the heritage aesthetic that prevails in Rajasthan's top-end

i ARRIVING IN JODHPUR

If a rickshaw driver is clamouring to take you to a particular guesthouse or hotel, it's probably because he is aiming to receive a commission from them. There's a growing anti-commission movement among hoteliers here, but some still pay your rickshaw or taxi driver an absurd 50% of what you pay for your room. Don't believe drivers, or strangers on the street, who tell you the place you want has closed, is full, is under repair, is far from the centre etc.

Many lodgings can organise a pick-up from the train station or bus stops, even at night, if you call ahead. Otherwise, for most places in the old city, you can avoid nonsense by getting dropped at the clock tower and walking from there. Some drivers might ask: 'Which clock tower?' to confuse you: the answer is Sardar Market.

hotels, Raas' clean, uncluttered style and subtle lighting are just the ticket. The red-stone-and-terrazzo rooms are not massive, but they're pleasing and come with plenty of luxury touches. Most have balconies with great Mehrangarh views – also enjoyed from the lovely pool in the neat garden-courtyard.

Haveli Inn Pal HERITAGE HOTEL $$
(☏2612519; www.haveliinnpal.com; Gulab Sagar; r incl breakfast ₹2050-2550; ❄@) The smaller, 12-room sibling of Pal Haveli. It's accessed through the same grand entrance, but is located around to the right in one wing of the grand *haveli*. It's a simpler heritage experience, with comfortable rooms and lake or fort views from the more expensive ones. It also has its own good rooftop restaurant, a mere chapati toss from Indique at Pal Haveli. Free pickups from Jodhpur transport terminals are offered, and discounts are often available for single occupancy.

Hill View Guest House GUESTHOUSE $
(☏2441763; r ₹150-400) Perched just below the fort walls, this is run by a friendly, enthusiastic, no-hassle, Muslim family, who'll make you feel right at home. Rooms are basic, clean and simple, all with bathrooms, and the terrace has a great view over the city. Good, home-cooked veg and non-veg food is on offer.

Blue House GUESTHOUSE $

(☎2621396; bluehouse36@hotmail.com; Dabgaron-ki-Gali, Moti Chowk; r ₹250-1800; ❄@) Certainly blue, this rambling old house run by a friendly Jain family is a reliable bet. It has a big range of individually decorated rooms and some very steep stairs. The two top-floor rooms (₹900 each) are good value. Free pick-ups available.

Shahi Guest House GUESTHOUSE $$

(☎2623802; www.shahiguesthouse.net; Gandhi St, City Police; r ₹900-2200; ❄❧) Shahi is an interesting guesthouse developed from a 350-year-old zenana (women's quarters). There's lots of cool stone, and narrow walkways surrounding a petite courtyard. The six rooms are individual and cosy, and the family is charming. There is a delightful rooftop restaurant with views, and they offer free train and bus station pickups.

Hotel Haveli HOTEL $$

(☎2614615; www.hotelhaveli.net; Makrana Mohalla; r ₹500-2200; ❄@❧) This 250-year-old building inside the walled city is a popular, efficient and friendly place. Rooms vary greatly and are individually decorated with colour themes and paintings; many have semibalconies and fort views. The rooftop vegetarian restaurant, Jharokha, has excellent views and nightly entertainment.

Yogi's Guest House GUESTHOUSE $

(☎2643436; www.yogiguesthouse.com; Naya Bass, Manak Chowk; r ₹350-1200; ❄@) Yogi's Guest House is a classic travellers' hangout that's moving upmarket. There are many refurbished rooms, but still plenty of budget options available. Set in a 500-year-old haveli near the base of the fort walls, it's a friendly place painted blue and other bright colours. The rooms are smart and clean; some have air-conditioning and/or views. There's also a lovely rooftop restaurant. The guesthouse offers free train station, bus station and airport pickups. It's signposted from the surrounding lanes.

Pushp Paying Guest House GUESTHOUSE $

(☎2648494; sanukash2003@yahoo.co.in; Pipli-ki-Gali, Naya Bass, Manak Chowk; r ₹200-600; ❄@❧) A small guesthouse with five clean, colourful rooms with windows. There's an up-close view of Mehrangarh from its rooftop restaurant, where owner Nikhil, an ex-five-star-hotel cook, rustles up great vegetarian fare (dishes ₹30 to ₹80).

Heritage Kuchaman Haveli HERITAGE HOTEL $$

(☎2547787; www.kuchamanhaveli.com; inside Merti Gate; r ₹1550-2950, ste ₹3750; ❄@❧≋) This recently renovated 19th-century haveli is a rare midrange option in the old city. It's a well-proportioned building, with a pool and multicuisine rooftop restaurant, but the rooms are rather dull.

Bristow's Haveli HOMESTAY $$

(☎2612736; www.bristowsindia.com; 136 Sutharkha-na-ki-Gali; d ste incl breakfast ₹3500) If you fancy immersing yourself in local culture or festivals for a few days, or learning crafts such as silversmithing, printing textiles or cooking with local artisans, consider Bristow's. Run by British orientalist Phil Porter, it organises fixed-date residential courses and can also set up **classes** (per day one/two people ₹1000/1200) for individual travellers. The house is a gorgeously peaceful retreat set around a walled garden just under Mehrangarh.

Shivam Paying Guest House GUESTHOUSE $

(☎2610688; shivamgh@hotmail.com; Makrana Mohalla; r ₹200-700, without bathroom ₹150; ❄) Near the clock tower, this quiet, hassle-free option run by a helpful family has cosy rooms, steep staircases and a lovely little rooftop restaurant.

Ganpati Guest House GUESTHOUSE $

(☎2631686; ganpatigh@yahoo.com.uk; Makrana Mohalla; r ₹300-1000; ❄) Clean, bright, airy rooms have modern bathrooms and there is a pleasant rooftop restaurant with an espresso machine.

Heaven Guest House GUESTHOUSE $

(☎2639283; nishajijain@yahoo.com; Manak Chowk Rd; r ₹300-850; ❄❧) A welcoming spot with good-sized, clean, colourful rooms, good-value food and an enthusiastic, helpful Jain hostess.

Discovery Paying Guest House GUESTHOUSE $

(☎2623156; discovery_pguesthouse@yahoo.com; Manak Chowk; r ₹150-600; ❄@❧) Discovery is run by a friendly family, has rooms with 24-hour hot showers and colourful wall paintings and serves good homemade food on the rooftop.

Gopal Guest House GUESTHOUSE $

(☎2615369; shakti_gopal@yahoo.com; Makrana Mohalla; r ₹150-300, without bathroom ₹100) Plain but spotless rooms, good-value home-cooked meals, nice terraces and a friendly family make this a good budget bet.

Laxmi Niwas Guest House GUESTHOUSE $
(📞9829237566; laxmi_niwas@hotmail.com; Makrana Mohalla; s ₹200-500, d ₹250-550; ❀@) Clean rooms with murals (fort views from some), and a decent rooftop restaurant.

Cosy Guest House
GUESTHOUSE $
(📞2612066; www.cosyguesthouse.com; Chuna-Ki-Choki, Navchokiya; r ₹150-900; ❀@🛈) A 500-year-old blue house with rooftop restaurant in quiet Navchokiya.

TRAIN STATION AREA
Govind Hotel HOTEL $
(📞2622758; www.govind-hotel.com; Station Rd; r ₹350-900; ❀@🛈) Well set up for travellers, with helpful management, an internet cafe, and a location convenient to the Jodhpur train station. All rooms are clean and tiled, with fairly smart bathrooms. There's a rooftop restaurant and coffee shop with excellent espresso and cakes.

SOUTH OF THE OLD CITY
TOP CHOICE **Devi Bhawan** HERITAGE HOTEL $$
(📞2511067; www.devibhawan.com; Ratanada; r ₹1800-2300; ❀@🛈❄) A charming hotel surrounding a verdant oasis shaded by majestic neem trees. As well as being the most peaceful place in Jodhpur it is also excellent value. There's a superb pool and a good **restaurant** (veg/non-veg thali ₹175/200; ☺7-10am & 8-10pm). Rooms are spacious, clean, comfortable and decorated with colourful textiles and traditional furnishings.

Ratan Vilas HERITAGE HOTEL $$
(📞2613011; www.ratanvilas.com; Loco Shed Rd, Ratanada; r ₹2000-2950; ❀@🛈) Built in 1920 by the great polo player Maharaj Ratan Singhji of Raoti, this beauty from a bygone era is the real deal. It's quintessential colonial India, with manicured lawns, spacious, spotless and solidly tasteful rooms, and exceptional staff who prepare wonderful meals. Free airport, train or bus station pickups available.

Durag Niwas Guest House GUESTHOUSE $
(📞2512385; www.durag-niwas.com; 1st Old Public Park Lane, Raika Bagh; rooftop per person ₹100, r ₹350-1000; ❀) A friendly place set away from the hustle of the old city. Good home-cooked veg and non-veg dishes are available, and there's a cushion-floored, sari-curtained area on the roof for relaxing. There are deals for long-termers: a double room with full board is ₹9000 per month. Management offers cultural tours and the opportunity to do volunteer work with the Sambhali Trust (see p357), helping to empower disadvantaged women and girls.

Newtons Manor GUESTHOUSE $$
(📞2670986; www.newtonsmanor.com; 86 Jawahar Colony, Ratanada; r ₹1395-1595; ❀🛈) Strictly Victorian, Newtons Manor is a family home with eight elegant guest rooms fussily decorated with lots of antique furniture. It offers excellent home cooking, though pride of place goes to the good-sized billiard table. There's an eternally ungrateful tiger in the sitting room.

Ajit Bhawan HERITAGE HOTEL $$$
(📞2513333; www.ajitbhawan.com; Circuit House Rd; r ₹10,000-17,000; ❀@❄) Ajit Bhawan is set back from dusty Circuit House Rd, 2km southeast of the centre, in splendid gardens. Behind the gracious main heritage building, built in 1927 for Maharajadhiraj Ajit Singh (younger brother of Maharaja Umaid Singh), the accommodation is a series of comfortable thatched stone cottages with traditional furnishings. There's a sensational swimming pool (nonguests ₹552) and a fine-dining restaurant with live Rajasthani folk music in the evenings.

Vivanta Hari Mahal HOTEL $$$
(📞2439700; www.vivantabytaj.com; 5 Residency Rd; r ₹14,500-16,500, ste ₹27,500; ❀@🛈❄) Run by the Taj Group, this is a luxurious modern hotel with traditional Rajasthani flourishes, 2km south of the train station. It has very spacious common areas including a bar, a big, inviting courtyard swimming pool, and some lovely artwork. The pricier rooms have a pool rather than garden view. Decent discounts are often available for online bookings.

Ranbanka Palace HERITAGE HOTEL $$$
(📞2512801; www.ranbankahotels.com; Circuit House Rd; r ₹5500-6500, ste ₹7500-8500; ❀@🛈❄) In a beautiful sandstone building right next to the higher-profile Ajit Bhawan, this was built for the same prince. It's cheaper than its Siamese sibling and less polished, with rooms that have soaring ceilings but lack charisma. Those set around the pool and garden are the best.

Umaid Bhawan Palace HERITAGE HOTEL $$$
(📞2510101; www.tajhotels.com; Umaid Bhawan Rd; r ₹26,500-43,500, ste ₹41,000-150,000; ❀@❄) This massive art deco palace, still the royal residence, is constructed from honey sandstone and white marble and is located 3km southeast of the old city. It's so immense it

feels rather like a parliament building or a university – that is, it's not all that cosy. The hotel section has luxurious rooms and numerous sporting facilities, including a magnificent indoor swimming pool.

Karni Bhawan HOTEL $$

(☑2512101; www.karnihotels.com; Palace Rd, Ratanada; s/d/ste ₹2200/2750/4000; ✳@🛜🐕) A remodelled colonial bungalow that feels eerily motel-like and is popular with groups. It is still good for families, thanks to the peaceful lawns, village-theme restaurant and large, though unshaded, pool. The rooms are heavy with traditional furnishings, but are clean and spacious.

✖ Eating

It's often convenient to eat in your guesthouse or hotel restaurant (which is usually on the roof, with a fort view), but there are also a number of places well worth going out to.

TOP CHOICE Indique INDIAN $$

(☑3293328; Pal Haveli, Gulab Sagar; mains ₹200-275) This candle-lit rooftop restaurant at the Pal Haveli hotel is the perfect place for a romantic dinner. Even murky Gulab Sagar glistens at night and the views to the fort, clock tower and Umaid Bhawan are superb. The food covers traditional tandoori, biryanis and North Indian curries, and you won't be disappointed by the old favourites – butter chicken and rogan josh. On your way up, drop into the delightful 18 Century Bar, with saddle stools and enough heritage paraphernalia to have you ordering pink gins.

Nirvana INDIAN $$

(1st fl, Tija Mata ka Mandir, Tambaku Bazar; mains ₹90-130, regular/special thali ₹160/250) Sharing premises with a Rama temple, 300m from the clock tower, Nirvana has both an indoor cafe covered in 150-year-old wall paintings of the Ramayana story, and a rooftop eating area with panoramic views. The Indian vegetarian food is among the most delicious you'll find in Rajasthan, and the thalis are wonderful. The special thali is truly enormous and easily enough for two. Continental as well as Indian breakfasts are served in the cafe.

Jharokha MULTICUISINE $

(Hotel Haveli, Makrana Mohalla; mains ₹60-90) The rooftop terraces of the Hotel Haveli host one of the best vegetarian restaurants in Jodhpur. As well as the excellent food and views there's nightly entertainment in the form of traditional music and dance. The dishes include Rajasthani specialities and traditional North Indian favourites, as well as pizza, pasta and pancakes for the homesick.

Jhankar Choti Haveli MULTICUISINE $

(Makrana Mohalla; mains ₹70-110; 🛜) Stone walls, big cane chairs, prettily painted woodwork and whirring fans set the scene at this semi-open-air travellers' favourite. It serves up good Indian vegetarian dishes plus pizzas, burgers and baked cheese dishes.

On the Rocks INDIAN $$

(☑5102701; Circuit House Rd; mains ₹115-325; ⊙12.30-3.30pm & 7.30-11pm) This leafy garden restaurant, 2km southeast of the old city, is very popular with locals and tour groups. It has tasty Indian cuisine, including lots of barbecue options and rich and creamy curries, plus a small playground and a cave-like bar (open 11am to 11pm) with a dance floor (for couples only).

Umaid Bhawan Palace MULTICUISINE $$$

(☑2510101; Umaid Bhawan Rd) This palace-hotel has a selection of elegant eateries. **Risala** (mains ₹650-2000; ⊙1-3pm & 7.30-11pm), celebrating the famous Jodhpur Lancers (Risala means cavalry), is a casual fine-dining experience with Indian and international dishes including New Zealand lamb and local Rajasthani specialities. Behind Risala on the colonnaded western verandah is the **Pillars**, a breezy coffee shop and informal à la carte eatery. There are sublime views across the lawn towards Mehrangarh.

Omelette Shop CAFE $

(Sardar Market; dishes ₹15-25) Located beside the northern gate of Sardar Market, this spot goes through 1000 to 1500 eggs a day. The egg man has been doing his thing here for over 30 years. Three tasty, spicy boiled eggs cost ₹15, and a two-egg masala and cheese omelette with four pieces of bread is ₹25.

Kalinga Restaurant MULTICUISINE $$

(off Station Rd; mains ₹105-270) This restaurant near Jodhpur train station is smart and popular. It's in a dimly lit setting and has AC, a well-stocked bar, and tasty veg and non-veg North Indian tandooris and curries. Try the *lal maans,* a mouthwatering Rajasthani mutton curry.

Mid Town INDIAN $

(off Station Rd; mains ₹70-120, thali ₹110-150; ⊙7am-11pm) This clean, AC restaurant does great veg food, including some Rajasthani specialities, and some particular to Jodhpur, such as *chakki-ka-sagh* (wheat dumpling cooked in rich gravy), *bajara-ki-roti pachkuta* (*bajara* wheat roti with local dry vegetables) and kabuli (vegetables with rice, milk, bread and fruit).

Janta Sweet Home SWEETS $
(sweets ₹10-15) Nai Sarak **(Nai Sarak)**; Station Rd (Station Rd) Both branches are hugely popular for their delectable Jodhpur specialities, such as the baklava-like *mawa ladoo,* the *malai* sandwich (a milk-and-almond sponge coated in silver leaf) and *mawa kachori* (similar to a large round samosa). They have a few tables but most people enjoy their treats standing and watching the street life go by.

Priya Restaurant INDIAN $
(181-182 Nai Sarak; mains ₹50-73) If you can handle the traffic fumes, this street-facing place has a certain cheerful clamour, and serves up reliable North and South Indian cuisine. The thalis (₹89) are good and there are sweets, too.

Drinking

While you're in Jodhpur, try a glass of *makhania* lassi, a thick and filling saffron-flavoured edition of that most refreshing of drinks.

Shri Mishrilal Hotel CAFE
(Sardar Market; lassi ₹20; ☺8am-10pm) Just inside the southern gate of Sardar Market, this place is nothing fancy but whips up the most superb creamy *makhania* lassis. These are the best in town, probably in all of Rajasthan, possibly in all of India.

Coffee drinkers will enjoy the precious beans and espresso machines at the deliciously air-conditioned **Cafe Sheesh Mahal** (Pal Haveli; ☺10am-9pm); the rooftop coffee shop at the **Govind Hotel** (Station Rd); and, for those who need their dose of double-shot espresso, a branch of **Cafe Coffee Day** (Ansal Plaza, High Court Rd; ☺10am-11pm).

For other forms of liquid refreshment, pull up an elephant-foot stool at the **Trophy Bar** (Umaid Bhawan Palace; Umaid Bhawan Rd; ☺11am-3pm & 6-11pm).

Shopping

Plenty of Rajasthani handicrafts are available, with shops selling textiles and other wares clustered around Sardar Market and along Nai Sarak (you'll need to bargain hard).

Jodhpur is famous for antiques, with a concentration of showrooms along Palace Rd, 2km southeast of the centre. These warehouse-sized shops are fascinating to wander around, but they're well known to Western antiques dealers, so you'll be hard-pressed to find any bargains. Also remember that the trade in antique architectural fixtures may be contributing to the desecration of India's cultural heritage (beautiful old *havelis* are often ripped apart for their doors and window frames). Restrictions apply to the export of Indian items over 100 years old; see the boxed text, p331. However, most of these showrooms deal in antique reproductions, and can make a piece of antique-style furniture and ship it home for you. The best bets for quality replica antiques are **Ajay Art Emporium** (Palace Rd), **Rani Handicrafts** (www.ranihandicrafts.com; Palace Rd), and **Rajasthan Arts & Crafts House** (www.rachindia.com; Palace Rd). These shops also have more portable and often less expensive items than furniture, such as textiles, carvings and silverware. Nearer the centre, the two facing shops of **Maharani Art Exporters** (Tambaku Bazar), one dealing in textiles and the other mainly in carvings, have some very attractive stuff, but you'll have to contend with a hard sell and tales about how Richard Gere bought 100 scarves here, etc.

MV Spices FOOD & DRINK
(www.mvspices.com) Sardar Market (209B Vegetable Market; ☺10am-9pm); Nai Sarak (107 Nai Sarak; ☺9.30am-10pm) The clock tower area has several tourist-oriented spice shops with tourist-oriented prices and copycat names. This one has genuine spices and good service – and they'll email you some recipes if you buy.

Sambhali Boutique
CLOTHING & ACCESSORIES
(Makrana Mohalla; ☺10.30am-8pm) This small but interesting shop sells goods made by women who have learned craft skills with the Sambhali Trust (see p357), which works to empower disadvantaged women and girls. Items include attractive *salwar* trousers, cute stuffed silk or cloth elephants, bracelets made from pottery beads, silk bags, and block-printed muslin curtains and scarves.

Kaman Art ART
(www.kamanart.blogspot.com; Old Fort Rd, Killikhana; ☺10am-8pm) This tiny contemporary art gallery features the work of about 40 top Rajasthani painters.

Krishna Art & Crafts HANDICRAFTS
(1st fl, Tija Mata ka Mandir, Tambaku Bazar) A good place to gain knowledge of traditional garments. It also has a large range of carpets and shawls.

Krishna Book Depot BOOKSTORE
(Sardar Market; ⊙10.30am-7.30pm) Stocks an impressive range of secondhand and new books.

ℹ Information

There are ATMs all over the city, including State Bank ATMs at Jodhpur train station, on Nai Sarak, next to the Tourist Reception Centre (High Court Rd) and near Shahi Guest House. There's also an ICICI Bank ATM on Nai Sarak.

Gucci's (Killikhana; internet per hr ₹30) Cold drinks and international phone calls too.

Main post office (Station Rd; ⊙9am-4pm Mon-Fri, 9am-3pm Sat, stamp sales only 10am-3pm Sun)

Net Hut (Makrana Mohalla; internet per hr ₹30; ⊙9.30am-11pm)

Om Forex (Sardar Market; internet per hr ₹30; ⊙9am-10pm) Also exchanges currency and travellers cheques.

Police (Sardar Market; ⊙24hr) Small police post inside the market's north gate.

State Bank of India (off High Court Rd; ⊙10am-4pm Mon-Fri, 10am-1pm Sat) Changes currencies and travellers cheques; east of Umaid Gardens.

Thomas Cook (Shop 1, Mahaveer Complex, Circuit House Rd; ⊙9.30am-6pm Mon-Sat) Changes cash and travellers cheques; 2km southeast of the centre.

Tourist Reception Centre (☑2545083; High Court Rd; ⊙9am-6pm Mon-Fri) Offers a free map and willingly answers questions.

ℹ Getting There & Away

Air

Jet Airways (☑5102222; www.jetairways.com; Residency Rd) and **Indian Airlines** (☑2510758; www.indian-airlines.nic.in; Circuit House Rd) both fly daily to Delhi and Mumbai, with Indian Airlines' Mumbai flights stopping at Udaipur on the way.

Bus

Destinations served from the Rajasthan State Road Transport Corporation (RSRTC) **Central Bus Stand** (Raika Bagh) include Ajmer (non-AC/AC ₹133/217, 4½ hours, half-hourly), Bikaner (₹145, 5½ hours, hourly), Delhi (₹379, 13 hours, four daily), Jaipur (express/deluxe/AC ₹197/239/346, seven hours, half-hourly), Jaisalmer (₹155, 5½ hours, 11 daily), Pushkar (₹125, five hours, five daily), Mt Abu (₹172, 5½ hours, three daily) and Udaipur (₹157, six to eight hours, 10 daily). Comfortable Volvo AC buses head off to Ajmer (₹300) and Jaipur (₹500) at 1am, and to Jaipur and Delhi (₹1100) at 4pm. The Central Bus Stand is 500m east of Umaid Gardens.

Numerous private bus companies, including Mahadev Travels, Jain Travels and VK Jain Travels, have offices on the street leading from Jodhpur train station to the Ranchodji Temple. They serve destinations such as Jaisalmer (₹150), Udaipur (₹160), Bikaner (₹140), Jaipur (₹180), Ajmer (₹120), Mt Abu (₹200) and Ahmedabad (₹260). Hotels and guesthouses will get you tickets for about ₹30 commission. Private buses leave from various locations around 2km southwest of Jodhpur train station, including Bombay Motors Circle, Kalpatru Cinema and Residency Rd – about ₹60 by autorickshaw from the clock tower.

Taxi

You can organise taxis for inter-city trips, or longer, through most accommodation places, or deal direct with drivers. There's a taxi stand outside Jodhpur train station. A reasonable price is ₹6 per kilometre (for a non-AC car), with a minimum of 250km per day. The driver will charge at least ₹100 for overnight stops and will charge for his return journey.

Train

The computerised **booking office** (Station Rd; ⊙8am-8pm Mon-Sat, 8am-1.45pm Sun) is 300m northeast of Jodhpur station. There's a tourist quota (Window 786).

Most trains from the east stop at the Raika Bagh station before heading on to the main station, which is handy if you're heading for a hotel on the eastern side of town.

To Jaisalmer, the *Delhi-Jaisalmer Express* (14059) departs at 6.10am, arriving in Jaisalmer (2nd class/sleeper/3AC/2AC/1AC ₹100/165/419/566/944) at 11.45am. The *Jodhpur-Jaisalmer Express* (14810) departs every night at 11pm, arriving at 5am.

To Delhi, the *Mandore Express* (12462) leaves Jodhpur at 7.30pm, reaching Jaipur (sleeper/3AC/2AC/1AC ₹188/458/608/1015) at 12.40am, and Delhi (₹282/723/975/1627) at 6.25am. The *Intercity Express* (12466) departs at 5.55am, reaching Jaipur (2nd class/sleeper/AC chair/3AC ₹110/188/369/458) at 10.45am, and Sawai Madhopur (₹133/227/453/567) at 1.15pm. There are several daily trains to Bikaner, including the *Ranakpur Express* (14708) departing at 10.45am and arriving in Bikaner (sleeper/3AC/2AC ₹156/395/531) at 4.40pm.

For Karachi (Pakistan), the *Thar Express* (14889), alias the *Jodhpur–Munabao Link Express*, leaves Bhagat Ki Kothi station, 4km south of the main station, at 1am on Saturday only, reaching Munabao on the India–Pakistan border at 7am. There you undergo lengthy border procedures before continuing to Karachi (assuming you have a Pakistan visa) in a Pakistani train, arriving about 2am on Sunday. Accommodation is 2nd-class and sleeper only, with a total sleeper fare of around ₹400 from Jodhpur to Karachi. In the other direction the Pakistani train leaves Karachi about 11pm on Friday, and Indian train 14890 leaves Munabao at 7pm on Saturday, reaching Jodhpur at 11.50pm. Schedules can be erratic, so check in Jodhpur for departure times and stations.

🛈 Getting Around

To/From the Airport

The airport is 5km south of the city centre, about ₹200/100 by taxi/autorickshaw.

Autorickshaw

Autorickshaws between the clock tower area and the train stations or Central Bus Stand should be about ₹35. Some drivers of course ask for absurd fares and even claim there is such a thing as a 'foreigner price' (complete garbage).

Around Jodhpur

The mainly arid countryside around Jodhpur is dotted with surprising lakes, isolated forts and palaces and intriguing villages. It's home to a clutch of fine heritage hotels where you can enjoy the slower pace of rural life.

MANDORE

Situated 7km north of the centre of Jodhpur, Mandore was the capital of Marwar prior to the founding of Jodhpur. It may have been founded as early as the 4th century, and passed to the Rathore Rajputs in 1381. Only a few traces of the ancient seat of power remain, but the lush **Mandore Gardens** (⊙9am-5.30pm), with their monuments and museum, make an appealing and relaxing excursion from Jodhpur (it's thronged with local tourists at weekends).

The gardens, complete with rock terraces and home to playful grey langurs, contain a variety of dark-red cenotaphs of Jodhpur's rulers. These include the soaring but unkempt **Chhatri of Maharaja Dhiraj Ajit Singh** (1793), which combines Buddhist and Jain elements in its architecture. It's an enormous edifice with a high *sikhara* (spire), a pillared and domed forechamber, and fine sculpture including small carved elephants and lions. The memorial also marks the spot where 64 queens and concubines committed *sati* on Ajit Singh's death in 1724.

Opposite is the 1720 **Chhatri of Maharaja Dhiraj Jaswant Singh I**, with a large pa-

vilion and a vast dome on an octagonal base. It achieves a remarkable symmetry, with a gallery supported by huge pillars. The remaining cenotaphs date to the 17th century.

At the top end of the gardens is the small **government museum** (Indian/foreigner ₹5/50, student ₹2/25; ⊙9.45am-5.15pm Tue-Sun), which is housed in the Abhay Singh Palace and shows relics of Mandore, including sculpture and inscriptions. A path winds 350m up from beside the museum entrance to quite extensive remains of Mandore's **fort** on the hill above, whose origins go back to the 6th century AD or possibly earlier – long before the Rathores. It's now inhabited mostly by langurs, dogs and cows. To the left of the museum is a **Ganesh temple** with its idols covered in bright coloured foil, and to the left of that is the 18th-century **Hall of Heroes & Divinities**, an array of nine Marwar heroes and six groups of deities, carved from the rock wall, coated with fine plaster and luridly painted.

🍽 Sleeping & Eating

Mandore Guest House GUESTHOUSE $$ (☎0291-2545210, 9983330865; www.mandore.com; s ₹1150-1250, d ₹1350-1550; ❄@) Fifteen delightful mud-walled cottages are set in a leafy garden, 300m along a small street opposite the gardens entrance. You'll find good home-cooked food here, and the guesthouse is connected with a local NGO working on education, health and environmental projects in Jodhpur district villages. For information on their volunteer programmes see p358.

🛈 Getting There & Away

Buses to Mandore (₹8) run about every five minutes from Jodhpur. You can catch them at a stop just east of the Tourist Reception Centre on High Court Rd.

You could get a rickshaw to take you there for around ₹50, or a taxi for ₹100.

BALSAMAND LAKE

Picturesque Balsamand Lake, 1.5km southwest of Mandore, is the oldest artificial lake in Rajasthan (it was built in 1159) and makes a refreshing escape from the city. On its banks the **Bal Samand Lake Palace & Garden Retreat** (☎0291-2572321; www.jodhana heritage.com; s/d ₹6200/7000, ste incl breakfast ₹17,000; ❄@❄), owned by the Jodhpur royal family, offers comfort in a lush and serene setting. The suites, in full traditional Jodhpur style and with large Jacuzzi baths, are in the main building – a deep-red sandstone palace built in the 17th century. The 'Garden Retreat' rooms sit in the former stables, among orchards and gardens, and are very comfortable, with exposed stone walls and private terraces. The hotel also features a spa, croquet lawn and nine-hole obstacle golf course.

SOUTHERN VILLAGES

A number of Bishnoi and other traditional villages are strung along and off the Pali road southeast of Jodhpur. Most hotels and guesthouses in Jodhpur offer tours to these villages. It's a well-worn trail and a lot depends on how good your guide is, but the tours do bring you into contact with a rural side of Rajasthan that's quite different from the cities where many travellers spend most of their time. Do remember that you are visiting private communities, and make sure you ask before taking photographs. A typical four-hour, 90km tour to the Bishnoi villages of Khejadali and Guda (east of the main road) and the non-Bishnoi craft-making villages of Salawas (west of the road) and Kakani (on the road) costs ₹500 or ₹600 per person (minimum two people). A recommended Jodhpur-based operator is **Bishnoi Village Safari** (☑9829126398; www.bishnoivillagesafari.com), run by Deepak Dhanraj.

Many villagers live in handmade thatched huts, in the traditions of their ancestors. Tours often include a meal cooked over the fire in one of the villages. Visitors are sometimes invited to share *amal*, an opium preparation which is traditionally offered to guests.

Many visitors are surprised by the density, and fearlessness, of wildlife such as blackbuck, bluebulls (nilgai), chinkara gazelles and desert fox around the Bishnoi villages. The relationship between the Bishnoi and the animals has been nurtured for hundreds of years. The 1730 sacrifice of 363 villagers to protect the khejri trees is commemorated in September at **Khejadali** village, where there is a memorial to the victims fronted by a small grove of khejri trees.

At **Guda Bishnoi**, the locals are traditionally engaged in animal husbandry. There's a small artificial lake where migratory birds, such as demoiselle cranes, and mammals such as blackbucks and chinkaras, can be seen, particularly at dusk when they come to drink. The lake is full only after a good monsoon (July and August).

The village of **Salawas** is a centre for weaving beautiful *dhurries* (rugs), a craft also practised in many other villages. A cooperative of 42 families here runs the efficient **Roopraj Dhurry Udyog** (☑0291-2896658; rooprajdurry@sify.com), through which all profits go to the artisans. A 3ft x 5ft *dhurrie* costs a minimum of ₹2800, a price based on two weavers working several hours a day for a month at ₹50 per day each. Prices depend on the intricacy of the design (there are more than 100 traditional designs), the number of colours used, and the material (which could be cotton, camel or goat hair, wool, jute or even silk). Some *dhurries* are stonewashed to give an antique effect. The weavers will send *dhurries* to your home country by sea or air, if you wish.

Several other Salawas families, mostly of the Muslim community, are engaged in block printing. The hand-woven, block-printed cloth is known as *fetia*. A single/double bed sheet costs around ₹400/500, but prices can vary according to the design. Other families are potters, using hand-turned wheels to produce big earthenware pots known as *mutka*, used for keeping water cool.

There are more potteries, and several other *dhurrie* outlets, including another branch of Roopraj Dhurry Udyog, in **Kakani**.

🛏 Sleeping & Eating

Fort Chanwa Luni   HERITAGE HOTEL **$$$**
(☑02931-284216; www.fortchanwa.com; r ₹6500-7500; ❄❀❁) In Luni village, 10km southwest of Kakani (35km from Jodhpur), this expansive red-stone *haveli* was built in 1895 by a Jodhpur state minister. Rooms are large, tasteful and comfy, with period furniture and photos, many boasting local *dhurries*. The five 'heritage deluxe' rooms have the most character. Good multicuisine meals are served and a Rajasthani folk dance, music and puppet show happens in the large central courtyard every evening. A range of village tours and horse, camel and camel-cart rides are on offer and there are bicycles for hire.

SARDAR SAMAND LAKE

The route to this charming and remote wildlife refuge, about 66km southeast of Jodhpur, passes through a number of colourful little villages. Blackbucks, chinkara and birds such as flamingos, pelicans, ducks, cranes, egrets and kingfishers may be spotted.

Atop a cliff above the lake is **Sardar Samand Palace** (☑02960-245001; www.jodhana heritage.com; s/d ₹5500/6600; ❀❁). This grey-stone art deco building with a domed turret was built in 1933 as a hunting lodge for the Maharaja of Jodhpur. Rooms are comfort-

Sar santey rookh rahe to bhi sasto jaan. (A chopped head is cheaper than a felled tree.)
Bishnoi saying

The Bishnoi are among the world's most dedicated conservationists. They hold all animal life sacred, in particular the endangered blackbuck (a type of antelope with long, spiralling horns). The Bishnoi sometimes bury dead blackbuck and mark their graves with stones, and the women are said to suckle blackbuck fawns that have been orphaned. They believe that they will be reincarnated as antelopes. They also have a long history of protecting the sacred khejri tree – sometimes with their lives. The men are recognisable by their large white turbans, while women usually wear red (or purple for mourning) and a large nose ring, a skirt with a white dot and a green-bordered red dupatta (long scarf).

The sect was founded in the 15th century, when a severe drought was crippling the desert regions near Jodhpur. A villager named Jambeshwar had a vision that the drought had been caused by humans meddling with the natural order. He laid down 29 tenets for conserving nature, including not killing animals, not felling trees and not using wood for funeral pyres (Bishnois bury their dead, unlike the majority of Hindus). Other commandments include taking early morning baths, not taking opium or cannabis or drinking alcohol, not indulging in unnecessary discussions, and not wearing blue (it's thought this was to save the indigo plant). Jambeshwar became known as Guru Jambhoji, and his followers became known as the Bishnoi (meaning '29') after the principles they followed.

In 1730 the most famous Bishnoi act of self-sacrifice occurred. The Maharaja of Jodhpur sent woodcutters into Bishnoi villages to cut down khejri trees for his lime kilns. A woman named Amritdevi clung to one of the trees and refused to be removed, crying: 'A chopped head is cheaper than a felled tree'. The axeman cut her head off. One by one, other Bishnoi villagers followed Amritdevi's lead, until 363 people lay dead. The maharaja, hearing of the carnage, declared a conservation zone around the Bishnoi villages, prohibiting tree felling or poaching in the area.

Today the site at Khejadali is a quiet grove of khejri trees, and a temple commemorates the sacrifice. The Bishnoi continue to live by their strict code and to defend native wildlife. In 1996 a Bishnoi villager named Nihal Chand Bishnoi was shot and killed by poachers near Bikaner as he tried to save the lives of some chinkara gazelles. In 1998 Bollywood superstar Salman Khan was arrested for killing two blackbucks near a Bishnoi village. The authorities were allegedly alerted to the crime by the villagers, who chased Khan from the scene and presented the dead blackbucks as evidence. Khan eventually faced court and spent short terms in jail in 2006 and 2007, between appeals and bail hearings, before the case disappeared into the black hole of bureaucracy. Reports from the Bishnoi suggest that the high profile of the case has resulted in a reduction in poaching activity. Today around 90% of the blackbucks in Rajasthan live under Bishnoi protection.

able and have great views. It has two restaurants, a swimming pool, tennis and squash courts and large lakeside grounds, and is a world away from the clamour of Jodhpur. Village safaris are available.

The only way to get here is by taxi (around ₹1000 round trip).

ROHET

Rohet Garh (☑02936-268231; www.rohetgarh. com; s/d ₹4000/5000, ste ₹7500; ※@🛜🏊), in Rohet village, 40km south of Jodhpur on the Pali road, is one of the area's most appealing heritage hotels. This 350-year-old, lovingly tended manor has masses of character and a tranquil atmosphere, which obviously helped Bruce Chatwin when he wrote *The Songlines* here, and William Dalrymple when he began *City of Djinns* in the same room, No 15. (Dalrymple writes about the hotel in *Nine Lives*.) Rohet Garh has a gorgeous colonnaded pool, charming green gardens, great food and lovely, individual rooms. It also possesses a stable of fine Marwari horses and organises rides from two-hour evening rides (₹1500) to six-day back-country treks, sleeping in luxury tents. Or you can take a camel safari, a village tour by jeep, or a birdwatching trip by bicycle.

THE MOTORBIKE TEMPLE

One of the strangest temples in all India stands 8km south of Rohet beside the Pali road, near Chotila village. The deity at **Om Bana Temple** is a garland-decked Enfield Bullet motorcycle, known as Bullet Baba. The story goes that local villager Om Bana died at this spot in the 1980s when his motorbike skidded into a tree. The bike was taken to the local police station, but then mysteriously twice made its own way back to the tree, and travellers along the road started seeing visions of Om Bana – inevitably leading to the machine's deification. Any time of day or night people can be seen at the open-air shrine here, praying for safe journeys and making offerings of liquor. Food and souvenir stalls line the road either side of the shrine and fatal tree.

Mihir Garh (📞9829023453; www.mihirgarh. com; ste incl full board & village safari ₹24,000; ✳@🛜🏊), the latest pride and joy of the family who own Rohet Garh, rises out of the plains 17km to the west of its sibling like a fantasy desert castle. Opened in 2009, this is the ultimate Rajasthan chill-out spot. It has just nine huge, all-different suites, equipped with contemporary amenities (including plunge pool or Jacuzzi) and beautiful Rajasthani artefacts. Three specialist chefs (Continental, Indian and desserts) cater to your personal culinary preferences, and you can relax in the infinity pool, the spa or the large, comfy lounge where local musicians play in the evenings – or enjoy the activities offered by Rohet Garh.

Buses to Rohet (₹29, one to 1½ hours) leave Jodhpur's Central Bus Stand about every 15 minutes. A taxi is around ₹800.

BHENSWARA

Bhenswara, which translates as 'the place where buffaloes were kept', is about 130km south of Jodhpur, on the banks of the Jawai River.

Ravla Bhenswara (📞02978-282187; r from ₹2600; ✳🏊), an unpretentious rural manor, is perfect if you want a cosy, welcoming respite from travelling. The quaint rooms are decorated with lots of personality. Vintage-jeep safaris to local villages and the hilly surrounding country can be arranged, as can visits to **Jalore Fort**, 16km west. The climb up to the fort takes about 45 minutes (carry water, as the ascent can be a hot one).

RSRTC buses run about half-hourly from Jodhour to Jalore (₹88, three hours), where you can catch a taxi to Bhenswara.

KHIMSAR

About 90km northeast of Jodhpur on the road to Nagaur and Bikaner, the palatial

Khimsar Fort (📞01585-262345; www.welcome heritagehotels.com; s ₹6000-10,000, d ₹6500-10,500; ✳@🏊) dates back to 1523 and is now a classy heritage hotel with spacious, well-appointed rooms, a pool (with nearby hammock to laze away the day), a good restaurant and pleasant gardens. It's possible to arrange a camel trip or a wildlife safari by jeep.

Bikaner-bound buses from Jodhpur's Central Bus Stand will stop here (₹70), while a taxi costs about ₹1000.

NAGAUR
📞01582 / POP 88,313

The busy town of Nagaur, situated 130km northeast of Jodhpur (slightly more than halfway to Bikaner), is built around the massive 12th-century **Ahhichatragarh** (Fort of the Hooded Cobra; Indian/foreigner ₹25/100, camera/video ₹50/150, English-speaking guide ₹100; ⊙9am-1pm & 2-5pm). In medieval times Nagaur was hotly contested between rival regional powers, falling at various times under the rule of Sind (whose governor Mohammed Bahlim founded the fort in 1122), the sultanate of Delhi, the Rathores, an independent local dynasty led by Shams Khan Dandani, the Lodi sultans of Delhi, the Mughals under Akbar, and the princes of Bikaner. It was finally acquired by Jodhpur in the early 18th century.

After many years of army occupation and despoliation, Ahhichatragarh has undergone a two-decade, award-winning restoration programme, with unique frescoes rescued from underneath military whitewash. The 1-sq-km fort complex is protected by its vast double walls. Inside, the focal point is the central Rajput-Mughal palace group, built around beautiful pools. You can admire the very ingenious system of channels and ducts that brought water to the fountains and bath-house of the Abha Mahal, palace of the Nagaur Maharaja Amar Singh (r 1634–44), from a well near the ramparts. The finest frescoes, depicting female courtly life, are in the Hadi Rani Mahal, palace of Amar Singh's wife. You can see the ladies brushing their hair in mirrors, swimming in one of the palace's pools and sitting on a garden swing. The ground-floor ceiling has a unique painting of eight animals sharing one pair of eyes. The Eye of Nagaur interpretation centre displays maps and photos of the site and information on its restoration (in English).

Just outside the fort but within the walls of the old city are several mosques, including the **Tarkin-ki-Dargah**, commissioned by the Mughal emperor Akbar for a disciple of the Sufi saint Khwaja Muin-ud-din Chishti (see p158). Its minarets can be seen from the fort's ramparts.

The colourful **Nagaur Fair** (p253) in January or February is a smaller but even more camel- and cattle-focused version of the Pushkar Camel Fair.

🛏 Sleeping & Eating

Ranvas   HERITAGE HOTEL **$$$**
(☏0291-2572321; www.jodhanaheritage.com; r incl breakfast ₹7500-15,000; ❋🐾❋) A newly opened luxury hotel within the fort, set within the former quarters of the 16 wives of the 18th-century Maharaja Bakht Singh. The 33 rooms occupy what were 10 separate *havelis,* each of which has its own courtyard. There are two restaurants.

Hotel Mahaveer International   HOTEL **$**
(☏243158; Vijai Vallabh Chowk; s/d ₹450/550, AC ₹950/1150; mains ₹45-85, thali ₹85-175; ❋) One kilometre from the fort, this hotel has uninspiring but comfortable rooms aimed at business travellers, and a relatively clean and cool vegetarian restaurant.

Royal Camp Nagaur   CAMPGROUND **$$$**
(☏0291-2572321; www.jodhanaheritage.com; tent s/d incl full board ₹7500/9000) Luxury tent accommodation inside the fort, set up when there is expected to be a demand. Tents are 4 sq metres and have bathrooms. Rates almost double during Nagaur Fair.

Hotel Bhaskar   HOTEL **$**
(☏240100; Station Rd; r ₹400-800; mains ₹50-90; ❋) This place near the train station, 1.5km from the fort gate, has worn-out and grim rooms, but it's friendly and a veg curry won't ruin the budget.

❶ Getting There & Away
Half-hourly RSRTC buses between Jodhpur and Bikaner stop at Nagaur (₹72, 2½ to three hours from either place). Trains between Jodhpur and Bikaner (at least four daily) also stop here.

Jodhpur to Jaisalmer

The most direct route by road to Jaisalmer is the southern route via Agolai, Dechu and Pokaran. But, if you have time, it's more rewarding to take the less-travelled northern route, which goes via Osian and Phalodi and meets up with the main route at Pokaran. The exquisite temples at Osian and the spectacular demoiselle cranes at Kichan lie on or just off this northern route, which numerous buses ply every day.

OSIAN
The ancient Thar Desert town of Osian, 65km north of Jodhpur, was an important trading centre between the 8th and 12th centuries. Known as Upkeshpur, it was dominated by the Jains, whose wealth left a legacy of exquisitely sculpted, well-preserved temples. Today it receives lots of pilgrims at certain times, and a smattering of tourists, some of whom come on day trips from Jodhpur. There are dunes just outside the town and sunset camel rides or longer safaris are available from here, making it a good place for a taste of the desert if you can't make it to Jaisalmer or Bikaner. Osian today is inhabited mostly by Brahmins – most of the houses here are painted blue (traditionally a Brahmin practice), as in Jodhpur.

◉ Sights
The finely carved ancient temples of Osian rival the Hoysala temples of Karnataka and the Sun Temple of Konark in Odisha (Orissa).

Sachiya Mata Temple   HINDU TEMPLE
(⊙6am-7.15pm) This hilltop temple, about 200m north of the bus stand, receives crowds of pilgrims, both Hindu and Jain. People usually come here after the marriage of their children, but the big crowds come for Navratri (nine nights of worship in March or April and October or November). Sachiya Mata (Mother of Truth) is the ninth and last incarnation of the goddess Durga. A long flight of steps, under fancifully decorated arches, takes you to the forechamber. Before the *mandapa* (pavilion in front of a

temple), and beyond the impressive *torana* (gateway), are sandstone statues of various incarnations of Durga that were excavated by archaeologists and installed here. The main temple, probably built in the 12th century, is flanked by nine smaller temples, each dedicated to an incarnation of the goddess.

Mahavira Temple   JAIN TEMPLE

(Indian/foreigner free/₹10, camera/video ₹50/100; ☺6am-8.30pm) Five minutes' walk from Sachiya Mata Temple, Mahavira Temple is dedicated to the last of the Jain *tirthankars* (great teachers). This is a more spacious temple than Sachiya Mata, featuring an open-air pavilion-style *mandapa* supported by carved pillars. As at the Sachiya Mata Temple, the drum of the dome features sculptures of *apsaras* (heavenly nymphs). There is also a beautiful *torana* before the temple, decorated with very intricate sculptural work.

The image of Mahavira glistens with piercing eyes. According to legend it's over 2000 years old, was found buried underground, and is made of sand and milk and coated in gold. In the right-hand corner there's an ancient frieze, which retains fragments of colour.

Other Sights   HINDU TEMPLES

Among the other temples in Osian are those dedicated to Surya, Shiva and Harihara. The temples are ruined, but they have some beautiful carving. The damaged 9th-century Katan *baori* (step-well) has more fine, worn sculptural work.

☞ Tours

☑ Gemar Singh (☑9460585154; www.hacra.org), a native of Bhikamkor village northwest of Osian, arranges camel safaris, homestays, camping, desert walks and jeep trips in the deserts around Osian and their Rajput and Bishnoi villages. The emphasis here is on channelling the benefits of tourism to local people and Gemar's trips receive rave reviews. The cost is around ₹1000 per person per day (minimum two people), including bus transfer from Jodhpur.

⊨ Sleeping & Eating

Reggie's Camel Camp   CAMPGROUND $$$

(☑0291-2437023; www.camelcamposian.com; tent s/d incl dinner, breakfast, camel ride & folk entertainment ₹10,000/11,000; ☒) This place offers expensive upmarket accommodation in tents on a secluded sand dune that over-

looks Osian. Champagne dinners and longer camel safaris can be arranged. Bookings are advised.

Guest House   GUESTHOUSE $

(☑02922-274331, 9414440479; s/d without bathroom ₹250/300) Prakash Bhanu Sharma, a personable Brahmin priest, has a basic, echoing guesthouse geared to pilgrims, opposite the Mahavira Temple. Rooms are simple, with shared bathroom and bucket hot water. Prakash can arrange jeep excursions and camel safaris, and he is also a knowledgeable guide to the nearby temples. You can usually find him sitting at the gateway to the temple.

Safari Camp Osian   CAMPGROUND $$

(☑9928311435; www.safaricamposian.com; tents s/d incl dinner, breakfast & camel ride ₹6000/7000) Offers a similar package to Reggie's on a slightly less luxurious but still comfortable basis.

ℹ Getting There & Away

RSRTC buses run about hourly to/from Jodhpur (local/express ₹33/36, 1½ hours) and Phalodi (local/express ₹44/49, two hours). Trains between Jodhpur and Jaisalmer (three daily each way) also stop here. A return taxi from Jodhpur costs about ₹900.

KICHAN & PHALODI

☑02925

Morning and afternoons in the winter months, huge flocks of graceful demoiselle cranes flock to the tiny village of Kichan (p273). The village is 5km east of Phalodi, a town at the junction of roads from Jodhpur (135km), Jaisalmer (165km), Bikaner (168km) and Nagaur (130km), and is a destination of long-distance camel treks from Bikaner.

Phalodi surrounds a crumbling 15th-century fort. The town rose to prominence during the 18th century when Jain business families trading in salt built impressive *havelis* and colourful, gaudy Jain temples, including the domed **Shri Parasnath temple** (camera ₹20), which glistens with gold and Belgian glass. The most prominent *haveli*, **Dadha Haveli**, now houses the Lal Niwas hotel and the small **Dadha Heritage Museum** (Indian/foreigner ₹10/50; ☺9am-5pm), which contains coins and Jain and Hindu manuscripts, paintings and silver, bronze and copper sculptures, from many parts of India.

THE DEMOISELLE CRANES OF KICHAN

From late August or early September to the end of March you can witness the extraordinary sight of hundreds of demoiselle cranes *(Anthropoides virgo)* wintering near Kichan. Numbers may reach several thousand by mid-winter. Around sunrise and in the late afternoon, the birds circle overhead, then make a dramatic descent for the grain that villagers spread for them at the 'Birds Feeding Home' on the west side of the village (turn left as you enter Kichan from Phalodi). It was the 18th-century French queen Marie Antoinette who dubbed the cranes 'demoiselle', for their grace, when some were taken to France from the Russian steppes. Here they're known as *kurja*.

Brown-grey birds with a black chest and throat, demoiselle cranes stand about 76cm high, and have a long neck and a short beak. In traditional Marwari songs, women beseech the cranes to bring back messages from their loved ones when they return from distant lands. The flock consumes a phenomenal 600kg of grain each day, which is funded by (very welcome) donations.

The feeding of the cranes dates back some 150 years. The sight of these wonderful birds in such large numbers descending on the feeding ground is truly awe-inspiring; and the noise of the assembly is amazing. It's an experience that shouldn't be missed if you're in the area. To avoid scaring the birds, keep your distance and refrain from making any noise. During the day, many of the cranes can be found around a small lake on the east side of Kichan.

The demoiselle cranes also winter in Pakistan and Africa. To migrate they must cross the Himalayas from their breeding range, which extends over a wide belt spanning eastern Europe, Central Asia and eastern China.

🛏 Sleeping & Eating

Lal Niwas (☎223813; www.lalniwas.com; Dadha St; s ₹2500-4000, d ₹2750-4500; ❄❖) is a splendid, carved, deep-terracotta *haveli* in the old part of Phalodi, with balconies, courtyards and a tangle of passages. All the rooms are different, decorated in the traditional style with heavy wooden furniture. The quaint room 200 has frescoes, a 200-year-old bed and an alcove with carved arches. The hotel has a multicuisine restaurant and a bar, and the management acts as the defacto information office for the region and can organise visits to Kichan. The little pool was disappointingly cloudy on our last check.

❶ Getting There & Around

There are RSRTC buses to/from Jodhpur (local/express ₹74/80, 2¼ to 2¾ hours, hourly), Jaisalmer (₹68/80, 3½ hours, four daily) and Bikaner (₹101, 3½ hours, hourly).

Phalodi has rail connections with Jodhpur (sleeper/3AC ₹130/263, 2½ hours, three daily), Jaisalmer (sleeper/3AC ₹130/288, 2½ to 3½ hours, five daily), and Bikaner (sleeper ₹130, 2¾ hours, two daily).

A return autorickshaw from Phalodi to Kichan costs about ₹100 including an hour's wait.

RAMDEVRA

This windswept desert village (also spelt Ramdeora), just off the Phalodi road and 12km north of central Pokaran, is home to an important temple dedicated to deified local hero Ramdev, who is revered by both Hindus and Muslims. Ramdev was born in Tanwar village to a Rajput family and was opposed to the caste system, believing instead that all human beings are equal. He achieved the ecstatic state of *samadhi* and departed his body in 1458. The **Ramdev Mandir**, built at the *samadhi* site in 1931 beside a ghat-lined lake, is approached through a bustling bazaar where terracotta wind-chimes are big sellers. The temple has a brightly coloured facade and is festooned with green, red, yellow, orange and purple flags, but isn't especially thrilling architecturally. However, the devotional activities of the hundreds of pilgrims who pay homage here daily are enthralling. Devotees place model horses in the temple in honour of the holy man's trusty steed, who carried him around while he was doing his good work. The temple is at its busiest during the festival devoted to the saint in August or September (p253), at which time you will see flag-carrying pilgrims walking towards Ramdevra along roads all over Rajasthan.

NUCLEAR SABRE-RATTLING

In May 1998 India detonated five nuclear devices underground in the Pokaran area. These included miniature devices to be used for missile warheads and a 40-kiloton device that was almost three times more powerful than the Hiroshima bomb. India also conducted its first nuclear test here, in 1974.

The 1998 tests, ordered by the Hindu-revivalist Bharatiya Janata Party (BJP) government of the day, heightened tension between India and neighbouring Pakistan. Hundreds of thousands of Hindu loyalists celebrated the controversial decision to hold the tests with parties in the street. The US was less impressed, imposing sanctions and suspending aid. Pakistan swiftly responded by detonating six nuclear devices, symbolically one more than India, igniting global concern about a nuclear arms race in South Asia. The rupee plummeted and visitors were scared away – Jaisalmer was rendered a virtual ghost town.

In late September 2001 the US lifted the sanctions against India. Analysts saw this as a reward for India's support in the 'war against terror' after the 9/11 attacks on the United States.

Neither India nor Pakistan has carried out any known nuclear tests since 1998. Today, some Indian nationalists consider the Indian tests to have marked the start of the country's rise to major power status. Other observers argue that they effectively nullified the military superiority in conventional forces that India held over Pakistan before the tests.

Worth seeking out is director Anand Patwardhan's award-winning 2002 documentary *War & Peace* (www.patwardhan.com). This fascinating, dark and funny film examines the nuclear standoff, the patriotism that followed and the human cost. It was banned in India for two years.

Should you need to stay overnight, the best bet is **Hotel Ramdev & Dining Hall** (☑02996-235069; r ₹200-800; ❄), beside the road as you enter Ramdevra from Pokaran, 800m before the temple. It's a modern place with clean, comfortable rooms and good food. Room rates can rise to ₹2000 at festival times. Most buses between Pokaran and Phalodi pass through Ramdevra; there are also jeep taxis between Pokaran and Ramdevra (₹5, 20 minutes).

POKARAN
☑02994

At the junction of roads from Jodhpur (160km), Jaisalmer (110km) and Bikaner (223km), this desert town is the site of another fort – a grand edifice the colour of dark plums. Pokaran Fort hotel is a popular lunch stop between Jodhpur and Jaisalmer. If you wander through the town, look for its well-known terracotta pottery products including animals, lamps, wind chimes and more.

Pokaran became notorious in 1998 as the site of India's controversial nuclear tests.

The private bus stand is beside Hwy 114 (the Jodhpur–Jaisalmer road) in the northern part of town. The fort is about 800m

south of here. The RSRTC bus stand is just off the Jodhpur road on the southeast edge of town, 700m east of the fort. There is a State Bank of India ATM in the bazaar on the main road, 150m southeast of the private bus stand.

☉ Sights

Pokaran Fort FORT
(Indian/foreigner ₹10/50, camera ₹50; ☺8am-6pm) The dark-red sandstone Pokaran Fort is an evocative place overlooking a tangle of narrow streets lined by balconied houses. Built between the 14th and 17th centuries, it once had charge of 108 villages. Part of it is now a heritage hotel. There's a small museum with an assortment of weaponry, some brocaded clothes, old wooden printing blocks and various games belonging to former rulers of Pokaran, including dice and dominoes. There are also 15 'living' temples or shrines, still attended by villagers, scattered around the fort, including a small shrine to Durga.

⛏ Sleeping & Eating

Fort Pokaran HERITAGE HOTEL **$$**
(☑222274; www.fortpokaran.com; r/ste ₹3500/7000; breakfast/lunch/dinner ₹300/600/700; ❄@≋)

The hotel in the fort offers 19 individual, atmospheric rooms that have been expertly restored yet changed as little as possible – many rooms boast their original floors, antique furniture, and teak and mirror ceilings. Of course there are also modern amenities such as tea and coffee makers, plus a superb swimming pool. It's a peaceful place to stay, and offers visits to local weavers who make stoles and cotton clothing on pit looms in and around Pokaran.

RTDC Motel Pokaran HOTEL $
(☑222275; s/d ₹650/800, AC ₹900/1150; ❋) Two kilometres west of town on the Jaisalmer road, this place offers clean rooms and cottages with colourful textiles. A lot better than many other Rajasthan Tourism Development Corporation (RTDC) hotels, it also has a restaurant.

❶ Getting There & Away

RSRTC buses head to Jaisalmer (ordinary/express ₹44/52, two hours, 20 daily), Jodhpur (₹101, three hours, 15 daily) and Bikaner (₹133, five hours, five daily). Many private buses between Jodhpur and Jaisalmer stop here too.

There are three trains a day each to Jodhpur (sleeper/3AC ₹130/316, 3¼ to 4¼ hours) and Jaisalmer (sleeper/3AC ₹130/250, 2¼ to 2¾ hours).

Jaisalmer

☑02992 / POP 58,286

The fort of Jaisalmer is a breathtaking sight: a massive sandcastle rising from the sandy plains like a mirage from a bygone era. No place better evokes exotic camel-train trade routes and desert mystery. Ninety-nine bastions encircle the fort's still-inhabited twisting lanes. Inside are shops swaddled in bright embroideries, a royal palace and numerous businesses looking for your tourist rupee. Despite the commercialism it's hard not to be enchanted by this desert citadel. Beneath the ramparts the narrow streets of the old city conceal magnificent *havelis,* all carved from the same golden-honey sandstone as the fort – hence Jaisalmer's designation as the Golden City.

A city that has come back almost from the dead in the past half-century, Jaisalmer may be remote but it's certainly not forgotten – indeed it's one of Rajasthan's biggest tourist destinations, and few people come here without climbing onto a camel in the surrounding Thar Desert. Competition to get *your* bum into a camel saddle can be fierce, with some operators adopting unpleasant hard-sell tactics. But by following a few basic guidelines you can fix yourself an enjoyable

---

A CASTLE BUILT ON SAND

What happens when you tip a bucket of water over a sand castle? Conservation group Jaisalmer in Jeopardy used this rhetorical question to describe the crisis that hung over Jaisalmer Fort a decade ago. In 1996, the fort had appeared on the World Monuments Fund's list of 100 endangered sites worldwide and there were fears it would steadily self-destruct.

The main problem was material progress, in the form of piped water for the fort's inhabitants – something not even dreamt about when the fort was built. With an estimated 12 times the antiquated drainage system's capacity flowing out of fort buildings, water leakage was threatening to undermine the whole structure. Three of the ancient bastions had collapsed and parts of the fort palace were leaning at an alarming rate.

British-based **Jaisalmer in Jeopardy** (www.jaisalmer-in-jeopardy.org) was established in 1996 and since then it and several Indian organisations, including the **Indian National Trust for Art & Cultural Heritage** (INTACH; www.intach.org) and the Jaisalmer Heritage Trust, have raised funds and carried out much-needed conservation works to save the fort. Most important has been the renewal of the fort's drainage system, including installation of toilets for 2500 inhabitants, and the repaving of the streets, as well as repair works inside the fort palace.

While the fort is no longer in imminent danger of subsiding, it remains a delicate structure that needs a lot of TLC. Thoughtless, often illegal, building work – in many cases encouraged by Jaisalmer's tourism bonanza – remains a threat to parts of its structure. It makes sense for any visitor to be aware of the fort's fragile nature and to conserve resources, especially water, as much as possible.

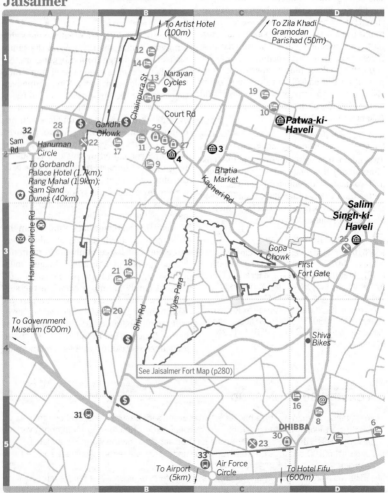

To Artist Hotel
(100m)

To Zila Khadi
Gramodan
Parishad (50m)

Chainpura St

Narayan
Cycles

Court Rd

19

10

**Patwa-ki-
Haveli**

32

28

Gandhi
Chowk

29

Sam
Rd

Hanuman
Circle

22

17

11 26

27

3

9

4

To Gorbandh
Palace Hotel (1.7km);
Rang Mahal (1.9km);
Sam Sand
Dunes (40km)

Bhatia
Market

Kacheri Rd

**Salim
Singh-ki-
Haveli**

25

Hanuman Circle Rd

Gopa
Chowk

First
Fort Gate

To Government
Museum (500m)

18

21

Shiv Rd

Vyas Para

20

See Jaisalmer Fort Map (p280)

Shiva
Bikes

16

@

8

31

30

DHIBBA

6

33

23

7

To Airport
(5km)

Air Force
Circle

To Hotel Fifu
(600m)

ride (see the boxed text, p291, for more on camel safaris).

Jaisalmer was once completely surrounded by an extensive wall, much of which has, sadly, been torn down for building material. Some of it remains, however, including the city gates. As long ago as 1975, Prime Minister Indira Gandhi expressed her horror at how beautiful old Jaisalmer buildings were being dismantled and sold off in parts. Today Jaisalmer seems much more aware of the importance of preserving appearances, at least, for the sake of tourism. Indeed many of the new buildings going up around

town boast beautifully carved sandstone in Jaisalmer's centuries-old tradition.

This is not a big city and most accommodation is within walking distance of the fort at its heart. The main market area, Bhatia Market, straggles along winding lanes not far north of the fort.

Jaisalmer celebrates its desert culture with the action-packed **Desert Festival** (p253) in January or February each year.

History

Jaisalmer was founded way back in 1156 by a leader of the Bhati Rajput clan named Jaisal.

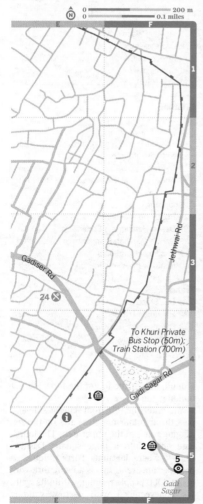

To Khuri Private
Bus Stop (50m);
Train Station (700m)

Gadi Sagar Rd

Gadiser Rd

Jethwai Rd

Gadi
Sagar

slaughtered his women himself after a surprise attack by a local rival while his knights were out of town.

By the 16th century Jaisalmer was prospering from its strategic position on the camel-train routes between India and Central Asia. It eventually established cordial relations with the Mughal empire. Maharawal Sabal Singh, in the mid-17th century, won the patronage of emperor Shah Jahan when he fought with distinction in a campaign at Peshawar. Sabal Singh expanded the Jaisalmer princedom to its greatest extents by annexing areas that now fall within the administrative districts of Bikaner and Jodhpur.

The Jaisalmer rulers continued to line their coffers with illicit gains from cattle rustling, as well as by imposing levies on the camel caravans that passed through the kingdom. As they fought to enlarge their territories, they won renown both for their valour and for their treachery.

Religion and the arts flourished. Though themselves Hindu, Jaisalmer's rulers were tolerant of Jainism, giving refuge to Jains fleeing persecution in Gujarat in the 15th century, and encouraging the construction of the beautiful Jain temples that now grace the fort. Sculptures of both Hindu and Jain deities and holy men stand side by side on the walls of these fine buildings. Jains in turn contributed heavily to the strengthening of Jaisalmer Fort. The rulers also commissioned scholars to copy precious sacred manuscripts and books of ancient learning that may otherwise have been lost during Muslim raids.

The merchants and prominent citizens built magnificent houses and mansions, all carved from wood and golden-yellow sandstone. Merchant *havelis* are found all over Rajasthan (notably in Shekhawati), but nowhere are they quite as exquisite as in Jaisalmer. Even the humblest of shops and houses display something of the Rajput love of the decorative arts in its most whimsical form.

Under British rule the rise of sea trade (especially through Mumbai) and railways saw Jaisalmer's commercial importance decline. Its population halved between 1890 and 1930, and Partition in 1947, with the cutting of trade routes to Pakistan, seemingly sealed the city's fate. Water shortages could then have pronounced the death sentence. But the 1965 and 1971 wars between India

The Bhatis, who trace their lineage back to Krishna, ruled right through to Independence in 1947.

The city's early centuries were tempestuous, partly because its rulers relied on looting for want of other income, and Jaisalmer suffered repeated revenge attacks. *Jauhar* (ritual mass suicide) is said to have happened here 2½ times – twice in the 14th century in the face of attacks by the Delhi sultans Ala-ud-din Khilji (who reputedly besieged Jaisalmer for nine years) and Tughlaq, with the half-*jauhar* coming in the 16th century when Maharawal Loonkaran

and Pakistan gave Jaisalmer new strategic importance, and since the 1960s the Indira Gandhi Canal to the north has brought revitalising water to the desert.

Today tourism and the area's many military installations are the pillars of the city's economy.

⊙ Sights

Jaisalmer Fort FORT
(Map p280) Founded in 1156 by the Rajput ruler Jaisal and reinforced by subsequent rulers, Jaisalmer Fort was the focus of a number of battles between the Bhatis, the Mughals of Delhi and the Rathores of Jodhpur. The lower of the fort's three layers of wall is composed of solid stone blocks, which reinforce the loose rubble of Trikuta Hill. The second wall snakes around the upper part of the fort, and between this and the third, inner wall, the warrior Rajputs hurled boiling oil and water, and massive round missiles on their enemies.

The Jaisalmer standard, which features a *chhatri* against a red-and-yellow background, flies at the top of the fort's highest building, the palace.

You enter the fort from its east side and pass through four massive gates on the zigzagging route to the upper part. The fourth gate opens into a large square, Dashera Chowk, where Jaisalmer Fort's uniqueness becomes apparent: this is a living fort, with about 3000 people residing within its walls. It's honeycombed with narrow, winding lanes, all of them paved in stone and lined with houses and temples – along with a large number of handicraft shops, guesthouses, restaurants and massage/beauty parlours, just to remind you that you are in the age of 21st-century tourism, not the middle ages. Fortunately cars cannot drive beyond the main square. The fort walls provide superb views over the city and surrounding desert – it's fantastic to stroll around the outer parts at sunset. From outside, the fort looks especially magical when it's lit up at night under a clear sky full of stars.

Watch your bags and pockets as you wander around the fort – there have been some incidents of theft.

Fort Palace

(Map p280; Indian/foreigner incl audio guide & camera ₹30/250; video ₹50/150; ☺8am-6pm Apr-Oct, 9am-6pm Nov-Mar) Towering over the fort's main square, and partly built on top of the Hawa Pol (the fourth fort gate), is the former rulers' elegant seven-storey palace.

Much of the palace is open to the public – floor upon floor of small rooms provide a fascinating sense of how such buildings were designed for spying on the outside world. The doorways connecting the rooms of the palace are quite low. This isn't a reflection on the stature of the Rajputs, but was a means of forcing people to adopt a humble, stooped position in case the room they were entering contained the maharawal.

The 1½-hour audio-guide tour, available in six languages, is worthwhile but you must deposit ₹2000 or your passport, driver's licence or credit card. Highlights include the mirrored and painted Rang Mahal (the bedroom of the 18th-century ruler Mulraj II), a gallery of finely wrought 15th-century sculptures donated to the rulers by the builders of the fort's temples, and the spectacular 360-degree views from the rooftop. One room contains an intriguing display of stamps from the former Rajput states. On the eastern wall of the palace is a sculpted pavilion-style balcony. Here drummers raised the alarm when the fort was under siege. You can also see numerous round rocks piled on top of the battlements, ready to be rolled onto advancing enemies.

The last part of the tour moves from the king's palace (Raja-ka-Mahal) into the queen's palace (Rani-ka-Mahal), which contains an interesting section on Jaisalmer's annual Gangaur processions in spring.

Jain Temples

(Map p280; admission ₹30, camera/video/cellphone ₹70/120/30; ☺7am-1pm) Within the fort walls is a maze-like, interconnecting treasure trove of seven beautiful yellow sandstone Jain temples, dating from the 15th and 16th centuries. Opening times have a habit of changing, so check with the caretakers. The intricate carving rivals that of the marble Jain temples in Ranakpur and Mt Abu, and has an extraordinary quality because of the soft, warm stone. Shoes and all leather items must be removed before entering the temples.

Chandraprabhu is the first temple you come to inside. No mortar was used in its construction; blocks of masonry are held together by iron staples. Dedicated to the eighth *tirthankar,* whose symbol is the moon, it was built in 1509 and features fine sculpture in the *mandapa,* whose intensely sculpted pillars form a series of *toranas.* Around the inside of the drum are 12 statues of Ganesh, and around the upper gallery are 108 marble images of Parasnath, the 23rd *tirthankar.* The inner sanctum holds four images of Chandraprabhu, and the hall around it is lined with statues of *tirthankars.* In Jain temples the statues are usually unclothed – a contrast to Hindu temples, where statues are elaborately dressed. The voluptuous women are tributes to female beauty and to the importance of carnal desire in human existence.

To the right of Chandraprabhu is the **Rikhabdev** temple, which has a lovely, tranquil atmosphere. There are some fine sculptures around the walls, protected by glass cabinets, and the pillars are beautifully sculpted with *apsaras* and gods. Behind the sanctum is a depiction of the Hindu goddess Kali, flanked by a Jain sculpture of an unclothed woman – a chance to compare the elaborately garbed Hindu statue with its less prim Jain equivalent.

Behind Chandraprabhu is **Parasnath**, which you enter through a beautifully carved *torana* culminating in an image of the Jain *tirthankar* at its apex. There is a voluptuous carving of an *apsara* balancing sets of balls on her raised forearm. The interior has a beautiful, brightly painted ceiling.

A door to the south leads to small **Shitalnath**, dedicated to the 10th *tirthankar.* The image of Shitalnath enshrined here is composed of eight precious metals. A door in the north wall leads to the enchanting, dim chamber of **Sambhavanth** – in the front courtyard, Jain priests grind sandalwood in mortars for devotional use. Steps lead down to the **Gyan Bhandar**, a fascinating, tiny, underground library founded in 1500 that houses priceless ancient illustrated manuscripts, some dating from the 11th century. Other exhibits include astrological charts and the Jain version of the Shroud of Turin: the Shroud of Gindhasuri, named for a Jain hermit and holy man who died in Ajmer. When his body was placed on the funeral pyre, the shroud remained miraculously unsinged. In a small locked cabinet are images of Parasnath that are made of ivory and various precious stones, including emerald and crystal.

Jaisalmer Fort

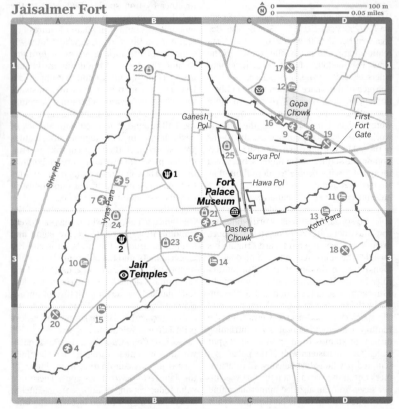

The remaining two temples are **Shanti-nath** and, below the library, **Kunthunath**, both built in 1536, with plenty of sensual carving. The enclosed gallery around Shantinath is flanked by hundreds of images of saints, some made of marble and some of Jaisalmer sandstone.

Laxminarayan & Surya Temples
(Map p280) The Hindu Laxminarayan Temple, in the centre of the fort, is simpler than the Jain temples and has a brightly decorated dome. Devotees offer grain, which is distributed before the temple. The inner sanctum has a repoussé silver architrave around its entrance, and a heavily garlanded image enshrined within.

There's also a small 16th-century Hindu temple devoted to Surya, the sun god, inside the fort.

Havelis
Inside the fort but outside it, too (especially in the streets to the north), Jaisalmer is replete with the fairy-tale architecture of *havelis* – gorgeously carved stone doorways, *jali* (carved lattice) screens, balconies and turrets. The are some outstanding examples of incredibly fine sandstone *havelis* built by wealthy merchants and local notables in the 18th to 20th centuries.

Patwa-ki-Haveli   HISTORIC BUILDING
(Map p276) The biggest fish in the *haveli* pond is Patwa-ki-Haveli, which towers over a narrow lane, its intricate stonework like honey-coloured lace. It is divided into five sections and was built between 1800 and 1860 by five Jain brothers who made their fortunes in brocade and jewellery. It's most impressive from the outside, though the first of the five sections is open as the privately owned **Kothari's Patwa-ki-Haveli Mu-**

Jaisalmer Fort

seum (Indian/foreigner ₹50/120, camera/video ₹40/70; ⊙8.30am-7pm), which richly evokes 19th-century life.

Salim Singh-ki-Haveli   HISTORIC BUILDING
(Map p276; admission incl guide ₹20, camera/video ₹20/50; ⊙8am-7pm May-Sep, 8am-6pm Oct-Apr) This 18th-century haveli has an amazing, distinctive shape. It's narrow for the first floors, and then the top storey spreads out into a mass of carving, with graceful arched balconies surmounted by pale blue cupolas. The beautifully arched roof has superb carved brackets in the form of peacocks. Amazingly, the building is constructed with

no mortar or cement – the stones are connected with visible iron joints.

Salim Singh was a notorious 19th-century prime minister of Jaisalmer. His father had been prime minister before him, and was murdered by some of the Jaisalmer nobility. Salim Singh eventually took revenge by poisoning numerous nobles in return. His was a stern, unpleasant rule, and his ill treatment of the area's Paliwal Brahmin community led them to abandon their 84 villages and move elsewhere. You can visit Kuldara and Khaba, two of the deserted villages, west of Jaisalmer. Salim Singh was eventually murdered on the orders of the maharawal.

Nathmal-ki-Haveli   HISTORIC BUILDING
(Map p276; admission ₹20; ⊙8am-7pm) This late-19th-century *haveli* also used to be a prime minister's house and is still partly inhabited. It has an extraordinary exterior, dripping with carvings and the 1st floor has some beautiful paintings using 1.5kg of gold. A doorway is surrounded by 19th-century British postcards and there's a picture of Queen Victoria. The left and right wings were the work of two brothers, whose competitive spirits apparently produced this virtuoso work – the two sides are similar, but not identical. Sandstone elephants welcome visitors/shoppers.

Museums

Desert Cultural Centre & Museum MUSEUM
(Map p276; Indian/foreigner ₹20/50, camera/video ₹20/50; ⊙9am-8pm) Next to the Tourist Reception Centre, this interesting little museum has material in English and Hindi on the history of Rajasthan's different princely states, and exhibits on traditional Rajasthani culture. Features include Rajasthani music (with video), textiles, a *kaavad* mobile temple (see the boxed text, p197), and a *phad* scroll painting depicting the story of the Rajasthani folk hero Pabuji, used by travelling singers as they recite Pabuji's epic exploits. The museum was founded and is looked after by local historian NK Sharma (author the informative booklet *Jaisalmer, the Golden City*), with the aim of preserving cultural heritage. It also hosts nightly half-hour **puppet shows** (Indian/foreigner ₹30/50, camera/video ₹20/50; ⊙6.30pm, 7.30pm) with English commentary. The museum ticket also gives admission to the Jaisalmer Folklore Museum, also founded by Mr Sharma.

Jaisalmer Folklore Museum
MUSEUM

(Map p276; ⊙8am-6pm) Also founded by NK Sharma, and included in the Desert Cultural Centre ticket, this small museum near Gadi Sagar has an eclectic collection ranging from camel decorations and printing blocks to camel-hide opium bottles. The hill nearby is a tremendous place to soak up the sunset.

Government Museum
MUSEUM

(Map p276; Indian/foreigner ₹5/10, Mon free; ⊙10am-4.30pm Sat-Thu) On the west side of town, this small museum has a well-captioned collection of fossils, some dating back to the Jurassic era (160 to 180 million years ago), plus examples of ancient script, coins, religious sculptures (some from the 11th century), puppets and textiles. There's even a stuffed great Indian bustard, the state bird of Rajasthan, which thrives in the Thar Desert but is declining elsewhere.

Thar Heritage Museum
MUSEUM

(Map p276; off Court Rd; admission ₹40) This privately run museum near Gandhi Chowk also has an intriguing assortment of Jaisalmer area artefacts, from turbans, musical instruments, fossils and kitchen equipment to displays on birth, marriage, death and opium customs. It's brought alive by the guided tour you'll probably get from its founder, local historian and folklorist LN Khatri. Opening hours are variable but if it's closed, you should find Mr Khatri at his shop, Desert Handicrafts Emporium, nearby on Court Rd.

Other Attractions

Gadi Sagar
LAKE

This stately tank, southeast of the city walls, was Jaisalmer's vital water supply until 1965, and because of its importance it is surrounded by many small temples and shrines. The tank was built in 1367 by Maharawal Gadsi Singh, taking advantage of a natural declivity that already retained some water. It's a waterfowl favourite in winter, but can almost dry up before the monsoon. A popular visitor activity here is feeding the lake's large catfish population, which swarms in a writhing mass to the shore whenever someone tosses breadcrumbs. **Boat hire** (⊙8am-9pm) costs ₹50 to ₹100 for 30 minutes.

The attractive **Tilon-ki-Pol** gateway that straddles the road down to the tank is said to have been built by a famous prostitute. When she offered to pay to have it constructed, the maharawal refused permission on the grounds that he would have to pass under it to go down to the tank, which would

be beneath his dignity. While he was away, she built the gate anyway, adding a Krishna temple on top so the king could not tear it down.

Vyas Chhatari
HISTORIC BUILDING

(admission ₹20, camera/video ₹20/30; ⊙4pm-30min after sunset) This atmospheric assemblage of golden sandstone *chhatris,* in an old Brahmin cemetery on a rise on the northwest edge of town, forms a popular sunset point from which to view the fort. Enter from Ramgarh Rd opposite the Himmatgarh Palace Hotel.

🏃 Activities

Massage & Beauty Treatment

After a camel trek you can soothe your jangled body with a spot of massage and herbal healing.

Guru Health Care
AYURVEDA

(Map p280; ✆252452; Vyas Para, Fort; ⊙8am-9pm) The most professional of the places in the fort, with qualified ayurvedic staff trained in Kerala. They offer a big range of massages, plus facials, aromatherapy, reflexology, and *kativasti* treatment for lower-back problems. A 30-minute/one-hour massage costs ₹250/500.

Panghat Spa
AYURVEDA, BEAUTY TREATMENT

(✆253801; Gorbandh Palace Hotel, Sam Rd) A luxurious spa at the top-end Gorbandh Palace Hotel, offering a variety of massages, therapies and beauty treatments. A 30-minute head, neck and back tension-reliever is ₹1800; one hour's full-body ayurvedic massage is ₹3800.

These following places offer henna painting and beauty treatments such as facials, manicures, pedicures and waxing, as well as massage:

Baiju Ayurvedic Beauty Parlour
MASSAGE & BEAUTY TREATMENT

(Map p280; ✆250803; ⊙10am-8pm) A friendly operation with two locations in the fort: one near the main square and other at the end of the street past the Jain temples.

Bobby Henna Painting & Herbal House
MASSAGE & BEAUTY TREATMENT

(Map p280; ✆251968; Vyas Para; ⊙10am-8pm) Bobby is an energetic lady serving women only.

Tours

The Tourist Reception Centre runs sunset tours to the Sam sand dunes (₹200 per person, minimum four people). Add ₹100 if you'd like a short camel ride too. Another tour visits Amar Sagar, Lodhruva and Bada Bagh for ₹500 per car.

🛏 Sleeping

While staying in the fort is the most atmospheric and romantic choice, you should be aware of the pressure tourism exerts on the fort's infrastructure (see the boxed text, p275).

There is a wide choice of good places to stay outside the fort. Rates at many places fluctuate with the seasons – if there's a festival on, rooms are expensive and scarce, but at slow times most places offer big discounts. You'll get massive discounts between April and August, because Jaisalmer is hellishly hot then. Unfortunately, a few budget hotels are heavily into high-pressure selling of camel safaris and things can turn sour if you don't take up their safari offers – see the boxed text, p283 for more on this. Some fly-by-night operators just rent hotels for the purpose of carrying out this kind of business, and their establishments can appear and disappear rapidly.

OUTSIDE THE FORT

 Desert Moon   GUESTHOUSE $
(☏250116, 9414149350; www.desertmoon guesthouse.com; Achalvansi Colony; s ₹700-800, d ₹800-1000; ❋) On the northwest edge of town, 1km from Gandhi Chowk, Desert Moon is in a peaceful location beneath the Vyas Chhatari sunset point. The guesthouse

is run by a friendly Indian-Kiwi couple who offer free pick-up from the train and bus stations. The 11 rooms are cool, clean and comfortable, with polished stone floors, tasteful decorations and sparkling bathrooms. The rooftop vegetarian restaurant has fort and *chhatari* views.

Hotel Pleasant Haveli   HOTEL $$
(☏253253; www.pleasanthaveli.com; Chainpura St; r ₹1200-2000, ste ₹2000-3250; ❋🛜) Recently renovated, this welcoming place has lots of lovely carved stone, a beautiful rooftop and just a handful of spacious, attractive, colour-themed rooms, all with bathroom and AC. Free pick-ups from transport terminals available.

Hotel the Royale Jaisalmer   HOTEL $$
(Map p276; ☏252601; www.royalejaisalmer.com; Dhibba; r ₹1850-2500; ❋@❋) South of the fort gate, this bright hotel is a good choice for its spacious, colourful, traditionally decorated rooms, multicuisine rooftop restaurant and neat pool in the rear courtyard.

Residency Centre Point   GUESTHOUSE $
(Map p276; ☏/fax 252883; residency_guesthouse@ yahoo.com; Kumbhara Para; r ₹450) Near the Patwa-ki-Haveli, this friendly, family-run guesthouse has five clean, spacious doubles in a lovely 250-year-old building. Rooms vary in size – budget by price but midrange in quality – and number 101 has a wonderful antique balcony. The rooftop restaurant has superb fort views and offers home-cooked food.

ℹ ARRIVAL IN JAISALMER

Touts work the buses heading to Jaisalmer from Jodhpur, hoping to steer travellers to guesthouses or hotels in Jaisalmer where they will get a commission. Some may even approach you before the bus leaves Jodhpur; others ride part or all of the way from Jodhpur, or board about an hour before Jaisalmer. On arrival in Jaisalmer, most buses are surrounded by a swarm of touts baying for your attention. If an autorickshaw driver has a sign with the name of the accommodation you want, by all means take the free ride offered (after checking that it is free). Otherwise, don't believe anyone who offers to take you 'anywhere you like' for just a few rupees, and do take with a fistful of salt any claims that the hotel you want is 'full', 'closed' or 'no good any more', and don't listen to people outside your chosen hotel telling you 'their' hotel is full. They have probably followed your rickshaw on a motorbike and are pretending to be associated with the hotel. Go inside to the reception where you may well find a vacancy.

Also be very wary of offers of rooms for ₹100 or similar absurd rates. Places offering such prices are almost certainly in the camel-safari hard-sell game and their objective is to get you out of the room and on to a camel as fast as possible. If you don't take up their safari offers, the room price may suddenly increase or you might be told there isn't a room available any more.

Touts are less prevalent on the trains, but the same clamour for your custom ensues outside the station once you have arrived.

Hotel Swastika
HOTEL **$**

(Map p276; ☑252483; swastikahotel@yahoo.com; Chainpura St; dm ₹100, s/d/tr ₹200/300/400, r with AC ₹600; ❀) In this well-run place the only thing you'll be hassled about is to relax. Rooms are plain, quiet, clean and very good for the price; some have little balconies. There are plenty of restaurants nearby.

Hotel Fifu
HOTEL **$$**

(☑254317; www.fifutravel.com; Bera Rd; r incl breakfast ₹2650; ❀☎) Down a dusty lane on the south edge of town, this hotel is a little out of the way, however, it offers free pickup from the train and bus stations. As well, the beautiful, colour-themed sandstone rooms afford a very peaceful and pleasant stay. The rooftop has tremendous views and a great vegetarian restaurant. The owners also run Jasmin Haveli next door, with the same rates.

Hotel Nachana Haveli
HERITAGE HOTEL **$$**

(Map p276; ☑252110; www.nachanahaveli.com; Gandhi Chowk; s/d ₹2500/3000; ❀@) This 280-year-old royal *haveli*, set around three courtyards – one with a tinkling fountain – is a fascinating hotel. The raw sandstone rooms have arched stone ceilings and the ambience of a medieval castle. They are sumptuously and romantically decorated, though some lack much natural light. The common areas come with all the Rajput trimmings, including swing chairs and bearskin rugs.

Hotel Gorakh Haveli
HOTEL **$$**

(Map p276; ☑9982657525; www.hotelgorakhhaveli.com; Dhibba; s/d ₹1000/1500, AC ₹1500/2500; ❀) A pleasantly low-key spot south of the fort, Gorakh Haveli is a modern place built with traditional sandstone and some attractive carving. Rooms are comfy and spacious, staff are amiable, and there's a reasonable multicuisine rooftop restaurant (mains ₹60 to ₹120), with fort views, of course.

Hotel Renuka
HOTEL **$**

(Map p276; ☑252757; hotelrenuka@rediffmail.com; Chainpura St; r ₹200-750; ❀@) Spread over three floors, Renuka has squeaky clean rooms – the best have balconies, bathrooms and AC. It's been warmly accommodating guests since 1988, so management knows its stuff. The roof terrace has great fort views and a good restaurant, and the hotel offers free pickup from the bus and train stations.

Artist Hotel
HOTEL **$**

(☑252082; www.artisthotel.info; Artist Colony; s ₹150-250, d ₹250-500, AC tr ₹1000; ❀)This friendly, Austrian-and-Indian–run establishment helps support and maintain the artistic traditions of formerly nomadic musicians and storytellers who are now settled in the same area of town. There are great fort views from the roof, where frequent musical events take place, and a very good range of European and Indian dishes (mains ₹85 to ₹220) is served. Rooms vary, but are clean and comfortable, with small bathrooms. The cheapest ones are in a nearby annex, the Artist Lodge.

Killa Bhawan Lodge
HOTEL **$$**

(Map p276; ☑253833; www.killabhawan.com; AC/AC r incl breakfast ₹1400/2000; ❀) Near Patwa-ki-Haveli, this small hotel is managed by the same group who run a luxury operation within the fort. There are five big and beautifully decorated rooms, a pleasant rooftop restaurant and free tea and coffee all day.

Shahi Palace
HOTEL **$**

(Map p276; ☑255920; www.shahipalacehotel.com; off Shiv Rd; r ₹550-2050; ❀@) Shahi Palace is a friendly and popular option and offers free pickup from the transport stations. It's a modern building in the traditional style with some lovely carved sandstone. It has attractive rooms with raw sandstone walls, colourful embroidery, and carved stone or wooden beds, though only a limited number have natural light. The cheaper rooms are mostly in two annexes along the street, **Star Haveli** and **Oasis Haveli**. The rooftop restaurant (mains ₹80 to ₹200) is excellent, with Indian veg and non-veg dishes plus some European fare, cold beer and a superb evening fort view.

Mandir Palace Hotel
HERITAGE HOTEL **$$$**

(Map p276; ☑252788; www.mandirpalace.com; Gandhi Chowk; s/d ₹4500/5000, ste ₹8000-10,000; ❀☎) Jaisalmer's erstwhile royal family still lives in this sprawling 18th-century palace just inside the town walls. Named for its many mandirs (temples), it has exquisite stone latticework and one of its towers (off-limits to guests) is Jaisalmer's highest building outside the fort. Some rooms are full of character, with antique furnishings, but the newer ones have less character, and staff can be distant. A small museum (₹20) exhibits a few royal trappings.

Jawahar Niwas Palace HERITAGE HOTEL $$

(☏252208; www.jawaharniwaspalace.co.in; 1 Bada Bagh Rd; s/d incl breakfast ₹4000/4500; ✷@✸) Like a desert mirage, this forlorn beauty stands in solitary splendour 1km west of the fort. Built around 1890 as a guesthouse for colonial officials, it's still owned by the Jaisalmer royal family. Rooms are elegant and spacious, with soaring ceilings and generous bathrooms. There's a fabulous pool sunk into a walled garden and you can ride horses in the hotel's own large grounds.

Hotel Fort View HOTEL $

(Map p280; ☏252214; Gopa Chowk; r ₹150-400) A friendly stalwart of the budget scene, close to the fort gate. The cheapest rooms are small and in the back, but clean. Rooms 21 and 31 have fort views. There's a popular fort-facing multicuisine restaurant (mains ₹50 to ₹80), but the 9am checkout is less popular!

Hotel Golden City HOTEL $

(Map p276; ☏251664; www.hotelgoldencity.com; r ₹300-1500, AC from ₹600; ✷✸) Off Gadi Sagar Rd, this busy hotel feels like a mini-budget resort, with a wide range of clean rooms, satellite TV, a decent multicuisine rooftop restaurant (mains ₹70 to₹190) and a pool (nonguests ₹100). Some travellers have been less than happy with their camel trips, however.

Pol Haveli HOTEL $

(☏250131; www.hotelpolhaveli.com; Dedansar Rd; r ₹500-1500; ✷@) Owned by the same family as the Shahi Palace. Similar to its sibling, Pol Haveli has sandstone walls and carving and rooms ranging from medium-sized without natural light to large and bright with window seats. Staff are helpful and there's a panoramic roof terrace and restaurant. It's in a newish residential area 500m north of Hanuman Circle.

Hotel Ratan Palace HOTEL $

(☏253615; Chainpura St; r ₹200-800; ✷@) The same friendly family that runs the Hotel Renuka operates Ratan Palace. It has a similar range of bright rooms.

Hotel Jaisal Palace HOTEL $

(Map p276; ☏252717; www.hoteljaisalpalace.com; near Gandhi Chowk; s ₹600-1050, d ₹750-1250; ✷) This is a well-run, good-value hotel, though the rooms tend to be on the small side and characterless.

Apollo Guest House GUESTHOUSE $

(Map p276; ☏252528; r ₹400-800; ✷) A friendly new guesthouse with helpful management in a nice new stone building in the south of town.

IN THE FORT

TOP CHOICE Hotel Killa Bhawan BOUTIQUE HOTEL $$$

(Map p276; ☏251204; www.killabhawan.com; 445 Kotri Para; r incl breakfast ₹3850-9400; ✷) A cute mini-labyrinth of a place combining three old houses set right on the fort walls. French-owned and designed, it has vividly coloured rooms, attractive little sitting areas and all sorts of intriguing arts and crafts. Rooftop yoga sessions can be arranged and there are especially fab views from the honeymoon suite.

Hotel Paradise HOTEL $$

(Map p280; ☏252674; www.paradiseonfort.com; r ₹300-2000, AC from ₹1050; ✷@) Right above the fort's southern walls, Paradise has great terraces for lounging, eating and drinking, and nice clean rooms, many with views and/or pretty little murals. Fourteen of the 23 have private bathroom.

Hotel Siddhartha HOTEL $

(Map p280; ☏253614; r ₹500-700) Just down the street past the Jain temples, little Siddhartha has well-kept, stone-walled rooms with attached bathrooms. Some have street views, some have panoramic views and some have no views.

Garh Jaisal HERITAGE HOTEL $$$

(Map p280; ☏253836; http://garhjaisal.com; Kotri Para; r incl breakfast US$125; ✷@) This old *haveli* right at the fort's eastern corner has seven well-decorated, stone-walled rooms with king-size beds and lovely window seats. There's also a fabulously positioned terrace and restaurant.

Desert Boy's Guest House GUESTHOUSE $

(Map p280; ☏253091; desert_p@yahoo.com; Vyas Para; r ₹500-1800; ✷) Assorted rooms with traditional artefacts, some with fine views, plus relaxing terraces and a restaurant.

OUTSIDE TOWN

There are a number of high-end hotels situated not far out of town.

Suryagarh HOTEL $$$

(☏269269; www.suryagarh.com; Kahala Fata, Sam Rd; s/d ₹11,000/12,000, ste from ₹16,000/17,000, incl breakfast; ✷@✺✸) The undisputed king in this category, Suryagarh rises like a fortress beside the Sam road, 14km west of town. It's a brand-new building in traditional Jaisalmer style centred on a huge palace-like courtyard with beautiful carved stonework. Features include a fabulous indoor pool (with separate kids' pool), a wood-panelled billiards room, and a multi-cuisine restaurant, Nosh (mains ₹650-800), where non-guests are welcome. Rooms follow the traditional/contemporary theme, with large LCD TVs and *jali*-screened dressing tables. It's a spectacular place but respect for nature doesn't seem to be its strong suit: Humvee desert trips are among the suggested outings, and a desert golf course and, yes, artificial dunes are in the pipeline.

Fort Rajwada HOTEL $$$
(☑253233; www.fortrajwada.com; Jodhpur-Barmer Link Rd; s/d ₹5400/7000, ste from ₹12,500; ✳@☎☲) Two kilometres east of town, off the Pokaran road, this large, modern but traditional-style place was built according to the ancient Indian design principles of *vaastu*, which is similar to feng shui. All materials in the hotel are natural. An opera designer created the interior, so it's suitably dramatic. Rooms are well equipped, though not huge, and there's a nice pool.

Gorbandh Palace Hotel HOTEL $$$
(off Map p276; ☑253801; www.hrhhotels.com; Sam Rd; r ₹6000; ✳@☎☲) Two kilometres west of Hanuman Circle, this grandiose modern hotel with large if unimaginative gardens is a good bet for families. It's constructed with traditional design elements from local sandstone, and the friezes around the hotel were sculpted by local artisans. There's a superb pool (nonguests ₹200), a classy spa and a good bookshop. Rooms aren't huge, though some have balconies or terraces.

Rang Mahal HOTEL $$$
(off Map p276; ☑250907; www.hotelrangmahal. com; Sam Rd; s ₹4000-9500, d ₹4500-10,000; ✳@☎☲) A close neighbour to the Gorbandh Palace, this is a dramatic, traditional building with big bastions. It's a big hotel catering mainly for groups, with fairly standard-issue top-end rooms, though it does have an excellent restaurant and a spectacular pool.

✗ Eating

As well as the many hotel-rooftop eateries, there's a good number of other places to enjoy a tasty meal, often with a view.

Desert Boy's Dhani INDIAN $
(Map p276; Dhibba; mains ₹70-90; ☉8am-10pm) This is a walled-garden restaurant where tables are spread around a large, stone-paved courtyard with a big tree. There's also

traditional cushion seating under cover. Rajasthani music and dance is performed from 8pm to 10pm nightly, and it's a very pleasant place to eat excellent, good-value Rajasthani and other Indian veg dishes.

Jaisal Italy ITALIAN $$
(Map p280; First Fort Gate; mains ₹120-170) Though it's run by the same family as the Bhang Shop, you won't have to worry about bhang pizzas. Instead you'll find superb all-veg bruschetta, antipasti, pasta, pizza, salad and desserts, plus Spanish omelettes. All this is served up in an exotically decorated indoor restaurant (cosy in winter, deliciously air-conditioned in summer) or on a delightful terrace atop the lower fort walls, with cinematic views.

Sun Set Palace MULTICUISINE $
(Map p280; mains ₹60-120) This restaurant has cushions and low tables on an airy terrace on (as the name implies) the fort's west side. Pretty good vegetarian Indian dishes are prepared, as well as Chinese and Italian options.

Natraj Restaurant MULTICUISINE $$
(Map p276; mains ₹110-270) This is an excellent place to eat, and the rooftop has a satisfying view of the upper part of the Salim Singh-ki-Haveli next door. The veg and non-veg food, including tandoori and curries, as well as Chinese and Continental dishes, is consistently excellent, as is the service.

Saffron MULTICUISINE $$
(Map p276; Gandhi Chowk; mains ₹70-180) On the spacious roof terrace of Hotel Nachana Haveli, the veg and non-veg food here is excellent and it's a particularly atmospheric place in the evening. The Indian food is hard to beat, though the Italian comes a close second.

Free Tibet MULTICUISINE $$
(Map p280; Fort; mains ₹70-140; ☉8am-9pm) It's multi-multicuisine here, with everything from French baguettes to moussaka, but the speciality is Tibetan, including good noodle soups and *momos* (dumplings). It's near the fort's southeast corner, with good views from window tables.

Trio MULTICUISINE $$
(Map p276; ☑252733; Gandhi Chowk; mains ₹100-190) Under a tented roof atop the wall of the Mandir Palace, this long-running Indian, Chinese and Continental restaurant offers reliably good veg and non-veg dishes. The thalis and tandoori items are excellent, and

the restaurant has a lot more atmosphere than most places in town. Traditional musicians play in the evening and there's a great fort view.

Chandan Shree Restaurant INDIAN $
(Map p276; near Hanuman Circle; mains ₹50-90, thalis ₹60-140) An always busy (and rightfully so) dining hall serving up a huge range of tasty, spicy South Indian, Gujarati, Rajasthani, Punjabi and Bengali dishes.

Dhanraj Bhatia Sweets SWEETS $
(Map p280; off Gopa Chowk; sweets per 100g ₹13) This place in Bhatia Marketthas been churning out traditional sweet treats for 10 generations. It's renowned in Jaisalmer and beyond for its local specialities, such as *ghotua ladoos* (sweetmeat balls made with gram flour) and *panchadhari ladoos* (made with wheat flour).

Kanchan Shree Ice Cream ICE CREAM $
(Map p276; Gadiser Rd; lassi ₹15-30; ⊙9am-10pm) This friendly little dairy whips up homemade ice cream (₹10) and delicious *makhania* lassis, as well as numerous other flavours. You can also order lassis with a dollop of ice cream or fizzy ice-cream sodas.

Bhang Shop CAFE $
(Map p280; Gopa Chowk; medium/strong lassi ₹50/60) Outside the First Fort Gate, this 'shop' (not the most attractive establishment in town) offers lassis of different strengths as well as bhang cookies, cakes and sweets; camel-safari packs are a speciality. Note that bhang doesn't agree with everyone (see p342).

🛍 Shopping

Jaisalmer is famous for its stunning embroidery, bedspreads, mirror-work wall hangings, oil lamps, stonework and antiques. Watch out when purchasing silver items: the metal is sometimes adulterated with bronze.

Hari Om Jewellers HANDICRAFTS
(Map p280; Chougan Para, Fort; ⊙10am-8.30pm) This family of silversmiths makes beautiful, delicate silver rings and bracelets featuring world landmarks and Hindu gods. Asking prices for rings start at ₹1800 (at a rate of ₹300 per day's work).

Jaisalmer Handloom HANDICRAFTS
(Map p276; Court Rd; www.jaisalmerhandloom. com; ⊙9am-8pm) This place had a big array of bedspreads, tapestries, clothing (ready-made and custom-made, including silk) and

other textiles, made by its own workers and others, and it doesn't belabour you with too much of a hard sell.

Light of the East SOUVENIRS
(Tewata Para, Fort; ⊙8am-9pm) An enthralling little shop selling crystals and rare mineral specimens. The owner will probably whip back a little curtain to reveal an amazing apophyllite piece – not for sale.

Desert Handicrafts Emporium
HANDICRAFTS
(Map p276; Court Rd; ⊙9am-8pm) With some unusual jewellery, paintings and all sorts of textiles, this is one of the most original of numerous craft shops around town.

Bellissima HANDICRAFTS
(Map p280; Fort; ⊙8am-9pm) This small shop near the Fort's main square sells beautiful patchworks, embroidery, paintings, bags, rugs, cushion covers and all types of Rajasthani art. Proceeds assist women.

Silk Route Art Gallery HANDICRAFTS
(Map p280; btwn 3rd & 4th Fort Gates; ⊙8am-10pm) A particularly good selection of patchwork quilts, cushion covers and wall hangings put together from village and tribal textiles.

Bhatia Newsagency BOOKSTORE
(Map p276; Court Rd; ⊙9am-9pm) Has an excellent selection of new and secondhand books in several languages and day-old newspapers. It buys books, too.

Rawal Handicraft & Book Store BOOKSTORE
(Map p280; Vyas Para, Fort; ⊙9am-8pm) Another good selection of new and used books.

There are several good *khadi* (homespun cloth) shops where you can find fixed-price tablecloths, rugs, clothes, cushion covers and shawls, with a variety of patterning techniques including tie-dye, block printing and embroidery. Try **Zila Khadi Gramodan Parishad** (Malka Prol Rd; ⊙10am-6pm Mon-Sat), **Khadi Gramodyog Bhavan** (Dhibba; ⊙10am-6pm Mon-Sat) or **Gandhi Darshan Emporium** (near Hanuman Circle; ⊙11am-7pm Fri-Wed).

ℹ Information

Internet Access

There are several internet cafes in the fort, but not so many outside it. Typical cost is ₹40 per hour.

SOCH it (Map p276; Dhibba; internet per hr ₹40; ⊙7.30am-10pm)

Money

ATMs include State Bank and SBBJ near Hanuman Circle, SBBJ and ICICI Bank on Shiv Rd, and State Bank outside the train station.

Thomas Cook (Map p276;Gandhi Chowk; ☺9.30am-7pm Mon-Sat, 10am-5pm Sun) A reliable moneychanger, changing travellers cheques and cash. Also provides credit- and debit-card advances.

Post

Main post office (Map p276; Hanuman Circle Rd; ☺10am-5pm Mon-Sat)

Post office (Map p280; Gopa Chowk; ☺10am-5pm Mon-Fri, 10am-1pm Sat) Just outside the fort gate; sells stamps and you can send postcards.

Tourist Information

Tourist Reception Centre (Map p276; ☑252406; Gadi Sagar Rd; ☺9.30am-6pm) This friendly office has a free (if rather old) town map and various brochures. Staff will helpfully answer all sorts of questions.

Getting There & Away

Air

The airport, 5km south of town, opens and closes intermittently due to border tensions with Pakistan. In early 2011 it was closed. The most recent flights were operated by **Kingfisher Airlines** (www.flykingfisher.com) to Jodhpur.

Bus

RSRTC buses leave from a stand just off Shiv Rd on the south side of town. There are buses to Pokaran (ordinary/express ₹44/52, two hours, 20 daily), Jodhpur (₹125/155, 5½ hours, 15 daily), Phalodi (₹68/80, 3½ hours, four daily), Bikaner (₹130/162, seven hours, four daily) and Jaipur (semi-deluxe ₹375, 12 hours, 5.30pm).

Private buses mostly leave from a yard near Desert Boy's Dhani, south of the fort. You can book through your accommodation (which adds ₹30 to the fare) or direct with the bus company ticket offices, most of which are at Hanuman Circle, including **Swagat Travels**, which has buses to Jodhpur (seat/sleeper ₹150/250, 16 daily), Bikaner (₹150/250, three daily), Ahmedabad (₹350/450, 12 hours, 5.30pm) and Udaipur (₹350/450, 12 hours, 3.30pm), and **Hanuman Travels**, with services to Jaipur (₹280/380, 4.30pm) and Bhuj (₹400/800, 15 hours, 2.30pm). These prices are for direct buses; some agencies may also sell tickets requiring a change of bus at Jodhpur, and some travellers have found themselves in Jodhpur with a useless onward ticket, so do clarify what you're getting.

Taxi

One-way taxis should cost about ₹1800 to Jodhpur, ₹2500 to Bikaner or ₹4500 to Udaipur. There is a stand on Hanuman Circle Rd.

Train

The **station** (☺ticket office 8am-8pm Mon-Sat, 8am-1.45pm Sun) is on the eastern edge of town, just off the Jodhpur road.

Two daily express trains leave for Jodhpur. The *Jaisalmer–Jodhpur Express* (14809; sleeper/3AC ₹165/419) departs at 11.15pm, reaching Jodhpur at 5.20am. The 14060 *Jaisalmer–Delhi Express* leaves at 4.30pm, reaching Jodhpur (sleeper/3AC/2AC ₹165/419/566) at 9.50pm, and continues to Jaipur (₹262/693/945, 10½ hours from Jaisalmer) and Delhi (₹331/888/1215, 18½ hours).

Trains 14703 and 14701 leave Jaisalmer at 10.40am and 10.45pm respectively for Ramdevra, Phalodi (sleeper ₹130, 2½ to 2¾ hours) and Bikaner (₹168, 5½ hours).

ⓘ Getting Around

Autorickshaw

Official rates (first kilometre ₹11, each subsequent kilometre ₹6, minute of waiting ₹0.20) are posted at some autorickshaw stands. That adds up to about ₹25 from the train station to Gandhi Chowk, for example, but you may have to bargain hard to get this price.

Bicycle

A good way to get around town is by bicycle. There are a number of hire places, including **Narayan Cycles** (near Gandhi Chowk; per hr/day ₹10/40).

Car & Motorcycle

It's possible to hire taxis or jeeps from the **stand** on Hanuman Circle Rd. To Khuri, the Sam sand dunes or Lodhruva, expect to pay ₹500 return including a wait of about an hour or so. A full day of sightseeing around Jaisalmer is around ₹1000.

Shiva Bikes (Dhibba; scooter/motorbike per day ₹300/400) is a licensed hire place with adequate motorbikes and scooters for exploring town and nearby sights (helmets and area maps included).

Around Jaisalmer

There are several fascinating places to visit in the desolate, wind-swept landscape around Jaisalmer. A few local buses trundle out to some of them, but you can combine several sights in a day trip by taxi, jeep or even motorcycle (see p288), or fix a tour through Jaisalmer's Tourist Reception Centre (p288).

Note that most of Rajasthan west of National Hwy 15 is a restricted area, requiring special permission from the **district magistrate** (☑02992-252201) in Jaisalmer, which is usually issued only in exceptional circumstances. However, Bada Bagh, Amar Sagar, Lodhruva, Kuldara, Khaba, Sam, Akal and Khuri are among places exempt from the restrictions.

BADA BAGH

Six kilometres north of Jaisalmer, Bada Bagh is a fertile oasis with a big old tank (now often dry) that was built by Maharawal Jait Singh II in the 16th century and completed after his death by his son.

Above the tank (closed to visitors) are picturesque **chhatris** (Indian/foreigner ₹20/50, camera/video ₹20/50; ⊙7am-6.307pm), monuments to Jaisalmer royals spanning the 16th to 20th centuries. Many *chhatris* have beautifully carved ceilings and sculptures of kings (often on horseback) and queens. On Maharawal Jait Singh's memorial there is an inscription stating that on his death his queen and 10 concubines committed *sati*.

AMAR SAGAR

This once-pleasant **formal garden** (admission ₹10; ⊙8am-5pm), 7km northwest of Jaisalmer and 4km west of Bada Bagh, is still Jaisalmer royal property but has fallen into decay. According to locals, the step-wells here were built by prostitutes.

On the far (west) bank of the lake here (2km by road) is a beautifully restored and finely carved 18th-century **Jain temple** (Indian/foreigner donation/₹30, camera/video/mobile-phone camera ₹70/120/30; ⊙dawn-dusk) that's well worth a look. The lake usually dries up in the dry season.

LODHRUVA

The Bhati Rajput capital before Jaisalmer, the deserted ruins of Lodhruva are 17km northwest of Jaisalmer and 10km beyond Amar Sagar. Lodhruva (also spelt Ludarva and several other variations), was probably founded by the Lodra Rajputs, and passed to Bhati Devaraja, ruler of Devagarh, in the 10th century. In 1025 Mahmud of Ghazni laid siege to the town and it was sacked various times over subsequent decades, prompting Bhati leader Jaisal to shift the capital to a new location – Jaisalmer – in 1156.

The Jain temples, rebuilt in the late 1970s, are the sole reminders of the city's former magnificence. The inner sanctum of the

main temple (Indian/foreigner donation/₹30, camera/video ₹70/120; ⊙dawn-dusk) enshrines a finely wrought, silver-crowned image of Parasnath, the 23rd *tirthankar,* surrounded by fine sculptures. The small sculptures around the lower course of the inner sanctum are badly damaged and bear the scars of Muslim raids long ago.

Before the temple, just inside the outer gate, is a beautiful *toran* arch. The ornate rosette in the centre of the drum of the dome over the *mandapa* was carved from a single piece of stone. Behind the inner sanctum is a 200-year-old carved stone slab that bears images of the *tirthankars'* feet in miniature. The temple compound is said to be home to a pair of cobras, sight of either of which brings good luck!

KULDARA

This abandoned **village** (admission ₹10, vehicle ₹50; ⊙dawn-dusk) is 19km west of Jaisalmer, 6km south of the Sam road. It was abandoned by its Paliwal Brahmin inhabitants – just like the area's 83 other Paliwal Brahmin villages – about 200 years ago. They were heavily taxed, their property was looted and the daughter of one family had been kidnapped, but there was no response to their complaints, so the entire community upped and left. Legend has it they buried the gold and silver they couldn't carry in Kuldara, which has attracted treasure hunters to the area.

Some of the houses are in remarkable condition as they have been restored for use as film sets – this is a popular Bollywood location.

KHABA

This is another of the abandoned Paliwal Brahmin villages, with a small, partly restored **fort** (admission ₹10; ⊙dawn-dusk) overlooking the ruins, which stand beside a seasonal lake. Khaba is about 12km south of Damodra, which is 20km west of Jaisalmer on the Sam road.

SAM SAND DUNES

The silky **Sam sand dunes** (admission vehicle/camel ₹50/80), 41km west of Jaisalmer along a good sealed road (maintained by the Indian army), are one of the most popular excursions from the city. The band of dunes is about 2km long and is undeniably one of the most picturesque in the region. Some camel safaris camp here, but many more people just roll in for sunset, to be chased across the sands by dressed-up dancing children and

JAISALMER CAMEL SAFARIS

Trekking around by camel is the most evocative and fun way to sample Thar Desert life. Don't expect dune seas, however – the Thar is mostly arid scrubland sprinkled with villages and wind turbines, with occasional dune areas popping out here and there. You will often come across fields of millet, and children herding flocks of sheep or goats whose neck-bells tinkle in the desert silence – a welcome change after the sound of belching camels.

The best time to go is from October to February. Temperatures top 40°C from mid-April to mid-July. If you're short on time, you can always join the crowds and take a one- or two-hour ride at Sam Dunes or Khuri, but spending at least one night out in the desert is much more memorable experience. Most trips now include jeep rides to get you to less frequented areas. An alternative to Jaisalmer is to base yourself in Khuri, 48km southwest, where some good safaris are available and you're already in the desert when you start.

Before You Go

Competition between safari organisers is cut-throat and standards vary. Most hotels and guesthouses are very happy to organise a camel safari for you. While many provide a good service, some may cut corners and take you for the kind of ride you didn't have in mind. A few low-budget hotels in particular exert considerable pressure on guests to take 'their' safari. Others specifically claim 'no safari hassle'.

You can also organise a safari direct with one of the several reputable specialist agencies in Jaisalmer. This removes one layer of middlemen from the arrangement. Since these agencies depend exclusively on safari business it's particularly in their interest to satisfy their clients. Neither hotels nor most of the agencies own their own camels – they're go-betweens between you and the camel owners.

Talk to other travellers and ask two or three operators what they're offering. If a hotelier makes you feel uneasy about this, that's reason to be uneasy about them. Don't let yourself be pressured by claims that places are available only if you sign up straight away.

Start with a basic idea of how long you want to go for, and what kind of area you want to head to, then check out prices and exactly what is included. Camels are generally pretty docile and all you really have to do is sit there and do a little steering, but you may well suffer stiff legs and/or back and get saddle sores. Be cautious of sun exposure, too.

A one-night safari, leaving Jaisalmer in the afternoon and returning next morning, with a night on some dunes, is a minimum to get a feel for the experience: you'll probably get 1½ to two hours riding each day. You can trek for several days or weeks if you wish. The longer you ride, the more you'll gain understanding of the desert's villages, oases, wildlife and people.

The best known dunes, at Sam (40km west of Jaisalmer) and Khuri, are always crowded in the evening and are more of a carnival than a back-to-nature experience. 'Non-touristy' safaris take you to other areas but some of these have almost become standard now, so 'off the beaten track' is the new catchphrase; these trips head southwest from Jaisalmer to the area between Sam and Khuri, or beyond Khuri.

With jeep transfers included, typical rates are between ₹550 and ₹750 per person per day. This should include three meals a day, plus as much mineral water and as many blankets as you need, and often thin mattresses. Check that there will be one camel for each rider. Stirrups can make the ride a lot more comfortable. You can pay for greater levels of comfort (eg tents, better food), but always get it all down in writing. If an operator is unwill-

tenacious camel owners offering short rides. Plenty more people stay overnight in one of the couple of dozen tent resorts near the dunes. All in all the place acquires something of a carnival atmosphere from late afternoon till the next morning, making it somewhere to avoid if you're after a solitary desert sunset experience. However, it is still just about possible to frame pictures of solitary camels against lonely, wind-rippled dunes.

The tent hotels cater primarily to group tourists with one-night packages that generally include a camel ride, cultural show (traditional Rajasthani music and dance), campfire, dinner and breakfast. Package rates for two people start at around ₹2500. One of the ing to write down what they have agreed to provide you, and the agreed price, you have a right be suspicious.

Establish what time you'll be leaving Jaisalmer and getting back. You shouldn't have to pay for a full day if you're returning after breakfast on the last day. One-night safaris starting in the afternoon and ending the following morning are normally charged as about 1½ days.

What to Take

Women should consider wearing a sports bra, as a trotting camel is a bumpy ride. A wide-brimmed hat (or Lawrence of Arabia turban), long trousers, long-sleeved shirt, insect repellent, toilet paper, torch, sunscreen, water bottle (with a strap), and some cash (for a tip to the camel men, if nothing else) are also recommended. It can get cold at night, so if you have a sleeping bag bring it along, even if you're told that lots of blankets will be supplied. During summer, rain is not unheard of, so come prepared.

Which Safari?

» **Ganesh Travels** (Map p280; ☑250138; ganeshtravel45@hotmail.com; Fort) Run by camel owners from the villages and has a good basic rate of ₹550 per day. Most shorter trips are in the Bersiala area, 50km to 60km southwest of Jaisalmer.

» **Sahara Travels** (Map p280; ☑252609; sahara_travels@yahoo.com; Gopa Chowk) Its office is just outside the First Fort Gate. This agency gets good reviews and is run by the proudly bearded and moustachioed LN Bissa, alias Mr Desert. Trips may circle the area around Sam, or head out beyond Khuri. The normal daily rate is ₹700.

» **Trotters** (Map p280; ☑9414469292; www.trotterscamelsafarijaisalmer.com; Gopa Chowk) Trotters has a daily rate of ₹750 but provides very reliable service. Its one-night, off-the-beaten-track option costs between ₹900 and ₹1500 depending on your departure and return times.

There are several other options, including hotel-organised safaris. Note that recommendations here should not be a substitute for doing your own research. Whichever agency you go for, insist that all rubbish is carried back to Jaisalmer.

In the Desert

Camping out at night, huddling around a tiny fire beneath the stars and listening to the camel drivers' songs, is magical.

There's always a long lunch stop during the hottest part of the day. At resting points the camels are unsaddled and hobbled; they'll often have a roll in the sand before limping away to browse on nearby shrubs, while the camel drivers brew chai or prepare food. The whole crew rests in the shade of thorn trees.

Take care of your possessions, particularly on the return journey. Any complaints you do have should be reported, either to the **Superintendent of Police** (☑252233), the **Tourist Reception Centre**, or the intermittently staffed **Tourist Assistance Force** posts inside the First Fort Gate and on the Gadi Sagar access road.

The camel drivers will expect a tip or gift at the end of the trip; don't neglect to give them one.

classier places, though still a pre-packaged experience, is **Chokhi Dhani** (☑9314879806; tent incl 2 meals & camel safari ₹6000), which is in a large 'ethnic village' compound about 1km before the dunes. The tents have carpets, brightly patterned bedspreads, big bathrooms with hot water, and nice blue linings with white stars. The entertainment

here encompasses archery, playground rides, a craft market, puppetry and a magician, as well as music and dance performances.

If you're organising your own camel ride on the spot, expect to pay ₹200 to ₹300 for a one-hour sunset ride, but beware tricks from camel men such as demanding more money en route.

AKAL WOOD FOSSIL PARK

About 1km off the road to Barmer, 17km from Jaisalmer, are the amazing fossilised remnants of a 180-million-year-old **forest** (Indian/foreigner ₹10/20; ◷8am-1pm & 2-6pm). They're a collection of fallen, broken logs protected by little corrugated-iron shelters. The largest fossil is 13.4m long and 0.4m wide. The climate here was once hot and humid – a stark contrast with today's dry desert. Near the entrance is a small display where you get the chance to stroke an ancient red wood tree-trunk fossil.

A return taxi will cost around ₹500.

KHURI

☏03014

The village of Khuri, 48km southwest of Jaisalmer, has quite extensive dune areas attracting their share of sunset visitors, and a lot of mostly smallish 'resorts' offering the same sort of overnight packages as Sam. It also has a number of low-key guesthouses where you can stay in tranquillity in a traditional-style hut with clay-and-dung walls and thatched roof, and venture out on interesting camel trips in the relatively remote and empty surrounding area. Khuri is within the Desert National Park, which stretches over 3162 sq km southwest of Jaisalmer to protect part of the Thar ecosystem, including wildlife such as the desert fox, desert cat, chinkara gazelle, nilgai or bluebull (a large antelope), and some unusual bird life including the endangered great Indian bustard.

Be aware that the commission system is entrenched in Khuri's larger accommodation options.

🛏 Sleeping & Eating

TOP CHOICE **Badal House** HOMESTAY $
(☏9660535389; per person incl full board r or hut ₹300) Here you can stay in a family compound in the centre of the village with a few spotlessly clean, mud-walled, thatch-roofed huts and equally spotless rooms (one with its own squat toilet), and enjoy good home cooking. Former camel driver Badal Singh is a charming, gentle man who charges ₹500 for a camel safari with a night on the dunes. He doesn't pay commission so don't let touts warn you away.

Gangaur Guest House GUESTHOUSE $
(☏7742547711, 9929296900; hameersingh@yahoo.com; huts without/with bathroom per person ₹500/00, tent per person ₹1000) One of the closest lodgings to the main dunes (on the south side of the village), this has yet an-

other circle of snug huts. Prices are for packages including a camel ride, dinner with traditional dance entertainment and breakfast. Wildlife **jeep tours** (per person per day ₹500) as well as overnight camel safaris in the less touristy area east of Khuri are on offer.

Arjun Family GUESTHOUSE $
(☏274132; arjunguesthouse@yahoo.co.in; per person incl full board huts/r ₹150/200) A couple of doors from Badal House, this is another friendly family offering very clean lodgings, home-cooked meals and inexpensive safaris. Rooms have attached bathroom, huts don't.

Mama's Guest House GUESTHOUSE $
(☏274042; gajendra_sodha 2003@yahoo.com; per person without bathroom incl half-board ₹500) A long-running place opposite Badal House with a circle of cosy, clean, whitewashed huts. A basic/luxurious overnight camel safari costs ₹650/900.

❶ Getting There & Away

Private buses to Khuri (₹30, one hour) leave from the Barmer road corner in the southeast of Jaisalmer at about 10.30am, 11.30am, 3.30pm and 5pm. You may be approached by camel-safari touts en route.

Bikaner

☏0151 / POP 529,007

Bikaner is a vibrant, dust-swirling desert town with a fabulous fort and an energising outpost feel. It's less dominated by tourism than many other Rajasthan cities, though it has plenty of hotels and a busy camel-safari scene, which is attracting more and more travellers looking to avoid the Jaisalmer hustle. Bikaner's atmospheric walled old city sits in what's now the southwest of the city, with the main train station (Bikaner Junction) and Junagarh fort to its northeast, in what's more or less the centre of town. The northern parts of town are more modern, with wider, straighter streets.

Few people come to Bikaner without taking a trip out to the notorious Karni Mata Temple at Deshnok, 30km south, where pilgrims worship thousands of holy rats. Less Brothers Grimm, but still fairy tale, is the small temple town of Kolayat, with its holy lake and religious fair, 51km to the southwest.

Around the full moon in January or very late December, Bikaner celebrates its three-day Camel Festival (p253), with one day of events at the Karni Singh Stadium and two days out at Ladera, 45km northeast of the city.

History

The city was founded in 1488 by Rao Bika, a son of Rao Jodha, Jodhpur's founder, though the two Rathore ruling houses later had a serious falling out over who had the right to keep the family heirlooms. It grew fast as a staging post on the great caravan trade routes from the late 16th century onwards, and flourished under a friendly relationship with the Mughals, but declined as they did in the 18th century. Its harsh desert surroundings fortunately spared it the Maratha attacks that then plagued many other cities. By the 19th century the area was markedly backward, but managed to turn its fortunes around by hiring out camels to the British during the Afghan War. In 1886 it was the first desert princely state to install electricity.

Maharaja Dungar Singh (r 1872–87) introduced new hospitals, police and schools and is considered the founder of modern Bikaner. Maharaja Ganga Singh (r 1887–1943) was one of Rajasthan's most notable and accomplished rulers. His clever diplomacy and canny economic sense helped develop Bikaner. He promoted the Ganga Canal, built between 1925 and 1927, which continues to irrigate a large area of arid land. He later led the Indian delegation to the League of Nations.

⊙ Sights

TOP CHOICE **Junagarh**   FORT
(Indian/foreigner ₹30/200, video ₹100, audio-guide incl camera ₹250; ⊙10am-5.30pm, last entry 4.30pm) This most impressive fort was constructed between 1589 and 1593 by Raja Rai Singh, ruler of Bikaner and a general in the army of the Mughal Emperor Akbar. Palaces and luxurious suites were added inside the fort by subsequent maharajas, making a picturesque ensemble of courtyards, balconies, *chhatris,* towers and windows, with superb stone carving. Unlike many Rajasthan forts, Junagarh doesn't command a hilltop position. But it's no less imposing for that and – a credit to its planners and architects – it has never been conquered. Its 986m-long wall, with 37 bastions, is surrounded by a (now dry) moat. You enter through the Karan Prole gate on the east side and pass through three more gates before the ticket office for the palace-museum. The carved handprints on the third gate, Daulat Prole, commemorate the wives of Rajput soldiers lost in battles, who committed *sati* on their husbands' funeral pyres.

The admission price includes a group tour in Hindi and/or English with an official guide. The one-hour tours leave every 15 to 20 minutes. The audio-guide (requiring an identity document as a deposit), available in English, French, German and Hindi, is very informative and allows you to visit at a more leisurely pace.

The beautifully decorated **Karan Mahal** was the palace's Diwan-i-Am (Hall of Public Audience), built in the 17th and 18th centuries, and the rulers' silver coronation throne can still be seen here. According to local lore, Maharaja Karan Singh (r 1631–69) was camping at Golkonda in southern India, in his capacity as a general in the Mughal army, when an artist named Ali Raza showed him fine works in gold. Ali Raza said his family was originally from Jaisalmer, but had migrated to southern India when a famine swept over his homeland. The maharaja invited the artist to return to Bikaner, where he was given royal patronage. His work, and that of his students, is now seen in the Karan Mahal and the Anup Mahal, which you visit a little later in the tour. The *sonakin* style, seen on the Karan Mahal's walls, features white plaster decorated with delicate patterns and painted with gold leaf; the *jangali sunthari* style, on the ceiling, features plaster with a green backing that depicts floral motifs; and the *manovat* style features plaster embossments on clay pillars, painted with gold leaf.

Anup Mahal Chowk has lovely carved *jarokhas* (balcony-windows) and *jali* screens, through which the women of the zenana could watch the activities below. It was commissioned in the late 17th century by Maharaja Anup Mahal, a noted patron of the arts in what is considered Bikaner's golden age. Off here are a room of Bikaner state heirlooms and royal insignia, the sumptuously decorated **Anup Mahal** – a hall of private audience with painted marble columns and walls lacquered in red and gold – and the **Badal Mahal** (Cloud Palace), whose walls are beautifully painted with blue cloud motifs, red and gold lightning, and rain at the foot of the walls.

The **Gaj Mandir**, the suite of Maharaja Gaj Singh (r 1745–87) and his two top wives, is a fantastic symphony of gold paint, colourful murals, sandalwood, ivory, mirrors, niches and stained glass. Its central bedroom is a *sheesh mahal* (hall of mirrors).

From here you head up to the palace roof to enjoy the views and, if it's open, have a

Bikaner

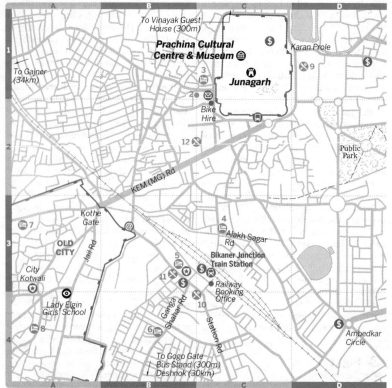

Bikaner

look at the **Hawa Mahal** (Palace of Winds – used in the summer). The mirror positioned over the bed here is said to have enabled Maharaja Dungar Singh to see the reflec- tions of people walking across the courtyard and thus alert him to potential enemies (al- though other motives might be suspected). The decorative blue tiles on some of the

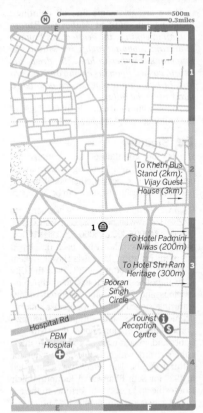

Prachina Cultural Centre & Museum
(Indian/foreigner ₹10/50, camera ₹20; ⊙9am-6pm) The museum, across the fort's main courtyard from the palace entrance, is fascinating and well labelled. It focuses on the Western influence on the Bikaner royals before Independence, including crockery from England and France and menu cards from 1936, as well as some exquisite costumes, jewellery and textiles, and intriguing everyday ephemera. There are also exhibits on contemporary Bikaner crafts.

Old City

The old city still has a medieval feel despite the motorbikes and autorickshaws. This labyrinth of narrow, winding streets conceals a number of fine old *havelis*, and a couple of notable Jain temples just inside the south wall, 1.5km southwest of Bikaner Junction train station. It makes for an interesting wander – we guarantee you will get lost at least once. The old city is encircled by a 7km-long, 18th-century wall with five entrance gates. The main entrance from the city centre is the triple-arched Kothe Gate, which is surrounded by a bustling commercial area.

Bhandasar Temple
(⊙5am-1pm & 5.30-11.30pm) Of the two Jain temples, Bhandasar is particularly beautiful, with yellow-stone carving and dizzyingly vibrant paintings. It's dedicated to the fifth *tirthankar*, Sumtinath, and was commissioned in 1468 by a wealthy Jain merchant, Bhandasa Oswal. It was completed after his death in 1514.

The interior of the temple is stunning. The pillars bear floral arabesques and depictions of the lives of the 24 Jain *tirthankars*. It's said that 40,000kg of ghee was used instead of water in the mortar, which locals insist seeps through the floor on hot days.

On the 1st floor of the three-storey temple are beautiful miniatures of the sentries of the gods. There are fine views over the city from the 3rd floor, with the desert stretching to the west. The priest will probably ask for a donation in excess of ₹100, of which half will go to your guide. In fact, a trust pays for the upkeep of the temples.

Sandeshwar Temple
(⊙6am-12.30pm & 4-7.30pm) The second Jain temple, smaller than Bhandasar and built around the same time, has good carving around the door architraves and columns, and ornately carved, painted pillars. Inside

roofs up here were imported from Europe and China.

Moving on, you reach **Ganga Niwas Chowk**, with its European-style columns, and then the arms galleries, before entering the superb **Ganga Durbar Hall** of 1896, designed by Sir Samuel Swinton Jacob (also responsible for Bikaner's Laxmi Niwas and Lallgarh Palaces). The hall's pink stone walls are covered in fascinating relief carvings, on themes of different deities, and include dozens of beautiful animal and plant figures.

You then move into **Maharaja Ganga Singh's office** and finally the **Vikram Vilas Durbar Hall**, which he had built in 1935. Pride of place here goes to a De Havilland DH-9 biplane bomber, pieced together from parts of two planes that were shot down during WWI and presented to Ganga Singh as war souvenirs by the British government.

the drum of the *sikhara* (spire) are almost ethereal paintings, and the sanctum itself has a marble image of Neminath, the 22nd *tirthankar,* flanked by smaller marble statues of other *tirthankars.*

Lakshminath Temple

(⊙5am-1pm & 7.30-11.30pm) Behind Bhandasar Temple, to the right, is the splendid Hindu Lakshminath Temple. It was built during the reign of Rao Lunkaran between 1505 and 1526. Lakshminath was the patron god of the rulers of Bikaner, and during major religious festivals a royal procession headed by the maharaja paid homage at the temple. The elaborate edifice was maintained with tributes received from five villages and several shops, which were granted to the temple by Maharaja Ganga Singh. Photography is prohibited here. Around 10.30am and 9.30pm you may witness praying in Sanskrit.

Sri Sadul Museum   MUSEUM

(Indian/foreigner ₹25/50; camera/video free/₹150; ⊙10am-5.30pm) In the grounds of the royal Lallgarh Palace (now a hotel) about 2km northeast of Junagarh, this well-presented museum celebrates the history of Bikaner's Rathore royal family. You can see Maharaja Sadul Singh's 1940s railway carriage, Maharaja Karni Singh's golf clubs and hairbrush, a nice collection of Bikaner school miniatures, and lots of shooting photos right down to the medals of contemporary Princess Rajyashree Kumari, who excelled in target shooting rather than wildlife shooting.

Ganga Government Museum   MUSEUM

(Indian/foreigner ₹10/50; ⊙10am-5pm Tue-Sun) This museum, on the Jaipur road, houses well-displayed, interesting exhibits including terracotta ware from the Gupta period, Rajasthani traditional musical instruments, rich gold paintings by local artisans, exquisite carpets and royal vestments, and miniature models of the Gajner and Lallgarh palaces and the Royal Bikaner train.

Also on show are decrees issued by the Mughals to the maharajas of Bikaner, including one advising Rai Singh to proceed to Delhi 'without any delay and with utmost expedition and speed, travelling over as great a distance as possible during the day time as well as by night' as 'Emperor Akbar is dying'. It was issued by Crown Prince (who would shortly become Emperor) Jehangir.

There are also some fine oil paintings, including one entitled *Maharaja Padam Singhji avenging...the death of his brother, Maharaja Mohan Singhji by killing the Emperor's brother-in-law...He drew his sword, rushed upon his enemy and severed him in two with a blow which also left a mark upon the pillar.*

The museum entrance is at the back of the building on the left-hand side.

🛏 Sleeping

Hotels and guesthouses are scattered all round town. If you're arriving by train in the early morning, check whether you'll have to pay extra for occupying the room before noon.

Bhanwar Niwas   HERITAGE HOTEL $$$

(☑2529323; www.bhanwarniwas.com; Rampuria St, Old City; s ₹4000-5000, d ₹5000-6000, ste ₹14,000; ❋@) This superb hotel has been developed out of the beautiful Rampuria Haveli – a gem in the old city, 300m southwest of the City Kotwali police station. It has 26 all-different, spacious and delightfully decorated rooms, featuring stencil-painted wallpaper, marble or mosaic floors and antique furnishings. Comfortable common rooms drip with antiques and are arranged around a large internal courtyard, which doubles as a venue for cultural events. The *haveli* was completed in 1927 for Seth Bhanwarlal Rampuria, heir to a textile and real-estate fortune. In the entrance gate is a stunning blue 1927 Buick.

Hotel Desert Winds   HOTEL $$

(☑2542202; www.hoteldesertwinds.in; s ₹900-1100, d ₹1100-1300; ❋@) This lovely hotel with spotless, spacious rooms and a friendly, relaxed atmosphere is 1km northeast of the fort. It's owned by a retired deputy director of Rajasthan Tourism and his family, who can give you plenty of info about the city. Located opposite Karni Singh Stadium.

Bhairon Vilas   HERITAGE HOTEL $$

(☑2544751, 9928312283; http://hotelbhaironvilas. tripod.com; s ₹1000-1800, d ₹1300-2100; ❋@⌨) This hotel on the west side of Junagarh is run by a former Bikaner prime minister's great-grandson. Rooms are mostly large and are eclectically decorated with antiques, gold-threaded curtains and old family photographs (some of the wiring and fittings seem to be of the same vintage). There's a bar straight out of the Addams Family, a restaurant in the garden (which is stalked by some fine poultry) and a boutique and art shop that specialises in beautiful, original wedding saris. Three-hour city tours with government-authorised guides (₹200) and a range of camel and jeep safaris are on offer.

Laxmi Niwas Palace HERITAGE HOTEL **$$$**
(☑2202777; www.laxminiwaspalace.com; s ₹7700-9900, d ₹8800-11,000, ste ₹18,000-25,000; ❋@🛜) Located two kilometres north of the city centre, this pink-sandstone hotel is part of the royal palace, dating from 1902. It has opulent interiors with lovely stone carving. Rooms are mostly large, elegant and evocative, and the bar and billiards room are overlooked by skins, heads and photos of deceased wildlife. A nightly dance show accompanies dinner in the central courtyard, beneath the palace's fabulously carved *zenana*.

Hotel Jaswant Bhawan HOTEL **$$**
(☑2548848; www.hoteljaswantbhawan.com; s/d ₹600/800, with AC ₹1000/1200; ❋@) This is a pleasant, quiet, welcoming place run by descendants of Bikaner prime ministers. It has a small garden and a nice, comfy, old-fashioned sitting room with historic family photos. The air-conditioned rooms are spacious, plain and airy, though some of the external paintwork needs attention. Good meals (Indian vegetarian unless you request otherwise) are available at ₹100/250/275 for breakfast/lunch/dinner. It's a two-minute walk from the main station (via the station's 'foot over bridge'); self-catering is also possible.

BIKANER SAFARIS

Bikaner is an excellent alternative to the Jaisalmer camel safari scene and increasingly popular with travellers. There are fewer people running safaris here, so the hassle factor is quite low. Camel trips tend to be in the areas east and south of the city and focus on the isolated desert villages of the Jat, Bishnoi, Meghwal and Rajput peoples. Interesting wildlife can be spotted here, such as bluebull antelopes (nilgai), chinkara gazelles, desert foxes, hares and cats, spiny-tailed lizards and plenty of birds including peacocks and winter visitors like the griffon vulture, demoiselle crane and steppe eagle.

Three days and two nights is a common camel-safari duration, but half-day, one-day and short overnight trips are all possible. If you're after a serious camel trek, go for a cross-country trip to Phalodi/Kichan (about six days) or Jaisalmer (two weeks). The best months to head into the desert on a camel are October to February. Avoid mid-April to mid-July, when it's searingly hot.

Typical costs are ₹1000 to ₹1200 per person per day including overnight camping, with tents, mattresses, blankets, meals, mineral water, one camel per person, a camel cart to carry gear (and sometimes tired riders), and a guide in addition to the camel men.

Many trips start at Raisar, about 8km east of Bikaner, or Deshnok, 30km south. Travelling to the starting point by bus rather than jeep is one way of cutting costs.

Many accommodation places in Bikaner can arrange camel trips but you can easily deal direct with the main operators, some of whom run their own Bikaner guesthouses too. The two most popular operators, both reliable and long-established, are the **Camel Man** (☑2231244, 9829217331; www.camelman.com; Vijay Guest House, Jaipur Rd), run by Vijay Singh Rathore, and **Vino Desert Safari** (☑2270445, 9414139245; www.vinodesertsafari.com; Vino Paying Guest House, Ganga Shahar), run by Vinod Bhojak.

Smaller operators worth checking out include **Desert Tours** (☑2521967; www.uniqueidea.org; Cyber Station), run by the experienced Kamal Saxena; **AFEV** (☑9829867323; www.afevinde.com; Pause Café, KEM Rd), a French-run NGO that (among other things) provides some medical, veterinary and financial support to camel men; and **Kaku Safari** (☑9829218237; www.kakusafari.com), which takes trips in the little-visited area around Kaku, 80km south of Bikaner – contact Bhagwan Singh, manager at **Bhanwar Niwas**, for further information.

You can also explore the Bikaner-area deserts and villages on other kinds of transport. AFEV offers one- or two-night horse-cart or bike trips; Desert Tours does jeep safaris to Phalodi (three days) or Jaisalmer (five days); and **Vinayak Desert Safari** (☑2202634; www.vinayakdesertsafari.com; Vinayak Guest House) does appealing jeep safaris (per person per day ₹1500) with zoologist Jitu Solanki. This safari focuses on desert animals and birds including the enormous cinereous vulture, with its 3m wingspan, which visits the area in numbers from November to March.

Vijay Guest House　　　　GUESTHOUSE $
(☑2231244, 9829217331; www.camelman.com; Jaipur Rd; s ₹300-1000, d ₹400-1200; a) About 4km east of the centre, this is a home away from home with 10 spacious, light-filled rooms and a friendly family. Owner Vijay is a camel expert and a recommended safari operator. This is an ideal base for taking a safari, with a comfortable common room and good home-cooked meals (₹125 to ₹200), which you can eat inside or in the garden. As well as camel trips, they offer free pickup and drop-off from the train and bus stations, jeep outings to Deshnok and other sights around Bikaner, and two-night tours to their house in the untouristy village of Thelasar, Shekhawati.

Hotel Padmini Niwas　　　　HOTEL $
(☑2522794; padmini_hotel@rediffmail.com; 148 Sadul Ganj; r without/with AC ₹850/1050; ❀@≋) A fabulous place to unwind away from the rush of the city. Padmini Niwas has clean, carpeted rooms and a chilled-out, helpful owner. The lawn area is a revelation, boasting one of the town's few outdoor pools.

Hotel Marudhar Heritage　　　　HOTEL $
(☑2522524; hmheritage2000@hotmail.com; Ganga Shahar Rd; s ₹400-1200, d ₹500-1500; ❀@) This is a friendly, well-run and good-value option a short walk from the main train station. There are plain and comfortable rooms with TV and phone to suit most budgets. You may wish to avoid the carpeted rooms which are a bit musty. Check-out is 24 hours after you check in. You can order veg meals in your room and there are nice views from the roof.

Hotel Meghsar Castle　　　　HOTEL $
(☑2527315, 9982249016; www.hotelmeghsar
castle.com; 9 Gajner Rd; r ₹300-1050; ❀@) This hotel is 900m north of Junagarh and has clean, old-fashioned rooms with terrazzo and tile surfaces, some echoingly large. It's a well-run, friendly place, with meals available in the garden. The front rooms can suffer from a bit of traffic noise.

Vinayak Guest House　　　　GUESTHOUSE $
(☑2202634; vinayakguesthouse@gmail.com; r ₹150-800, s without bathroom ₹100; ❀@) This place offers six varied and clean rooms in a quiet family house with a little sandy garden (hot water only by bucket in some rooms). On offer are a free pickup service, good home-cooked food, cooking lessons, bicycles (per day ₹25) and camel safaris and wildlife trips with Vinayak Desert Safari. It's just 400m north of Junagarh fort.

Vino Paying Guest House　　　　GUESTHOUSE $
(☑2270445, 9414139245; www.vinodesertsafari.
com; Ganga Shahar; s ₹150-200, d ₹250-350; @≋) This guesthouse is in a family home 3km south of the main train station. It's a cosy choice and is the base of one of Bikaner's best camel-safari operations. They have six rooms in the house and six in cool adobe huts around the garden, where there's also a plunge pool. It's excellent value, and the family is enthusiastic, helpful and welcoming. They also serve up good home-cooked food and offer free cooking classes. It's opposite Gopeshwar Temple; they'll pick you up for free from the train station.

Shanti House　　　　GUESTHOUSE $
(☑2543306, inoldcity@yahoo.com; New Well, near City Kotwali; r ₹250-400; @) This tiny old-city *haveli* has a narrow staircase and four bargain rooms with squat toilets, bucket hot water and some nice wall paintings. The bustle of old Bikaner is at your doorstep. The helpful owner, Gouri, is knowledgeable and can walk you around the old city (per person per hour ₹30). Free cooking classes and station pickups (a good idea as it's not the easiest place to find – call the day before) are offered.

Hotel Palace View　　　　HOTEL $
(☑2543625; hotelpalaceview@gmail.com; Lallgarh Palace Campus; s/d ₹500/600, AC ₹700/800; ❀) This place is in the north of town, close to the bus station and Lallgarh Palace, with, yes, some palace views. It's a spotless place, whose hosts take pride in accommodating their guests. The decoration is spare and the ambience subdued, but is a good choice for those looking for a little peace.

Lallgarh Palace　　　　HERITAGE HOTEL $$$
(☑2540201; www.lallgarhpalace.com; s/d ₹5000/6000, ste ₹14,000-25,000; ❀@≋) Occupying another section of the same royal palace as the Laxmi Niwas Palace hotel, Lallgarh Palace has less atmosphere but still offers huge, well-appointed suites in the main building and the more modern Sajjan Niwas wing. There is an indoor pool (₹350 per hour for nonguests), as well as a billiard room, tennis facilities and in-house astrologer.

Hotel Shri Ram Heritage　　　　HOTEL/HOSTEL $
(☑2522651; www.hotelshriram.com, www.yhaindia.
org; 228 Sadul Ganj; hostel s ₹200-600, d ₹300-800, hotel s ₹500-1100, d ₹700-1500; ❀☏) In a quiet area 2km east of the main train station, Shri Ram Heritage is a combination of a YHA-affiliated youth hostel and a guesthouse-like hotel. Despite its diversity, it retains a fam-

ily atmosphere, with home-cooked meals available. Rooms vary in size and comfort and are clean, with solar-heated water. Free pickup from the train and bus stations is offered, and note the 9am checkout.

Karni Bhawan Palace Hotel
HERITAGE HOTEL **$$**

(2524701; www.hrhhotels.com; Gandhi Nagar; ste ₹5000; ❀@☎) This hotel is about 500m east of Lallgarh Palace and was briefly the residence of Maharaja Karni Singh. It's a red-and-white 1940s edifice in art deco style, which may or may not be to your taste, but the suites are huge, high-ceilinged and well equipped, and the place is well run. A visit to the stunning Gajner Palace hotel and Gajner Wildlife Sanctuary outside Bikaner can be arranged.

Hotel Harasar Haveli
HOTEL **$$**

(2209891; www.harasar.com; near Karni Singh Stadium; r ₹500-2000) Most rickshaw-wallahs will want to bring you to this hotel, 1km northeast of Junagarh fort, which is notorious for its commission-paying tactics. So it's a good place to meet other travellers. The 38 plain rooms cover a big range in price, size and cleanliness. There's a decent rooftop restaurant.

Mohan Kunj
GUESTHOUSE **$**

(9461246154; mohangkunj@yahoo.com; behind Prakash Chitra, near Dauji Rd, Old City; r ₹150-750; ❀) Opened in 2011 by the family behind Shanti House, this has bigger rooms, seat toilets and hot showers.

Hotel Joshi
HOTEL **$**

(2527700; Station Rd; s ₹375-900, d ₹500-1000; ❀) Hotel Joshi's unexciting, well-used rooms are the best of the Station Rd cheapies (the alternatives are quite depressing). It's friendly, conveniently near the station and with 24-hour checkout.

✗ Eating

Bikaner is noted for its *bhujiya*, a special kind of *namkin* (spicy nibbles), sold in the shops along Station Rd among other places.

Gallops
MULTICUISINE **$$**

(mains ₹200-400; ⊙10.30am-10pm) This fairly modern cafe and restaurant close to the Junagarh entrance is known as 'Glops' to rickshaw-wallahs. There are snacks such as pizzas, pakoras and sandwiches, and a good range of Indian and Chinese veg and non-veg dishes. You can sit outside or curl up in an armchair in the air-conditioned interior with a cold beer, espresso coffee or fuming hookah.

Pause Café
CAFE **$**

(KEM Rd; dishes ₹30-70; ⊙10am-10pm; ☎) A travellers' hangout with a nice garden setting and internet (per hr ₹20, wi-fi per hr ₹10), French-run Pause serves up soups, chips, cheese toast, salads, rice and dhal, a daily vegetarian dish, banana lassi and real coffee. It's run by the NGO AFEV (p357) and is also the contact point for AFEV's 'equitable-tourism' camel safaris. Located next to Ratan Bihari Temple.

Heeralal's
INDIAN **$**

(Station Rd; mains ₹50-110; ⊙noon-10.30pm) This bright and hugely popular 1st-floor restaurant serves up pretty good veg and non-veg Indian dishes, plus a few Chinese and pizzas (but unfortunately no beer), amid large banks of plastic flowers. The ground-floor fast-food section is less appetising but it has a good sweets counter.

Palace Garden Restaurant
INDIAN, CHINESE **$$**

(Hotel Laxmi Niwas; mains ₹110-240; ⊙7.30-10pm) This excellent garden restaurant at one of Bikaner's best hotels is a lovely place to eat – at least until the nights become too chilly. The fare spans South Indian, veg and non-veg North Indian, and Chinese, and if you're lucky there will be live music.

Bhanwar Niwas
INDIAN **$$**

(2529323; Rampuria St, Old City; set lunch/dinner ₹350/375; ⊙lunch & dinner) A splendid place to eat, this beautiful hotel welcomes nonguests to its veg dining hall (reservations are essential). You can have a drink before dinner in the courtyard.

Laxmi Hotel
INDIAN **$**

(Station Rd; mains ₹40-80, thali ₹60-100) A simple place, Laxmi is open to the street and dishes up tasty, fresh vegetarian thalis. You can see the roti being flipped in front of you.

Amber Restaurant
INDIAN **$**

(Station Rd; mains ₹75-115, thali ₹51-105; ⊙8am-10.30pm) It has a staid, no-nonsense look, but Amber is well regarded and popular for veg fare. To one side is an Indian sweets counter, to the other an ice-cream parlour.

🛍 Shopping

Abhivyakti
HANDICRAFTS

(Ganganagar Rd; ⊙8.30am-6.30pm Mon-Sat, 8.30am-1pm Sun) Run by the Urmul Trust, a local NGO supported by Urmul Dairy (whose office is next door), Abhivyakti sells blankets, bags, shirts and cushion-covers produced by skilled village artisans. The Urmul Trust, founded in 1986, promotes women's rights and funds girls' colleges and an eye hospital for desert people. It welcomes volunteers (see p357). Abhivyakti pays no commission to touts or drivers so don't be dissuaded by them if you want to go here. The shop is 1.4km northeast of Junagarh fort.

Rajasthan Handicrafts HANDICRAFTS
(11A Lallgarh Palace Campus; ⊙10am-9pm) Opposite Hotel Sagar, about 2km north of Junagarh fort, this is a more conventional crafts emporium, with a good stock of silverware, textiles and paintings.

 Information

For an online guide to Bikaner, check out www.realbikaner.com. You'll find a State Bank ATM outside the main train station, and Bank of Baroda ATMs opposite the station and next to the Tourist Reception Centre. There are several cybercafes on Ganga Shahar Rd.

Cyber Station (internet per hr ₹20; ⊙6.30am-11pm) Located behind main post office; also the home of Desert Tours (p297).

Lake Palace Trade & Travels (Junagarh; ⊙9am-6pm Mon-Sat) Just inside the fort entrance; changes currency and travellers cheques.

Main post office (⊙9am-4pm Mon-Fri, 9am-2pm Sat) Near Bhairon Vilas hotel.

Modi Cyber Cafe (Station Rd; internet per hr ₹20; ⊙9.30am-9.30pm) Under a Vadilal (ice cream) sign.

PBM Hospital (☑2525312; Hospital Rd) One of Rajasthan's best government hospitals, with 24-hour emergency service.

State Bank of Bikaner & Jaipur (⊙10am-2pm & 3-4pm Mon-Fri) Train station area (Ambedkar Circle); near Junagarh (Public Park) Both branches change cash and travellers cheques.

Tourist Reception Centre (☑2226701; ⊙9.30am-6pm Mon-Fri) This very helpful and friendly office (near Pooran Singh Circle) can answer most tourism-related questions and provide transport schedules and a map and brochure. A branch office was due to open opposite the east side of Junagarh fort.

 Getting There & Away

Bus

The RSRTC's Central Bus Stand is 1.5km northeast of Junagarh fort, almost opposite the road leading to Lallgarh Palace. If your bus is coming from the south, you can ask the driver to let you out closer to the city centre. RSRTC buses depart for Jodhpur (₹143, 5½ hours, half-hourly) via Nagaur (₹72, 2½ hours), Jaipur (₹191, seven hours, hourly 5am to 6pm) via Fatehpur and Sikar, Udaipur (₹289, 13 hours, 4.30pm), Delhi

(₹287, 11 hours, three daily) via Mandawa (₹117, five hours), Jhunjhunu (₹130, five hours, two daily), Ajmer (₹156, seven hours, seven daily), Phalodi (₹101, 3½ hours, about hourly 5am to 5pm) and Pokaran (₹133, five hours, five daily).

Private buses and their ticket offices mostly congregate along the southern wall of the fort. Destinations include Jaisalmer (seat/sleeper ₹140/200, seven hours, 5.30am, 3pm and 10pm), Jodhpur (₹150/200, six daily), Jaipur (₹150/200, 11 daily), Delhi (₹250/300, 7.30pm, 8pm and 8.30pm), Ajmer (₹150/200, 10pm and 11pm), Pushkar (₹150/180, seven hours, 9pm, 10pm and 11pm). Private buses to Fatehpur, Nawalgarh and Mandawa leave about every half-hour, 10am to 7pm, from a stop on the Jaipur road known as the Khetri bus stand. A private bus to Amritsar (seat/sleeper ₹300/350, 15 hours, 5.45pm) leaves from Ambedkar Circle.

Train

The main station is Bikaner Junction station on Station Rd. However, a couple of other useful services go from Lalgarh Junction station in the north of the city. At Bikaner Junction the **computerised reservations office** (⊙8am-8pm Mon-Sat, 8am-2pm Sun) is in a separate building just east of the main station building. The foreigners' window is number 2931.

To Jaipur, the 09733 *Hanumangarh–Kota Special* leaves at 10.17pm (sleeper/3AC/2AC ₹188/487/659, seven hours) and the 12467 *Intercity Express* leaves at 5.30am (2nd class ₹123, 6¾ hours), both from Bikaner Junction. For Jodhpur the 14707 *Ranakpur Express* departs Bikaner Junction at 9.30am (sleeper/3AC/2AC ₹156/395/531, five hours). The 15610 *Avadh–Assam Express* leaves Lalgarh Junction at 7.45pm for Delhi (sleeper/3AC/2AC ₹262/693/945, 11½ hours). To Jaisalmer (sleeper ₹168, six hours), via Phalodi and Ramdevra, the 14702 *Bikaner–Jaisalmer Express* leaves Bikaner Junction at 11.35pm, and the 14704 *Lalgarh–Jaisalmer Express* leaves Lalgarh Junction at 7.20am.

 Getting Around

An autorickshaw from the train station to Junagarh palace should cost ₹30, but you'll probably be asked for more.

Bikaner Motorbikes & Bicycle Hire (www.bikanermotorbikesbicyclehirerentalcenter.com; ⊙9am-7pm), by the roundabout 600m northeast of Junagarh fort, rents out 18-gear mountain bikes for ₹300 per day, ordinary gearless bikes for ₹50, 125cc and 150cc motorbikes for ₹400 and 180cc motorbikes for ₹600. Motorbikes come with a clean helmet! Guided day/half-day desert rides by bike or motorbike are available.

You can also hire old clunker bicycles outside the main post office for ₹25 a day.

The camels reared at Bikaner's National Research Center on Camels are of three breeds. The long-haired camels with hairy ears are the local Bikaner variety and are renowned for their strength. The light-coloured camels are from Jaisalmer and are renowned for their speed. The dark-coloured camels are from Kachchh (Kutch) in Gujarat, and the females are renowned for the quantity of milk they produce.

Camel milk tastes a little salty and is reputedly good for the liver. If you have a cup of chai in a small desert village, you're quite possibly drinking camel milk. The stout of heart might even like to try fresh, warm camel milk at the farm. The camels on the farm are crossbred so, in theory, they should be the strongest, fastest and best milk-producing camels you'll find anywhere. Breeding season is from around December to March, and at this time the male camels froth at the mouth disconcertingly.

Locals bring their female camels here to be serviced free of charge. Female camels can give birth every one and a half years, depending on their age and health, following a 13-month gestation period. A male camel can inseminate up to five cows per day.

Adult camels drink around 30L of water per day in summer, and about 20L in winter. In winter a healthy camel can work up to one month without food or water, but in summer not more than one week.

Around Bikaner

DEVI KUND

The marble and red-sandstone royal cenotaphs of the Bika dynasty rulers, with some fine frescoes, are located 8km east of the centre of Bikaner. The white-marble *chhatri* of Maharaja Surat Singh is among the most imposing.

It costs ₹150 return by rickshaw to get to this quiet spot.

NATIONAL RESEARCH CENTRE ON CAMELS

The National Research Centre on Camels (☎0151-2230183; Indian/foreigner ₹10/20, camera ₹20, rides ₹20; ☺2-6pm) is 8km southeast of central Bikaner, beside the Jodhpur–Jaipur Bypass. While here you can visit baby camels, go for a short ride and look around the small museum. There are about 400 camels, of three different breeds. The British Army had a camel corps drawn from Bikaner during WWI. Guides are available for ₹50-plus. The on-site Camel Milk Parlour doesn't look much but can whip up a lassi for ₹5. The round trip, including a half-hour wait at the camel farm, is around ₹150 for an autorickshaw or ₹300 for a taxi.

GAJNER WILDLIFE SANCTUARY

The lake and forested hills of this 24-sq-km, privately owned reserve (admission per jeep ₹2000), 32km from Bikaner on the Jaisalmer road, are inhabited by chinkara gazelles, blackbuck, nilgai (bluebulls), wild boar, desert foxes, and wildfowl that include winter visitors such as the demoiselle crane. Gajner was once a royal hunting ground – many British luminaries have killed wildlife here. The reserve is accessible only by vehicle from Gajner Palace Hotel, where nonguests may hire vehicles.

🛏 Sleeping & Eating

Gajner Palace Hotel   HERITAGE HOTEL $$$
(☎01534-275061; www.hrhhotels.com; r/ste ₹6000/8000; ☒) On the edge of the lake is the magnificent erstwhile royal winter palace and hunting lodge. The pink-sandstone palace is set in lush surroundings and the rooms are lavishly furnished. The 13 suites in the main building have lake views; the others have garden views. Some of the rugs in the main palace were woven by prisoners of the Bikaner jail. You can pop in for lunch (₹750) or dinner (₹1000) or just a visit with tea or coffee (₹150), and eat indoors or outdoors, watching the birds bobbing on the lake.

ⓘ Getting There & Away

RSRTC buses (₹30) run about hourly, 5am to 5pm, from Bikaner to Gajner village, about 1km away from the hotel. A return taxi from Bikaner costs ₹800 to ₹1000, including two hours' waiting time.

KOLAYAT

With its temples and 52 ghats around its lake, Kolayat, 51km southwest of Bikaner, is a beautiful, holy and untouristed town. Visiting here is considered a worthy Hindu pilgrimage, with one day here being worth up to 10 years at another sacred place. Like Pushkar, it has a (rare) Brahma temple. The

DON'T MISS

THE TEMPLE OF RATS

The resident mass of holy rodents at Deshnok's **Karni Mata Temple** is not for the squeamish. Karni Mata lived in the 14th century and performed many miracles during her lifetime. When her youngest son, Lakhan, drowned, she ordered Yama, the god of death, to bring him back to life. Yama replied that he was unable to do this, but that Karni Mata, as an incarnation of Durga, could restore Lakhan's life. This she did, decreeing that members of her family would no longer die but would be reincarnated as *kabas* (rats). Around 600 families in Deshnok claim to be descendants of Karni Mata and that they will be reincarnated as *kabas*.

The temple is an important place of pilgrimage; Karni Mata is the patron goddess of the Bikaner royal family and pilgrims are disgorged here from buses every few minutes. Once at the village, they buy *prasad* (holy food offerings) in the form of rice, milk or sugar balls to feed to the rats. Eating *prasad* covered in holy rat saliva is also claimed by believers to bring good fortune, although most travellers are willing to take their word for it.

Before the temple is a beautiful marble facade with solid silver doors, donated by Maharaja Ganga Singh. The doors of the inner sanctum are of repoussé silver – one panel shows the goddess with her charges at her feet. Inside the inner sanctum pilgrims are anointed with a tikka made with ash from a holy fire, while the objects of their devotion may run over their toes (sorry, no shoes permitted). There are special holes around the sides of the temple courtyard to facilitate the rats' movements, and a wire grille has been placed over the courtyard to keep out birds and other predators.

It's considered highly auspicious to have a *kaba* run across your feet – you may be graced in this manner whether you want it or not. Sighting one of the few white *kabas* at the temple also augurs well for your spiritual progress.

What may seem unusual to foreigners' eyes is believed devoutly by pilgrims – remember that this isn't a sideshow but a place of worship. And don't conveniently forget to remove your shoes!

---

main temple is the **Kapil Muni** (⊘closed 3-5pm), dedicated to a Vedic sage who, legend tells, shed his body under a banyan tree here.

There are some very basic *dharamsalas* (pilgrims' rest houses), but most won't accept tourists. **Bhaheti Dharamsala** (r without bathroom ₹35), on the main ghat by the lakeside, is a reasonable place. Otherwise Kolayat is a good day trip from Bikaner.

The **Kapil Muni Mela** (fair) is held here in October or November, around the same time as the Pushkar Camel Fair (with fewer camels and cattle, but with plenty of sadhus).

RSRTC buses (₹33, one hour) leave Bikaner about hourly from 5am to 5pm, or there's train 14704 from Lalgarh Junction station at 7.20am (sleeper ₹130, 45 minutes), with the 14703 heading back at 3.21pm.

DESHNOK

Karni Mata Temple (camera/video ₹20/50; ⊘4am-10pm) at the village of Deshnok, 30km south of Bikaner, is extraordinary even by Indian standards. Most travellers coming to Bikaner make a beeline here. The holy rats of Karni Mata are considered to be incarna-

tions of storytellers, and they run riot over the temple complex.

Two special festivals take place at the Karni Mata Temple in March/April and September/October. Ask at Bikaner's Tourist Reception Centre for exact dates.

◉ Sights

Temple Museum   MUSEUM
(admission by donation; ⊘7am-7pm) The pictorial display in this pink building across the square from the temple is worth a look. It tells the story of Karni Mata's life, with descriptions in English and Hindi.

❶ Getting There & Away

Buses to Deshnok (₹20, 40 minutes) leave the main and Gogo Gate bus stands in Bikaner every 20 minutes. There are also several trains from Bikaner Junction station, including the 59705 *Suratgarh–Jaipur Passenger* at 10.45am (2nd-class ₹5, 35 minutes) and the 14887 *Kalka–Haridwar Express* at 11.15am (₹18, 30 minutes); the 14888 *Barmer–Jkalka Express* heads back from Deshnok at 2.57pm. The temple is 200m from the train station.

A return taxi/autorickshaw from Bikaner with a one-hour wait costs ₹500/280.

Understand Rajasthan, Delhi & Agra

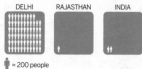

population per sq km

DELHI · RAJASTHAN · INDIA

👤 ≈ 200 people

Rajasthan, Delhi & Agra Today

A Populated Desert

Covering an area 342,236 sq km, Rajasthan represents roughly 10% of the Indian landmass. Much of it embraces the vast Thar Desert, which is populated with rural villages, trade-route towns and burgeoning cities of princely states.

The desert supports life because of the monsoon rains that percolate through the sands into the water table to be tapped throughout the year at the ubiquitous wells scattered across the country. In recent years, Rajasthan's life-giving monsoon has become less and less predictable, however, and the scarcity of rain and rapid drop in the water table has affected people's livelihoods as well as the greater environment. Chronic droughts have accelerated migration from the parched agricultural lands to the already overburdened cities. For those who remain on the land, it has become a battle for survival. No wonder then, that there were tears of joy as the waters from the Sardar Sarovar dam, part of the controversial Narmada River Project in Gujarat, finally trickled into deserts around Barmer and Jalore in 2008. Bringing drinking and irrigation water to millions of people affected by drought was a political triumph, but the ultimate financial, social and environmental costs have yet to be counted.

Tourism State & Hi-Tech City

Around 40% of all visitors to India come to Rajasthan, bringing in foreign revenue and providing much needed employment throughout the states. Tourism is the most important industry in Rajasthan, funding the conservation of Rajasthan's magnificent heritage and revitalising the region's splendid arts and crafts. The surge in tourism has provided many locals from all walks of life with alternative and promising career options. A large number of young Rajasthanis now earn a living by working

» Population Rajasthan: 68.1 million

» Population Delhi: 12.6 million

» Population Agra: 1.7 million

» Rajasthan Population Growth Rate: 2.1%

» National GDP growth rate: 8.3%

» Life expectancy (women/men): 68/65 years

Top Reads

Desert Places Robyn Davidson travels by camel through the Thar Desert.

City of Djinns William Dalrymple's fascinating study of Delhi.

The Last Mughal William Dalrymple on the dying days of the Mughal Empire.

Twilight in Delhi Ahmed Ali's novel paints a revealing picture of pre-independent Delhi.

Maharanis Lucy Moore's delightful account of the lives and loves of three generations of Indian princesses.

Top Indian Films

Pyaasa (Thirst; 1957)

Kaagaz Ke Phool (Paper Flowers; 1959)

Gandhi (1982)

Fire (1996)

Earth (1998)

Water (2005)

belief systems
(% of population)

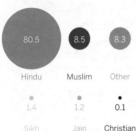

80.5	8.5	8.3
Hindu	Muslim	Other

1.4	1.2	0.1
Sikh	Jain	Christian

if India were 100 people

30 would be 14 years or younger
65 would be aged between 15 and 64 years
5 would be older than 65 years

in hotels, driving taxis, manning counters at souvenir shops or sprucing up their knowledge of history to become tourist guides.

Over in Delhi, another cog in the Indian economic juggernaut continues to spin and the business process outsourcing (BPO) industry has emerged as a lucrative industry. Scores of outsourcing firms dot the skylines of Delhi's suburbs, providing employment to hordes of urban graduates. Easy money has predictably bumped up living standards, bringing previously unaffordable luxuries within arm's reach of urban India's generation next.

Trending Now

Rajasthan's population has more than quadrupled since 1951. There are several contributing factors, such as vastly improved medical facilities and availability of medicines, which have led to a big drop in the mortality rate. The local mindset has not always kept pace with these changes, which is why procreation still follows the norm of having 'an heir and a spare' – at least two male offspring. The reluctance to practise contraception is another reason behind the sharp rise in the headcount; government-sponsored family-planning programmes are fighting a losing battle on this front.

The economy, whether you are talking about Rajasthan or the entire country, has undeniably made giant strides in recent years; however, the challenges for today's politicians – redistribution of wealth and environmental conservation – remain unresolved. Rajasthan continues to lose its wildlife, fertile soils and vegetation, and India is expected to become the world's third-largest emitter of carbon by 2015. In a land where juxtaposition of old and new has become a hackneyed slogan, the visitor must still marvel at the scene of ancient cenotaphs of silk-route nobility standing shoulder-to-shoulder with state-of-the-art wind turbines, which are helping to address India's burgeoning energy and pollution crisis.

Saying 'namaste' with hands together in a prayer gesture is a traditional, respectful Hindu greeting and a universally accepted way to say hello – handy since not all people shake hands with the opposite gender.

Your right hand is for eating and shaking hands; don't use the left (aka 'toilet') hand!

Nonfiction

India After Gandhi: The History of the World's Largest Democracy Ramachandra Guha.
The Elephant, the Tiger and the Cellphone Shashi Tharoor.

Dos & Don'ts

» Dress conservatively – avoid tight clothes; keep shoulders and knees covered.

» Public kissing, cuddling or holding hands is not condoned.

» Be respectful at holy places.

» Remove shoes before entering people's homes and holy sites.

» Always ask before photographing people or holy places.

» Taking photos of funeral proceedings, religious ceremonies or of people bathing publicly can be considered invasive and offensive.

History

A popular Indian saying goes that the state of Rajasthan alone has more history than the rest of the country put together. Given that its name literally translates as 'the land of kings', perhaps the idea holds some truth. Strewn with fascinating palaces, forts and ruins, with a colourful and diverse culture to boot, Rajasthan is an exotic land that intrigues as much as it enthrals. Throw in the neighbouring medieval capitals of Delhi and Agra, and you've got a heady cocktail laced with a thousand royal legends, potent enough to work its charm on even the most prosaic of imaginations.

But all good things come at a price. And Rajasthan, along with its neighbouring areas, has had to pay heavily in the past in order to inherit the rich heritage it calls its own today. Over the centuries, the province has had to cope with waves of ruthless invasions lashing in from the geographically vulnerable northwest, and later the south. These raids, undertaken by everyone from treasure hunters to religious crusaders, have brought along their own share of carnage, vandalism and desecration.

Uncertainty and political turmoil have been a way of life here. Delhi, for instance, has been razed and rebuilt by different dynasties at least nine times throughout the ages. And the crisis has often been compounded by severe infighting among princely states in the area. Ironically, it is this very streak of collective unrest that has contributed immensely towards shaping the character of the terrain and its people, leaving behind a legacy unparalleled by any other part of the nation.

The subcontinent saw Brahmanical empires and Hindu-Buddhist dynasties ebb and flow for over a millennium before the arrival of the Islamic sultanates, which, along with the Mughals, established Muslim control over much the region for another several hundred years. Princely states in Rajasthan mushroomed along trade routes, and they alternated between bickering and tying allegiances with neighbours, but mostly they just fought. The Mughals were overtaken by the British, who managed to conquer the entire peninsula. But this potted chronology is

Top History Reads

» *A History of India,* Romila Thapar and Percival Spear

» *A History of Jaipur,* Jadunath Sarkar

» *India: A History,* John Keay

» *The Great Moguls,* Bamber Gascoigne

» *A History of Rajasthan,* Rima Hooja

TIMELINE

10,000 BC

Stone Age paintings first made in the Bhimbetka rock shelters, in what is now Madhya Pradesh; the art continues here for many centuries. Settlements thought to exist across subcontinent.

CHRIS BEALL

» Prehistoric rock painting

deceptive: small dynasties emerged, passed away and emerged again in the shadow of larger empires.

Back Where It All Began

Archaeologists have discovered that the desert and scrub areas of Rajasthan have been home to humans for several thousand years. Excavations in Kalibangan, near Ganganagar in northern Rajasthan, have unearthed terracotta pottery and jewellery that date back to around 3000 BC, conclusively dating the earliest spread of settlements in the state to that time. Some of these urban centres were presumably absorbed into the Harappan segment of the Indus Valley civilisation, where they flourished until the settlement was mysteriously abandoned 3700 years ago. The mass exodus, possibly triggered by flooding or a severe climatic change, rendered the region devoid of human settlement for some time, until indigenous tribes such as the Bhils and the Minas moved in to set up their own squabbling small kingdoms, thereby commencing the long history of argumentative neighbours in the region.

But even as the tribes tore away at each other, another civilisation was sprouting in the fertile plains to the east of Rajasthan, between the rivers Yamuna and Ganga (Ganges). Though their exact origins are difficult to determine, the settlers in this fledgling colony are widely assumed to belong to a seminomadic race of Indo-European origin, who were known as Aryans or 'noblemen'. It was in this civilisation that Hinduism first evolved as a religious tradition and a way of life, along with a complex patriarchal social structure and the tiered caste system that the greater Indian society adheres to even today. By 1000 BC, the province had seen the establishment of at least two prominent kingdoms: the Matsya territory of Viratnagar encompassing Alwar, Bharatpur, Dholpur and Karauli; and Indraprastha, the earliest-known incarnation of Delhi, which was successively built on by several dynasties to come.

Little is known of Rajasthan's development at this time. However, it was an era that saw few incursions, as the mighty empires which were then strengthening their hold on the subcontinent, surprisingly, chose to pass on the state for one reason or another. Alexander the Great, who came to Asia on his epic conquest, was forced to return when his troops, homesick and weary after the campaign, convinced him to retreat. The Mauryan empire (323–185 BC) had minimal impact too, largely due to its most renowned emperor, Ashoka, taking to nonviolent ways after he converted to Buddhism. In stark contrast to the atrocities he had inflicted on the eastern Indian kingdom of Kalinga, the only evidence Ashoka left of his reign in Rajasthan were Buddhist caves and stupas (Buddhist shrines) near Jhalawar, rock-cut edicts at Bairat, an ancient Buddhist site near Sariska Tiger Reserve, and a 13m-high pillar he inscribed in Delhi.

The oldest natural relics in Rajasthan are fossilised remains of a 180-million-year-old forest, located at the Akal Wood Fossil Park in the Thar Desert near Jaisalmer.

The website www.harappa.com provides an illustrated yet scholarly coverage of everything you need to know about the ancient Indus Valley civilisation, including the significance of recent archaeological finds.

Rajput armies primarily consisted of cavalries. They were known to breed pedigree horses such as the Marwari and Kathiawari, which were inducted into their forces.

c 2600–1700 BC	c 1500 BC	1500–1200 BC	c 1000 BC
The heyday of the Indus Valley civilisation; the settlement spans parts of Rajasthan, Gujarat and the Sindh province in Pakistan.	The Indo-Aryan civilisation takes root in the fertile plains of the Indo-Gangetic basin. The settlers speak an early form of Sanskrit, from which several Indian languages later evolve.	The Rig-Veda, the first and longest of Hinduism's canonical texts, the Vedas, is written; three more books follow. Earliest forms of priestly Brahmanical Hinduism emerge.	Indraprastha, Delhi's first incarnation, comes into being. Archaeological excavations at the site where the Purana Qila now stands continue even today.

Marauding Huns & the Advent of Kings

The insulation that Rajasthan enjoyed through its early years came to an abrupt end during the 5th century AD, when armies of fierce Hun warriors rode in from Central Asia to carry out a series of pillaging raids across north India. These raids were to alter the course of the region's history in two major ways. To begin with, they resulted in the disintegration of the Gupta dynasty, which had taken over from the Mauryas as a central power and had reigned over the country 320–550. But more importantly, they triggered a parallel invasion, as the Rajputs finally came to make Rajasthan their home and, in the absence of an overarching monarchy, grew from strength to strength to usher in the golden age of Rajasthan.

Historical evidence suggests that the Rajputs (their name meaning 'children of kings') fled their homelands in Punjab, Haryana, Gujarat and Uttar Pradesh to settle in Rajasthan, primarily to escape the wrath of the White Huns (and later the Arabs) who had begun to storm in from Pakistan and Afghanistan. Once they had arrived in Rajasthan, the Rajputs trampled over the Bhils and Minas, and set up their own small fiefdoms in the face of mounting local chaos. Though they largely belonged to the lower rungs of Hindu society, volatile circumstances demanded that the Rajputs don the role of warriors, if only to fend off further advances by foreign invaders. So in spite of rigid social norms, which didn't allow for any kind of self-promotion, early Rajput clans such as the Gurjara Pratiharas crossed the caste barriers to proclaim themselves Kshatriyas, members of the warrior class, who came second only to the Brahmins (priests) in the caste hierarchy.

To facilitate their smooth transition through social ranks, and to avoid stinging criticism from the Brahmins, these early Rajput clans chose to jettison their worldly ancestry and took to trumpeting a mythological genealogy that supposedly evolved from celestial origins. From the 6th century onward, some of the clans began calling themselves Suryavanshis (Descendants of the Sun), while others chose to be known as Chandravanshis (Descendants of the Moon). A third dynasty, on the other hand, traced their roots to the sacrificial fire that was lit on Mt Abu during the Mauryan era, thereby naming themselves Agnivanshis (Fire-Born).

As the Rajputs slowly consolidated their grip over Rajasthan, they earned a reputation for their chivalry, noble traditions and strict code of conduct. Their sense of honour matched perhaps only by Arthurian knights or the Japanese samurai, the Rajputs gave rise to several well-known dynasties, who in turn established some of the most renowned princely states of Rajasthan. The largest of these kingdoms, and the third

ZERO

The concepts of zero and infinity are widely believed to have been devised by eminent Indian mathematicians, such as Aryabhatta and Varahamihira, during the reign of the Guptas.

The 24-spoke wheel, an emblem designed by Ashoka, has been adopted as the central motif on the national flag of India, where it is rendered in blue against a white background.

c 540 BC

The writing of the Mahabharata begins. The longest epic in the world, it takes nearly 250 years to complete, and mentions settlements such as Indraprastha, Pushkar and Chittorgarh.

599–528 BC

The life of Mahavir, the 24th and last *tirthankar* (enlightened teacher) who established Jainism. Like the Buddha, he preaches compassion and a path to enlightenment for all castes.

BRENT WINEBRENNER

» Sculpture inside Jain temple, Jaisalmer Fort (p278)

largest in India after Kashmir and Hyderabad, was Marwar. Founded by the Suryavanshi Rathores who rode in from Uttar Pradesh, it was initially ruled from Mandore, before the seat of power was relocated to the Mehrangarh Fort in nearby Jodhpur. The Sisodias migrated from Gujarat to assemble in the folds of the Aravalli Hills to the south, where they formed the state of Mewar encompassing Chittorgarh and Udaipur. The Kachhwahas, from Gwalior in Madhya Pradesh, settled in Jaipur in eastern Rajasthan, their capital nestled in the twin fort complex of Amber and Jaigarh. Meanwhile, a fourth kingdom, called Jaisalmer, was established in the Thar Desert by the Bhattis, who belonged to the lunar dynasty. Obscured by the dunes, the Bhattis remained more or less entrenched in their kingdom until Jaisalmer was integrated into the state of Rajasthan after Independence.

Over the years, Rajasthan saw the mushrooming of many other smaller dynasties, each of which staked claim to its own patch of territory in the region and ruled with complete autonomy, often refusing to submit to the whims of the bigger kingdoms. A few temporary alliances forged through cosmetic treaties or marriages didn't help much, as their fierce sense of pride and independence kept these states from growing and functioning as a unified force. Besides, the clans were so content with their tiny fiefdoms that they rarely thought of looking beyond their borders to explore and conquer newer territories.

One dynasty, however, proved to be an exception. The Chauhans, who belonged to the Agnivanshi dynasty, moved in from Gujarat around the 8th century to settle in the city of Ajmer, from where they gradually extended their empire across the neighbouring states of Haryana and Uttar Pradesh. Within Rajasthan, the Hada offshoot of the Chauhans crossed over to the Hadoti region and captured the cities of Bundi and Kota, while the Deora branch took over the nearby Sirohi area, making way for successive generations to zero in on the provinces of Ranthambore, Kishangarh and Shekhawati. The most illustrious of the Chauhan kings, Prithviraj III, went a notch further by leading his troops to invade Delhi, which had been reduced to insignificance after the fall of Indraprastha and was being governed by local chieftains. Keen to set up a new capital here, Prithviraj Chauhan commissioned the building of a settlement called Qila Rai Pithora, the ramparts of which can still be seen near the Qutb Minar in Mehrauli. One of the few Hindu kings to hold fort in Delhi, Prithviraj Chauhan administered his empire from the twin capitals of Qila Rai Pithora and Ajmer, before his reign was put to an end by Islamic warriors, who galloped in by the thousands to change the face of the region forever.

Upon losing Delhi to the Afghans, Prithviraj Chauhan was captured and taken back to Mohammed of Ghori's court in Ghazni, where he was later blinded and killed.

Best Rajput Monuments

» Amber Fort, Jaipur

» Mehrangarh, Jodhpur

» Jaisalmer Fort

» Chittorgarh, Chittor

» Kumbalgarh

» Ranthambhore Fort

563–483 BC	326 BC	323–185 BC	1st century
The life of Siddhartha Gautama. The prince attains enlightenment beneath the Bodhi Tree in Bodhgaya (Bihar), thereby transforming into the Buddha (Awakened One).	Alexander the Great invades India. He defeats Porus in Punjab to enter the subcontinent, but a rebellion keeps him from advancing beyond the Beas River in Himachal Pradesh.	India comes under the rule of the Maurya kings. Founded by Chandragupta Maurya, this Pan-Indian empire is ruled from Pataliputra (Patna), and briefly adopts Buddhism.	International trade booms: the region's elaborate overland trade networks connect with ports linked to maritime routes. Trade to Africa, the Gulf, Socotra, Southeast Asia, China and Rome thrives.

The Sword of Islam

Some 400 years after Prophet Mohammed had introduced Islam into Arabia, northern India saw the arrival of Muslim crusaders. It was to be expected. With the banner of Islam fluttering high, the crusaders had taken over the province of Sindh (in Pakistan) long ago, and, once they had managed to occupy Ghazni in neighbouring Afghanistan, it

THE INDOMITABLE SISODIAS

In a region where invasions and political upheavals were historical norms, the Sisodias of Mewar stood out as an exception, using everything from diplomacy to sheer valour to retain an iron grip over their land. Pillage and blood baths notwithstanding, the dynasty administered its kingdom in southern Rajasthan without a hiatus for some 1400 years. Lorded over by 76 monarchs throughout the ages, the Sisodias also enjoy the rare distinction of having had one of the longest-serving dynasties in the world.

While they claim to be Suryavanshis, the lineage of the Sisodia kings can be traced back to a prince named Guhil, born to a Rajput queen in the 6th century AD. Orphaned soon after birth and his kingdom ransacked by Huns, Guhil grew up among native Bhils in the forests of the Aravalli Hills. At age 11, he forged an alliance with a Bhil chieftain to establish a dynasty called the Guhilots. The chieftain also granted Guhil a tract of forested land in the mountains, which later expanded and flourished as the state of Mewar.

The Guhilots shifted base from the hills in the 12th century to a place called Ahar. It was here that the family split, resulting in a breakaway faction that relocated to the town of Sissoda and rechristened themselves Sisodias. The separatists soon took over Chittorgarh, an ancient garrison that remained under their control (despite being attacked by Ala-ud-din Khilji) until it was sacked by Mughal emperor Akbar in 1568. Though it came as a major military setback, the Sisodias lost no time in retreating into the Aravalli Hills, where they put together a new capital called Udaipur. A serenely beautiful city, Udaipur was never lost to the enemy, and remained the capital of Mewar until the kingdom was absorbed into the state of Rajasthan following India's Independence.

Known for their resilience and courage, the Sisodias have been credited with producing some of the most flamboyant kings ever to have reigned in Rajasthan. The family boasts names such as Rana Sanga, who died a valiant death in 1527 while fending off Mughal troops under Babur, and Maharana Pratap (1540–97), who made several daring though unsuccessful attempts to win Chittorgarh back from Akbar during his time in power. Being prolific builders, the Sisodias also gave Mewar some of its finest structures, including the Victory Tower at Chittorgarh, the grand City Palace in Udaipur, the elegant Monsoon Palace atop Sajjangarh Hill and the spectacular Lake Palace, which stands on an island amid the placid waters of Lake Pichola, also in Udaipur. A part of the City Palace now houses a museum, open to the public, which contains countless artefacts showcasing and documenting the glorious heritage of Mewar.

» Rajput sun symbol

AD 320–550

The period of the Gupta dynasty, the second of India's great monarchies after the Mauryas. This era is marked by a creative surge in literature and the arts.

500–600

The emergence of the Rajputs in Rajasthan. Stemming from three principal races supposedly of celestial origin, they form 36 separate clans who claim their own kingdoms across the region.

610

Prophet Mohammed establishes Islam. He soon invites the people of Mecca to adopt the new religion under the command of God, and his call is met with eager response.

ANDERS BLOMQVIST

was obvious that India would figure next on their agenda. So at the beginning of the 11th century, zealous Turk warriors led by the fearsome Sultan Mahmud of Ghazni descended upon India, razing hundreds of Hindu temples and plundering the region to take away vast amounts of wealth to fill their coffers back home. The Turks made their raids into India almost an annual affair, ransacking the northern part of the country 17 times in as many years. Jolted out of their internal bickering, the Rajput princes organised some hasty defence, but their army was torn to shreds even before they could retaliate. Rajasthan had been lost to Islam.

Delhi, located further east, was initially spared the wrath of the crusaders, as the Sultan largely confined his raids to Rajasthan and parts of Gujarat. Trouble, however, came by the name of Mohammed of Ghori, governor of Ghazni, who invaded India in the late 12th century, taking up where his predecessor had left off. He was thwarted on his first campaign by Prithviraj Chauhan, but the resolute Ghori returned a year later to defeat the Rajput king in the Second Battle of Tarain. Having convincingly stamped his victory over the region, Ghori trotted back to Ghazni, leaving Delhi under the governorship of Qutb-ud-din Aibak, a former Turk slave who had risen to command forces in India. When news of Ghori's death arrived in Delhi a decade and a half later, Qutb-ud-din shrugged off competition from rivals to stake claim to the Indian part of Ghori's empire. He declared himself Sultan of the region, and founded the Mamluk or Slave dynasty, giving Delhi the first of its many Islamic monarchies.

An Age of Treachery & Exploits

The enthronement of Qutb-ud-din Aibak flagged off the Sultanate era of Delhi, which lasted for about 350 years. Throughout this period, Delhi was ruled by six different Islamic dynasties, with a break between 1526 and 1540, when Delhi was captured by the Mughals. The six dynasties produced a line of 38 rulers, who gradually pushed the boundaries of their kingdoms to conquer new land. The whole of the Gangetic basin soon came under the Sultanates' control, as did Rajasthan and Gujarat – the princely states there had little option but to bow down to their might.

Apart from expanding their empire, the Sultanate kings also significantly urbanised Delhi. The Mamluks created the city of Mehrauli, whose most famous monument is the Qutb Minar. The Khiljis, on their part, seated their capital at Siri. The Tughlaqs constructed the forts of Tughlaqabad and Firoz Shah Kotla, while Sher Shah Suri, the most renowned of the Sur kings, chose to rule from Shergarh, built on the site of the Purana Qila, which he had won from the Mughal emperor Humayun.

The eccentric Tughlaq emperor Mohammed bin Tughlaq reduced Delhi to a ghost town for two years by moving the entire population to a new capital called Daulatabad, more than 1100km away in the Deccan.

While the construction of the Qutb Minar in Delhi was started by Qutb-ud-din Aibak in 1193, it was completed during the reign of Firoz Shah, more than 150 years later.

1024	1192	1206	1303
Mahmud of Ghazni raids India for the last time, ransacking on this occasion the Somnath Temple in Gujarat, where he purportedly smashes the idol with his own hands.	Prithviraj Chauhan loses Delhi to Mohammed of Ghori. The defeat effectively ends Hindu supremacy in the region, exposing Rajasthan and the subcontinent to subsequent Muslim invaders.	Ghori is murdered during a prayer session while returning to Ghazni from a campaign in Lahore. In the absence of an heir, his kingdom is usurped by his generals. The Delhi Sultanate is born.	Ala-ud-din Khilji sacks Chittorgarh with the intention of carrying away the beautiful Sisodia queen Padmini. The queen immolates herself to escape humiliation – the first recorded instance of *sati* in Rajasthan.

Despite the glorious developments, however, the Sultanate era was marked by prolonged phases of political turmoil and administrative tension. Having become the jewel of foreign eyes, Delhi was persistently being attacked from the northwest by Mongol, Persian, Turk and Afghan raiders, who all wanted to set up their own outposts in the city. Within the empire, stability had given way to turncoat politics, conspiracy and internal strife, as deceitful kings contrived bloody assassinations and coups to either remove or upstage their predecessors. Things got murkier with time, until two noblemen who were disgraced by Emperor Ibrahim Lodi decided to get even with the Sultan by inviting Babur, prince of Kabul, to invade Delhi. Ironically, in plotting their revenge, the two men unknowingly paved the way for the most celebrated Islamic dynasty to roll into India.

William Dalrymple's *City of Djinns* is a wonderful book that draws upon his personal experiences in Delhi, and chronicles the fascinating history of the city in its many incarnations.

Enter the Mughals

Babur, whose Turkic-Mongol lineage included great warriors such as Genghis Khan and Timur the Lame, marched into India through Punjab, defeating Ibrahim Lodi in the First Battle of Panipat (1526) to establish the Mughal dynasty in the country. Once he had seized Delhi, Babur focused his attention on Rajasthan, where many princely states, anticipating his moves, had already banded together to form a united front under the Sisodia king Rana Sanga. Taking advantage of the chaos in Delhi, the Rajputs had meanwhile clawed back in the power race, and states such as Mewar had become formidable enough to pose a considerable threat to the rulers of Delhi. Babur, however, squared everything by defeating the Rajput alliance in a blood-spattered battle where several Rajput chiefs, including Rana Sanga, fell to the enemy's wrath. The defeat, which shook the foundations of the Rajput states, also left the Mughals as the undisputed rulers of northern India.

Mughal supremacy was briefly cut back in the mid-16th century by Sher Shah Suri, who defeated Babur's successor Humayun to give Delhi its sixth and final Sultanate. Humayun reclaimed Delhi 14 years later, and was succeeded upon his accidental death by his 13-year-old son Akbar. Known as the greatest of the Mughal emperors, Akbar ruled for a period of 49 years, and, being a master diplomat, used both tact and military force to expand and consolidate the Mughal empire in India. Realising that the Rajputs could not be conquered on the battlefield alone, Akbar arranged a marriage alliance with a princess of the important Kachhwaha clan which held Amber (and later Jaipur), and even chose Rajput warriors to head his armies. Honoured by these gestures, the Kachhwahas, unlike other Rajputs, aligned themselves with the powerful Mughals, as Akbar indirectly succeeded in winning over one of the biggest Rajput states.

Best Mughal Monuments

» Taj Mahal, Agra
» Fatehpur Sikri
» Humayun's Tomb, Delhi
» Jama Masjid, Delhi
» Agra Fort, Agra
» Red Fort, Delhi

1321	1336	1345	1398
The Tughlaqs come to power in Delhi. Mohammed bin Tughlaq expands his empire but becomes known for inelegant schemes such as creating forgery-prone currency.	Foundation of the mighty Vijayanagar empire, named after its capital city, the ruins of which can be seen today in the vicinity of Hampi (in modern-day Karnataka).	Bahmani Sultanate is established in the Deccan following a revolt against the Tughlaqs of Delhi. The capital is set up at Gulbarga, in today's northern Karnataka, later shifting to Bidar.	Timur the Lame invades Delhi, on the pretext that the Sultans of Delhi are too tolerant with their Hindu subjects. He executes more than 100,000 Hindu captives before the battle for Delhi.

Of course, when diplomacy didn't work, Akbar resorted to war; he conquered Ajmer, and later proceeded to take the mighty forts of Chittorgarh and Ranthambhore. Gradually, all the important Rajput states except Mewar had acknowledged Mughal sovereignty to become vassal states. But even as he was well on his way to becoming the supreme ruler of India, Akbar became more tolerant in many ways. He married a Hindu Rajput princess and encouraged good relations between Hindus and Muslims, giving Rajputs special privileges so that they were embraced within his empire. A monarch with great social insight, he discouraged child marriage, banned *sati* (ritual suicide of a widow on her husband's funeral pyre) and arranged special market days for women. Akbar's reign also saw an unprecedented economic boom in the country, as well as great development in art and architecture.

Known for his religious tolerance, Akbar propounded a cult called Din-I-Ilahi, which incorporated the best elements of the two principal religions of his empire, Hinduism and Islam.

The Last of the Mughal Greats

Jehangir, Akbar's son, was the next Mughal emperor (1605–27), and he ruled alongside his adored Persian wife, Nur Jahan, who wielded considerable power and brought Persian influences to the court. Nur Jahan also commissioned the beautiful Itimad-ud-Daulah, the first Mughal structure to be built in marble, in Agra for her parents. The Rajputs maintained cordial relationships with the Mughals through Jehangir's rule, a notable development being that Udai Singh, king of Udaipur, ended Mewar's reservations about the Muslims by befriending Jehangir.

Good times, however, came to an end soon after Jehangir's period in office, as his descendants' greater emphasis on Islam began to rock the relative peace in the region. Upon Jehangir's death, the prince Khurram took over, assuming the title Shah Jahan, which meant 'monarch of the world'. His reign was the pinnacle of Mughal power. Like his predecessors, Shah Jahan was a patron of the arts, and some of the finest examples of Mughal art and architecture were produced during his reign, including the Taj Mahal, an extravagant work of extreme refinement and beauty. Shah Jahan also commenced work on Delhi's seventh incarnation, Shahjahanabad, constructing the Red Fort and the Jama Masjid.

Unfortunately, the emperor harboured high military ambitions, and often bled the country's financial resources to meet his whims. His exhaustion of the state treasury didn't go down well with the Rajputs, and towards the end of Shah Jahan's rule, the Rajputs and the Mughals had resigned to accept each other as unsatisfactory bedfellows. Things worsened when Aurangzeb became the last great Mughal emperor in 1658, deposing his father who died in imprisonment at the Musamman Burj in Agra eight years later. An Islamic hardliner, Aurangzeb quickly made enemies in the region. His zeal saw him devoting all his resources to ex-

The Great Mughals

» Babur
(1483–1530)
r. 1526–1530

» Humayun
(1508–1556)
r. 1530–1556

» Akbar
(1542–1605)
r. 1556–1605

» Jehangir
(1569–1627)
r. 1605–1627

» Shah Jahan
(1592–1666)
r. 1627–1658

» Aurangzeb
(1618–1707)
r. 1658–1707

1469	1498	1504	1526
Guru Nanak, founder of the Sikh faith, which has millions of followers within and beyond India to the present day, is born in a village near Lahore (in modern-day Pakistan).	Vasco da Gama, a Portuguese voyager, discovers the sea-route from Europe to India. He arrives in Kerala and engages in trade with the local kings.	Agra is founded on the banks of the Yamuna River by Sikandar Lodi. Its glory days begin when Akbar makes it his capital, and the city is briefly called Akbarabad during his reign.	Babur conquers Delhi and stuns Rajasthan by routing its confederate force, gaining a technological edge on the battlefield due to the early introduction of matchlock muskets in his army.

tending the Mughal empire's boundaries. His government's emphasis on Islam alienated his Hindu subjects. Aurangzeb imposed punitive taxes, banned the building of new temples, even destroying some, and forbade music and ceremonies at court. Challenges to his power mounted steadily as people reacted against his dour reign. And when he claimed his rights over Jodhpur in 1678, his relations with the Rajputs turned into full-scale war. Before long, there was insurgency on all sides, which only increased as Aurangzeb died in 1707 to leave the empire in the hands of a line of inefficient successors given to Bohemian excesses, who had little or no interest in running the state. The Mughal empire was on a one-way journey towards doom.

The British Drop Anchor

The British invaders came by the sea, following the Portuguese explorer Vasco da Gama, who had first discovered the sea route from Europe to India around Africa in 1498. The British East India Company, a London trading firm that wanted a slice of the Indian spice trade (having seen how well the Portuguese were doing), landed in India in the early 1600s. Granted trading rights by Jehangir, the company set up its first trading outpost in Surat in Gujarat, and gradually went about extending its in-

DELHI'S TWILIGHT YEARS

The death of Aurangzeb marked the beginning of Delhi's Twilight Years, a period through which the degenerating Mughal empire was laid to waste by the Marathas and the Persians. The Marathas had risen to prominence between 1646 and 1680 led by the heroic Shivaji, under whom their empire was administered by the *peshwas,* or chief ministers, who later went on to become hereditary rulers. At a time when the Mughals were struggling to hold their empire together, the Marathas trooped in from the south and gained a stranglehold on Delhi, primarily by supplying regiments to the Mughal army who soon went out of control and began to take possession of the land. Contemporary Mughal rulers, who were both ineffective and cowardly, failed to curb their unruly behaviour. The resulting confusion was capitalised on by the Persian invader Nadir Shah, who sacked Delhi in 1739 and robbed the city of much of its wealth. When the Marathas were unable to put up any resistance on behalf of the Mughals, they joined the Persians in pillaging the capital. They soon sucked Delhi dry of all its treasures, and when there was nothing left to rob, the Marathas turned their eyes on Rajasthan. Raids and skirmishes with the Rajputs followed; cities were sacked, lives were lost, and the Marathas began to win large tracts of Rajput land in the state. The absence of a central Indian authority only contributed to the mayhem, so much so that India had to wait till the early 19th century for another invasion to bring the country under a single umbrella once again.

1540	1556	1568
The Sur dynasty briefly captures Delhi from the Mughals – the loss forces the Mughals to temporarily seek help from the Rajputs.	Hemu, a Hindu general in Adil Shah Suri's army, seizes Delhi after Humayun's death. He rules for barely a month before losing to Akbar in the Second Battle of Panipat.	Akbar leads his army to Chittorgarh and wrests it from the Sisodias. Udai Singh, then king of Mewar, survives the onslaught and transfers his capital to the new city of Udaipur.

ANDERS BLOMQVIST

» Tower of Victory (p194)

fluence across the country, harbouring interests that went beyond mere trade. Extraordinarily enough, this commercial firm ended up nominally ruling India for 250 years.

Sooner or later, all leading European maritime nations came and pitched tent in India. Yet none managed to spread out across the country as efficiently as the British. The early English agents became well assimilated in India, learning Persian and intermarrying with local people, which gave them an edge over other European hopefuls. When the Mughal empire collapsed, they made a calculated political move, filling the power vacuum and taking over the reins of administration through a series of battles and alliances with local rulers. By the early 19th century, India was effectively under British control, and the British government in London had begun to take a more direct role in supervising affairs in India, while leaving the East India Company to deal with day-to-day administrative duties.

Outside British territory, the country was in a shambles. Bandits were on the prowl in the rural areas, and towns and cities had fallen into decay. The Marathas' 32 raids in Rajasthan continued, and though the British at first ignored the feuding parties, they soon spotted an opportunity for expansion and stepped into the fray. They negotiated treaties with the leaders of the main Rajput states, offering them protection from the Marathas in return for political and military support. The trick worked. Weakened by habitual wrangling and ongoing conflicts, the rulers forfeited their independence in exchange for protection, and British residents were installed in the princely states. The British ultimately eliminated the Maratha threat, but, in the process, the Rajputs were effectively reduced to puppets. Delhi's prominence as a national capital dwindled too, as the British chose to rule the country from Calcutta (now Kolkata).

The later British authorities had an elitist notion of their own superiority that was to have a lasting impact on India. The colonisers felt that it was their duty to civilise the nation, unlike the first agents of the East India Company who had seen and recognised the value in India's native culture. During the first half of the 19th century, the British brought about radical social reforms. They introduced education in the English language, which replaced Persian as the language of politics and governance. New roads and canal systems were installed, followed by the foundation of schools and universities modelled on the British system of education. In the later stages, they brought in the postal system, the telegraph and the railways, introductions that remain vital to the Indian administrative system today.

But at the same time, British bureaucracy came with controversial policies. Severe taxes were imposed on landowners and, as raw materials from India were used in British industry, cheap British-produced

HISTORY THE BRITISH DROP ANCHOR

The Doctrine of Lapse, a policy formulated by Lord Dalhousie, enabled the East India Company to annex any princely state if its ruler was either found incompetent or died without a direct heir.

Captain James Tod's *Annals and Antiquities of Rajasthan* (published 1829–32) is a historical masterpiece, with the captain's fascinating observations on a region previously undocumented by Europeans.

1608	1631	1674	1707
Granted trading rights by way of a royal charter, the first ships of the British East India Company sail up the Arabian Sea to drop anchor at Surat in Gujarat.	Construction of the Taj Mahal begins after Shah Jahan, devastated by the death of his wife Mumtaz Mahal, vows to build the most beautiful mausoleum in the world in her memory.	Shivaji establishes the Maratha kingdom, spanning western India and parts of the Deccan and north India. He assumes the supercilious title of Chhatrapati ('Lord of the Universe').	Death of Aurangzeb, the last of the Mughal greats. His demise triggers the gradual collapse of the Mughal empire, as anarchy and rebellion break out across the country.

MEANWHILE IN AGRA

As Delhi's light began to shine again, Agra, sadly, slid further from recognition. Being predominantly a satellite capital, where power occasionally spilt over from Delhi, the city had lost most of its political importance after the Mughals had departed. In the modern context, it made little sense to invest it with any kind of government machinery, so much so that it lost out to Lucknow when it came to selecting a state capital for Uttar Pradesh. Nonetheless, Agra continues to be high up on the tourism map of India, as travellers throng the city to visit its many historic sites and monuments.

The Proudest Day – India's Long Road to Independence by Anthony Read and David Fisher is an engaging account of India's pre-Independence period.

goods began to flood Indian markets and destroy local livelihoods. Mass anger in the country began to rise, and found expression in the First War of Independence (Indian Uprising) in 1857. Soldiers and peasants took over Delhi for four months and besieged the British Residency in Lucknow for five months before they were finally suppressed by the East India Company's forces. Rajasthan also saw uprisings among the poor and middle classes, but there was little effect in the royal circles as Rajput kings continued to support the British, and were rewarded for their loyalty after the British government assumed direct control of the country the following year.

Independence, Partition & After

Following a lengthy freedom movement, India finally freed itself of British domination in 1947. The road to Independence was an extraordinary one, influenced by Mohandas Karamchand Gandhi, later known as the Mahatma (Great Soul), who galvanised the peasants and villagers into a nonviolent resistance that was to spearhead the nationalist movement. A lawyer by qualification, he caused chaos by urging people to refuse to pay taxes and boycott British institutions and products. He campaigned for the Dalits (the lower classes of Hindu society, who he called Harijans or the 'Children of God'), and the rural poor, capturing public imagination through his approach, example and rhetoric. The freedom struggle gained momentum under him such that the British Labour Party, which came to power in 1945, saw Indian independence as inevitable. The process of the handover of power was initiated, but Hindu–Muslim differences took their toll at this crucial moment, and saw the country being divided on religious lines, with Pakistan being formed to appease the Muslim League, which sought to distance itself from a Hindu-dominated country.

Prior to the change of guard, the British had shifted their capital out of Calcutta (now Kolkata) and built the imperial city of New Delhi

Mahatma Gandhi argued that the leader of the Muslim League, Mohammed Ali Jinnah, should lead a united India if that would prevent the partition of the country.

1739	1747	1756	1757
Nadir Shah plunders Delhi, and carries away with him the Peacock Throne, as well as the Kohinoor, a magnificent diamond which eventually becomes property of the British royalty.	Afghan ruler Ahmad Shah Durrani sweeps across northern India, capturing Lahore and Kashmir, sacking Delhi and dealing another blow to the rapidly contracting Mughal empire.	The rise of the notorious Jat dynasty of Bharatpur in Rajasthan. Under the leadership of Suraj Mahl and his son Jawahar Singh, the Jats join the Marathas and Persians in looting Delhi and Agra.	Breaking out of its business mould, the East India Company registers its first military victory on Indian soil. Siraj-ud-Daulah, nawab of Bengal, is defeated by Robert Clive in the Battle of Plassey.

through the early 1900s, work on which was overseen by architect Edwin Lutyens. Meant to be an expression of British permanence, the city was speckled with grand structures such as the Rashtrapati Bhavan, the Central Vista and hundreds of residential buildings that came to be known as Lutyens Bungalows. After Independence, many of these Colonial buildings were used to house the brand-new Indian government, as Delhi was reinstated to its former status as the administrative and political capital of the country.

The long history of insurgency and unrest in India did not end with Independence. In 1962, India had a brief war with China over disputed border territories, and went on to engage in three battles with Pakistan over similar issues. Political assassinations didn't recede into history either. Mahatma Gandhi was slain soon after Independence by a Hindu extremist who hated his inclusive philosophy. Indira Gandhi, India's first

The 2005 film *The Rising* retells the story of the 1857 rebellion through the life and death of its most celebrated hero, the soldier Mangal Pandey, played by Aamir Khan.

THE FIRST WAR OF INDEPENDENCE: THE INDIAN UPRISING

In 1857, half a century after having established firm control of India, the British suffered a serious setback. To this day, the causes of the Uprising (known at the time as the Indian Mutiny and subsequently labelled by nationalist historians as the War of Independence) are the subject of debate. The key factors included the influx of cheap goods, such as textiles, from Britain that destroyed many livelihoods, the dispossession of territories from many rulers and taxes imposed on landowners.

The incident that's popularly held to have sparked the Uprising, however, took place at an army barracks in Meerut in Uttar Pradesh on 10 May 1857. A rumour leaked out that a new type of bullet was greased with what Hindus claimed was cow fat, while Muslims maintained that it came from pigs; pigs are considered unclean to Muslims, and cows are sacred to Hindus. Since loading a rifle involved biting the end off the waxed cartridge, these rumours provoked considerable unrest.

In Meerut, the situation was handled with a singular lack of judgment. The commanding officer lined up his soldiers and ordered them to bite off the ends of their issued bullets. Those who refused were immediately marched off to prison. The following morning, the soldiers of the garrison rebelled, shot their officers and marched to Delhi. Of the 74 Indian battalions of the Bengal army, seven (one of them Gurkhas) remained loyal, 20 were disarmed and the other 47 mutinied. The soldiers and peasants rallied around the ageing Mughal emperor in Delhi. They held Delhi for some months and besieged the British Residency in Lucknow for five months before they were finally suppressed. The incident left festering scars on both sides.

Almost immediately the East India Company was wound up, and direct control of the country was assumed by the British government, which announced its support for the existing rulers of the princely states, claiming they would not interfere in local matters as long as the states remained loyal to the British.

1857	1858	1869	1885
The short-lived First War of Independence breaks out across India. In the absence of a national leader, the rebels coerce the last Mughal king Bahadur Shah Zafar to proclaim himself emperor of India.	British government assumes control over India – with power officially transferred from the East India Company to the Crown – beginning the period known as the British Raj.	The birth of Mohandas Karamchand Gandhi in Porbandar (Gujarat) – the man who would later become popularly known as Mahatma Gandhi and affectionately dubbed 'Father of the Nation'.	The Indian National Congress, India's first home-grown political organisation, is set up. It brings educated Indians together and plays a key role in India's freedom struggle.

MAHARAJA METAMORPHOSIS

The fate of the royal families of Rajasthan since Independence has been mixed. A handful of the region's maharajas have continued their wasteful ways, squandering away their fortunes and reducing themselves to abject poverty. A few zealous ones, who hated to see their positions of power go, have switched to politics and become members of leading political parties in India. Some have skipped politics to climb the rungs of power in other well-known national institutions, such as sports administration bodies or charitable and nonprofit organisations in the country. Only a few have chosen to lead civilian lives, earning a name for themselves as fashion designers, cricketers or entertainers.

The majority of kings, however, have refused to let bygones be bygones, and have cashed in on their heritage by opening ticketed museums for tourists and converting their palaces to lavish hotels. With passing time, the luxury hospitality business has begun to find more and more takers from around the world. The boom in this industry can be traced back to 1971, when Indira Gandhi, then India's Prime Minister, abolished the privileges granted to the Rajasthan princes at the time of accession. Coming as a massive shock to those at the top of the pile, the snipping of the cash cord forced many kings to inadvertently join the long list of heritage hotel owners.

In spite of the abolition, many kings choose to continue using their royal titles for social purposes till this day. While these titles mean little more than status symbols in the modern context, they still help in garnering enormous respect from the common public. On the other hand, nothing these days quite evokes the essence of Rajput grandeur as much as a stay in palatial splendour surrounded by vestiges of the regal age, in places such as the Rambagh Palace in Jaipur and the Umaid Bhawan Palace in Jodhpur. Not all the royal palaces of Rajasthan are on the tourist circuit, though. Many of them continue to serve as residences for erstwhile royal families, and some of the mansions that were left out of the tourism pie are crumbling away, ignored and neglected, their decaying interiors home to pigeons and bats.

woman prime minister, was gunned down by her Sikh bodyguards in retaliation to her ordering the storming of the Golden Temple, the holiest of Sikh shrines, in 1984. Her son, Rajiv, who succeeded her to the post of prime minister was also assassinated by Tamil terrorists protesting India's stance on Sri Lankan policies. Rajiv's Italian-born widow, Sonia, was the next of the Gandhis to take up the dynastic mantle of power. In 2004, she was chosen as president of the Congress Party, which has fed on the reputation and charisma of the Gandhis since its formative years and is currently a principal political alliance in one of the world's largest democracies.

1906	1911	1940	1947
All-India Muslim League is formed, following an education conference in Dhaka, in response to concerns that a Hindu majority would not recognise Islam or serve Muslim interests.	Architect Edwin Lutyens begins work on New Delhi, the newest manifestation of Delhi, subsequently considered in architectural circles as one of the finest garden cities ever to have been built.	The Muslim League adopts its Lahore Resolution, which champions greater Muslim autonomy in India. Subsequent campaigns for a separate Islamic nation are spearheaded by Mohammed Ali Jinnah.	India gains independence on 15 August. Pakistan is formed a day earlier. Thousands of Hindus and Muslims brave communal riots to migrate to their respective nations.

Rajasthan Is Born

Ever since they swore allegiance to the British, the Rajput kingdoms subjugated themselves to absolute British rule. Being reduced to redundancy, they also chose to trade in their real power for pomp and extravagance. Consumption took over from chivalry and, by the early 20th century, many of the kings were spending their time travelling the world with scores of retainers, playing polo and occupying entire floors of expensive Western hotels. Many maintained huge fleets of expensive cars, a fine collection of which can be seen in the automobile museum in Udaipur. While it suited the British to indulge them, the maharajas' profligacy was economically and socially detrimental to their subjects, with the exception of a few capable rulers such as Ganga Singh of Bikaner. Remnants of the Raj (the British government in India before 1947) can be spotted all over the region today, from the Mayo College in Ajmer to the colonial villas in Mt Abu, and black-and-white photographs, documenting chummy Anglo-Rajput hunting expeditions, which deck the walls of any self-respecting heritage hotel in the state.

Discover the bygone days of Rajasthan's royalty in *A Princess Remembers*, the memoirs of Gayatri Devi, maharani of Jaipur. Cowritten by Santha Rama Rau, it's an enthralling read.

After Independence, from a security point of view, it became crucial for the new Indian union to ensure that the princely states of Rajasthan were integrated into the new nation. Most of these states were located near the vulnerable India–Pakistan border, and it made sense for the government to push for a merger that would minimise possibilities of rebellion in the region. Thus, when the boundaries of the new nation were being chalked out, the ruling Congress Party made a deal with the nominally independent Rajput states to cede power to the republic. To sweeten the deal, the rulers were offered lucrative monetary returns and government stipends, as well as being allowed to retain their titles and property holdings. Having fallen on hard times, the royals couldn't but agree with the government, and their inclination to yield to the Indian dominion gradually brought about the formation of the state of Rajasthan.

To begin with, the state comprised only the southern and southeastern regions of Rajasthan. Mewar was one of the first kingdoms to join the union. Udaipur was initially the state capital, with the maharaja of Udaipur becoming *rajpramukh* (head of state). The Instrument of Accession was signed in 1949, and Jaipur, Bikaner, Jodhpur and Jaisalmer were then merged, with Jaipur as the state's new capital. Later that year, the United State of Matsya was incorporated into Rajasthan. The state finally burgeoned to its current dimensions in November 1956, with the additions of Ajmer-Merwara, Abu Rd and a tract of Dilwara, originally part of the princely state of Sirohi that had been divided between Gujarat and Rajasthan. Rajasthan is now India's largest state.

ROYALTY

1948	1948–56	1952
Mahatma Gandhi is assassinated during a public walk in New Delhi by Nathuram Godse on 30 January. Godse and his co-conspirator Narayan Apte are later tried, convicted and executed.	Rajasthan takes shape, as the princely states form a beeline to sign the Instrument of Accession, giving up their territories which are incorporated into the newly formed Republic of India.	The first elections are held in Rajasthan, and the state gets its first taste of democracy after centuries of monarchical rule. The Congress is the first party to be elected into office.

ANDERS BLOMQVIST

» Painting of Gandhi

Rajasthani Way of Life

First Impressions

It's not the turbaned maharajas, or the call-centre graduates, or even the stereotypical beggars, for that matter. The first people you run into upon your arrival in Rajasthan or Delhi are a jostling bunch of overly attentive locals, who ambush you the moment you step out of the airport or the railway station to drown you in a sea of unsolicited offers. Great hotels, taxi rides at half-price, above-the-rate currency exchange... the list drags on, interspersed with beaming smiles you would usually only expect from long-lost friends. Famed Indian hospitality at work? This is no reception party; the men are touts out on their daily rounds, trying to wheedle a few bucks off unsuspecting travellers, and most of them can lie through their teeth. There's no way you can escape them, though a polite but firm 'no thank you' often stands you in good stead under such circumstances. It's a welcome each and every newcomer is accorded in India.

It's hard not to get put off by the surprise mobbing, but don't let the incident make you jump to the hasty conclusion that every local is out to hound the daylights out of you. Walk out of the terminal and into the real India, and things suddenly come across as strikingly different. With little stake in your activities, the people you now meet are genuinely warm (even if overtly curious), hospitable and sometimes helpful beyond what you'd call mere courtesy. For example, someone might volunteer to show you around a monument expecting absolutely nothing in return. And while it's advisable to always keep your wits about you, going with the flow often helps you understand the Indian psyche better, as well as making your trip to the region all the more memorable.

Contemporary Life

Urbanity and exposure to the outside world notwithstanding, North Indian society remains conservative at heart. Cities such as Delhi and Jaipur may have acquired a liberal sheen on the outside, thanks to globalisation, but within the walls of a typical home, little has changed through time. The man of the house still calls the shots; conversations relating to sex don't make it to the dinner table; and moving in with a partner is considered immoral, if not a sign of blatant promiscuity. Western influences are apparent in the public domain: satellite TV rules the airwaves, mobile phones are nothing short of a necessity, and coffee shops are jam-packed on the weekends. But ask a young man in front of his parents what his girlfriend does, and you needn't look beyond several pairs of flushed cheeks to realise you've made a faux pas. Urban India prefers to wallow in a state of conscious denial. Some things are best left unsaid.

Opium was traditionally served to guests at social functions by several indigenous communities of Rajasthan. Though the sale of opium is now illegal, it continues behind law-enforcers' backs.

OPIUM

In the region's backyard, the scene is rather stark. Rural Rajasthan remains one of the poorest areas in the country. Being in close proximity to the Thar Desert, the climate here is harsh, and people dwelling in the region's villages are locked in a day-to-day battle for survival, as they have been for ages. Unemployment is rife, which in turn has led to problems such as debt, drug abuse, alcoholism and prostitution. Indigenous tribes have been the worst affected and it isn't uncommon to see members from their communities begging or performing tricks at Delhi's traffic signals in return for loose change.

Rajasthan also lags behind on the education front, its literacy rate being about 4% behind the national average of 65.4%. In 2001, the government implemented a nationwide 'education-for-all' programme, which aims to impart elementary education to all Indian children. The project focuses on the education of girls, who have historically been deprived of quality schooling. Rajasthan is expected to benefit immensely from the programme, and the authorities are optimistic that the 2011 census will throw up positive results and set the record straight.

Marriage & Divorce

Indian marriages were always meant to unite families, not individuals. In rural Rajasthan, the case remains much the same today. Unlike in cities, where people now find love through online dating sites, weddings in villages and small towns are still arranged by parents. Those getting married have little say in the proceedings and cross-caste marriages are still a no-no. Few move out of their parents' homes after tying the knot; setting up an independent establishment post-marriage is often considered an insult to the elderly.

By and large, marriages in rural areas are initiated by professional matchmakers who strike a suitable match based on family status, caste and compatible horoscopes. Once a marriage is finalised, the bride's family arranges for a dowry to be paid to the groom's parents, as an appreciation of their graciously accepting the bride as a member of their family. Sometimes running into hundreds of thousands of rupees, dowries can range from hard cash to items such as TVs, motorcycles, household furniture, utensils and even toiletries. Despite the exact amount of dowry being finalised at the time of betrothal, there have been sporadic cases reported where the groom's family later insists that the girl's parents cough up more, failing which the bride might be subjected to abuse and domestic violence. Stories of newly married girls dying in kitchen 'accidents' are not uncommon either. In most cases, they leave the grooms free to remarry and claim another dowry.

Indian law sets the marriageable age of men and women at 21 and 18 respectively, yet child marriages continue to be practised in rural Rajasthan. It is estimated that one in every two girls in the state's villages

Matchmaking has embraced the cyber age, with popular sites including www.shaadi.com, www.bharatmatrimony.com and, more recently, www.secondshaadi.com – for those seeking a partner again.

CRICKET

Cricket is a national obsession in India and Rajasthan is no exception. Nearly everybody claims to understand the game down to its finer points, and can comment on it with endless vigour. Shops down shutters and streets take on a deserted look every time India happens to be playing a test match or a crucial one-day game. The arrival of the Twenty20 format and new domestic leagues such as the Indian Premier League (IPL) has only taken the game's popularity a notch further.

Keep your finger on the cricketing pulse at www.espncricinfo.com and www.cricbuzz.com. Cricket tragics will be bowled over by *The Illustrated History of Indian Cricket* by Boria Majumdar and *The States of Indian Cricket* by Ramachandra Guha.

are married off before they turn 15. Divorce, on the other hand, remains forbidden, thereby complicating things if marriages don't work out. Even if a divorce is obtained, it is difficult for a woman to find another husband; as a divorcee, she is considered less chaste than a spinster. Given the stigma associated with divorce, few people have the courage to walk out on each other, instead preferring to silently live through a botched marriage.

Women in Rajasthan

Mala Sen's *Death by Fire: Sati, Dowry Death & Female Infanticide in Modern India* is a disturbing and impassioned account, written from the perspective of three different women.

Traditionally objectified to the extent of being seen as child-bearing machines, women in rural Rajasthan are yet to rub shoulders with their menfolk in several ways. Being socially disadvantaged, their freedom has been seriously clipped, and, as keepers of a family's honour, they have been forbidden from mingling freely with strangers. If you tried approaching a village belle on the street, you'd probably see her beat a quick retreat into the privacy of her home, her face hidden behind her sari. A Rajasthani woman's beauty, after all, is only for her family to appreciate.

Screened from the outside world, most women in rural Rajasthan are sentenced to a lifetime of strenuous household chores. If they are allowed to work at all, they are paid less than their male counterparts. Besides all this, the radically patriarchal society still doesn't recognise them as inheritors of family property, which almost always goes to male heirs. The birth of a girl child is often seen as unlucky, since it not only means an extra mouth to feed but a generous dowry that needs to be given away at the time of her marriage. Embryonic sex determination, despite being illegal, is practised on the sly, and local newspapers occasionally blow the lid off surgical rackets where conniving surgeons charge huge amounts of money to carry out female-foeticide operations.

Progress has been made, however, in the form of development programmes run by the central and state governments, as well as nongovernmental organisations (NGOs) and voluntary outfits that have swung into action. Organisations such as the Barefoot College, URMAL Trust and Seva Mandir all run grass-roots programmes in Rajasthan, devoted to awareness, education, health issues and female empowerment, and volunteering opportunities are never lacking; see p357.

In the cities, the scene is much better. Urban women in Delhi and Jaipur have worked their way to social and professional recognition, and feminists are no longer dismissed as fringe lunatics. Even so, some of India's first-generation female executives recall a time not very long ago when employers would go into a tizz every time a woman put in a request for maternity leave, as motherhood had been precluded as an occasion that merited time off from work.

HIJRAS – THE THIRD SEX

India's most visible nonheterosexual group is the *hijras*, a caste of transvestites and eunuchs who dress in women's clothing. Some are gay, some are hermaphrodites and some were unfortunate enough to be kidnapped and castrated. Since it has long been traditionally frowned upon to live openly as a gay man in India, *hijras* get around this by becoming, in effect, a third sex of sorts. They work mainly as uninvited entertainers at weddings and celebrations of the birth of male children, and also possibly as prostitutes.

Read more about *hijras* in *The Invisibles* by Zia Jaffrey and *Ardhanarishvara the Androgyne* by Alka Pande.

Peoples of Rajasthan

Demographically speaking, much of the region's population still lives in its villages but they are on the move. The cities attract people from all walks of life to creating a high-density, multiethnic population. Religious ghettos can be found in places such as Ajmer and Jaipur, where a fair number of Christian families live; the Ganganagar district, which is home to a large number of Sikhs; and parts of Alwar and Bharatpur, where the populace is chiefly Muslim. Though most Muslims in Rajasthan belong to the Sunni sect, the state also has a small but affluent community of Shiite Muslims, called the Bohras, living to the southeast.

Tribes & Indigenous Communities

Rajasthan has a large indigenous population, comprising communities that are native to the region and have lived there for centuries. Called Adivasis (ancient dwellers), most of these ethnic groups have been listed as Scheduled Tribes by the government. The majority of the Adivasis are pagan, though some have either taken to Hindu ways or converted to Christianity over time.

Bhils

The largest of Rajasthan's tribes, the Bhils live to the southeast, spilling over into Madhya Pradesh. They speak their own distinct native language and have a natural talent for archery and warfare. Witchcraft, magic and superstition are deeply rooted in their culture. Polygamy is still practised by those who can afford it, and love marriages are the norm.

Originally a hunter-gatherer community, the Bhils have survived years of exploitation by higher castes to finally take up small-scale agriculture. Some have left their villages to head for the cities. Literacy is still below average and not too many Bhil families have many assets to speak of, but these trends are slowly being reversed. The Baneshwar Fair (see p177) is a huge Bhil festival, where you can sample the essence of their culture first hand.

Minas

The Minas are the second-largest tribal group in Rajasthan and live around Shekhawati and eastern Rajasthan. The name Mina comes from *meen* (fish), and the tribe claims it evolved from the fish incarnation of Vishnu. Minas once ruled supreme in the Amber region, but their miseries began once they were routed by the Rajputs. To make matters worse, they were outlawed during the British Raj, after their guerrilla tactics earned them the 'criminal-tribe' label. Following Independence, the criminal status was lifted and the Minas subsequently took to agriculture.

Festivities, music and dance form a vital part of Mina culture; they excel in performances such as swordplay and acrobatics. Minas view marriage as a noble institution, and their weddings are accompanied by enthusiastic celebrations. They are also known to be friendly with other tribes and don't mind sharing space with other communities.

Bishnois

The Bishnois are the most progressive of Rajasthan's indigenous communities, and even have their presence on the internet (http://bishnoi. org). However, they can't be strictly classified as a tribe. The Bishnois owe their origin to a visionary named Jambho Ji, who in 1485 shunned the Hindu social order to form a casteless faith that took inspiration from nature. Credited as the oldest environmentalist community in India, the Bishnois are animal-lovers and take an active interest in preserving forests and wildlife. Felling of trees and hunting within Bishnoi territory is strictly prohibited.

For comprehensive information on India's native and tribal communities, check out the website www.tribal.nic.in, maintained by the Ministry of Tribal Affairs under the Government of India.

Sacred India

Hindus comprise nearly 90% of Rajasthan's population. Much of the remaining 10% are Muslims, followed by decreasing numbers of Sikhs, Jains, Christians and Buddhists respectively. In spite of this religious diversity, tolerance levels are high and incidents of communal violence are rare, at least in comparison to the volatile nature of things in the neighbouring state of Gujarat.

Hinduism & the Caste System

Hinduism is among the world's oldest religious traditions, with its roots going back at least 3000 years. Theoretically, Hinduism is not a religion; it is a way of life, an elaborate convention that has evolved through the centuries, in contrast to many other religions which can trace their origins to a single founder. Despite being founded on a solid religious base, Hinduism doesn't have a specific theology, or even a central religious institution. It also has no provision for conversion; one is always born a Hindu.

Being an extremely diverse religion, Hinduism can't be summed up by a universal definition. Yet, there are a few principal tenets that most Hindu sects tend to go by. Hindus believe that all life originates from a supreme spirit called Brahman, a formless, timeless phenomenon manifested by Brahma, the Hindu lord of creation. Upon being born, all living beings are required to engage in dharma (worldly duties) and samsara (the endless cycle of birth, death and rebirth). It is said that the road to salvation lies through righteous karma (actions which evoke subsequent reactions), which leads to moksha (emancipation), when the soul eventually returns to unite with the supreme spirit.

If that's not complex enough, things are convoluted further by the caste system, which broadly divides Hindus into four distinct classes based on their mythical origins and their occupations. On top of the caste hierarchy are the Brahmins, priests who supposedly originated from Brahma's mouth. Next come the Kshatriyas, the warriors who evolved from the deity's arms – this is the caste that the Rajputs fit into. Vaishyas, tradespeople born from the thighs, are third in the pecking order, below which stand the Shudras. Alternatively called Dalits or Scheduled Castes, the Shudras comprise menial workers such as peasants, janitors or cobblers and are known to stem from Brahma's feet. Caste, by the way, is not changeable.

Hindu Sacred Texts & Epics

Hindu sacred texts fall under two categories: those believed to be the word of God (*shruti,* meaning 'hearing') and those produced by people (*smriti,* meaning 'memory').

Introduced in the subcontinent by the Aryans, the Vedas are regarded as *shruti* knowledge and are considered to be the authoritative basis for Hinduism. The oldest works of Sanskrit literature, the Vedas contain mantras that are recited at prayers and religious ceremonies. The Vedas are divided into four Samhitas (compilations); the Rig-Veda, the oldest of the Samhitas, is believed to be written more than 3000 years ago. Other Vedic works include the Brahmanas, touching on rituals; the Aranyakas whose name means the 'wilderness texts', meant for ascetics who have renounced the material world; and the Upanishads, which discuss meditation, philosophy, mysticism and the fate of the soul.

The Puranas comprise a post-Vedic genre that chronicles the history of the universe, royal lineages, philosophy and cosmology. The Sutras, on the other hand, are essentially manuals, and contain useful information on different human activities. Some well-known Sutras are Griha

OM

In Hinduism, the syllable 'Om' is believed to be a primordial sound from which the entire universe takes shape. It is also a sacred symbol, represented by an icon shaped like the number three.

Shiva is sometimes characterised as the lord of yoga, a Himalaya-dwelling ascetic with matted hair, an ash-smeared body and a third eye symbolising wisdom.

Sutra, dealing with the nuances of domestic life; Nyaya Sutra, detailing the faculty of justice and debate; and Kamasutra, a compendium of love and sexual behaviour. The Shastras are also instructive in nature, but are more technical as they provide information pertaining to specific areas of practice. Vaastu Shastra, for example, is an architect's handbook that elaborates on the art of civic planning, while Artha Shastra focuses heavily on governance, economics and military policies of the state.

HINDU GODS & GODDESSES

According to Hindu scriptures, there are around 330 million deities in the Hindu pantheon. All of them are regarded as a manifestation of Brahman (the supreme spirit), which otherwise has three main representations, known as the Trimurti – the trio of Brahma, Vishnu and Shiva.

Brahman

The One; the ultimate reality. Brahman is formless, eternal and the source of all existence. Brahman is *nirguna* (without attributes), as opposed to all the other gods and goddesses, which are manifestations of Brahman and therefore *saguna* (with attributes).

Brahma

The only active role that Brahma ever played was during the creation of the universe. Since then, he has been immersed in eternal meditation and is therefore regarded as aloof. His vehicle is a swan and he is sometimes shown sitting on a lotus.

Vishnu & Krishna

Being the preserver and sustainer of the universe, Vishnu is associated with 'right action'. He is usually depicted with four arms, each holding a lotus, a conch shell, a discus and a mace respectively. His consort is Lakshmi, the goddess of wealth, and his vehicle is Garuda, a creature that's half bird, half beast. Vishnu has 10 incarnations, including Rama, Krishna and Buddha. He is also referred to as Narayan.

Krishna, the hugely popular incarnation of Vishnu, was sent to earth to fight for good and combat evil, and his exploits are documented in the Mahabharata. A shrewd politician, his flirtatious alliances with *gopis* (milkmaids) and his love for Radha, his paramour, have inspired countless paintings and songs.

Shiva & Parvati

Although he plays the role of the destroyer, Shiva's creative role is symbolised by his representation as the frequently worshipped lingam (phallus). With snakes draped around his neck, he is sometimes shown holding a trident while riding Nandi the bull. With 1008 names, Shiva takes many forms, including Pashupati, champion of the animals, and Nataraja, performer of the *tandava* (cosmic dance of fury). He is also the lord of yoga.

Shiva's consort is the beautiful goddess Parvati, who in her dark side appears as Kali, the fiercest of the gods who demands sacrifices and wears a garland of skulls. Alternatively, she appears as the fair Durga, the demon slayer, who wields supreme power, holds weapons in her 10 hands and rides a tiger or a lion.

Ganesh

The pot-bellied, elephant-headed Ganesh is held in great affection by Indians. He is the god of good fortune, prosperity and the patron of scribes, being credited with writing sections of the Mahabharata. Ganesh is good at removing obstacles, and he's frequently spotted above doorways and entrances of Indian homes.

Hanuman

Hanuman is the hero of the Ramayana and is Rajasthan's most popular god. He is the loyal ally of lord Rama, and the images of Rama and his wife Sita are emblazoned upon his heart. He is king of the monkeys and thus assures them refuge in temple complexes across the country.

The Mahabharata is a 2500-year-old rip-roaring epic that centres on the conflict between two fraternal dynasties, the Pandavas and the Kauravas, overseen by Krishna. Locked in a struggle to inherit the throne of Hastinapura, the Kauravas win the first round of the feud, beating their adversaries in a game of dice and banishing them from the kingdom. The Pandavas return after 13 years and challenge the Kauravas to an epic battle, from which they emerge victorious. Being the longest epic in the world, unabridged versions of the Mahabharata incorporate the Bhagavad Gita, the holy book of the Hindus, which contains the worldly advice given by Krishna to Pandava prince Arjuna before the start of the battle.

Two recommended publications containing English translations of holy Hindu texts are *The Bhagavad Gita* by S Radhakrishnan and *The Valmiki Ramayana* by Romesh Dutt.

Composed around the 2nd or 3rd century BC, the Ramayana tells of Rama, an incarnation of Vishnu, who assumed human form to facilitate the triumph of good over evil. Much like the Mahabharata, the Ramayana revolves around a great war, waged by Rama, his brother Lakshmana and an army of apes led by Hanuman against Ravana, the demon king who had kidnapped Rama's wife Sita and had held her hostage in his kingdom of Lanka (Sri Lanka). After slaying Ravana, Rama returned to his kingdom of Ayodhya, his homecoming forming the basis for the important Hindu festival of Dussehra.

RAJASTHANI FOLK GODS & GODDESSES

Folk deities and deified local heroes abound in Rajasthan. Apart from public gods, families are often known to pay homage to a *kuladevi* (family idol).

Pabuji is one of many local heroes to have attained divine status. His is a particularly violent and chivalrous tale: Pabuji entered a transaction with a woman called Devalde, in which, in return for a mare, he vowed to protect her cows from all harm. The time to fulfil this obligation came, inconveniently, during Pabuji's own marriage. However, Pabuji immediately went to the aid of the threatened livestock. During the ensuing battle, he, along with all the male members of his family, perished at the hands of a villain called Jind Raj Khinchi. To preserve the family line, Pabuji's sister-in-law cut open her own belly and produced Pabuji's nephew, Nandio, before committing *sati* (a widow's act of self-immolation on her husband's funeral pyre).

A community of professional storytellers called Bhopas have traditionally paid homage to the hero by performing *Pabuji-ka-phad,* in which they recite poetry in praise of Pabuji while unfurling *phad* (cloth-scroll) paintings that chronicle the life of the hero. You can attend these performances at places such as Chokhi Dhani or Jaisalmer, if they happen at a time when you're around.

Gogaji was a warrior who lived in the 11th century and could cure snakebite; today, victims are brought to his shrines by both Hindu and Muslim devotees. Also believed to cure snakebite is Tejaji who, according to tradition, was blessed by a snake which decreed that anyone honouring Tejaji by wearing a thread in his name would be cured of snakebite.

Goddesses revered by Rajasthanis include incarnations of Devi (the Mother Goddess), such as the fierce Chamunda Mata, an incarnation of Durga; Sheetala Mata, the goddess of smallpox who is invoked by parents who want their children to be spared from the affliction; and Karni Mata, worshipped at Deshnok near Bikaner. Women who have committed *sati* on their husband's funeral pyres are also frequently worshipped as goddesses, such as Rani Sati, who has an elaborate temple in her honour in Jhunjhunu, in Shekhawati. Barren women pay homage to the god Bhairon, an incarnation of Shiva, at his shrines, which are usually found under khejri trees. In order to be blessed with a child, the woman is required to leave a garment hanging from the branches of the tree. The deified folk hero Ramdev also has an important temple at Ramdevra, near Pokaran in western Rajasthan.

Islam

Islam was founded in Arabia by the Prophet Mohammed in the 7th century AD. The Arabic term 'Islam' means 'surrender', and believers undertake to surrender to the will of Allah (God), which is revealed in the Quran, the holy book of Islam. A devout Muslim is required to pray five times a day, keep daylong fasts through the month of Ramadan, and make a pilgrimage to the holy city of Mecca in Saudi Arabia, if possible.

Islam is monotheistic. God is held as unique, unlimited, self-sufficient and the supreme creator of all things. God never speaks to humans directly; his word is instead conveyed through messengers called prophets, who are never themselves divine. The religion has two prominent sects, the minority Shiites (originating from Mohammed's descendants) and the majority Sunnis, who split soon after the death of Mohammed owing to political differences, and have since gone on to establish their own interpretations and rituals. The most important pilgrimage site for Muslims in Rajasthan is the extraordinary dargah (burial place) of the sufi saint Khwaja Muin-ud-din Chishti at Ajmer.

Sikhism

Now among the world's largest religions, Sikhism was founded on the sermons of 10 Sikh gurus, beginning with Guru Nanak Dev (1469–1539). The core values and ideology of Sikhism are embodied in the Guru Granth Sahib, the holy book of the Sikhs which is also considered the eternal guru of Sikhism. The Sikhs evolved as an organised community over time, and devoted themselves to the creation of a standing militia called the Khalsa, which carried out religious, political and martial duties and protected the Sikhs from foreign threats. The religion, on its part, grew around the central concept of Vaheguru, the universal lord, an eventual union with whom is believed to result in salvation. The Sikhs believe that salvation is achieved through rigorous discipline and meditation, which help them overcome the five evils – ego, greed, attachment, anger and lust.

> Sufism is a mystic tradition derived from Islam, which originated in medieval times. Being largely secular, it has attracted followers from other religions and is widely practised in North India.

Jainism

The Jain religion was founded around 500 BC by Mahavira, the 24th and last of the Jain *tirthankars* (path finders). Jainism originally evolved as a reformist movement against the dominance of priests in Hindu society. It steered clear of complicated rituals, rejected the caste system, and believed in reincarnation and eventual moksha by following the example of the *tirthankars*.

Jains are strict vegetarians and revere all forms of life. The religion has two main sects. The Svetambaras (White Clad) wear unstitched white garments; the monks cover their mouths so as not to inhale insects and brush their path before they walk to avoid crushing small creatures. The monks belonging to the Digambaras (Sky Clad), in comparison, go naked. Jainism preaches nonviolence, and its followers are markedly successful in banking and business, which they consider nonviolent professions.

Arts, Crafts & Architecture

Arts

If the Rajputs knew how to fight, they also knew how to create art. Rajasthan's culture is a celebration of beauty, manifested through its, literature, poetry, music, dance, painting and architecture. The state also has a rich legacy of handicrafts, which are prized the world over, both for their intricate craftsmanship and ornamental appeal.

Dance

Ghungroos are anklets made of metallic bells strung together, worn by Indian classical dancers to accentuate their complex footwork during performances.

Folk dance forms in Rajasthan are generally associated with indigenous tribes and communities of nomadic gypsies. Each region has its own dance specialities. The *ghoomer* (pirouette) is performed by Bhil women at festivals or weddings, and its form varies from one village to another. The Bhils are also known for *gair,* a men-only dance, that's performed at springtime festivities. Combine the two, and you get *gair-ghoomer,* where women, in a small inner circle, are encompassed by men in a larger circle, who determine the rhythm by beating sticks and striking drums.

Among other popular forms, the *kachhi ghori* dance of eastern Rajasthan resembles a battle performance, where dancers ride cloth or paper horses and spar with swords and shields. To the south, the *neja* is danced by the Minas of Kherwara and Dungarpur just after Holi. A coconut is placed on a large pole, which the men try to dislodge, while the women strike the men with sticks and whips to foil their attempts. A nomadic community called the Kalbelias, traditionally associated with snake charming, performs swirling dances such as the *shankaria,* while the Siddha Jats of Bikaner are renowned for their spectacular fire dance, performed on a bed of hot coals, which supposedly leaves no burns.

Painting & Sculpture

Miniatures

The website www. artindia.net keeps enthusiasts in tune with the best of classical music and dance happening around India, and has an excellent repository of articles on performing arts.

Rajasthan is famed for its miniatures – small-scale paintings that are executed on small surfaces, but cram in a surprising amount of detail by way of delicate brushwork. Originating in the 16th and 17th centuries, they led to the emergence of eminent schools such as Marwar, Mewar, Bundi-Kota, Amber and Kishangarh, among others. Each school had its own stylistic identity; while paintings from the Mewar school depicted court life, festivals, ceremonies, elephant fights and hunts, those from the Marwar school featured vivid colours and heroic, whiskered men accompanied by dainty maidens. Miniatures gained immense value as souvenirs with the coming of the tourism boom.

India has the world's biggest film industry. Films come in all languages, the majority pumped out by the Hindi tinsel town of Bollywood in Mumbai, and Mollywood, its Tamil counterpart, in Chennai. Most productions, however, are formulaic flicks that seize mass attention with hackneyed motifs – unrequited love, action that verges on caricature, slapstick humour, wet saris and plenty of sexual innuendo. Nonetheless, the past 10 years have seen upscale productions aimed at a burgeoning multiplex audience. Check out the cricket extravaganza *Lagaan*, the patriotic *Rang De Basanti*, or Shakespearean adaptations such as *Maqbool* (Macbeth) and *Omkara* (Othello). Although it garnered a bit of criticism from the local industry, the British-Indian production and huge international hit, *Slumdog Millionaire*, finally won over the locals with its Hindi-dubbed version, *Slumdog Crorepati*.

India also has a critically acclaimed art-house movement. Pioneered by the likes of Satyajit Ray, Adoor Gopalakrishnan, Ritwik Ghatak and Shyam Benegal, the tradition now boasts directors such as Mira Nair (*Salaam Bombay, Monsoon Wedding, The Namesake*) and Deepa Mehta (*Earth, Water, Fire*).

Phad & Fresco

Apart from miniatures, Rajasthan is also renowned for a kind of scroll painting called *phad,* which is done on cloth and portrays deities, mythology and legends of Rajput kings. Bhilwara, near Udaipur, is one of the better-known centres for *phad* scrolls.

Fresco painting, originally developed in Italy, arrived in Rajasthan with the Mughals, and its finest examples can be seen in the exquisitely muralled *havelis* of Shekhawati. The region's *havelis* form an open-air art gallery, with work in a kaleidoscope of colour and styles. Other kinds of painted houses can be seen in certain tribal areas, where earthen walls are decorated with *pithoras* – naive, appealing designs rendered in white – which were believed to bring luck and keep away evil spirits.

Crafts

Paper making

Paper making is centred in Sanganer, near Jaipur, whose paper has traditionally been the most celebrated in India. The process makes environmentally friendly use of discarded fabric rags, which are soaked, pulped, strained, beaten and then spread out to dry on frames. Though some of the town's factories nowadays use machines, there are plenty of places that still perform the entire process by hand – view the racks of paper spread out to dry along Sanganer's river, or pop in for a visit at one of the town's 10 or so paper-making factories.

Jewellery, Gems & Enamelwork

Two jewellery-making styles particularly prevalent in Rajasthan are *kundan* and *meenakari* work. *Kundan* involves setting gemstones into silver or gold pieces; one symbolic variation is known as *navratan,* in which nine different gems are set into an item of jewellery, corresponding to the nine planets of Indian astrology. This way, it's an eternally lucky item to have about your person, since you will always be wearing, at any given time, the symbol of the ruling planetary body. *Meenakari,* meanwhile, is a gorgeous type of enamelwork, that is usually applied to a base of silver or gold. Jaipur's pieces of *meenakari* are valued for their vibrant tones, especially the highly prized rich ruby-red; a fantastic selection can be found on sale at the city's Johari Bazaar.

Get arty with *Indian Art* by Roy Craven, *Contemporary Indian Art: Other Realities* edited by Yashodhara Dalmia, and *Indian Miniature Painting* by Dr Daljeet and Professor PC Jain.

BANDHANI

Leatherwork

Leatherworking has a long history in Rajasthan. Leather shoes known as jootis are produced in Jodhpur and Jaipur, often featuring *kashida* (ornate embroidery). Strange to Western eyes and feet, there is no 'right' or 'left': both shoes are identical but after a few wears they begin to conform to the wearer's feet. Jaipur is the best place to buy jootis; try the marvellous UN-supported *mojari*.

Textiles

Rajasthan is renowned for the blazing colour of its textiles. Riotously woven, dyed, block- or resist-printed and embroidered, they are on sale almost everywhere you look throughout the state. You can also seek out specialist favourites, such as the *kota doria* (gold-woven) fabric from the village of Kaithoon near Kota, with silk, cotton and pure-gold thread used to create exquisite, delicate saris.

During the Mughal period, embroidery workshops known as *kaarkhanas* were established to train artisans so that the royal families were ensured an abundant supply of richly embroidered cloth. Finely stitched tapestries, inspired by miniature paintings, were also executed for the royal courts.

Today, Bikaner specialises in embroidery with double stitching, which results in the pattern appearing on both sides of the cloth. In the Shekhawati district, the Jat people embroider motifs of animals and birds on their *odhnis* (headscarves) and *ghaghara* (long cotton skirts), while tiny mirrors are stitched into garments in Jaisalmer. Beautifully embroidered cloth is also produced for domestic livestock, and ornately bedecked camels are a wonderfully common sight, especially at the Pushkar camel fair.

Intricate *bandhani* (tie-dye) often carries symbolic meanings when used to make *odhnis* (headscarves). A yellow background indicates that the wearer has recently given birth, while red circles on that background means she's had a son.

Carpets & Weaving

Carpet weaving took off in the 16th century under the patronage of the great Mughal emperor Akbar, who commissioned the establishment of various carpet-weaving factories, including one in Jaipur. In the 19th century Maharaja Ram Singh II of Jaipur established a carpet factory at the Jaipur jail, and soon other jails introduced carpet-making units. Some of the most beautiful *dhurries* (flat-woven rugs) were produced by prisoners, and Bikaner jail is still well known for the excellence of its *dhurries*. Recent government training initiatives have seen the revival of this craft, and fine-quality carpets are once again being produced across Rajasthan.

PUPPETRY

Puppetry is one of Rajasthan's most acclaimed, yet endangered, performing arts. Puppeteers first emerged in the 19th century, and would travel from village to village like wandering minstrels, relaying stories through narration, music and an animated performance that featured wooden puppets on strings called *kathputlis*. Puppetry is now a dying art; waning patronage and lack of paying audiences has forced many puppeteers to give up the art form and switch to agriculture or menial labour. Those that frequent tourist hotels in the evening usually have a 'day job' and are not paid by the hotel but rather hope for donations after the performance and maybe to sell a puppet or two. The colourful puppets have certainly retained their value as souvenirs. Organisations such as the Barefoot College (see p161) now make use of puppetry as a medium to spread useful information on health, education and human rights.

ANTIQUE SHOPPING RULES

Rajasthan (and Delhi) really is one of the easiest places to spend money, with its busy bazaars, colourful arts and crafts, gorgeous fabrics, miniature paintings, and much more. The cardinal rule is to bargain and bargain hard.

» Be careful when purchasing items that include delivery to your home country – you may well be given assurances that the price includes all charges, but this is not always the case.

» Be aware that sellers often claim that miniature paintings are antiques; this is rarely the case. For other important warnings also read p131.

» Avoid buying products that further endanger threatened species and habitats. It's illegal to export ivory products or any artefact made from wild animals. Articles over 100 years old are not allowed to be exported from India without an export clearance certificate. If you have doubts about any item and think it could be defined as an antique, you can check with branches of the Archaeological Survey of India. In Delhi, contact the Director of Antiquities, **Archaeological Survey of India** (☏011-23017443; Janpath; ☺9.30am-1.30pm & 2-6pm Mon-Fri), located next to the National Museum.

Pottery

Of all the arts of Rajasthan, pottery has the longest lineage, with fragments recovered in Kalibangan dating from the Harappan era (around 3000 BC). Before the beginning of the 1st millennium, potters in the environs of present-day Bikaner were already decorating red pottery with black designs.

Today, different regions of Rajasthan produce different types of pottery, and most villages in Rajasthan have their own resident potter. The most famous of Rajasthan's pottery is the blue pottery of Jaipur. The blue-glazed work was first evident on Mughal palace and cenotaph tiling, and later applied to pottery. Though, over the centuries, the tradition declined, it was revived in Jaipur in the mid-19th century, and a wide range of blue pottery is still available here.

The most famous marble quarries were located in Makrana, from where the marble used in the Taj Mahal and the Dilwara Temples was sourced.

Architecture

The magnificence of Delhi, Agra and Rajasthan's architectural heritage is astounding, and the province is home to some of India's best-known buildings. From temples and mosques to mansions and mausoleums, the region has it all. Most spectacular, however, are the fairy-tale forts and palaces built by Rajputs and Mughals, which bear testimony to the celebrated history of North India.

Temples

Rajasthan's earliest surviving temples date from the Gupta period. Built between the 4th and 6th century, these temples are small and their architecture restrained – the Sheetaleshvara Temple at Jhalrapatan is a notable example. Temple architecture (both Hindu and Jain) developed through the 8th and 9th centuries, and began to incorporate stunning sculptural work, which can be seen on temples at Osiyan and Chittorgarh. Structurally, the temples usually tapered into a single *sikhara* (spire) and had a *mandapa* (pillared pavilion before the inner sanctum). The Dilwara complex at Mt Abu epitomises the architecture of this era. Built in the 11th century, it has marble carvings that reach unsurpassed heights of virtuosity.

Delhi, traditionally an Islamic stronghold, has few ancient temples to boast of. Nevertheless, the city is known for two spectacular modern structures. The Lotus Temple, built in 1986 as a place of worship

The Royal Palaces of India by writer George Michell and photographer Antonio Martinelli is a comprehensive guide including maps to the grand residences of the Indian royalty.

for the Bahai community, is a magnificent modern building mimicking a nine-sided lotus with marble-clad petals. It has won several architectural awards for its design. In 2005, Delhi got its second grand temple, Swaminarayan Akshardham, which holds a Guinness record for being the world's largest comprehensive Hindu temple.

Forts & Palaces

The fabulous citadels of Rajasthan owe their origins to reasons ranging from mandatory fortification to the realisation of royal whims.

Best Forts & Palaces

» Mehrangarh, Jodhpur

» Udaipur City Palace

» Jaisalmer Fort

» Amber Fort

» Agra Fort

» Delhi's Red Fort

» Chittorgarh

Most of Rajasthan's forts and palaces were built between the 15th and 18th centuries, which coincided with the Mughal reign in Delhi and saw the Rajputs borrowing a few architectural motifs from the Mughals. The concept of the *sheesh mahal* (hall of mirrors) was adopted from Islamic architecture, as was the use of pillared arches. Another ornamentation that was widely used across Rajasthan was the spired Bengal roof, shaped like an inverted boat. Magnificent examples of Rajput architecture across the state include the Amber Fort and the Hawa Mahal in Jaipur, and the City Palace in Udaipur.

The forts and palaces of Delhi and Agra, conversely, adhere to the Islamic style, with intricate marblework, ornate *pietre dura* (stone inlay) panels, arched entrances and symmetrical, four-square gardens. Mausoleums and mosques, such as the Taj Mahal and the Jama Masjid, are capped by onion-shaped domes and flanked by minarets. Almost every dynasty that ruled in Delhi built its own fort and monuments in the city. Though they all follow Islamic architectural style, subtle differences exist among these structures due to their having been built centuries apart from each other.

Towards the end of the British era, a novel architectural style called the Indo-Saracenic school emerged in India, which blended Victorian and Islamic elements into a highly wrought, frilly whole. Some striking buildings were produced in this style, including Albert Hall in Jaipur and Lallgarh Palace in Bikaner.

The Kumbalgarh Fort, a former Mewar stronghold in the Rajsamand district of Rajasthan, has the second-longest fortification in the world after the Great Wall of China.

Havelis

Rajasthani merchants built ornately decorated residences called *havelis,* and commissioned masons and artists to ensure they were constructed and decorated in a manner befitting the owners' importance and prosperity. The Shekhawati district of northern Rajasthan is riddled with such mansions that are covered with extraordinarily vibrant murals (see p239). There are other beautiful *havelis* in Jaisalmer, constructed of sandstone, featuring the fine work of renowned local *silavats* (stone carvers).

Step-Wells & Chhatris

Given the importance of water in Rajasthan, it's unsurprising that the architecture of wells and reservoirs rival other structures in the region. The most impressive regional *baoris* (step-wells) are Raniji-ki-Baori in Bundi and the extraordinary Chand Baori near Abhaneri.

Chhatris (cenotaphs) are a statewide architectural curiosity, built to commemorate maharajas, nobles, and, as is the case in the Shekhawati district, wealthy merchants. In rare instances, *chhatris* also commemorate women, such as the Chhatri of Moosi Rani at Alwar. Literally translating to 'umbrella', a *chhatri* comprises a central dome, supported by a series of pillars on a raised platform, with a sequence of small pavilions on the corners and sides.

Naturally Rajasthan

The Lie of the Land

The rugged Aravalli Range splits Rajasthan like a bony spine, running from the northeast to the southwest. These irregular mountains form a boundary between the Thar Desert to the west and the relatively lusher vegetation to the east. With an average height of 600m, in places the range soars to over 1050m; the highest point, Guru Shikhar (1722m), is near Mt Abu. It's thought to be the oldest mountain range in the world. A second hilly spur, the Vindhya Range, splays around the southernmost regions of Rajasthan.

The state's sole perennial river is the wide, life-giving swell of the Chambal. Rising in Madhya Pradesh from the northern slopes of the Vindhyas, the river enters Rajasthan at Chaurasigarh and forms part of Rajasthan's eastern border with Madhya Pradesh. The south is drained by the Mahi and Sabarmati Rivers; the Luni, which rises about 7km north of Ajmer in the Aravalli, is the only river in western Rajasthan. Seasonal and comparatively shallow, the Luni sometimes billows out to over 2km wide.

DESERT – JUST ADD WATER

It sounds too simple and it probably is. Irrigating India's vast arid lands has long been the dream of rulers and politicians. The Indira Gandhi Canal was initiated in 1957 and, though it is still incomplete, it includes an amazing 9709km of canals, with the main canal stretching 649km. Critics suggest that the massive project, connected with Bhakra Dam in Punjab, was concerned with short-term economics and politics to the detriment of the long-term ecology of the region.

The canal has opened up large tracts of the arid western region for cash crops, but these tracts are managed by wealthy landowners rather than the rural poor. Environmentalists say that soil has been destroyed through over-irrigation, and indigenous plants have suffered, adding to the degeneration of the arid zone. Furthermore, sections of the Indira Gandhi Canal are built on traditional grazing grounds, to which graziers are now denied access. The canal has also been blamed for breeding malaria-carrying mosquitoes.

In 2008, the waters from India's largest westward flowing river, the Narmada, which were dammed in highly controversial circumstances, trickled into Rajasthan's drought-ravaged regions of Jalore and Barmer. The miraculous appearance of the water brought untold joy to the long-suffering villagers. However, the entire Narmada River project has been heavily criticised both on environmental grounds and for displacing a large number of tribal people in the Narmada Valley. The search is underway for the next river to dam and tap.

The arid region in the west of the state is known as Marusthali or Marwar (the Land of Death), which gives some idea of the terrain. Sprawling from the Aravallis in the east to the Sulaiman Kirthar Range in the west is the Thar Desert, which covers almost three-quarters of the state. It's a dry, inhospitable expanse – the eastern extension of the great Saharo-Tharian Desert – forming 61% of the area covered by desert in India.

Low, rugged hills occasionally punctuate the parched plains. About 60% of the region is also made up of sand dunes, which are formed by the erosion of these low hills and from sand blown from Gujarat's vast desert, the Great Rann of Kutch.

It's hard to believe, but this desolate region was once covered by massive forests and populated by huge animals. In 1996 two amateur palaeontologists working in the Thar Desert discovered animal fossils, some 300 million years old, that included dinosaur fossils. At the Akal Wood Fossil Park, near Jaisalmer, you can visit the incredible remains of fossilised trees that are around 180 million years old. Plant fossils from 45 million years ago show that Rajasthan's metamorphosis into desert is relatively recent – and ongoing.

It's hard to make out where the desert ends and becomes semiarid. The semiarid zone nestles between the Aravallis and the Thar Desert, extending west from the Aravallis and encompassing the Ghaggar River Plain, parts of Shekhawati and the Luni River Basin.

Delhi lies on the vast flatlands of the Indo-Gangetic Plain, though the northernmost pimples of the Aravallis amount to the Ridge, which lies west of the city centre. The Yamuna River flows southwards along the eastern edge of the city. To the south, Agra lies on the banks of the Yamuna, in the neighbouring state of Uttar Pradesh.

Desert Plants

Vegetation in the desert zone is sparse – only a limited range of grasses and slow-growing thorny trees and shrubs can grow here. The most common tree species are the ubiquitous khejri *(Prosopis cineraria)* and varieties of acacia. Rajasthan also has some dry teak forest, dry mixed deciduous forest, bamboo brakes and subtropical hill forests. Forest stocks are dwindling as inhabitants scour the landscape for fuel and fodder.

The hardy khejri, which is held sacred by the Bishnoi tribes of Jodhpur district, is drought resistant on account of its very deep roots and is heavily utilised. No part of the plant goes to waste: the thorny twigs are used to build barriers to keep sheep and goats away from crops, the leaves are dried and used for fodder, and the bean-shaped fruit can be eaten. The latter, when cooked, is known as *sangri*. The wood is used to make furniture and the branches are burnt for fuel. The khejri twigs are used in the sacred fire that's lit during marriage ceremonies. When you see the heavily pruned khejri trees around Jodhpur you will be amazed by their staying power.

Wild Rajasthan

For a place apparently so inhospitable, Rajasthan hosts an incredible array of animals and birds; the stars are the dwindling numbers of tigers now virtually restricted to Ranthambhore National Park and the magnificent migratory bird show of Keoladeo Ghana National Park.

Animals

Arid-zone mammals have adapted to the lack of water in various resourceful ways. For example, some top up their fluids with insects that are composed of between 65% and 80% water, and water-bearing plants, while others retain water for longer periods. Faced with the incredible heat, many creatures burrow in the sand or venture out only at night.

The Thar Desert is the most densely populated desert in the world, with an average of over 60 people per square kilometre.

GERBILS

Desert gerbils are small, but they're big trouble: they descend on crops in vast numbers, causing untold damage. In the arid zone an incredible 12,000 to 15,000 burrows per hectare have been identified.

Antelopes & Gazelles

Blackbuck antelopes, with their amazing long spiralling horns, are most common around Jodhpur, where they are protected by local Bishnoi tribes. Bishnoi conservation has also helped the chinkaras (Indian gazelles); these delicate, small creatures are extremely fast and agile and are seen in small family herds.

Also notable is the extraordinary nilgai (or blue bull), which is the largest of the antelope family – only the males attain the blue colour. It's a large, muscular animal whose front legs appear longer than its rear legs, giving it a rather ungainly stance.

Big Cats

Tigers were once found along the length of the Aravallis. However, royal hunting parties, poachers and habitat destruction have decimated the population, and the only viable tiger population in Rajasthan can be found in Ranthambhore National Park. Although occasionally tigers do decide to move beyond the park boundaries, as was the case with four intrepid felines in the winter of 2010. The radio collars sported by all adult tigers at Ranthambhore allowed authorities to watch their movements.

Between 2008 and 2009 a handful of Ranthambhore's tigers were relocated to the much larger Sariska Tiger Reserve, but by 2010 one had already been poisoned, highlighting the conflict between the ever-expanding village populations and tiger conservation. The last of Sariska's original tigers were killed by poachers in 2004-05.

The mainly nocturnal and rarely seen leopard (panther) inhabits rocky declivities in the Aravallis, and parts of the Jaipur and Jodhpur districts.

Dogs

Jackals are renowned for their unearthly howling. Once common throughout Rajasthan, they would lurk around villages, where they scavenged and preyed on livestock. Habitat encroachment and hunting (for their skins) have reduced their numbers, though they are still a very common sight in Keoladeo Ghana, Ranthambhore and Sariska parks.

The wolves once roamed in large numbers in the desert, but farmers hunted them almost to the point of extinction. Wolves have begun to reappear over recent decades, due to concerted conservation efforts. The wildlife sanctuary at Kumbhalgarh is known for its wolves.

The Tiger's Destiny, by Valmik Thapar, with photographs by Fateh Singh Rathore, is all about the besieged tigers of Ranthambhore National Park.

Fund for the Tiger (www.fundfor thetiger.com) and Save the Tiger Fund (www.save thetigerfund.org) are non-profit fundraisers who finance initiatives to assist tiger conservation in India and elsewhere.

NATURALLY RAJASTHAN WILD RAJASTHAN

RETURN OF THE CHEETAH?

India's last wild cheetahs were likely shot by the Maharaja of Surguja in 1947. This fellow who also had the dubious distinction of having shot the most tigers in India.

India's ambitious plans for cheetah reintroduction had been drawn out for years and included requests for cell samples from Iran's Asiatic cheetahs to start a cloning program. But it seems India's ministry for the environment and forests may finally have found a way to reintroduce cheetahs from South Africa. There were three reserves being prepared for the reintroduction in 2011: the Kuno-Palpur Wildlife Sanctuary and Nauradehi Wildlife Sanctuary in Madhya Pradesh, and the Shargarh bulge grassland near Jaisalmer, Rajasthan. There remains considerable scepticism about whether these releases are a good idea and whether they will eventuate. Critics need only point to the tiger's plight to show how problematic it is to conserve big cats in India. Furthermore, studies have revealed that most of the potential cheetah habitat is severely overgrazed by livestock and subject to relentless poaching pressure. Meanwhile, it is reported that during the past two decades as many as 30 Cheetahs brought to zoos in India from various countries for breeding purposes have died here.

The sandy-coloured desert fox is a subspecies of the red fox and was once prolific in the Thar Desert. As with wolves, the fox population has shrunk due to human endeavours. Keep your eyes open for them scavenging roadkill on the highway near Jaisalmer.

Elephas maximus – A Portrait of the Indian Elephant by Stephen Alter, reveals the princely pachyderm in all its wild grandeur as well as describing its influence in art, warfare and ceremony.

Monkeys

Monkeys seem to be everywhere in Rajasthan. There are two common types: the red-faced and red-rumped rhesus macaque and the shaggy grey, black-faced langur, with prominent eyebrows. Both types are keen on hanging around human settlements, where they can get easy pickings. Both will steal food from your grasp at temples, but the macaque is probably the more aggressive and the one to be particularly wary of.

Bears

In forested regions you might see a sloth bear – a large creature covered in long black hair with a prominent white V on its chest and peculiar muzzle with an overhanging upper lip. That lip helps it feed on ants and termites dug out with those dangerous-looking claws on its front paws. Sloth bears feed mostly on vegetation and insects but aren't averse to a bit of carrion. The bears are reasonably common around Mt Abu and elsewhere on the western slopes of the Aravalli Range.

A Guide to the Wildlife Parks of Rajasthan, by Dr Suraj Ziddi, with photographs by Subhash Bhargava, is a comprehensive guide to Rajasthan's reserves.

Birds

Keoladeo Ghana National Park, a wetland in eastern Rajasthan, is internationally renowned for birdwatching. Resident and winter migrants put on an amazing feathery show. Migratory species include several varieties of storks, spoonbills, herons, cormorants, ibis and egrets. Wintering waterfowl include the common, marbled, falcated and Baikal teal; pintail, gadwall, shoveler, coot, wigeon, bar-headed and greylag geese; common and brahminy pochards; and the beautiful demoiselle crane. Waders include snipe, sandpipers and plovers. Species resident

TOP NATIONAL PARKS & WILDLIFE SANCTUARIES

NAME	LOCATION	FEATURES	BEST TIME TO VISIT
Desert National Park	western Rajasthan	great Indian bustards, blackbuck, nilgai, wolves, desert foxes, crested porcupines	Sep–Mar
Keoladeo Ghana National Park	eastern Rajasthan	400 bird species, including migratory birds & waterbirds (wetlands)	Oct–Mar, Jul–Aug
Kumbhalgarh Wildlife Sanctuary	southern Rajasthan	wolves in packs of up to 40, chowsinghas, four-horned antelopes, leopards, horse riding	Oct–Jun
Mt Abu Wildlife Sanctuary	southern Rajasthan	forest, sloth bears, wild boar, sambars, leopards	Mar–Jun
Ranthambhore National Park	eastern Rajasthan	tigers, chitals, leopards, nilgai, chinkaras, bird life, ancient fort	Oct–Apr
Sariska Tiger Reserve	eastern Rajasthan	leopards, chitals, chinkaras, birdlife, fort, deserted city & temples	Nov–Jun
Tal Chhapar Wildlife Sanctuary	northern Rajasthan	blackbuck, chinkaras, desert foxes, antelopes, harriers, eagles, sparrowhawks	Sep–Mar

GOING, GOING, GONE...

Some of Rajasthan's endangered wildlife is disappearing due to ongoing encroachment on its habitat, but poaching is also a serious problem.

From numbers in excess of 40,000 in the early 20th century, wild tigers in India have crashed to an official count of 1400 estimated in 2010. Tiger watchers say this number is a gross exaggeration and that the real number is somewhere around 800, and many of these are in small, isolated and unsustainable populations. It's estimated that during the 1990s more than 20 tigers were slaughtered at Ranthambhore National Park and the tigers of Sariska Tiger Reserve were all gone by 2005.

National parks and sanctuaries are proving to be lucrative hunting grounds for poachers. Frequently, only main roads in parks are patrolled by (often poorly paid) guards, so poachers can trespass without fear of detection.

Numbers of the great Indian bustard have also dwindled alarmingly due to hunting and because the bird's eggs are trampled by livestock. However, in Rajasthan, where the bird is the emblem of the state, there is no program for conservation and this has led to calls for a national program similar to Project Tiger to protect this majestic bird.

Three types of vulture have become endangered in recent years. Once common, they joined the endangered ranks after the population in south Asia fell by 95%. The cause was exposure to a veterinary drug, which the vultures absorbed while feeding from livestock carcasses. The reduction in numbers has had knock-on ecological and health effects, as the birds once disposed of many carcasses, thus reducing risks of disease.

throughout the year include the monogamous sarus crane, moorhens, egrets, herons, storks and cormorants. Birds of prey include many types of eagles (greater spotted, steppe, imperial, Spanish imperial and fishing), vultures (white-backed and scavenger), owls (spotted, dusky horned and mottled wood), marsh harriers, sparrowhawks, kestrels and goshawks.

The remaining forests and jungles that cling to the rugged Aravalli Ranges harbour orioles, hornbills, kingfishers, swallows, parakeets, warblers, mynahs, robins, flycatchers, quails, doves, peacocks, barbets, beeeaters, woodpeckers and drongos, among others. Birds of prey include numerous species of owls (great horned, dusky, brown fishing and collared scops, and spotted owlets), eagles (spotted and tawny), white-eyed buzzards, black-winged kites and shikras.

Common birds of the open grasslands include various species of lark. Quails can also be seen, as can several types of shrike, mynahs, drongos and partridges. Migratory birds include the lesser florican, seen during the monsoon, and the Houbara bustard, which winters at the grasslands. Birds of prey include falcons, eagles, hawks, kites, kestrels and harriers.

The Thar Desert also has a prolific variety of birdlife. At the small village of Kheechan, about 135km from Jodhpur, you can see vast flocks of demoiselle cranes descending on fields from the end of August to the end of March. Other winter visitors to the desert include Houbara bustards and common cranes. As water is scarce, waterholes attract large flocks of imperial, spotted, pintail and Indian sandgrouse in the early mornings. Other desert dwellers include drongos, common and bush quail, blue-tailed and little green bee-eaters, and grey partridges. Desert birds of prey include eagles (steppe and tawny), buzzards (honey and long-legged), goshawks, peregrine falcons and kestrels. The most notable of the desert and dry grassland dwellers is the impressive Indian bustard.

The website of India's premier wildlife magazine, *Sanctuary* (www.sanctuaryasia.com) highlights the latest conservation issues and has numerous related links.

Rajasthani Food

Wherever you go in this region of India, you'll never be far away from something tempting and delicious. From the sweet, decadent deep-fry of a Jaipur street-food stall, to the bliss of a hot cardamom-scented chai (tea) on a freezing Delhi January morning, food is all around you. Moreover, food is never just food here – it marks celebrations and festivals, honours guests, and accompanies births, marriages and deaths.

Rajasthan's cuisine has developed in response to its harsh climate. Fresh fruit and vegetables are rare commodities in desert zones, but these parts of the state overcome the land's shortcomings by serving up an amazing and creative variety of regional dishes, utilising cereals, pulses, spices, milk products and unusual desert fruits in myriad ways. Rajasthan, Delhi and Agra's regal feasts, meanwhile, are the stuff of legend. And modern Delhi ranks as one of the best restaurant destinations in the country, with scores of establishments serving up everything from butter chicken to international fusion cuisine.

> The eating reviews in this book are divided into three categories: budget (**$**) for meals less than ₹100, midrange (**$$**) for meals between ₹100 and ₹300, and top end (**$$$**) for meals over ₹300.

Making a Meal of It

Bread of Life

A meal is not complete in north India unless it comes with a bountiful supply of roti, little round circles of unleavened bread (also known as chapati), made with fine wholemeal flour and cooked on a *tawa* (hotplate). In Rajasthan you'll also find *sogra,* a thick, heavy chapati made from millet; *makki ki* roti, a fat cornmeal chapati; and *dhokla,* yummy balls of steamed maize flour cooked with coriander, spinach and mint, and eaten with chutney. Yet another kind of roti is a pastry-like *purat* roti, made by repeatedly coating the dough in oil, then folding it to produce a light and fluffy result. *Cheelre,* meanwhile, is a chapati made with gram (chickpea) powder paste, while *bhakri* is a thick roti made from barley, millet or corn, eaten with pounded garlic, red chilli and raw onions by working-class Rajasthanis, and said to prevent sunstroke.

Alongside the world of roti come *puris, parathas* and naans. A *puri* is a delicious North Indian snack of deep-fried wholemeal dough that puffs up like a soft, crispy balloon. *Kachori* is similar, but here the dough is pepped up with potato, corn or dhal masala. Flaky *paratha* is a soft, circular bread, deliciously substantial and mildly elastic, which makes for a scrumptious early morning snack, and is often jazzed up with a small bowl of pickle and a stuffing of *paneer* (unfermented cheese), *aloo* (potato), or grated vegetables. Naan bread, made with leavened white flour, is distinguished from roti by being larger, thicker and doughier, cooked on the inner walls of a tandoor (oven) rather than on a *tawa.* Best plain, it is also delicious when laced with garlic and lashings of butter, and filled with *paneer, aloo,* or coconut and raisins.

> For the full foodie experience whilst in Delhi, pick up the Times of India's *Times Food Guide.*

TERRIFIC THALIS

Thalis are the traditional cheap and filling meals made up of a combination of curried dishes, served with relishes, pappadams, yogurt, *puris* and rice. The term 'thali' also covers the characteristic metal tray-plate on which the meal is frequently served. If you're strapped for cash, thalis are a saviour, especially at local hole-in-the-wall restaurants and railway-station dining halls, since they're far heavier on the stomach than the wallet. In southern Rajasthan, many restaurants serve more sophisticated, sweet and lightly spiced Gujarati thalis – one of the best ways to sample a taste of Gujarati cuisine.

Rice

Basmati rice is considered the cream of India's crop, its name stemming from the Hindi phrase for 'queen of fragrance'. Aside from the plain steamed rice variety, you'll find pilau (aka pilaf), a tasty, buttery rice dish, whose Rajasthani incarnations frequently include cinnamon, cardamom, cloves, and a handful or two of almonds and pistachios.

Spotlighting rice, *Finest Rice Recipes* by Sabina Sehgal Saikia shows just how versatile this humble grain is, with classy creations such as rice-crusted crab cakes.

Dhal & Cereals

India has around 60 different varieties of dahl. In Rajasthan, the dhal of choice is *urad,* black lentils boiled in water, then cooked with garam masala, red chillies, cumin seeds, salt, oil and fresh coriander.

The state's most popular dhal-based dish is *dhal-bati-choorma,* which mixes dhal with *bati,* buttery hard-baked balls of wholemeal flour, and *choorma,* sweet fried wholemeal-flour balls mixed with sugar and nuts.

Gram-flour dumplings known as *gatta* are a delicious dish usually cooked in yogurt or masala and *mangodi* are lentil-flour dumplings served in an onion or potato gravy. A speciality of Jodhpur is *kabuli Jodhpuri,* a dish made with meat, vegetables and yet more fried gram-flour balls. *Govind gatta* offers a sweet alternative: lentil paste with dried fruit and nuts rolled into a sausage shape, then sliced and deep-fried. Pakora (fritters), *sev* (savoury nibbles) and other salted snacks generally known as *farsan* are all equally derived from chickpea gram.

For a taste of the desert, try out a few dishes from the recipe collection, *Classic Cooking of Rajasthan* by Kaira Jiggs and Raminder Malhotra.

Meat Matters

While Rajasthan's Brahmins and traders stuck to a vegetarian diet, the Rajputs have a far more carnivorous history. Goat (known as 'mutton' since the days of the British Raj), lamb and chicken are the mainstays; religious taboos make beef forbidden to Hindus, and pork to Muslims.

In the deserts of Jaisalmer, Jodhpur and Bikaner, meats are often cooked without the addition of water, instead using milk, curd, buttermilk and plenty of ghee. Cooked this way, dishes keep for days without refrigeration, a practical advantage in the searing heat of the desert. *Murg ko khaato* (chicken cooked in a curd gravy), *achar murg* (pickled chicken), *kacher maas* (dry lamb cooked in spices), *lal maas* (a rich red dish, usually mutton) and *soor santh ro sohito* (pork with millet dumplings) are all classic desert dishes.

Maas ka sule, a Rajput favourite, is a dry dish that can be made from partridge, wild boar, chicken, mutton or fish. Marinated chunks of meat are cooked on skewers in a tandoor, then glazed with melted butter and a tangy masala spice mix. Mughlai meat dishes, meanwhile, include rich korma and rogan josh, the former mild, the latter cooked with tomatoes and saffron, and both generously spiked with thick, creamy curd.

There's really no such thing, in India, as a 'curry'. The term is thought to be an anglicisation of the Tamil word *kari* (black pepper), coined by bewildered Brits for any dish that included spices.

Vegetarians will have no problem maintaining a varied and exciting diet in India.

Vegetarian food is sometimes divided up in India into 'veg' and 'pure veg', a frequently blurred and confusing distinction. As a general rule of thumb, 'veg' usually means the same as it does in the West: without meat, fowl or seafood, but possibly containing butter (in India's case, ghee), dairy products, eggs or honey. 'Pure veg' often refers to what the West knows as vegan food: dishes containing no dairy products, eggs or honey. Other times, 'pure veg' might also mean no onions, garlic or mushrooms (which some Hare Krishna believe can have a negative effect on one's state of consciousness) or even no root vegetables or tubers (since many Jains, according to the principles of ahimsa, are loathe to damage plants).

Though it's extremely easy to be vegetarian in India, finding vegan food – outside 'pure veg' restaurants – can be trickier. Many basic dishes include a small amount of ghee, so ask whether a dish is 'pure veg', even in a vegetarian restaurant.

Fruit & Vegetables

Rajasthan's delicious *sabji* (vegetable) dishes have to be admired for their inventiveness under frequently hostile growing conditions. Dishes you might come across include *papad ki sabzi,* a simple pappadam made with vegetables and masala (a mixture of spices), and *aloo mangori,* ground lentil paste sun-dried then added with potato to a curry. Once rolled by hand, the paste is now often forced through a machine in a similar way to making macaroni. A common vegetarian snack is *aloo samosa,* triangular pastry cones stuffed with spicy potato, while another scrumptious local snack is *mirch bada,* a large chilli coated in a thick layer of deep-fried potato and wheatgerm.

There are a few vegetables specific to the deserts of Rajasthan. These include *mogri,* a type of desert bean, which is made into *mogri mangori,* (similar to *aloo mangori*) or a sweeter version which is known as *methi mangori – methi* being the leaf of a green desert vegetable. Another use for these *methi* leaves is in *dana methi,* where they are boiled with *dana* (small pea-shaped vegetables) and mixed with sugar, masala and dried fruit.

With developments in infrastructure, more vegetable dishes are now available in Rajasthan than during its barren, warrior-filled past. Heads of cauliflower are usually cooked dry on their own, with potatoes to make *aloo gobi.* Fresh green peas turn up stir-fried with other vegetables in pilaus and biryanis, in samosas along with potato, and in one of North India's signature dishes, *mattar paneer* (peas and fresh, firm white cheese). Brinjal (eggplant or aubergine), *bhindi* (okra or ladies' finger) and *saag* (a generic term for leafy greens) are all popular choices.

The desert bears a handful of fruits, too. The small, round *kair* is a favourite of camels as well as people, to whom it is usually served with mango pickle; *kachri* is frequently made into chutney. If you order something that arrives looking like a plate of dry sticks, these are s*angri* (dried wild desert beans). The seeds and beans are soaked overnight in water, boiled, and then fried in oil with masala, dried dates, red chillies, turmeric powder, shredded dried mango, salt, coriander and cumin seeds.

Pickles, Chutneys & Relishes

You're in a pickle without a pickle, or *achar:* no Indian meal is complete without one or two *chatnis* (chutneys) and relishes on the side. A relish can be anything from a roughly chopped onion to a delicately crafted fusion of fruit, nuts and spices. The best known is raita (mildly spiced

To find out more about veganism in India, take a look at www. indianvegan.com. For recipe ideas, pick up a copy of *Spicy Vegan* by Sudha Raina.

Even deities have their favourite dishes. Krishna likes milk products, and Ganesh is rarely seen without a bowl of *modak* (sweet rice-flour dumplings).

yogurt or curd often containing cucumber, tomato or pineapple), which makes a refreshing counter to spicy meals.

Other regional variations include *goonde achar*, *goonde* being a green fruit that is boiled and mixed with mustard oil and masala. *Kair achar* is a pickle with desert fruit as its base, while *lahsun achar* is an onion pickle. *Lal mirch* is a garlic-stuffed red chilli and *kamrak ka achar is* a pickle made from *kamrak*, a type of desert vegetable with a pungent, sour taste. The most widely served are made of raw mango, mixed with spices and mustard oil, with lime, shredded ginger, or with tiny whole shallots.

Dairy

Milk and milk products make a staggering contribution to Indian cuisine (hence the sanctity of the cow), and in Rajasthan they're even more important: *dahi* (curd) is served with most meals and is handy for countering heat in terms of both temperature and spiciness of dishes; firm, unmeltable *paneer* cheese is a godsend for the vegetarian majority and is used in apparently endless permutations; popular lassi (yogurt and iced-water drink) is just one in a host of nourishing sweet or savoury drinks, often with fruit such as banana or mango added; ghee (clarified butter) is the traditional and pure cooking medium; and the best sweets are made with plenty of condensed, sweetened milk or cream.

Sweets & Desserts

Indians have a heady range of tooth-achingly sweet *mithai* (sweets), made from manifold concoctions of sugar, milk, ghee, nuts and yet more sugar. Rajasthani varieties include *badam ki barfi*, a type of fudge made from sugar, powdered milk, almonds and ghee, and *chakki*, a *barfi* (fudge) made from gram flour, sugar and milk. Gram flour, sugar, cardamom, ghee and dried fruits combined make *churma*, while *ladoo* comes in ball-form.

Ghewar is a paste based on *urad* (a mung-bean type pulse) that's crushed, deep-fried and dipped in sugar syrup flavoured with cardamom, cinnamon and cloves. It's served hot, topped with a thick layer of unsweetened cream and garnished with rose petals.

Kheer is perhaps India's favourite dessert, a delectable, fragrant rice pudding with a light flavour of cardamom, saffron, pistachios, flaked almonds, and cashews or dried fruit. *Gulab jamun* are spongy deep-fried balls of milk dough soaked in rose-flavoured syrup. *Kulfi* is addictive once experienced; delicious, substantially firm-textured, made with reduced milk and flavoured with nuts, fruits and berries, and especially tasty in its pale-green pistachio incarnation, *pista kulfi*.

Alongside these more sophisticated offerings are food-stall sweets such as *jalebis* (orange-coloured whirls of fried batter dipped in syrup), which melt in the mouth and hang heavy on the conscience.

Gorge yourself by reading about the extravagant royal recipes of Rajasthan in *Royal Indian Cookery* by Manju Shivraj Singh, the niece of the late Maharaja Bhawani Singh of Jaipur.

PAAN

Meals are often rounded off with *paan*, a fragrant mixture of betel nut (also called areca nut), lime paste, spices and condiments wrapped in an edible, silky *paan* leaf. Peddled by *paan*-wallahs, *paan* is a digestive and mouth-freshener. The betel nut is mildly narcotic and some aficionados eat *paan* the same way heavy smokers consume cigarettes, which can cause these people's teeth can rot.

There are two basic types of *paan*: *mitha* (sweet) and *saadha* (with tobacco). A parcel of *mitha paan* is a splendid way to finish a satisfying meal – pop the whole parcel in your mouth and chew slowly.

Drinks

Tea & Coffee

India runs on chai (tea). It's a unique and addictive brew: more milk than water, stewed for a long time and frequently sugary enough to give you an energy boost. A glass of steaming, sweet chai is the perfect antidote to the heat and stress of Indian travel.

If you just crave a simple cuppa, many cafes and restaurants can serve up 'tray tea' or 'English tea'. Coffee used to be fairly unusual in the region, but Delhi and the well-travelled parts of Rajasthan have caught up with the double-mocha-latte ways of the West. At bus and train stations, coffee is still almost indistinguishable from chai: the same combination of water, boiled milk and sugar, but with a dash of instant-coffee powder.

Cooling Off

Aside from the usual gamut of Pepsis and 7Ups, India has a few of its own sugary bottled drinks: the vaguely lemonish Limca and orange Mirinda. *Masala soda* is the quintessential Indian soft drink, but it's an acquired taste. Freshly squeezed orange juice is also widely available, though the most popular street juices are made from sweet lemon and sugar cane, pressed in front of you by a mechanised wheel complete with jingling bells.

Jal jeera is made with lime juice, cumin, mint and rock salt and is sold in large earthenware pots by street vendors as well as in restaurants. *Falooda* is a sweet rose-flavoured Muslim speciality made with milk, cream, nuts and strands of vermicelli.

By far the most popular of all Indian cold drinks, however, is a refreshing sweet or salty lassi (yogurt drink). Jodhpur is famous for its sweet *makhania* lassis, flavoured with saffron and hearty enough to stand in for a meal. *Chach* is a thin, salted lassi and *kairi chach* is unripe mango juice with water and salt added, widely available in summer and allegedly a good remedy for sunstroke.

Learn more about Sula Wines and their environmentally-friendly sustainable agriculture programmes at their website, www.sulawines.com.

SULA WINES

Cheers

Most travellers champion Kingfisher beer; other brands include Royal Challenge, Foster's, Dansberg, London Pilsner and Sandpiper. Served ice-cold, all are equally refreshing. But if you can find draught beer, such as Kingfisher and Golden Peacock, you will certainly notice the better taste over the bottled beer, which has glycerine added as a preservative.

Though the Indian wine industry is still in its infancy, there are signs that Indian wines are slowly being accepted into local markets. One of the best-known Indian wine producers is Sula Wines, which creates a whole slew of different varieties with grapes grown in northern Maharashtra. Meanwhile, Grover Vineyards, established in 1988 near Bangalore, also has a solid reputation, with a smaller range of wines than Sula.

At the other end of the scale, arak is what the poor drink to get blotto, poignantly called *asha* (hope) in the north of India. The effects of this distilled rice liquor creep up on you quickly and without warning. Only ever drink this from a bottle produced in a government-controlled distillery. *Never* drink it otherwise – hundreds of people die or are blinded every year in India as a result of drinking arak produced in illicit stills.

BEWARE OF THOSE BHANG LASSIS!

It's rarely printed in menus, but some restaurants in Rajasthan clandestinely whip up bhang lassi, a yogurt and iced-water beverage laced with bhang, a derivative of marijuana. This 'special lassi' can be a potent concoction – some travellers have been stuck in bed for several miserable days after drinking it; others have become delirious.

Survival Guide

344

Scams & Touts

India has its fair share of scams, particularly in cities such as Delhi, Agra and Jaipur, but most problems can be avoided with some common sense and caution. Scams change as tricksters try to stay ahead of the game, so chat with travellers and tourism officials to keep abreast of the latest cons. Look at the India branch of Lonely Planet's **Thorn Tree Travel Forum** (www.lonely planet.com/thorntree) for timely warnings from on-the-road travellers.

Contaminated Food & Drink

» Some private medical clinics have given patients more treatment than necessary to procure larger payments from travel insurance companies – get a second opinion.

» The late 1990s saw a dangerous scam in Agra and Varanasi when several travellers died after being fed food spiked with bacteria from restaurants linked to dodgy clinics. This scam has been quashed, but there's always the chance it could reappear.

» Most bottled water is legit, but always check that the lid

seal is intact and the bottom of the bottle hasn't been tampered with.

» Crush plastic bottles after use to prevent them being misused later.

» Use your own water bottle and water-purification tablets or a filtration system.

Gem Scams

» This long-running scam involves charming con artists who promise foolproof 'get rich quick' schemes.

» Travellers are asked to carry or mail gems (or sometimes carpets) home and then sell them to the trader's (non-existent) overseas representatives at a profit.

» Without exception, the goods – if they arrive at all – are worth a fraction of what you paid, and the 'representatives' never materialise.

» Don't believe hard-luck stories about an inability to obtain an export licence, and don't believe the testimonials they show you from other travellers – they are all fake.

» This scam is particularly prevalent in Jaipur (p131).

Transport Scams

» Agree on prices beforehand when flagging down an autorickshaw or arranging an airport pick-up from your hostel or hotel.

» Make sure you're completely clear what is included in the price of any tour to avoid charges for hidden 'extras' later on; get this in writing.

» Be extremely wary of anyone offering tours to Kashmir.

» Some travel agents exploit travellers' safety concerns to make extra money from

TOP SCAMS

These long-running scams have been separating travellers from their money for years.

» Gunk (dirt, paint, poo) suddenly appears on your shoes, only for a shoe cleaner to magically appear and offer to clean it off – for a price.

» Shops and restaurants 'borrow' the name of their more successful and popular competitor.

» Taxi drivers insist that they don't know the way to your hotel, or that it has moved or is closed – but will happily take you to their 'friend's' place (where they'll receive a nice commission).

» Touts claim to be 'government-approved' guides or 'tour operators' and sting you for large sums of cash. Inquire at the local tourist office about recommended guides and ask to see evidence from the guides.

KEEPING SAFE

» A good travel-insurance policy is essential (p350).

» Email copies of your passport identity page, visa page and airline ticket to yourself; keep copies on you.

» Keep your money and passport in a concealed money belt or a secure place under your shirt and never keep your wallet in your back pocket.

» Store at least US$100 separately from your main stash but keep the rest of your cash and other valuables on your person.

» Separate big currency notes from small bills so you don't publicly display large wads of cash when paying for services or checking into hotels.

» Consider using your own padlock at cheaper hotels where doors are locked with a padlock.

» If you cannot lock your hotel room securely from the inside at night, stay somewhere else.

tours that you can do just as easily (and safely) on public transport.

» When buying a bus, train or plane ticket anywhere other than the registered office of the transport company, make certain you're getting the ticket class you paid for. It's not uncommon for travellers to book a deluxe bus or AC train berth and arrive to find a bog-standard ordinary bus or a less comfortable sleeper seat.

» Ignore tricksters that pose as India Rail officials and insist you pay to have your e-ticket validated.

» Ignore taxi drivers outside airports who say they are prepaid taxi drivers; your prepaid taxi receipt includes the designated drivers' licence plate number.

Theft & Druggings
Druggings

» Very occasionally, tourists (especially solo travellers) are drugged and robbed during train or bus journeys. A spiked drink is the most commonly used method.

» Use your instincts if offered drinks or food by strangers; if you're unsure then politely decline (stomach upsets are a convenient excuse).

Theft

» Keep luggage securely locked on buses and trains.

» Be extra alert just before the train departs; thieves often take advantage of the confusion and crowds.

» Take extra care in dormitories and never leave your valuables in your room when you go out unless there is a safe.

» For lost credit cards call the international lost/stolen number; for lost/stolen travellers cheques, contact the American Express or Thomas Cook office in Delhi (p80).

Touts & Commission Agents

» Many hotels and shops drum up extra business by paying commission fees to local fixers who bring in tourists. The prices in these places will invariably be raised to allow for the fixer's commission.

» Train and bus stations are often swarming with touts – if anyone asks if this is your first trip to India, say you've been here several times, even if you haven't.

» Touts can be particularly bothersome in major tourist centres such as Agra and Jaipur.

» Telling touts that you have already prepaid your journey can help dissuade them.

» Where possible, arrange hotel pick-ups, particularly in big cities.

» You'll often hear stories about hotels that refuse to pay commissions as being 'full' or 'closed' – check things out yourself.

» Be very sceptical of phrases like 'my brother's shop' and 'special deal at my friend's place'.

» Touts *can* be beneficial if you arrive in a town without a hotel reservation when a big festival is on, or during the peak season – they'll know which places have beds.

CARD CON

Be careful when paying for souvenirs with a credit card. While government shops are usually legitimate, private shops have been known to surreptitiously run off extra copies of the credit-card imprint slip, to be used for phoney transactions later. Insist that the trader carries out card transactions in front of you. Alternatively, take out cash from an ATM to avoid this risk altogether.

Directory A–Z

Accommodation

Accommodation ranges from grungy backpacker hostels with concrete floors and cold 'bucket' showers to opulent palaces fit for a maharaja. In this guide, we've listed reviews by author preference; standout options are indicated by the top choice icon .

Categories & Price Icons

As a general rule, budget covers everything from basic hostels and railway retiring rooms to simple guesthouses in traditional village homes.

Midrange hotels tend to be modern-style concrete blocks that usually offer extras such as cable/satellite TV and air-conditioning (although some just have noisy 'air-coolers' that simply cool air by blowing it over water).

Top-end places stretch from gorgeous heritage hotels to luxury five-star international chains.

The budget breakdown given here is a loose guide; many places have rooms covering a variety of categories – their upper-priced rooms are midrange, lower-priced ones are budget, etc. The price indicators in this book refer to the cost of a double room, including private bathroom, unless otherwise noted.

PRICE ICON & CATEGORY	COST
$ budget	<₹1000
$$ midrange	₹1000–5000
$$$ top end	>₹5000

Reservations

» The majority of top-end and some midrange hotels require a deposit at the time of booking, which can usually be done with a credit card.

» Some midrange places may ask for a cheque or cash deposit into a bank account to secure a reservation – this is usually more hassle than it's worth.

» Some budget options won't take reservations as they don't know when people are going to check-out. Call ahead to check.

» Some places may ask for a deposit at check-in – ask for a receipt and be wary of any request to sign a blank impression of your credit card. If the hotel insists, consider going to the nearest ATM and paying cash.

» Verify the check-out time when you check-in – some hotels have a fixed check-out time (usually 10am or noon), while others give you 24-hour check-out.

» Reservations by phone without a deposit are usually fine, but call to confirm the booking the day before you arrive.

Seasons

» Rates in this guidebook are full price in high season (although not for the Christmas to New Year peak). High season coincides with the best weather (October to mid-February).

» In areas popular with foreign tourists there's an additional peak period over Christmas and New Year – make reservations well in advance.

» At other times you may find significant discounts; if the hotel seems quiet, ask for a discount.

» Many temple towns have additional peak seasons around major festivals and pilgrimages (eg Pushkar); for festival details see the Month by Month chapter (p24) and the Festivals boxed texts near the start of the regional chapters.

BOOK YOUR STAY ONLINE

For more reviews by Lonely Planet authors, check out hotels.lonelyplanet.com/india. You'll find independent reviews, as well as recommendations on the best places to stay. Best of all, you can book online.

PRACTICALITIES

» **Newspapers & Magazines** Major English-language dailies include the *Hindustan Times, Times of India, Indian Express, Hindu, Statesman, Telegraph, Daily News & Analysis (DNA)* and *Economic Times*. Regional English-language and local-vernacular publications are found nationwide. Incisive current-affairs magazines include *Frontline, India Today,* the *Week, Tehelka* and *Outlook*.

» **Radio** Government-controlled All India Radio (AIR) is India's national broadcaster with more than 220 stations broadcasting local and international news. There are also private FM channels broadcasting music, current affairs, talkback and more.

» **TV & Video** The national (government) TV broadcaster is Doordarshan. Most people watch satellite and cable TV; English-language channels include BBC, CNN, Star World, HBO and Discovery.

» **Weights & Measures** Officially India is metric. Terms you're likely to hear are: lakhs (one lakh = 100,000) and crores (one crore = 10 million).

Taxes & Service Charges

» At most budget places you won't have to pay any taxes. Once you get into the mid-range and top-end accommodation, you will usually have to pay a 10% 'luxury' tax on rooms over ₹1000 plus 12.5% on food and beverages in hotels that attract the luxury tax on their rooms.

» On top of taxes, many midrange and upmarket hotels have a 'service charge' (usually 10%). This may be restricted to room service and telephone use, or may be levied on the total bill.

» Rates quoted in this book's regional chapters exclude taxes unless otherwise noted.

Budget & Midrange Hotels

Most budget and midrange hotels are modern-style concrete blocks. Some are charming, clean and good value, others less so.

» Room quality can vary considerably within hotels so try to inspect a few rooms first, and avoid carpeted rooms at cheaper hotels unless you like the smell of mouldy socks.

» Shared bathrooms (often with squat toilets) are usually only found at the cheapest lodgings.

» Most rooms have ceiling fans, and better rooms have electric mosquito-killers and/or window nets, though cheaper rooms may lack windows altogether.

» If staying at the very cheapest of hotels bring your own sheet or sleeping-bag liner.

» Sound pollution can be irksome (especially in urban hubs); pack good-quality earplugs and request a room that doesn't face a busy road.

» It's wise to keep your door locked, as some staff (particularly in budget accommodation) may knock and automatically walk in without first seeking your permission.

» Blackouts from load shedding is common so check that the hotel has a back-up generator if you're paying for electronic 'extras' such as air-conditioners and TVs.

» Note that some hotels lock their doors at night. Members of staff may sleep in the lobby but waking them up can be a challenge. Let the hotel know in advance if you'll be arriving or returning to your room late in the evening.

Dormitory Accommodation

» A number of hotels have cheap dormitories though these may be mixed and, in less touristy places, full of drunken drivers – not ideal conditions for women. More traveller-friendly dorms are found at the handful of hostels run by the YMCA, YWCA and Salvation Army as well as at HI-associated hostels.

Paying Guest House Scheme (Homestays)

» Rajasthan pioneered the Paying Guest House Scheme, so it's well developed in the state. Prices range from budget to upper midrange – contact the local Rajasthan Tourism Development Corporation (RTDC) tourist reception centres for details (see the individual regional chapters). Jaipur also has a reputable private scheme called Jaipur Pride (p119).

Railway Retiring Rooms

» Most large train stations have basic rooms for travellers holding an ongoing train ticket or Indrail Pass. Some are grim, others are surprisingly pleasant, but all are noisy from the sound of trains and passengers. Nevertheless, they're useful for early-morning train departures and there's usually a choice of dormitories or private rooms (24-hour checkout).

Palaces, Forts & Havelis

» Rajasthan is famous for its wonderful heritage hotels created from palaces, forts and *havelis*, most famous being the Lake Palace in

Udaipur, Rambagh Palace in Jaipur and Umaid Bhawan Palace in Jodhpur. But there are hundreds of others, and it often doesn't cost a fortune: some are the height of luxury and priced accordingly, but many are simpler, packed with character and set in stunning locations.

» As palaces and forts were not originally designed for tourism, the size and quality of rooms can vary, so look at a few rooms first.

Top-End Hotels

» As major tourist centres, Rajasthan, Delhi and Agra have a bevy of top-end hotels, ranging from five-star chains such as the Oberoi, Taj and Welcomgroup, to slightly less glamorous four-star options.

» Note that US dollar rates often apply to foreigners, including to nonresident Indians (NRIs).

» If you're interested in staying at a top-end hotel, it's often cheaper to book it online. Nevertheless, unless the hotel is busy, you can nearly always score a discount from the rack rates.

Activities

From exploring the desert on camelback, to being covered in ayurvedic oils, Rajasthan has an exhilarating range of activities on offer.

Remember that travel agents often take a cut of what you pay and sell you on as clients to someone else. The end provider gets only part of what you paid and so you may get poor equipment, insufficient food or poor safety standards. If you are using an agent, try to deal with companies that are the end provider and ask if they're registered with the state government and an accredited travel agent association. Best of all get recommendations from fellow travellers.

Business Hours

» Official business hours are from 9.30am to 5.30pm Monday to Friday.

» Most offices have an official lunch hour from around 1pm.

» Bank opening hours vary from town to town, so check locally; foreign-exchange offices may open longer and operate daily.

» Some larger post offices have a full day on Saturday and a half-day on Sunday.

» In reviews, we only list business hours where they differ from the following standards.

BUSINESS	OPENING HOURS
airline offices	9.30am-5.30pm Mon-Sat
banks	9.30 or 10am-2 or 4pm Mon-Fri, to noon or 1pm Sat
government offices	9.30am-1pm & 2-5.30pm Mon-Fri, to noon Sat, closed alternative Sat (usually 2nd and 4th)
post offices	9am-6pm Mon-Fri, to noon Sat
museums	10am-5pm Tue-Sun
restaurants	lunch: noon-2.30 or 3pm; dinner: 7-10 or 11pm
sights	10am-5pm
shops	10am-7pm, some closed Sun

Customs Regulations

Technically you're supposed to declare any amount of cash/travellers cheques over US$5000/10,000 on arrival. Indian rupees shouldn't be taken out of India. Officials very occasionally ask tourists to enter expensive items such as video cameras and laptop computers on a 'Tourist Baggage Re-export' form to ensure they're taken out of India at the time of departure.

Electricity

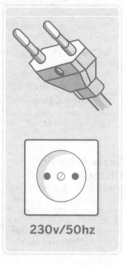

230v/50hz

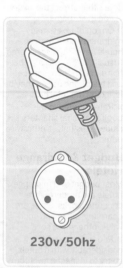

230v/50hz

Many foreign diplomatic missions have certain timings for visa applications (usually mornings), so phone for details. The following consulates are all based in Delhi.

COUNTRY	TELEPHONE	WEBSITE	ADDRESS
Australia	011-41399900	www.india.highcommission.gov.au	1/50G Shantipath, Chanakyapuri
Bangladesh	011-24121394	www.bhcdelhi.org	EP39 Dr Radakrishnan Marg, Chanakyapuri
Bhutan	011-26889230	www.bhutan.gov.bt	Chandragupta Marg, Chanakyapur
Canada	011-41782000	www.canadainternational.gc.ca/india-inde	7/8 Shantipath, Chanakyapur
France	011-24196100	http://ambafrance-in.org/	2/50E Shantipath, Chanakyapuri
Germany	011-44199199	www.new-delhi.diplo.de	6/50G Shantipath, Chanakyapuri
Ireland	011-24626733	www.irelandindia.com	203 Jor Bagh
Israel	011-30414500	http://delhi.mfa.gov.il	3 Aurangzeb Rd
Italy	011-26114355	www.ambnewdelhi.esteri.it	50E Chandragupta Marg, Chanakyapur
Japan	011-26876564	www.in.emb-japan.go.jp	50G Shantipath, Chanakyapuri
Malaysia	011-26111291/97	www.kln.gov.my/web/ind_new-delhi/home	50M Satya Marg, Chanakyapuri
Maldives	011-41435701	www.maldiveshighcom.in/	B2 Anand Niketan
Myanmar (Burma)	011-24678822		3/50F Nyaya Marg
Nepal	011-23327361		Barakhamba Rd
Netherlands	011-24197600	http://india.nlembassy.org/	6/50F Shantipath, Chanakyapur
New Zealand	011-46883170	www.nzembassy.com/india	Sir Edmund Hillary Marg, Chanakyapuri
Pakistan	011-24676004		2/50G Shantipath, Chanakyapuri
Singapore	011-46000915	www.mfa.gov.sg/newdelhi	E6 Chandragupta Marg, Chanakyapuri
Sri Lanka	011-23010201	www.newdelhi.mission.gov.lk	27 Kautilya Marg, Chanakyapuri
Switzerland	011-26878372	www.eda.admin.ch	Nyaya Marg, Chanakyapuri
Thailand	011-26118103-4	www.thaiemb.org.in	56N Nyaya Marg, Chanakyapuri
UK	011-24192100	http://ukinindia.fco.gov.uk	Shantipath, Chanakyapuri
USA	011-24198000	http://newdelhi.usembassy.gov/	Shantipath, Chanakyapuri

Gay & Lesbian Travellers

In July 2009, Delhi's High Court overturned India's antihomosexuality law. Prior to this landmark ruling, homosexual relations for men were illegal with penalties for transgression theoretically up to life imprisonment (there's no law against lesbian sexual relations).

However, the country remains largely conservative and public displays of affection are generally frowned upon for heterosexual couples as well as gay and lesbian couples.

There are low-key gay scenes in cities such as Delhi.

Insurance

» Comprehensive travel insurance to cover theft, loss and medical problems (as well as air evacuation) is strongly recommended; also see p371.

» Some policies specifically exclude potentially dangerous activities such as scuba diving, skiing, motorcycling, paragliding and trekking – read the fine print.

» Some trekking agents may only accept customers who have cover for emergency helicopter evacuation.

» If you plan to hire a motorcycle in India, make sure the rental policy includes at least third-party insurance; see p367.

» Check in advance if your insurance policy will pay doctors and hospitals directly or reimburse you later for overseas health expenditures (keep all documentation for your claim).

» It's crucial to get a police report in India if you've had anything stolen; insurance companies may refuse to reimburse you without one.

» Worldwide travel insurance is available at www.lonely planet.com/travel_services.

You can buy, extend and claim online anytime – even if you're already on the road.

Internet Access

Internet cafes are widespread and connections are usually reasonably fast, except in more remote areas. Wireless (wi-fi) access is available in an increasing number of hotels and some coffee shops in larger cities. In this book, hotels offering internet access are marked by @ and wireless by 📶.

Practicalities

» Internet charges vary regionally (see regional chapters); charges fall anywhere between ₹15 and ₹90 per hour and often with a 15- to 30-minute minimum.

» Power cuts are not uncommon; avoid losing your email by writing and saving messages in a text application before pasting them into your browser.

» Bandwidth load tends to be lowest in the early morning and early afternoon.

» Some internet cafes may ask to see your passport; carrying photocopies of the relevant pages (information and visa) saves you having to dig your passport out each time.

» See p17 for useful India-specific web resources.

Security

» Be wary of sending sensitive financial information from internet cafes; some places can use keystroke-capturing technology to access passwords and emails.

» Avoid sending credit-card details or other personal data over a wireless connection; using online banking on any nonsecure system is generally unwise.

Laptops

» Many internet cafes can supply laptop users with internet access over an Ethernet LAN cable; alternatively join an international roaming service with an Indian dial-up number, or take out an account with a local Internet Service Provider (ISP).

» Make sure your modem is compatible with the telephone and dial-up system in India (an external global modem may be necessary).

» Companies including Reliance, Airtel and Vodafone offer 3G Data Cards, which can be plugged into the USB port of your laptop and will allow you to access the internet.

» Tariffs range from ₹800 per month for 3GB to ₹1500 per month for 15GB.

» Check that the area you're travelling to is covered by your service provider.

» Consider purchasing a fuse-protected universal AC adaptor to protect your circuit board from power surges.

» Plug adaptors are widely available throughout India, but bring spare plug fuses from home.

Legal Matters

If you're in a sticky legal situation, contact your embassy as quickly as possible. However, be aware that all your embassy may be able to do is monitor your treatment in custody and arrange a lawyer. In the Indian justice system, the burden of proof can often be on the accused and stints in prison before trial are not unheard of. Travellers should note that they can be prosecuted under the law of their home country regarding age of consent, even when abroad.

Antisocial Behaviour

» Smoking in public places is illegal throughout India but this is very rarely enforced; if caught you'll be fined ₹200.

» People can smoke inside their homes and in most open spaces such as streets (heed any signs stating otherwise).

» A number of Indian cities have banned spitting and littering, but this is also variably enforced.

Drugs

» Indian law does not distinguish between 'hard' and 'soft' drugs; possession of any illegal drug is regarded as a criminal offence.

» If convicted, the minimum sentence is 10 years, with very little chance of remission or parole.

» Cases can take months, even several years, to appear before a court while the accused may have to wait in prison. There's also usually a hefty monetary fine on top of any custodial sentence.

» Be aware that travellers have been targeted in sting operations in some backpacker enclaves.

» Marijuana grows wild in various parts of India, but consuming it is still an offence, except in towns where bhang is legally sold for religious rituals.

» Police are getting particularly tough on foreigners who use drugs, so you should take this risk very seriously.

Police

» You should always carry your passport; police are entitled to ask you for identification at any time.

» If you're arrested for an alleged offence and asked for a

bribe, the prevailing wisdom is to pay it, as the alternative may be a trumped-up charge; although there are no 'rules' guiding how much you should pay.

» Corruption is rife, so the less you have to do with local police the better; try and avoid potentially risky situations in the first place.

Maps

Maps available inside India are of variable quality. Throughout Rajasthan, most state-government tourist offices stock basic local maps. The following maps are available at good bookshops, or you can buy them online from Delhi's **India Map Store** (www.indiamapstore.com).

» **Eicher** (http://maps.eicher world.com/) Road, state and city maps

» **Nelles** (www.nelles-verlag. de) Western India

» **Survey of India** (www. surveyofindia.gov.in) Decent city, state and country maps but some titles are restricted for security reasons.

Money

The Indian rupee (₹) is divided into 100 paise (p), but paise coins are becoming increasingly rare. Coins come in denominations of ₹1, ₹2 and ₹5; notes come in ₹5, ₹10, ₹20, ₹50, ₹100, ₹500 and ₹1000. The Indian rupee is linked to a basket of currencies and has been subject to fluctuations in recent years; see p17 for exchange rates.

ATMs

» ATMs are found in most urban centres and Visa, MasterCard, Cirrus, Maestro and Plus are the most commonly accepted cards.

» Some banks in India that accept foreign cards include Citibank, HDFC, ICICI, Standard Chartered, HSBC, State

Bank of India (SBI) and State Bank of Bikaner & Jaipur (SBBJ).

» Before your trip, check whether your card can reliably access banking networks in India and ask for details of charges.

» Notify your bank that you'll be using your card in India (provide dates) to avoid having your card blocked; take along your bank's phone number just in case.

» The ATMs listed in this book's regional chapters accept foreign cards (but not necessarily all types of cards).

» Always keep the emergency lost-and-stolen numbers for your credit cards in a safe place, separate from your cards, and report any loss or theft immediately.

» Away from major towns, always carry cash or travellers cheques as back-up.

Black Market

» Black-market moneychangers exist but legal moneychangers are so common that there's no reason to use them. Exceptions may be to change small amounts of cash at land border crossings. As a rule, if someone approaches you on the street and offers to change money, you're probably being set up for a scam.

Cash

» Major currencies such as US dollars, British pounds and Euros are easy to change throughout India, although some bank branches insist on travellers cheques only. Some banks also accept other currencies such as Australian and Canadian dollars, and Swiss francs.

» Private moneychangers deal with a wider range of currencies, but Pakistani, Nepali and Bangladeshi currency can be harder to change away from the border.

» When travelling off the beaten track, always carry an adequate stock of rupees.

» Whenever changing money, check every note. Don't accept any filthy, ripped or disintegrating notes, as these may be difficult to use.

» It can be tough getting change in India so keep a stock of smaller currency; ₹10, ₹20 and ₹50 notes are helpful.

» Officially, you cannot take rupees out of India, but this rule is laxly enforced. You can change any leftover rupees back into foreign currency, most easily at the airport (some banks have a ₹1000 minimum). You may be required to present your encashment certificates or credit-card/ATM receipts, and show your passport and airline ticket.

Credit Cards

» Credit cards are accepted at a growing number of shops, upmarket restaurants, and midrange and top-end hotels, and they can usually be used to pay for flights and train tickets.

» Cash advances on major credit cards are also possible at some banks.

» MasterCard and Visa are the most widely accepted cards.

Encashment Certificates

» Indian law states that all foreign currency must be changed at official money-changers or banks.

» For every (official) foreign-exchange transaction, you'll receive an encashment certificate (receipt), which will allow you to exchange rupees back into foreign currency when departing India.

» Encashment certificates should total the amount of rupees you intend changing back to foreign currency.

» Printed receipts from ATMs are also accepted as evidence of an international transaction at most banks.

International Transfers

» If you run out of money, someone back home can wire you cash via money-changers affiliated with **Moneygram** (www.moneygram.com) or **Western Union** (www.westernunion.com). A fee is added to the transaction. To collect cash, bring your passport and the name and reference number of the person who sent the funds.

Moneychangers

» Private moneychangers are usually open for longer hours than banks, and are found almost everywhere (many also double as internet cafes and travel agents). Upmarket hotels may also change money, but their rates are usually not as competitive.

Tipping, Baksheesh & Bargaining

» In tourist restaurants or hotels, a service fee is usually already added to your bill and tipping is optional. Elsewhere, a tip is appreciated.

» Hotel bellboys and train/airport porters appreciate anything around ₹20 to ₹50, and hotel staff should be given similar gratuities for services above and beyond the call of duty.

» It's not mandatory to tip taxi or rickshaw drivers, but it's good to tip drivers who are honest about the fare.

» If you hire a car with driver for more than a couple of days, a tip is recommended for good service – details on p364.

» Baksheesh can loosely be defined as a 'tip'; it covers everything from alms for beggars to bribes.

» Many Indians implore tourists not to hand out sweets, pens or money to children, as it encourages them to beg. To make a lasting difference, donate to a reputable school or charitable organisation (see p357).

» Unless shopping in fixed-price shops (such as government emporiums and fair-trade cooperatives), bargaining is the norm.

Travellers Cheques

» All major brands are accepted, but some banks may only accept cheques from American Express (Amex) and Thomas Cook.

» Pounds sterling and US dollars are the safest currencies, especially in smaller towns.

SECURE IT OR LOSE IT

» The safest place for your money and your passport is next to your skin, in a concealed moneybelt or pouch. Never, ever carry these things in your luggage or a shoulder bag. Bum bags are not recommended either, as they advertise that you have a stash of goodies.

» Never leave your valuable documents and travellers cheques in your hotel room (including under your mattress). If the hotel is a reputable one, you should be able to use the hotel safe.

» It's wise to peel off at least US$100 and keep it stashed away separately from your main horde, just in case.

» Separate your big notes from your small ones so you don't display large wads of cash when paying for things.

» Keep a record of the cheques' serial numbers separate from your cheques, along with the proof-of-purchase slips, encashment vouchers and photocopied passport details. If you lose your cheques, contact the American Express or Thomas Cook office in Delhi (see p80).

» To replace lost travellers cheques, you need the proof-of-purchase slip and the numbers of the missing cheques (some places require a photocopy of the police report and a passport photo). If you don't have the numbers of your missing cheques, the company that issued them will contact the place where you bought them.

Photography

For useful tips and techniques on travel photography, read Lonely Planet's guide to *Travel Photography.*

Digital

» Memory cards for digital cameras are available from photographic shops in most large cities and towns.

» Expect to pay upwards of ₹500 for a 1GB card.

» To be safe, regularly back up your memory card to CD; internet cafes may offer this service for ₹100 to ₹120 per disk.

» Some photographic shops make prints from digital photographs for roughly the standard print-and-processing charge.

Restrictions

» India is touchy about anyone taking photographs of military installations – this can include train stations, bridges, airports, military sites and sensitive border regions.

» Photography from the air is officially prohibited, although airlines rarely enforce this.

» Many places of worship, such as monasteries, temples and mosques, also prohibit photography. Taking photos inside a shrine, at a funeral, at a religious ceremony or of people publicly bathing (including rivers) can also be offensive – ask first.

» Flash photography may be prohibited in certain areas of a shrine, or may not be permitted at all.

» Exercise sensitivity when taking photos of people, especially women, who may find it offensive – obtain permission in advance.

» When photographing people use your instincts; some people may demand money afterwards.

Post

India has the biggest postal network on earth, with over 155,500 post offices. Mail and poste-restante services are generally good, although the speed of delivery will depend on the efficiency of any given office. Airmail is faster and more reliable than sea mail, although it's best to use courier services (such as DHL) to send and receive items of value – expect to pay around ₹3000 per kilogram to Europe, Australia or the USA. Private couriers are often cheaper, but goods may be repacked into large packages to cut costs and things sometimes go missing.

Receiving Mail

» Ask senders to address letters to you with your surname in capital letters and underlined, followed by poste restante, GPO (main post office), and the city or town in question. To claim mail you'll need to show your passport.

» Many 'lost' letters are simply misfiled under given/first names, so check under both your names and ask senders to provide a return address.

» Letters sent via poste restante are generally held for around one to two months before being returned.

» It's best to have any parcels sent to you by registered post.

Sending Mail
LETTERS

» Posting letters/aerogrammes to anywhere overseas costs ₹20/15.

» International postcards cost around ₹7.

» For postcards, stick on the stamps *before* writing on them, as post offices can give you as many as four stamps per card.

» Sending a letter overseas by registered post adds ₹15 to the stamp cost.

PARCELS

» Posting parcels can be relatively straightforward or involve multiple counters and a fair amount of queuing; get to the post office in the morning.

» Prices vary depending on weight (including packing material).

» A small package (unregistered) costs ₹40 (up to 100g) to any country and ₹30 per additional 100g (up to a maximum of 4000g; different charges apply for higher weights than this).

» Parcel post has a maximum of 20kg to 30kg depending on where it is being sent.

» There is the choice of airmail (delivery in one to three weeks); sea mail (two to four months); or Surface Air-Lifted (SAL), a curious hybrid where parcels travel by both air and sea (around one month). Another option is EMS (express mail service; delivery within three days) for around 30% more than the normal airmail price.

» Parcels must be packed up in white linen and the seams sealed with wax – local tailors offer this service if the post office doesn't.

» The post office can provide the necessary customs declaration forms and these must be stitched or pasted to the parcel. If the contents are a gift under the value of ₹1000, you won't be required to pay duty at the delivery end.

» Carry a permanent marker to write on the parcel any information requested by the desk.

» Books or printed matter can go by international book post for ₹350 (maximum 5kg), but the package must be wrapped with a hole that reveals the contents for inspection by customs – tailors can do this in such a way that nothing falls out.

» **India Post** (www.indiapost .gov.in) has an online calculator for domestic and international postal tariffs.

Public Holidays

There are officially three national public holidays. Every state celebrates its own official holidays, which cover bank holidays for government workers as well as major religious festivals. Most businesses (offices, shops etc) and tourist sites close on public holidays, but transport is usually unaffected. It's wise to make transport and hotel reservations well in advance if you intend visiting during major festivals.

Public Holidays

Republic Day 26 January

Independence Day 15 August

Gandhi Jayanti 2 October

Major Religious Festivals

Mahavir Jayanti (Jain) February

Holi (Hindu) March

Easter (Christian) March/ April

Buddha Jayanti (Buddhist) April/May

Eid al-Fitr (Muslim) August/September

Dussehra (Hindu) October

Diwali (Hindu) October/ November

Nanak Jayanti (Sikh) November

Christmas (Christian) 25 December

Safe Travel

Travellers to India's major cities may fall prey to petty and opportunistic crime; see p344 for information on dealing with touts and avoiding scams. Also have a look at the India branch of Lonely Planet's **Thorn Tree Travel Forum** (www.lonelyplanet. com/thorntree), where travellers often post timely warnings about problems they've encountered on the road.

Indian cities have occasionally been targeted by bombers, typically associated with the situation in Kashmir. In May 2008 Jaipur suffered such an attack. However rare such attacks may be, it makes sense to check the security situation with embassy travel advisories and local newspapers. Always check your government's travel advisory warnings.

Telephone

» Useful online resources include the **Yellow Pages** (www.indiayellowpages.com) and **Justdial** (www.justdial. com).

Call Booths

» Private PCO/STD/ISD call booths offer inexpensive local, interstate and international calls at lower prices than calls made from hotel rooms.

» These booths are found around the country, many open 24 hours.

» A digital meter displays how much the call is costing and usually provides a printed receipt when the call is finished.

» Costs vary depending on the operator and destination but can range from ₹1 per minute for local calls

GOVERNMENT TRAVEL ADVICE

The following government websites offer travel advice and information on current hot spots.

» **Australian Department of Foreign Affairs** (www.smarttraveller.gov.au)

» **British Foreign Office** (www.fco.gov.uk/en)

» **Canadian Department of Foreign Affairs** (www.voyage.gc.ca)

» **Ministry of Foreign Affairs Netherlands** (www.government.nl/Subjects/Advice_to_ travellers)

» **German Foreign Office** (www.auswaeriges-amt.de)

» **Japan Ministry of Foreign Affairs** (www.mofa.go.jp)

» **Switzerland** (www.eda.admin.ch)

» **US State Department** (http://travel.state.gov)

and between ₹5 and ₹10 for international calls.

» Some booths also offer a 'call-back' service – you ring home, provide the phone number of the booth and wait for people at home to call you back, for a fee of around ₹10 on top of the cost of the preliminary call.

Mobile Phones

» Indian mobile phone numbers usually have 10 digits typically beginning with ☏9.

» There's roaming coverage for international GSM phones in most cities and large towns.

» To avoid expensive roaming costs (often highest for incoming calls), get hooked up to the local mobile-phone network.

» Note that mobiles bought in some countries may be locked to a particular network; you'll have to get the phone unlocked, or buy a local phone (available from ₹2000) to use an Indian SIM card.

GETTING CONNECTED

» Getting connected is inexpensive but increasingly complicated owing to security concerns and involves a lot of paperwork.

» Foreigners must supply between one and five passport photos, their passport, and photocopies of their passport identity and visa pages.

» You must also supply a residential address, which can be the address of the hotel where you're staying (ask the hotel to write a letter on your behalf by way of confirmation).

» Some phone companies send representatives to the listed address, or at the very least call to verify that you are actually staying there.

» Some travellers have reported their SIM card being suspended once the phone company realised that they had moved on from the hotel where they registered their phone. Others have been luckier and used the same SIM card throughout their travels.

» Another option is to get a friendly local to register the phone using their local ID.

» Prepaid mobile-phone kits (SIM card and phone number, plus an allocation of calls) are available in most Indian towns from around ₹200 from a phone shop or local PCO/STD/ISD booth, internet cafe or grocery store. You must then purchase new credits on that network, sold as scratch cards in shops and call centres.

» Credit must usually be used within a set time limit and costs vary with the amount of credit on the card.

» The amount you pay for a credit top-up is not the amount you get on your phone – state taxes and service charges come off first.

» For some networks, recharge cards are being replaced by direct credit, where you pay the vendor and the credit is deposited straight to your phone – ask which system is in use before you buy.

CHARGES

» Calls made within the state or city in which you bought the SIM card are cheap – ₹1 per minute – and you can call internationally for less than ₹10 per minute.

» SMS messaging is even cheaper – usually, the more credit you have on your phone, the cheaper the call rate.

» The most popular (and reliable) companies include Airtel, Vodafone and BSNL.

» Most SIM cards are state specific; they can be used in other states, but you pay for calls at roaming rates and you'll be charged for incoming calls as well as outgoing calls.

» If you buy a SIM card in Delhi, calls outside Delhi will be around ₹1.50 per minute, while the charge to receive a call from anywhere in India (ex-Delhi) is ₹1 per minute.

» Be aware that unreliable signals and problems with international texting (with messages or replies being delayed or failing to get through) are not uncommon.

Phone Codes

Note that the government is slowly trying to bring all numbers in India onto the same system, so area codes may change and new digits may be added to numbers with limited warning.

Calling India from abroad Dial your country's international access code, then ☏91 (India's country code), then the area code (without the initial zero), then the local number.

Calling internationally from India Dial ☏00 (the international access code), then the country code of the country you're calling, then the area code (without the initial zero if there is one) and the local number.

Toll-free numbers begin with ☏1800.

Time

India uses the 12-hour clock and the local standard time is known as IST (Indian Standard Time). IST is 5½ hours ahead of GMT/UTC. The floating half-hour was added to maximise daylight hours over such a vast country.

CITY	NOON IN DELHI
Beijing	2.30pm
Dhaka	12.30pm
Islamabad	11.30am
London	6.30am
Kathmandu	12.15pm
New York	1.30am
San Francisco	10.30pm
Sydney	5.30pm
Tokyo	3.30pm

Toilets

Public toilets are most easily found in major cities and tourist sites and the cleanest toilets (usually with sit-down and squat choices) are most reliably found at modern restaurants, shopping complexes and cinemas. Beyond urban centres toilets are of the squat variety and locals will use the 'hand-and-water' technique, which involves cleaning one's bottom with a small jug of water and the left hand. It's always a good idea to carry your own toilet paper, just in case.

Tourist Information

In addition to the Government of India tourist offices (also known as 'India Tourism') each state maintains its own network of tourist offices. In Rajasthan, the Rajasthan Tourism Development Corporation (RTDC) operates Tourist Reception Centres in most places of interest. These vary in their efficiency and usefulness – some are run by enthusiastic souls who go out of their way to help, others are little more than a means of drumming up business for RTDC tours. Most have free brochures and often a free (or inexpensive) local map (for further map information see p351).

The first stop for information should be the tourism website of the Government of India, **Incredible India** (www.incredibleindia.org). For details of its regional offices around India, click on the 'Help Desk' tab at the top of the homepage.

There is a **RTDC Tourist Reception Centre** (☑011-3381 884; Tourist Reception Centre, Bikaner House, Pandara Rd, Delhi) in Delhi, and **Government of India tourist offices** (Delhi ☑011-23320005; 88 Janpath; Jaipur

☑0141-2372200; Hotel Khasa Kothi; ⊙9am-6pm Mon-Fri) in Delhi and Jaipur. See regional chapters for contact details of relevant tourist offices.

Travellers with Disabilities

India's crowded public transport, hectic urban life and variable infrastructure can test even the hardiest able-bodied traveller. If you have a physical disability or you are vision impaired, these factors can pose even more of a challenge. If your mobility is considerably restricted you may like to ease the stress by travelling with an able-bodied companion.

Accommodation Wheelchair-friendly hotels are almost exclusively top end. Make pre-trip inquiries and book ground-floor rooms at hotels that lack adequate facilities.

Accessibility Some restaurants and offices have ramps; most tend to have at least one step. Staircases are often steep; lifts frequently stop at mezzanines between floors.

Footpaths Where pavements exist, they can be riddled with holes, littered with debris and packed with pedestrians. If using crutches, bring along spare rubber caps.

Transport Hiring a car with a driver will make moving around a lot easier (see p364); if you use a wheelchair, make sure the car-hire company can provide an appropriate vehicle to carry it.

For further advice pertaining to your specific requirements, consult your doctor before heading to India.

Internet resources for further information:

Access-Able Travel Source (www.access-able.com).

Accessible Journeys (www.disabilitytravel.com).

Global Access News (www.globalaccessnews.com).

Mobility International USA (MIUSA; www.miusa.org).

Royal Association for Disability & Rehabilitation (RADAR; www.radar.org.uk).

Visas

A pilot scheme is currently in place to provide visas on arrival to nationals of Japan, New Zealand, Singapore, Luxembourg and Finland at Mumbai, Chennai, Kolkata and New Delhi airports. This scheme has been introduced on a one-year 'experimental' basis so double-check before you fly. All other nationals – except Nepal and Bhutan – must get a visa *before* arriving in India; these are available at Indian embassies worldwide. Note that your passport needs to be valid for at least six months beyond your intended stay in India with at least two blank pages.

Entry Requirements

» In 2009 a large number of foreigners were found to be working in India on tourist visas so regulations surrounding who can get a visa and for how long have been tightened. These rules are likely to change however, so check with the Indian embassy in your country prior to travel.

» Most people travel on the standard six-month tourist visa.

» Student and business visas have strict conditions (consult the Indian embassy for details).

» Tourist visas are valid from the date of issue, not the date you arrive in the country. You can spend a total of 180 days in the country.

» Five- and 10-year tourist visas are available to US citizens *only* under a bilateral arrangement, but you can still only stay in the country for up to 180 days continuously.

» An onward travel ticket is a requirement for most visas, but this isn't always enforced (check in advance).

» There are additional restrictions on travellers from Bangladesh and Pakistan, as well as certain Eastern European, African and Central Asian countries. Check any special conditions for your nationality with the Indian embassy in your country.

» Visas are priced in the local currency and may have an added service fee.

» Extended visas are possible for people of Indian origin (excluding those in Pakistan and Bangladesh) who hold a non-Indian passport and live abroad.

» For visas lasting more than six months, you're supposed to register at the Foreigners' Regional Registration Office (FRRO) within 14 days of arriving in India; inquire about these special conditions when you apply for your visa.

Re-entry Requirements

» Current regulations dictate that when you leave the country, you will receive a stamp in your passport indicating you may not re-enter India for two months, regardless of how much longer your visa may be valid for.

» If you wish to return to India before the two-month period has passed, you will have to visit the Indian High Commission or Consulate in the country where you've travelled to, or are resident, and apply for a Permit to Re-enter. This permit is only granted if urgent or in extreme cases.

» If you're travelling to multiple countries and your trip follows an itinerary (eg transiting back through India from Nepal on your way home), a permit is not needed – show your itinerary details at immigration.

» If granted a permit, you must register with the FRRO/FRO within 14 days.

Visa Extensions

At the time of publication, the **Ministry of Home Affairs** (☏011-23385748; Jaisalmer House, 26 Man Singh Rd, Delhi; ⊙inquiries 9-11am Mon-Fri) were not granting visa extensions. The only circumstances where this might conceivably happen are in *extreme* medical emergencies or if you were robbed of your passport just before you planned to leave the country (at the end of your visa).

In such cases, you should contact the **Foreigners' Regional Registration Office** (FRRO; ☏011-26195530; frrodelhi@hotmail.com; Level 2, East Block 8, Sector 1, Rama Krishna (RK) Puram, Delhi; ⊙9.30am-5.30pm Mon-Fri), just around the corner from the Hyatt Regency hotel. This is also the place to come for a replacement visa if you need your lost/stolen passport replaced (required before you can leave the country). Note that regional FRROs are even less likely to grant an extension.

Assuming you meet the stringent criteria, the FRRO is permitted to issue an extension of 14 days (free for nationals of most countries; inquire on application). You must bring your confirmed air ticket, one passport photo (take two, just in case) and a photocopy of your passport identity and visa pages. Note that this system is designed to get you out of the country promptly with the correct official stamps, not to give you two extra weeks of travel.

Volunteering

Many charities and international aid agencies work in India and there are numerous opportunities for volun-

teers. It may be possible to find a placement after you arrive in India, but charities and NGOs normally prefer volunteers who have applied in advance and been approved for the kind of work involved.

There are some excellent local charities and NGOs, some of which have opportunities for volunteers; for listings check www.indianngos.com.

The **Concern India Foundation** (☏011-26224482/3; www.concernindiafoundation.org; Room A52, 1st fl, Amar Colony, Lajpat Nagar 4, Delhi) may be able to link volunteers with current projects around the country; contact them well in advance for information. Delhi's *First City* magazine lists various local NGOs that welcome volunteers and financial aid.

Overseas Volunteer Placement Agencies

For long-term posts and information on volunteering check out the following organisations:

Action Without Borders (www.idealist.org)

AidCamps International (www.aidcamps.org)

Co-ordinating Committee for International Voluntary Service (www.unesco.org/ccivs)

Ethical Volunteering (www.ethicalvolunteering.org)

Global Volunteers (www.globalvolunteers.org)

Indicorps (www.indicorps.org)

Voluntary Service Overseas (www.vso.org.uk)

Volunteer Abroad (www.volunteerabroad.com)

Working Abroad (www.workingabroad.com)

World Volunteer Web (www.worldvolunteerweb.org)

Worldwide Volunteering (www.worldwidevolunteering.org.uk)

Aid Programs in Rajasthan, Delhi & Agra

The following programs may have opportunities for volunteers; it's best to contact them before turning up on their doorstep. Donations may also be welcomed.

DELHI

» **Hope Project** (☎011-24353006; www.hopeproject india.org; 127 Basti Hazrat, Nizamuddin) Runs a community health centre, a crèche, a non-formal school, vocational training courses, a thrift and credit program, and a women's microenterprise unit.

» **Missionaries of Charity** (☎011-65731435; www. motherteresa.org; 1 Magazine Rd) Welcomes volunteers (weekdays only).

» **Salaam Baalak Trust** (☎011-23681803; www. salaambaalaktrust.com; Chandiwalan, Main Bazaar, Paharganj) Provides shelter, food, education and other support to Delhi's homeless street children. There's opportunities to sponsor a child for ₹28,500 per year, fund individual projects or donate clothes, toys, blankets, books and computers. Volunteer English teachers, doctors and computer experts are welcome. Another way you can help is by taking a tour with a street child.

RAJASTHAN

» **Action Formation Education Voyage** (AFEV; ☎9829867323; www.afevinde. com; Pause Cafe, Bihari Temple, KEM Rd, Bikaner) An NGO working on projects in and around Bikaner including plastic-bag recycling, a small orphanage, street cleaning and equitable tourism. It's run by a local French resident and foreign volunteers can work with children, on information services or other projects, with food and accommodation provided.

» **Animal Aid Unlimited** (☎9784005989, 9950531639; www.animalaidunlimited.com; Badi Village, Udaipur) Volunteers can help rescue, treat and care for injured, abandoned or stray animals (mostly dogs, cows and donkeys) at its spacious premises a few kilometres outside Udaipur. Make an appointment before going to see them. There's no minimum period, but volunteers are encouraged to stay long enough to learn the routines and develop relationships with individual animals. See p204.

» **Disha** (☎0141-2393319; www.dishafoundation.org; Disha Path, Nirman Nagar-C, Jaipur) Operates a centre providing special education, home management, staff training, counselling and advocacy. Volunteers are needed in the fields of physiotherapy, speech therapy, special education, sports, arts and crafts and vocational counselling.

» **Help in Suffering** (☎0141-3245673; www.his-india.in; Maharani Farm, Durgapura, Jaipur) Welcomes qualified voluntary vets (three-/six-/12-month commitments). Apply first in writing.

» **Ladli** (☎9829011124; www. ladli.org; 74 Govindpuri, Rakdi, Sodala, Jaipur) Vocational training for abused, orphaned and destitute children. Volunteers work in child care and teach English; placements last from a week to a year.

» **Marwar Medical & Relief Society** (☎0291-2545210; www.mandore.com; c/o Mandore Guesthouse, Dadwari Lane, Mandore) Runs educational, health, environmental and other projects in villages in the Jodhpur district. Guests at its guesthouse in Mandore and other short- or long-term volunteers are welcomed.

» **Missionaries of Charity** (☎0141-2365804; Vardhman Path, C-Scheme, Jaipur).

» **Sambhali Trust** (☎0291 2512385; www.sambhali-trust. org; c/o Durag Niwas Guest House, 1st Old Public Park, Raika Bagh, Jodhpur) Organisation aiming to empower disadvantaged women and girls in Jodhpur city and Setrawa village, primarily through textile production, literacy and English-language learning. Volunteers can teach and help organise workshops on topics such as health, women's rights and nutrition.

» **Seva Mandir** (☎0294-2451041; www.sevamandir. org; Old Fatehpura, Udaipur) A long-established NGO working with rural and tribal people in southern Rajasthan on a host of projects including afforestation, water resources, health, education and empowerment of women and village institutions. Volunteers and interns can get involved in a wide range of activities.

» **Shikshantar** (☎2451303; www.swaraj.org/shikshantar; 83 Adinath Nagar, Kharol Colony, Udaipur) Volunteers can work on issues such as slow food, healthy lifestyles, herbal medicines, urban and organic farming, alternative technologies and zero waste design. See p212 for more information.

» **URMUL Trust** (☎0151-2523093; urmultrust@datain fosys.net; Urmul Bhawan, Ganganagar Rd, Bikaner) Provides primary health care and education to desert dwellers in arid western Rajasthan, as well as promoting their handicrafts and women's rights. Volunteer placements (minimum one month) are available in English-teaching, health care, documentation and other work.

Women Travellers

Although Bollywood might suggest otherwise, India remains a largely conservative society. As such, female travellers should be aware that their behaviour and dress code are under scrutiny, particularly away from the more touristed areas.

Attention

» Be prepared to be stared at – this is just something you'll have to live with so don't allow it to get the better of you.

» Refrain from returning male stares as this may be considered a come-on.

» Avoid unwanted conversations by wearing dark glasses or focusing on books or MP3 players.

Clothing

» Steer clear of sleeveless tops, shorts, miniskirts (ankle-length skirts are recommended) and anything else that's skimpy, see-through or tightfitting.

» Draping a dupatta (long scarf) over T-shirts is a good way of staving off unwanted stares – it's also handy if you visit a shrine that requires your head to be covered.

» Wearing a salwar kameez (traditional tunic and trouser combination) will show your respect for local dress etiquette; it's also surprisingly cool in the hot weather. A smart alternative is a kurta (long shirt) worn over jeans or trousers.

» Going out in public wearing a choli (sari blouse) or a sari petticoat (which some foreign women mistake for a skirt) is rather like strutting around half-dressed – avoid it.

» Most Indian women wear long shorts and a T-shirt whenever swimming in public view.

Health & Hygiene

» Sanitary pads are widely available but tampons are usually restricted to pharmacies in big cities and some tourist towns (even then, the choice may be limited). Carry additional stocks for travel off the beaten track.

Sexual Harassment

» Most cases of sexual harassment are reported in urban centres of North India and prominent tourist towns elsewhere, and have involved lewd comments, invasion of privacy and sometimes groping.

» Exuberant special events such as the Holi festival can be notorious for harrassment.

» Women travelling with a male partner are less likely to be hassled.

Taxis & Public Transport

» Being a woman has some advantages; women are able to queue-jump for buses and trains without consequence and on trains there are special ladies-only carriages.

» Solo women should prearrange an airport pick-up from their hotel if their flight is scheduled to arrive after dark.

» Delhi (and some other cities) have prepaid radio cab services such as Easycabs. They cost more than regular prepaid taxis, but are promoted as a safe service, with drivers that have been vetted as part of their recruitment.

» If you get a regular prepaid taxi, make a point of writing down the car registration and driver's name – in front of the driver – and giving it to one of the airport police.

» Avoid taking taxis alone late at night and never agree to have more than one man (the driver) in the car – ignore claims that this is 'just my brother' or 'for more protection'.

» Solo women have reported less hassle by opting for the more expensive classes on trains, especially for overnight trips.

» If you're travelling overnight in a three-tier carriage, try to get the uppermost berth, which will give you more privacy (and distance from potential gropers).

» On public transport, don't hesitate to return any errant limbs, put some item of

SOLO TRAVELLERS

Travellers often move in roughly the same direction throughout Rajasthan, so it's not unusual to see the same faces over and over again on your trip. Tourist hubs are good places to meet fellow travellers, get up-to-the-minute travel tips and find others to travel with. You may also be able to find travel companions on Lonely Planet's **Thorn Tree Travel Forum** (www.lonely planet.com/thorntree).

» Single-room rates at guesthouses and hotels are sometimes not much lower than double rates; some midrange and top-end places don't offer a single tariff. Always try negotiating a lower rate for single occupancy.

» Save money by sharing taxis and autorickshaws, as well as when hiring a car for longer trips.

» Solo bus travellers may be able to get the 'co-pilot' (near the driver) seat on buses, which not only has a good view out front, but is also handy if you've got a big bag.

» Solo travellers, particularly women, are advised against hitching rides.

» There have been muggings on single men wandering around isolated areas, even during the day. Don't be paranoid, but it's wise to stay on your toes in unfamiliar surroundings.

HANDY WEBSITES

You can read some personal experiences proffered by fellow women travellers at www.journeywoman .com and www.wander lustandlipstick.com.

luggage in between you, be vocal (so as to attract public attention, thus shaming the fellow) or simply find a new spot.

Staying Safe

» Keep conversations with unknown men short – getting involved in an inane conversation with someone you barely know can be misinterpreted as a sign of sexual interest.

» Questions and comments such as 'Do you have a boyfriend?' or 'You're very beautiful' are indicators that the conversation may be taking a dubious tangent.

» Some women wear a wedding ring, or announce early on in the conversation that they're married or engaged (regardless of the reality).

» If you get the feeling that a guy is encroaching on your space, he probably is. A firm request to keep away usually does the trick, especially if your tone is loud and curt enough to draw the attention of passers-by.

» The silent treatment can be very effective.

» Follow local women's cues and instead of shaking hands say *namaste* – the traditional, respectful Hindu greeting.

» Avoid wearing expensive-looking jewellery.

» Check the reputation of any teacher or therapist before going to a solo session; seek out some recommendations from other travellers – some women have reported being molested by masseurs and other therapists. If you feel uneasy at any time, leave.

» Female filmgoers will probably feel more comfortable (and lessen the chances of potential harassment) by going to the cinema with a companion.

» At hotels, keep your door locked, as staff (particularly at budget places) can knock and automatically walk in without waiting for your permission.

» Try to arrive in towns before dark. Don't walk alone at night and avoid wandering alone in isolated areas even during daylight.

Transport

GETTING THERE & AWAY

Getting to India is increasingly easy, with plenty of international airlines servicing the country and overland routes open between India and Nepal, Bangladesh, Bhutan and Pakistan. The following sections contain information on transport to, from and around India. Flights, tours and other tickets may also be booked online at www.lonelyplanet.com/bookings.

Entering India

Entering India by air or land is relatively straightforward, with standard immigration and customs procedures; see p348.

Passport

To enter India you need a valid passport, visa (p356) and an onward/return ticket. Your passport should be valid for at least six months beyond your intended stay in India. If your passport is lost or stolen, immediately contact your country's representative (p349). Keep photocopies of your airline ticket and the identity and visa pages of your passport in case of emergency. Better yet, scan and email copies to yourself. Check with the Indian embassy in your home country for any special conditions that may exist for your nationality.

Airports & Airlines

India has four main gateways for international flights (see the following list). Most Rajasthan-bound travellers fly into Delhi or Mumbai. A small number of international flights, mostly from the Middle East, serve Jaipur – for details, inquire at travel agencies and see www.indianairports.com.

Chennai (Madras; MAA; Anna International Airport; ☎044-22560551; www.chennaiairportguide.com)

Delhi (DEL; Indira Gandhi International Airport; ☎91-124-3376000.; www.newdelhiairport.in)

Kolkata (Calcutta; CCU; Netaji Subhash Chandra Bose International Airport; ☎033-25118787; www.calcuttaairport.com)

Mumbai (Bombay; BOM; Chhatrapati Shivaji International Airport; ☎022-2626 4000; www.csia.in)

India's national carrier is **Air India** (www.airindia.com), of which the former state-owned domestic carrier, Indian Airlines, is now a part, following a merger deal. Air India has had a relatively decent air safety record in recent years.

Tickets

An onward or return air ticket is usually a condition of the Indian tourist visa, so few visitors buy international tickets inside India. Only designated travel agencies can book international

---

CLIMATE CHANGE & TRAVEL

Every form of transport that relies on carbon-based fuel generates CO_2, the main cause of human-induced climate change. Modern travel is dependent on aeroplanes, which might use less fuel per person than most cars but travel much greater distances. The altitude at which aircraft emit gases (including CO_2) and particles also contributes to their climate-change impact. Many websites offer 'carbon calculators' that allow people to estimate the carbon emissions generated by their journey and, for those who wish to do so, to offset the impact of the greenhouse gases emitted with contributions to portfolios of climate-friendly initiatives throughout the world. Lonely Planet offsets the carbon footprint of all staff and author travel.

flights, but fares may be the same if you book directly with the airlines. Departure tax and other charges are included in airline tickets. You are required to show a copy of your ticket or itinerary in order to enter the airport, whether flying internationally or within India.

Land

Rajasthan to Pakistan

The weekly *Thar Express* (aka 14889 *Jodhpur–Munabao Link Express*) runs from Jodhpur to Karachi. In Jodhpur it leaves from Bhagat Ki Kothi station on Saturday at 1am and reaches Munabao on the border at 7am. There you undergo lengthy border procedures before continuing to Karachi in a Pakistani train, arriving there about 2am on Sunday. The Pakistan side of the border is Khokhraparker.

You must have a valid visa to Pakistan from India to travel on this train. Ticketing is 2nd-class and sleeper only, with a total sleeper fare of around ₹400 from Jodhpur to Karachi. In the other direction the Pakistani train leaves Karachi about 11pm on Friday, and Indian train 14890 leaves Munabao at 7pm on Saturday, reaching Jodhpur at 11.50pm. Schedules can be erratic, so check locally in Jodhpur for departure times and stations. Tickets can only be booked at Jodhpur

(ie not online) and have to be booked less than 15 days before departure.

GETTING AROUND

Air

Within Rajasthan, there are airports in Jaipur, Jaisalmer, Jodhpur and Udaipur. However, Jaisalmer is often closed, usually when tensions are high along the Pakistan border.

Security at airports is generally stringent. All hold baggage must be x-rayed prior to check-in and every item of cabin baggage needs a baggage label, which must be stamped as part of the security check (don't forget to collect tags at the check-in counter). The recommended check-in time for domestic flights is one hour before departure. The usual baggage allowance is 20kg (10kg for smaller aircraft) in economy class, and 30kg in business.

Airlines in India

The following airlines operate across various destinations in India, including Rajasthan, Delhi and Agra – see regional chapters for specifics about routes, fares and booking offices. Keep in mind, however, that the competitive nature of the aviation industry means that fares fluctuate dramatically.

Air India (☑1800 1801407; www.airindia.com) India's national carrier operates many domestic and international flights.

GoAir (☑1800 222111; www.goair.in) Reliable low-cost carrier servicing Goa, Kochi (Cochin), Jaipur, Delhi and Bagdogra among other destinations.

IndiGo (☑1800 1803838; www.goindigo.in) Good, reliable budget airline flying to numerous cities including Kolkata, Mumbai, Delhi and Chennai.

Jet Airways (☑011-39893333; www.jetairways.com) Rated by many as India's best airline, with growing domestic and international services.

JetLite (☑1800 223020; www.jetlite.com) Jet Airways' budget carrier flies to numerous destinations including Amritsar, Chennai and Jodhpur.

Kingfisher Airlines (☑1800 2093030; www.flyingfisher.com) Domestic and international flights; Kingfisher Red is their low-cost option.

Spicejet (☑1800 1803333; www.spicejet.com) Budget carrier to destinations including Bengaluru (Bangalore), Varanasi, Srinagar, and Colombo, Sri Lanka and Kathmandu, Nepal.

Bicycle

Rajasthan offers an immense array of experiences for a long-distance cyclist. Nevertheless, long-distance cycling is not for the faint of heart or weak of knee. You'll need physical endurance to cope with the roads, traffic and climate.

There are no restrictions on bringing a bicycle into the country. However, bicycles sent by sea can take a few weeks to clear customs in India, so it's better to fly bikes in. It may actually be cheaper (and less hassle) to hire or buy a bicycle in

---

PREPAID TAXIS

Most Indian airports and many train stations have a prepaid taxi booth, normally just outside the terminal building. Here, you can book a taxi for a fixed price (which will include baggage) and thus avoid commission scams. However, officials advise holding on to the payment coupon until you reach your chosen destination, in case the driver has any other ideas! Smaller airports and stations may have prepaid autorickshaw booths instead.

India itself. Read up on bicycle touring before you travel – Rob Van Der Plas' *Bicycle Touring Manual* and Stephen Lord's *Adventure Cycle-Touring Handbook* are good places to start. Consult local cycling magazines and cycling clubs for useful information and advice. The **Cycling Federation of India** (📞011- 23753529; www.cyclingfederationofindia.org; 12 Pandit Pant Marg; ⊙10am-5pm Mon-Fri) can provide local information.

Hire

» Tourist centres and traveller hang-outs are the easiest spots to find bicycles for hire.

» Prices vary between ₹40 and ₹100 per day for roadworthy, Indian-made bicycles. Mountain bikes are usually upwards of ₹350 per day.

» Hire places may require a cash security deposit (avoid leaving your airline ticket or passport).

Practicalities

» Roadside cycle mechanics abound but you should still bring spare tyres and brake cables, lubricating oil and a chain repair kit, and plenty of puncture-repair patches.

» Bikes can often be carried for free, or for a small luggage fee, on the roof of public buses – handy for uphill stretches.

» Contact your airline for information about transporting your bike and customs formalities in your home country.

Purchase

» Delhi's Jhandewalan Cycle Market has new and second-hand bikes and spare parts.

» Indian mountain bikes such as Hero and Atlas start at around ₹3500.

» Reselling is easy – ask at local cycle or hire shops or put up an advert on travel noticeboards.

Road Rules

» Vehicles drive on the left side in India but otherwise road rules are virtually non-existent. Cities and national highways can be hazardous places to cycle, so, where possible, stick to the back roads.

» Be conservative about the distances you expect to cover – an experienced cyclist can manage around 60km to 100km a day on the plains and 40km or less on dirt roads.

Tours

» If you want to splash out, **Butterfield & Robinson** (www.butterfield.com) offer upmarket biking expeditions through Rajasthan.

Bus

» The Rajasthan state government bus service is **Rajasthan State Road Transport Corporation** (RSRTC; www.rsrtc.gov.in), otherwise known as Rajasthan Roadways.

» Often there are privately owned local bus services as well as luxury private coaches running between major cities – these can be booked through travel agencies.

» Avoid night buses unless there's no alternative, as driving conditions are more hazardous and drivers may be suffering from lack of sleep.

» All buses make snack and toilet stops (some more frequently than others), providing a break but possibly adding hours to journey times.

Bus Types & Classes

» On the main routes in Rajasthan you have a choice of ordinary, express and deluxe. Express and deluxe buses make fewer stops than ordinary buses – they're still usually crowded though. The fare is marginally higher than

ordinary buses, but worth every rupee.

» On selected routes there are RSRTC Gray Line (sleeper) buses – these have beds and make overnight trips more comfortable. Beds have a bunk-bed arrangement, with rows of single beds, each with a curtain for privacy.

» Silver Line is a so-called superdeluxe service and the buses have a reasonable level of comfort.

» Air-conditioned Volvo and Gold Line buses are the best bus options and serve the Jaipur–Delhi and Agra–Udaipur routes.

» Private buses also operate on most Rajasthan routes; apart from often being quicker and usually more comfortable, the booking procedure is much simpler than for state-run buses. However, private companies can often change schedules at the last minute to get as many bums on seats as possible.

Luggage

» Luggage is either stored in compartments underneath the bus (sometimes for a small fee) or it can be carried on the roof.

» Arrive at least an hour ahead of the scheduled departure time – some buses cover the roof-stored bags with a large sheet of canvas, making it inconvenient/impossible for last-minute additions.

» If your baggage is stored on the roof, make sure it is securely locked, and tied tightly to the metal baggage rack – some unlucky travellers have seen their belongings go bouncing off the roof on bumpy roads!

» Theft is a minor risk – keep an eye on your bags at snack and toilet stops and *never* leave your daypack or valuables unattended inside the bus.

ROAD DISTANCES (KM)

	Agra	Ahmedabad	Ajmer	Alwar	Bharatpur	Bikaner	Bundi	Chittorgarh	Delhi	Jaipur	Jaisalmer	Jodhpur	Kota	Mt Abu	Mumbai
Ahmedabad	889														
Ajmer	388	526													
Alwar	172	798	272												
Bharatpur	56	658	332	116											
Bikaner	665	754	233	462	497										
Bundi	438	485	163	347	382	396									
Chittorgarh	579	364	191	463	523	424	121								
Delhi	195	916	392	163	251	470	465	583							
Jaipur	232	657	138	143	174	354	205	345	259						
Jaisalmer	853	296	490	762	822	333	653	657	882	543					
Jodhpur	568	511	205	477	537	243	368	372	597	317	285				
Kota	453	522	200	383	418	432	36	158	504	242	690	405			
Mt Abu	737	221	375	647	707	569	418	297	767	465	572	326	455		
Mumbai	1204	554	1071	1343	945	1299	1041	928	1461	1202	1341	1056	1005	766	
Udaipur	637	252	274	551	581	506	233	112	664	347	545	260	270	185	797

Reservations

» Most deluxe buses can be booked in advance – usually up to a month in advance for government buses – at the bus station or local travel agencies.

» Reservations are rarely possible on 'ordinary' buses and travellers often get left behind in the mad rush for a seat. To maximise your chances of securing a seat, either send a travelling companion ahead to grab some space, or pass a book or article of clothing through an open window and place it on an empty seat.

» Many buses only depart when full – you may find your bus suddenly empties to join another bus that's ready to leave before yours.

» At many bus stations there's a separate women's queue, although this isn't always obvious because signs are often in Hindi and men frequently join the melee. Women travellers should sharpen their elbows and make their way to the front,

where they will get almost immediate service.

Car

Few people bother with self-drive car rental – not only because of the hair-raising driving conditions, but also because hiring a car with a driver is wonderfully afford-able in India, particularly if several people share the cost. International rental companies with representa-tives in India include **Budget** (www.budget.com) and **Hertz** (www.hertz.com).

Hiring a Car & Driver

» Most towns have taxi stands or car-hire companies where you can arrange short or long tours (see regional chapters).

» Use your hotel to find a car and driver – this achieves a good level of security and reliability and often a better rate.

» Not all hire cars are licensed to travel beyond their home state. Even those

vehicles that are licensed to enter different states have to pay extra (often hefty) state taxes, which will add to the rental charge.

» Ask for a driver who speaks some English and knows the region you intend visiting, and try to see the car and meet the driver before paying any money.

» Ambassador cars look great but are rather slow and uncomfortable if travelling long distances – consider them for touring cities.

» For multiday trips, the charge should cover the driver's meals and accom-modation. Drivers should make their own sleeping and eating arrangements.

» It is *essential* to set the ground rules with the driver from day one, in order to avoid anguish later.

Costs

» The price depends on the distance and sometimes the terrain (driving on mountain roads uses more petrol, hence the 'hill charges').

» One-way trips usually cost the same as return ones (to cover the petrol and driver charges for getting back).

» To avoid potential misunderstandings, ensure you get *in writing* what you've been promised (quotes should include petrol, sightseeing stops, all your chosen destinations, and meals and accommodation for the driver).

» If a driver asks you for money to pay for petrol en route (reasonable on long trips), keep a record (he will do the same).

» Rates with the Rajasthan Tourism Development Corporation (RTDC) are from ₹5.75/7 per kilometre for a non-AC/AC Ambassador, with a 250km minimum per day (plus 10.3% service tax), and an overnight charge of ₹150 to ₹300.

» For sightseeing day trips around a single city, expect to pay anywhere upwards of ₹800/1000 for a non-AC/AC car with an eight-hour, 80km limit per day (extra charges apply beyond this).

» A tip is customary at the end of your journey; ₹125 to ₹150 per day is fair (more if you're really pleased with the driver's service).

Local Transport

» Buses, cycle-rickshaws, autorickshaws, taxis and urban trains provide transport around cities.

» On any form of transport without a fixed fare, agree on the price *before* you start your journey and make sure that it covers your luggage and every passenger.

» Fares usually increase at night (by up to 100%) and some drivers charge a few rupees extra for luggage.

» Carry plenty of small bills for taxi and rickshaw fares as drivers rarely have change.

» Carry a business card of the hotel in which you are

staying, as your pronunciation of streets, hotel names etc may be incomprehensible to drivers. Some hotel cards even have a sketch map clearly indicating their location.

» Some taxi/autorickshaw drivers are involved in the commission racket – for more information see p344.

Autorickshaw & Tempo

» The Indian autorickshaw is basically a three-wheeled motorised contraption with a tin or canvas roof and sides, providing room for two passengers (although you'll often see many more bodies squeezed in) and limited luggage.

» They are also referred to as autos, tuk-tuks, Indian helicopters, or Ferraris.

» Autorickshaws are mostly cheaper than taxis and are often metered, although getting the driver to turn on the meter can be a challenge.

» Tempos and *vikrams* (large tempos) are outsized autorickshaws with room for more than two passengers, running on fixed routes for a fixed fare.

Bus

Urban buses, particularly in the big cities, are fume-belching, human-stuffed mechanical monsters that travel at breakneck speed (except during morning and evening rush hours, when they can be endlessly stuck in traffic). It's usually far more convenient and comfortable to opt for an autorickshaw or taxi.

Cycle-Rickshaw

» A cycle-rickshaw is a pedal cycle with two rear wheels, supporting a bench seat for passengers. Most have a canopy that can be raised in wet weather, or lowered to provide extra space for luggage.

» Many of the big cities have phased out (or reduced) the

number of cycle-rickshaws, but they are still a major means of local transport in many smaller towns.

» Fares must be agreed upon in advance – speak to locals to get an idea of what is a fair price. A typical distance for a cycle-rickshaw ride is between 1km and 3km and costs roughly between ₹20 and ₹40. Remember this is extremely strenuous work and the wallahs are among India's poorest, so a tip is appreciated and haggling over a few rupees unnecessary.

Share Jeep

Share jeeps supplement the bus service in many parts of Rajasthan, especially in areas off the main road routes, such as many of the towns in Shekhawati. Jeeps leave when (very) full, from well-established 'passenger stations' on the outskirts of towns and villages; locals should be able to point you in the right direction. They are usually dirt cheap and jam-packed and tend to be more dangerous than buses.

Taxi

» Taxis are usually metered, but drivers often claim that the meter is broken and proceed to request a hugely elevated 'fixed' fare instead – threatening to get another taxi will often miraculously fix the meter.

» Meters are almost always outdated, so fares are calculated using a combination of the meter reading and a complicated 'fare adjustment card'. Predictably, this system is open to abuse.

» In tourist areas in particular, some taxis flatly refuse to use the meter – if this happens, get out and find another cab.

» To avoid fare-setting shenanigans, only use prepaid taxis where possible (regional chapters contain details).

Motorcycle

Cruising solo around India by motorcycle offers the freedom to go when and where you desire. There are also some excellent motorcycle tours available, which take the hassle out of doing it alone.

Helmets, leathers, gloves, goggles, boots, waterproofs and other protective gear are best brought from your home country, as they're either unavailable in India or are of variable quality.

Driving Licence

To hire a motorcycle in India, you're required to have a valid international drivers' permit in addition to your domestic licence. In tourist areas, some places may rent out a motorcycle without asking for a driving permit/licence, but you won't be covered by insurance in the event of an accident, and may also face a fine.

Hire

» The classic way to motorcycle round India is on an Enfield Bullet, still built to many of the original 1940s specifications. As well as making a satisfying sound, these bikes are easy to repair (parts can be found almost everywhere in India). On the other hand, Enfields are less reliable than the newer, Japanese-designed bikes.

» Plenty of places rent out motorcycles for local trips and longer tours. Japanese- and Indian-made bikes in the 100cc to 150cc range are cheaper than the big 350cc and 500cc Enfields.

» As a deposit, you'll need to leave a large cash lump sum (ensure you get a receipt that also stipulates the refundable amount), your passport or your air ticket. It's strongly advisable to avoid leaving your air ticket and passport, the latter of which you'll need to check in at hotels and which the police can demand to see at any time.

» For three weeks' hire, a 500cc Enfield costs from ₹22,000; a European style is ₹23,000; and a 350cc costs ₹15,000. The price includes excellent advice and an invaluable crash course in Enfield mechanics and repairs.

» See the regional chapters for other recommended rental companies and their charges.

Purchase

» Secondhand bikes are widely available and the paperwork is a lot easier than buying a new machine.

» Finding a secondhand motorcycle is a matter of asking around, checking travellers' noticeboards and approaching local motorcycle mechanics.

» A looked-after, secondhand 350cc Enfield will cost anywhere from ₹25,000 to ₹50,000. A more modern version, with European-style configuration, costs ₹45,000 to ₹65,000. The 500cc model costs anywhere from ₹60,000 to ₹85,000. You will also have to pay for insurance.

» It's advisable to get any secondhand bike serviced before you set off.

» When re-selling your bike, expect to get between half and two-thirds of the price you paid if the bike is still in reasonable condition.

» Shipping an Indian bike overseas is complicated and expensive – ask the shop you bought the bike from to explain the process.

» Helmets are available for ₹500 to ₹2,000 and extras like panniers, luggage racks, protection bars, rear-view mirrors, lockable fuel caps, petrol filters and extra tools are easy to come by. One useful extra is a customised fuel tank, which will increase the range you can cover between fuel stops. An Enfield 500cc gives about 25km/L; the 350cc model gives slightly more.

» A good site for Enfield models is www.royalenfield.com.

» The following dealers come recommended:

Delhi Run by the knowledgeable Lalli Singh, Lalli Motorbike Exports (☏011-28750869; http://lallisingh. com; 1740-A/55 (basement), Hari Singh Nalwa St, Abdul Aziz Rd, Karol Bagh) sells and rents out Enfields and parts, and buyers get a crash course in running and maintaining these lovable but temperamental machines. He can also recommend other reputable dealers in the area.

Jaipur Rajasthan Auto Centre (☏0141-2568074; Sanjay Bazaar, Sanganeri Gate) comes recommended as a place for hiring, fixing or purchasing a motorcycle. To hire a 350cc Bullet costs ₹500 per day (including helmet); if you take the bike outside Jaipur, it costs ₹600 per day. Ask for Saleem, the Bullet specialist.

OWNERSHIP PAPERS

» There's plenty of paperwork associated with owning a motorcycle; the registration papers are signed by the local registration authority when the bike is first sold and you'll need these papers when you buy a secondhand bike.

» Foreign nationals cannot change the name on the registration. Instead, you must fill out the forms for a change of ownership and transfer of insurance. If you buy a new bike, the company selling it must register the machine for you, adding to the cost.

» For any bike, the registration must be renewed every 15 years (for around Rs5000) and you must make absolutely sure that it states the 'fitness' of the vehicle, and that there are no outstanding debts or criminal proceedings associated with the bike.

» The process is complicated and it makes sense

to seek advice from the company selling the bike – allow two weeks to tackle the paperwork and get on the road.

Fuel, Spare Parts & Extras

» If you're going to remote regions it's also important to carry basic spares (valves, fuel lines, piston rings etc). Spare parts for Indian and Japanese machines are widely available in cities and larger towns and Delhi's Karol Bagh is a good place to find parts.

» Make sure you regularly check and tighten all nuts and bolts, as Indian roads and engine vibration tend to work things loose quite quickly.

» Check the engine and gearbox oil level regularly (at least every 500km) and clean the oil filter every few thousand kilometres.

» Given the road conditions, the chances are you'll make at least a couple of visits to a puncture-wallah – start your trip with new tyres and carry spanners to remove your own wheels.

» It's a good idea to bring your own protective equipment (helmet, jackets etc).

Insurance

» Only hire a bike with third-party insurance – if you hit someone without insurance, the consequences can be very costly. Reputable companies will include third-party cover in their policies; those that don't probably aren't trustworthy.

» You must also arrange insurance if you buy a motorcycle (usually you can organise this through the person selling the bike).

» The minimum level of cover is third-party insurance – available for ₹300 to ₹600 per year. This will cover repair and medical costs for any other vehicles, people or property you might hit, but no cover for your own machine.

Comprehensive insurance (recommended) costs upwards of ₹800 per year.

Road Conditions

Given the varied road conditions, India can be challenging for novice riders. Hazards range from cows and chickens crossing the carriageway to broken-down trucks, pedestrians on the road, and perpetual potholes and unmarked speed humps. Rural roads sometimes have grain crops strewn across them to be threshed by passing vehicles – a serious sliding hazard for bikers.

Try not to cover too much territory in one day and avoid travelling after dark – many vehicles drive without lights and dynamo-powered motorcycle headlamps are useless at low revs while negotiating around potholes.

On busy national highways expect to average 45km/h without stops; on winding back roads and dirt tracks this can drop to 10km/h.

Organised Motorcycle Tours

Dozens of companies offer organised motorcycle tours around India with a support vehicle, mechanic and guide. Below are some reputable outfits (see websites for contact details, itineraries and prices):

Blazing Trails (www.blazingtrailstours.com)

Classic Bike Adventure (www.classic-bike-india.com)

Ferris Wheels (www.ferriswheels.com.au)

H-C Travel (www.hctravel.com)

Indian Motorcycle Adventures (www.indianmotorcycleadventures.com)

Lalli Singh Tours (www.lallisingh.com)

Moto Discovery (www.motodiscovery.com)

Royal Expeditions (www.royalexpeditions.com)

Saffron Road Motorcycle Tours (www.saffronroad.com)

Shepherds Realms (www.asiasafari.com)

Wheel of India (www.wheelofindia.com)

Tours

Organised tours can be an inexpensive way to see several places on one trip, although you rarely get much time at each place. If you arrange a tailormade tour, you'll have more freedom about where you go and how long you stay.

Drivers may double as guides, or you can hire a qualified local guide for a fee. In tourist towns, be wary of touts claiming to be professional guides. See the Tours sections in the regional chapters for details about local tours.

International Tour Agencies

Many international companies offer tours to Rajasthan, Delhi and Agra, from straightforward sightseeing trips to adventure tours and activity-based holidays. Some good places to start your tour hunt:

Dragoman (www.dragoman.com) One of several reputable overland tour companies offering trips on customised vehicles.

Exodus (www.exodustravels.co.uk) A wide array of specialist trips, including tours with a holistic, wildlife and adventure focus.

India Wildlife Tours (www.india-wildlife-tours.com) All sorts of wildlife tours, plus jeep/horse/camel safaris and birdwatching.

Indian Encounter (www.indianencounters.com) Special-interest tours that include wildlife spotting, river-rafting and ayurvedic treatments.

Intrepid Travel (www.intrepidtravel.com) Endless possibilities from wildlife tours to sacred rambles.

Peregrine Adventures
(www.peregrine.net.au)
Popular cultural and trekking
tours.

Sacred India Tours
(www.sacredindia.com) In-
cludes tours with a holistic
focus such as yoga and
ayurveda, as well as architectural and cultural tours.

Shanti Travel (www.shanti
travle.com) A range of tours
including family and adventure tours, run by a Franco-
Indian team.

World Expeditions (www.
worldexpeditions.com.au) An
array of options that in-
cludes trekking and cycling
tours.

Train

Travelling by train is a quintessential Indian experience.
Trains offer a smoother
ride than buses, and are
especially recommended for
long journeys that include
overnight travel. India's rail
network is one of the largest and busiest in the world

and Indian Railways is the
largest utility employer on
earth, with roughly 1.5 million
workers. There are around
6900 train stations scattered
across the country.

We've listed useful trains
throughout this book but
there are hundreds more
services. The best way of
sourcing updated railway
information is to use relevant internet sites such
as **Indian Railways** (www.
indianrail.gov.in) and the
useful www.seat61.com/
India.htm. There's also
Trains at a Glance (₹35),
available at many train station bookstands and good
bookshops/newsstands, but
it's published annually so it's
not as up-to-date as web-
sites. Nevertheless, it offers
comprehensive timetables
covering all the main lines.

Booking Tickets Online

Booking online is the easiest
way to buy train tickets. The
railway reservation system
is open from 1.30am to

11.30pm every day (IST) so
keep this in mind when trying
to book online, particularly if
you are abroad. The following
websites all issue e-tickets,
which are valid for train
travel. You may have to show
your passport as ID along
with the printout of your
booking reference when you
are on the train. The following
websites all accept international credit cards:

**Indian Railway Catering
and Tourism Corporation
Limited** (www.irctc.co.in)
Set up by the Ministry of
Railways, here you can book
regular trains as well as tourist trains such as the Deccan
Odyssey. The site can often
be overloaded.

Cleartrip (www.cleartrip.com)
An excellent, easy-to-use and
reliable website that charges
a small fee (₹20) on top of
the regular ticket price.

Make My Trip (www.make
mytrip.com) Similar to Cleartrip with very good reports
from travellers.

Yatra (www.yatra.com) This
travel booking website has
an Indian version (www.yatra.
in) and a UK site (www.yatra.
com/UK/index.html).

Booking Tickets in India

You can either book tickets
through a travel agency or
hotel (for a commission) or
in person at the train station.
Big stations often have
English-speaking staff who
can help with choosing the
best train. At smaller stations, midlevel officials such
as the deputy station master
usually speak English. It's
also worth approaching tourist office staff if you need
advice about booking tickets,
deciding train classes etc.
The nationwide railways
inquiries number is ☑139.

» **At the station** Get a
reservation slip from the
information window, fill in the
name of the departure station, destination station, the
class you want to travel and
the name and number of the

PALACES ON WHEELS

To travel maharaja style, try the RTDC *Palace on
Wheels* and *Royal Rajasthan on Wheels* services.

The *Palace on Wheels* (www.palaceonwheels.net)
operates one-week tours of Rajasthan, departing
from Delhi. The itinerary includes Jaipur, Jaisalmer,
Jodhpur, Ranthambore National Park, Chittorgarh,
Udaipur, Keoladeo Ghana National Park and Agra. Fit-
for-a-maharaja carriages are sumptuously decked out
and there are dining cars, a bar, a lounge and a library.
The train runs from August to April and the total fare
(seven nights) per person is US$4830/3610/3250 for
single/double/triple cabins, except for August when it's
US$3605/2708/2456. Book ahead – tickets can sell
out 10 months in advance for peak periods.

The *Royal Rajasthan on Wheels* (www.royalrajast-
hanonwheels.com) is even more luxurious and runs
one-week trips from September to April starting and
finishing in Delhi. The route takes in Jodhpur, Udaipur,
Chittorgarh, Ranthambore National Park, Jaipur, Khajuraho, Varanasi and Agra. The total fare (seven nights)
per person is US$11,200 for a super deluxe suite and
US$6370/9100 for single/twin occupancy of deluxe
suites.

TRAIN CLASSES

» **Air-Conditioned First Class (1AC)** The most expensive class of train travel; two- or four-berth compartments with locking doors and meals included.

» **Air-Conditioned 2-Tier (2AC)** Two-tier berths arranged in groups of four and two in an open-plan carriage. The bunks convert to seats by day and there are curtains for some semblance of privacy.

» **Air-Conditioned 3-Tier (3AC)** Three-tier berths arranged in groups of six in an open-plan carriage; no curtains.

» **AC Executive Chair** Comfortable, reclining chairs and plenty of space; usually found on Shatabdi express trains.

» **AC Chair** Similar to the Executive Chair carriage but with less fancy seating.

» **Sleeper Class** Open plan carriages with three-tier bunks and no AC; the open windows afford great views.

» **Unreserved 2nd Class** Wooden or plastic seats and *a lot* of people – but cheap!

train. Join the long queue to the ticket window where your ticket will be printed. Women should avail of the separate women's queue – if there isn't one, go to the front of the regular queue.

» **Tourist Reservation Bureau** Larger cities and major tourist centres have an International Tourist Bureau, which allows you to book tickets in relative peace – check www.indianrail.gov.in for a list of these stations.

Reservations

» Bookings open 90 days before departure and you must make a reservation for all chair-car, sleeper, and 1AC, 2AC and 3AC carriages. No reservations are required for general (2nd class) compartments. Trains are always busy in India so it's wise to book as far in advance as possible; advanced booking for overnight trains is strongly recommended. Train services to certain destinations are often increased during major festivals but it's still worth booking well in advance.

» Reserved tickets show your seat/berth number

and the carriage number. When the train pulls in, keep an eye out for your carriage number written on the side of the train (station staff and porters can also point you in the right direction). A list of names and berths is also posted on the side of each reserved carriage.

» Be aware that train trips can be delayed at any time of the journey, so, to avoid stress, factor some leeway into your travel plans.

» Also be mindful of potential passenger drugging and theft – see p345.

If the train you want to travel on is sold out, make sure to inquire about the following:

» **Reservation Against Cancellation (RAC)** Even when a train is fully booked, Indian Railways sells a handful of RAC seats in each class. This means that if you have an RAC ticket and someone cancels before the departure date, you will get his or her seat (or berth). You'll have to check the reservation list at the station on the day of travel to see where you've been allocated to sit. Even

if no one cancels as an RAC ticket holder you can still board the train, and even if you don't get a seat, you can still travel.

» **Taktal Tickets** Indian Railways holds back a limited number of tickets on key trains and releases them at 8am two days before the train is due to depart. A charge of ₹10 to ₹300 is added to each ticket price. First AC and Executive Chair tickets are excluded from the scheme.

» **Tourist Quota** A special (albeit small) tourist quota is set aside for foreign tourists travelling between popular stations. These seats can only be booked at dedicated reservation offices in major cities (see regional chapters for details), and you need to show your passport and visa as ID. Tickets can be paid for in rupees (some offices may ask to see foreign exchange certificates – ATM receipts will suffice), British pounds, US dollars or Euros, in cash or Thomas Cook and American Express travellers cheques.

» **Waitlist (WL)** Trains are frequently overbooked, but many passengers cancel and there are regular no-shows. So if you buy a ticket on the waiting list you're quite likely to get a seat, even if there are a number of people ahead of you on the list. Check your booking status at www.indianrail.gov.in/pnr_stat.html by entering your tickets' PNR number. A refund is available if you fail to get a seat – ask the ticket office about your chances.

Refunds

» Tickets are refundable but fees apply. If you present more than one day in advance, a fee of ₹20 to ₹70 applies. Steeper charges apply if you seek a refund less than four hours prior to departure, but you can get some sort of refund as late as 12 hours afterwards.

Classes & Costs

Shatabdi express trains are same-day services between major and regional cities. These are the fastest and most expensive trains, with only two classes; AC Executive Chair and AC Chair. Shatabdis are comfortable, but the glass windows cut the views considerably compared to non-AC classes on slower trains, which have barred windows and fresh air.

Rajdhani express trains are long-distance express services running between Delhi and the state capitals, and offer air-con 1st class (1AC), 2-tier air-con (2AC), 3-tier air-con (3AC) and 2nd class. Two-tier means there are two levels of bunks in each compartment, which are a little wider and longer than their counterparts in 3-tier. Costing respectively a half and a third as much as 1AC, 2AC and 3AC are perfectly adequate for an overnight trip.

For an excellent description of the various train classes (including pictures) see www.seat61.com/India.htm; scroll down to the 'What are Indian trains like?' heading.

Fares are calculated by distance and class of travel; Rajdhani and Shatabdi trains are slightly more expensive, but the price includes meals. Most air-conditioned carriages have a catering service (meals are brought to your seat). In unreserved classes it's a good idea to carry portable snacks. Seniors (those over 60) get 30% off all fares in all classes on all types of train. Children below the age of five travel for free; those aged between five and 12 are charged half price.

Health

While the potential dangers of travelling in India can seem quite ominous, in reality few travellers experience anything more than an upset stomach. Hygiene is generally poor throughout the country, so food- and waterborne illnesses are common. Travellers tend to worry about contracting infectious diseases, but infections are a rare cause of *serious* illness or death in travellers. Pre-existing medical conditions such as heart disease, and accidental injury (especially traffic accidents), account for most life-threatening problems.

Fortunately, most travellers' illnesses can either be prevented with some common-sense behaviour or be treated easily with a well-stocked traveller's medical kit. The following advice is a general guide only and does not replace the advice of a doctor trained in travel medicine.

BEFORE YOU GO

» Pack medications in their original, clearly labelled containers.

» A signed and dated letter from your physician describing your medical conditions and medications, including generic names, is very useful.

» If you are carrying syringes or needles, be sure to have a physician's letter documenting their medical necessity.

» If you have a heart condition, bring a copy of your ECG taken just prior to travelling.

» If you take any regular medication, bring double the amount you need in case of loss or theft.

» You'll be able to buy many medications over the counter in India without a doctor's prescription, but it can be difficult to find some of the newer drugs.

Insurance

» Even if you're fit and healthy, don't travel without health insurance – accidents do happen.

» You may require extra cover for adventure activities such as rock climbing.

» Make sure you are covered for emergency evacuation.

» Ask in advance if your insurance plan will make payments directly to providers or reimburse you later for overseas health expenditures. (In many countries doctors expect payment in cash.)

» If you have to claim later, make sure you keep all documentation.

» Some policies ask you to call (reverse charges) a centre in your home country, where an immediate assessment of your problem is made.

Medical Checklist

Recommended items for a personal medical kit:

» antibacterial cream, eg Muciprocin

» antibiotic for skin infections, eg Amoxicillin/ Clavulanate or Cephalexin

» antifungal cream, eg Clotrimazole

» antihistamine – there are many options, eg Cetrizine for daytime and Promethazine for night

» antiseptic, eg Betadine

HEALTH ADVISORIES

It's a good idea to consult your government's travel-health website before departure, if one is available:
Australia (www.dfat.gov.au/travel/)
Canada (www.travelhealth.gc.ca)
New Zealand (www.mfat.govt.nz/travel)
South Africa (www.dfa.gov.za/consular/travel _advice.htm)
UK (www.doh.gov.uk/traveladvice/)
USA (www.cdc.gov/travel/)

» antispasmodic for stomach cramps, eg Buscopan
» contraceptive(s)
» decongestant, eg Pseudoephedrine
» DEET-based insect repellent
» diarrhoea medication – consider an oral rehydration solution (eg Gastrolyte), diarrhoea 'stopper' (eg Loperamide) and anti-nausea medication (eg Prochlorperazine); antibiotics for diarrhoea include Norfloxacin and Ciprofloxacin, for bacterial diarrhoea Azithromycin, and for giardia or amoebic dysentery Tinidazole
» first-aid items such as scissors, Elastoplasts, bandages, gauze, thermometer (but not mercury), sterile needles and syringes, safety pins and tweezers
» Ibuprofen or another anti-inflammatory
» indigestion tablets, eg Quick Eze or Mylanta
» iodine tablets (unless you are pregnant or have a thyroid problem) to purify water
» laxative, eg Coloxyl
» migraine medication if you suffer from them
» paracetamol
» permethrin to impregnate clothing and mosquito nets
» steroid cream for allergic or itchy rashes, eg 1% to 2% hydrocortisone
» sunscreen and hat
» throat lozenges
» treatment for thrush (vaginal yeast infection), eg Clotrimazole pessaries or Diflucan tablet
» Ural or equivalent if you are prone to urine infections

Vaccinations

Specialised travel-medicine clinics are your best source of information; they stock all available vaccines and will be able to give specific recommendations for you and your trip. The doctors will take into account factors such as past vaccination

REQUIRED & RECOMMENDED VACCINATIONS

Yellow fever is the only vaccine required by international regulations. Proof of vaccination will only be required if you have visited a country in the yellow-fever zone within the six days prior to entering India. If you are travelling to India from Africa or South America you should check to see if you require proof of vaccination. The World Health Organization (WHO) recommends that travellers to India be up to date with measles, mumps and rubella vaccinations. Other vaccinations it recommends:

» **Adult diphtheria and tetanus** Single booster recommended if none given in the previous 10 years.

» **Hepatitis A** Provides almost 100% protection for up to a year; a booster after 12 months provides at least another 20 years' protection.

» **Hepatitis B** Now considered routine for most travellers. Given as three shots over six months.

» **Polio** Only one booster is required as an adult for lifetime protection.

» **Typhoid** Recommended for all travellers to India, even if you only visit urban areas. The vaccine offers around 70% protection, lasts for two to three years and comes as a single shot. Tablets are also available; however, the injection is usually recommended as it has fewer side effects.

» **Varicella** If you haven't had chickenpox, discuss this vaccination with your doctor.

Immunisations recommended for long-term travellers (those going away for more than one month) or those at special risk:

» **Japanese B Encephalitis** Three injections in all. Booster recommended after two years.

» **Meningitis** Single injection. There are two types of vaccination: the quadrivalent vaccine gives two to three years' protection and the meningitis group C vaccine gives around 10 years' protection. Recommended for longterm backpackers aged under 25.

» **Rabies** Three injections in all. A booster after one year will then provide 10 years' protection.

» **Tuberculosis (TB)** Adult long-term travellers are usually advised to have a TB skin-test before and after travel, rather than vaccination. Only one vaccine needs to be given in a lifetime.

history, the length of your trip, activities you may be undertaking, and underlying medical conditions, such as pregnancy.

Most vaccines don't give immunity until at least two weeks after they're given, so visit a doctor four to eight weeks before departure. Ask your doctor for an International Certificate of Vaccination (otherwise known as the yellow booklet), which will list all the vaccinations you've received.

Websites

There's a wealth of travel-health advice on the internet. **LonelyPlanet.com** (www.lonelyplanet.com) is a good place to start. Some other suggestions:

Centers for Disease Control and Prevention (CDC; www.cdc.gov) Good general information.

MD Travel Health (www.mdtravelhealth.com) Provides complete travel-health recommendations for every country; updated daily.

World Health Organization (WHO; www.who.int/ith/) Its superb book *International Travel & Health* is revised annually and is available online.

Further Reading

Lonely Planet's *Asia & India – Healthy Travel* is pocket-sized and packed with useful information about pre-trip planning, emergency first aid, immunisation and disease information, and what to do if you get unwell while on the road. Other recommended references include *Traveller's Health*, by Dr Richard Dawood and *Travelling Well* (which is also online at www.travellingwell.com.au) by Dr Deborah Mills.

IN INDIA

Availability & Cost of Health Care

» Most hotels have a doctor on call – if you're staying at a budget hotel and they can't help, try contacting an upmarket hotel to find out which doctor they use.

» Some cities now have clinics catering specifically to travellers and expats. These are usually more costly than local facilities but are worth it, as they offer a superior standard of care. Additionally, staff at these clinics understand the local health system, and can also liaise with insurance companies should you require evacuation.

» It is difficult to find reliable medical care in rural areas. If you're seriously ill, contact your country's embassy (see p349), which usually has a list of recommended doctors and dentists.

» Treatment at public hospitals is generally reliable, though private clinics offer the advantage of shorter queues.

» Many pharmaceuticals sold in India are manufactured under licence from multinational companies, so you'll probably be familiar with many brand names.

» Before buying medication over the counter, always check the expiry date and ensure the packet is sealed.

Infectious Diseases

Coughs, Colds & Chest Infections

Around 25% of travellers to India will develop a respiratory infection. This usually starts as a virus and is exacerbated by environmental conditions such as pollution

in the cities or cold and altitude in the mountains. A secondary bacterial infection, marked by fever, chest pain and coughing up discoloured or blood-tinged sputum, will commonly intervene. If you have the symptoms of an infection, seek medical advice or commence a general antibiotic.

Dengue

This mosquito-borne disease is becoming increasingly problematic in the tropical world, especially in the cities. As there is no vaccine available it can only be prevented by avoiding mosquito bites. The mosquito that carries dengue bites day and night, so use insect avoidance measures at all times.

Symptoms of dengue fever include high fever, severe headache and body ache (dengue was previously known as 'breakbone fever'). Some people develop a rash and experience diarrhoea. There is no specific treatment – just rest and paracetamol. Do not take aspirin as it increases the chance of haemorrhaging. See a doctor to be diagnosed and monitored.

Hepatitis A

A problem throughout the region, this food- and water-borne virus infects the liver and causes jaundice (yellow skin and eyes), nausea and lethargy. There is no specific treatment for hepatitis A; you need to rest and allow time for the liver to heal itself. All travellers to India should be vaccinated against hepatitis A.

Hepatitis B

The only sexually transmitted disease that can be prevented by vaccination, hepatitis B is spread by body fluids (eg by sexual contact). The long-term consequences can include liver cancer and cirrhosis.

TRAVELLER'S DIARRHOEA

Traveller's diarrhoea is the most common problem that affects travellers – between 30% and 70% of people will suffer from it within two weeks of starting their trip. In over 80% of cases, traveller's diarrhoea is caused by a bacteria, and therefore responds promptly to antibiotics. Treatment with antibiotics will depend on your situation – how sick you are, how quickly you need to get better etc.

Traveller's diarrhoea is defined as the passage of more than three watery bowel actions within 24 hours, plus at least one other symptom such as fever, cramps, nausea, vomiting or feeling generally unwell. Treatment consists of staying well hydrated; rehydration solutions such as Gastrolyte are best for this. Antibiotics such as Norfloxacin, Ciprofloxacin or Azithromycin will kill the bacteria quickly. Loperamide is just a 'stopper' and doesn't get to the cause of the problem. It can be helpful, though, for example if you have to go on a long bus ride. Don't take Loperamide if you have a fever, or blood in your stools. Seek medical attention quickly if you do not respond to an appropriate antibiotic.

Hepatitis E

Hepatitis E is transmitted through contaminated food and water. It has similar symptoms to hepatitis A but is far less common. It is a severe problem in pregnant women and can result in the death of both mother and baby. There is currently no vaccine, and prevention is by following safe eating and drinking guidelines.

HIV

HIV is spread via contaminated body fluids. Avoid unsafe sex, unsterile needles (including in medical facilities) and procedures such as tattoos. The growth rate of HIV in India is one of the highest in the world.

Japanese B Encephalitis

This viral disease is transmitted by mosquitoes and is rare in travellers. Like most mosquito-borne diseases, it's becoming a more common problem in affected countries. Most cases occur in rural areas, and vaccination is recommended for travellers spending more than one month outside cities. There is no treatment, and a third of infected people will die, while another third will suffer permanent brain damage.

Malaria

Considering it's such a serious and potentially deadly disease, there is an enormous amount of misinformation about malaria. You must get expert advice as to whether your trip will put you at risk. For most rural areas, the risk of contracting malaria far outweighs the risk of any tablet side effects. Before you travel, seek medical advice on the right medication and dosage for you.

Malaria is caused by a parasite transmitted by the bite of an infected mosquito. The most important symptom of malaria is fever, but general symptoms such as headache, diarrhoea, cough or chills may also occur. Diagnosis can only be made by taking a blood sample.

Two strategies should be combined to help prevent malaria – mosquito avoidance and antimalarial medications. Most people who catch malaria are taking inadequate or no antimalarial medication.

Travellers are advised to take to the following steps to prevent mosquito bites:

» Use an insect repellent that contains DEET on exposed skin. Wash this off at night, as long as you're sleeping under a mosquito net. Natural repellents such as citronella can be effective but must be applied more frequently than products containing DEET.

» Sleep under a mosquito net impregnated with permethrin.

» Choose accommodation with screens and fans (if not air-conditioned).

» Impregnate clothing with permethrin in high-risk areas.

» Wear long sleeves and trousers in light colours.

» Use mosquito coils.

» Spray your room with insect repellent before going out for your evening meal.

A variety of medications are available:

» The effectiveness of the Chloroquine and Paludrine combination is now limited in many parts of south Asia. Common side effects include nausea (in 40% of people) and mouth ulcers.

» Doxycycline is a broad-spectrum antibiotic with the added benefit of helping to prevent a variety of tropical diseases such as leptospirosis, tick-borne disease and typhus. The potential side effects include photosensitivity (a tendency to sunburn), thrush in women, indigestion, heartburn, nausea and interference with the contraceptive pill. More serious side effects include ulceration of the oesophagus – you can help prevent this by taking your tablet with a meal and a large glass of water, and never lying down within half an hour of taking it. It must be taken for four weeks after leaving the risk area.

» Lariam (Mefloquine) has received much bad press, some of it justified, some not. This weekly tablet suits many people. Serious side effects are rare but include depression, anxiety, psychosis and fits. Anyone with a history of depression, anxiety, any other psychological disorder or epilepsy should not take Lariam. It is considered safe in the second and third trimesters of pregnancy. Tablets must be taken for four weeks after leaving the risk area.

» Malarone is a combination of Atovaquone and Proguanil. Side effects are uncommon and mild, most commonly nausea and headache. It is the best tablet for beach-goers and for those on short trips to high-risk areas. It must be taken for one week after leaving the risk area.

Rabies

This uniformly fatal disease is spread by the bite or lick of an infected animal – most commonly a dog or monkey. You should seek medical advice immediately after any animal bite and commence postexposure treatment. If an animal bites you, gently wash the wound with soap and water, and apply an iodine-based antiseptic.

Having a pre-travel vaccination means the post-bite treatment is greatly simplified. If you are not prevaccinated, you will need to receive rabies immuno-globulin as soon as possible, and this is very difficult to obtain in much of India.

STDs

Sexually transmitted diseases most common in India include herpes, warts, syphilis, gonorrhoea and chlamydia. People carrying these diseases often have no signs of infection. Condoms will prevent gonorrhoea and chlamydia but not warts or herpes.

If after a sexual encounter you develop any rash, lumps, discharge or pain when passing urine, seek immediate medical attention. If you have been sexually active on your travels, have an STD check when you return home.

Tuberculosis

While TB is rare in western countries, it is not rare in India and long-term travellers should take precautions. Vaccination is usually only given to children under the age of five, but adults at risk are advised to undergo pre- and post-travel TB testing. The main symptoms are fever, cough, weight loss, night sweats and tiredness.

Typhoid

This serious bacterial infection is also spread via food and water. It gives a high and slowly progressive fever and a headache. It may also be accompanied by a dry cough and stomach pain. It is diagnosed by blood tests and treated with antibiotics. Be aware that vaccination is not 100% effective, so you must still be careful with what you eat and drink. Vaccination is recommended for travellers spending more than a week in India.

Amoebic Dysentery

Amoebic dysentery is rare in travellers but often mis-

diagnosed by poor-quality labs. Symptoms are similar to bacterial diarrhoea: fever, bloody diarrhoea and generally feeling unwell. You should always seek reliable medical care if you have blood in your diarrhoea. Treatment involves two drugs: Tinidazole or Metronidazole to kill the parasite in your gut and then a second drug to kill the cysts. If left untreated, complications such as liver or intestinal abscesses can occur.

Giardiasis

Giardia is a parasite that is relatively common in travellers. Symptoms include nausea, bloating, excess gas, fatigue and intermittent diarrhoea. The parasite will eventually go away if left untreated, but this can take months. The treatment of choice is Tinidazole, with Metronidazole being a second-line option.

Environmental Hazards

Air Pollution

Air pollution, particularly vehicle pollution, is an increasing problem in most of India's major cities. If you have severe respiratory problems, speak with your doctor before travelling to any heavily polluted urban centres.

TAP WATER

» Never drink tap water.
» Bottled water is generally safe – check the seal is intact at purchase.
» Avoid ice.
» Avoid fresh juices that have been watered down.
» Boiling water is the most efficient method of purifying it.
» The best chemical purifier is iodine. It should not be used by pregnant women or those with thyroid problems.
» Water filters should also filter out viruses. Ensure your filter has a chemical barrier such as iodine and a small pore size, eg less than four microns.

Food

Eating in restaurants is the biggest risk factor for contracting traveller's diarrhoea. Ways to avoid it include eating only freshly cooked food, and avoiding shellfish and food that has been sitting around on buffets. Peel all fruit, cook vegetables and soak salads in iodine water for at least 20 minutes (avoid iodine if you are pregnant or have thyroid problems).

Heat

With temperatures hitting 45°C and over in the summer months, heatstroke and heat exhaustion are serious dangers for travellers used to cooler climes; for most people it takes at least two weeks to adapt.

Swelling of the feet and ankles is common, as are muscle cramps caused by excessive sweating. Prevent these by avoiding dehydration and excessive activity in the heat.

Drink rehydration solution or eat salty food. Treat cramps by stopping activity, resting, rehydrating with double-strength rehydration solution and gently stretching.

Dehydration is the main contributor to heat exhaustion. Symptoms include a feeling of weakness, headache, irritability, nausea or vomiting, sweaty skin, a normal or slightly elevated body temperature, and a fast, weak pulse. Treatment involves getting the sufferer out of the heat and/or sun, fanning them and applying cool wet cloths to the skin. Lay the sufferer flat with their legs raised, and rehydrate them with water containing a quarter of a teaspoon of salt per litre.

Heatstroke is a serious medical emergency. Symptoms come on suddenly and include weakness, nausea, a hot, dry body with a body temperature of more than 41°C, dizziness, confusion, loss of coordination, fits and eventually collapse and loss of consciousness. Seek medical help, and cool the person by getting them out of the heat, removing their clothes, fanning them and applying cool wet cloths or ice to their body, especially to the groin and armpits.

Prickly heat is a common skin rash caused by excessive perspiration getting trapped under the skin. Treat it by moving out of the heat and into an air-conditioned area for a few hours and by having cool showers. Creams and ointments clog the skin, so they should be avoided. Locally bought prickly-heat powder can be helpful.

Insect Bites & Stings

Bedbugs don't carry disease, but their bites are very itchy. They live in the cracks of furniture and walls, and then migrate to the bed at night to feed on you. You can treat the itch with antihistamines.

Lice inhabit various parts of your body but most commonly your head and pubic area. Transmission is via close contact with an infected person. Lice can be difficult to treat, and you may need numerous applications of an anti-lice shampoo such as permethrin. Pubic lice are usually contracted from sexual contact.

Ticks are contracted after walking in rural areas. They're commonly found behind the ears, on the belly and in the armpits. If you have had a tick bite and experience symptoms such as a rash at the site of the bite or elsewhere, fever or muscle aches, you should see a doctor. Doxycycline prevents tick-borne diseases.

Bee and wasp stings mainly cause problems for people who are allergic to them. Anyone with a serious bee or wasp allergy should carry an injection of adrenaline (eg an Epipen) for emergency treatment. For others, pain is the main problem – apply ice to the sting and take painkillers.

WANT MORE?

For in-depth language information and handy phrases, check out Lonely Planet's *Hindi, Urdu & Bengali Phrasebook* and *India Phrasebook*. You'll find them at **shop.lonelyplanet.com**, or you can buy Lonely Planet's iPhone phrasebooks at the Apple App Store.

Language

India's linguistic landscape is varied – 23 languages (including English) are recognised in the constitution, and more than 1600 minor languages are spoken. This large number of languages certainly helps explain why English is still widely spoken in India and why it's still in official use. Despite major efforts to promote Hindi as the national language of India, phasing out English, many educated Indians speak English as virtually their first language. For the large number of Indians who speak more than one language, it's often their second tongue. Although you'll find it very easy to get around India with English, it's always good to know a little of the local language.

While the locals in Rajasthan, Agra and Delhi may speak Punjabi, Urdu, Marwari, Jaipuri, Malvi or Mewati to each other, for you, Hindi will be the local language of choice. Hindi has about 600 million speakers worldwide, of which 180 million are in India. It developed from Classical Sanskrit, and is written in Devanagari script. In 1947 it was granted official status along with English.

PRONUNCIATION

Most Hindi sounds are similar to their English counterparts. The main difference is that Hindi has both aspirated consonants (pronounced with a puff of air, like saying 'h' after the sound) and unaspirated consonants, as well as retroflex (pronounced with the tongue bent backwards) and nonretroflex ones. Our simplified pronunciation guides don't include these distinctions – if you read them as if they were English, you'll be understood.

Pronunciation of vowels is important, especially their length (eg a and aa). The consonant combination ng after a vowel indicates nasalisation (ie the vowel is pronounced 'through the nose'). Note also that au is pronounced as the 'ow' in 'how'.

Word stress in Hindi is very light; we've indicated the stressed syllables with italics.

BASICS

Hindi verbs change form depending on the gender of the speaker (or the subject of the sentence in general) meaning it's the verbs, not the pronouns 'he' or 'she', which show whether the subject of the sentence is masculine or feminine. In these phrases we include the options for male and female speakers, marked 'm' and 'f' respectively, as needed.

Hello./Goodbye.	नमस्ते ।	na·ma·*ste*
Yes.	जी हाँ ।	jee haang
No.	जी नहीं ।	jee na·*heeng*
Excuse me.	सुनिये ।	su·ni·ye
Sorry.	माफ़ कीजिये ।	maaf *kee*·ji·ye
Please ...	कृपया ...	kri·pa·*yaa* ...
Thank you.	थैंक्यू ।	*thayn*·kyoo
You're welcome.	कोई बात नहीं ।	*ko*·ee baat na·*heeng*

How are you?
आप कैसे/कैसी हैं?
aap *kay*·se/*kay*·see hayng (m/f)

Fine. And you?
मैं ठीक हूँ ।
आप सुनाइये ।
mayng teek hoong
aap su·*naa*·i·ye

What's your name?
आप का नाम क्या है?   aap kaa naam kyaa hay

My name is ...
मेरा नाम ... है।   *me·*raa naam ... hay

Do you speak English?
क्या आपको अंग्रेज़ी   kyaa aap ko an·*gre·*zee
आती है?   *aa·*tee hay

I don't understand.
मैं नहीं समझा/   mayng na·*heeng* sam·jaa/
समझी।   sam·jee (m/f)

ACCOMMODATION

Where's a ...?	... कहाँ है?	... ka·*haang* hay
guesthouse	गेस्ट हाउस	gest *haa·*us
hotel	होटल	*ho·*tal
youth hostel	यूथ हास्टल	yoot *haas·*tal

Do you have a ... room?	क्या ... कमरा है?	kyaa ... *kam·*raa hay
single	सिंगल	*sin·*gal
double	डबल	da·*bal*

How much is it per ...?	... के लिये कितने पैसे लगते हैं?	... ke li·ye *kit·*ne *pay·*se *lag·*te hayng
night	एक रात	ek raat
person	हर व्यक्ति	har *vyak·*ti

air-con	ए० सी०	e see
bathroom	बाथरूम	*baat·*room
hot water	गर्म पानी	garm *paa·*nee
mosquito net	मसहरी	*mas·*ha·ree
washerman	धोबी	*do·*bee
window	खिड़की	*kir·*kee

DIRECTIONS

Where's ...?
... कहाँ है?   ... ka·*haang* hay

How far is it?
वह कितनी दूर है?   voh *kit·*nee door hay

What's the address?
पता क्या है?   pa·*taa* kyaa hay

Can you write it down, please?
कृपया यह लिखिये?   kri·pa·*yaa* yeh li·*ki·*ye

Can you show me (on the map)?
(नक्शे में) दिखा   (nak·she meng) di·*kaa*
सकते है?   *sak·*te hayng

Turn left/right.
लेफ्ट/राइट मुड़िये।   left/*raa·*it mu·ri·ye

at the corner	कोने पर	*ko·*ne par
at the traffic lights	सिगनल पर	*sig·*nal par
behind ...	... के पीछे	... ke *pee·*che
in front of ...	... के सामन	... ke *saam·*ne
near ...	... के पास	... ke paas
opposite ...	... के सामने	... ke *saam·*ne
straight ahead	सीधे	*see·*de

EATING & DRINKING

What would you recommend?
आपके ख़्याल में   aap ke kyaal meng
क्या अच्छा होगा?   kyaa *ach·*chaa ho·gaa

Do you have vegetarian food?
क्या आप का खाना   kyaa aap kaa *kaa·*naa
शाकाहारी है?   shaa·kaa·*haa·*ree hay

I don't eat (meat).
मैं (गोश्त) नहीं   mayng (gosht) na·*heeng*
खाता/खाती।   *kaa·*taa/*kaa·*tee (m/f)

I'll have ...
मुझे ... दीजिये।   mu·je ... *dee·*ji·ye

That was delicious.
बहुत मज़ेदार हुआ।   ba·*hut* ma·ze·*daar* hu·aa

Please bring the menu/bill.
मेन्यू/बिल लाइये।   *men·*yoo/bil *laa·*i·ye

Key Words

bottle	बोतल	*bo·*tal
bowl	कटोरी	ka·*to·*ree
breakfast	नाश्ता	*naash·*taa
dessert	मीठा	*mee·*taa
dinner	रात का खाना	raat kaa *kaa·*naa
drinks	पीने की चीज़ें	*pee·*ne kee *chee·*zeng
food	खाना	*kaa·*naa
fork	काँटा	*kaan·*taa
glass	गिलास	glaas
knife	चाकू	*chaa·*koo
local eatery	ढाबा	*daa·*baa
lunch	दिन का खाना	din kaa *kaa·*naa
market	बाज़ार	*baa·*zaar
plate	प्लेट	plet
restaurant	रेस्टोरेंट	*res·*to·rent
set meal	थाली	*taa·*lee
snack	नाश्ता	*naash·*taa
spoon	चम्मच	*cham·*mach
with/without	के साथ/बिना	ke saat/bi·*naa*

Meat & Fish

beef	गाय का गोश्त	gaai kaa gosht
chicken	मुर्ग़ी	*mur*·gee
duck	बतख़	ba·*tak*
fish	मछली	*mach*·lee
goat	बकरा	*bak*·raa
lobster	बड़ी झींगा	*ba·ree jeeng*·gaa
meat	गोश्त	gosht
meatballs	कोफ़्ता	*kof*·taa
pork	सुअर का गोश्त	*su*·ar kaa gosht
prawn	झींगी मछली	*jeeng*·gee *mach*·lee
seafood	मछली	*mach*·lee

Fruit & Vegetables

apple	सेब	seb
apricot	ख़ुबानी	ku·*baa*·nee
banana	केला	*ke*·laa
capsicum	मिर्च	mirch
carrot	गाजर	*gaa*·jar
cauliflower	फूल गोभी	pool go·*bee*
corn	मक्का	*mak*·kaa
cucumber	ककड़ी	*kak*·ree
date	खजूर	ka·*joor*
eggplant	बैंगन	*bayng*·gan
fruit	फल	pal
garlic	लहसुन	*leh*·sun
grape	अंगूर	*an*·goor
grapefruit	चकोतरा	cha·*kot*·raa
lemon	निम्बू	*nim*·boo
lentils	दाल	daal
mandarin	संतरा	*san*·ta·raa
mango	आम	aam
mushroom	खुंभी	*kum*·bee
orange	नारंगी	naa·*ran*·gee
papaya	पपीता	pa·*pee*·taa
peach	आड़ू	*aa*·roo
peas	मटर	ma·*tar*
pineapple	अनन्नास	a·*nan*·naas
potato	आलू	*aa*·loo
pumpkin	कद्दू	*kad*·doo
spinach	पालक	*paa*·lak
vegetables	सब्ज़ी	*sab*·zee
watermelon	तरबूज़	*tar*·booz

Other

bread	चपाती/ नान/रोटी	cha·*paa*·tee/ naan/*ro*·tee
butter	मक्खन	*mak*·kan
chilli	मिर्च	mirch
chutney	चटनी	*chat*·nee
egg	अंडे	*an*·de
honey	मधु	*ma*·dhu
ice	बर्फ़	barf
ice cream	कुल्फ़ी	*kul*·fee
pappadams	पपड़	pa·*par*
pepper	काली मिर्च	*kaa*·lee mirch
relish	अचार	a·*chaar*
rice	चावल	*chaa*·val
salt	नमक	na·*mak*
spices	मिर्च मसाला	mirch ma·*saa*·laa
sugar	चीनी	*chee*·nee
tofu	टोफू	to·*foo*

Drinks

beer	बियर	bi·*yar*
coffee	काईफ़ी	*kaa*·fee
juice	रस	ras
milk	दूध	dood
red wine	लाल शराब	laal sha·*raab*
sugarcane juice	गन्ने का रस	*gan*·ne kaa ras
sweet fruit drink	शरबत	*shar*·bat
tea	चाय	chaai
water	पानी	*paa*·nee
white wine	सफ़ेद शराब	sa·*fed* sha·*raab*
yogurt	लस्सी	*las*·see

EMERGENCIES

Help!
मदद कीजिये! — ma·*dad kee*·ji·ye

I'm lost.
मैं रास्ता भूल गया/गयी हूँ। — mayng *raas*·taa bool ga·*yaa*/ga·*yee* hoong (m/f)

Go away!
जाओ! — *jaa*·o

There's been an accident.
दुर्घटना हुई है। — dur·*gat*·naa hu·*ee* hay

Call a doctor!
डॉक्टर को बुलाओ! — *daak*·tar ko bu·*laa*·o

Call the police!
पुलिस को बुलाओ! pu·*lis* ko bu·*laa*·o

I'm ill.
मैं बीमार हूँ। mayng *bee*·maar hoong

It hurts here.
इधर दर्द हो रहा है। i·*dar* dard ho ra·*haa* hay

I'm allergic to (antibiotics).
मुझे (एंटीबायोटिकिस) mu·*je* (en·tee·baa·*yo*·tiks)
की एलर्जी है। kee e·*lar*·jee hay

SHOPPING & SERVICES

I'd like to buy ...
मुझे ... चाहिये। mu·*je* ... *chaa*·hi·ye

I'm just looking.
सिर्फ़ देखने आया/ sirf *dek*·ne aa·*yaa*/
आयी हूँ। aa·yee hoong (m/f)

May I look at it?
दिखाइये। di·*kaa*·i·ye

Do you have any others?
दूसरा है? *doos*·raa hay

How much is it?
कितने का है? *kit*·ne kaa hay

It's too expensive.
यह बहुत महंगा/ yeh ba·*hut* ma·han·gaa/
महंगी है। ma·*han*·gee hay (m/f)

Can you lower the price?
क्या आप दाम kyaa aap daam
कम करेंगे? kam ka·*reng*·ge

There's a mistake in the bill.
बिल में गलती है। bil meng *gal*·tee hay

bank	बैंक	baynk
post office	डाक ख़ाना	daak *kaa*·naa
public phone	सार्वजनिक फ़ोन	*saar*·va·ja·nik fon
rupee	रुपया	ru·pa·*yaa*
tourist office	पर्यटन ऑफ़िस	*par*·ya·tan aa·fis

Question Words		
How?	कैसे?	*kay*·se
What?	क्या?	kyaa
Which?	कौनसा?	*kaun*·saa
When?	कब?	kab
Where?	कहाँ?	ka·*haang*
Who?	कौन?	kaun
Why?	क्यों?	kyong

TIME & DATES

What time is it?
टाइम क्या है? *taa*·im kyaa hay

It's (10) o'clock.
(दस) बजे हैं। (das) ba·je hayng

Half past (10).
साढ़े (दस)। *saa*·re (das)

morning	सुबह	su·*bah*
afternoon	दोपहर	*do*·pa·har
evening	शाम	shaam
Monday	सोमवार	*som*·vaar
Tuesday	मंगलवार	man·*gal*·vaar
Wednesday	बुधवार	*bud*·vaar
Thursday	गुरुवार	gu·ru·*vaar*
Friday	शुक्रवार	*shuk*·ra·vaar
Saturday	शनिवार	sha·ni·*vaar*
Sunday	रविवार	ra·vi·*vaar*
January	जनवरी	*jan*·va·ree
February	फ़रवरी	*far*·va·ree
March	मार्च	maarch
April	अप्रैल	a·*prayl*
May	मई	ma·*ee*
June	जून	joon
July	जुलाई	ju·*laa*·ee
August	अगस्त	a·*gast*
September	सितम्बर	si·*tam*·bar
October	अक्टूबर	ak·*too*·bar
November	नवम्बर	na·*vam*·bar
December	दिसम्बर	di·*sam*·bar

TRANSPORT

Public Transport

When's the ... (bus)?	... (बस) कब जाती है?	... (bas) kab *jaa*·tee hay
first	पहली	*peh*·lee
next	अगली	*ag*·lee
last	आखिरी	*aa*·ki·ree
bicycle rickshaw	साइकिल रिक्शा	*saa*·i·kil *rik*·shaa
boat	जहाज़	ja·*haaz*
bus	बस	bas
plane	हवाई जहाज़	ha·*vaa*·ee ja·*haaz*
train	ट्रेन	tren

Numbers			
1	१	एक	ek
2	२	दो	do
3	३	तीन	teen
4	४	चार	chaar
5	५	पाँच	paanch
6	६	छह	chay
7	७	सात	saat
8	८	आठ	aat
9	९	नौ	nau
10	१०	दस	das
20	२०	बीस	bees
30	३०	तीस	tees
40	४०	चालीस	chaa·lees
50	५०	पचास	pa·chaas
60	६०	साठ	saat
70	७०	सत्तर	sat·tar
80	८०	अस्सी	as·see
90	९०	नब्बे	nab·be
100	१००	सौ	sau
1000	१०००	एक हज़ार	ek ha·zaar

I'd like a/an ... seat.
मुझे ... सीट चाहिये। — mu·je ... seet chaa·hi·ye

   aisle किनारे — ki·naa·re
   window खिड़की के पास — kir·kee ke paas

bus stop बस स्टॉप — bas is·taap
ticket office टिकटघर — ti·kat·gar
timetable समय सारणी — sa·mai saa·ra·nee
train station स्टेशन — ste·shan

Driving & Cycling

I'd like to hire a ...
मुझे ... किराये पर लेना है। — mu·je ... ki·raa·ye par le·naa hay

   4WD फ़ोर व्हील ड्राइव — for vheel draa·iv
   bicycle साइकिल — saa·i·kil
   car कार — kaar
   motorbike मोटर साइकिल — mo·tar saa·i·kil

At what time does it leave?
कितने बजे जाता/जाती है? — kit·ne ba·je jaa·taa/jaa·tee hay (m/f)

How long does the trip take?
जाने में कितनी देर लगती है? — jaa·ne meng kit·nee der lag·tee hay

How long will it be delayed?
उसे कितनी देर हुई है? — u·se kit·nee der hu·ee hay

Does it stop at ...?
क्या ... में रुकती है? — kyaa ... meng ruk·tee hay

Please tell me when we get to ...
जब ... आता है, मुझे बताइये। — jab ... aa·taa hay mu·je ba·taa·i·ye

Please go straight to this address.
इसी जगह को फ़ौरन जाइए। — is·ee ja·gah ko fau·ran jaa·i·ye

Please stop here.
यहाँ रुकिये। — ya·haang ru·ki·ye

A ... ticket (to ...).
(...) के लिये ... टिकट दीजिये। — (...) ke li·ye ... ti·kat dee·ji·ye

   1st-class फ़र्स्ट क्लास — farst klaas
   2nd-class सेकंड क्लास — se·kand klaas
   one-way एक तरफ़ा — ek ta·ra·faa
   return आने जाने का — aa·ne jaa·ne kaa

Is this the road to ...?
क्या यह ... का रास्ता है? — kyaa yeh ... kaa raas·taa hay

Can I park here?
यहाँ पार्क कर सकता/सकती हूँ? — ya·haang paark kar sak·taa/sak·tee hoong (m/f)

Where's a service station?
पेट्रोल पम्प कहाँ है? — pet·rol pamp ka·haang hay

I need a mechanic.
मुझे मरम्मत करने वाला चाहिये। — mu·je ma·ram·mat kar·ne vaa·laa chaa·hi·ye

The car/motorbike has broken down at ...
कार/मोटर साइकिल ... में ख़राब हो गयी है। — kaar/mo·tar saa·i·kil ... meng ka·raab ho ga·yee hay

I have a flat tyre.
टायर पंक्चर हो गया है। — taa·yar pank·char ho ga·yaa hay

I've run out of petrol.
पेट्रोल ख़त्म हो गया है। — pet·rol katm ho ga·yaa hay

(m) indicates masculine gender, (f) feminine gender and (pl) plural

ahimsa – nonviolence and reverence for all life

apsara – celestial maiden

Aryan – Sanskrit word for 'noble'; people who migrated from Persia and settled in northern India

ashram – spiritual community or retreat

autorickshaw – a noisy three-wheeled device with a motorbike engine and seats for two passengers behind the driver

Ayurveda – the ancient and complex science of Indian herbal medicine and healing

bagh – garden

baithak – salon in a *haveli* where merchants received guests

baksheesh – tip, donation (alms) or bribe

bandhani – tie-dye

baori – well, particularly a step-well with landings and galleries

betel – nut of the betel tree; chewed as a stimulant and digestive in a concoction know as *paan*

bhang – dried leaves and flowering shoots of the marijuana plant

Bhil – tribal people of southern Rajasthan

bindi – forehead mark

Bishnoi – tribe known for their reverence for the environment

Bodhi Tree – *Ficus religiosa,* under which Buddha attained enlightenment

Brahmin – member of the priest caste, the highest Hindu caste

Buddha – Awakened One; the originator of Buddhism; also regarded by Hindus as the ninth incarnation of Vishnu

bund – embankment, dyke

chajera – mason employed by Marwari businessmen of Shekhawati to build *havelis*

charpoy – simple bed made of ropes knotted together on a wooden frame

chaupar – town square formed by the intersection of major roads

chhatri – cenotaph (literally 'umbrella')

choli – sari blouse

chowk – town square, intersection or marketplace

chowkidar – caretaker; night watchman

crore – 10 million

cycle-rickshaw – three-wheeled bicycle with seats for two passengers behind the rider

dacoit – bandit

Dalit – preferred term for India's *Untouchable* caste

dalwar – sword

dargah – shrine or place of burial of a Muslim saint

dharamsala – pilgrims guest house

dhobi – laundry

dhurrie – cotton rug

Digambara – Sky Clad; a Jain sect whose monks show disdain for worldly goods by going naked

Diwan-i-Am – hall of public audience

Diwan-i-Khas – hall of private audience

dupatta – long scarf for women often worn with the *salwar kameez*

durbar – royal court; also a government

garh – fort

ghat – steps or landing on a river; range of hills or road up hills

ghazal – Urdu song derived from poetry; sad love theme

ghoomer – dance performed by women during festivals and weddings

gopis – milkmaids; Krishna was very fond of them

guru – teacher or holy person

Harijan – name (no longer considered acceptable) given by Gandhi to India's *Untouchables,* meaning 'children of god'

hathi – elephant

haveli – traditional, ornately decorated rseidence

hijra – eunuch

hookah – water pipe

howdah – seat for carrying people on an elephant's back

jali – carved marble lattice screen; also refers to the holes or spaces produced through carving timber

Jats – traditionally people who were engaged in agriculture; today Jats play a strong role in administration and politics

jauhar – ritual mass suicide by immolation, traditionally performed by *Rajput* women after military defeat to avoid dishonour

jootis – traditional leather shoes of Rajasthan; men's *jootis* often have curled-up toes; also known as *mojaris*

kabas – the holy rats believed to be the incarnations of local families at Karni Mata Temple at Deshnok

Kalbelias – nomadic tribal group associated with snake charming

karma – Hindu, Buddhist and Sikh principle of retributive justice for past deeds

kashida – embroidery on *jootis*

kathputli – puppeteer

khadi – homespun cloth; Mahatma Gandhi encouraged people to spin *khadi* rather than buy English cloth

khadim – Muslim holy servant or mosque attendant

kotwali – police station

Kshatriya – warrior or administrator caste, second in the caste hierarchy; Rajputs claim lineage from the Kshatriyas

kundan – type of jewellery featuring *meenakari* on one side and precious stones on the other

kurta – long cotton shirt with either a short collar or no collar

lakh – 100,000

lingam – phallic symbol; symbol of Shiva

madrasa – Islamic college

Mahabharata – Vedic epic poem of the Bharata dynasty; describes the battle between the Pandavas and the Kauravas

mahal – house, palace

maharaja – literally 'great king'; princely ruler; also known as maharana, maharao and maharawal

maharani – wife of a princely ruler or a ruler in her own right

Mahavir – the 24th and last *tirthankar*

mahout – elephant driver/keeper

mandapa – chamber before the inner sanctum of a temple

mandir – temple

mantra – sacred word or syllable used by Buddhists and Hindus to aid concentration; metric psalms of praise found in the *Vedas*

Marathas – warlike central Indians who controlled much of India at times and fought against the *Mughals* and *Rajputs*

marg – major road

masjid – mosque

Marwar – kingdom of the Rathore dynasty that ruled from Mandore, and later from Jodhpur

meenakari – type of enamelwork used on ornaments and jewellery

mehfilkhana – Islamic building in which religious songs are sung

mehndi – henna; intricate henna designs applied by women to their hands and feet

mela – fair, festival

Mewar – kingdom of the Sisodia dynasty; ruled Udaipur and Chittorgarh

moksha – release from the cycle of birth and death

monsoon – rainy season; June to October

mosar – death feast

Mughal – Muslim dynasty of Indian emperors from Babur to Aurangzeb (16th to 18th centuries)

nawab – Muslim ruling prince or powerful landowner

nilgai – antelope

niwas – house, building

NRI – nonresident Indian

odhni – headscarf

Om – sacred invocation that represents the essence of the divine principle

paan – chewable preparation made from betel leaves, nuts and lime

PCO – public call office

pol – gate

prasad – sacred food offered to the gods

puja – literally 'respect'; offering or prayer

purdah – custom among some conservative Muslims (also adopted by some Hindus, especially the Rajputs) of keeping women in seclusion; veiled

raga – any conventional pattern of melody and rhythm that forms the basis for free composition

raj – rule or sovereignty; British Raj (sometimes just

Raj) refers to British rule before 1947

raja – king; also *rana*

Rajputs – Sons of Princes; Hindu warrior caste, former rulers of western India

rana – see *raja*

rani – female ruler; wife of a king

rawal – nobleman

Road – railway town that serves as a communication point to a larger town off the line, eg Mt Abu and Abu Road

RSRTC – Rajasthan State Road Transport Corporation

RTDC – Rajasthan Tourism Development Corporation

sadar – main

sadhu – ascetic, holy person, one who is trying to achieve enlightenment; usually addressed as 'swamiji' or 'babaji'

sagar – lake, reservoir

sahib – respectful title applied to a gentleman

sal – gallery in a palace

salwar kameez – traditional dresslike tunic and trouser combination for women

sambar – deer

sati – suicide by immolation; banned more than a century ago, it is still occasionally performed

Scheduled Tribes – government classification for tribal groups of Rajasthan; the tribes are grouped with the lowest casteless class, the Dalits

shikar – hunting expedition

Sikh – member of the monotheistic religion Sikhism, which separated from Hinduism in the 16th century and has a military tradition; Sikh men can be recognised by their beards and turbans

sikhara – temple-spire or temple

silavat – stone carvers

Singh – literally 'lion'; a surname adopted by Rajputs and Sikhs

Sufi – Muslim mystic

tabla – pair of drums

tempo – noisy three-wheeled public transport; bigger than an autorickshaw

thakur – Hindu caste; nobleman

tikka – a mark devout Hindus put on their foreheads with *tikka* powder; also known as a *bor* or *rakhadi*

tirthankars – the 24 great Jain teachers

tonga – two-wheeled passenger vehicle drawn by horse or pony

toran – shield-shaped device above a lintel, which a bridegroom pierces with his sword before claiming his bride

torana – elaborately sculpted gateway before temples

tripolia – triple gateway

Vaishya – merchant caste; the third caste in the hierarchy

Vedas – Hindu sacred books; collection of hymns composed during the 2nd millennium BC and divided into four books: Rig-Veda, Yajur-Veda, Sama-Veda and Atharva-Veda

wallah – man; added onto almost anything, eg *dhobi-wallah, chai-wallah, taxi-wallah*

yagna – self-mortification

zenana – women's quarters

behind the scenes

SEND US YOUR FEEDBACK

We love to hear from travellers – your comments keep us on our toes and help make our books better. Our well-travelled team reads every word on what you loved or loathed about this book. Although we cannot reply individually to postal submissions, we always guarantee that your feedback goes straight to the appropriate authors, in time for the next edition. Each person who sends us information is thanked in the next edition – and the most useful submissions are rewarded with a free book.

Visit **lonelyplanet.com/contact** to submit your updates and suggestions or to ask for help. Our award-winning website also features inspirational travel stories, news and discussions.

Note: We may edit, reproduce and incorporate your comments in Lonely Planet products such as guidebooks, websites and digital products, so let us know if you don't want your comments reproduced or your name acknowledged. For a copy of our privacy policy visit lonelyplanet.com/privacy.

OUR READERS

Many thanks to the travellers who used the last edition and wrote to us with helpful hints, useful advice and interesting anecdotes:

Felipe Perez Agustin, Donald Aitchison, Carrie Bartlett, Liz Bate, Sarah Carden, Tiffany Care, Rachel Century, Rory Chapple, John Ciosk, Emily Clayson, Stuart and Pamela Davis, Natalie De Oliveira, Matthias Dehner, Fabienne Deiss, Marije Erkens, Hamish Gillespie-Jones, Gina Gurung, Leanne Hart, Johann Karl Held, Jonathan Holubecki-France, Lauren Hubbard, Katy Kennedy, Genine Keogh, Tobias Krank, Eva Langhammer, Xingkai Loy, Niccolò Rangoni Machiavelli, Michaela Markert, Dennis Mogerman, Heather Monell, Ruben Mooijman, Vincent Morello, Brenda Nagy, Eleonora Palilla, Nathan Pan, Simone Panato, Costantino Piergiuseppe, Leszek Raschkowski, James Sabin, Robert Schofield, Markus Schwegler, Tim Simpson, Carmen Stanley, Duncan Thomas, Simone Tobler, Sabine Turek, David Valls, Jan Verbeeck

AUTHOR THANKS

Lindsay Brown

Thanks to the many people in Rajasthan who shared their interest and expertise. In particular, I would like to thank Satinder and Ritu and Dicky and Kavita in Jaipur, Ramesh Jangid in Nawalgarh, Laxmi Kant Jangid in Jhunjhunu, Goverdhan and Usha and Abhay, Deepak and Rahul in Rhanthambhore, and Shoryavardhan in Alwar. For his wide smile and prowess on the road, a huge thanks to Vinod. Thanks to fellow author John Noble, and thanks to Jenny, Pat and Sinead at home.

Abigail Hole

Many thanks to all at Lonely Planet, especially to Suzannah Shwer. Thanks very much to Rajinder, as well as to all the readers who wrote in with useful advice and updates. Many, many thanks to the baby-sitting team: Luca, Mum, Ant and Karen, and to Gabriel and Jack for being so good.

Daniel McCrohan

Special thanks for help with my Agra research to Ramesh. Thanks to travellers I met on the road for good tips and great company. Most of all, thank you to Taotao, Dudu and Yoyo, and to all my family in the UK and Belgium, for your love, patience and endless support.

John Noble

So many people gave generously of their time and knowledge to assist my research. Especially Kanhaiya Lal Gurjar (driver, guide, interpreter and research assistant extraordinaire), Sue Carpenter, Mukesh and Manish Mehta, Piers Helsen and Phil Porter. Many thanks to ever-helpful and understanding coordinating author Lindsay Brown, to commissioning editor Suzannah Shwer for her help, enthusiasm and answers to many questions, and to Sarina Singh for general good advice on Rajasthan. Not least, Izzy and Jack, my ideal travelling companions.

ACKNOWLEDGMENTS

Climate map data adapted from Peel MC, Finlayson BL & McMahon TA (2007) 'Updated World Map of the Köppen-Geiger Climate Classification', *Hydrology and Earth System Sciences*, 11, 163344.

Cover photograph: Man and camel in Yamuna River near the Taj Mahal, Agra/Guylain Doyle/ Lonely Planet Images. Many of the images in this guide are available for licensing from Lonely Planet Images: www.lonelyplanet images.com.

Illustrations: pp14-15 and pp42-3 by Javier Zarracina.

THIS BOOK

This edition of Rajasthan, Delhi & Agra was coordinated by Lindsay Brown, who also wrote the Jaipur, Eastern Rajasthan and Northern Rajasthan chapters. John Noble wrote the Southern Rajasthan and Western Rajasthan chapters, Abigail Hole wrote Delhi and Daniel McCrohan wrote the Agra chapter. Dr Trish Batchelor wrote the Health chapter. The 1st and 2nd editions were coordinated by Abigail Hole and Lindsay Brown respectively. This guidebook was commissioned in Lonely Planet's Melbourne office, and produced by the following:

Commissioning Editor Suzannah Shwer

Coordinating Editor Chris Girdler

Coordinating Cartographer Andrew Smith

Coordinating Layout Designer Jessica Rose

Managing Editors Sasha Baskett, Brigitte Ellemor

Managing Cartographers Alison Lyall, Adrian Persoglia

Managing Layout Designers Jane Hart, Celia Wood

Assisting Editors Elisa Arduca, Alice Barker, Janice Bird, Cathryn Game, Beth Hall, Carly Hall, Matty Soccio

Assisting Cartographer Alex Leung

Cover Research Naomi Parker

Internal Image Research Sabrina Dalbesio

Language Content Branislava Vladisavljevic

Thanks to Sharara Ahmed, Andras Bogdanovits, Nigel Chin, Helen Christinis, Ryan Evans, Lisa Knights, Anna Metcalfe, Mark Milinkovic, Averil Robertson, Peter Shields, Sarina Singh

index

how to use this book

These symbols will help you find the listings you want:

👁 Sights 　　🎏 Festivals & Events 　　☆ Entertainment

🏃 Activities 　　🛏 Sleeping 　　🔒 Shopping

🍵 Courses 　　✕ Eating 　　ℹ Information/Transport

👉 Tours 　　🍷 Drinking

Look out for these icons:

TOP CHOICE Our author's recommendation

🌿 A green or sustainable option

Our authors have nominated these places as demonstrating a strong commitment to sustainability – for example by supporting local communities and producers, operating in an environmentally friendly way, or supporting conservation projects.

These symbols give you the vital information for each listing:

📞	Telephone Numbers	📶	Wi-Fi Access	🚌	Bus
☺	Opening Hours	🏊	Swimming Pool	🚢	Ferry
P	Parking	🥗	Vegetarian Selection	Ⓜ	Metro
☺	Nonsmoking	📖	English-Language Menu	Ⓢ	Subway
❄	Air-Conditioning	👪	Family-Friendly	⊖	London Tube
@	Internet Access	🐾	Pet-Friendly	🚃	Tram
				🚆	Train

Reviews are organised by author preference.

Map Legend

Sights
- 🏖 Beach
- 🛕 Buddhist
- 🏰 Castle
- ✝ Christian
- 🕉 Hindu
- ☪ Islamic
- ✡ Jewish
- 🗿 Monument
- 🏛 Museum/Gallery
- Ruin
- 🍷 Winery/Vineyard
- 🦁 Zoo
- Other Sight

Activities, Courses & Tours
- Diving/Snorkelling
- Canoeing/Kayaking
- Skiing
- Surfing
- Swimming/Pool
- Walking
- Windsurfing
- Other Activity/Course/Tour

Sleeping
- Sleeping
- Camping

Eating
- Eating

Drinking
- Drinking
- Cafe

Entertainment
- Entertainment

Shopping
- Shopping

Information
- Bank
- Embassy/Consulate
- Hospital/Medical
- Internet
- Police
- Post Office
- Telephone
- Toilet
- Tourist Information
- Other Information

Transport
- Airport
- Border Crossing
- Bus
- Cable Car/Funicular
- Cycling
- Ferry
- Metro
- Monorail
- Parking
- Petrol Station
- Taxi
- Train/Railway
- Tram
- Other Transport

Routes
- Tollway
- Freeway
- Primary
- Secondary
- Tertiary
- Lane
- Unsealed Road
- Plaza/Mall
- Steps
- Tunnel
- Pedestrian Overpass
- Walking Tour
- Walking Tour Detour
- Path

Geographic
- Hut/Shelter
- Lighthouse
- Lookout
- Mountain/Volcano
- Oasis
- Park
- Pass
- Picnic Area
- Waterfall

Population
- Capital (National)
- Capital (State/Province)
- City/Large Town
- Town/Village

Boundaries
- International
- State/Province
- Disputed
- Regional/Suburb
- Marine Park
- Cliff
- Wall

Hydrography
- River, Creek
- Intermittent River
- Swamp/Mangrove
- Reef
- Canal
- Water
- Dry/Salt/Intermittent Lake
- Glacier

Areas
- Beach/Desert
- Cemetery (Christian)
- Cemetery (Other)
- Park/Forest
- Sportsground
- Sight (Building)
- Top Sight (Building)

OUR STORY

A beat-up old car, a few dollars in the pocket and a sense of adventure. In 1972 that's all Tony and Maureen Wheeler needed for the trip of a lifetime – across Europe and Asia overland to Australia. It took several months, and at the end – broke but inspired – they sat at their kitchen table writing and stapling together their first travel guide, *Across Asia on the Cheap*. Within a week they'd sold 1500 copies. Lonely Planet was born.

Today, Lonely Planet has offices in Melbourne, London and Oakland, with more than 600 staff and writers. We share Tony's belief that 'a great guidebook should do three things: inform, educate and amuse'.

OUR WRITERS

Lindsay Brown
Coordinating Author, Jaipur, Eastern Rajasthan and Northern Rajasthan (Shekhawati)

After completing a PhD on evolutionary genetics, and following a stint as a science editor, Lindsay started working for Lonely Planet. Lindsay is a former Publishing Manager of the Outdoor Activity Guides at Lonely Planet and he returns to the subcontinent to trek, write and photograph whenever possible. He has also contributed to Lonely Planet's *India, South India, Nepal, Bhutan,* and *Pakistan & the Karakoram Highway* guides, among others.

Abigail Hole
Delhi

Abigail was first bewitched by India around 15 years ago, when she travelled around the north on a hot and bewildering summer trip. She has returned at least every couple of years with increasingly regularity – visiting three times in 2010 alone. She wrote the very first edition of *Rajasthan, Delhi & Agra* and has written on India for various newspapers and magazines, including *Lonely Planet Magazine*.

Daniel McCrohan
Agra & the Taj Mahal

Daniel has been travelling to India on and off for almost 20 years. His writing career began in London in the late 1990s, and he worked there as a news and sports reporter for seven years before switching to travel. He now specialises in India and China, and has cowritten six Lonely Planet guidebooks for this part of the world, including *India, China* and *Tibet*. He now lives in China, but never tires of returning to India thanks to the gems it throws up each visit.

John Noble
Udaipur & Southern Rajasthan and Jaisalmer, Jodhpur & Western Rajasthan

John, from England, lives in Spain and has written about 20 countries for Lonely Planet. He first experienced India in the days of Rajiv Gandhi but has never written about it until now. Best on-the-road decision in Rajasthan: to blow his budget on a night at Udai Bilas Palace, Dungarpur. Best surprise: discovering that camels are a lot easier to ride than horses.

Published by Lonely Planet Publications Pty Ltd
ABN 36 005 607 983
3rd edition – Aug 2011
ISBN 978 1 74179 460 1
© Lonely Planet 2011   Photographs © as indicated 2011
10 9 8 7 6 5 4 3 2 1
Printed in China